The Van Nostrand Series in
Business Administration and Economics
JOHN R. BEISHLINE, *General Editor*
**Professor and Chairman,
Department of Management and Industrial Relations
New York University**

WAGE DETERMINATION: An Analysis of Wage Criteria
By JULES BACKMAN, *Professor of Economics, New York University*

ACCOUNTING PRINCIPLES
By ANDREW D. BRADEN, *Assistant Dean, School of Business, Western Reserve University,* and ROBERT G. ALLYN, *Executive Secretary, Board of C.P.A. Examiners, New York State*

AN INTRODUCTION TO AUTOMATIC COMPUTERS: A Systems Approach for Business, 2nd Ed.
By NED CHAPIN, *Associate Professor, San Francisco State College*

THE AMERICAN ECONOMY
By LEO FISHMAN, *Professor of Economics and Finance,* and BETTY G. FISHMAN, *Lecturer in Economics, both at West Virginia University*

FUNDAMENTALS OF BUSINESS ENTERPRISE
By PAUL G. HASTINGS, *Professor of Finance, Real Estate and Insurance, Sacramento State College*

THE MANAGEMENT OF BUSINESS FINANCE
By PAUL G. HASTINGS

AN INTRODUCTION TO ELECTRONIC DATA PROCESSING FOR BUSINESS
By LEONARD W. HEIN, *Associate Professor of Business Administration, Los Angeles State College*

BUSINESS, GOVERNMENT AND PUBLIC POLICY
By ASHER ISAACS, *late Professor of Economics, University of Pittsburgh,* and REUBEN E. SLESINGER, *Professor of Economics, University of Pittsburgh*

INTERNATIONAL ECONOMICS
By HUGH B. KILLOUGH, *Former Professor of Economics, Brown University,* and LUCY W. KILLOUGH, *A. Barton Hepburn Professor of Economics, Wellesley College*

MARKET THEORY AND THE PRICE SYSTEM
By ISRAEL M. KIRZNER, *Associate Professor of Economics, New York University*

MANAGERIAL ACCOUNTING
By MARY E. MURPHY, *Professor of Accounting, Los Angeles State College*

Additional titles will be listed and announced as published.

THE MANAGEMENT

OF

D. VAN NOSTRAND COMPANY, INC.

Princeton, New Jersey

BUSINESS

FINANCE

By Paul G. Hastings

Professor and Head
Department of Finance, Real Estate
and Insurance
Sacramento State College

Toronto . New York . London

D. VAN NOSTRAND COMPANY, INC.
120 Alexander St., Princeton, New Jersey (*Principal office*)
24 West 40 Street, New York 18, New York

D. VAN NOSTRAND COMPANY, LTD.
358, Kensington High Street, London, W.14, England

D. VAN NOSTRAND COMPANY (Canada), Ltd.
25 Hollinger Road, Toronto 16, Canada

Published simultaneously in Canada by
D. VAN NOSTRAND COMPANY (Canada), LTD.

To my nephews
CHRIS AND PAUL

Preface

This text is designed for the first course in Business or Corporation Finance. It is intended to provide students with the information and management techniques necessary to a fundamental understanding of the financial problems basic to most business firms.

A business manager's chief function is making decisions. Whether he is the chief financial officer or a minor executive in a nonfinancial position, his decisions will affect the finances of his company. Although it is not the purpose of this book to make accomplished financial executives of its readers, it will serve as a useful first step in that direction. Emphasis is given to the relationship of the finance function with related functions of management: how sales policy, inventory policy, depreciation techniques, and policy decisions in other areas affect financial policy and vice versa.

To a considerable extent, the book serves as a source of information. It is not, however, intended to be exhaustive. The readings at the end of each chapter are listed for the purpose of providing more extensive information on each area of business finance. Reference to particular corporations is occasionally made for the purpose of illustrating principles discussed in the book.

While this book is intended to be informative, its prime purpose is to develop the powers of judgment and analysis of the reader. Descriptions of financial practices, policies, the instruments of finance, and the legal aspect of business finance are presented as a background to decision-making. Business, however, is dynamic. Institutions and practices change. For that reason, the information here is not presented for itself alone, but as a means of maturing the financial judgment of the reader, whether he be a college student or a businessman. If, after reading this book, the critical faculties of the reader have been sharpened, its prime purpose will have been accomplished.

Suggestions and criticism from many persons have aided in the preparation of the book. However, the responsibility for the manuscript in its final form remains mine. I am grateful to Professors George L. Marrah, Chester F. Healy, Herbert J. Chruden, Norbert J. Mietus, and others for the time and encouragement they gave. I am particularly indebted to Dr. Constantine Danellis for his critical reading of portions of the manuscript and proofs. To my son, David, and my daughter, Margery, I owe special thanks for the many acts of helpfulness while I was working on the book.

PAUL G. HASTINGS

Contents

Part I

Introduction

1. THE PLACE OF FINANCE IN THE ECONOMY

1

The Place of Finance
in the Economy

THE IMPORTANCE OF FINANCE IN MODERN LIFE

Man throughout his long history has struggled to organize a society in which his efforts and intelligence can be directed toward the good of all. In the economic sphere of life human activity has been coordinated through business organizations. Some have been owned and operated by governments, some by private individuals. This book deals with privately owned business organizations, which account for most of the production, distribution, and service enterprises in the United States. Upon them rests our standard of living and our expectation that it will continue to improve.

In our modern economy people depend upon each other for most of life's necessities and for specialized services; it is thus possible for each person to contribute the maximum of his capabilities to society. It is for this reason that specialization and exchange have been highly developed in industrial societies. Although exchange of goods and services is possible without money (known as barter) in simple societies where each person produces most of what he consumes, money and claims to money are essential to an economy of sophisticated type. In modern society exchange is accomplished in two steps: selling one's goods or services for money and buying goods or services with money.

Finance is one aspect of an economy based on money. It is the art of raising and spending money. Finance, which Webster's dictionary calls the "management of monetary affairs," is of central importance in any organization whose affairs involve the use of money. It is important to governments, to colleges and religious bodies, and to profit and nonprofit organizations. In nearly all decisions made by such organizations, financial considerations are paramount.

3

THE ROLE OF INVESTMENT

Investment means many things to many people. To a businessman it may mean the extent of his ownership of a company; to a farmer the value of his land, buildings, and machinery; to a banker the bonds and notes in the bank's investment portfolio; to an economist a net increase in buildings, machinery, and other productive assets of a nation. In this book, however, we shall define investment as the expenditure of money to acquire property for a business purpose. Property includes items as long lasting as land and buildings or as transitory as materials in process of production. As time passes, the proportion of total spending for different classes of assets changes. Fig. 1-1 shows how investment in plant and equipment has declined relative to investment in current assets in recent years.

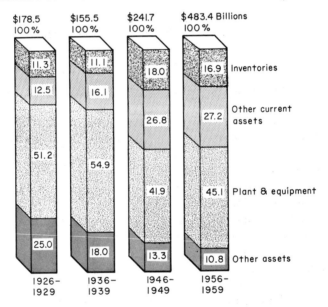

Fig. 1-1   *Structure of assets.* (*Sources:* U. S. Department of Commerce; Treasury Department; The Conference Board. *Road Maps of Industry*, No. 1377, copyright 1962 by National Industrial Conference Board, Inc.)

Payments have to be made to purchase the tools of production and to finance research on new products and techniques. Investment requires more and more money, and the financial officer of every business must concern himself with raising the necessary funds. To supply the funds for the capital goods needed by business, people in the economy must produce more than they consume. Although investment is the broad channel by which the efforts and property of people are directed to business purposes, managers of firms cannot buy the labor and property they need until they first secure the necessary money.

Sources of the money required by business are many. A classification of the leading sources is given in Fig. 1-2, where the liabilities indicate corporate borrowing and the investment of stockholders is shown by the net worth. Business itself is one of the important sources of funds through depreciation allowances and retained earnings which constitute the *internal* sources of funds. Depreciation allowances are made in recognition that capital in business operations is consumed and that this consumption must be recorded as one of the expenses of doing business. Accounting for

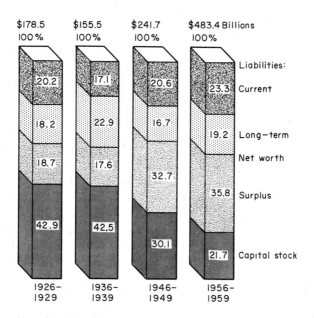

Note: Data exclude finance, insurance, and real estate corporations

Fig. 1-2 *Liabilities and net worth.* (*Sources:* U. S. Department of Commerce; Treasury Department; The Conference Board. *Road Maps of Industry,* No. 1377, copyright 1962 by National Industrial Conference Board)

depreciation does not result, however, in channeling part of the company revenue into cash reserves, to remain idle until spent to replace worn out assets. Rather, depreciation allowances permit an increase in investment in various assets of the company as a result of earnings retained.

Retained earnings are used as a source of funds for investment by nearly all businesses. In most corporations, large or small, and in most unincorporated businesses, the systematic retention of earnings is a fixed policy that stems mainly from a desire to reduce the taxable income of stockholders or to finance expansion through a plowback of earnings.

THE FUNCTION OF PROFITS

When an accountant speaks of profit, he distinguishes between two kinds: *gross* and *net*. Gross profit usually designates the amount remaining after the cost of making and selling goods is subtracted from the sales the company has made. Net profit is usually the term applied to what remains after deductions for materials, labor, interest, depreciation, and all other expenses have been made. In either case, profit is a concept of residual income. To both the stockholder of a corporation and the owner of an unincorporated firm, profit is a prime goal of business endeavor. Profit—or more precisely the expectation of profit—compensates the individual for the use of the funds he has invested in the firm and for the risk he has undertaken in committing his funds to a particular enterprise. In our capitalistic society, where investment is largely voluntary, the goal of profit is of prime importance in attracting investment funds.

Because profits are a residual payment, business owners, to whom the payment belongs, strive to make the residual as large as possible. The pursuit of profits takes many forms. Some, like price reduction, research, informative advertising, cost reductions resulting from increased efficiency, and customer service, are beneficial to society. Others that exploit the ignorance of consumers, take advantage of the weak bargaining position of some customers, use predatory tactics to destroy competitors, or secure undeserved favors from government are harmful to society. Competition generally helps to channel the pursuit of profit into beneficial ways. The existence of monopoly power, on the other hand, tends to make the pursuit of profit destructive. Although competition in a highly complex society cannot be depended upon as the sole protection of the consumer, it is usually considered to be the primary force beneficial to the consumer in a predominantly capitalistic economy.

Since profits are a residual, they fluctuate more during the course of business cycles than payments for labor, materials, and other business expenditures. As a matter of fact, business profits have risen and fallen sharply during recent decades. In years of deep depression (such as 1921, 1931, 1932, and 1933) business profits were practically eliminated. In years of prosperity (such as 1951, 1955, and 1959) profits reached very high levels.

For many years most economists have assumed that businessmen seek to maximize the profits of their firms. Where competition is intense and profit margins low, as in many retail stores, the pursuit and maximization of profits appear to be single-minded. However, in industries where competition is less intense than in retailing—say, aircraft manufacture—profit maximization appears to be less dominant in shaping management policy. Where elements of monopoly are present—say, utilities—a goal of satisfactory rather than maximum profits seems to guide management. Recent economic literature refers to such behavior as *satisficing* rather than *maximizing* profits.

Profit maximization is nevertheless accepted by most business managers as an axiom of economic life, and is often a guide in measuring departmental efficiency within a firm. Even in satisficing, the usual explanation is that company policy is the maximization of long-run rather than short-run profits. Any action, however long maintained, could be explained as being of "short-run" rather than "long-run" significance, since each person can define the long run to be as long as he chooses.

Whether maximizing or satisficing is the criterion applied to the pursuit of profits, an attempt is made to fit the manufacturing, pricing, advertising, and other policies of a firm into the over-all company policy designed to achieve the economic goals of the company. The principal financial officer must test his financial plans for consistency with company profit policy. His recommendations on long-term borrowing, selling stock, declaring dividends, dealing with bankers, and leasing equipment—to name a few—must be made to coordinate with the requirements of other divisions of management. The directors set the goals, and the financial manager helps determine the contribution of finance in reaching the goals.

ORGANIZATION FOR FINANCE

Development of Finance in Company Organization Management is not an art that can be broken down into compartments, each separate and unrelated to the others. Personnel management is not unrelated to production management. Traffic management is not separate from marketing management. Problems of price, product design, inventory, and taxation affect all divisions of management. In a very small business, one man may make all the management decisions. However, in large businesses, requiring many management men, a division of responsibility and the compartmentalization of management are necessary to handle the large volume of work.

Finance in the Organization Chart Finance is one of the functions of management. Financial decisions affect wage policy, inventory policy, pricing, and every other area of decision-making. The reverse is also true. Management decisions are made at every level of business organization from president to foreman, and nearly every management decision involves the finances of the company.

Theoretically as shown in Fig. 1-3, the shareholders control the conduct of a corporation by electing the board of directors, to whom the management is then responsible. During the early history of the corporation as a business organization, the shareholders as a group often exercised considerable control over the policies of the companies they owned. The number of company shareholders was generally small, stockholder meetings were usually well attended, and most stockholders were sophisticated in business matters. In these circumstances the owners participated actively in formulating basic policy. More recently, however, the shareholder has almost been eliminated from the formulation of policy, at least in large corporations with widely scattered stockholders. Two developments have been largely responsible for the decline in the power of the shareowner in policy-making: the scattering of stock ownership and the limitation of voting power.

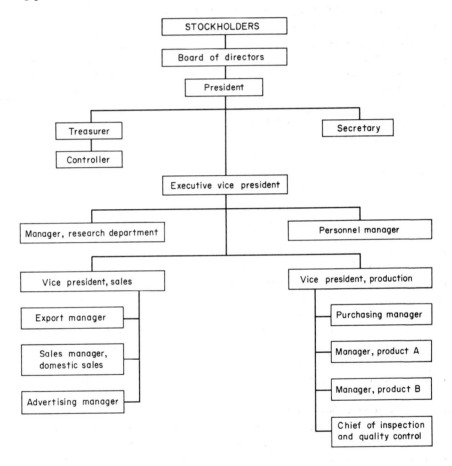

Fig. 1-3 *Organization chart of a corporation.*

The Chief Financial Officers A typical organizational structure for finance is shown in Fig. 1-4. The vice president for finance exercises authority over the finance function. Often he will be a member of the board of directors, and he is usually chairman of the finance committee of the board. As a board member his recommendations on financial policy will have considerable weight with other members of the board. As chief financial officer of the corporation he has the responsibility to carry out the financial policy decisions made by the board. The three officers of the corporation that share responsibility in the financial area with the financial vice president are the *treasurer, controller* (also called *comptroller*), and the *secretary*. If there is no financial vice president, the treasurer is usually the chief financial officer.

The treasurer's responsibilities include custody of such assets as cash, bank accounts, the investment portfolio of the corporation, and insurance policies. Cash receipts and disbursements fall within his jurisdiction, as do the management of bank accounts and the shifting of company funds from one bank to another. Checks drawn on company bank accounts generally bear his signature and are usually cosigned by another officer. If there is no controller, the treasurer's department usually includes accounting functions.

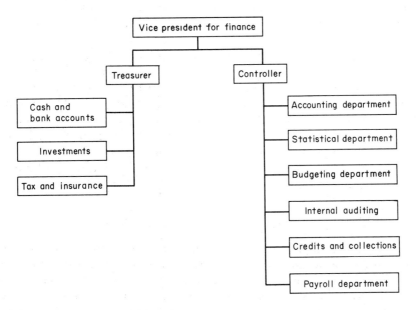

Fig. 1-4 *Organization for finance in a corporation.*

The controller is the chief accounting officer of the company. If the company is small, he may have the help of only a few bookkeepers. In a large company his authority extends to several hundred employees organized into departments with such names as Accounts Receivable, Accounts Payable, General Ledger, Internal Audit, Payroll, Tax, and Credits and Collections. Approval by the controller may be required of all payments made by the treasurer, as part of the routine designed to prevent unauthorized disbursements of cash. In some companies the preparation of budgets and their periodic review are undertaken by the treasurer; other companies relegate these duties to the controller. Regardless of how his functions may be defined in any particular company, the controller has duties which bring him into contact with the manufacturing, selling, and other activities of the company. The scope of responsibilities and the importance of the office of controller have increased substantially in recent years. As a matter of fact, the office of controller in some companies has become that of right-hand adviser to the president. Indeed, some controllers have become company presidents.

The secretary's principal responsibility is recording the minutes of meetings of the stockholders and of the board of directors. He also announces stockholders' meetings, issues proxy forms, and keeps the list of stockholders. The official seal of the corporation is kept in his office and is used on documents that require the seal's formality. Legal papers, such as contracts, franchises, and leases, are frequently kept by the secretary. The functions of the secretary of the corporation, while important, do not normally permit much decision-making latitude, at least in the United States. In Great Britain the corporation secretary frequently has managerial authority.

Where the number of directors on the board of a corporation is large, committees are frequently formed to consider at length whatever problems fall within their jurisdiction. Officers of the corporation and specialists hired for particular problems may be consulted or may attend certain meetings of the committees. After deliberation, a committee recommendation is generally referred to the whole board of directors at its next regular meeting. Directors recognize the importance of financial policy, because whenever committees are established at the board level, a committee on finance is nearly always included.

STOCKHOLDERS' MEETINGS

The stockholders are the sole owners of their corporation. Although they do not participate (unless they are also directors) in the management of the company, stockholders nevertheless retain certain powers. Their approval must be secured before the corporation may issue bonds, amend the charter, enter into a merger, or dissolve the company. To secure approval for these actions, to elect (usually re-elect) the directors, and to report on company operations, stockholders' meetings are called. Usually a meeting is held once a year to hear reports on the past year's operations and to elect directors for another year. If approval of a merger or the issuance of a bond is needed before the next regular meeting date, a special meeting is called.

Rarely is approval denied for any action requested by the directors. At a stockholders' meeting of a corporation with widely scattered stock, 80 or 90 per cent of the stock not held by members of the board of directors is represented at the meeting by proxy, a written authorization signed by a stockholder appointing a representative to vote his stock at the meeting. In most circumstances the proxies are sent by the directors themselves authorizing the stock to be voted in support of all actions desired by the directors. It is rare for a dissident group of stockholders to attempt to unseat the existing board of directors or to enlist support of fellow stockholders against a management proposal by sending out its own proxy forms. One reason for this is that letters, brochures, personal visits by proxy solicitors to holders of large blocks of shares, and other expenses of presenting the position of existing management on an issue are charged to the corporation and paid out of company funds. Similar expenses incurred by a group opposing the management are paid out of the pockets of the members of the opposition group.

Questions

1. Why is the finance function likely to be centralized, even in a large business that decentralizes manufacturing and distribution?
2. In modern society, exchange is accomplished by selling one's goods or services for money and then buying other goods and services with money. Discuss the advantages of this in comparison with barter.
3. What does *investment* mean to a banker? A farmer? A businessman?
4. How can accounting for depreciation make funds available for investment in a business?
5. Why is profit called a residual payment? Why does profit fluctuate during the course of business cycles more than payments for wages and materials?
6. Companies sometimes take actions that limit profits. Why do they do this?
7. What are the responsibilities of the treasurer? Of the controller? Of the secretary?
8. Should stockholders be encouraged to attend annual meetings of corporations? Give your reasons.
9. Why is it difficult for a dissident group of stockholders to unseat the existing board of directors of a large publicly held corporation?
10. Suggest reasons why the external sources of funds for corporations fluctuate more wildly over the years than internal sources.

Problem

Get a copy of the post-meeting report of a publicly held corporation, such as the Standard Oil Company of New Jersey. Analyze the types of questions asked by the stockholders. Do they seem relevant to company affairs? What votes, if any, other than for re-election to the board were taken? Can you suggest improvements in the handling of the meetings?

Selected Readings

Berle, Adolf A., and William C. Warren, *Cases and Materials on the Law of Business Organizations,* The Foundation Press, Inc., Houston, 1948.

Robinson, Joan, *The Accumulation of Capital,* Books I and IV, Richard D. Irwin, Inc., Homewood, Ill., 1956.

Weston, J. Fred, "The Finance Function," *The Journal of Finance,* September 1954.

Wright, David McCord, *Capitalism,* McGraw-Hill Book Co., Inc., New York, 1951, Chap. 5.

Part II

Financial Planning and Analysis

2

Financial Statements

THE NEED FOR STATEMENT ANALYSIS

An important reason for having financial records is to enable the chief financial officers to determine the degree of past performance of the business and to make future plans on this basis. However, financial records are not used by the financial officers or the other executives of the company alone. They are also needed by governmental regulatory agencies in attempting to determine whether a given set of rates in regulated companies is within the limits prescribed by law. Owners of businesses need them to determine the quality of management and to serve as a basis for investment decisions. Where taxes are based on financial records, taxing agencies depend upon the adequacy of the records in determining the amount of taxes. Some taxing agencies, especially at the municipal level, will accept the tax returns based on the financial records of the business, and will not attempt to determine whether they are accurate and complete. In other cases, particularly at the state and federal levels, the adequacy and accuracy of financial records used in preparing tax returns are checked by the taxing agency. Some regulatory agencies, for example the Federal Power Commission, prescribe the keeping of records and preparation of financial statements according to standards published by the agency.

Financial records prepared for the use of certain groups are frequently not in a form suitable for others. Statements prepared for taxing agencies and regulatory bodies must contain information required by the agencies; statements for the use of company executives usually require a detail not demanded by others that need financial data about the company; and statements for stockholders or the general public are usually in summary form. In the latter case the financial information is frequently prepared with liberal use of bar charts, pie charts, and other statistical methods of presentation to enable persons not financially sophisticated to understand the data presented.

15

TOOLS OF FINANCIAL ANALYSIS

The Balance Sheet The basic tools of financial analysis are the balance sheet, profit and loss statement, and statement of surplus. The *balance sheet,* also known as the *statement of condition,* pictures the financial condition of a business at an instant of time, as of the close of business December 31, 1964. It reveals the property owned by the business, the *assets,* and the debts owed by the company, the *liabilities.* The difference between the assets and the liabilities is the *net worth* of the company. Figure 2-1 shows a visualized presentation of a balance sheet and a profit and loss statement. By custom the assets are listed first and are usually classified according to categories such as current assets, also called the working capital, fixed assets, investment assets, and intangible assets. Net working capital, shown as a separate bar on Fig. 2-1, is defined as the difference between the current assets (cash, receivables, and inventories) and the current liabilities (current debt, taxes payable, and other short-term debt). The length of the bar representing working capital, therefore, is the length of the portion of the asset bar representing current assets minus the length of the portion of the liabilities bar representing the current debt. Ordinarily, the assets are listed on the balance sheet in direct order of liquidity; cash is generally listed first, with the fixed assets at the bottom.

   Although the balance sheet is a useful picture of a firm's financial condition, it is not necessarily an exact reflection of the firm's economic worth. The balance sheet is prepared according to rather rigid rules that are encrusted in long-standing customs of the accounting profession. A bank's balance sheet, for example, might list real estate owned at a value of $1, furniture and fixtures also at $1, and possibly some other assets at purely nominal figures. Frequently intangible assets, such as patents, franchises, or good will, if they are carried on the balance sheet at all, are listed at $1. Accountants are by nature financially conservative, and traditionally will list assets on an understated basis wherever there is any doubt as to their value. In many cases the market value of an asset cannot be ascertained unless it is sold, and even then the price received would accurately indicate the value only on the day that the sale was made. Some leeway must be allowed in the valuation of many assets listed on balance sheets, particularly those which have a long life and are sold infrequently.

   A balance sheet represents the condition of a business at an instant of time. Each day the business will make purchases, sell goods or services, the dollar value of inventories will change, the cash account will rise or fall, and accounts payable and accounts receivable will increase or decrease. Because there is change in the business, the value of a balance sheet decreases in utility as time passes. A balance sheet prepared last week is of considerable value in guiding the actions of company officers; one prepared a year ago is of less value. Balance sheets of prior years, however, are useful in preparing charts or other indications of trends in the financial affairs of the

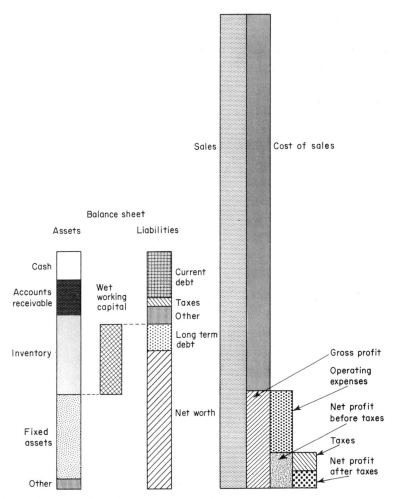

Fig. 2-1 *Visualized financial statement of the Noname Manufacturing Company, December 31, 1964. (Source: Small Business Reporter, Bank of America)*

company. Many businesses have quarterly balance sheets, while others prepare monthly or even weekly ones. It is not now feasible to prepare a daily balance sheet, although the great advance in the use of electronic machines in accounting may make such a policy practical in the future.

The Profit and Loss Statement and Surplus Statement The income of a company can be pictured as a stream of earnings, as shown in Fig. 2-2, that is diverted to various channels to cover operating expenses, pay taxes and dividends, and provide funds for investment. To furnish a financial measure of the stream of earnings a *profit and loss statement* or *statement of income* is prepared which shows the change in the financial condition of a business over a period of time. Statements of income are most often prepared on a quarterly or annual basis.   The first item on the statement is customarily sales, from which are deducted the various expenses incurred in making the sales.   Various operating expenses, administrative expenses, other income, and taxes are accounted for, until what is usually the last item, the figure of net income after taxes, is reached.   A profit and loss statement in the form of a bar chart (see Fig. 2-1) shows first what portion of the sales bar remains after deduction of the cost of goods sold, next what remains after operating expenses are deducted, and finally what is left after taxes on income are subtracted.   Some of the expenses listed on the income

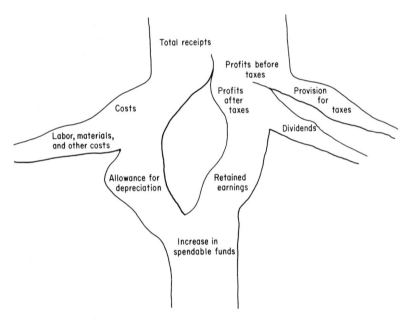

Fig. 2-2   *Revenue flow chart.*

statement will be accounted for by expenditures of cash, so that their value in terms of money can be accurately determined.   Other expenses not paid for in cash at the time the expense is incurred must in many cases be estimated.   Frequently judgment or arbitrary decision is the basis for making the estimate.   One example is depreciation.   If the method of determining depreciation is not consistent between two companies, the income statement of one must be modified to conform to the method of determining depreciation in the other.   It is, of course, highly useful for a company to be consistent in the treatment of expenses when preparing its income statements year after year.   It can then accurately determine the trend of its income and expense over a period of time, which would not be possible if the basis for determining depreciation and other expenses were changed.   During the 1950's the income tax laws of the federal government were amended to permit a more rapid rate of depreciation on the machinery and other productive assets of businesses. The published profit and loss statements of most corporations in the late 1950's reflected the larger expense for depreciation permitted by the tax laws compared with the less generous depreciation allowances used in the early 1950's. The net income after tax figure shown on the income statements of many corporations was a smaller figure than would have been shown had depreciation expense been figured on the pre-1950 basis. During years of changing accounting standards a valid trend of profits is obtained by modifying the income statements to achieve uniformity.

The *surplus statement* shows the changes in the surplus account of a corporation during a stated period which is usually the same period as is covered by the profit and loss statement. The surplus account is credited with the amount of net income earned by the corporation and debited with any dividends declared by the directors. If stock is sold for more than its par value, the difference is credited to surplus. Uninsured damage to company property, operating losses, and expenses of organization of the corporation are debited to surplus.

Financial Ratios   Although other statements may be prepared, the balance sheet and the profit and loss statement are the two that are basic to financial analysis. It is largely from them that the ratios and other tools of financial analysis are derived. Table 2-1 lists the ratios most commonly used in financial analysis.

TABLE 2-1

Ratios Applying to the Balance Sheet	*Ratios Applying to the Income Statement or to the Income Statement and Balance Sheet*
Current ratio	Ratio of income to equity
Acid test ratio	Ratio of income to sales
Ratio of equity (net worth) to debt	Merchandise inventory turnover
	Turnover of receivables
	Invested capital turnover
	Times interest earned
	Times dividends earned

The *current ratio* is determined by the following formula:

$$\text{Current ratio} = \frac{\text{current assets}}{\text{current liabilities}}$$

This ratio is intended to measure the capacity of a business to meet its short-term debt. A popular rule of thumb is that the current ratio should be at least two to one. If the ratio is low, it generally indicates that the business is likely to have difficulty in meeting on time its payment of current liabilities. On the other hand, if the current ratio is unusually high, it can be concluded that the business is probably not making the most efficient use of its current assets. The possible reasons are an unnecessarily large amount of cash on hand, more than adequate inventories, and the slow collection of accounts receivable. The financial manager must use care in avoiding the extremes of too high or too low a current ratio. It is useful for one company to compare its ratio with that for the industry as a whole and to compare the most recent ratio with ratio figures for the company in the past.

The purpose of the *acid test ratio* is similar to that of the current ratio. It measures the ratio of cash and receivables to current liabilities, as indicated below:

$$\text{Acid test ratio} = \frac{\text{cash and receivables}}{\text{current liabilities}}$$

Here, too, there is a popular rule of thumb that says the acid test ratio should be one to one. If so, it is presumed that the company could meet with cash, notes receivable, and accounts receivable any demand for payment of current liabilities. The acid test ratio is also sometimes called the *quick ratio*.

The *ratio of equity* (also known as net worth, which includes preferred and common stock and surplus) *to debt* shows at a glance the relative importance of equity and debt in the financing of a company. It is expressed in the following equation:

$$\text{Equity-debt ratio} = \frac{\text{net worth}}{\text{total liabilities}}$$

There is no rule of thumb to indicate the proper ratio of equity to debt. Useful in indicating to the financial manager the trend of financing of his company, it also provides a quick and easy means of comparing the structure of one company with another or with the industry average. Generally, if a ratio is low, the return of profit to the owners will increase rapidly in times of rising prosperity for the company and will decrease rapidly in times of declining business activity. A low ratio increases the risk of insolvency for the company but also increases the possibility of accelerating the rate of return on the owners' investment. Conversely, a high ratio of equity to debt indicates that the company's financial position is relatively safe from insolvency, but that the return on the owners' investment will be less than could be achieved in times of prosperity compared with what might have been yielded with a lower ratio. The ratio of equity to debt measures the degree of conservatism in financing a company. Typically this ratio is high for companies with variable and unpredictable earnings, such as mining companies. On the other hand, such companies as public utilities that can predict with a high degree of accuracy their earnings in the future show a low ratio of equity to debt.

The ratio of income to equity (net worth) is derived from the following equation:

$$\text{Ratio of income to equity} = \frac{\text{net income}}{\text{net worth}}$$

For example, if a company had a net income of $30,000 and a net worth of $400,000, the ratio would be $\frac{\$30,000}{\$400,000} = 0.075$ or 7.5 per cent. The ratio is usually expressed as a percentage. One of the most important ratios to company owners, it provides the information essential to any decision with respect to disbursement of dividends in a corporation or the withdrawal of funds by owners in an unincorporated business. This ratio will be strongly affected by the valuation of expenses on the income statement of the company.

Another measure of profitability is the *operating profit ratio*, also known as the *ratio of income to sales*. It compares total sales with what is left (net income before taxes, or operating profit) after the cost of goods sold and operating expenses have been deducted from sales. The ratio is expressed in the following equation:

$$\text{Operating profit ratio} = \frac{\text{net income}}{\text{sales}}$$

For example, if total sales of a company for a year are $250,000 and the net income is $10,000, the ratio of income to sales is 0.04 or, as it is most often expressed, 4 per cent. A high ratio of income to sales does not mean that there will be a high ratio of income to equity or profitable return to owners' investment. Instead, it may represent a managerial policy of demanding a high markup on merchandise sold. Such a policy would make for a relatively low rate of turnover of inventory, a policy which, as indicated later, managers usually seek to avoid. It might be possible for a company to increase the return on the owners' investment by reducing the price of its goods. This might increase total sales considerably, although it would reduce the profit per unit of sale and reduce the ratio of income to sales. It should be emphasized that the goal of business is usually considered to be the maximization of the owners' investment rather than the maximization of profit per unit of sale.

The *merchandise inventory turnover* may be obtained by using the following equation:

$$\text{Merchandise inventory turnover} = \frac{\text{cost of goods sold}}{\text{average inventory}}$$

One method of determining the average inventory is by adding the beginning inventory to the ending inventory for the period, usually a year, and dividing by two. In company financial management it is generally a goal to increase the merchandise inventory turnover to as high a figure as possible. Like other ratios, this one is useful in comparing present performance of a company with its past performance and in comparing its performance with that of other companies in the industry. The merchandise inventory turnover figure will vary considerably from one industry to another, because of the different sales patterns of different industries.

The *turnover of accounts receivable* is determined by dividing the annual credit sales by the average accounts receivable for the period, usually one year:

$$\text{Turnover of accounts receivable} = \frac{\text{sales on credit}}{\text{average accounts receivable}}$$

Just as the turnover of inventory is a means of measuring the capability of inventory management, the receivables turnover figure is a means of measuring the capability of the management of accounts receivable. If annual sales on credit are $1,200,000 during a year and the average accounts receivable for the year is $200,000, the receivables turnover figure is six times. If comparison of the receivables turnover figure for the most recent period compared with that for previous periods shows a decline, it may mean that the corporation has been lax in collecting overdue accounts, or at least that the policies of extending credit to the company's customers merit some attention. The receivables turnover figure is also a useful indicator of the liquidity of the asset accounts receivable. For the preceding example, if the receivables turnover figure is six times, it means that the average account remains outstanding for a period of two months. In other words, the turnover figure of six times per year means that the accounts receivable are on the average two months away from being turned into cash. If the turnover figure should decline to three times, it would mean that on the average the company has to wait four months before realizing cash on its accounts receivable.

Although the turnover of accounts receivable provides a quick picture of the relative liquidity of this asset, it does not indicate the extent to which accounts are overdue. This is best shown by means of a schedule posting the relative age of outstanding accounts and classifying them according to the number of days, weeks, or months that they may be overdue. Such a schedule helps to determine whether particular accounts should be written off or attempts be made to collect them.

The *invested capital turnover* is calculated by the following equation:

$$\text{Invested capital turnover} = \frac{\text{sales}}{\text{invested capital}}$$

The figure generally used for invested capital is the sum of the bonds and other long-term debt, the preferred stock, the common stock, and the surplus. This measure indicates the vigor with which the capital in the business is being applied. Its usefulness is restricted largely to comparing different years of the same company or different companies having similar capital structures.

A useful ratio relating income and interest charges is the ratio of *times interest earned*. This may be obtained by taking the earnings of the company before interest and income taxes and dividing the figure by annual interest charges. The figure representing income before payment of interest and taxes is generally used, because the payment of interest is a business expense, and like other expenses, reduces the net income figure on which income taxes are levied. If net income is $450,000 and the interest charges for the same period are $150,000, the interest is earned three times. This means that the net income of the corporation could decline to one-third before there would be insufficient income to cover the interest expense. This ratio is one that is examined closely by any institution considering a long-term loan to a borrowing company, and it is particularly important in planning the issuance of bonds. Where the times-interest-earned figure is low, it would be very difficult to market a bond issue at favorable rates of interest. Because this ratio has a very strong effect on the borrowing capacity of a corporation, it is a ratio that most managements watch closely. Where the earnings pattern of a company over a period of years is steady, a relatively low times-interest-earned ratio is considered safe. This is true of most public utilities. On the other hand, a company which shows an erratic earnings pattern particularly when characteristic of most companies in the same industry, a times-interest-earned ratio has to be much higher before the company will find it easy to borrow on a long-term basis.

If a company has more than one bond issue outstanding, it is necessary in determining the times-interest-earned figure to add the interest of the particular bond issue (or other debt being considered) to the interest of all other debt having equal priority and to all debt which is senior to the debt under consideration. If this is not done, an erroneous picture may result, as illustrated below:

Gross income	$20,000,000
Operating expenses	15,000,000
Operating profit	5,000,000
Interest on mortgage bonds	2,000,000
Income after mortgage interest	3,000,000
Interest on debenture bonds	1,000,000
Net income (before income taxes)	$ 2,000,000

If the times-interest-earned ratio is computed separately for each bond, the ratio for the mortgage bond is $\dfrac{\$5,000,000}{\$2,000,000} = 2.5$ times. For the debenture bond it is $\dfrac{\$3,000,000}{\$1,000,000} = 3$ times. Thus it appears that the junior bond is better protected than the senior bond, which is obviously erroneous. The computation of the ratio for the debenture bond should combine the interest expense of the debenture bond with that of other debt having equal or prior claim to earnings. For the debenture bond the computation is as follows:

$$\frac{\$5,000,000}{\$2,000,000 \ + \ \$1,000,000} \ = \ 1.67 \ \text{times}$$

Thus a decline in earnings of 67¢ out of $1.67 (or a decline of 40 per cent) places the payment of interest on the debenture bonds in jeopardy.

Just as the times-interest-earned figure is useful in managing the long-term debt of a company and is very important to creditors in determining any risk in making long-term loans, so the *times-dividends-earned* figure is used with respect to a corporation's capability to make regular payment of dividends on preferred stock. In this case it is the figure representing preferred stock dividends that is compared to net income. To prepare this ratio the analyst may take the figure representing net income after payment of interest and taxes and divide it by the dividened requirement for the preferred stock under study plus the dividend requirements of other preferred stock issues having equal or senior position. The use of the times-dividends-earned ratio is subject to the same criticism as that stated in discussing the junior bond, in that the preferred stock might appear to be better protected than bond issues of the same company. Some authorities suggest using an overall coverage figure for preferred stock which involves adding the preferred dividend to all interest and other charges to income having priority over the preferred stock dividend.

The payment of dividends on preferred and common stocks is not a contractual payment on the part of the corporation as is the payment of interest on debt. The nonpayment of dividends on the preferred will not put the corporation into insolvency. Nevertheless, this figure is very important to the investor considering the purchase of the preferred stock and to the company in its efforts to raise funds through the sale of preferred stock. Furthermore, this figure is important to the owners of a corporation, the common stockholders, because it indicates how well the corporation is able to pay dividends on the common. Like the times interest earned, the times dividends earned may be low and still be reasonably safe, if the corporation has a very steady pattern of earnings. If, however, the earnings pattern is erratic, then it is difficult for a corporation to raise funds by the sale of preferred stock, simply because an investor would be loath to purchase such a stock unless the dividends were generous enough to offset the risk that earnings would not cover dividend requirements on the preferred.

HAZARDS IN THE USE OF FINANCIAL STATEMENTS

The analysis of financial data of a business involves a number of hazards. The use of the various ratios and other tools of financial analysis helps to reduce the amount of time involved in financial analysis and makes it easier for the financial manager to pinpoint certain financial aspects of the corporation's position. These could be compared with similar ratios representing the average in the industry as a whole, but each business must be treated as an individual entity. A permissible figure representing the current ratio for one business would not necessarily be appropriate for the industry as a whole. On the other hand, the average current ratio figures for a whole industry might not be safe ones to apply to a particular business. It is not always possible to use industry data as a standard for the financial analysis of a particular company, since many companies are not confined to a single industry. For example, a chemical company might manufacture plastics, paints, toothbrushes, and explosives besides chemical products. The question immediately raised is *which* industry's average financial ratios should be considered representative for such a company. As a matter of fact, it would be difficult to get a set of representative financial ratios for the chemical industry as a whole, because many companies in that industry derive a substantial proportion of their sales from products other than chemicals.

Another hazard lies in the use of hidden surplus by some companies. The term *hidden surplus* (or *secret reserve*) is applied to the deliberate understatement of income or undervaluation of assets. This can be accomplished by charging excessive depreciation expense or by carrying on the balance sheet of the corporation assets at a nominal figure rather than at the estimated true value. The result of such a practice is that surplus is also understated, and therefore part of the surplus is "hidden." Sometimes this is done to make the corporation appear to be less profitable than it actually is, a device intended to reduce stockholder demand for increased dividends. Mostly, however, it is a result of applying conservative accounting principles to the valuation of assets. For example, it is accepted accounting procedure to value inventory at cost or market value, whichever is lower, and to give nominal values of $1 to such assets as patents and goodwill. Another source of hidden surplus has resulted from the taxation policy of the federal government. Efforts by businessmen to reduce the tax rate on corporation income during the 1950's were unsuccessful. However, businessmen were successful in getting Congress to permit companies to increase depreciation expense, which had the effect of reducing business income subject to the corporation income tax, thus reducing the tax burden without reducing the tax rate. It also had the effect of increasing hidden surplus.

Still another danger in comparing the financial ratios of one company with those of other companies is the variation in size of companies within an industry. Typically, small companies have a simpler financial structure, while large companies have outstanding not only common stock but also preferred stock and bonds. Smaller corporations frequently have only one class of stock outstanding and no bonded indebtedness at all. Not only are the financial structures of companies dissimilar, but the pattern of both current and fixed assets is also different. It is safer, therefore, to compare the financial ratios of one company with others in the same industry that are approximately equal in size. Consideration should also be given in some industries to the geographical location of the company. It is less hazardous to analyze the financial data of a company by comparing its recent figures with its historical figures. Nevertheless caution should be exercised. Past conditions are rarely the same as conditions in the future. A financial ratio that was legitimate in the past may not be so in the future. On the other hand, the financial managers might restrict profit opportunities by applying too rigidly to the future certain financial standards which perhaps were necessary in the past, but are no longer relevant to the changed conditions of the present.

Furthermore, the typical company goes through a number of stages in its life cycle. During the first few years after its organization, a company is usually in a rather critical stage of development. Conservative operation, considering the greater risk of insolvency during the early life of a business, dictates a policy of caution in financial operation to the extent that competitive conditions and financial resources permit. After a company has become well established, it may then be possible to relax the standards applied to past financial operations. It might be possible for a company to increase its long-term indebtedness during such a phase because of a greater stability in the pattern of earnings compared with the early years. This increase in debt might permit a more rapid rise in the earnings per common share than would have been possible had the debt not been incurred.

Finally, the philosophy of the owners of a small company or of the board of directors of a large publicly held corporation should be considered in deciding upon financial policies and in the analysis of financial data. Some companies are operated by managements that are very conservative and others by managements much more willing to take financial risks. Which is better in a particular situation is difficult to say. Under certain circumstances a conservative approach would be better, while under others the acceptance of calculated risk might prove to be superior. One must use judgment in analyzing financial data and in selecting polices to be followed by a company. Financial statements are an aid in arriving at useful decisions, but not a substitute for judgment.

Financial tools of analysis are very useful in guiding judgment and in presenting financial data in such forms that important features can be readily grasped at a glance. Data are often presented in graphic form. Although the careful preparation of financial statements and the use of ratios and other tools of financial analysis can save time, common sense is still essential to good financial control and management.

Questions

1. As the size of a company increases, the amount of record keeping tends to rise more rapidly. Why is this so?
2. Why can large companies make better use of electronic computers than small

companies? Explain how the disadvantage of small size in using electronic computers has become less as time passes.

3. Why do some companies prepare different income statements or balance sheets for tax returns, company directors, and stockholders?
4. Why are some assets, such as goodwill, valued at $1?
5. How is it possible that two equally capable accountants may arrive at different figures for the net income of a company?
6. Why are adjustments sometimes necessary in comparing current statements of a company with those prepared ten years ago for the company?
7. What information does the current ratio provide?
8. "The ratio of equity to debt is a measure of the degree of conservatism in financing a company." Explain and criticize the statement.
9. Should management strive for a high ratio of income to sales or a high ratio of income to the owners' investment? Can the two goals be in conflict? Explain.
10. What conflict of interest might arise between the sales manager and the credit manager in handling accounts receivable? Of what use is the turnover of accounts receivable measure in resolving such a conflict?
11. What is the measure times-interest-earned? If the figure is 4 for a particular company, what does this mean?
12. What are the hazards in the uncritical examination and use of financial statements?

Selected Readings

Foster, Louis A. O., *Understanding Financial Statements and Corporate Annual Reports,* Chilton Co., Philadelphia, 1961.

Foulke, Roy A., *Practical Financial Statement Analysis,* 4th ed., McGraw-Hill Book Co., Inc., New York, 1957.

Helfert, Erich A., *Techniques of Financial Analysis,* Richard D. Irwin, Inc., Homewood, Ill., 1963.

Kelley, Pearce C., and Kenneth Lawyer, *How to Organize and Operate a Small Business,* Prentice-Hall, Inc., Englewood Cliffs, N. J., Chap. 20 and 21.

The Use of Financial Ratios and Other Financial Techniques and Services, Bureau of Economic and Business Research, Temple University, Philadelphia, 1962.

Wessel, Robert H., *Principles of Financial Analysis,* The Macmillan Company, New York, 1961, Chaps. 3-6.

3

Depreciation and Depletion

THE CONCEPT OF DEPRECIATION

If a farmer buys a truck, presumably he has convinced himself that its use will enable him to earn an amount which is at least equivalent to its cost. If he expects the truck's useful life to be eight years, he knows that at the end of that period he will have to purchase another truck. He may annually set aside a portion of income from the sale of crops to build up a fund in his savings account so that at the end of eight years he will have enough to purchase a new truck. Or, knowing that in eight years time he will have to purchase a new truck, he may use part of his cash income to reduce his total indebtedness, so that at the end of eight years he will be in a good position to borrow money from the bank to purchase the vehicle. In any case, he recognizes that the truck will deteriorate through use and the passage of time. He also knows that he will have to have the cash, or be able to borrow the money, to buy a new truck.

Nearly every asset owned by a company deteriorates over time, although land is an exception. Its contours may be changed by erosion, leveling processes, or by other means. Gravel, clay or other substances may be extracted from it. But the land itself remains—its acreage is the same regardless of what is done with it. The life of some assets may be so long as to appear timeless. There are many examples throughout the world of buildings constructed hundreds of years ago that remain in usable condition. Highways and aqueducts built during Roman times continued in service long after Rome fell to the barbarians. Nevertheless, the fact remains that practically every physical asset of a business loses value as time passes. This fact must be recognized in the financial planning for the company. The accountant views the loss in value through the passage of time as one of the expenses of business operation. If it is not recognized as an expense, which is the case in some small family held enterprises, the business may find itself in a financial condition unable to replace a worn-out asset when it is

28

necessary to do so. The inclusion of depreciation expense among the other expenses of operation is the financial expression of the fact that practically all assets of a business are "consumed" in the course of time. Of course, the "consumption" rate varies considerably from one asset to another. An automobile used by a salesman may need to be replaced each year. The transmission lines of an electric power company may need to be replaced every twenty years. The life of a factory building may be forty years. The life of an office building may be as long as seventy or eighty years. The use of these assets creates income for the company. The net income, however, will be overstated if it does not include the expense of using up of the assets of the enterprise, regardless of the asset's longevity.

Depreciation charges differ from other expenses in two important respects. They are related to the consumption of assets that have a life longer than one year, or more specifically one accounting period. If an asset has a useful life of seven years, it is reasonable to charge this cost to expenses over the seven-year period. During this period the asset will be both generating income for the company and adding to the expense of the company. In the second place, depreciation charges differ from other expenses in that they are not cash expenses. If a machine with an estimated useful life of five years is purchased at a cost of $10,000 and is estimated to have a scrap value of $2,000, the decline in value of the machine over the five-year period will be $8,000. This loss in value could be charged as an expense equally over the five-year period, at the rate of $1,600 per year. Depreciation expense, however, is not paid out in cash, as are the costs of wages and materials. Nevertheless, it is an expense which must be recognized and must be covered, if the company is to maintain solvency. Moreover, in the previous example, at the end of the five-year period the company must be in a position to replace the worn-out machine with a new one. The inclusion of depreciation charges in the profit and loss statement is a recognition of the fact that to operate at a profit a company must generate sufficient income to cover both cash and non-cash expenses. If it were not for depreciation charges, cash might be removed from the company by the owners or distributed in dividends by the directors in excess of the true earnings of the enterprise. Depreciation charges thus serve to prevent the dissipation of earnings that are needed to replace the asset when it is worn out.

Although depreciation represents one form of a company's retained earnings, it does not follow that part of the cash received by a company through sales or the collection of accounts receivable must be retained in the form of cash. Indeed, it would be poor financial management to build up a fund of cash for a period of five years to replace an asset with an estimated life of the same period. Much better use could be made of the cash during the five years than idle accumulation. The allowance for depreciation, like net income retained by a company, represents a source of funds that may be used by the company. Unlike retained net income, however, allowance for depreciation represents a source of funds which have a temporary use.   The use of funds generated by depreciation allowances is subject to the necessity that the company prepare itself to replace the worn-out assets at the end of their useful lives.   Depreciation allowances on an asset with a life of five years may be treated in a manner similar to a loan which must be repaid in five years.   In both cases the funds must be used in such a way that the company is in a position to replace the funds used at the end of five years.

In the narrow sense *depreciation* refers to the physical wear and tear on man-made assets, such as buildings, machinery, or trucks, through use or as a result of exposure to weather.   In the broad sense, however, and in the sense used in this chapter, the word refers to the loss of value of a long-term asset as a result of the passage of time.   In determining the base on which depreciation charges are figured, accountants in general and tax authorities in particular insist on using the original cost rather than replacement cost of the asset.   Original cost has therefore been assumed in the examples used later in this chapter.   However, in periods of rising prices, the accumulated allowance for depreciation will not cover the cost of replacing the worn-out asset.   To meet this financing problem some companies annually set aside a portion of earned surplus equal to the estimated gap between depreciation allowances and replacement cost.

Obsolescence refers to the loss of value of a long-term asset because it becomes outdated or because more efficient models are available.   Coal-burning locomotives become obsolete before they are worn out and are replaced by diesel locomotives.   Piston engines become obsolete in airplanes as jet engines come into use.   Dies used to stamp out fenders for 1963 model automobiles may be physically capable of being used for several years.   If the fender design of an automobile is changed each year, however, the dies become obsolete each year.

Depletion refers to the using up of assets that cannot be replaced, such as oil, limestone, coal, and ores.   The more rapid the rate of extraction of such an asset, the more rapidly it is finally depleted.

Amortization is the process of recovering through periodic charges to income the cost of an intangible asset.   Such assets as copyrights, patents, franchises, and leases lose value as time passes, and this loss must be recognized as a charge against income.   If the intangible asset is given a purely nominal value, such as $1, it need not be amortized.   The accounting treatment of depreciation, obsolescence, depletion, and amortization is similar. The cost of the asset must be determined, the period of years over which the asset is written off must be decided, and the residual value, if any, at the end of the period must be estimated.   With this information, the loss in value of the asset can be charged to income over the years of its use on whatever basis of allocation of cost is used by the company.

METHODS OF CALCULATING DEPRECIATION AND DEPLETION

Until 1950 the most common method of determining depreciation on an asset was to estimate the useful life of the asset, subtract the estimated scrap or trade-in value at the end of its life from the original cost, and divide the difference between these two sums by the number of years the asset is used. This figure was then used as the annual depreciation expense for the asset. This method, called the straight line method of depreciation, was required until the 1950's by the Federal Internal Revenue Service in determining depreciation costs for most business assets. It is still used for determining depreciation charges for many assets today, but not nearly to the extent that it was prior to 1950. There are many other ways of determining depreciation charges. The more commonly used methods will be discussed here.

Straight Line Depreciation It is logical to apply the straight line method to an asset that loses the same dollar amount of value each year of its life. It is also logical to apply this method where the rate of loss of value per year cannot readily be determined. If a building is purchased at a cost of $100,000, if its useful life is estimated at forty-five years, and if the building is expected to have a value of $10,000 at the end of the period, the amount to be depreciated is $90,000. The straight line method results in a charge amounting to $2,000 for each of the forty-five years of the building's use. It is typical of most assets that expenses for repairs and maintenance increase with age. Under the straight line method, the combined expense for depreciation, maintenance, and repairs generally increases each year as the asset grows older. This fact is sometimes used as an argument against the straight line method. On the other hand, this method is easy to understand and easy to compute. It is extensively used as a means of charging depreciation against buildings and other long-term assets. The great majority of electric power companies use this method of depreciation on those assets having a long life.

Fixed Percentage of Declining Balance Under the method of fixed percentage of declining balance, a steady rate of depreciation is charged each year. The straight line method charges a fixed percentage of the original cost, resulting in the same dollar charge for depreciation each year. The declining balance method, on the other hand, applies a fixed percentage not to the original cost, but to the book value which declines each year. Under this method, the rate charged each year to the book value of the depreciating asset is larger than it is under the straight line method. Typically, it is double the percentage applied each year under the straight line method. For example, an asset having an estimated useful life of twenty years with no scrap value would have a depreciation charge of 5 per cent of the original cost each year under the straight line method and a charge of 10 per cent of the declining book value each year under the declining balance method. The principal advantage under the declining balance method is that the depreciation charges during the early years are higher than the charges during the later years, thus approximating more closely the actual loss in value of many assets than the straight line method.

The main disadvantage of the declining balance method is that the sum of the annual charges for depreciation never equals the original cost of the asset, no matter how many years the depreciation charges are computed. This weakness is serious if the asset being depreciated is estimated to have no scrap value. For those assets that do have a scrap value at the end of

TABLE 3-1. DEPRECIATION COMPUTATION UNDER THREE METHODS
(A. Straight Line; B. Fixed Percentage; C. Sum-of-the-Years' Digits)
Original Cost of Asset: $100 (No Scrap Value)
Useful Life: 10 Years (Income Tax Rate: 50%)

A. STRAIGHT LINE METHOD *

Year	Annual Depreciation	Annual Reduction in Income Tax	Cumulative Depreciation Charges	Cumulative Reduction in Income Tax	Book Value of Asset at End of Year
1	$10.00	$5.00	$10.00	$ 5.00	$90.00
2	10.00	5.00	20.00	10.00	80.00
3	10.00	5.00	30.00	15.00	70.00
4	10.00	5.00	40.00	20.00	60.00
5	10.00	5.00	50.00	25.00	50.00
6	10.00	5.00	60.00	30.00	40.00
7	10.00	5.00	70.00	35.00	30.00
8	10.00	5.00	80.00	40.00	20.00
9	10.00	5.00	90.00	45.00	10.00
10	10.00	5.00	100.00	50.00	0

* Annual depreciation at 10% of original cost.

B. FIXED PERCENTAGE OF DECLINING BALANCE *

Year	Annual Depreciation	Annual Reduction in Income Tax	Cumulative Depreciation Charges	Cumulative Reduction in Income Tax	Book Value of Asset at End of Year
1	$20.00	$10.00	$20.00	$10.00	$80.00
2	16.00	8.00	36.00	18.00	64.00
3	12.80	6.40	48.80	24.40	57.20
4	10.24	5.12	59.04	24.52	40.96
5	8.19	4.10	67.23	33.62	32.77
6	6.56	3.28	73.79	36.90	26.21
7	5.24	2.62	79.03	39.52	20.97
8	4.19	2.10	83.22	41.62	16.78
9	3.36	1.68	86.58	43.30	13.42
10	2.68	1.34	89.26	44.64	10.74

* Annual depreciation at 20% of book value.

C. SUM-OF-THE-YEARS' DIGITS

Year	Annual Depreciation	Annual Reduction in Income Tax	Cumulative Depreciation Charges	Cumulative Reduction in Income Tax	Book Value of Asset at End of Year
1	$18.18	$9.09	$18.18	$ 9.09	$81.82
2	16.36	8.18	34.54	17.27	65.46
3	14.55	7.28	49.09	24.55	50.91
4	12.73	6.36	61.82	30.91	38.18
5	10.91	5.46	72.73	36.37	27.27
6	9.09	4.54	81.82	40.91	18.18
7	7.27	3.64	89.09	44.55	10.91
8	5.45	2.72	94.54	47.27	5.46
9	3.64	1.82	98.18	49.09	1.82
10	1.82	.91	100.00	50.00	0

their useful lives, the percentage to be applied to the declining balance can be adjusted so as to reduce the book value to approximately its scrap value at the end of the asset's estimated useful life. The effect of using the two methods of calculating depreciation can be seen in Table 3-1. At the end of five years, the straight line method has charged off fifty per cent of the original cost of the asset to depreciation expense, while the declining balance method has charged two thirds off the original cost during the same period. At the end of ten years, the straight line method has charged off to depreciation expenses the full cost of the asset, while the declining balance method has charged off 89 per cent of the asset's original value. If the scrap value of the asset is estimated to be approximately one tenth of its original cost at the end of ten years, the declining balance method, as used in this illustration, can usefully be applied. If the scrap value of the asset in Table 3-1 is estimated at the end of ten years to be one tenth of its original value, the rate of depreciation under the straight line method to be charged each year should be 9 per cent rather than 10 per cent of the original cost. This would leave a book value of one tenth the original value at the end of ten years.

Sum-of-the-Years' Digits The major criticism of the fixed percentage of the declining balance method is that regardless of the number of years a rate of depreciation is applied to the declining balance, a balance always remains. The chief attraction of this method, however, is that it charges a higher amount to depreciation expense during the early years of life of the asset. The sum-of-the-years' digits method provides higher depreciation charges during the early life of the asset and, like the straight line method, depreciates the entire value of the asset at the end of the depreciation period. The mechanics of this method are simple. The number of years of estimated useful life of the asset is added together to form the denominator of the fraction used in determining the depreciation to be charged each year. For example, if the estimated useful life of the asset is five years, the denominator is $1+2+3+4+5$, which equals 15. The numerator of the this fraction is the number of years of useful life remaining at the beginning of each year. If the useful life of the asset is five years, the numerator of the fraction for the first year is five. The depreciation charge for the first year, therefore, would be $\frac{5}{15}$ or $\frac{1}{3}$ of the original value of the asset. The depreciation charge for the second year would be $\frac{4}{15}$ of the original cost of the asset, for the third year $\frac{3}{15}$, and so on. In the illustration of this method in Table 3-1, the useful life of the asset is estimated at ten years. The denominator in this case is the sum of the digits one through ten, which equals fifty-five. The depreciation charge for the first year is calculated by multiplying the fraction $\frac{10}{55}$ by the original value of the asset. The charge for the second year is $\frac{9}{55}$ times the original value of the asset, for the third year $\frac{8}{55}$ times the original value of the asset, and so on. The depreciation charge for the last year is $\frac{1}{55}$ multiplied by the original value of the asset.

Other Methods In addition to the methods of determining depreciation discussed above, other methods are occasionally used. Three of these deserve mention: the compound interest method, depreciation based on use, and depreciation charges contingent upon earnings.

If an asset costs $100,000 and is expected to be replaced at the end of twenty years at a cost of $100,000, a sum of money can be withdrawn from earnings each year, invested at 5 per cent or some other rate of interest, and accumulated to equal $100,000 at the end of twenty years. Annuity tables are available which will give the sum of money that must be withdrawn each year and invested at 5 per cent, for example, to equal $100,000 at the end of twenty years. The amount so determined is the yearly depreciation expense for the asset. In this example, the amount that must be set aside each year is $3,024.50. This amount invested each year at 5 per cent will at the end of twenty years equal $100,000. This method of calculating depreciation results in a smaller annual charge than the straight line method, which ignores the earning value of the amount allocated each year to depreciation expense. Although this method is logical in that it assumes that the amount of depreciation expense deducted from income will be put to work to earn money for the company, it is not a method which finds much favor, chiefly because the annual depreciation expense is lower than it is for the methods discussed above.

During World War II, some equipment was put to use around the clock. Understandably, such equipment wore out in a much shorter period than had similar equipment that had previously been used only during daylight hours. In such a situation it was more logical to base depreciation charges on use than on the number of years the equipment was in the factory. There was some reluctance on the part of the Bureau of Internal Revenue to accept depreciation charges based on use during World War II, unless the more rapid deterioration of equipment based on accelerated use could be supported by strong evidence. Since 1954, depreciation charges based on use have in most instances been accepted by the Bureau of Internal Revenue. There are two bases on which use can be applied in determining depreciation expense. One is in terms of the number of hours that a machine is in use, and the other is in terms of the number of units produced by the machine. For example, if a machine costs $2,400 and has an expected life of 8,000 hours of use, the depreciation cost per hour would be 30¢ ($2,400 divided by 8,000 hours). If the machine were used for 3,000 hours during one year, the depreciation cost charged to the machine would be $900. If, on the other hand, the depreciation charge for the above machine were determined on the basis of the number of units produced by the machine, the useful life in terms of units produced would have to be determined. If it were estimated that the machine could produce 12,000 units before replacement, the depreciation charge per unit of production would be 20¢. In this case, if the machine produced 4,000 units in one year, the depreciation charge for the year would be $800. If the item to be depreciated is a vehicle, its annual mileage sometimes serves as the basis for calculating depreciation charges.

If depreciation charges are based on use, the charges tend to be low during periods of low business activity and higher during periods of improved business conditions. Depreciation charges calculated on the basis of use, therefore, help to stabilize the earnings pattern of a company, since earnings usually are low during slow business periods and high during periods of intensive business activity. In those companies where depreciation expense is a large element of cost, depreciation charges are sometimes manipulated for the purpose of stabilizing the earnings pattern of the company. Depreciation expense is sometimes calculated on the basis of a certain percentage of sales per month or per year. In other cases, depreciation expense is calculated as a certain percentage of profits before taxes. In a few cases, the calculation of depreciation charges for a company is entirely arbitrary, having no relationship to time, use, sales, or anything else. Where depreciation charges are calculated on an entirely arbitrary basis, the explanation in most cases is the desire on the part of the directors to overstate profits or understate losses in times of recession and to understate profits in times of prosperity. During the depression of the 1930's, arbitrary methods of determining depreciation were sometimes used in calculating net profits reported to stockholders, while more orthodox methods of calculating depreciation were used for income tax purposes. In some companies, a method of calculating depreciation is used which has the appearance of being arbitrary but actually has a logical basis. This is the calculation of depreciation on the basis of inspection of machinery and equipment by engineers, who estimate the amount of wear suffered by each piece of equipment during the year. The cost of this estimated wear then becomes the basis for determining depreciation expenses.

Depletion   Although depreciation and depletion charges may appear to be similar, they are fundamentally different. Depreciation represents the wearing out of an asset in use—deterioration through use and also through the passage of time. Depletion represents the consumption of an asset such as coal, oil, gravel, and other natural resources. Depletion does not reflect any deterioration in the asset through the passage of time. As a matter of fact, the assets that are subject to depletion are those that are unaffected by time. Coal and oil, for example, remain in the ground for millions of years before they are brought to the surface, and any delay of a few years in their extraction does not affect the value of the resource. If a machine is not used, it continues to depreciate as time passes, unless it is stored in such a way as to make it secure from the deteriorating effects of weather. If extraction of coal from a coal mine ceases, the coal remaining in the ground is not subject to deterioration; therefore, no depletion results.

Since depletion accounts for the rate of use of "wasting assets" (those assets that are physically transformed into salable products) of the corporation, the failure to account for depletion overstates the income of the corporation. The logical method of calculating depletion involves the following three steps: the calculation of the cost of acquisition or estimate of the total value of the assets to be depleted; the calculation of the cost per barrel, ton, or other unit of measurement; and the multiplication of the cost per unit by the number of units extracted during the year or other accounting period. If a coal mine is purchased at a cost of $8 million, and the quantity of coal recoverable is estimated at 10 million tons, the cost of depletion per ton is 80¢. If 200,000 tons of coal are extracted from a mine during the year, the charge for depletion amounts to $160,000. If the coal-bearing land is undeveloped, to the cost of acquiring the land may be added the cost of drilling test holes to determine the extent and thickness of the coal seams, the cost of cutting mine shafts, and other development expenses that may have to be incurred before the coal can be extracted. Furthermore, the estimate of the amount of coal in the ground may have to be revised upward as additional seams of coal are discovered underground, or revised downward if later estimates indicate that the original survey overstated the amount of coal that could be recovered profitably. It is frequently very difficult to determine the amount of a natural resource that can ultimately be recovered from an area of land. Changes in technology have made profitable some mineral-bearing land once considered of little value, as new technological processes have been applied. Land containing iron ore with a relatively low content of iron, once considered worthless, is now being exploited for the production of iron ore. Mechanical methods of mining coal have made profitable again mines once considered "played out." The technology of drilling for oil and gas has permitted profitable extraction of these minerals from wells 15,000 to 20,000 feet deep and deeper. It is obviously difficult at the time of acquisition of the property to estimate the total amount of minerals that might ultimately be recovered.

Nevertheless, this is the logical basis on which to calculate depletion costs.

Although some companies determine depletion costs on the basis of computations explained above, most companies in the extractive industries calculate depletion on the basis of gross income. The Federal Internal Revenue Code permits annual depletion charges ranging from 5 per cent of gross annual income for sand and gravel, 10 per cent for coal, and 27.5 per cent for petroleum and natural gas. The amount that can be charged to depletion costs may not exceed 50 per cent of the net income from the coal mine, gas well, or other property as calculated prior to deducting the depletion charge.

Because the charge for depletion based on a percentage of gross income in most cases results in a higher amount than the charge for depletion based on the number of units extracted from the estimated total available for extraction, determining depletion charges on the basis of gross income has proved to be popular. The percentage of gross income method bears no relation to the number of units extracted or to the cost per unit of extraction. Depreciation expense, regardless of the method used, cannot be charged to income after the asset has been fully depreciated. Depletion, on the other hand, calculated as a percentage of gross income can, under the Internal Revenue Code, continue to be charged to income long after the cost of acquisition or the development of the property has been fully recovered. Depletion charges can continue to be taken indefinitely, with all the advantages in reducing income taxes which depletion allowances measured as percentage of gross income permits. The poor logic of this method of computing depletion is attacked by a number of authorities. Concerning this, Dewing says:

> Any method of computing depletion as a percentage of income, rather than as a unit cost deduction from the capital assets, is illogical. The income tax authorities have, however, permitted its computation on the basis of the annual income of the corporation; and the entirely erroneous assumption has become current that depletion is a deduction from income that varies in amount in accordance with the amount of income.[1]

At the end of the Korean War in 1953, considerable pressure was exerted on Congress to reduce the tax on business income. At the same time, Congress was reluctant to reduce taxes in view of the continued high level of federal spending. These conflicting pressures resulted in the 1954 Federal Income Tax Code which retained the 52 per cent tax rate on corporation income, but permitted depreciation charges to be based on either the fixed percentage of the declining balance method or the sum-of-the-years' digits method, in addition to the straight line method that had been required previously. (The effects of the three methods of depreciation on the tax liability of a corporation are shown in Table 3-1.) The fixed percentage of the declining balance method provides a greater reduction in

---

[1] Arthur Stone Dewing, *The Financial Policy of Corporations*, The Ronald Press Company, New York, 1953, p. 557.

the annual income tax during the first four years as compared with the straight line method, and a smaller reduction in income tax liability during the balance of the ten-year period compared to the straight line method. The sum-of-the-years' digits method also provides a greater reduction in the income tax each year during the first five years than the straight line method, and a smaller reduction than the straight line method during the asset's last five years of life.

From the standpoint of reducing the income tax burden of the corporation, the sum-of-the-years' digits method in determining depreciation is preferred in this instance over the fixed percentage of the declining balance method, because it provides a larger reduction in the income tax liability during the first five years and a larger cumulative reduction in the income tax during the ten-year life of the asset than does the fixed percentage of the declining balance method. In Table 3-1 it is assumed that there is no change in the income tax rate on corporation income during the life of the asset.

Since a change in accounting which increases depreciation allowances will reduce net income, some corporations have prepared two different income statements. One, using the traditional straight line method, is prepared for distribution to the stockholders of the company. The other, using the sum-of-the-years' digits method or the fixed percentage of the declining balance method is used in determining income for tax purposes. A study made in 1961 indicated that 87 per cent of corporations continued to use the straight line method exclusively in determining depreciation, even through the 1954 Income Tax Code permitted depreciation expense to be calculated on the fixed percentage of declining balance method or the sum-of-the-years' digits method.[2] The preparation of two income statements using different depreciation calculations is much less common now than it was shortly after 1954. Most companies now use the same income statement for distribution to the stockholders that is prepared for the tax collector. The statement for the stockholders, however, may be a summarized version of the one prepared for reporting taxable income.

In 1960 the Federal Treasury asked 3,300 corporations for information about their current depreciation methods and their suggestions on changes in the tax laws regarding depreciation. The answers from most corporations indicated a desire for greater freedom from federal tax regulations in determining depreciation expense. In their replies corporation executives particularly criticized the federal schedule of "useful lives" of the various assets used by business, which in nearly all cases were based on an estimate of the physical life of the machinery, buildings, or other assets. Textile cards, for example, were required by tax regulations to be depreciated over a period of forty years, textile blending machines thirty years, and textile

2 Sherwood W. Newton, "The 1962 Depreciation Reform," *Kansas Business Review*. January 1963, p. 3. Those continuing the use of the straight line method appeared to be mostly small companies.

looms twenty-five years. Many corporation executives felt that one reason for the accelerating industrial growth in the western European nations during the latter part of the 1950's was the rapid rate at which assets could be depreciated in computing income tax liabilities. In Italy and Sweden, for example, machinery and equipment could be written off in five years regardless of the physical life of the asset. It was almost unanimously argued by industry spokesmen that modernization and industrial development in the United States would be encouraged if the federal income tax laws regarding depreciation were changed to permit assets to be depreciated over a shorter period of life.

The Revenue Act of 1962 and the regulations of the Treasury Department issued in that year simplified the determination of the minimum life over which an asset could be depreciated and reduced the number of years over which depreciable assets could be written off. Prior to 1962 the assets in each industry were divided into several hundred classes each of which had a minimum depreciable life for tax purposes. In the chemical industry, there were 201 asset classifications, each of which had an assigned life for depreciation purposes. The equipment used by manufacturers of ice cream included 111 separate items, ranging from a four-year life for ice cream cans to a twenty-five year life for cast iron flavoring kettles. The depreciation classifications published by the Treasury Department in 1962 set up seventy-five broad classifications of assets for all industry, rather than a hundred or more different classes for each of the items used by a company. The assets owned by a business in the 1962 depreciation schedule could be distributed over four or five classes. All the production machinery for each industry generally fell into one class for that industry. Items used by most industries, such as trucks and automobiles, were placed in a single classification, and such equipment as office machines and furniture was similarly grouped together into one classification. More important

Assets	Former Depreciable Life (years)	Depreciable Life 1962 Code (years)
Office equipment	15	10
Water transport equipment	30-60	18
Electrical equipment	15	8
Pulp and paper machinery	17-28	16
Printing and publishing equipment	10-25	11
Rubber processing machinery	17	14
Shipbuilding machinery	20-25	12
Automobiles	3-5	3
Petroleum drilling equipment	16	6
Iron and steel manufacturing equipment	25	18
Nonferrous metal manufacturing equipment	17-30	14
Saw mills	20-25	10

was the shortening in the life of assets in the broad classes, permitting a considerable increase in depreciation expense charged to gross income. Corporations could recover the cost of machinery, equipment, and other assets much more quickly than was the case prior to 1962; they could also reduce their tax payments as a result of the larger depreciation allowances permitted. The list above gives some examples of the reduced period of time over which assets could be written off through depreciation allowances. The effect of the reclassification of items into seventy-five broad groups and the average reduction in the minimum life over which the asset may be depreciated increases the depreciation expense which may be charged to gross income and, therefore, reduces the tax liability of corporations.

PRICE INFLATION AND DEPRECIATION

It is frequently suggested, as was noted earlier in the chapter, that the base on which depreciation charges are calculated should be the replacement cost of the asset rather than the acquisition cost, particularly if the replacement cost is higher. This raises the question of the fundamental nature of depreciation charges. If the depreciation charges are accompanied by the building up of reserves out of which the asset is to be replaced, the reserve can be easily built up to the point where it equals the original cost of the asset but is still below the amount necessary to replace it. Accountants have generally considered that the purpose of the depreciation charge is to amortize the cost of the asset over the period of its estimated useful life. They consider the charge for depreciation as a recognition of the gradual consumption of the asset in the process of business operations.

It may be argued, however, that during a period of inflation of prices the dollar volume of gross income rises even if there is no increase in the physical quantity of goods produced, and the costs of doing business go up even if there is no increase in the number of units produced. Since in a period of rising prices, labor, materials, and most other business costs rise, it is logical to assume that the value of depreciable assets increases also; and depreciation charges should therefore be raised to reflect this increase in asset value. It follows that if higher depreciation charges are not included among the costs of doing business during a period of rising prices, the net income of the company will be overstated. If all net earnings are paid out in dividends, the overstatement of corporate income resulting from using depreciation charges based on original cost rather than replacement value has the effect of distributing to the owners not only income in the form of dividends but part of the capital of the company as well. Conversely, in a period of declining prices depreciation charges based on original cost understate net income. Therefore, charges should be reduced to reflect the declining value of assets and their lower replacement price. During the depression of the 1930's, some corporations revalued their assets at a lower figure than during the period before 1930 and reduced their depreciation charges to reflect the reduction in the value of the assets. The result was to increase the net profit reported by the corporations.

Although accountants have endorsed the practice of carrying depreciating assets on the books of the corporation at their original acquisition value, they recognize that an adjustment must be made for rising replacement costs in a period of inflation. An annual appropriation or earmarking of part of the surplus account as a reserve for replacement of assets has the same result as an increase in depreciation allowances. An adjustment in the surplus account to take into consideration rising replacement cost does not affect the income statement. One attraction of the practice of increasing the value of assets on the books of the corporation during the period of rising prices, and raising the depreciation charges accordingly, is that it leads to a lower reported net income subject to income taxes. The depreciation regulations of the Bureau of Internal Revenue, however, require that original acquisition costs be used as the basis for calculating depreciation. Yet, if the inflation is a gradual one, the shorter life on which depreciation is charged (that is permitted under the tax code of 1962) probably has the effect of reducing reported income for tax purposes to a greater degree than would the alternative of basing depreciation on replacement costs and using a longer life to determine annual depreciation charges.

OBSOLESCENCE

The distinction between obsolescence and depreciation is that the latter is a physical deterioration of an asset while the former is a loss in value caused by technological change. Obsolescence has been defined by the United States Internal Revenue Service as follows: "Obsolescence is that which is brought about by the progress of the arts and sciences, changed economic conditions, legislation or otherwise, whereby it can be predicted with reasonable accuracy that property used in the trade or business will be useless at a definite future date prior to the expiration of the normal useful life of the property." A machine may become obsolete because a more efficient model has been invented. Obsolescence in the form of styling changes may make the value of a passenger car decline more rapidly than it would from use alone. Assets may become obsolete as a result of legislation as were whiskey stills and brewery equipment with the passage of the Eighteenth Amendment.

In a dynamic economy, obsolescence is present in varying degrees in nearly every industry. In the early period of development of an industry, assets tend to become obsolete at a particularly rapid rate. Following World War II, for example, television, electronic computers, and airplane manufacture were characterized by a rapid rate of development and consequently by a high degree of obsolescence. However, in any industry, regardless of its age, technological change may make existing facilities obsolete. The change from coal-burning to diesel locomotives induced the directors of many railroads to scrap usable steam engines before they were worn out and to replace them with the more efficient diesel locomotives. The development of jet airplanes has made propeller-driven airplanes obsolete on most airlines, even though the propeller-driven airplanes were capable of several additional years of flight. In some industries, obsolescence is predictable. In the American automobile industry, for example, the annual styling change in passenger cars results from an industry policy to make passenger cars of previous years outdated as soon as current year models are introduced. This policy makes some of the tools and dies that shape the fenders and other body contours of passenger cars obsolete after only one year's use. In the airline industry, the development of new airplane designs and new engines for military use is followed in a predictable pattern by the application of these designs to passenger and cargo aircraft. In most industries, however, the rate of future technological change cannot be measured with any degree of accuracy. In such industries the time when equipment now in use will become obsolete can only be guessed.

There is considerable difference of opinion as to how obsolescence should be treated in financial computations. It is recognized by all that the causes of obsolescence and depreciation are different, and that depreciation is an expense which must be included in computing net income. But should a charge for obsolescence be recognized in financial statements as a cost separate from depreciation? Should depreciation charges be increased to include an estimate for obsolescence? Or should obsolescence be recognized by earmarking a portion of the surplus as a reserve for obsolescence? Companies usually do not make a calculation for obsolescence as a cost of doing business in computing company income. Where obsolescence is recognized as a cost in the accounts of a company, it is usually lumped together with depreciation in an account called obsolescence and depreciation. In the comparatively rare instances where obsolescence is recognized as an expense separate from depreciation, the expense is handled in the same manner as depreciation. An account for obsolescence expense is debited with the estimated cost of obsolescence, and an account labeled allowance for obsolescence is credited. The allowance for obsolescence is generally shown on the balance sheet, if it is shown at all, as a deduction from the particular fixed asset subject to obsolescence. Since obsolescence and depreciation are caused by different factors, it is logical to separate them in the accounts of a company. Businessmen generally agree, however, that obsolescence is more difficult to predict than depreciation. The difficulty of prediction is usually the cause they give for not including obsolescence as a cost of doing business or for lumping it with more generous depreciation charges in their accounts.

Because federal tax officials do not recognize obsolescence as a legitimate deduction from gross income in computing net income subject to taxes, there is no tax advantage to be obtained in reporting obsolescence as an expense. Yet by implication, obsolescence is recognized in the shorter life permitted under the tax law of 1962 in depreciating many classes of assets. Companies may list charges for depreciation and for obsolescence separately, if they wish. As far as a determination of the net income of a corporation subject to income taxes is concerned, it matters not whether separate accounts are carried for depreciation and for obsolescence, as long as the total of the two does not exceed the permitted rate of depreciation in the 1962 tax law.

DEPRECIATION AS A SOURCE OF FUNDS

Depreciation is often spoken of as a source of funds. Strictly speaking, it is not. Accounting for depreciation is merely a bookkeeping transaction having the effect of reducing the net income and of reducing net asset value. Expenditure for such expense items as wages and purchase of material are a drain on cash. Charges for depreciation, on the other hand, are not. The cash that is conserved as a result of including depreciation charges in the income statement is available for whatever business use the company management chooses. The source of the funds made available through depreciation charges is the receipt of cash from sales rather than from depreciation. Table 3-2 illustrates this point. As the table shows, if no depreciation charge is made in the income statement, the amount of the net income available for distribution to the owners and the amount of cash remaining are identical. If the net income were distributed to the owners in the form of cash dividends, the fixed assets would gradually be liquidated in cash payments to the owners. If depreciation charges are included in the income statement, the amount of net income before income taxes is lowered by the amount of depreciation charges made, and is also lower after income taxes are paid. The amount of income available for distribution to the owners, if depreciation charges are made, is $1,040,000. If all this were distributed in cash dividends to the owners, unexpended cash generated from sales in the amount of $1 million, equal to the amount of depreciation expense, would remain. Since depreciation charges do not constitute expenses that are paid in cash, they have the effect of making cash available for company use rather than for distribution to the owners. If there is no legitimate business use for the cash retained as a result of including depreciation charges as an expense, the money can be used for investment.

Since depreciation charges have the effect of retaining part of the cash generated by sales, depreciation charges and other noncash expenses may be added to net income after taxes to indicate the amount of cash flow available to the company in each accounting period. Any increase in depreciation expenses reduces the stated net income and so decreases the income tax liability of the corporation. An increase in depreciation expense, however, does not reduce the cash flow to the corporation. It is most likely to increase the amount of cash flow, because increased depre-

TABLE 3-2. EFFECT ON CASH OF TAKING DEPRECIATION

	No Depreciation Taken		Depreciation Taken	
	Income Statement	Cash Receipts from Sales and Cash Drain from Expenses	Income Statement	Cash Receipts from Sales and Cash Drain from Expenses
Sales	$10,000,000	$10,000,000	$10,000,000	$10,000,000
Operating and other costs	7,000,000	7,000,000	7,000,000	7,000,000
Depreciation expense	—	—	1,000,000	—
Income before income taxes	3,000,000	3,000,000	2,000,000	3,000,000
Income taxes (48%)	1,440,000	1,440,000	960,000	960,000
Net income	1,560,000		$1,040,000	
Cash available		$ 1,560,000		$ 2,040,000

ciation expense reduces the cash payment of income taxes by the corporation. Any federal legislation that permits larger depreciation expenses, such as the Revenue Codes of 1954 and 1962, has the effect of both reducing net income reported and increasing the cash flow. The increase in depreciation allowances and the increase in cash flow to corporations from 1947 to 1962 is shown in Fig. 3-1.

Although depreciation charges conserve cash by reducing the income tax liability of the corporation and by reporting a lower net income out of

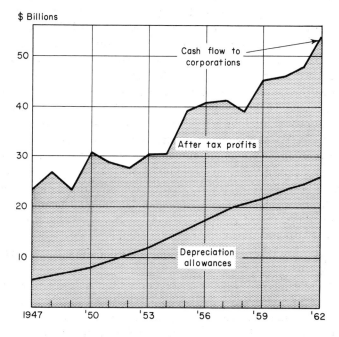

Fig. 3-1 *Rising flow of cash to corporations.* (*Source:* U. S. Department of Commerce)

which dividends may be declared, care must be used in putting the cash to work. The amount of cash conserved by depreciation charges can be viewed as a liquidation of depreciable assets by transforming them into cash. Eventually each capital asset will gradually be turned into cash. Whatever the use made of the cash retained as a result of charging depreciation expense, businessmen must recognize the need for replacement of the depreciating assets. This does not mean that cash must be accumulated year after year to purchase replacement for worn-out assets. It does mean that each company must plan for the replacement of depreciating assets. This can be accomplished, for example, by reducing the indebtedness of the corporation to enable it to borrow money on better terms when necessary to replace assets no longer of use to the company.

AMORTIZATION

Businesses often have assets of an intangible nature that are of considerable value to the company. These include patents, copyrights, licenses, leaseholds, trademarks, and goodwill. Assets of this nature that have a limited life should be gradually charged off to the expenses of doing business. A patent, for example, has a life of seventeen years in the United States. The full value of the patent should be charged off to business expense during this period. Although the bookkeeping entries are similar to those involving depreciation of tangible assets, such as machinery and equipment, the charging off of intangible assets is called amortization. If a patent has been purchased at a price of $1 million and has fifteen years of life left to run at the time of purchase, the amortization cost charged to income each year should be $66,666.67. If a valuable invention is developed in the laboratory of a company and the patent issued on the invention, the value of the patent may be difficult to determine. If the laboratory expenses attributable to the invention can be determined, such costs may be taken as the value of the patent. In many cases, however, the scientists and technicians in the laboratory will be engaged in a number of different projects, and the allocation of laboratory costs to each project may be a mere matter of conjecture. Furthermore, some of the most revolutionary laboratory discoveries are the result of accidents or chance, and the value of the patents given to such discoveries is a matter of guess work. It may be the policy of a company to assign a purely nominal value, such as $1, in such cases. If a nominal value is assigned, it need not be amortized.

A copyright has a life of twenty-eight years, with the privilege of extending the copyright for an additional twenty-eight years. A copyright awarded to a company is usually carried on the books at a nominal figure, and is not amortized. However, if the copyright is purchased, the purchase price is generally amortized over the remaining life of the copyright in the same manner as the amortization of a patent right. The purchase price of the copyright may be amortized over the full remaining life of the copyright including the extension of twenty-eight years. In many cases, however, it will be obvious that the value of the copyright will approach zero long before its legal life expires. A song, a novel, or a play may enjoy considerable popularity in the year it is introduced, and may be all but forgotten three years later. If a value has been assigned to such an item of more than a nominal figure, it would be prudent to amortize the dollar figure over the years that it is expected to produce revenue for the company. A franchise or a leasehold usually generates income throughout its life. In such a case, it would be reasonable to amortize the value of the franchise or leasehold over its full life.

Amortization is usually calculated on a straight line basis. Amortization expense, like depreciation, is charged to income. Unlike depreciation, however, an amortization reserve is generally not set up as a deduction from the asset value of the item being amortized. Rather, the book value of the asset is reduced each year by the amount of the amortization expense charged against the asset for the year.

A trademark, unlike a patent or a copyright, does not have a life limited by law. Trademarks, therefore, are not amortized. In any case, the trademarks are almost always carried on the books of the corporation at a nominal figure of $1, and for that reason as well are not subject to amortization. Goodwill is similar to a trademark in enjoying a life that is not limited by law. If goodwill has been purchased, it is usually carried on the books of the company at the cost of acquisition. Goodwill, like land, does not necessairly decline in value through the passage of time, although it may decline due to competitive forces. If goodwill is purchased, conservative accounting dictates that its purchase price be amortized over a reasonable number of years. In such cases the number of years chosen for the amortization of goodwill is generally arbitrary. The expenses of organization of a corporation may be carried as an asset on the first balance sheet of the new company. Since organizational expenses are not an asset in the usual sense of the word, sound accounting requires their elimination from the balance sheet as quickly as possible. Prior to 1954 the amortization of organizational expenses could be charged against income to reduce the income tax liability of the corporation only if the charter of the corporation specified a limited life for the company. Such expenses incurred after 1954, however, may be charged against income in computing the income tax of the corporation, provided that the organizational expenses are amortized over a period of not less than five years.

Questions

1. What is the purpose of accounting for depreciation?
2. Explain how the allowance for depreciation constitutes a source of funds for a company.
3. How does obsolescence differ from depreciation?
4. What industries need to account for depletion?
5. Explain the purpose of amortization, indicating the types of assets to which it might be applied.
6. Explain and illustrate the following methods of calculating depreciation:
   (a) Straight line
   (b) Fixed percentage of declining balance
   (c) Compound interest
   (d) Sum-of-the-years' digits
   (e) Depreciation based upon use
   (f) Depreciation charges contingent upon earnings
7. How can the rate of depletion be calculated?
8. Explain the fact that depletion charges are based upon a percentage of gross income rather than on the basis of cost of acquisition or development divided by number of units extracted.
9. In general terms, what were the changes in accounting for depreciation introduced in the Revenue Act of 1962?

10. What problems are created in accounting for depreciation during periods of unstable prices? What can be done to meet these problems?
11. Why is obsolescence more rapid in some industries than in others?
12. How is obsolescence treated in those companies that account for obsolescence?
13. Why are patents and copyrights often listed at $1 on the books of a company?
14. To what assets are amortization charges applicable? What is the purpose of amortization?
15. How does accounting for trademarks and goodwill differ from accounting for organizational expenses?

Selected Readings

Caplin, Mortimer M. (U.S. Commissioner of Internal Revenue), *New Depreciation Guide Lines—Realistic and Flexible,* Management Aids for Small Manufacturers, Small Business Administration, Washington, D.C., November 1962.
Jensen, Carl P. N., *Depreciation Costs—Don't Overlook Them,* Small Marketers Aids, Small Business Administration, Washington, D.C., June 1961.
Morrisey, E. C., *The Many Sides of Depreciation,* Amos Tuck School of Business Administration, Dartmouth College, Hanover, N. H., 1960.
Newton, Sherwood W., "The 1962 Depreciation Reform," *Kansas Business Review,* University of Kansas, January 1963.

The following two articles present arguments in favor of liberalized tax treatment of depreciation:
"Needy Industries Get Tax Break," *Business Week,* October 14, 1961, p. 32.
"Let's Not Eat the Goose that Lays the Golden Eggs," *Business Week,* July 21, 1962, pp. 130B-130C.

The following article presents arguments attacking liberalized tax treatment of depreciation:
"Exploding the Profit Squeeze Myth," *AFL-CIO American Federationist,* June 1962, pp. 1-8.

4

Budgeting and the Management of Cash

THE CIRCULAR FLOW OF CURRENT ASSETS

ONE OF THE characteristics of current assets is that they are in a state of continual change. A manufacturing business, for example, changes its cash into raw materials, supplies, and other elements needed for production, and a retailer changes cash into inventory and inventory back into cash. Whenever there is a decrease in an asset account or an increase in a liability account, there tends to be an increase in spendable funds; and an increase in an asset account or a decrease in a liability account usually results in a decrease in spendable funds. Stated in another way, increases in liabilities are sources of funds, and increases in assets are uses of funds. In some instances an increase in liabilities will increase the asset cash, as when a company borrows money from a bank. In other cases an increase in liabilities is the source of an increase in some other asset, as when a company purchases supplies for which payment may be made later. In the first instance the cash account is immediately involved. In the second instance the cash account is not involved when the purchase is transacted, but later when cash is used to liquidate the liability by payment to the supplier.

During the production process raw materials are changed into goods in process of manufacture, with the goods in process of manufacture in turn becoming finished goods. The inventory of finished goods then becomes accounts receivable. The collection of accounts receivable transforms this asset into cash. Thus there is a cycle of change in the form of current assets. The rapidity of change depends upon what is manufactured, the methods of manufacture, and the season of the year. For some businesses the complete cycle starting and ending with cash will require only a few days; at the other extreme are those processes of manufacture that require several years. If aging is necessary in transforming raw materials into finished products, as happens with some beverages and cheeses, the cycle of current assets will last for months or years. In any case, the cycle (see Fig. 4-1) is present in virtually every business.

It is an art to manage assets in such a way that there is a smooth flow from one stage to another over a period of time. At any moment there should be some current assets in the forms of cash, raw materials, goods in process, finished goods inventory, and accounts receivable. In other words, at any

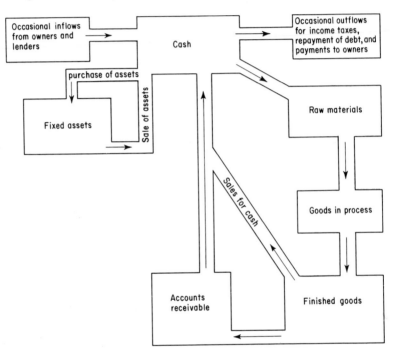

Fig. 4-1   *Circular flow of current assets.*

one time current assets should be found in all stages of the cycle. If there is not the smooth circuit flow of assets, there will be shortages of some current assets and overabundance of others, both being inefficient for company operations. If anything can be done to increase the rate of circuit flow of current assets, without sacrificing quality of production or service to customers, it will help to increase the company's income.

The current assets cannot of themselves be transformed from one form to another; the fixed assets must be applied to the current assets. In the process of applying fixed assets to current assets, the fixed assets are gradually used up. Machinery, buildings, and other assets, except for land, are slowly consumed in the process of adding value to the current assets. In the successful management of current assets, business operations will generate a larger amount of cash than was present at the beginning of the circuit. This is essential to profitable business. It is necessary to offset the drain on cash that is found in any enterprise. The circuit flow of current assets must generate sufficient cash to purchase additional raw materails to continue the cycle and to pay for all the other expenses of business operations.

THE PURPOSE OF BUDGETING

Planning for the Future   If current assets are to form the smooth circuit flow, there must be close coordination between all the processes of production and distribution. The chief financial officer shares in this responsibility. As the cycle progresses, there is considerable variety in the demand for cash and in the receipt of cash. It is essential to predict as accurately as possible the future variations in this demand so that the company's assets and its work force are used most efficiently. The more accurately the chief financial officer is able to determine when the cash needs of the company will be below the cash resources and when the cash will be in excess of current needs, the better he will be able to manage the cash accounts of the company and prevent them from becoming larger than necessary or—what is worse—insufficient to meet disbursement requirements. Therefore, he must provide a system for forecasting future cash needs and expected cash receipts.

The importance of budgeting for short-term funds applies equally to long-term funds. Planning for the purchase of long-term assets, the issuance and retirement of bonds and other long-term debts, the depreciation of buildings and machinery, and their replacement is as vital to the profitable operation of the firm as careful planning of the use of cash. To simplify financial administration, planning the flow of both long-term and short-term funds is undertaken separately. In this chapter, budgeting for short-term funds is treated; Chapter 19 deals with budgeting for long-term funds. It must be emphasized that short-term and long-term budgeting must each be carried out with due consideration for the other, so that the flow of funds planned in the capital budget will be coordinated with the flow planned in the cash budget.

Development of Performance Standards   Our economy is one of constant change. As the years pass, there are changes in prices, the degree and character of competition in an industry and between industries, the character and direction of government regulation, the level of taxes and the administration of tax laws, public tastes in consumer goods, and costs and methods of operation. Business is perhaps not as changeable as the weather, but certainly the course of business in the future appears to be just as hard to predict. Yet present decisions must be based on predictions of the future. Budgeting improves the quality of predictions by systematizing future planning.

Budgeting also helps in the development of performance standards for the company executives. The simplest means of measuring the standard of performance of a particular department or of the business as a whole is to compare it with a similar period in the past. If the sales for the current year are 10 per cent higher than they were for the previous year, it would appear that the sales manager and the sales department had improved their performance by 10 per cent. Such a conclusion would, however, not follow. Prices might have risen during the current year, and a rise in the dollar volume of sales might reflect no increase in the unit volume of items sold. General business activity might have risen, and the performance of the sales department may have been no better than the improvement in the economy as a whole, and might even have been less than what should have been expected in view of the increase in economic activity. If a sales budget for a year is prepared, it should reflect the calculations of management regarding the course of prices in the coming year, the expected rise or fall of general business activity, any change in incomes of customers buying the company's products, and any other factors that might revise the expectation of sales compared to the past. It is only the extent that the information on which the sales budget is based is accurate that the sales budget itself will be accurate. Using the budget to measure the performance of the sales department can improve the standards of managerial competence and departmental efficiency; what has been said about the sales department and the sales budget is also applicable to other departments and their budgets.

Coordinating Departmental Goals The forecast of sales is an important element in the forecast of receipts of cash. The forecast of the cost of raw materials and the cost and availability of labor is necessary in planning for the future prices of the company products. Changes in prices in the future will in turn affect the prediction of sales. The various departmental or subordinate budgets cannot be prepared without considering their effect on the budgets of other departments or divisions. One of the great advantages of the budgeting process is that it enforces a degree of coordinated planning. Although the preliminary preparation of departmental budgets is frequently undertaken prior to consultation with other departments, the approved budget for a particular department is prepared only after it is considered in the light of its effect on the other budgets and of other budgets on it. Budgeting thus makes department heads and the lower managerial echelons aware of the importance of the overall goals of the business and the necessity of planning individual actions so that together they will further the company goals.

Control of Internal Operations Once the series of budgets has been adopted for a company they serve as a constant guide to the operations of each of the phases of business activity. Once adopted, a budget serves as a very important control, analogous to a battle plan for an army. Once a battle plan has been adopted all the military units subject to the plan must make their unit orders conform to it. Similarly, once a budget has been adopted, the orders given by the executives and the departmental policies and decisions made during the budget period must conform to the budget.

A serious question arises with respect to the use of a budget as a means of controlling the activities of departments and workers: how rigidly should a budget be followed? One extreme position is that a budget be rigidly adhered to and that no decisions be taken which will alter the budget. At the other extreme is a policy which permits such frequent deviations that the budget is hardly of any value in guiding the activities of a business. To seek the compromise obviously needed, we can once again compare a budget to a battle plan. If no initiative whatsoever is given to unit commanders within the theater of military operations, those opportunities unexpectedly presenting themselves could not be exploited to the advantage of the army, because they would not have been foreseen at the time the battle plan was drawn up. In using a budget as a means of control of internal operations, a certain amount of latitude must be permitted. The range of individual decision should be stated clearly at the time the budget is adopted. If the budget is not viewed as a substitute for executive control, but rather as a means of implementing it in a more systematic manner, it can serve a useful purpose in the internal control of a company's activities.

In addition to the latitude permitted executives and workers in operating within the terms of a budget, a question must be answered regarding budget revisions during the budget period. Since it is impossible to predict the future with perfect accuracy, it is inevitable that the future will be somewhat different from our expectations. Should the budget be changed when the actual future proves to be different from that predicted? Again the extreme positions should be avoided. The budget should not be modified or changed to conform to relatively minor and unimportant differences between the predicted and the actual. On the other hand, drastic changes call for a modified budget. In this respect as in others, the budget should serve as a useful guide to executive judgment, but not as a substitute for it.

THE CASH BUDGET

The Importance of Budgeting for Cash   One of the most important budgets, and the principal one with which the chief financial officer is concerned, is the cash budget. This is essentially an estimate of the future receipts and disbursements of cash, and the future level of the cash account for each month, week, or other division of time. Specifically, the cash budget is prepared to provide the following information for the financial officer:

1. An estimate of the amount of cash expected to be received during each time division of the budget.
2. The estimated cash disbursements during each time division of the budget.
3. The estimated cash balance at the end of each time division of the budget.

4. The difference at the end of each time division between the amount of cash expected to be on hand and the amount considered to be "normal" or necessary.

5. A prediction of whether additional cash must be raised to bring the predicted cash balance up to the required level for each time division of the budget.

6. A prediction of when additional funds must be borrowed to bring up the level of the cash account and for how long the borrowed funds are needed.

7. A prediction as to when and in what amounts borrowed cash can be repaid out of expected cash receipts.

8. A comparison, as time passes during budgetary time divisions, of actual receipts and disbursements with projected receipts and disbursements, so that control of cash can be better managed.

With the information provided by the cash budget the financial officer can proceed to plan the borrowing necessary to bring the cash account up to the required levels during those periods when the budget predicts deficiencies in cash. It is never advisable either for an individual or a business to be in the position of having to borrow on short notice. A company in such a position does not have the maneuverability to raise the money needed on the best possible terms. Under such conditions bargaining with lenders would be akin to emergency negotiations, and the borrowing company would have to accept whatever terms were demanded by the lender. If the cash budget has been carefully prepared, the financial officer can anticipate the need for raising short-term funds, and can make arrangements with commerical banks or other sources of loans in an unhurried atmosphere more conducive to businesslike discussion.

In addition to permitting more careful deliberation, the cash budget also promotes greater accuracy in determining the length of time for which various amounts must be raised. It is not only inefficient but also costly if a company borrows money for a period either shorter or longer than necessary. Although the length of time that a loan is needed and the exact amount of money needed cannot be predicted perfectly, a cash budget permits a greater degree of accuracy than would be possible without it. Furthermore, the length of time for which a loan is needed will be an important factor in helping the financial officer decide from what sources the loan can most advantageously be raised.

The importance of the cash budget in aiding the financial officer to borrow money under circumstances most favorable to the company also helps him in handling the excess cash. If the cash budget guides the financial officer in predicting with reasonable accuracy the amount of excess cash generated by the operations of the company and the length of time that the cash will be available, he can most effectively invest it so that it will bring in additional income to the company. The amount of extra cash and the length of time available will obviously be of considerable importance in deciding the type of investment. The example of the cash budget in Table 4-1 shows how cash needs are estimated for a budget period of one year with subdivisions of one month. To aid in financial planning, an income statement and balance sheet for the coming year may be prepared, based on estimates of future sales, expenses, and changes in balance sheet accounts. Financial statements for future periods are called *pro forma* statements. It is important, however, to distinguish between the cash budget and the pro forma income statement. There are certain transactions included in a pro forma income statement that are not included in the cash budget and vice versa. Table 4-2 lists transactions included in the cash budget alone, the income statement alone, in both, or in neither.

The Preparation of a Cash Budget   In the preparation of a cash budget four different types of financial data are included:

1. Cash receipts and disbursements relating to the regular business operations of the company.
2. Transactions involving cash having to do with nonoperating items of the company, such as the receipt of cash as a result of interest payments to the company or payments of cash on interest owed by the company.
3. Cash received from the sale of capital assets.
4. Cash paid out for the purchase of capital assets and for those cash transactions resulting from any increase or decrease in the long-term indebtedness of the company or in the equity of the company.

The period for which a cash budget may be prepared varies from a month to a year, the most common being three months, six months, and a year. A decision must also be made as to the length and number of the budget-period divisions. The most common segment into which the cash budget is divided is one month, as it is done in Table 4-1. If the amount of the cash balance to be maintained is small relative to the dollar volume of transactions during the budget period, a division of the budget into weekly segments may be necessary to provide tighter control over the cash balance. In other words, if the business is to be operated "on a shoestring" with respect to the amount of cash maintained, it is necessary to keep very close check on the cash account. In these circumstances, dividing the cash budget into many small segments will be very useful. If, on the other hand, the reserves of cash on hand and in the bank are ample and if expected cash receipts and disbursements can be predicted with considerable accuracy and are expected to be fairly even throughout the year, such a division will serve no purpose.

The next preparatory step is the listing of items involving cash transactions during the coming budgetary period. Most of this information will be available from departmental budgets. Indeed, much of the work in

TABLE 4-1. SMITH AND DREXEL COMPANY: CASH BUDGET FOR YEAR ENDING DECEMBER 31, 1965

	Jan.	Feb.	March	April	May	June	July	Aug.	Sept.	Oct.	Nov.	Dec.
Cash balance (beginning of month)	$30,000	$43,000	$19,000	$10,000	$10,000	$10,000	$10,000	$10,000	$10,000	$10,000	$10,000	$10,000
Receipts from receivables	100,000	60,000	70,000	70,000	80,000	80,000	90,000	90,000	120,000	160,000	150,000	130,000
Total available cash	130,000	103,000	89,000	80,000	90,000	90,000	100,000	100,000	130,000	170,000	160,000	140,000
Less disbursements:												
Accounts payable	40,000	40,000	45,000	45,000	60,000	80,000	75,000	65,000	45,000	35,000	35,000	35,000
Direct labor	8,000	9,000	9,000	12,000	16,000	15,000	13,000	8,000	7,000	7,000	7,000	8,000
Other manufacturing expenses	12,000	13,000	13,000	18,000	24,000	22,000	19,000	14,000	10,000	10,000	11,000	12,000
Sales expenses	20,000	15,000	15,000	15,000	15,000	15,000	15,000	15,000	15,000	15,000	15,000	15,000
Administrative expenses	7,000	7,000	7,000	7,000	7,000	7,000	7,000	7,000	7,000	7,000	7,000	7,000
Additions to fixed assets				10,000	10,000	10,000						
Repayment of bank loans									36,000	86,000	75,000	29,000
Total disbursements	$87,000	$84,000	$89,000	$107,000	$132,000	$149,000	$129,000	$109,000	$120,000	$160,000	$150,000	$106,000
Cash shortage			10,000	27,000	42,000	59,000	29,000	9,000				
Bank loans to be obtained			10,000	37,000	52,000	69,000	39,000	19,000				
Cash balance (end of month)	$43,000	$19,000	$10,000	$10,000	$10,000	$10,000	$10,000	$10,000	$10,000	$10,000	$10,000	$34,000

TABLE 4-2. TRANSACTIONS INCLUDED IN OR EXCLUDED FROM
PRO FORMA INCOME STATEMENT AND CASH BUDGET

Anticipated Transactions	Included in Pro Forma Income Statement	Included in Cash Budget
Payment of current expenses	X	X
Cash sales	X	X
Payments received on accounts receivable		X
Prepayment of expenses charged to subsequent periods		X
Cash purchase of fixed assets		X
Purchase of fixed assets, payment in subsequent period		
Receipt of loan from bank		X
Payment of loan to bank		X
Sales on account, payment receivable in subsequent period	X	
Provision for income taxes, payment in subsequent period	X	
Depreciation expense	X	
Sale of fixed assets, payment receivable in subsequent period		

preparing the cash budget is simply the transferral of figures from other budgets. Generally, the first item to be listed in the cash budget is cash received from operations. In most businesses this is the sum expected from cash sales and collection of accounts and notes receivable. This figure depends, of course, upon the forecast of sales for the coming budgetary period. The estimate of future sales, probably the most important single estimate made by a business in the budgeting process, must be made with great care because of its extreme importance upon the entire budget.

Not only must the total sales for the coming complete budgetary period be predicted as accurately as possible, but the predicted sales must be divided for each division of the budgetary period, so that the expected receipts from cash sales and collection of receivables can be allocated according to the time divisions of the budgetary period. If the company sells only for cash, the cash arising from sales will be simpler to predict in preparing the cash budget. However, it will not be sufficient in most cases simply to forecast the sales for each time division of the budget. Most companies will have to estimate the dollar amount for returns and allowances to customers. If the company sells on a credit basis as well as for cash, an estimate must be made of the amount of sales for cash and those for credit. Sales that are made on credit require an estimate of the length of time that accounts will remain outstanding. Allowance in the cash budget must, of course, be made for the expected percentage of uncollectable accounts predicted by the credit manager of the company. Furthermore, most companies that sell on credit provide for cash discounts to those customers paying their accounts within ten days or some other period. The percentage of credit sales which will be paid by customers taking advantage of the cash discount must be estimated, because this will have a bearing on the cash receipts from accounts receivable.   The past record of credit customers in making payments is used to predict the receipts of cash on accounts receivable.

The receipt of cash from transactions other than those in the regular course of business are relatively rare.   Nevertheless, they must be included in the cash budget.   Receipts of interest and dividends on investments owned by the company, as well as rental income, can generally be estimated accurately both as to time and amount.   On the other hand, royalty payments on patents owned by the company and leased to others frequently cannot be accurately predicted, particularly where the amount of the royalty depends upon the number of units produced in each period by the companies licensed under the patent.   If a corporation controls a number of subsidiaries, it may also be difficult to predict accurately the timing and amount of cash transactions between the corporation and its subsidiaries.

If it is known that any capital assets of the company will be sold at the time the cash budget is being prepared, the expected receipt of cash should be included in the cash budget.   In many cases this type of transaction is rather difficult to predict.   While, for example, the budgeting for depreciation allowances for machinery is relatively easy and can be determined by standardized methods, the actual rate of wearing out and the need for replacement are a little more difficult to predict.   If a worn-out machine must be replaced and is traded in for a newer one, cash is not involved in the trade.   However, if a worn-out machine or any other asset is sold for cash, then the cash account is involved, and the transaction should be included in the cash budget.   In many businesses, however, the infrequent nature of such transactions and the irregularity with which they take place make it extremely difficult to predict the amount and timing of such cash receipts.

When the cash budget is prepared, estimates of the amount of borrowing required and changes in the equity accounts of the company are generally forecast.   As a matter of fact, the preparation of the cash budget aids in making these estimates more accurate.   The cash budget will, therefore, include the cash receipts from loans to be negotiated from banks and other sources of funds, any long-term loans to be made or bonds sold, any cash expected from the sale of stock or cash invested by the owners, and any other cash transactions involving financing during the budgetary period. The cash budget is often prepared before the amount of changes in the debts of the company and in the equity accounts is determined.   It will indicate the budgetary period for bank loans to be negotiated, bonds to be sold, or additional stock to be marketed.   Where this is done, the financial officer generally prepares a supplementary budget under the title "loan schedule" or "needed financing."

In the preparation of the cash budget the estimate of cash disbursements is of equal importance to the estimate of cash receipts.   The largest volume of cash payments will, of course, result from the operations of the company. The estimate of such cash payments will depend upon the estimate of sales, because most businesses attempt to gear their operations as closely as possible to sales. Generally, it can be said that the estimate of cash disbursements during the budgetary period can be made with greater accuracy than the estimates of cash receipts. For the most part, the company must make payments on wages, accounts payable, money borrowed, and cash purchases on definite dates. For purposes of analysis the cash disbursements included in the cash budget will be divided into the following categories:

1. Materials and supplies.
2. Wages.
3. Other manufacturing expenses.
4. Expenditures incurred to secure sales.
5. Expenditures for administration.
6. Expenditures covering nonoperating expenses.
7. Purchase of capital assets.
8. Payments to owners.
9. Payments to governmental agencies.

Materials and supplies. In most cases a close relationship exists between the purchase of a company's raw materials and supplies and the sales of its products. If the company decides to make its purchases of materials and supplies on a "hand to mouth" basis, the amounts purchased will be tied very closely to expected sales for the period. This practice, however, can be costly if operations are interrupted due to delays in the receipt of ordered materials. Most companies prefer to keep on hand a sufficient supply of raw materials and supplies to guard against any of these interruptions. It may also be company policy to make purchases whenever raw material prices are low. Whatever the purchasing policy of the company, the purchase of materials and supplies will be coordinated in greater or lesser degree with the production schedule of the company, and the production schedule in turn will be coordinated with the forecast of sales. It is very important for the company to take advantage of discounts allowed on early payments, which must then be provided for in the cash budget. If payment terms of 2/10, net 30 are offered by a supplier, the cost to the company in making payment of the full amount of the invoice at the end of thirty days rather than deducting 2 per cent from the invoice and paying in ten days is considerable (amounting to 36 per cent interest per annum). It is, therefore, usually advisable for the company to borrow from its bank, if necessary, in order to take advantage of such terms.

Wages. The calculation in the cash budget for the cash expended for wages and the dates that these expenditures must be made depends upon the character of the business. In manufacturing enterprises labor is paid either on a piecework or an hourly basis. The calculation for the cash expenditures for direct labor in production may be estimated by determining the amount of labor cost per unit of production multiplied by the number of units to be produced during each period of the budget. If salesmen are employed by the company, they may be paid in part or in whole on commissions based on the number or dollar volume of products sold. The commissions of the salesmen depend upon the estimate of sales for the period, and the cash disbursements to the salesmen are estimated on that basis. Cash payments for the labor of office workers and executives are usually made semimonthly or monthly. The expenditures are typically steady, and there is no particular problem in determining them in advance. If the divisions of the cash budget are made on a basis of months and if the laborers in a factory are paid on a weekly basis, the number of pay periods occurring each month will vary between four and five. In other instances, wages accrued during one month may become a cash disbursement during the following month. There will, therefore, often be a difference between the labor expense for a month and the expenditure of cash for wages during the same month. In addition to cash expenditures for wages, salaries, and commissions, provision must be made in the cash budget for overtime work, paid holidays and vacations, payment into the company pension fund, bonuses and other incentives. Finally, it is important to predict any changes in wage payments, officers' salaries, and fringe benefits having an effect on cash disbursements.

Other manufacturing expenses. In a manufacturing concern there is a variety of cash expenditures over and above the cost of materials and direct labor. They include those made for repairs, maintenance, light and power, heat, and insurance. The cash expenditures for such items will not usually coincide with the cost per month of these same items, because the cash expenditures will be made on a variety of bases. The cash expenditure for insurance, for example, is generally made in advance of the allocation of the cost of insurance to various units of manufacture and to various time periods. Insurance may be bought in advance for a three-year period, and is then charged to manufacturing expense over the time covered by the insurance, even though the expenditure of cash occurs only when the actual payment of the premium is made.

Expenditures incurred to secure sales. If a sales budget has been prepared by the sales department, it will include such items as an estimate of total sales for the coming year if that is the budgetary period, an estimate of salesmen's salaries and commissions, and an estimate of other expenses involved in making sales. From this information the items in the cash budget estimating the expenditures to be made for the purpose of selling the products or services of the company are prepared. Some of these expenditures, such as salaries and commissions, may be calculated rather simply from the projected estimate of sales. In other cases, the estimate of cash expenditures may not be so directly dependent upon the estimated sales. Traveling expenses, delivery expenses, advertising allowances to customers, advertising expenditures by the company, and expenditures for entertainment of customers will generally show a less direct correlation with the sales pattern than is shown by the salesmen's commissions.

Expenditures for administration. The administrative expenses of the company include such items as property taxes, property insurance, office expenses, and executive salaries. They do not vary with the fluctuations in the volume of plant production but remain relatively fixed. In preparing the cash budget, one must recognize that the expenditures of cash for administrative expenses is made less frequently than for those expenses that vary with the rate of production, such as wages and materials. As in the case of other expense items the allocation of expenses to each month or another accounting period does not coincide with the cash disbursement for the expense during the period.

Expenditures covering nonoperating expenses. Nonoperating expenses include such items as interest payable and income taxes payable. Payments on these items are usually made on a quarterly basis, although interest payments are sometimes made semiannually, annually, or monthly. As in the case of administrative or overhead expenses, the cash disbursement involved with the expense is generally made with less frequency than the monthly divisions into which expense calculations are usually divided.

Purchase of capital assets. The purchase of a factory building or other capital asset is obviously not an expense chargeable to the year of purchase. Nevertheless, the cash outlay must be included in the cash budget. The purchase of capital assets often involves such a large amount that the decision to buy is made only after long deliberation. In any case, at the time that the cash budget is prepared the probable purchase of capital assets during the period covered by the cash budget is known. If the full amount of the capital asset is not paid by the company at the time of purchase, only the amount expended is included in the cash budget. If the expenditure of cash required at the time the capital asset is purchased is considerable, it is obvious that the financial officer must provide for an accumulation of cash in anticipation of the large withdrawal necessary to complete the purchase. Planning for such large cash disbursements is one purpose for drawing up a cash budget.

Payments to owners. In a proprietorship, the withdrawals of cash as the payment to the owner of the business may be done whenever the owner feels that the cash account is sufficiently high to permit it, or may be carefully planned to provide him with a systematic payment. In a partnership, the withdrawals of the partners can be handled on similar bases. However, the advantages of regularity of payment are considerable, since agreement among all the general partners is necessary with respect to the amount and timing of withdrawals.

In a corporation the payments to the owners are in the form of dividends. Where a corporation has preferred stock outstanding, the dividend payments usually come to a definite annual amount. Some corporations, particularly the utility companies, pay regular dividends on their common stock. The American Telephone and Telegraph Company, for example, paid for many years a dividend of $2.25 per share four times a year, maintaining this quarterly payment during the depression of the 1930's, World War II, and the postwar readjustment period. It is certainly true that it simplifies the preparation of a cash budget if the dividends to be paid on the common stock are regular in amount and frequency. For the most part, the directors of those corporations whose stock is listed on the major exchanges of the United States attempt to achieve regularity in the payment of dividends on common stock. Nevertheless, there is greater variation in the amount of cash paid out for common stock dividends than that for preferred stock dividends.

Payments to government agencies. The principal payments are the quarterly payments to the federal government of money withheld each pay day from the employees to cover their approximate income tax, and each employer's and employee's contributions to the social security fund.[1] If the company is a corporation, quarterly payments to the federal government are also made on the estimated income tax liability of the company. Tax payments to state and local governments and payments of other kinds to various governmental bodies can generally be predicted with accuracy when the cash budget is prepared. Although an estimate must be made of the expected income of a corporation so that its income tax liability can in turn be predicted and the quarterly income tax payments budgeted, the actual net income may vary considerably from the estimate. If this is the case, the corporation officers are permitted to file a revised estimate of income, and change the payments on estimated income tax accordingly. Furthermore, at the time that the statement of profit and loss is prepared, if the actual net income earned by the corporation differs from the estimated income on which the quarterly tax payments were based, the corporation either makes an additional payment or files a claim for refund of part of the tax already paid. In such a case, the provision in the cash budget for payment on income tax may differ from the amount of cash actually expended for the tax.

---

[1] The amount withheld each pay day plus the employer's contribution is due on the last day of the month following each quarter: April 30, July 31, and so on (1954 Federal Revenue Code, Sec. 3827).

PRO FORMA STATEMENTS

The cash budget is very useful in attaining that most important goal of a business enterprise: the generating of profits. In addition, the pro forma income statement and the pro forma balance sheet are in widespread use in financial planning. As stated earlier, the pro forma income statement is a forecast in the form of a profit and loss statement of the operations of a company for a future period.

It is easier to see whether any modifications in the plans or requests of the various departments are necessary if the tentative plans for the coming year of the manufacturing divisions, the advertising department, the sales department, and others are translated into actual figures from which a pro forma income statement is prepared. For example, the statement may reveal that if the tentative plans of the various departments are carried out without modification, the company will suffer a net loss during the coming period. Obviously, then, some drastic revisions will be necessary to insure a continued profit. The pro forma statement may reveal hidden defects in planning, as well as a lack of appreciation by one department of the effect of its plans upon operations in another.

The pro forma balance sheet provides an estimate of the results of changes during the coming year in assets, liabilities, and net worth. It shows the results of any major purchases of assets that are contemplated for the coming year, it will show major financing that is planned, and it will reflect in the net worth section the expected results of operations projected in the pro forma income statement. By means of ratios prepared from the pro forma balance sheet, it can be seen whether any contemplated financing should be postponed or additional financing required.

LIQUIDITY VERSUS PROFITABILITY

In the financial planning of any business there are two considerations to be kept in mind: liquidity and profitability. To some extent each is in conflict with the other. Liquidity is a measure of the capability of a firm in meeting its maturing financial obligations. The cash flow statement is a means of organizing the financial actions planned for the company's future so as reasonably to insure that when financial obligations are due the needed cash will be available. It is not possible to coordinate perfectly the expected receipts of cash with expected disbursements. Because of this uncertainty there must be a "cushion," which generally takes the form of availability of cash in excess of the anticipated needs. The size of this cushion will vary according to the accuracy with which cash receipts and cash expenditures have been predicted in the past and the speed with which money can be raised by the company in emergencies. If the company, for example, owns marketable securities and other assets that can be rapidly turned into cash, its cash account can be held at a level lower than would otherwise be safe.   A line of credit (explained in Chapter 6) from a bank permits borrowing with a minimum of delay, thus allowing company officers to reduce safely the size of the cushion.   The two commonly used measures of liquidity are the current ratio and the acid test ratio.   An increase in liquidity of a company gets a favorable reception from most creditors, generally resulting in an enhanced credit rating, and thus strengthens the company's ability to increase its short-term borrowing whenever necessary. The goal of liquidity is the goal of safety, security, and peace of mind.

However, risk cannot be entirely eliminated from business or personal life.   The hope of profits involves the risk of loss.   In order to increase the profits of a company, chances must be taken, which usually means a compromise between the goal of liquidity and that of profitability.   Whether the compromise will be in the direction of safety and liquidity or of profit and risk depends largely upon the temperament of the owners.   In a large business with scattered stockholders, the compromise depends upon the temperament of the directors of the company.   The executives of some companies are noted for their willingness to accept a high degree of risk, while those of other companies have a reputation for financial conservatism and caution.   Just as a military commander may, because his strategic position is inferior with respect to his opponent, adopt a bold policy as the only hope of victory open to him, so may the directors of a company resort to a policy containing a higher degree of risk than usual when conditions favor their major competitors rather than themselves.   In order to increase the return on the funds invested by owners, the company executives must employ the funds so that a larger volume of profits is generated with a given level of investment.   This might mean channeling fewer funds into those assets providing a moderate return, such as marketable securities, and more into those assets providing a higher rate of return, such as inventories and machinery.   It is easy to say that money should be put to work in such a way that the rate of return of the funds invested is as great as possible without involving a dangerous reduction in liquidity.   The financial officer must emphasize to the other executives of the company and to its owners the conflict between the goals of liquidity and profitability. The compromise between these two goals is so fundamental that it must be resolved at the highest policy-making level.

Questions

1. What is meant by the circuit flow of current assets?   Why may one circuit take a long period in some cases and a short period in other cases?
2. What is a budget?   How does its use help in improving financial operations?
3. Show how the preparation and use of departmental budgets can raise the degree of coordination between departments.
4. How is a budget similar to a battle plan for an army?
5. What information does the cash budget provide the chief financial officer?
6. What is a pro forma income statement?   How does it help in financial planning?

7. How does regularity of dividend payments aid in budgeting cash?
8. Should a budget, once adopted, be followed strictly, or should it be changed as often as unexpected developments occur during the budget period?
9. How are the goals of profitability and liquidity in conflict?
10. "The hope of profit involves the risk of loss." Criticize the statement.

Selected Readings

Boros, Theodore E., *Cash Management in Small Plants*, Management Aids for Small Manufacturers #124, Small Business Administration, Washington, D.C., 1961.

———, "Flow of Funds in the American Economy," *Business in Brief*, Chase Manhattan Bank, New York, January-February 1963.

Kaiser, Harry M., *Getting Results from Your Budget*, Management Aids for Small Manufacturers, Small Business Administration, Washington, D.C., 1961.

Kempner, Jack J., "Clarifying the Mysteries of the Source and Application of Funds," *Montana Business Review*, Montana State University, February, 1962.

5

Sources and Uses of Funds

THE CONCEPT OF FLOW OF FUNDS

THE OPERATIONS of a business firm are conducted with the assets owned by the firm. At any given instant a company has a certain amount of assets in a variety of forms that undergo change during each working day. If a balance sheet could be prepared at the close of each day's operations, it would show the daily transformation of business property from the form of one asset into another, with some assets increasing and others decreasing in value as the result of the day's business activities. The transformation of assets can be pictured as a flow, somewhat like a river. Controlling the flow so that it will produce profits for the company is essentially the art of management.

In order for management to be effective, the value of the assets must be known as they change in form. Since the measure of value in the United States is the dollar, the assets of a company, whatever their form, are listed on the financial records in terms of dollar values. The logic of assigning dollar values to the assets of the business is twofold: it provides a uniform standard for comparing asset values; and it implies that assets, whatever their form, are merely stages in the transformation of property into cash.

In the transformation of assets from one form to another, the financial manager deals with changes in the dollar values of the assets. Changes in the physical form of assets are the primary concern of the production manager. Neither the financial manager nor the production manager can afford to ignore either the physical composition of the assets or their dollar value. It is simply that each tends to look at assets from a different viewpoint. To repeat, the financial manager looks at assets in terms of their dollar value. To him, assets are funds. As a term, *funds* is an abstraction representing a concept separate from physical property. It is a concept of the value imbedded in assets rather than the physical characteristics distinguishing one asset from another. The total amount of funds used in a firm's operations is equal to the total assets employed in the enterprise.

66

From the standpoint of the financial manager, funds take such forms as cash, accounts receivable, finished goods inventories, raw materials, machinery and equipment, factory buildings, warehouses, land, and notes receivable. Funds are not the same as cash; cash is a *form* of funds. It is easiest to measure the value of funds in the form of cash, since cash in the United States is dollars and cents, and they are used to measure value. However, all the other assets used in a business represent a form of funds also, even though their value in dollars is more difficult to estimate and the accuracy of measurement more uncertain.[1]

From the standpoint of financial management, the flow of funds in terms of the amount and form of total assets permits a logical approach to financial problems. It is not just the current assets but all the assets that must be considered in the concept of flow of funds. The advantage in including all assets is seen when one considers borrowing as one of the sources of funds. Money can be borrowed on a short-term or a long-term basis. But the use to which money borrowed on a short-term basis is put is not restricted to the acquisition of current assets nor is the use of long-term borrowing restricted to the acquisition of fixed assets. For example, a company may raise $10 million through the sale of twenty-year bonds. Part of this money may be used to purchase machinery and part to increase inventories. At the time that the bonds were first sold, cash was received by the corporation. If the concept of funds is restricted to current assets, it is necessary to conclude that part of what was funds (cash) at the time of the sale of the bonds has changed in character and is no longer funds, since the cash was transformed in part into fixed assets (machinery). The retirement of the bond issue in this example becomes one of coordinating the management of short-term assets and long-term assets, so that cash will be available in the amounts needed to pay interest when due and to retire the bonds at maturity. Financial management is simplified, therefore, by use of the funds concept as one embracing the total resources of the firm.

Our study of the flow of funds focuses on the process by which cash is

---

[1] Some of the literature of finance limits the meaning of the term *funds* to current assets. Under this definition funds represent the purchasing power inherent in cash, receivables, inventories, and other current assets available to meet the current operating needs of the firm and the claims of the short-term creditors represented by the current liabilities. This definition may be useful in focusing upon one aspect of financial management, the financing of current operations. From the standpoint of total financial planning, the financial problems associated with machinery, buildings, patents, and other long-term assets are equally important. The distinction between short-term finance and long-term finance is arbitrary. It is more logical to consider all assets as forms of funds than to restrict use of the term to short-term assets. Accountants disagree as to the definition of the term *funds*. Among those that use it to denote total resources are L. Goldberg, "Funds Statement Reconsidered," *Accounting Review*, October 1951; W. A. Paton and R. A. Stevenson, *Principles of Accounting*, The Macmillian Company, New York; E. O. Edwards, "Funds Statements for Short- and Long-Run Analyses," *Journal of Business*, July 1952; R. L. Boyd and R. I. Dickey, *Basic Accounting*, Rinehart, New York. With some reservations, these accountants consider the concept of funds to be a measure of the total purchasing power inherent in the total resources of the firm.

generated and used in total business operations. Cash on hand or in the bank is the fundamental means of payment for goods and services. Because the financial manager must be able to pay company bills as they become due, cash management is one of his principal responsibilities. Having cash available to meet obligations permits the company to maintain its credit. The concept of flow of funds permits better cash planning and reduces the risk of insolvency, while permitting operations to be conducted on a lower average cash balance. Cash is thereby conserved and turnover of current assets increased, the advantage of which was explained in Chapter 4. Cash planning involves the use of cash budgets, a topic which was also discussed in that chapter.

SOURCES OF FUNDS

Keeping in mind that funds include all the assets of the firm, one can picture available funds as a tank in which the quantity of funds rises and falls like the level of water in a water tank. Sources of funds replenish the quantity in the tank while uses of funds deplete it, as shown in Fig. 5-1.

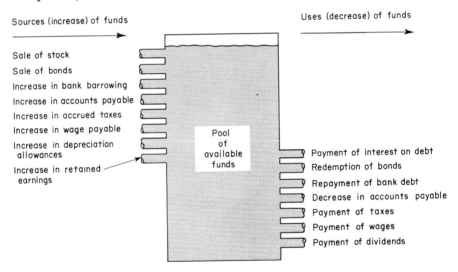

Fig. 5-1   *Flow of funds chart.*

Note that the sources of funds are many. For purposes of analysis, it is useful to divide the sources into different categories. They may be classified into short-term sources, such as bank borrowing, and long-term sources, such as sale of bonds or sale of stock. This is useful, since funds from short-term sources are usually more quickly obtainable, if a need for funds develops unexpectedly. It should be emphasized that such a classification does not imply that short-term funds are devoted only to short-term uses, as in increasing inventories, and that long-term funds are devoted only to long-term uses, as in the purchase of machinery. Figure 5-1 intentionally shows no direct connection between short-term sources and short-term uses. It is probably more useful to classify sources of funds according to internal sources and external sources.

Internal sources of funds

Retained Earnings. Figure 21-2 (p. 365) shows the amount of net income earned by corporations annually since the end of World War I. The policy during the 1920's was to pay out most of the net income in dividends, retaining a small part for investment in the business. During the 1930's, practically all net earnings were distributed in dividends. It was not until the outbreak of World War II that corporations began retaining a substantial portion of net income. Since 1939, roughly half of all earnings after taxes have been retained by corporations, thereby constituting an important source of funds. In 1963, for example, net income after taxes for business corporations was over $25 billion after payment of income taxes, of which roughly $10 billion was retained.

Although retained earnings have been and probably will continue to be an important source of funds for business, it has become less important in recent years. In 1951, for example, retained earnings accounted for half of the internally generated funds for business. In 1963, on the other hand, only 24 per cent of internally generated funds were from retained earnings; the remainder came from depreciation allowances. It is not so much a change in dividend policies that has accounted for this decline as it is changes in the tax laws with regard to accounting for depreciation. As Fig. 5-2 shows, retained earnings have fluctuated between $7 billion and $13 billion from 1947 to 1962. The fluctuations that have occurred during that period have been largely a result of differences in profitability for corporations during those years.

Depreciation Allowances. By far the chief source of funds at this time is depreciation allowances, as Fig. 5-2 shows. In 1947, retained earnings accounted for $11.4 billion of funds and depreciation allowances for $5.2 billion. In 1963, retained earnings accounted for $9.4 billion and depreciation allowances $29.4 billion.

The primary purpose of depreciation allowances is to reflect the expense resulting from the wearing out of assets, such as machinery and buildings. The depreciation allowances preserve a portion of the excess of gross income over expenses, so that fixed assets, once having worn out, may be replaced. When a machine or building must be replaced, it does not follow that it will be replaced with a newer model of the same machine or a newer building of the same construction and dimensions, since the requirements and technology of the business are likely to have changed in the meantime. The new assets may differ considerably in design, operation, and construction. During the lifetime of some machines, technology may have changed so rapidly that the old machines are retired without being replaced. In any case, it is difficult to determine when a fixed asset is acquired how long it will be used in the enterprise and what will be the cost of replacing it at the end of its useful life.

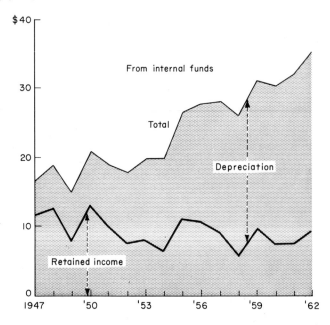

Fig. 5-2 *Internal sources of funds for nonfinancial corporations. (Source:* U. S. Department of Commerce)

The actual amount of funds retained in the form of depreciation allowances is determined by financial managers according to how much depreciation expense may be charged to operations under the provisions of the corporation income tax laws of the federal government. The maximum depreciation expense charged to the use of each asset that may be permitted is indicated in the United States Internal Revenue Code. As indicated in Chapter 3, the Code has been changed on several occasions since the end of World War II to permit an ever larger expense for depreciation to be charged against gross income, which permits more generous depreciation allowances. Since depreciation allowances are a source of funds that escape the payment of corporation income taxes, in contrast to retained earnings, this liberalization of the corporation income tax laws has made depreciation allowances an increasingly attractive source of funds. The corporation income tax, on the other hand, remained at 52 per cent of net income during the decade of the 1950's, dropped to 50 per cent in 1964, and to 48 per cent beginning with 1965. The more favorable treatment of depreciation expense under the income tax laws than retained income explains the increased use of depreciation allowances as a source of funds. In 1963, of every $1 of retained net income only 48¢ could be re-invested in the business or paid out to the owners in dividends, and 52¢ was paid in income taxes. For every $1 of depreciation allowances, on the other hand, the full $1 could be reinvested in the business.

Depreciation allowances have become by far the largest single source of funds, external or internal. In meeting the need for funds, the financial manager will devote a great deal of time to maintaining and increasing, if possible, this source of funds. It will be essential for him to be acquainted with the most recent legislation regarding depreciation accounting under the Internal Revenue Code and the most recent court decisions interpreting the Code.

External Sources of Funds Figure 5-3 shows the volume of funds received annually from external sources by corporations since World War II. As can be seen from the graph, external funds constitute a far more erratic source of funds than internal sources. It is apparent that since World War II most firms have looked to depreciation allowances and retained income as the prime source of funds and have considered external funds as a supplementary source to be used only to the extent that internal sources have been inadequate. Part of the explanation lies in the comparative cost of the two. It is easy to see that payment must be made for funds secured·from external sources. When money is borrowed, either on a short-term or long-term basis, interest is paid. When preferred stock is sold, dividends

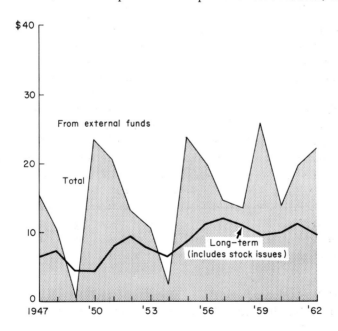

Fig. 5-3 *External sources of funds for nonfinancial corporations. (Source:* U. S. Department of Commerce)

are expected by the purchasers of the stock. When common stock is sold, the expectation of dividend payments is also present even though stockholders are often willing to wait many years before receiving them. Because the financial managers of some companies consider internal funds to be costless, they exhibit a strong preference for this source. It is, of course, an error to consider internal funds as "free" (see Chapter 19). It is generally accepted that internal funds are a less costly source than most if not all sources of external funds. Particularly for smaller businesses, internal funds are more attractive than external funds because the cost of external funds is generally greater and the variety of sources is more limited for smaller businesses than for larger ones.

Long-Term Borrowing and Owners' Investment. The principal external source of long-term funds is debt. As Table 5-1 shows, bonds and other long-term debt account in most years for well over half the external sources of funds. In 1962, for example, bonds and other long-term debt amounted to $7.5 billion out of the total of $9.6 billion of funds raised externally. In recent years, funds secured by the sale of stock have been smaller in total than funds raised by bonds. To some extent, this is due to defining interest on bonds as an expense that reduces the taxable income of a corporation, whereas dividends paid on stock does not receive such favorable treatment. To some extent, the relative unpopularity of stock as a means of securing funds is due to the desire on the part of owners of firms not to dilute the ownership through sale of stock to the public. The owners of small businesses appear to be particularly reluctant to share in the ownership of their firms, sometimes making it difficult to raise needed finances.

Bonds and other debt, no matter how far from the future of their maturity, must be repaid.[2] For this reason, they are both a source and a use of funds: a source at the time the bonds are sold, and a use when repayment is made. Furthermore, interest payments on debt represent a use of funds. Stocks, on the other hand, do not have a maturity date. The sale of common stock to raise funds does not involve considerations of redemption of the stock, inasmuch as the retirement of common stock is rarely undertaken except in a merger, consolidation, reorganization in bankruptcy, or voluntary dissolution. (These aspects will be discussed in later chapters.) Although preferred stock, like common stock, does not have a maturity date, it is sometimes treated as a temporary means of financing. If this is the case, one of the uses of funds resulting from preferred stock financing is the systematic retirement of preferred stock, much in the manner of retirement of bonds.

Short-Term Sources of Funds. As Fig. 5-3 and Table 5-1 show, the external sources of short-term funds fluctuate much more widely from year

---

[2] A few issues of bonds have no maturity date. These bonds are so rare that in the present discussion they can be ignored.

to year than long-term funds from external sources. The short-term sources of external funds represent debt in one form or another. Short-term sources may be designated as negotiated or non-negotiated. Loans from banks and other lending institutions, loans on the basis of promissory notes or drafts, and any loans resulting from bargaining between the borrower and lender are classed as negotiated loans. Debts created as an incidental part of business operations, such as trade payables and accrued expenses, are non-negotiated. An increase in accrued taxes is in effect an increase in the funds borrowed from government, and an increase in wages payable is an increase in funds borrowed from employees. Debt resulting from the delay in payment for goods purchased usually represents the largest part of total short-term external sources of funds. Individual accounts and notes payable are paid as they are due, and new ones are created as purchases are made. Payment for accounts payable and notes payable is a use of funds. Although payments and purchases are made daily, they are rarely in the same amount, thus causing the volume of outstanding accounts and notes payable to fluctuate constantly.

TABLE 5-1. EXTERNAL SOURCES OF FUNDS FOR NONFINANCIAL CORPORATIONS FOR SELECTED YEARS (BILLIONS OF DOLLARS)

	1947	1950	1955	1960	1961	1962
External Long-Term Sources, Total	6.3	4.2	8.6	9.8	11.1	9.6
Stocks	1.4	1.7	2.7	3.0	4.5	2.1
Bonds	3.0	2.0	4.2	5.0	5.1	5.0
Other debt	1.9	.5	1.7	1.7	1.4	2.5
External Short-Term Sources, Total	9.5	19.2	15.1	3.9	8.7	12.6
Bank loans	1.4	2.1	3.7	1.3	.4	3.0
Trade payables	4.5	8.8	5.5	2.6	6.0	5.5
Federal income tax liabilities	2.1	7.3	3.8	—1.5	.6	1.0
Other	1.5	1.0	2.1	1.6	1.7	3.1

Source: Department of Commerce

When purchases on account are greater than payments on account, there is a net increase in the inflow of funds, and the level in the pool of available funds is raised. When the reverse is true, there is a net increase in the out-flow of funds, and the pool of available funds is lowered. The same is true of the other sources of external short-term funds. The incurring of bank loans represents a source of funds, and the repayment of bank loans a use of funds. The financial manager will recognize that an increase in the pool of funds can be accomplished by delaying payment of, or increasing the volume of, short-term debt. Short-term debt as a source of funds is more flexible than long-term sources. Increases and decreases in short-term debt can be accomplished more rapidly in most cases than similar action in long-term debt. A company that has a pattern of seasonal peaks and valleys of operations must increase its pool of funds during the peak period and reduce the pool during the season of slack operations. By increasing its accounts and notes payable outstanding or by increasing its borrowing from banks the company can increase its pool of funds to meet the increase required by the period of peak operations. The increase in the flow of funds into the pool as a result of the short-term borrowing creates the requirement of an outflow of funds to repay the loans. The outflow of funds required to pay off the short-term borrowing can be arranged to take place when the outflow resulting from operations is at a seasonal low, or at least can be delayed until after the outflow associated with the peak of operations is passed. Thus, although the operations of a company may be highly seasonal, the flow of funds, because of short-term borrowing and repayment, may be smoothed out over a period of a year.

If the company is expanding its sales year after year, it will find that its pool of funds at seasonal peaks is higher each year and that the pool during seasonal valleys is also higher each year. Short-term debt will not only be higher at succeeding peaks than previous peaks but will be higher during successive seasonal valleys. Thus, the financial manager may find it advisable to shift from one source of funds to another. For example, he may increase his supply of funds from long-term sources and use the supply to replace part of the funds from short-term sources, to bring the dependence of the company upon short-term sources back to the approximate level of earlier years.

USES OF FUNDS

As we have seen in Fig. 5-1, the uses of funds are many and include uses for operations, capital expenditures, and payments to owners. The operational uses of funds include repaying short-term debt, meeting payrolls and taxes, and paying for raw materials and supplies, heat, light, power, and rent. The uses of funds for operations can be pictured as a constant flow, rising and falling as a result of seasonal influences, but nevertheless continuing in a steady stream. By contrast, the use of funds for capital expenditures, retirement of long-term debt, or payments to owners is occasional, like the occasional opening and closing of a water tap.

The aspect of operations of particular concern to the financial manager is the continual change in the form of the assets known as current assets, which include cash, accounts receivable, notes receivable, inventories, and supplies. Because the volume of each of these assets changes daily, so does the dollar value of each. (It might be pictured as a circular flow, and is so treated in Chapter 4.) Since the outflow of funds for operations must generally be in the form of cash, an important aspect of financial management is making sure that adequate funds in the form of cash are available to meet the continual outflow. If more funds are in the form of cash than is necessary to meet the expected outflow of funds, the profits of the firm will be reduced. The problem of maintaining sufficient cash while avoiding an overabundance is an art that distinguishes the efficient financial manager from the mediocre one.

Capital Expenditures Such capital assets as machinery, buildings, and land are acquired infrequently. From a financial standpoint, this is the most important aspect distinguishing capital assets from current assets. Although capital assets, except for land, change in form as they are used (worn out) in operations, they do so at a much slower rate than current assets.[3] The volume of capital assets, also known as fixed assets, does not show the seasonal pattern of increases and decreases in volume exhibited by the current assets. Although a seasonal pattern is not evident, a cycle of change similar to the seasonal circuit of current assets is a useful concept in the financial management of fixed assets. In the latter case, the circuit would be brief for some and lengthy for others depending upon the number of years during which the acquisition cost of the asset under consideration may be recovered. In the case of machinery, it might be two or three years; in the case of a warehouse building, forty or fifty years.

Because the life of capital assets runs into years, careful replacement or expansion planning is sometimes not undertaken, particularly in some small businesses. Nevertheless, it is just as important to plan carefully the acquisition and retirement of fixed assets as it is to plan the acquisition and use of current assets. It is more difficult to do, because the planning involves extending further into the future than in the case of current assets. As a cash budget is a useful tool in planning the efficient use of current assets, so is a capital budget in working with fixed assets. Such budgeting is undertaken by well-managed firms and is found in nearly all large enterprises. (See Chapter 19.)

Business enterprise as a whole has expanded rapidly in the United States since World War II. The inflow of funds from operations, borrowing, and owners' equity has been transformed into physical assets, particularly plant and equipment, in order to support a larger volume of operations. Increases in plant and equipment, as shown in Fig. 5-4, account for a large part of the use of funds. Competitive pressures, the rapid rate of technological change in many industries, and increased depreciation allowances due to liberalized tax regulations are also responsible for a high level of expenditures for plant and equipment.

Payments to Owners Although the pursuit of profits is not the only motivation in business decisions, it is a primary one. If the inflow of funds

---

[3] It was stated earlier that the distinction between current assets and fixed or capital assets is arbitrary. As a matter of fact there are exceptions to the generalization that capital assets are used up more slowly than current assets. Inventories are classed as current assets, but inventories of cheese might be kept in storage for months and whiskey for years before being tranformed into accounts receivable or cash. Similarly machines are classed as fixed assets, but some machines or parts of machines, such as cutting tools, may wear out in a few days. Tools that wear out rapidly may be classed as supplies (current assets) simply because they are used up rapidly. Again the distinction, though useful, is arbitrary.

from payments for sales and from other receipts from operations is greater than the outflow of funds for wages, materials, and other payments, the pool of funds rises as operations progress.   Part of this increase in the level of funds can be used for capital expenditures.   It is the expectation of the owners of the enterprise, however, that operations will succeed in raising the pool of funds sufficiently to permit them to share in the outflow; this is in the form of dividends to stockholders of corporations or withdrawals by partners or the proprietor in an unincorporated business.

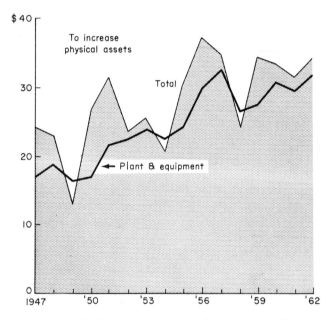

Fig. 5-4 *Principal uses of nonfinancial corporation.* (*Source:* U. S. Department of Commerce)

Like capital expenditures, payments to owners represent an occasional use of funds, and in a well-managed firm are carefully planned for the future.   In proprietorships and partnerships, in most of which the owners are also the principal officers of the firm, payments to owners are apt to be included with the salary of the officer-owners.   In corporations, payments to owners in the form of dividends are segregated from payments of salaries to officers, even where officers might also be owners.   In corporations, the choice of a dividend policy and the maintenance of the policy in good times and bad are actions that are carefully considered and frequently reviewed by the board of directors.   Unlike a proprietorship or a partnership, a large corporation may be owned by hundreds or thousands of people who vary considerably in economic status, age, willingness to take financial risks, and knowledge about business in general and the problems of their company in particular.   For example, wealthy owners, whose dividend income would be taxed at a high rate, often prefer a policy of paying no dividends or paying out only a very small percentage of net earnings each year. Stockholders living on a retirement income generally prefer a generous dividend policy. The directors must reconcile the conflicting desires of owners of the company in establishing dividend policy and must consider the needs of the company for retained earnings as well as the desires of the owners for dividend income. As we shall see in Chapter 21, to resolve such conflicts is not easy.

Uses of Funds in 1963 During prosperous years the pool of funds rises for most companies at a more rapid rate than in less prosperous ones. It would obviously be poor financial management to permit the increase to be in the form of cash. The chief alternatives open to the corporation directors are to increase capital expenditures, transform the cash into income paying securities, and increase the dividends.

To illustrate, the year 1963 may be considered. The flow of funds to corporations rose steadily during the year, reaching a rate of flow higher than for any previous year. The level of funds available to corporations in the United States reached record heights. As one publication expressed it, "If there is one thing American business has plenty of this year, it is money." [4] This presented a problem—certainly not an unwelcome one— of what to do with the money. The consensus of business managers was to divide most of the excess funds between capital expenditures, payments to owners, and loans to customers. There are many factors involved in the decision to make capital expenditures, as is described in Chapter 19. The availability of funds from operations is one of the most important factors in some companies and is less important in others. Companies often have more capital spending projects considered worthy than there are funds available to finance them. For this reason, if funds from operations for a given year are greater than expected, many managers will use them for projects rejected during the preparation of the most recent capital budget. Alternatively, the availability of more funds than expected will often cause managers to increase the size of the next capital budget. For 1963, *Business Week* stated that the "sheer weight of available cash is tipping the scales in favor of more capital spending." [5]

The surge in the flow of funds during 1963 permitted payments to owners in larger amounts than previously. However, directors are reluctant to raise the dividend rate of their corporation unless they feel that it can be maintained; uncertainty in this area will cause the directors frequently to distribute at the end of the year a dividend labeled an "extra dividend." If conditions the following year require eliminating the extra dividend, stockholders have fewer objections to it than to the reduction of the regular dividend.

---

[4] *Business Week,* October 19, 1963, p. 166.
[5] *Ibid.,* p. 168.

The third major use for the swollen flow of funds in 1963 was an increase in customer loans, i.e., a substantial increase in accounts receivable. The amount of funds in the form of accounts receivable increased rapidly from 1958 to 1962, and increased sharply in 1963. Automobile manufacturers, for example, used to require payment in cash by dealers upon receipt of shipment of new cars. By 1963 dealers were permitted to wait fifteen days before making payment—in effect, receiving a two-week loan in the amount of the invoice for the cars delivered. This policy change resulted in an increase of $300 million in accounts receivable for General Motors Corporation alone.[6]

Part of the increased flow of funds to businesses during 1963 was used to increase inventories, to retire debt, and to finance the acquisition of subsidiary companies. Part of the funds were simply transformed into holdings of commerical paper, bank deposits, and securities of the United States Treasury. Funds in these forms could be quickly liquidated when needed for other uses.

THE EFFECT OF FLOW OF FUNDS ON FINANCIAL STATEMENTS

The use of a series of balance sheets shows the effect the flow has on financial statements. Some transactions will raise the level of funds, others will lower it, and still others will not change the level but will alter the composition of items comprising the pool of funds. The reader should keep in mind that the term *funds* as defined in the beginning of this chapter includes all the assets of a firm, not just the current ones. Suppose that the financial condition of a corporation is shown by the following simplified balance sheet:

Assets			Liabilities and Net Worth		
Cash	$60,000		Accounts payable	$100,000	
Receivables	160,000		Notes payable	30,000	
Inventories	110,000				
		$330,000			$130,000
Machinery	80,000		Bonds payable	100,000	
Buildings	300,000		Capital stock	200,000	
Land	40,000		Retained earnings	320,000	
		$420,000			$620,000
		$750,000			$750,000

The company now makes a cash purchase of a piece of machinery for $30,000. After the purchase is completed, the balance is changed to the following:

[6] *Ibid.* This source quotes an economist in Washington, D.C., in these words: "Companies are financing larger amounts of receivables relative to current assets, and they're financing more of this with internally generated funds."

Assets			Liabilities and Net Worth		
Cash	$ 30,000		Accounts payable	$100,000	
Receivables	160,000		Notes payable	30,000	
Inventories	110,000				
		$300,000			$130,000
Machinery	$110,000		Bonds payable	$100,000	
Buildings	300,000		Capital stock	200,000	
Land	40,000		Retained earnings	320,000	
		$450,000			$620,000
		$750,000			$750,000

Notice that there is no alteration of the level of funds available, but that there is a change in their composition. After the machine is purchased, the amount of cash is reduced to $30,000 while the value of the machinery is increased to $110,000. Idle cash has been put into a form in which the operations of the company can be expanded, made more efficient, or both, depending upon the character of the machine purchased. The benefit to the company of the change in the composition of funds is offset by the fact that the company is no longer in a position to make a similar purchase. It is obvious that cash must be conserved and not used unless the advantages outweigh the disadvantage of greater inflexibility resulting from the expenditure of cash.

To show the effect of sales on the flow of funds, suppose the corporation makes a sale of $10,000 of goods. To simplify computation it will be assumed that no profit is made on the transaction. Inventories will be reduced by $10,000 and receivables increased by $10,000. Again, there will be no change in the level of funds, only in the composition. When the customer makes payment for the invoice of $10,000, receivables will be reduced by $10,000 and cash increased by the same amount. Thus the transaction will help in replenishing the cash account. The balance sheet following the two transactions will appear as below:

Assets			Liabilities and Net Worth		
Cash	$ 40,000		Accounts payable	$100,000	
Receivables	160,000		Notes payable	30,000	
Inventories	100,000				
		$300,000			$130,000
Machinery	$110,000		Bonds payable	$100,000	
Buildings	300,000		Capital stock	200,000	
Land	40,000		Retained earnings	320,000	
		$450,000			$620,000
		$750,000			$750,000

Suppose the company purchases a building for $100,000, paying $25,-000 in cash and giving a bond for the remainder. After the transaction the balance sheet will appear as follows:

Assets			*Liabilities and Net Worth*		
Cash	$ 15,000		Accounts payable	$100,000	
Receivables	160,000		Notes payable	30,000	
Inventories	100,000				
		$275,000			$130,000
Machinery	$110,000		Bonds payable	$175,000	
Buildings	400,000		Capital stock	200,000	
Land	40,000		Retained earnings	320,000	
		$550,000			$695,000
		$825,000			$825,000

The effect of the above transaction was to tranform $25,000 of cash into the form of a fixed asset (buildings). The cash account has been severely reduced, and, presumably, the company will have to seek means to replenish this account. The level of the pool of funds has been raised from $750,000 to $825,000, but the increase in the long-term debt of the company puts it in a weaker position to borrow additional money. Yet this may be remedied by selling additional common stock to retire some of the long-term indebtedness, using cash from future operations to reduce indebtedness, or by similar transactions. The point to be remembered is that debt is not a limitless source of funds. The financial manager is in a position somewhat similar to that of a farmer who must depend upon well water for his farm operations—too much pumping will make the well run dry.

A transaction that reduces the pool of funds may be illustrated by the liquidation of an asset to eliminate a liability or by a payment of cash to the owners of the company. Suppose the company sells a portion of its land that is not needed in the business and receives $20,000 in the sale. If the money is used to reduce the notes payable, the land account will fall to $20,000 and the notes payable account will fall to $10,000. If a distribution of $5,000 in cash is made to the owners, the cash account will be reduced to $10,000 and the retained earnings will fall to $315,000. Both of these transactions will reduce the pool of funds, and the balance sheet will be as follows:

Assets			*Liabilities and Net Worth*		
Cash	$ 10,000		Accounts payable	$100,000	
Receivables	160,000		Notes payable	10,000	
Inventories	100,000				
		$270,000			$110,000
Machinery	$110,000		Bonds payable	$175,000	
Building	400,000		Capital stock	200,000	
Land	20,000		Retained earnings	315,000	
		$530,000			$690,000
		$800,000			$800,000

To summarize the flows resulting from the transactions described above, a statement of balance sheet changes may be prepared. The statement below shows the changes resulting from the transactions during the period, a net increase in the level of funds (assets), the source of this increase as the rise in long-term debt (bonds), and a change in the working capital position.

CHANGES IN BALANCE SHEET DURING PERIOD

Assets	Beginning of Year	End of Year	Change
Cash	$ 60,000	$ 10,000	— 50,000
Receivables	160,000	160,000	.....
Inventories	110,000	100,000	— 10,000
Machinery	$ 80,000	110,000	+ 30,000
Buildings	300,000	400,000	+100,000
Land	40,000	20,000	— 20,000
Total	$750,000	$800,000	+ 50,000
Liabilities and Net Worth			
Accounts payable	$100,000	$100,000	.....
Notes payable	30,000	10,000	— 20,000
Bonds payable	100,000	175,000	+ 75,000
Capital stock	$200,000	$200,000	.....
Retained earnings	320,000	315,000	— 5,000
Total	$750,000	$800,000	+ $50,000

Working capital is the sum of the current assets of a firm. Net working capital is the sum of the current assets minus the sum of the current liabilities (see Fig. 2-1). The effect upon working capital of the transactions described above is given in the following statement, which shows that while net working capital cannot be increased by a corresponding increase in current liabilities, an increase in current liabilities permits an increase in total working capital:

	Beginning of Year	End of Year	Change
Current assets (working capital)	$330,000	$270,000	— $60,000
Current liabilities	$130,000	$110,000	— $20,000
Net working capital	$200,000	$160,000	— $40,000

IMPLICATIONS FOR MANAGEMENT

The implications for management of the sources and uses of funds can best be understood by keeping in mind the diagram in Fig. 5-1. One aspect of financial management is directed toward increasing the flow into the pool of funds and decreasing the outflow from the pool, although this does not imply that every means of increasing the inflow or decreasing the outflow is beneficial to the company. The sale of bonds, increase in bank borrowing, and increases in inventories purchased on account will all raise the level of funds. But payments on debt must be made sooner or later. If the increase in funds made available through borrowing cannot efficiently be used by the company, the action to increase the level is unwise. Similarly, the outflow of funds can be decreased by payment on accounts payable past the date that they are due, by renewing bank loans rather than retiring them, or by being niggardly in the repair of machinery and equipment. In most cases such actions would be unwise, even though they would reduce, temporarily at least, the outflow of funds. However, if the schedule of payment of wages can be changed from a weekly to a monthly basis, the account wages payable will rise to a higher figure, and the level of available funds will be increased concomitantly. If a change in the method of computing depreciation is adopted which results in increasing depreciation expense, depreciation allowances will rise and so will available funds. Under most circumstances, the result of these two actions in increasing funds will benefit a company. Also, if earnings can be increased by means of greater efficiency of operations or more intensive selling efforts, the pool of funds will be increased and the means by which the increase was caused will obviously be beneficial to the company.

If any change in the composition of assets can be accomplished that will increase the efficiency of operations, it will improve the profits of the company. The goal is to keep the components of the pool of funds in the best proportions possible in pursuing the goals of the company. The considerable increase in accounts receivable of corporations since 1958 appears to be an example of a shift in the proportion of funds in order to obtain the goal of greater sales. Another example of changing the pool components is found in the following quotation:

> To earn a return on corporate funds not immediately needed for operations, financial executives for some years have been putting cash into a variety of short-term money instruments of high quality, including U. S. Treasury bills, promissory notes of leading corporations, and, more recently, interest-bearing time deposits in commercial banks. Lately, however, more and more corporate funds are being put into investments that carry larger yields but may involve greater risks. Among them: Mexican commercial paper, time deposits in Japanese banks, and preferred stocks of U. S. corporations.[7]

The financial manager together with the other managers should strive to increase the rate of flow of funds, which is affected by the volume of available funds. Stated in other terms, the volume of funds should be kept as low as possible in relation to sales. If the sales volume can be maintained with a smaller inventory of finished goods, funds in the form of finished goods should be reduced. If more careful scheduling of purchases allows a smaller supply of raw materials to support the same volume of operations as before, funds in the form of raw material inventory can be

---

[7] *The Wall Street Journal,* November 5, 1963, p. 1.

cut down. The existence of the pool of funds is necessary to the survival of the firm. However, like a pool of water in a stream, it reduces the rate of flow of the funds. Therefore, the financial manager should attempt to make the size of the pool as small as possible with respect to the rate of flow necessary to support the sales volume of the company.

An important aspect of flow of funds is cash management (see also Chapter 4). When the pool of funds rises, the inflow is sometimes in cash, sometimes in assets other than cash, as in the receipt of supplies on account. When the level of the pool falls, the outflow is usually in the form of cash. Careful cash management will anticipate the outflows in time to make cash funds available to meet the expected outflow. This will require either transforming some existing funds into cash or increasing cash by bringing in additional money from external sources. In connection with the management of that portion of the pool of funds in the form of cash the circular flow of current assets should be considered. If a firm is profitable a larger amount of cash will be returned to the pool of funds than was spent during business operations.[8]

In looking at Fig. 4-1, it can be seen that there are in fact several pools of funds in the form of different assets in the circular flow. The flow from one pool to another indicates diagrammatically the changes taking place during operations. Where the total assets are represented as a single large pool of funds, as in Fig. 5-1, the circular flow is not seen. Nevertheless, the continual change in the form of the components of the pool, referred to as churning above, must be visualized if the funds are to be efficiently managed.

The concept of the flow of funds is presented in this chapter as a framework upon which to build an understanding of the various aspects of financial management. The concept of the flow of funds also serves a practical purpose as a frame of reference upon which to base financial decisions in a firm. The concept will emphasize the importance of increasing the rate of flow of funds, of keeping the level of funds as low as possible consistent with the volume of operations, and of adjusting the mix of components in the pool of funds to maintain the proportions best suited to achieve the company's goals.

Questions

1. Explain the twofold purpose of assigning dollar values to the assets of a firm.
2. What is the meaning of the term *funds?* What is the usefulness in considering all assets of the firm as various forms of funds?

---

[8] If the reader wishes to connect the Funds Flow Chart of Fig. 5-1 with the Circular Flow Chart of Fig. 4-1, the pool of cash of Fig. 4-1 can be shown to flow into the pool of funds of Fig. 5-1. The two channels through which the flow from the pool of cash to the pool of funds takes place is by way of increases in depreciation allowances and increases in retained earnings, through the channel in Fig. 4-1 labeled *Occasional outflows.* Both channels in Fig. 5-1 are shown as sources of funds.

3. Explain the rapid rise in depreciation allowances as a source of funds in recent years.
4. Why has there been such an erratic change from year to year in the volume of funds derived from external sources?
5. Why have bonds been relatively more important than stocks in raising funds for corporations in recent years?
6. Explain how short-term sources of funds are more flexible than long-term sources in meeting the seasonal fluctuation in the need for funds.
7. What is a cash budget? What is a capital budget? What is their purpose, how are they similar, and how are they different?
8. To what uses was the surge of funds to businesses in 1963 put?
9. Why is it beneficial to a company for the financial manager to strive to increase the inflow of funds and curtail the outflow? Explain how some methods of achieving this can be detrimental to the company.
10. Should the financial manager try to raise the rate of flow of funds in his firm? Discuss critically.

Selected Readings

Anton, Hector, *Accounting for the Flow of Funds,* Houghton Mifflin Company, Boston, 1962.

Helfert, Erich A., *Techniques of Financial Analysis,* Richard D. Irwin, Inc., Homewood, Ill., 1963.

O'Donnell, John L., and Milton S. Goldberg, *Elements of Financial Administration,* Charles E. Merrill Books, Inc., Columbus, Ohio, 1962.

Smith, Caleb A., *The Flow of Funds in Small and in Large Businesses,* Brown University Press, Providence, R.I., 1963.

Part III

The Sources of Short-Term Funds

6

Borrowing From the Bank

THE STRUCTURE OF BANKING IN THE UNITED STATES

The Development of Banking in the United States

COMMERCIAL BANKS are only one of many lending institutions in the United States, but their importance to our economic life can hardly be overestimated. Inactive funds are accumulated and loaned by them, they provide for the transfer of funds, they act as trustees for issues of bonds sold to the public, and they act as transfer agents for the stock of corporations. Although these activities are not performed by commercial banks alone, there is one function unique to them. Only commercial banks are authorized by government to create part of the money supply of the nation by extending loans in the form of deposits subject to check.

The American banking system developed in response to the historical forces shaping the economic and political structure of the nation. In banking more than in other industries the long standing opposition to centralized power has shaped today's largely localized banking structure. The first half century of national history witnessed a struggle between the advocates of strong central authority and those of local authority in economic and political affairs. In 1791, the Bank of the United States was created with a federal charter of twenty years, being authorized to issue bank note currency, transfer funds between different parts of the country, and to act as fiscal agent for the federal government. Despite the success of the bank in providing stable, conservative banking to the new nation, or perhaps because of it, opposition to the bank was intense. Its enemies, particularly the banks chartered by the states, succeeded in preventing the renewal of the charter in 1811. After five years of rapid increase in the number of banks with state charters, lax bank supervision, price inflation, and war, a new Bank of the United States was created by Congress in 1816, again with a twenty-year charter. As in the case of the first Bank, the

Second Bank of the United States after an unsteady start, brought responsible, conservative management to the industry of banking, and restrained the profligate issuance of bank notes by the state chartered banks; and, as happened before, when the charter of the Second Bank came up for renewal, it was killed, this time by the veto of President Andrew Jackson.

The pattern of banking during the balance of the nineteenth century was one of continual growth in the number of banks, most of them small and serving a local area. The state laws under which banks were permitted to operate prohibited or restricted the growth of branch banking. Although Congress passed acts in 1863 and 1864 permitting organizers of banks to receive federal charters, the administration of the federal banking laws bowed to the limitations on branch banking imposed by each of the states. As a result, the industry of banking did not, like other industries, consolidate into a few companies with nationwide operations. In contrast to Canada's ten commercial banks and Great Britain's "Big Five," with branches distributed nationwide, the United States had over 25,000 commercial banks in 1929 and over 13,000 in 1962. Some of these are large in asset size, a few have branches extending locally or statewide, and some in port cities have foreign branches, but the vast majority are small banks serving a local area.

Bank Organization   Commercial banks operate as corporations with charters issued either by the state government or the federal government. The former are called state banks and the latter national banks. In order for a proposed bank to receive a federal charter it is necessary for the promoters to convince the Comptroller of the Currency that there is enough demand for banking services to make its operation profitable, that the proposed directors and officers are capable and experienced, and that the financial standing of the applicants for the charter is strong. Although the necessary qualifications for a state charter are of the same type, the standards are usually less strict. Charters for national banks and for most state banks are now perpetual.

A charter is not forfeited merely because a bank meeting strict managerial and financial standards at the time of organization has later come under the control of persons unqualified to receive a charter for a new bank. Because the ownership and management of banks change as years pass, it is important for the financial officer of a business firm to select a bank with care.

The organizational structure of a bank is similar to that of most corporations: a board of directors, a president, several vice presidents, one cashier, perhaps several assistant cashiers, tellers, and, for a bank with a trust department, trust officers and assistants. The number of directors of a national bank may be as low as five or as high as twenty-five. Business interests often have a broad representation on these boards. Because the board determines the basic policies of the bank, the financial officer of a business firm should examine the names and affiliations of the board members before choosing a bank connection.

The Federal Reserve System The money panic of 1907 made it painfully obvious that the economic welfare of the United States could not be left to the haphazard and uncoordinated activities of thousands of independent banks. As a result of this catastrophe, Congress, following the recommendations of a bipartisan monetary commission, passed a bill establishing a central banking system for the United States, thereby creating the Federal Reserve System in 1913. Among its many responsibilities was that of maintaining the stability and availability of credit throughout the country, which it did through its power to influence the reserves of commercial banks. The size of the bank reserves in turn constituted a very important element in the volume of bank loans. When inflation of prices threatened, the Federal Reserve System generally tried to curtail the expansion of bank credit, usually known as a "tight money" policy. In face of a threatened decline in business activity, on the other hand, the Federal Reserve followed the opposite policy of encouraging expansion of credit. Monetary policy does not, however, strike the reserves of all commercial banks in the country with equal force. Some banks may find that the tight money policy affects their lending almost not at all, while other banks find that such a policy severely restricts the loans that the bank was otherwise making. In general, it can be said that where a restrictive monetary policy of the central banking system results in the curtailment of the volume of loans of a particular bank, this policy will affect the marginal customers of the bank considerably, and the strong borrowers much less or not at all.

Most of the industrial nations of the world have a central bank.[1] The United States is unique, however, in having a regional central banking system. There are twelve Federal Reserve Banks, each serving as a central bank for a district of the United States. Although the Federal Reserve System was created primarily to serve the commercial banking industry and the federal government, issue paper currency, and aid in stabilizing financial conditions of the country, it serves business both directly and indirectly. The System has eliminated the wild fluctuations in the availability of bank credit, reduced the seasonal and cyclical variation in interest rates, and made the cost of loans more nearly uniform throughout the United States. Of more direct benefit to business is the efficient clearing and collection of checks and the rapid transfer of funds through the System.

Government Regulation of Banking Associated with the structure of the banking industry, composed as it is of thousands of local banks, the United

---

[1] A brief description of the Federal Reserve System of the United States and the functions of central banking are given in Chapter 31 of Paul G. Hastings, *Fundamentals of Business Enterprise*, D. Van Nostrand Company, Inc., Princeton, N. J., 1961. A fuller description is given in Edwin W. Kemmerer and Donald L. Kemmerer, *The ABC of the Federal Reserve System*, Harper and Row, New York, 1950.

States has had a history of numerous bank failures.[2]   The growth of government regulation of banking has been largely the result of efforts to provide protection to the users of bank facilities.   State banks are examined by auditors from the state capital.   National banks are examined by examiners from the Comptroller of the Currency in Washington.   In addition, all insured banks are subject to examination by the Federal Deposit Insurance Corporation, and member banks [3] of the Federal Reserve System are subject to examination by the Reserve Bank of their district.   Most banks are subject to examination and regulation by at least two regulatory agencies.

Given the localized structure of banking in the United States, the high degree of regulation serves as a measure of protection against the results of mismanagement and embezzlement in banks, particularly small ones. The regulations, however, reduce the freedom and flexibility with which bankers can meet their customers needs.   The regulations apply equally to competent, capable bank management and the inexperienced, incompetent bank management, to which the regulations are primarily directed. This may explain to some degree why during the last few decades businesses have turned more to alternative lending institutions as a source of funds.

THE CHARACTER OF BANK LENDING

The loans outstanding on the books of banks in the United States December 20, 1963, were divided as follows:

	Millions
Loans to commerce and industry	$52,947
Loans to purchase and carry securities	7,862
Loans to financial institutions	13,084
Agricultural loans	7,470
Real estate loans	39,056
Other loans to individuals	34,550
Other loans	4,034
Total	$159,003

SOURCE: *Federal Reserve Bulletin.*

Even though the dominance of banks as a source of business loans has decreased, business borrowers still turn most often to their banks when a loan is needed.   Even when a loan is secured from another source, the bank loan is used as a standard against which to measure its cost and convenience.

Although a larger dollar volume of loans is accounted for by the process of businesses purchasing supplies on open book terms, the commercial

---

2 More than 5,000 banks failed in the Nation from 1930 to 1933.   Because of the absence of bank failures in Great Britain and Canada, there is greater freedom from regulation by government in those two countries than there is here.

3 All national banks and those state banks voluntarily joining the Federal Reserve System constitute the member banks of the Federal Reserve System.

banking system has historically been the most important source of short-term business borrowing and is today the first source of loans considered by most businessmen when short-term borrowing is contemplated.

Banks are not merely lending institutions; they also provide the following services for businessmen: (1) a safe place to deposit funds, (2) an efficient and rapid means of collecting checks and others items of exchange, (3) counseling on financial problems, (4) a source of foreign exchange, (5) a most important credit reference, and (6) a transfer agent or registrar for the stocks of a corporation.

The range and variety of services offered by commercial banks are greater than many businessmen, particularly small businessmen, realize. The banks also provide services for noncommercial institutions, such as colleges, municipal governments, and philanthropic organizations. The range of services offered and the variety of customers served have sometimes resulted in the commercial bank being called a "department store of credit." Although the services are many and varied, making loans and offering checking accounts remain the distinguishing features of the commercial bank. Nearly every business maintains a checking account as a convenient means of making payments. Since the typical bank loan to a businessman is in the form of a credit to his checking account, loans from the bank constitute one of the most convenient sources of lending to business.

The character of commercial banking has changed considerably during the last thirty years. Prior to World War II, the amount loaned by commercial banks to the federal government was approximately three times as much as that loaned to business borrowers. Their loans to consumers were relatively insignificant. During World War II, the volume of bank loans to the federal government through purchasing government bonds increased with great rapidity, while loans to commercial and industrial borrowers increased only moderately. Following the war, however, commercial and industrial loans increased very rapidly, while bank holdings of government bonds declined, as Table 6-1 shows.

TABLE 6-1. LOANS AND INVESTMENTS OF ALL INSURED BANKS

(Loans outstanding end of year)	1941	1945	1947	1958	1960	1962
Commercial and industrial loans	9,214	9,461	18,012	40,289	42,957	48,673
Agricultural loans	1,450	1,314	1,610	4,913	5,628	7,097
Loans to individuals		2,361	5,654	20,589	26,263	30,553
Real estate loans	4,773	4,677	9,266	25,148	28,602	34,259
Holdings of U.S. government bonds and other obligations	21,046	88,912	67,941	65,669	60,468	66,434

Source: Federal Reserve Bulletin.

During the post-World War II era, the most spectacular increase in the type of loans made by commercial banks occurred in the financing of real estate and durable goods by consumers. Prior to World War II, it could be stated with justification that the commercial banking system was primarily an agency for providing credit to the federal government. Following World War II, banks became a credit agency devoted largely to providing loans to commercial and industrial borrowers and government borrowers. Although the volume of borrowing by the federal government from the banking system was substantial in 1961, there has been a notable decline in this use of commercial bank credit.

By tradition, commercial banks have been a source of self-liquidating loans for industry and commerce.[4] In recent decades, however, the variety of purposes for which different borrowers have sought loans from commercial banks has increased considerably. Furthermore, the types of loan contracts and the various methods of extending loans have increased. To some extent businesses have become less dependent upon banks as a source of financing, chiefly by relying instead on internal sources of funds. There has also been an increase in alternative external sources of funds due to the development of lending institutions other than commercial banks. In order to increase their volume of loans, banks have made loan contracts more flexible than they used to be, and have sought to make their policies suitable to a wider variety of business requirements than before.

The loan agreement between the bank and the borrowing company is a contract containing a number of clauses. As stated earlier, there is considerable variation in the characteristics of bank loans, but they also have certain common characteristics. All bank loan agreements describe the size of the loan, the method of repayment and the times that the payments must be made, the rate of interest and whether it is to be deducted at the beginning or at the end, whether any security is required, the size of the minimum balance to be maintained in the borrower's checking account, and the extent of any limitations on financial freedom during the life of the loan.

If loans are in considerable demand and it is relatively easy for a bank to lend to the extent of its capacity, bank officers tend to be more restrictive in the terms demanded than they are during periods when the demand for bank loans is slack. Some banks refuse to make loans on an unsecured basis for periods in excess of one year, while other banks make such loans frequently. Some banks will accept greater risk in making loans than others. Some banks acquire a reputation for specializing in certain types of loans, such as financing agricultural projects, oil well operations, international transactions, or retail operations. From the standpoint of the business borrower, therefore, it is important that the officers of the business consider carefully the "personality" of the bank with which they intend to maintain relations.

---

4 A loan is said to be self-liquidating when it is used for a purpose which provides the means of repaying the loan. An example of this would be to borrow $10,000 from a commercial bank to purchase a new stock of goods for a retail store; the resale of the goods to the store's customers would provide the means of loan repayment.

TYPES OF BANK LOANS

The borrowers and depositors are the customers of the bank without whose goodwill the bank would not be able to earn a profit. The credit needs of the business borrowers of a bank vary considerably. In order to satisfy them, a commercial bank offers many kinds of loans. Loans are designed to meet the needs of business borrowers while, at the same time, providing due consideration for the necessities of safeguarding the funds of the bank.

The Size of Bank Loans   The amount requested by the borrower in the loan application is limited by what the borrower feels can be profitably used by the company. Some business borrowers are in the fortunate position of being able to borrow more than they can effectively put to use at a given time, but most, particularly small companies, usually have to get along with less bank credit than they want. From the standpoint of the commercial bank, the limit on the size of a loan that the bank is willing to make is conditioned by the degree of risk involved and the likelihood of default on payment of interest and principal. Another factor conditioning the size of the loan is the size of the borrowing business, the size of loan usually varying with the size of the company. A large proportion of a bank's customers are small businesses. Thirty-nine per cent of all business loans made by member banks of the Federal Reserve System in 1957 were to businesses having assets of less than $50,000 each, and the average size of these loans was $2,900.[5]

The size of the loan that a commercial bank is willing to make to a business borrower is affected by the balance sheet presented by the borrower as part of the loan application. If the balance sheet shows considerable short-term indebtedness already in existence, the bank will limit the size of the loan. Furthermore, if the borrower has already outstanding one or more loans from other commercial banks, an application for the loan would probably be restricted in amount more than if no loans from other banks were on the borrower's balance sheet. Although most commercial banks do not refuse to make loans to medium and small companies already in debt to other banks, the general attitude is one of considerable caution. The financial data furnished by a small business borrower are not always complete or entirely accurate. Since indebtedness to other banks is sometimes omitted in the application, banks in many cities maintain a central credit and loan file operated by the local clearing house association of the banks. A daily report of all bank loans is made by each bank, giving the name of the borrower, the amount of the loan, and other items of informa-

[5] *Federal Reserve Bulletin*, April 1958, p. 396. The member banks of the Federal Reserve System include the largest commercial banks in the country. Approximately two-thirds of the commercial banks in the United States are nonmembers and are mostly small banks. It is evident that the percentage of loans of the nonmember banks to business borrowers with less than $50,000 in total assets is considerably higher than that of member banks.

tion. Each of the banks can then check the total amount of the indebtedness of a borrower to all the banks in the community.

The size of the bank loan is also limited by the capacity of the bank to make loans. Banks are limited by state or national bank regulations in the size of the loan that each can make to a borrower. A national bank may lend no more than 10 per cent of its unimpaired capital and surplus to any one borrower. There are, however, certain loans exempt from this limitation, such as loans secured by the deposit of United States government bonds or loans secured by commodities in process of shipment. The legal limitation on the size of bank loans makes it inconvenient for large businesses to borrow from small banks. Not only that, but, because corporations sometimes find it difficult to borrow the full amounts that they need from larger banks, they will occasionally borrow from several banks at one time under a single loan agreement.

Maturity Although banks make loans running for several years, two-thirds of the dollar volume of all bank loans have a maturity of less than one year. The commercial bank, therefore, is primarily a source of short-term funds for business. In this connection, however, it should be pointed out that the average maturity of promissory notes signed by businesses borrowing from banks is shorter than the average length of loans from all sources. Provided the financial condition and the credit standing of the borrower does not deteriorate during the life of the loan, most banks will look with favor on an application for a renewal of the loan to replace the matured note. Thus a business borrower might obtain loans from a bank by means of notes all of which have a maturity of thirty or sixty days, even though the borrower might be continuously in debt to the bank for a period considerably longer than sixty days. Although most banks are quite willing to renew loans for those maintaining their credit rating, they also attempt to eliminate the tendency to substitute continuous renewal of short-term loans for a long-term loan. The usual means for accomplishing this is the requirement that each borrower "get out of the bank" at least once each year —in other words, the business borrower must repay all outstanding indebtedness to the bank at least once each year. If this were not done, some businesses would probably rely on bank credit to furnish part of the permanent working capital of the business. Another reason is that banks recognize that most businesses have a pattern of seasonal fluctuation of sales. The annual cleanup rule assumes that if the business is in sound condition, it will have no difficulty in repaying the loans negotiated to finance the seasonal peak of operations during the part of the season that the short-term borrowing is not needed. Some banks consider this annual cleanup as proof that the borrower is not using the bank as a source of permanent investment funds. Where a business borrower is in debt to several banks, the attitude of the banks regarding the annual cleanup of loans differs. Some banks will require that each of its loan customers clean up all the bank indebtedness at least once a year. Others have no objection to a borrower cleaning up its loans to the bank while remaining in debt to other banks. The justification for this policy is that it shows evidence that the business borrower has alternative sources of bank loans, and, therefore, a degree of flexibility in meeting its credit requirements. If the annual cleanup of bank loans results in an increase in the trade accounts payable to the borrower, most banks will have no objection.

Costs of Borrowing In extending loans, it costs money to interview an applicant for a loan, to review the written application and credit file of the applicant, to prepare the ledger cards and other forms necessary in placing the loan on the books of the lender, and to collect the installments during the life of the loan or the repayment of the principal plus interest at the maturity of the loan. All these costs are involved regardless of the size of the loan and, in most cases, cannot be reduced below a certain minimum. It is partly for this reason that the costs of small loans is substantially higher as a percentage of the amount loaned than is the cost of large loans. The charges lenders make to borrowers may be simple or complex. In the case of installment financing of consumer goods, the charges paid by the consumer frequently are so complex that it is almost impossible for him, unless he is a professional mathematician, to determine what is the full cost of borrowing the money. Charges made by lenders to business borrowers are usually simpler. This is true of the charges for bank loans. The simplest is an interest charge on the unpaid balance of a single payment loan. An example of this is 6 per cent interest on a $1,000 loan payable in one payment at the end of twelve months: $1,000 is used for one year, and $1,060 is paid in at the end. Although this type of loan is sometimes made by banks to business borrowers, more commonly banks discount the promissory notes of their customers. Thus, if a $1,000 note payable in one year is discounted at 6 per cent, the borrower receives the use of $940 for one year and repays $1,000 to the bank at the end of that time. The actual cost of the loan in this case is 6.38 per cent per annum.

Where the loan contract requires the repayment of the principal in installments during the life of the loan (this is becoming increasingly common as a method used by banks to finance the purchase of machinery by their customers), there are two ways the bank makes the charge for the loan. One method requires that the customer sign a promissory note for the amount he wishes to borrow plus the interest charged by the bank, the sum of the two then being divided by the number of installments needed to retire the loan. The other method requires the borrower to sign a promissory note for a given figure from which the discount is then deducted, the face amount of the note being repayable in equal installments during the life of the loan. Under the first method the borrower receives $1,000 and is obligated to repay twelve installments of $88.33 each, if the life of the loan is one year. Under the second method the borrower receives only $940 and pays twelve monthly installments of $83.33. If the borrower wishes to approximate the true cost of the loan in terms of annual interest, he may do so by doubling the amount of the interest charged on the loan, the justification being that the average amount of the loan outstanding is half of the amount at the beginning of the period. If the borrower prefers a more sophisticated method of determining the cost of the loan in terms of true annual interest, he may use the following formula:

$$I = \frac{2Ni}{P(n+1)}$$

I is the interest rate per annum
N is the number of payments per year (usually 12)
i is the total of interest and other charges in dollars for the loan
P is the principal of the loan (the amount of money available for use by the borrower at the beginning of the loan period)
n is the total number of payments required by the loan contract

One important element in the cost of borrowing from commercial banks is their requirement that a *compensating balance* of a minimum amount be kept with the bank. The compensating balance, in the form of a demand deposit (checking account) with the bank, typically is maintained at 15 to 20 per cent of the amount owed the bank by the borrower. Banks vary considerably in administering this requirement. Where the business borrower has a line of credit (discussed below) with his bank, he might be required to maintain a compensating balance of 20 per cent of the line of credit whether the credit is fully used or only partly used. Other banks require that the compensating balance be maintained at 20 per cent of the line of credit when the line is being used and only 10 per cent when the line is not in use. In addition to the lack of uniformity in applying these rules, there is also considerable difference in enforcing them. In general, when the demand for loans runs high, banks enforce more strictly the compensating balance requirements; on the other hand, when business is slack and the demand for bank loans is slow, banks typically relax these rules.

There is quite a bit of controversy as to the legitimacy of the compensating balance requirement. The argument of the banks is that if they arrange under a line of credit to stand ready on demand to make loans to a customer, the customer should "insure" the line of credit by maintaining an adequate checking account balance with the bank. Another justification given by banks is that any business concern must maintain a checking account in some bank in order to make payments and that it is reasonable to require loan customers to maintain their balance in lending banks.

The compensating balance rule has been criticized by some business borrowers on the argument that it adds to the cost of bank loans by not permitting the borrower to make full use of the amount on which the borrower is required to pay interest. The extent of the added borrowing from the bank undertaken by the borrower to meet the compensating balance rule depends upon the additional deposit that must be maintained, if any, above that which would be maintained anyway by the borrower. It is certainly true that a properly managed business would have a balance in its checking account whether the business were in debt to the bank or not. For example, if a business maintains a $10,000 average balance in its checking account and receives a loan of $50,000 at 6 per cent interest on which a compensating balance of 20 per cent is required, there is then no additional cost to the company from the compensating balance requirement. However, if the borrowing company maintains an average balance of $5,000 at the time that a $50,000 loan is received from the bank at 6 per cent interest, the compensating balance requirement does impose an added cost. In this case, the borrower must bring up his balance to $10,000 in order to meet the minimum balance requirement. In other words, $5,000 of the $50,000 loan must remain in the account and only $45,000 is usable by the borrower. If the loan is for one year, the interest of $3,000 on the usable portion of the $45,000 loan represents a rate of 6.67 per cent. The balance maintained by a business concern does not, of course, remain constant day after day. If the lending bank does not insist upon strict maintenance of the compensating balance rule, then it probably does not impose much of a burden on business borrowers. It is only where a compensating balance rule is strictly enforced by the bank and where the minimum balance is in excess of what the financial officer of the borrowing company feels is necessary that the compensating balance rule imposes an added cost to the borrowing company.

Secured Loans If the position of the borrower is not sufficiently strong to qualify for an unsecured bank loan, the loan officer of the bank may require a pledge of assets as collateral securing the loan. Almost any marketable asset may qualify as collateral. Those most frequently pledged are accounts receivable, inventories, and stocks and bonds owned by the borrower. The demand for security is made more frequently against small borrowers than large ones. A study made by the Federal Reserve System in 1957 indicated that business borrowers with assets of less than $50,000 had 78 per cent of the dollar amount of their bank loans secured by the pledge of assets; borrowers having $100,000 or more in assets had only 17½ per cent secured.[6]

Although banks will make loans on the security of a wide variety of assets, they prefer security that is easily turned into cash. If the business borrower can offer marketable stocks or bonds or the cash surrender value of a life insurance policy, the conditions of the loan are generally easier on

---

[6] *Federal Reserve Bulletin,* April 1958, p. 403.

the borrower than if accounts receivable or inventory are offered. A bank prefers not to have to liquidate a loan by foreclosing on a herd of cattle, nor do bankers relish becoming the owners of 20,000 dozen eggs in storage. The main reason that bankers require security is that it imposes a discipline on a borrower that increases somewhat his efforts to meet repayment schedules on time. This explains the greater use of collateral to secure bank loans made to small businesses than to large businesses.

Repayment of Bank Loans Checking accounts constitute the bulk of the deposits of most commercial banks. Since these are subject to withdrawal without prior notice to the banks, the banks prefer to keep their earning assets as liquid as possible. For this reason they prefer to make business loans of short-term maturity. It is also for this reason that banks are more insistent upon prompt repayment of loans than are most trade creditors. If the loan contract provides for the repayment of the loan in installments, it is essential in the financial planning of the debtor company that provisions be made to assure that the company will have funds available in the bank ready to meet the loan payments when due. If the loan is repayable in one payment, the company must build up its account in the bank prior to this date so that the bank loan can be liquidated. If the amount of the repayment is large relative to the financial resources of the borrowing company, it may be necessary for the financial officer of the company to make arrangements to borrow sufficient funds from sources other than the bank to which the loan is repayable. While the alternate sources of credit may not be necessary, it is advisable that they be available in the event that the expected buildup of cash in the bank does not materialize in time for the loan repayment.

With respect to repayment requirements, some banks are very strict and spell out in detail the repayment provisions of the loans they make to business borrowers. Other banks, chiefly the smaller banks, are less exact in their repayment requirements. As a matter of fact, one bank examining agency has stated that "the one management weakness which is most prevalent [among banks] is the granting of credit with no firm understanding as to its repayment—how or when. Conversely, those bankers who require a firm understanding with borrowers as to the terms and means of repayment maintain the soundest loan portfolios." [7]

Restrictions Imposed on the Borrower As stated above, one of the main reasons a bank requires loan security is to impose a degree of discipline to help insure repayment. There are other ways of imposing discipline on the borrower. These are found in bank loans whether the loans are secured or unsecured. It is not uncommon for a bank to restrict the payment of dividends by a corporation to not more than a stated percentage of the net income of the corporation earned after the beginning date of the loan, or

---

[7] Homer J. Livingston, *Management Policies in American Banks*, Harper & Row, Publishers Inc., New York, 1956, p. 22.

...., California

Bank of America
NATIONAL TRUST AND SAVINGS ASSOCIATION
(hereinafter called BANK)

...., 19..........

....Branch

...., Calif.

Gentlemen:

The undersigned..

(hereinafter referred to as CREDITOR), a creditor of...

....(hereinafter referred to as BORROWER) desires that BANK continue to extend or extend such financial accommodations to BORROWER as BORROWER may require and as BANK may deem proper. For the purpose of inducing BANK to grant, continue or renew such financial accommodation, and in consideration thereof, the undersigned CREDITOR agrees as follows:

That at the present time BORROWER is indebted to CREDITOR in the sum of $.................................

That all claims of CREDITOR against BORROWER now or hereafter existing are and shall be at all times subordinate and subject to any and all claims now or hereafter existing (and renewals or extensions of the same) which BANK may have against BORROWER so long as any such claim or claims of BANK shall exist.

CREDITOR agrees not to sue upon, or to collect, or to receive payment of any claim or claims now or hereafter existing, (nor interest thereon) which CREDITOR may hold against BORROWER, and not to sell, assign, transfer, pledge, hypothecate, or encumber such claim or claims except subject expressly to this Agreement, and not to enforce or apply any security now or hereafter existing, nor to join in any petition in bankruptcy or any assignment for the benefit of creditors, or any creditors' agreement, nor to take any lien or security on any of BORROWER'S property, real or personal, so long as any such claim or claims of BANK against BORROWER shall exist.

In case of any assignment by BORROWER for the benefit of creditors, or in case of any bankruptcy proceedings instituted by or against BORROWER, or in case of the appointment of any receiver for BORROWER'S business or assets, or in case of any dissolution or winding up of the affairs of said BORROWER, BORROWER and any assignee, trustee in bankruptcy, receiver, or other person or persons in charge, are hereby directed to pay to BANK the full amount of BANK'S claims against BORROWER before making any payment of principal or interest to CREDITOR, and in so far as may be necessary for that purpose, CREDITOR hereby assigns and transfers to BANK all security or the proceeds thereof, and all rights to any payments, dividends or other distributions. If CREDITOR does not file a proper claim or proof of debt in the form required in such proceeding prior to 30 days before the expiration of the time to file such claim in such proceeding, then BANK has the right to and is hereby authorized to file an appropriate claim or claims for and on behalf of CREDITOR.

It is further agreed that until all such claims of BANK against BORROWER, now or hereafter existing, shall be paid in full, no gift or loan shall be made by BORROWER to CREDITOR.

For violation of this Agreement, CREDITOR shall be liable for all loss and damage sustained by reason of such breach, and upon any such violation BANK at its option may accelerate the maturity of its claims against BORROWER.

This Agreement shall be binding upon the heirs, successors and assigns of CREDITOR, BORROWER and BANK. This Agreement and any claim or claims of BANK may be assigned by BANK, in whole or in part, without notice to CREDITOR or BORROWER.

....
CREDITOR

ACCEPTANCE OF SUBORDINATION AGREEMENT BY BORROWER

The undersigned being the BORROWER named in the foregoing Subordination Agreement, hereby accepts and consents thereto and agrees to be bound by all the provisions thereof and to recognize all priorities and other rights granted thereby to BANK OF AMERICA NATIONAL TRUST AND SAVINGS ASSOCIATION, its successors and assigns, and to perform in accordance therewith.

Dated: ...., 19.........

....
BORROWER

TPL-12 9-59

Fig. 6-1 *Subordination agreement.*

in some cases may prohibit the payment of dividends entirely during the life of the loan.   Applied to unincorporated businesses, such a restriction limits the amount of withdrawals the partners or the proprietor may make from their businesses. The bank may require that the current ratio be kept above a stated minimum. Failure to do so might make the loan to the bank immediately due and payable. Furthermore, before the managers of the business take certain actions affecting the financial condition of the business, the bank may require approval, such as any major purchase of company assets or any other major expenditure by the company, any increase in officers' salaries, or any decision to repay debts ahead of their maturity.   The bank might require its approval before the borrowing company may seek additional loans from other sources.

As a further condition, banks and some other lenders require that existing indebtedness be subordinated. This is most commonly required where stockholders of closely held companies have made loans to the corporations they own.   By making these loans rather than increasing their stock investment, the stockholders can enjoy certain tax advantages. To receive favorable consideration from a lender, however, often requires that the loans from the stockholders be subordinated to the loans extended by the bank or other lenders. The subordination agreement is drawn up as a written document, as illustrated in Fig. 6-1. It will state, for example, that no payments on debts owed by the corporation to the stockholders may be made until the bank loan has been retired and that, in the event of bankruptcy, the bank loan will be paid in full before the subordinated debt is discharged.

Most of the above restrictions would be dictated by prudent financial management in the absence of any requirement by the bank. The purpose of the bank in making such restrictions is not to tell the borrower how to run his business but rather to decrease the risk in lending. Banks in making loans do not want to become "a partner of the business enterprise" to which the loan is made. Although banks occasionally find themselves in the position of being a "participant in the business," this is a position which they studiously try to avoid. What banks seek in making such restrictions is safety, not management prerogatives.

Lines of Credit   In Great Britain and some other European countries the typical method of extending bank loans is by means of an *overdraft*. The borrower receives from the bank an authority to overdraw his account up to a certain maximum figure during the period of the extension of credit. The authority to overdraw indicates the maximum amount that is permitted. Although the amount of the overdraft rises and falls, in most cases the total of the overdraft remains below the maximum figure permitted by the bank. The overdraft is very rarely used by United States banks as a means of lending.

However, a somewhat similar arrangement is the use of the *line of credit.* After a thorough credit investigation of the applicant, the bank issues a line of credit to the borrower, which establishes the maximum total of loans that the bank is willing to extend at any one time to him. It also indicates the general terms under which the bank is willing to make loans. The line of credit may state what security, if any, is required, the length of time for which loans may remain outstanding, the restrictions imposed on the use of the money lent, and possibly the rate of interest to be charged. Commonly, however, the bank reserves to itself the right to set the interest rate from time to time under the line of credit according to changing monetary conditions. As is true of the overdraft, the line of credit offered by American banks permits the borrower to receive funds with a minimum of uncertainty and delay.

Lines of credit are generally extended for periods of one year or less. If the borrower wishes to extend the line of credit for another year, the line must be re-established. In the case of borrowers with excellent credit ratings, such re-establishment is a routine matter. Possibly some changes might be made in the terms under which the bank is willing to make the loans. For example, if the business of the borrower has expanded since the time that the previous line of credit was granted, it is quite likely that the bank would be willing to increase the maximum amount of the line. If the borrowing needs of a large customer of the bank become too great for the bank to handle, it may suggest he establish a line of credit with several participating banks. Under such an arrangement, which is known as a *multiple line of credit,* the borrowing company receives authority to borrow from a group of banks under a uniform line of credit. This is particularly useful to large corporations in having their short-term borrowing needs met through bank lending.

In most cases the granting of a line of credit by the bank is not a contractual obligation on its part, but rather is in the nature of an informal understanding. The bank reserves the right to change the terms of the line of credit if it finds it necessary to do so, or even to revoke it entirely. A commercial bank, of course, is in business to serve its customers, and attempts to provide as good service as possible. If it did not do so, it would find that most of its loan customers would go to other banks. Therefore, while the bank does reserve the right to modify the line of credit at any time, it will usually do so for a good reason. It is possible for a business borrower to get a line of credit which is in the nature of a contract and which requires the payment of a fee by the borrower. The additional assurance of the availability of credit on demand provided by a firm contract may be important to some borrowers. For most business borrowers, however, the informal assurance provided by the usual line of credit is sufficient guarantee on which to base the financial planning of the company. The fee usually charged by a bank for a contract line of credit is based on the total amount of the line, and runs generally from one-half of one per cent to one per cent of the line. Loans actually extended under the line are charged at rates of interest in addition to that charged on the inactive line.

CHOOSING A BANK

A commercial bank is much more than a source of loans. The variety of services offered to the businessman has been suggested above. In addition to its advertised services, the bank stands ready to help its customers in many other ways. Generally, the extent to which a banker is willing to go out of his way to serve a customer depends upon the length of the particular customer-banker relationship, which makes it important for a businessman to establish a secure and lasting relationship with a bank. Because the customer-banker relationship is a continuing one, the company must choose its bank with great care. Of the many considerations involved in such a choice, the more important ones are discussed below.

Size and Location   A businessman should choose a bank that is "large enough to serve you but small enough to care," to paraphrase typical bank advertisements. In many cases, the financial officer of the company should be careful to select a bank that is not too small to meet the needs of a growing business, particularly if the business is one that expects to experience rapid growth. To a reasonably large business the legal loan limit of the bank is a very important criterion. Most of the large banks in the United States are national ones, operating under charters issued by the federal government and regulated by the Comptroller of the Currency. As we already know, one of these regulations sets a maximum amount that may be loaned to any one borrower.

In addition to being able to accommodate the loan requirements of a large borrower, a large bank can offer a wider variety of specialized services than a smaller bank. Small banks typically do not have trust departments, which would prove inconvenient to some customers. To a company having export or import operations, the advantage of a large bank may be considerable. Many large banks, even those located in inland cities, will have facilities for handling the numerous transactions involved in exporting and importing. A large bank has many more correspondent banks than does a small bank. These may provide important services, where the customer has many transactions involving clients located at a considerable distance. Large banks are able to employ specialists with an intimate knowledge of and experience in many different types of businesses. Large banks in Texas employ, for example, petroleum engineers and experts in cattle raising, cotton production, real estate management, and manufacturing. Their counsel is available not only to the bank in making loans and to the trust department in managing property under trust agreements but also to customers in advising them on better management of their business operations. In other parts of the country, the specialists vary in accordance with the industries in their area. Because of the volume of lending, a large bank can afford to make greater use of a wide variety of specialists. In some cases, the officers of a company may feel that there is some prestige in being associated with a large bank, though in the majority of cases this is probably not an important factor.

However, the advantages in dealing with a small bank must not be overlooked. Partly to offset the obvious ones of large banks, the officers of a small bank may go out of their way to provide a higher degree of attention to their customers. Although a small bank cannot afford to have as many specialists as a large bank, small banks sometimes are themselves specialists. One bank's specialty may be in agricultural loans, while another bank's may be directed to retailers. In 1960, a new bank was organized in San Francisco with officers almost entirely of Chinese ancestry and able to speak Chinese as well as English. The location of the bank was, understandably, in the Chinatown section of the city.

Bank Lending Policies Lending policies among banks show considerable variation. There are those banks that have highly conservative managements, while others have aggressive and vigorous ones. Some banks are noted for rapidly adopting innovations in lending money or offering new services, while others follow suit only after the more daring banks have introduced and tested them. Some banks are very reluctant to make loans of longer term than one year; others are reluctant to make loans on the security of inventory or accounts receivable. Some large banks vigorously promote the loans and deposits of small businessmen, while other large banks welcome such accounts but do not actively seek them. The considerable variation shown in service charges, compensating balance requirements, and restrictions imposed on marginal borrowers frequently causes a borrower to be turned down by one bank and eagerly accepted by another.

Financial Counseling and Other Services While it is true that large banks can provide a greater variety of services than small banks, the range of services offered by banks of any size is considerable. In addition to the loan and deposit services, provision is made for safe deposit boxes, cashier's checks, commercial drafts, telegraphic transfer of funds, and the purchase of government bonds. There is also credit information for the business customers. Some banks, particularly the large ones, employ an economist, who prepares studies of economic conditions of the region served by the bank or for the nation as a whole and provides economic forecasts, tax studies, and other data for the bank's business customers. Other banks, again the larger ones for the most part, provide a series of industry studies that are usually published and available not only to the bank customers but also to the public. If some of these services are important to a particular company, it should choose a bank with due consideration to the availability of such services.

Since all banks are interested in building up their business, it is to their advantage for their customers to become better managers. If the banker is able to help a customer in becoming a better businessman, the banker will do so. If a bank connection is chosen with care, the bank officers can be persons in whom the businessman can confide with assurance, and whose advice can be confidently taken. This is particularly important for the small business concern that is not able to hire a full-time financial officer.

In choosing a bank, the chief financial officer of the company should appraise its board of directors. In appraising the board of directors of a commercial bank, the businessman should consider whether the directors represent a broad spectrum of experience or a restricted view of a few industries or interest groups. It might be well for the financial officer to note whether or not the commercial bank has on its board any persons representing companies that are in sharp competition with his firm.

Community Standing of the Bank   The reputation of a bank in the community is a very important factor in the choice of a bank. Some have a reputation for being more interested in the growth and development of a community than do others. Some have a reputation for vigorously seeking out new business possibilities and aiding in the development of new and growing concerns. Some bank presidents will spend quite a bit of time in calling on business concerns to become better acquainted with their problems and to try to aid them in developing their business. Other bankers rely more on the age of their bank in the community. The style of advertising and public relations activity can frequently furnish clues to the character of the bank.

Loyalty to Customers   Since the careful selection of a bank takes time, it should be made with the expectation that the banking connection will be a long one. The bank officers' loyalty toward those of its customers that experience temporary distress must be appraised. When a company is enjoying substantial sales, when its profit position is good, when it is able to meet its trade payables within the cash discount period—in short, when a company is in a strong financial position, the financial officer will experience little difficulty in getting loans. It is axiomatic that a wider variety of sources of loans will be available to a strong borrower than to a weak borrower. Obviously, a bank would prefer that all its loan customers be strong. It is a rare company, however, that can maintain a constant strong position, and can disregard the changing economic conditions of the region. A banking connection, like friendship, is tested during adversity. A bank's first responsibility is to safeguard its depositors' funds, so it is unreasonable to expect that a bank would continue to make loans to improvident borrowers. Nevertheless, there is much that a bank can do without taking undue risks to aid its loan customers in times of temporary distress: renewal of loans, the granting of term loans, a temporary increase in the line of credit or the granting of emergency credit, additional credit granted on marketable securities or the cash surrender value of life insurance policies, or perhaps merely financial counseling. On some occasions, a bank unwilling to make a particular type of loan will arrange for another bank, perhaps a considerable distance away, to extend credit to a customer.

Safety Practically all commercial banks in the United States are covered by deposit insurance.[8] Present insurance coverage of bank deposits provides for a maximum of $10,000 of insurance on each depositor in each bank. The insurance was intended to provide protection to small depositors, both businessmen and consumers. For a business that has more than $10,000 deposited in a bank, the safety of the bank is a factor deserving careful consideration.

In appraising the safety of a bank the criterion applied in examining the financial stability of any business can be applied to a bank. To some extent, it is more difficult to make such an appraisal of a bank, however. Although banks require detailed financial information from the business companies to which they make loans, their own financial statements that are published are highly condensed and often uninformative. The most frequent failures among banks are the small in size and young in age. Any evidence of poor management or lack of proper supervision of bank operations should be considered a reason for rejecting a particular bank. Some banks do not employ an auditor on their staff and, in some cases, do not even employ the services of an outside auditing firm.[9] Some banks do not have any examining directors' committee to oversee the operations of bank officers, some fail to charge off uncollectible debts on their books, some permit improvident expenditures in the conduct of bank business, and others allow investments made without careful analysis.[10]

Although bank policies are adhered to rather strictly, they contain sufficient leeway to permit some bargaining between the bank and a potential borrower. Thus, it can be generally established how the bank's services will be provided and under what conditions the loans granted. The businessman is in his best bargaining position when he opens his account. Furthermore, it is important both to the bank and to the loan customer, at the time of arranging the banking connection, that there be a clear understanding of all the factors likely to be important in their future relationship.

Once a banking connection has been established, good relations ought

---

[8] This was necessitated by frequent bank failures in the present century. During the relatively prosperous 1920's, the number of bank failures annually was in the hundreds. When the two postwar depressions are included, the number from 1920 to 1933 totals 11,000. By comparison, the most recent bank failure in Canada was in 1923, when one bank closed its doors. In Great Britain, the last bank failure was in the 1890's. Since the establishment of the Federal Deposit Insurance Corporation in 1933, the number of failures has been small. However, nearly every year witnesses a few; between 1934 and 1960, over 400 banks failed in the United States.

[9] Homer J. Livingston, *op. cit.*, p. 78.

[10] *Ibid.*, p. 114.

to continue between the bank and the customer. Not only does the bank have a responsibility here, which arises from its desire to increase its business, but the customer must also convince the bank that it is worthwhile to continue the lender-borrower relationship. The financial officer of the business should keep the banker informed on any new developments in his business and supply the bank with complete and up-to-date financial statements as they are prepared for the company executives. This is important to the banker even during periods when the customer has no loans in the bank's loan portfolio. In order to make intelligent replies to requests for credit information about the company and in order to reduce any delay in approving loan requests, the banker always should have available up-to-date information about the financial condition of the business of his customers. If the businessman has the confidence and respect of the banker, and the banker the confidence and respect of the businessman, the banker-customer relationship can be cordial and profitable to both.

Questions

1. What is the difference in the structure of the banking industry between the United States and Canada? How do you account for this difference?
2. Is it possible for persons to become officers and directors who do not meet the standards to qualify them as directors or officers of a proposed bank seeking a charter? Explain.
3. Explain the greater amount of bank regulation in the United States than in Canada and Great Britain.
4. In addition to acting as a source of loans, what services do commercial banks provide?
5. What is meant by a "self-liquidating" loan? Give several examples of such loans.
6. Why do banks in many cities maintain central credit files?
7. How do large corporations avoid the inconvenience of legal limitations on the size of loans that may be made by banks?
8. Why do banks usually require that a borrower "get out of the bank" once each year?
9. What is the compensating balance requirement? Do banks enforce it rigidly or not? Explain.
10. What assets are most frequently used in getting a secured loan from the bank?
11. What restrictions are sometimes imposed by banks on borrowers as a condition to receiving the loan? Why are these restrictions imposed?
12. What is a line of credit? How may it be useful to businessmen borrowing from the bank?
13. What are the advantages to a company in choosing a large bank? In choosing a small bank?
14. In choosing a bank connection, why should a businessman be concerned about what persons serve on the board of directors?
15. If a bank carries deposit insurance, is the degree of risk of bankruptcy of the bank of any concern to a business customer of the bank? Explain.

Selected Readings

American Bankers Association, *The Commercial Banking Industry,* Prentice-Hall, Inc., Englewood Cliffs, N. J., 1962, Chaps. 1, 2, 4.

Kemmerer, Edwin W., and Donald L. Kemmerer, *The ABC of the Federal Reserve System,* Harper and Row, Publishers, Inc., New York, 1950.

Livingston, Homer J., *Management Policies in American Banks,* Harper and Row, Publishers, Inc., New York, 1956.

Robinson, Roland I., *The Management of Bank Funds,* McGraw-Hill Book Co., New York, 1951, Chaps. 1, 6, 7, 8, 9, 11.

Trescott, Paul B., *Financing American Enterprise, The Story of Commercial Banking,* Harper and Row, Publishers, Inc., New York, 1963.

7

Trade Credit and Other Sources of Credit

THE IMPORTANCE OF TRADE CREDIT

Trade credit is granted by sellers to their customers to aid the customer in financing his purchases. It is intercompany credit, extended by one company to another. On the books of the creditor company, it appears as accounts receivable; on the books of the debtor company, as accounts payable. Nearly all business uses trade credit to some extent in purchasing supplies and inventory. The relative importance of accounts payable to other forms of current financing is shown in Table 7-1. Considering the total volume of short-term credit supplied to business, trade credit ranks ahead of bank credit in volume. However, small companies depend upon trade credit as a means of short-term financing more often than do large corporations (see Table 7-2). The extent of this dependence varies not only with the size of the company, but also with the type of industry. Wholesale and retail companies and construction firms depend upon trade credit to a greater degree than do public utility and transportation companies. In manufacturing, the companies in the apparel fields use trade credit to a greater extent than do other firms.

Trade credit starts from an agreement between purchaser and supplier in ordering inventory and supplies. The purchase of the goods and the extension of credit to finance the purchase are both undertaken at the time of the transaction. The amount of the trade credit depends not only on the volume of credit purchases of a company but also on the length of terms granted by the suppliers. For example, a company making average purchases of $3,000 daily on terms which require payment within thirty days will have outstanding an average of $66,000, if the average thirty-day period contained twenty-two working days. Sometimes a company will increase its borrowing from suppliers by slow payment of its accounts payable. If

108

TABLE 7-1. TYPES OF CURRENT FINANCING AS PERCENTAGE OF TOTAL ASSETS
OF CORPORATIONS BY INDUSTRY GROUPS IN THE UNITED STATES

	Accounts Payable (%)	Notes Payable (%)	Accrued Expenses (%)	Other Current Liabilities (%)	Total Current Liabilities (%)
All corporations	5.6	3.5	2.1	13.8	25.0
Agriculture	8.6	11.9	1.9	4.2	26.6
Mining	9.4	4.2	4.1	2.0	19.7
Construction	22.3	7.6	4.0	18.7	52.6
Manufacturing	9.3	3.5	4.7	3.5	21.0
Transportation and utilities	3.1	1.8	3.5	3.0	11.4
Wholesale and retail trade	23.1	11.1	3.2	3.9	41.3
Services	13.0	9.7	4.1	5.5	32.3

Source: Statistics of Income, Corporations, U.S. Treasury Department, Washington, D.C., 1961, *passim.*

TABLE 7-2. TRADE CREDIT RELATED TO SIZE OF FIRMS
IN THE MANUFACTURING FIELD

Asset Size	Ratio of Trade Credit to Total Assets (%)
Less than $1,000,000	19.8
$1,000,000 to $4,999,999	12.4
$5,000,000 to $9,999,999	8.2
$10,000,000 to $24,999,999	7.4
$25,000,000 to $49,999,999	6.3
$50,000,000 to $99,999,999	6.7
$100,000,000 to $249,999,999	6.2
$250,000,000 to $999,999,999	6.8
$1,000,000,000 and over	6.0

Source: Federal Trade Commission and Securities and Exchange Commission, *Quarterly Financial Report for Manufacturing Corporations,* Third Quarter 1961, *passim.*

the credit terms extended by suppliers require payment within thirty days, but the company makes a habit of paying forty days after the invoice date, and if the average forty-day period contains thirty working days, daily purchases on credit of $3,000 would result in an average of $90,000 in accounts payable outstanding. A permanent policy of slow payment would damage a company's credit rating. However, if the company is a valued customer to most of its suppliers and its late payments are either occasional or, if habitual, small in amount, most suppliers will not pressure the company to be more prompt. On the other hand, some companies will make it virtually essential for a customer to pay for goods ordered within ten days of the invoice date rather than waiting until the thirty-day payment period has expired. This can be accomplished by offering discount terms of 1 or 2 per cent for payment within ten days. If this discount is offered by suppliers, the cost of obtaining credit from suppliers for an additional twenty days is prohibitive. Under such circumstances, it would be advisable for a company to borrow money from its bank in order to take advantage of cash discount terms rather than wait until the net amount of the invoice is due in thirty or forty days.

Some businesses, particularly in the wholesale and retail fields, have a rate of inventory turnover which may be so rapid that the average length of time that inventory remains with the business is less than the average length of payment terms. For example, if the average rate of a wholesaler's inventory turnover is twelve times a year, then the average item remains in inventory thirty days. If the payment terms, for the average purchase from suppliers, is sixty days, then the payment terms are thirty days longer than the average length of time that the inventory remains in stock. As a result of such a situation, the accounts payable can become a source of financing not only for the goods purchased from suppliers, but also for other short-term financial requirements.

It ought to be pointed out that trade and bank credit differ in a number of ways. Probably the most important distinction is that banks lend cash while trade creditors ordinarily do not. The extension of credit by a trade creditor is used in order to increase the sales of his product. The extension of credit by a commercial bank, however, does not involve any attempt to use credit in order to increase the services of the bank. For the extension of credit to be profitable to a bank, it must charge a rate of interest sufficiently high to cover all the costs in making the credit available to the customer. For the extension of credit to be profitable to a trade creditor, he must make a sufficient profit on the sale of the item to cover the cost of the credit. The extension of credit by trade creditors is purely incidental to their primary function of selling goods. The credit requirements of a commercial bank are usually stricter than those of a supplier selling to his credit customers. The credit investigation by a bank of a new loan customer is usually much more thorough than the credit investigation of a supplier making sales to a new customer on credit. Furthermore, a bank will review the credit standing of its loan customers more frequently and with greater thoroughness than will trade creditors. Banks typically consider themselves a source of short-term funds rather than a source of permanent capital and, for this reason, may require that a customer liquidate its debts to the bank at least once a year. A trade creditor, on the other hand, is not concerned if his customers remain in debt to him continuously for years at a time, as long as the individual invoices are paid within the period required in the payment terms. If the payment terms of the supplier are net thirty days, a customer that pays each invoice within the thirty-day period but makes daily purchases from the supplier might be several thousands of dollars in debt to the supplier for several years. In other words, the trade creditor does not wish to have any of his customers get out of debt to him if this involves any reduction in sales made to the customer. Since the accounts payable of a company usually do not fall to zero at any time of the year, the trade credit furnished to the company by its suppliers constitutes a source of permanent investment in the company. If the accounts payable outstanding of a corporation fall to $100,000 during the firm's slack season, this figure would represent a permanent investment resulting from the purchase of goods and supplies on credit. If during the peak season of operations the accounts payable rise to $180,000, it would then constitute a temporary source of credit in the amount of $80,000.

THE INSTRUMENTS OF TRADE CREDIT

The instruments of trade credit are the open book account, the promissory note, and the trade acceptance. Although all of these are important, particularly in wholesale and retail trade, the most extensively used is the open book account.

The Open Book Account Since the primary purpose of offering open book terms to customers is to induce them to place orders with the company, the

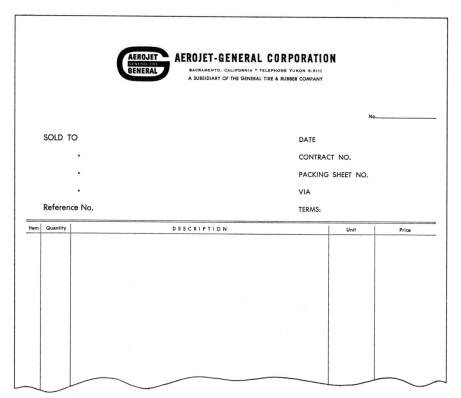

Fig. 7-1 *Sample invoice.*

basis on which the credit is extended is generally much less strict than in the case of bank loans. The credit terms (discussed below) extended to customers generally appear in the catalogue or other sales literature of the company. When an open book order is received from a new customer, the credit department of the company generally investigates the customer's credit standing before approving acceptance of the order. If the order is accepted, an invoice similar to the one in Fig. 7-1 is issued. This invoice indicates the date of the order, the amount of the order, and the credit terms. Usually, at least three copies are typed, one going to the credit department, one to the accounts receivable department, and the original to the customer. The customer receives the goods and is given the privilege of making payment later, according to the terms of the invoice. The customer company enters the amount of the invoice on its accounts payable ledger.

The instruments involved in open book credit are the purchase order, invoice, entry in the seller's accounts receivable ledger, and the entry in the buyer's accounts payable ledger. There is no formal acknowledgment of debt to the seller signed by the buyer. This type of trade credit is far more dependent upon confidence (i.e., credit standing) than are others forms of credit. A customer's credit standing is measured according to the ratings given him by credit agencies. High credit ratings are thus eagerly sought and jealously guarded by companies wishing to make maximum use of open book credit as a means of financing.

The Promissory Note The promissory note is a written promise to pay a specified sum of money on a stated date in the future either to the bearer of the note or to the order of a named person. For it to be negotiable, the promissory note must be an unconditional promise to pay.[1] Promissory notes are used to a much smaller extent than book credit in financing the movement of goods. Where a buyer has a credit rating so low that suppliers are unwilling to extend credit on open book terms, credit may be secured by means of promissory notes in the amount of orders placed by the buyer. If competition among suppliers is strong, it frequently happens that purchasers of dubious credit standing will be able to get open book terms from suppliers even though other suppliers will be unwilling to make such an extension of credit. Where, however, the preferred sources of supply deny open book terms to a customer, the customer has no choice but to pay cash, borrow from a bank to make payment, or sign promissory notes to finance the purchase of goods. In such a situation, a company will often prefer to sign promissory notes payable to its suppliers than to borrow from the bank in order to pay cash for purchases.

The promissory note, the open book account, and the draft are unsecured debt. The promissory note, therefore, does not give the creditor

---

[1] Demand notes are payable not at some future time but immediately upon demand. Demand notes, however, are very rare in trade transactions.

any stronger claim on the assets of the borrower in the event of nonpayment than does the existence of open book debt. The advantage to the creditor in demanding promissory notes as compared to extending credit on an open book basis is in the formality of the promissory note. The signature of the maker of the note is his formal acknowledgment of the existence of the debt, an acknowledgment lacking in open book credit. Where such credit is used, the purchaser may deny the existence of the debt. Where goods are ordered on an open book basis by placing the order in person with the supplier or by telephone, a denial by the purchaser may be difficult to refute. The existence of a promissory note properly drawn and signed by the purchaser at the time that the order for the goods is placed prevents him from denying the existence of the debt. In a few lines of business, such as jewelry and furs, wholesalers are in the habit of demanding promissory notes in financing the movement of goods.

The Trade Draft and Acceptance   The trade draft is an order written by the *maker* addressed to the *drawee* ordering him to pay a certain sum of money on a particular date to the *payee* or to his order. To a company which plans to purchase goods from a supplier unwilling to offer open book credit, the use of the trade acceptance is a convenient device. After receipt of the company's order, the supplier ships the goods under an *order bill of lading*. The goods can be picked up only when the order bill of lading is presented to the firm that transported the goods. A trade draft, drawn up by the supplier ordering the customer to pay, and the order bill of lading, are then mailed to a bank designated by the customer, usually in the town in which the customer is located. The bank is authorized to release the bill of lading only when the customer acknowledges the draft. A trade draft properly accepted becomes a *trade acceptance*. On acceptance of the trade draft with the signature of an authorized officer of the customer company, the bill of lading is released to the customer, who can then claim the shipment. The acceptance is returned to the supplier or sold in the money market, according to the instructions of the supplier to the bank. If the terms of shipment involve no extension of credit, the trade bill must be paid by the customer at the time that the bill of lading is released by the bank to him. If, on the other hand, the supplier is willing to extend credit to the customer, the draft will permit payment to be made at a later date. In such a case, the draft would be payable in thirty days, ninety days, or some other time period after the date of the draft.

The trade acceptance is an important means of financing the movement of goods in international trade. Like the promissory note, the trade acceptance eliminates any dispute as to the existence of the credit or the legal responsibility of the customer in making payment when the acceptance matures and becomes payable. In international trade, the hazard of selling on open book terms is greater than in domestic trade. The formal evidence of debt provided by the trade acceptance and the control over the goods that this device gives to the supplier during shipment make its use particularly well adapted to international transactions. Illustrations of a trade acceptance and a uniform order bill of lading are given in Figs. 7-2 and 7-3.

CREDIT TERMS

The most important element in the terms of trade credit is the length of time permitted to the customer in making payment. Commonly a period of thirty days is provided within which to make payment of the net amount of the invoice, although in some cases sixty days or longer is permitted, as shown in Fig. 7-4. Usually, the payment period includes the time used in shipping the goods to the customer. For example, a shipment requiring five days in transit under credit terms permitting payment in thirty days would actually give the customer the use of the goods for twenty-five days before payment had to be made, since the payment period is calculated from the date of the invoice rather than the date of receipt of the goods. Obviously, this provides a longer extension of credit to customers located close to the supplier. By the same token, this gives a competitive advantage to a supplier close to a customer over a supplier located at a distance. In some industries, competitive pressures have resulted in

Fig. 7-2 *A trade acceptance.*

No._____   Houston, Texas_____19_____

To_____

On_____19_____ Pay to the order of   ABC RUG COMPANY, INC.

_____Dollars ($_____)

The obligation of the acceptor arises out of the purchase of goods from the drawer. The drawee may accept this bill payable at any bank, banker, or trust company in the United States which such drawee may designate.

Accepted at_____on_____ 19___   (NO PROTEST)

Payable at_____ Bank

Bank Location_____   ABC RUG COMPANY, INC.

Buyer's Signature_____

By Agent or Officer_____   By_____
                                                         Treasurer

payment terms permitting the customer credit dating from the day of arrival of the goods rather than the invoice date. Credit terms including the letters A.O.G. (arrival of goods) or R.O.G. (receipt of goods) give the privilege of dating credit from the receipt of goods at his warehouse or plant. Such terms are frequently found in international transactions and in shipment of goods over considerable distances by water.

(Uniform Domestic Order Bill of Lading, adopted by Carriers in Official, Southern, Western and Illinois Classification territories, March 15, 1922, as amended August 1, 1930, and June 15, 1941.)

UNIFORM ORDER BILL OF LADING—Original

S-1564

Southern Pacific Company

Shipper's No._____

Agent's No.

RECEIVED, subject to the classifications and tariffs in effect on the date of the issue of this Bill of Lading.

At_____, 19____

FROM_____

the property described below, in apparent good order, except as noted (contents and condition of contents of packages unknown), marked, consigned, and destined as indicated below, which said company (the word company being understood throughout this contract as meaning any person or corporation in possession of the property under the contract) agrees to carry to its usual place of delivery at said destination, if on its own road or its own water line, otherwise to deliver to another carrier on the route to said destination. It is mutually agreed, as to each carrier of all or any of said property over all or any portion of said route to destination, and as to each party at any time interested in all or any of said property, that every service to be performed hereunder shall be subject to all the conditions not prohibited by law, whether printed or written, herein contained, including the conditions on back hereof, which are hereby agreed to by the shipper and accepted for himself and his assigns.
The surrender of this Original ORDER Bill of Lading properly indorsed shall be required before the delivery of the property. Inspection of property covered by this bill of lading will not be permitted unless provided by law or unless permission is indorsed on this original bill of lading or given in writing by the shipper.

CONSIGNED TO ORDER OF_____

DESTINATION_____STATE OF_____COUNTY OF_____
(Mail or street address of consignee—For purposes of notification only.)

NOTIFY_____

AT_____STATE OF_____COUNTY OF_____

ROUTE_____

DELIVERING CARRIER_____ CAR INITIAL_____ CAR NO._____

No. Pkgs.	DESCRIPTION OF ARTICLES, SPECIAL MARKS AND EXCEPTIONS	*Weight (Subj. to Corr.)	Class or Rate	Check Col.	
					Subject to Section 7 of conditions, if this shipment is to be delivered to the consignee without recourse on the consignor, the consignor shall sign the following statement:
					The carrier shall not make delivery of this shipment without payment of freight and all other lawful charges.
					(Signature of Consignor)
					If charges are to be prepaid, write or stamp here, "To be Prepaid."
					Received $_____ to apply in prepayment of the charges on the property described hereon.
					(Agent or Cashier)
					Per_____ (The signature here acknowledges only the amount prepaid.)
					Charges Advanced:

*If the shipment moves between two ports by a carrier by water, the law requires that the bill of lading shall state whether it is"carrier's or shipper's weight."
NOTE—Where the rate is dependent on value, shippers are required to state specifically in writing the agreed or declared value of the property. The agreed or declared value of the property is hereby specifically stated by the shipper to be not exceeding_____per_____ $_____

_____Shipper. _____Agent

Per_____ Per_____

Permanent post-office address of shipper_____

(This Bill of Lading is to be signed by the shipper and agent of the carrier issuing same.)

Fig. 7-3 *A uniform order bill of lading.*

Fig. 7-4   *Typical credit payment terms extended by wholesalers.*

Butter, eggs, and cheese: net 10 days, invoice usually dated Friday for sales
  during week
Tobacco and tobacco products: net 7 days
Candy: 2% 30 days
Drugs: 1/10/EOM (1% deductible 10 days after *end of month* in which
  invoice is dated)
Dry goods: 3/10/EOM or 2/10/60
Electrical supplies: 2/10/30
Hosiery: 10 days EOM or net 30 days
Building materials: 2/10/30
Knitted outerwear: 8/10/EOM
Plumbing supplies: 2/10/30
Shoes—men's, women's, children's: net 30 days
Woolen goods: 1/10/60 or net 30 days

As Fig. 7-4 illustrates, discounts for advance payment of invoices are
very common.   Where a discount from the amount of the invoice is given
for prompt payment, the extension of credit is most commonly limited to a
ten-day period from the date of the invoice.   The discount is usually 1 or
2 per cent of the amount of the invoice, and has the effect of charging the
customer for the privilege of using the full credit period permitted by the
terms on the invoice.
   Some suppliers sell on "cash" terms, a misnomer since "cash" terms usually involve the privilege of delay of a few days in making payment on invoices.   In "cash" payment terms the invoice is generally due and payable
in ten days or less from the date of the invoice.   This gives enough time to
the customer to inspect the goods, check the accuracy of the invoice and the
shipping documents, and make payment.   Sometimes payment terms designated as *bill to bill* are used.   Under such terms, the supplier and the customer agree that the receipt of each bill designates the date that the previous
bill is due and payable.   Most commonly this involves the equivalent of
seven to ten days credit to the customer, since such terms are commonly
used where deliveries are made weekly.
   Where no discount from the invoice is permitted by the supplier for
prompt payment, the cost of extending credit is absorbed by the seller and
included in his cost of doing business.   In such cases, it would generally be
to the advantage of the customer to wait until the end of the payment term
before sending his check for payment of the invoice, since no saving would
result from payment in advance.   Where a discount for advance payment is
given by the supplier, the customer determines the advantage of taking the
discount compared to the advantage of delaying payment until the net
amount of the invoice is due.   If payment terms of 2/10/30 are offered by
the supplier, the customer would be paying 2 per cent of the face amount
of the invoice to delay making payment for twenty days.   This is paying
for the use of funds at the rate of 36 per cent per annum.   The cost in

terms of annual interest involved in delaying payment until the net amount of the invoice is shown below for other payment terms in common use:

Payment Terms	Interest Rate per Annum
1/10/30	18
2/10/60	14
3/10/30	54
3/30/60	36
2/30/60	24
2/15/30	48
2/20/30	72
2/20/60	18

Discounts of 5, 10, 30 or more per cent are found in trade. Such terms are trade discounts, and are usually listed separately from the cash discount. Suppliers that permit an extended period during which discounts may be taken sometimes allow customers an additional discount if the invoice is paid prior to the expiration of the cash discount. For example, suppose that an invoice for $1,000 is dated March 31, terms 2/10/60 extra, and "anticipation" at the rate of 6 per cent per annum is permitted by the seller. Under the "extra" terms, the 2 per cent cash discount is extended for a sixty-day period in addition to the ten-day period for a total of seventy days from the date of the invoice. If payment is made within seventy days from March 31—that is, by June 10—the invoice is subject to a discount of 2 per cent or $20, leaving a net amount of $980 payable. If, however, payment is made on May 2, it has been made thirty-nine days before the end of the discount period. Therefore, the customer is entitled to reduce the $980 balance by 6 per cent interest for thirty-nine days. The discount resulting from "anticipation" is $6.37 (6 per cent per annum on $980 for thirty-nine days). The payment remitted by the customer is $973.63.

Suppliers sometimes state on their invoices that 6 per cent interest per annum will be charged on all past due accounts, in order to encourage buyers to pay their bills before they become overdue. The success of this policy is dubious: if the supplier is unable to collect payments from a customer within the credit period, it is also unlikely he can collect an additional 6 per cent interest.

MAINTAINING A GOOD CREDIT STANDING

A company that is able to purchase goods on favorable terms from suppliers is less dependent upon bank borrowing and other means of securing credit. Because trade credit is such an important source of credit for business concerns, it should be carefully managed. The best way to assure that trade credit will continue to be a source of funds is to maintain the credit standing of the company at as high a level as possible. Occasional late payment of bills will frequently be overlooked by the credit department of suppliers, but a company that has become "slow pay" has seriously damaged its credit. Indeed, the reputation of a company is greatly enhanced, if it becomes known that the company regularly pays its bills within the cash discount terms wherever they are offered.

Keeping suppliers furnished with up-to-date financial statements and promptly answering legitimate inquiries from the credit departments of suppliers also raises the reputation of a company. It is important to keep credit rating agencies, such as Dun & Bradstreet, supplied with all information requested by them, in addition to furnishing up-to-date financial statements. Finally, it should be emphasized that it is much easier to maintain a high rating than it is to restore a damaged one.

It is the responsibility of the credit manager to decide whether or not the customers of a company are worthy of credit. Decisions on extending credit to customers are sometimes made as a result of investigation by the company credit department but, to a considerable extent, they are based on information collected by specialized credit reporting agencies. The most important of these is Dun & Bradstreet, Inc.[2] Data are compiled by reporters on the staff of Dun & Bradstreet who visit businesses periodically to get financial information necessary in preparing credit reports. In addition, financial statements are received from business firms and reports about business firms from their suppliers. With all this information, Dun & Bradstreet compiles a *Reference Book* of more than 4,000 pages that lists nearly all the retailers, wholesalers, and manufacturers who purchase on open book terms from their suppliers—some three million companies in all. Since the credit rating assigned by Dun & Bradstreet is particularly significant in determining the extent of credit that any credit manager is willing to allow, each company listed by Dun & Bradstreet does all it can to maintain its credit rating and, if possible, to raise it. If a subscriber to Dun & Bradstreet services wishes to get more detailed information on a particular company, this is available in a series of reports. A report can be highly detailed, covering several typewritten pages, or it can be in synopsis form of one page or less, whichever is requested by the subscriber. For example, see Fig. 7-5.

Although Dun & Bradstreet is the oldest and most important of the credit rating agencies, it is by no means the only one. Others that compile credit information for businesses are as follows:

1. Special credit agencies confined to a particular industry or trade, such as the Lyon Furniture Mercantile Agency or the Jewelry Board of Trade.

2. Trade credit departments of certain trade associations, such as the

---

2 Dun & Bradstreet, Inc. was formed in 1933 when Bradstreet Company merged with R. G. Dun and Company. Both of these companies originated in the last century as credit reporting companies.

SIC	NAME & ADDRESS		STARTED	RATING

CD 13 NOV 4 19-- N

59 12	KENT STORE	DRUGS	1949	E 2

124 KENT ROAD
ST BERNICE MICH

	TRADE	DISC-PPT
	SALES	$89,232
	WORTH	$22,901
	EMPLS	2 P T

MILES GROSS   )
HANNAH (MRS MILES) GROSS) PARTNERS

SUMMARY   SALES ARE INCREASING AND FINANCIAL CONDITION IS SOUND.

TRADE

HC	OWE	P DUE	TERMS	Oct 21 19--		SOLD
2431	2000		2-10-30	Disc		Over 3 yrs
300			2-10-30	Disc		Over 2 yrs
250			2-10-30	Disc		Over 3 yrs
136	136		2-10	Disc		Over 3 yrs
75			2-10-30	Disc		Over 3 yrs
15			30	Ppt		Over 2 yrs

FINANCE

Statement Sept 30 19--

Cash on hand	$ 304	Accts Pay	$ 3,724
Cash in bank	1,872		
Mdse	14,450		
	------		-----
Total Current	16,626	Total Current	3,724
Fixt & Equip	9,913		
Deposits	86	NET WORTH	22,901
	------		-------
Total Assets	26,626	Total	26,626

Sales from Oct 1 19-- to Sept 30 19-- $89,232; gross profit $26,181;
salaries and drawings of partners $6,732; net profit over and above salaries
and drawings of partners $3,457. Monthly rent $150 on a five year lease.
Fire insurance on Mdse $10,000; fixt $7,000.
Signed Oct 20 19-- KENT STORE by Miles Gross, Partner

-----O-----

Residential construction has stepped up in this section with the result that both sales and profits of this business have mounted steadily.
Part of earnings have been reinvested in the business every year to finance
its steady growth.
On Nov 4, 19-- Miles Gross stated that sales are now picking up
slightly, as is usual in the Fall. Some thought has been given to opening
a second store, he said, but so far he has not been able to find the right
location.

OPERATION   Operates a pharmacy and soda fountain. Drugs and prescriptions account
for 50% of sales, with the remainder equally divided among fountain, sundries
and confectionery. Fixtures and a twenty-foot soda fountain are new. Both
partners are active and there are two employed part time. LOCATION: Rents
first floor of a two story building in good condition. Store measures about
20 x 50 feet. It is located in a residential section developed during the
past ten years.

HISTORY   The style Kent Store was registered by the partners on April 30, 1949.
This firm was formed April 1949. Starting capital consisted of $10,500
savings, a $3,500 loan from Teachers Credit Union, and a $3,000 loan from the
partners' families, making a total of $17,000. Loans have since been repaid.
Miles Gross, native born 19--. He was graduated from Columbia College
of Pharmacy. He then was employed as a pharmacist by Wark Pharmacy and by
Ray Drug Co., until this business was started.
Hannah (Mrs. Miles) Gross was born 19--. She was a school teacher
prior to formation of this firm.
11-4 (158 85)

Fig. 7-5 *A synopsis report.*

American Fur Merchants Association. Approximately 400 national trade associations provide their members with credit information.

3. Individual inquiry agencies that compile reports on demand wherein the clients feel that special attention is needed and information is more likely to be obtained by such agencies than by the general credit reporting agencies. These companies are in a sense detective agencies in the field of credit information.

4. Many companies cooperate with each other by exchanging data on their credit experience with customers.

5. In many cities there is a mercantile credit agency either operating as a cooperative owned by retailers of the city or as an independent company providing information for retailers. Although such agencies exist largely to furnish information about customers of retail firms in the city, they also provide information about business customers, which may be useful to suppliers of all kinds.

6. Banks are a very useful source of credit information. There is, however, little uniformity in the practice of furnishing credit information to companies requesting it. Some banks furnish, at no charge, information about their depositors which is very useful and detailed. Others provide no information other than the statement that the customer maintains an account with the bank. Still others will charge a fee for any requested credit appraisal.

ACCRUED EXPENSES

All companies receive a variety of services for which they make payment periodically. Until such a payment is made, the services rendered represent a source of credit that in some cases may be quite substantial. This source, which is sometimes called "volunteer credit," is listed as accrued expenses on the books of the company. Companies furnishing such items as electricity, telephone, water, building maintenance, and consulting services generally provide the service first and then collect payment on a monthly, quarterly, or some other time basis. Thus the liability of a company for payment of services rendered rises daily between payment dates. On any day the amount of accrued expenses may be considerable.

The most important accrued expense to many corporations is the federal corporation income tax. Since the collection of income taxes is periodic, a liability for federal income taxes is accrued between payment dates. This is an important source of funds for many corporations. For some manufacturing and retail companies it amounts to 10 per cent or more of the total liabilities and net worth of the company. The amount of this liability depends upon the net income of the corporation. Formerly, the federal government collected the income tax payable once a year on the income earned the previous year. The 1954 Internal Revenue Code (Sec. 1.6016-1) now requires each corporation whose tax liability can reasonably be expected to exceed $100,000 for the current year, and whose accounts are kept on a calendar-year basis, to file an estimate of its tax liability by September 15 of the current year based on the company's estimate of its income for the full year. On September 15 the corporation must also pay 25 per cent of the estimated tax liability and an additional 25 per cent on December 15. At the end of the year when the actual income of the corporation is determined, the actual liability for income tax is known. Half of the remaining tax liability is payable March 15 of the following year, and the balance is due June 15. At the end of the year, if the amount of quarterly payments on income tax has resulted in payment of a sum greater than the tax liability, a refund may be requested. On the other hand, if the net income tax at the end of the year is more than the income estimated earlier by the corporation, the corporation must pay an additional sum to the federal government.

Because payments on the federal income tax are made quarterly, the company in effect has the benefit of the various federal services for three months before payment is made. In this sense, accrued federal income taxes are similar to accrued wages. In order to be in a position to make the quarterly payments on federal income tax, the financial managers of some corporations accumulate the funds during the quarter and invest them in securities that can be liquidated when the tax payment is made. Frequently, such funds are invested in short-term government obligations, such as ninety-day treasury bills, or in commercial paper of such date that it matures just before the tax payment is due.

Many business concerns act as collectors of taxes owed to governmental bodies by their employees and customers. Part of the income earned by the employees is withheld by the company employing them and is later forwarded to the collector of internal revenue, where it is applied to the income tax liability of the individual employee. The amount withheld from each employee's paycheck depends upon the size of the income of the employee, the number of deductions available to him, and other factors. For many companies, this averages between 8 and 10 per cent of their wage bills. The amount is deducted from each paycheck regardless of how frequently wages are paid. However, the amount withheld from the employee is not forwarded to the government as frequently as it is withheld from the employee, since payments to the federal government are made quarterly. Although most company executives complain of being forced to act as tax collectors for government agencies, companies do receive some benefits to compensate for the inconvenience and bookkeeping expense involved.

Like the accrued expenses discussed above, taxes collected from employees and customers represent a sizable source of short-term credit to companies. Also, like accrued expenses, they represent interest-free short-term funds. To some companies, the availability of these funds is not worth the inconvenience and bookkeeping expense involved; to others, frequently small businesses, this source is a very welcome one. In addition to the withholding tax on employees' income, the social security taxes deducted from employees' paychecks add to the short-term funds available to companies until such time as the quarterly payments must be made to the federal government.

The most important tax collected by companies from its customers is the retail sales tax, which is usually a state tax, although some municipal governments also levy it. The tax is collected from retail customers whenever a sale is made, but the payment is commonly made to the state or local tax collector in quarterly periods. The company collecting sales taxes from its customers thus has the interest free use of the funds for periods as long as three months. Excise taxes, like retail sales taxes, are collected at various stages in the distribution of goods, and may similarly be a source of short-term funds for business concerns.

It was mentioned earlier that by delaying payment of accounts payable beyond the payment terms extended by suppliers, a company could increase the amount of credit received from its suppliers. Companies sometimes delay payment to the government of the money which they collect from their customers and employees. However, late payment of taxes collected by a company like slow payment of accounts payable may damage its reputation. Still, some companies in stringent financial straits, either temporarily or chronically, will resort to this device to increase the funds which they need in operating the businesses. Wherever this occurs, it is an evidence of unsound financial management.

COMMERCIAL PAPER HOUSES

As mentioned above, one method of borrowing short-term funds is for the borrower to make out a promissory note payable on a future date and then discount it at the bank. Another means is to prepare promissory notes and sell them at a discount, not to the company's own bank, but to other investors. Many corporations have idle funds that are available for investment in short-term securities maturing in a few days to six months or more. Other companies wish to borrow money for similar periods. If a corporation wishes to raise funds for a period of a few days or a few months, it can prepare promissory notes and sell them to other corporations that have idle funds to invest in short-term securities. The market for such promissory notes is the commercial paper market. In existence well before the Civil War, this market continued as an important alternative to bank borrowing from that war until the end of World War I. Following World War I, however, the volume of commercial paper declined steadily until the end of World War II. In 1945, for example, less than $160 million in commercial paper was marketed to commercial paper dealers. Since that time, though, the commercial paper market has expanded greatly, as Table 7-3 shows.

In raising money from the commercial paper market, the financial officer of the corporation must prepare promissory notes in convenient denominations of anywhere from $2,500 each to as high as $100,000 each, totaling approximately the sum of money which the corporation needs to raise. No interest is added to the face of the promissory note. The purchaser of the notes buys them at a discount and earns interest from his investment by being paid the face amount upon the maturity of the note. In order to enhance the salability of the notes, they must be made negotiable. Their negotiability is generally accomplished by making the notes payable to the corporation issuing them, which then endorses the notes prior to selling them.

TABLE 7-3. COMMERCIAL PAPER MARKET, 1957-1963

	Volume of commercial paper outstanding at end of year (millions)	Average interest rate during year on prime commercial paper (% per annum)
1955	$2,020	
1956	$2,166	
1957	$2,672	
1958	$2,751	2.46
1959	$3,202	3.97
1960	$4,497	3.85
1961	$4,686	2.97
1962	$6,000	3.26
1963 (April)	$7,359	3.32

Source: Federal Reserve Bulletin, various issues.

In order to make commercial paper an attractive way of raising funds, it is necessary that the cost to the borrowing corporation be equal to or less than the cost of borrowing from the bank. This generally makes it difficult for any but large, well-known, corporations to take advantage of the commercial paper market. Small corporations do sell their promissory notes directly to other corporations, but this is not done often enough to warrant any dependence upon this means of raising funds.

The purchasers of commercial paper include banks, business corporations, and financial institutions. Commercial banks constituted the bulk of the market for commercial paper until recently, when business corporations and financial institutions began investing in commercial paper. According to The Wall Street Journal,[3] in 1962 approximately 60 to 70 per cent of all commercial paper issued was purchased by business corporations. Approximately 15 to 20 per cent was purchased by commercial banks, mostly smaller banks in cities outside of the main money centers of the United States. The balance of commercial paper was purchased by

---

[3] The Wall Street Journal, August 8, 1962, p. 10.

college endowment funds, charitable foundations, a few governmental bodies, the United Nations, and foreign investors.

Commercial paper is issued by all types of large companies, including textile companies, food processors, wholesalers, manufacturers, and financial institutions. Sales finance companies, consumer finance companies, and other corporations in the financing field make considerable use of commercial paper in raising short-term funds. Some finance companies issue commercial paper in such large volume and on such a regular basis that they undertake their own marketing directly to investors. Most companies issuing commercial paper, however, do so on an infrequent basis and in volume insufficient to permit them effectively to market the paper themselves. To aid such companies in marketing commercial paper, there are financial organizations known as commercial paper dealers.

If a corporation wishes to raise money by selling its promissory notes through the commercial paper market, it will first contact one of the commercial paper houses. Before such a house undertakes to distribute the commercial paper of a new client, it will thoroughly investigate the credit of the client. The name of the corporation must be very well known, its size substantial, and credit rating high. A number of promissory notes are then prepared by a financial officer of the corporation in convenient denominations, endorsed by the corporation, and sold to the commercial paper house. These will be resold to investors at a discount from the face value of the note. In addition, the commercial paper dealer will subtract from the amount paid to the corporation an amount equal to one-eighth of one per cent or one-quarter of one per cent, depending upon the conditions of the market and the amount of the issue. This represents the charge for the house's services in distributing the commercial paper of its client. In some cases, the commercial paper house will act as a selling agent for the corporation issuing the commercial paper, and will not take title to the notes. Most commonly, however, the commercial paper house will buy outright the paper of its client, and then resell the paper to investors. Because commercial paper houses do not usually endorse the paper which they resell, the purchaser cannot look to them for reimbursement in the event that the issuer of the paper fails to pay the full amount. When banks purchase commercial paper, they generally purchase it on a ten-day option. Under such an option the bank may investigate the credit of the corporation issuing the commercial paper, and, if unsatisfied with its findings, can return the paper to the commercial paper house for a full refund. Other investors in commercial paper generally do not require such an option. The fact that the rate of loss to investors in purchasing commercial paper has been extremely low, so low as to be practically negligible, has made commercial paper one of the safest short-term investments available to investors. The mechanics of a commercial paper transaction can be seen in the following illustration:

A company sells 180-day notes with a face value of $10,000,000 at a discount of 4% per annum plus a commission to the commercial paper house of one-quarter of 1%.

Maturity value		$10,000,000
Interest, 180 days, 4% per annum	$200,000	
Selling commission at 0.25%	25,000	
Interest plus commission		$ 225,000
Amount received by company		$ 9,775,000
Effective rate of interest on loan		4.6% per annum
(including selling commission)		

To some extent, commercial paper supplements bank credit and other sources of credit and, to some extent, supplants bank credit. The main advantage to the large corporation of using the commercial paper market is cost. During 1962, the rate charged by commercial banks to their prime borrowers fluctuated between 4.5 and 5 per cent. However, because banks require a compensatory deposit as a condition to extending credit, the effective rate on the usable funds borrowed from banks by corporations with the highest credit rating has often been higher than the stated rate.[4] Partly because the discount of commercial paper is less than the discount of notes to the commercial bank and also because there is no compensatory balance requirement in commercial paper transactions, the cost of borrowing through commercial paper dealers has averaged between 1 and 2 percentage points less than the cost of bank borrowing.

The increasing volume of borrowing through the commercial paper market has been so marked in recent years as to cause concern to commercial banks:

> Indeed, the shift to commercial paper has been so pronounced that it amounts to a revolution in financing, but such a quiet revolution that even some corporate treasurers appear to have missed it. It has had two important consequences: The short-term loan business of many commercial banks has suffered, and many companies now issuing commercial paper have reduced their borrowing costs significantly.[5]

LOANS FROM CUSTOMERS, STOCKHOLDERS, AND OTHERS

In special situations, a company may secure funds from its customers. Where goods are to be made according to specifications demanded by the customer, it is logical that the customer advance funds to the manufacturer or aid in financing the manufacture of the goods. Automobile manufacturers sometimes provide advances to small machine-tool manufacturers or suppliers of equipment to aid them in completing the contract. A mail-order house or other large retailer will sometimes furnish short-term funds

---

[4] According to *The Wall Street Journal*, August 8, 1962, p. 10, "Many business borrowers calculate the true charge on bank loans as about one percentage point more than the stated rate." On this basis of calculation, the actual rate of bank borrowing to prime business borrowers in 1962 fluctuated between 5.5 and 6 per cent per annum.

[5] *Ibid.*, p. 1.

to a manufacturer that sells all or most of its output to the retailer. Such an advance of funds is frequently very welcome to a company that may not be able to secure sufficient financing from banks or other sources. The inducement to the customer in lending funds is that it can frequently secure a concession in price as a result of this financial service. Governmental agencies, particularly at the federal level, sometimes make advance payments under contracts submitted by the government agency to private manufacturers to aid them in completing the contract.

Small companies frequently borrow money from their officers, directors, stockholders, and friends. Occasionally, a company has borrowed money from its own employees or from the labor union representing its employees. This happens, for example, in the garment industry, where the size of individual companies and their financial condition does not always permit them to borrow from other sources at favorable rates. Loans from such sources are made to companies for other than financial reasons, and the rates of interest charged on such loans are not the result of strictly financial factors. In addition to making purchases on account, a company may under exceptional circumstances receive cash loans from a supplier which are generally in exchange for a promissory note from the company receiving the money.

Questions

1. Account for the fact that small companies use trade credit to a greater extent than large companies.
2. What are the differences between credit extended by a supplier to a customer and credit extended by a bank to a borrower?
3. What are the instruments used in trade credit?
4. Under what circumstances will a supplier require promissory notes in payment of invoices instead of open book credit?
5. What is a trade acceptance? For what kinds of transactions is it chiefly used?
6. When "cash" terms are extended, when is payment of an invoice expected?
7. What is the difference between cash discounts and trade discounts?
8. What services do Dun & Bradstreet offer to its subscribers?
9. What sources of information on the credit standing of companies are available to the credit manager of a firm?
10. Explain how accrued expenses can act as a source of credit.
11. How does a commercial paper house aid in securing short-term funds for a company?
12. What reasons are there for the rapid increase in the volume of commercial paper in recent years?

Selected Readings

Common Sale and Payment Terms, Small Marketers Aids, Small Business Administration, Washington, D.C., 1960.

Phelps, Clyde William, *Improving Collections from Credit Sales,* Small Marketers Aids #49, Small Business Administration, Washington, D.C., 1959.

Schultz, William J., and Hedwig Reinhardt, *Credit and Collection Management,* Prentice-Hall, Inc., Englewood Cliffs, N. J., 1954.

Seiden, Martin H., *The Quality of Trade Credit,* National Bureau of Economic Research, Inc., Washington, D.C., 1964.

8

Short-Term Secured Loans

THE REASONS LENDERS DEMAND SECURITY

THE ULTIMATE SOURCE of repayment of loans is profits. So long as there is no disagreement as to the amount of the loan and the terms of repayment, the lender can be reasonably assured of collecting the amount due him if the borrower's business is profitable. An excess of cash disbursements over cash receipts is frequently encountered in a profitable business, but can generally be foreseen if the business is well run. Plans can be made to borrow money to meet such contingencies and to repay them out of the later excess of cash receipts over cash disbursements. As long as the business is financially well organized and generates profits, the problems of making loan payments when they are due can be planned for and met.

Not all businesses, however, are profitable. Some are unprofitable from the moment of their organization; some may have been profitable for a considerable period, only to become unprofitable later; and others are unprofitable for a few years and then become profitable. If it seems that a business may become unprofitable, the borrower may be unable to meet payments in full when his debts are due. Lenders, of course, usually make careful investigation of the credit standings of their potential clients. Such investigations seek to determine primarily whether the business will be able to meet its loan commitments when due, which is closely tied to an estimate of the borrowing company's prospects for profit. No lender willingly makes a loan to a company or extends credit to it if he feels that too great a risk is involved. But conditions change as time passes, and as a result loans are sometimes defaulted. It has often been stated by bankers that "our bank has never made a bad loan, but some of the good loans we make do turn sour."

Besides making a careful investigation of the credit standing of borrowing companies a demand for security also serves to reduce the possibility of loss as a result of nonpayment of loans. If an asset of the borrowing company is pledged to assure the repayment of the loan, the asset becomes collateral. If there is a default in the payment of the loan or if the borrower violates any of the terms of the loan, the assets pledged as security may be liquidated in order to provide the means for retiring the loan. This process involves inconvenience, uncertainty, delay, and expense, all of which both debtor and creditor prefer to avoid. Creditors of business borrowers in all but rare cases would prefer to collect a debt by repayment when due to collecting through liquidation of the pledged security. The fact that a loan is secured, however, gives the creditor a preferred position in the event the debtor becomes bankrupt. Furthermore, the borrower is under stronger discipline, which frequently impels him to strive harder to meet the loan payments when due.

Since security for a loan exists to protect the lender, the borrower realizes no direct benefit. Why, then, should the borrower contract for a loan in which he offers his assets as security? The answer is that better terms can usually be obtained by a borrower who offers security for the loan. In some cases a company may not be able to secure credit at all unless security is offered. In most cases, however, credit can be obtained but not on as good terms as might be available where security is offered. A lender or creditor may be willing to extend credit for a short period without security; for a longer term he might require that the loan be secured. Finally, a creditor may be willing to offer low interest rates and freedom from clauses in the loan contract limiting management discretion only if the loan is secured. Companies with very high credit standing are naturally not required to resort to offering security for credit to the extent that companies without strong credit ratings are. Furthermore, large corporations do not offer security when they borrow as frequently as do small companies. In short, security is to some extent a substitute for a strong credit rating.

Some assets are more readily accepted by the lender than are others. The following general characteristics are considered attractive in accepting security for short-term loans: (1) mobility, (2) durability, (3) marketability, (4) identifiability, and (5) steadiness of price.

Unfortunately, relatively few assets have all these characteristics: precious metals, expensive furs, bonds, bank passbooks, marketable securities, and promissory notes admirably fulfill these requirements. However, if such items were demanded in all cases where loans were secured, the volume of secured loans would remain rather small. Creditors extend credit on a secured basis by accepting the pledge of almost any asset that has value, including accounts receivable, raw materials, finished goods, supplies, life insurance policies, and equipment. Assets which have few of the above characteristics may still be acceptable to creditors because of the discipline that is imposed upon debtors where credit is secured and the position of priority thereby given to the creditor. A creditor can expect payment on his loan in the event of default or bankruptcy up to 100 per cent of the liquidation value of the pledged asset. In addition, the creditor can expect to participate along with unsecured creditors in the distribution made to all unsecured creditors.

A large proportion of loans by banks to small businesses are secured loans. Among the many other sources of short-term loans for businesses are some that make a specialty of extending credit only or largely on a secured basis, the most important being the commercial finance companies and factors. Commercial finance companies make loans secured by the pledge of almost any asset owned by a business. However, the bulk of loans by commercial finance companies are secured by accounts receivable and inventory. Sales finance companies make loans to retailers dealing largely in automobiles and other durable goods. Loans from sales finance companies are secured by the pledge of inventory carried by retailers. They also purchase the installment notes used by the retailers of automobiles and durable goods signed by customers of these companies. Although sales finance companies exist chiefly to finance the operations of retailers in durable goods, some also extend credit to wholesalers.

The business of factors is confined largely to making loans secured by accounts receivable. Those factors that are known as *old-line factors* specialize in the purchase of accounts receivable from their clients rather than making loans secured by such assets. Those that are not old-line factors are not so restricted in their method of making loans; they are willing to accept the accounts receivable of their clients as security for loans extended to them.

FINANCING ACCOUNTS RECEIVABLE

Accounts Receivable as Security When the financial officer of a company wishes to borrow money on the security of the accounts receivable, he can turn to three main lenders: commercial banks, commercial finance companies, and factors. Not all banks, however, are willing to make loans on accounts receivable. Small commercial banks are particularly reluctant to do so, partly because many are unfamiliar with the mechanics of accounts receivable financing and partly because they cannot make loans secured by accounts receivable in sufficient volume to cover the costs involved in handling such loans.

The volume of loans on accounts receivable made by commercial finance companies is greater than the volume handled by commercial banks. The finance companies are not subject to the strict regulations imposed on commercial banks with respect to lending activities. As a result, commercial finance companies are better able to adjust the terms under which they make loans secured by accounts receivable to suit the requirements of particular customers. Although there are many commercial finance companies, the business is largely concentrated among a few. In 1960, 52 per cent of the financing of receivables undertaken by the 100 largest finance companies in the United States was accounted for by the three giants of the industry:

C.I.T. Financial Corporation, Commercial Credit Corporation, and General Motors Acceptance Corporation.[1]

The *factor* is a financial company specializing in accounts receivable. It can, like the commercial finance company, make loans secured by accounts receivable. However, the term *factoring* is confined to the purchase of accounts receivable, the function that is characteristic of the factor. The history of factoring is a long one, having developed in the textile industry to aid many small textile manufacturers with their financing. For many years, the factor was one of the few sources of dependable credit open to these small manufacturers. Eventually banks, commercial finance companies, and other lending organizations increased their loans to textile companies, and the relative importance of factors declined. The last twenty years, however, has witnessed a reversal in the situation, with an increase in the lending activity of factors to include oil-well equipment financing, general manufacturing, and other activities in addition to textile manufacturing.

Steps in Lending on Security of Accounts Receivable. To get a loan on the security of accounts receivable, a company enters into a contract or agreement with a bank or finance company, specifying the acceptance of the company's accounts receivable as collateral for loans. The contract will include in most cases the following clauses:

1. *The amount available from the bank or finance company* expressed in terms of a percentage of the dollar amount of pledge accounts receivable at any time. In the case of commercial finance companies, 85 per cent is a typical figure.

2. *A statement as to which customer accounts of the borrowing company are to be included as security for the loan.* The bank or the finance company may reserve the right to specify which particular customer accounts are acceptable as collateral. Occasionally, only a portion of the accounts receivable are included under the loan agreement. If so, the lending institution usually specifies that the accounts be selected at random to eliminate the possibility of the borrowing company choosing only the weaker accounts as receivables for security.

3. *The mechanics of adding to and subtracting from the dollar volume of accounts receivable pledged as security for the loan from the bank or finance company.* Additions are made to the dollar volume of accounts serving as security by sending to the finance company or bank copies of invoices representing sales made on credit to customers of the borrowing company. Subtractions are made from pledged accounts when invoices are paid by customers of the borrowing company and when allowances or refunds are credited by the company to its customers for defective or returned mechandise. Thus, the dollar amount in the fund of pledged accounts, changing daily with these additions and subtractions, at any

---

[1] *American Banker,* May 31, 1961, p. 9.

time determines the value on which the lending institution is willing to make loans up to the agreed percentage as stated above.

4. *The time period of each loan under the agreement.* Whenever the financial officer of the borrowing company wishes to borrow under the terms of the agreement, he prepares short promissory notes or demand notes for the amount needed. After the notes are presented to the finance company or bank for payment, they are discounted and the proceeds given to the officer of the borrowing company. Where demand notes are used, however, the charges may be made on the basis of calculating the average daily balance over a specified period of time and charging interest on it at the agreed upon rate. Occasionally, and this is more often found where finance companies make loans, both an interest charge and a service charge are levied on the borrower. The service charge may be based on the total number of accounts and the interest charge on the total dollar amount in the average balance. The cost of loans secured by accounts receivable varies widely. In general, it is a greater percentage of the amount of the loan where loans are small and where the percentage of loan to pledged accounts receivable is high. Translated into annual interest terms, the cost of borrowing on the security of accounts receivable varies in most cases between 10 and 15 per cent, though costs as high as 18 or even 20 per cent are not unknown.

5. *Credit insurance.* The agreement may specify that the accounts pledged as security for the loan carry credit insurance. Where this is done, the bank or finance company is generally willing to lend an amount equal to a larger percentage of the pledged accounts receivable and to reduce the interest costs or service charges. Where credit insurance is purchased, the insurance covers losses to the companies that amount to more than the average credit losses. For example, if the experience of the industry is that one-quarter of 1 per cent of credit sales results in uncollectible accounts, the credit insurance will reimburse the company for losses suffered in excess of this percentage. Where credit insurance is specified under the loan agreement, the bank or finance company is named the beneficiary.

Notification. Loans from banks and finance companies secured by accounts receivable are generally of the non-notification type. Under this plan, the customers of the company pay their invoices directly to the company, and usually have no knowledge that their accounts serve as security for a loan. As the borrowing company receives payments from its customers, the checks are usually endorsed and sent to the bank or finance company. Alternatively, the checks may be deposited in a special agency account, from which withdrawals may only be made by the lender.

Credit Risks. Lenders do not lend an amount of money equal to the full dollar value of the accounts receivable securing the loan. The amount will range from a low of about 50 per cent to a high of about 90 per cent of the dollar value of the pledged accounts receivable. Generally, commercial banks lend an amount equal to 70 to 80 per cent, while finance companies lend between 80 and 85 per cent. The reason for such caution is the possibility that the liquidation value of the pledged accounts may not be equal to their value on the books of the borrowing company. There are three main factors that contribute to the reduction in the book value of accounts receivable: (1) returns for defective merchandise; (2) demands for reductions in the invoice charge because poor quality was received, incorrect merchandise was shipped, or merchandise allegedly was not up to the specifications in the customer's order; or (3) nonpayment of accounts by customers of the borrowing company.

In determining the amount to lend on the security of accounts receivable, the lender takes a number of considerations into account. The bank or finance company investigates not only the credit of the borrowing company but also that of each customer of the company seeking the loan. If the borrowing company has been forced to make frequent allowances to its credit customers because the merchandise was defective or was not in accordance with the customer's order, the lending company will permit a smaller amount to be lent than would otherwise be the case.

Advantages and Disadvantages of Accounts Receivable Financing. As stated earlier, lenders demand security in those circumstances where the risk of nonpayment of the loan is considered too great to permit loans to be made on an unsecured basis. Companies in such a position may find that the best way to secure funds from lenders is to offer accounts receivable as collateral for the loan. In other words, the pledging of accounts receivable permits companies to obtain better credit terms from lenders than they could otherwise receive. Another benefit of this type of borrowing is that interest on the loan is based only upon the amount of funds actually used by the borrowing company. As checks are received from the customers of the borrowing company and are deposited, the amount of the outstanding indebtedness is reduced, and the interest is accordingly reduced. Where competitive conditions require that a company extend long credit terms, they may find that its investment in accounts receivable is very high. This asset then becomes a logical one to offer as security for a loan. Stated another way, where lengthy credit terms are necessitated by competitive conditions the pressure for borrowing money to finance the investment in accounts receivable is great, and the investment, in turn, becomes the security on which the loan can be obtained.

The chief disadvantage of accounts receivable financing is cost. This is true whether accounts receivable are used as security for a loan or the accounts are factored. If security is demanded, it is evidence that the seller considers the risk greater than in a loan where security is not demanded. Because the book work of the lender is increased where the pledge of accounts is involved, the rate is higher. Where the accounts are factored (explained below), the charges for handling the accounts plus the interest on money provided by the factor are much higher than the discount on a typical promissory note used to obtain money. The factoring charges amount to two or three times the cost of obtaining a bank loan. In the case of factoring, there might be some customer dissatisfaction in dealing with a factor rather than the seller in making payments on account.

Factoring Instead of seeking a loan secured by the pledge of accounts receivable, the financial officer of the company may elect to sell the accounts receivable for cash. To do this, he must make a contractual arrangement with a financial company called a *factor*. It is important to distinguish between the function of factoring and that of making loans secured by accounts receivable. Where loans are secured by accounts receivable, the accounts remain as an asset on the books of the borrowing company. The borrowing company makes the decision whether to extend credit to a particular customer, endeavors to collect the accounts when they are due, and suffers any losses from uncollectible debts. In other words, the company must maintain a department or at least an officer to handle credits and collections.

Where cash is received by a company as a result of selling accounts receivable rather than borrowing on the security of the accounts, the company not only exchanges the accounts for cash but also gets rid of the problems incidental to handling and collecting them. The accounts receivable sold to the factor do not appear on the books of the company, nor is there a liability on the books of the corporation in the form of a note payable, as would be the case where a loan is extended on the security of accounts receivable. Generally, the contract with the factor is made for a period of a year and renewed annually.

Each order received from a customer is referred to the factor for credit approval. If the factor refuses to approve the order, the company may make the sale at its own risk, bearing any loss resulting from nonpayment by that particular customer. Where a customer is approved by the factor, orders may be filled by the company up to the limit prescribed by the factor. On the invoices a statement will appear that payment is to be made directly to the factor rather than to the company receiving the order for the goods. If any shipments made to the customer approved by the factor result in nonpayment because of the customer's financial conditions, the factor stands the loss rather than the company selling the account. The factor buys the receivables without recourse. If, however, there is a dispute between the company and its customer relative to price, quality, or return of merchandise for credit, it must be resolved by the company and its customer. The factor, in other words, assumes all losses resulting from uncollectible debts but does not assume losses resulting from valid claims by customers for defective merchandise, returns, and similar allowances.

The factor charges a commission for collecting the accounts from customers and absorbing any credit losses. The commission rate depends upon the costs of collection of the accounts and the degree of risk involved. Where the volume of sales is large, the rate generally is small in relation to the volume. Where the quality of accounts is high, the commission rate generally is low. Where the credit terms are long, the commission rate is generally higher. If a cash discount is allowed by the company selling the accounts receivable, the customers generally take advantage of it. An invoice for $200 with a 2 per cent discount for payment in cash in ten days means that the payment usually will be $196. The commission of the factor then is based on $196 rather than $200. Commission rates in existence in 1962 varied from 0.25 per cent to as high as 4 per cent of all credit sales. This great range, of course, included exceptional charges. Most commission rates varied between 1 and 2.75 per cent. For example, if the commission charged by a factor is one per cent of net receivables and the invoice terms are 2/10/30, the following represents the transaction for a $100 invoice:

Face amount of invoice	$100.00
Cash discount taken by customer	2.00
Check received from customer	98.00
Commission deducted by factor at the rate of	
1 per cent	0.98
Net proceeds to company	$ 97.02

Factors also make a charge for interest. When the copy of each invoice representing a credit sale is received by the factor, he credits the account of the company selling the goods. The amount of money represented by this credit, however, is not immediately available unless the company pays an interest charge. Frequently, a company will prefer to wait for the amount of money representing the account sold until such time as the factor receives payment on the account. The length of time that the average account remains outstanding determines the interest charge. If the average length of time is thirty days, the amount represented by each credit sale may be withdrawn by the company thirty days after the date of each invoice. In this case, there is no interest charge by the factor for the money received. If, on the other hand, the company wishes to receive payment for the accounts sold to the factor before the date the factor receives payment from the customers, an interest charge is levied. This is based on the number of days in advance that the factor makes his money available to the client.

The advantages of factoring are as follows:

1. The most important attraction of factoring is that the credit and collections department of the client company is eliminated. Particularly advantageous to small businesses that might have difficulty in recruiting experienced and capable credit personnel, it is also important to those companies with a seasonal sales pattern, for the credit and collections departments of the companies might otherwise be very busy during part of the year and largely idle during the remainder.

2. Credit risks are eliminated. This might be a minor factor in some cases and a major factor in others. In effect, the sale of accounts receivable without recourse to a factor substitutes a calculated cost for an unpredictable loss.

3. Credit losses are reduced where credit sales of a company are divided among many accounts. The credit risk, however, is mostly confined to those situations where a company's credit sales are concentrated largely in one or a few big accounts. The risk of carrying such accounts is minimized for a factor that handles many accounts of many clients.

4. Unlike bank loans, there is no requirement that the client company "clean up his account once each year."

5. The financial condition of the company as represented by its balance sheet may be improved as a result of factoring its accounts receivable. This can be illustrated by the following example:

CURRENT POSITION BEFORE SALE OF ACCOUNTS RECEIVABLE

Cash	$ 50,000	Note payable	$200,000
Accounts receivable	400,000	Accounts payable	450,000
Inventories	500,000		
	$950,000		$650,000

Surplus of current assets over current liabilities	$300,000
Current ratio	1.46 to 1

CURRENT POSITION AFTER SALE OF ACCOUNTS RECEIVABLE

Cash	$ 50,000	Note payable	$100,000
Inventories	500,000	Accounts payable	150,000
	$550,000		$250,000

Surplus of current assets over current liabilities	$300,000
Current ratio	2.2 to 1

For simplicity, the above assumes that all the accounts receivable are sold for $400,000 and that $100,000 of the amount received from the sale is used to reduce the note payable and the remainder to reduce accounts payable.

Some factors, called *old-line factors,* restrict their financial services to the purchase of accounts receivable. These are in the minority, numbering probably no more than a score in the United States. Most factors provide services in addition to the purchase of accounts receivable. Many factors make loans on the security of inventory. Most will either purchase accounts receivable outright or will make loans secured on the pledge of accounts receivable. Some will make loans secured by mortgages on plant and equipment. Many will make loans without any security other than the general credit of the borrower. Many factors make short-term and also long-term loans. A few factors will invest in the business of their client through the purchase of preferred stock, common stock, or a partnership interest.

Among the services many factors will furnish, other than financial, are the following examples: [2]

1. Because factors are in a better position to obtain credit information than are most individual companies, they can help a company to expand to new territories and accounts unfamiliar to the company.

2. Some factors will conduct market studies to determine if a company is getting its share of the market and, if not, to find out why and suggest corrective measures.

3. Being familiar with the industry and having a broader outlook on the economy than would most individual companies, factors can be helpful in advising firms on general economic conditions and trends.

4. Some factors have been instrumental in rendering more efficient distribution setups.

5. Progressive, reliable factors seek to aid their accounts on the basis of personal service, almost as a management consultant. In addition to helping a company in long-range financial planning, they will counsel clients on production, sales, distribution plans, organizational matters, streamlining office procedures, and setting up a budget.

6. They have helped with work load analyses and other industrial engineering functions, surveyed production facilities, and advised on machinery replacement and modernization programs.

7. Some companies have found factors useful in establishing contacts with a good selling agency, enabling companies, for example, to enter the export market.

8. Factors help arrange banking connections and offer suggestions on tax matters, pension plans, trust funds for company officers, and other financial problems. Much of this counseling is provided free of charge.

LOANS ON INVENTORY

Types of Liens on Inventory   Inventory constitutes a large proportion of the total assets of many businesses. If the credit standing of a firm is very high, the existence of inventory may be one of the factors persuading a lending institution to extend unsecured loans to the company. On the other hand, if the credit of a company is not sufficiently high to warrant loans on that basis, the lending institution may be willing to make loans secured by inventory.[3] The loan may be secured by a *trust receipt*, a *fac-*

---

[2] Adapted from Clyde William Phelps, *The Role of Factoring in Modern Business Finance,* Commercial Credit Co., Baltimore, Md., 1956, pp. 49-50.

[3] Lenders, particularly commercial banks, have urged the adoption by states of the "Uniform Commercial Code." This law replaces the many separate laws governing the use of warehouse receipts, trust receipts, chattel mortgages, conditional sales, and other statutes governing loans secured by personal property, and replaces them with a single

tor's lien, or a *warehouse receipt.* If a trust receipt is used, the lender obtains title to the goods, retaining it until the goods are removed from inventory for processing or are sold by the borrower. Whenever the borrower needs to use any portion of the inventory to which the lender has title, it is necessary either for him to repay a portion of the loan or to substitute the inventory that was removed. At the time that the loan is negotiated and the title to the inventory is transferred from the borrower to the lender, the contract specifies the means by which the borower may remove items from inventory.

Where a factor's lien is used, the lien blankets all inventories and often receivables as well. The lien may be long-term, covering several cycles of production and turnover of accounts receivable. As in the case of the trust receipt, the factor's lien permits the borrower the use of the assets pledged. Over half of the states have laws specifying the conditions under which factor's liens may be used. Loans under this type of security may be obtained from factors, commercial banks, and other lenders.

A warehouse receipt may also be used to secure a loan. For various reasons, a company may find it advisable to have large inventory of certain items:

1. If there is a *seasonal demand* for a company's products, it must build up a large inventory in anticipation. If the production pattern is seasonal, the goods produced must be stored so as to be available during the season that the production is either absent or slow.

2. Frequent savings can be achieved if the inventory needed by a company is *purchased in large quantities.* One may take advantage of quantity discounts, savings in transportation, and purchasing at times when prices may be low.

3. Another reason is *safeguarding the supply of needed material.* Where interruptions in the supply of a particular material would be costly to a company, it can reduce them by maintaining a large enough inventory of the needed materials to carry over a considerable period.

4. Certain items improve with age. Where *aging* is required in improving the quality of a product (for example, whiskey or cheese), it is necessary to keep a large inventory of the product during the process.

5. It is necessary in some industries for a company to maintain a large inventory of repair parts to *service its customers.* Also, companies are sometimes required for competitive reasons to maintain a wide variety of styles and sizes. In either case, these circumstances may require a company to maintain a large inventory, in order to fill orders promptly.

Maintaining Inventories Secured for Loans Whenever inventories have

---

security agreement, a copy of which is filed with a public officer designated by the law. It makes lending on the security of inventory and other personal property far simpler than formerly, and reduces the variety of forms of secured loans used for generations. The Uniform Commercial Code was first enacted into law by Pennsylvania in 1954. By 1964, 28 states had adopted it.

to be maintained, there is the problem of where to maintain them. Our concern here, however, is not with the physical problem of inventory management but with the associated financial problems. From a financial standpoint, there are three types of inventory maintenance that deserve mention: *public warehousing*, *field warehousing*, and *floor-planning*. Public warehouses are found in all important cities and towns in the United States, and in other parts of the world as well. Some are highly specialized, handling only a few related items, while others are capable of handling a wide variety of goods. Public warehouses are independently owned, are licensed, and are bonded in order to assure customers of responsible and dependable storage.

A receipt from a bonded and licensed warehouse will enable a company to borrow on the security of the warehouse inventory on favorable terms from a bank or other lending source. The warehouse receipt may be either negotiable or non-negotiable. A negotiable one may be endorsed by the holder over to another person in a manner quite similar to the endorsement of a bank check or promissory note. If the receipt is non-negotiable, the goods may be delivered only to the person specifically named in the receipt. If a warehouse receipt is used as security for a bank loan and if the receipt is non-negotiable, the bank is named in the receipt, and authorization for the release of the warehoused goods must come from this bank. For an example of this type of receipt, see Fig. 8-1.

Making loans on inventory deposited in a public warehouse and covered by a warehouse receipt offers a high degree of security to the lender. This is reflected in more favorable terms to the borrower than would be available on unsecured loans. However, it would be unwise in many cases for a borrower to deposit inventory in a public warehouse in the process of arranging a loan, because of the cost and inconvenience of transporting inventory. Frequently, a borrower wishes to borrow money on the security of a type of inventory that is not suitable for public warehousing. The convenience to the borrower of having a public warehouse located on his premises is obvious. These advantages can be had by establishing a *field warehouse*. A portion of the premises of a company is leased or otherwise made available to a public warehousing company. This area is physically separated from the remainder of the property of the company usually by means of a fence, sometimes merely a temporary one. A sign is erected stating that this area is a field warehouse supervised by a named public warehousing company. The inventory items kept in the field warehouse are under the custody of employees of the public warehousing company, and deposits into and withdrawals from it are under the supervision of the warehousing company. Warehouse receipts are issued for items kept in the field warehouse in the same manner as similar receipts for materials deposited in the regular warehouses of the warehousing company. Occasionally an employee of the company on whose premises the field warehouse is located is hired on a part-time basis by the public warehousing company to

NON-NEGOTIABLE WAREHOUSE RECEIPT AND CONTRACT

BEKINS VAN & STORAGE CO.

Receipt & Lot Number

eceived *for the Account of* .... on ....
(hereinafter called Depositor) (Date)

....by Bekins Van & Storage Co. the goods described in
est known address) City State (hereinafter called the Company)

list below (contents and condition unknown) to be handled on monthly storage in depository located at................................

.... Calif. subject to the conditions printed on the face and reverse side hereof, all of which are agreed and assented
by Depositor for himself and his heirs, and to be delivered to Depositor upon payment of all charges. The storage rate is $.....................
month or fraction thereof. The storage rate may be changed upon 30 days written notice to the Depositor. Total drayage, packing, wrap-
g and labor charges are $...................... for placing these goods in storage.

ORAGE RATE—DECLARED VALUE—LIMIT OF COMPANY'S LIABILITY ▬◀ **READ CAREFULLY**
The Company's rates are based upon the value of the stored goods as declared herein by the Depositor, regardless of actual known value,
upon the space occupied by the goods. The basic (or lowest available) rate is based upon a declared value not to exceed **TEN cents per**
nd per article, which shall be the value for all purposes and in no event shall the Company's liability, if any, for loss or damage, exceed
declared value. Actual weight of the goods shall govern if ascertained; if not, the goods will be deemed to weigh seven pounds per cubic
, which is the average weight of household goods.
Should Depositor declare higher values than TEN cents per pound per article, such values must be declared by Depositor in writing by
rting the higher declared values opposite each article listed on the Original Non-Negotiable Warehouse Receipt and returning the same
he Company within fifteen (15) days of the date of the issue of such Receipt and Contract, for reissue with corrected values and recal-
ted rates of storage. In the latter event the rate is computed by taking the Company's basic rate and adding thereto TEN cents per month
each $100.00 valuation, or fraction thereof, specifically set forth. Until such return and reissue the declared value of **TEN cents per pound**
article shall govern.
OSITOR'S DECLARATION OF VALUE: After having an opportunity to declare higher values and pay a higher rate, Depositor, for the pur-
of this contract and irrespective of actual value, hereby declares the value of all goods stored, including contents of any container, and
goods hereafter stored for Depositor's account to be **TEN cents per pound per article.**
**he Depositor contracts and agrees, by the acceptance of this Receipt and Contract, to all the previsions, limi-
ions, terms and conditions printed on the face and on the reverse side hereof.**

Bekins Van & Storage Co.

.... By..
UR GOODS ARE NOT INSURED UNLESS THE INSURANCE CERTIFICATE BELOW IS FILLED IN AND COUNTERSIGNED.

THE GLOBE SECURITY INSURANCE COMPANY
309 West Jackson Boulevard, Chicago 6, Illinois
INSURANCE CERTIFICATE
THIS IS TO CERTIFY that under Open Household Goods Carrier and Warehousemen's Policy **No. 00045 — 29** issued to Bekins, $.......................
insurance has been extended to the goods held by Bekins under the Warehouse Receipt of which this Certificate is made a part while said goods are on
deposit in, or in transit to or from a warehouse operated by Bekins. The protection afforded is only with respect to the risks and perils assumed under optional
Coverage No. 5, of said policy, as set forth in the attached Insurance Conditions form. Indemnification for physical loss or damage is payable to the Depositor
named above or his order.
Insurance is applied as set forth herein in consideration of the payment by the Depositor or Owner of a monthly premium of $................until the goods
are removed from storage or this insurance is cancelled as provided in the Conditions.
Articles of extraordinary value are hereby specifically declared to the Company as follows: ....

This Certificate is made and accepted subject to the foregoing stipulations and conditions and of the Insurance Conditions form attached which are
specifically made a part of this certificate.
THE GLOBE SECURITY INSURANCE COMPANY
This Certificate is not valid
unless countersigned by:
Bekins Van & Storage Co.

By.......................................

SCHEDULE OF GOODS

Fig. 8-1 *A non-negotiable warehouse receipt.*

supervise the field warehouse. This practice, however, is considered unsatisfactory by most banks and other lending institutions.

The use of field warehousing as a means of securing inventory loans
is particularly common in those companies with seasonal operations. Suppose a fruit canner wishes to pack a large amount of fruit during its relatively brief ripening season. The storage sheds where the boxes of canned
fruit are stored can be set apart as a field warehouse. As the boxes of
canned fruit are moved to the warehouse, the custodian issues warehouse
receipts giving the number of each box deposited. The bank or other
lender makes loans to the canner on the basis of warehouse receipts. By
this means, 70 or 80 per cent of the entire fruit pack of the canner may be

financed by a bank. As sales are made, the canner will be in a position to repurchase the warehouse receipts from the lender. Thus he can move the inventory out of the field warehouse and send the cans on their way to his customers. As the selling season progresses, the canner will deplete the inventory of goods in the field warehouse, and will be able to repay the lender.

A type of inventory financing common in retail trade is called *floor-plan financing*. In floor-planning, a lender, usually a bank, retains title to the items in the showrooms of the retailer. The retailer has physical possession of the goods by means of a *trust receipt*. This is a formal document indicating that the bank has title to the goods which remain in possession of the retailer in trust for the bank while awaiting sale to customers of the retailer. In a typical transaction the loan is extended by the bank to the retailer by means of a demand note signed by the retailer and payable to the bank. As sales are made by the retailer, the amount advanced by the bank on the items sold must be repaid to the bank. This type of financing is confined largely to retailers of automobiles and household appliances. Each automobile or appliance is listed by its serial number, which is then recorded on the appropriate trust receipt held by the bank. At all times the retailer must have in his possession those items of which the serial numbers are on the outstanding trust receipts held by the bank. From time to time, usually unannounced, a representative of the bank will make a visual check of the items on which trust receipts are outstanding. If there is any material discrepancy between the items listed in the trust receipts and those identified on the premises of the retailer, the bank may present all the demand notes it holds against the retailer for immediate payment. The frequency of the unannounced physical check by a representative of the bank, of course, depends upon circumstances. A dealer that has had a long and trusted association with a bank may expect to have the representative of the bank call infrequently. On the other hand, a retailer possessing a less impeccable or a recently acquired reputation may expect to have a representative call frequently, sometimes daily, at his store.

Borrowers seeking loans secured by inventory are generally small- or medium-sized firms. The size of the loan secured by inventory varies from around $10,000 to $100,000 in most cases. The costs of financing by means of security on inventory varies considerably, depending upon the size of the loan, the credit standing of the borrower, the amount of book work, inspections, and other handling involved, and by the general level of interest rates prevailing at the time. The costs of this financing, if secured from banks, ranges from about 6 per cent to more than 12 per cent. Loans from other sources sometimes run higher.

Factors in the Suitability of Goods for Inventory Loans
It is axiomatic that borrowers would prefer to receive funds on an unsecured basis if this can be accomplished without increasing the cost of borrowing. Borrowers agree to loans secured by inventory either because they cannot otherwise

obtain the needed funds or because they can get them at lower cost than is possible on an unsecured basis. Accepting pledged inventory places the lender in a preferred position in the event the borrower defaults on his debts. The lender is particularly interested in the characteristics of the inventory offered for security. Some kinds of inventory are more attractive than others as collateral. Inventory characteristics that are examined by the lender include the probable cost of selling the goods if the lender should have to do that to liquidate the loan, the perishability of the inventory, the degree of stability of the product price, the costs involved in transportation to the market, and the sorting, grading, and brokerage involved in selling the goods.

Costs of Marketing the Product. Some commodities may be sold in a matter of minutes, such as grains sold through a broker who telephones an organized exchange handling the product. The price of the product can be determined at any moment, and the cost and inconvenience involved in making the sale is low relative to the value of the commodity.

Perishability. The perishability of different inventories varies considerably—that of coal is low, while that of eggs is high. Although modern storage techniques have greatly reduced the perishability of many products, there still is considerable variation. From the standpoint of the lender, those inventory items that have a low degree of perishability are preferred as security.

Price Stability. Prices of all products vary, but some vary considerably more than others. The variation in price of style goods, for example, is relatively high. If the inventory securing a loan has a high degree of price instability, the lending institution must exercise greater caution than is necessary where the price is stable.

Brokerage, Sorting, Grading, and Transporting Costs. The variation in costs of handling and maintaining commodities is taken into consideration by the lender in accepting inventory as security for a loan. Grains and other agricultural products must be graded before they are ready for marketing. In order to sell grains and other staple commodities a brokerage fee must be paid. The costs of transporting some commodities, such as coal and ores, is high relative to value, while the costs of transporting items of high value relative to weight is generally smaller. Account must be taken of this by the lender as well as the distance of the inventory item from the principal market.

Although the above factors are considered by the lender in preparing the loan contract on an inventory loan, it does not mean that only those commodities that have favorable characteristics are accepted. Loans are made on almost any inventory item. However, if a particular item is difficult to sell, has a high degree of price instability, or is perishable, the lender's terms would not be as favorable as on an item which does not suffer from these deficiencies. On items that are not very attractive as security, the lender may be willing to lend a maximum of only 50 or 60 per cent of the estimated value of the inventory. Alternatively, he may be willing to lend 70 to 80 per cent of the estimated value but will charge a high rate of interest for the loan. On the other hand, if the inventory has a ready market, is stable in price, and the costs of liquidation are low, the bank or other lending institution may be willing to lend as high as 90 per cent of the estimated value of the inventory and charge a low rate of interest. The financial officer of the borrowing company would do well to shop around among alternative sources of loans in order to find what best meets the requirements of the company as to amount and cost.

LOANS ON OTHER SECURITY

Short-term loans secured by assets other than accounts receivable and inventories are rare in business finance. Short-term loans are, however, occasionally made on such security as stocks and bonds, life insurance policies, and even savings accounts belonging to owners of businesses. Short-term loans secured by the pledge of such assets are confined almost entirely to small businesses.

Securities Stocks and bonds are often used by large corporations as security for long-term bond issues. However, businesses do infrequently offer stocks and bonds as security for short-term loans. If its credit rating is not high enough to warrant getting a loan on an unsecured basis at favorable terms, it is unlikely that the business will have an investment in stocks and bonds. Instead, such an investment would be liquidated in order to provide the funds needed. In some cases, however, a business may find it advisable to borrow on the security of stocks and bonds held rather than liquidating them, since the market for the stocks or bonds may be low and expected to recover in the near future. Also, if the company holds stocks as a means of control over another corporation, it probably will prefer not to liquidate the securities.

Life Insurance Policies Every businessman has or should have a life insurance policy. Most policies build up an increasing cash surrender value as the years pass, the major exceptions being group and term insurance. This is the amount that the insured would receive if he were to cancel his policy. In order to discourage the cancellation of policies to meet temporary emergency requirements for funds, life insurance companies provide for loans to be made to their policyholders up to the amount of the cash surrender value at low rates of interest. However, the delay involved in arranging the loan and the inflexibility of its provisions are sometimes inconvenient. An alternative is to use the cash surrender value of a policy as collateral for a bank loan. This is accomplished by assigning to the bank the rights under the insurance policy. The usual assignment form employed by banks is based upon the model prepared by the American Bankers Association, which provides for the signature of the insured and his beneficiary, thereby obtaining the consent of each of these parties to the assignment of the policy. A copy of this assignment is sent to the insurance company for the signature of an authorized officer of the company. As long as the loan is outstanding, the bank keeps the insurance policy in its vaults. If the businessman expects that he will borrow frequently on the security of the life insurance policy, the bank will generally advise him to keep the loan agreement in effect at all times by leaving a token amount, commonly one dollar, unpaid. If this is done, later loans can be negotiated at the bank with no delay. The terms offered by the bank are generally more flexible than can be obtained from the insurance company, although the interest charged by the bank may be higher than that charged by the insurance company.

Questions

1. For what reasons do lenders demand security for their loans?
2. Why may a lender sometimes prefer borrowing money by a secured loan rather than by an unsecured loan?
3. What are the characteristics that make an asset good collateral for a loan?
4. Why do lenders accept as collateral, assets that do not have the characteristics of good collateral?
5. What is factoring? In what industry did it first develop?
6. Explain how credit insurance serves to reduce the risk of loss in accounts receivable financing.
7. Give three reasons that collections of accounts receivable may be less than the value of the accounts on the books.
8. Show how the current ratio of a company may be improved by factoring its accounts receivable.
9. What services in addition to financing may be furnished by factors?
10. Distinguish between public warehousing, field warehousing, and floor-planning.
11. If a company holds stocks or bonds, why may it prefer to pledge them as security for a loan instead of selling them for cash?
12. A businessman can borrow money from his insurance company on the security of his life insurance policy or from his bank on the same security. What are the advantages of each source of money?

Selected Readings

The Financial Gap—Real or Imaginary? Industrial Economic Division, Denver Research Institute, University of Denver, Denver, Colo., 1962.

Goldsmith, Raymond W., *Financial Intermediaries in the American Economy Since 1900,* National Bureau of Economic Research, Inc., Washington, D.C., 1958.

Phelps, Clyde W., *Accounts Receivable Financing as a Method of Business Finance,* Commercial Credit Co., Baltimore, Md., 1957.

Sweetser, Albert G., *Financing Goods,* Albert G. Sweetser, Eau Claire, Wis., 1957.

9

Intermediate Credit

T<small>HE</small> P<small>ROBLEMS</small> of intermediate and short-term financing are similar, yet they also differ in several important respects: the length and purposes of credit, and the sources and methods of repayment.

Writers disagree about the length of intermediate credit, but most will place the dividing line between short-term and intermediate credit at one year. However, the dividing line between intermediate and long-term credit is far from uniform, having been placed at five, ten, and even fifteen years. Most commonly, however, intermediate credit extends over one year and changes into long-term credit anywhere between five and fifteen years. But in the analysis of financial statements, intermediate credit is generally classed as long-term debt, since no separate classification for intermediate credit is used.

There has been a rapid growth of intermediate credit (also referred to as term loans, particularly in bank lending) in the period following World War II. In 1946, member banks of the Federal Reserve System had outstanding $4.5 billions in term loans, representing 19.6 per cent of all their outstanding loans. In 1957, the volume had grown to $15.5 billions, representing 38 per cent of total outstanding loans.[1]

FINANCING EQUIPMENT PURCHASES

Financing of Sales of Equipment by Manufacturers   The chief function of intermediate credit is to finance the purchase of equipment. For this reason the decision to buy needed equipment is conditioned by the terms and availability of intermediate financing. If the financing is considered to be too expensive, the company may decide to postpone the purchase for a few months.

---

[1] *Federal Reserve Bulletin,* April 1959.

There are two methods by which intermediate credit is offered to customers of a company. (1) The company can take a single note or a series of notes with different maturities, secured by the machinery or equipment sold, and either hold these until they mature or discount them at a bank or another lending institution. The company may be in a position to secure long-term financing at low rates to finance its investment in the intermediate term notes of its customers. (2) The company can establish a subsidiary corporation for the purpose of handling customers' notes. If the volume of intermediate term receivables is large, the advantages of a separate corporation are considerable. The primary purpose of the financing subsidiary is the facilitation of the sale of goods by the parent company to its customers. Nevertheless, the problems of finance are different from those of selling. In a subsidiary company credit analysis, repossessions, and collecting installments or payments of notes when due can in most cases be handled better through independent judgment exercised by officers of a subsidiary than by a department within a company. Furthermore, the costs of offering financing to customers can be more easily determined if a subsidiary handles the financing than if the financing is done by a department of the company itself. This does not mean that a financing subsidiary of a manufacturer must under all circumstances try to operate at a profit. In a time of slack business, the best method of maintaining or improving sales might be an offer of more liberal credit rather than a price change or a change in the design of the products themselves. If such is the case, the financing subsidiary might offer credit to the customers of the parent company at a rate below cost, with the losses of the subsidiary offset by the profits of the parent.[2]

Leasing of Equipment   Three alternative means of securing equipment are: purchasing the equipment on a cash basis, financing a purchase by means of an installment contract, and leasing the equipment. Leasing is a technique applied both to intermediate and long-term finance. It is used to secure the use of a piece of land for ninety-nine years and the use of a truck or piece of machinery for one year. In Chapter 14, the use of the lease as an instrument of long-term finance will be discussed, but here leasing as a means of securing the use of equipment is emphasized. The effects of leasing equipment and the installment purchase of equipment are similar. In both cases, a periodic payment is made for the equipment while it is being used. The dissimilarities between leasing and installment purchasing are as follows:

1. In the case of an installment purchase, a down payment, between one fifth and one third of the purchase price of the equipment, must be made. In the case of a lease, no down payment is required.

2. With an installment purchase, the payment schedule is usually ar-

---

[2] An example of a financing subsidiary is the General Electric Credit Corporation, subsidiary of General Electric Company.

ranged to be completed before the end of the useful life of the equipment. For example, if the equipment is expected to have a useful life of five years, the installment contract would complete payment within three to four years. With leasing, the terms of payment are not necessarily shorter than the life of the equipment.

3. The risk of obsolescence is reduced if equipment is leased in contracts where the lessor agrees to replace obsolete equipment with more up-to-date equipment.

4. Because maintenance and repair are in many lease contracts shifted to the company owning the equipment, the problems of maintaining a fleet of trucks, highly specialized equipment, or even ordinary machine tools are lightened. A company leasing equipment to many other companies can usually afford to maintain a staff of specialists in repair and maintenance, which frequently is beyond the capability of the company that uses only one or two models of particular items of equipment. Highly specialized maintenance service on electronic computors is a good example.

5. A tax advantage is gained by leasing, because the total lease payments are deductible from business income as a cost of doing business.

6. Since a lease is not a liability listed on the balance sheet, a corporation leasing rather than financing the purchase of equipment by means of installments shows a better balance sheet position. This does not mean, of course, that the company is less obligated to make its lease payments than its installment payments. Instead, the total liabilities of the company leasing equipment are less than if the company purchased the equipment on an installment basis.

The main disadvantage of leasing as compared to owning equipment is the cost, which is in most cases significantly higher than financing by means of installment purchases. The recommendation of the financial officer of whether to lease or purchase equipment on the installment plan must be made after weighing carefully the advantages of one against the other. In many cases, the decision is not made on the basis of financial factors alone, but rather on considerations of convenience, freedom from the problems of maintenance, and the advantage found in many lease contracts of being assured the replacement of obsolete equipment with the latest models.

A new type of lease was pioneered by the Equitable Life Assurance Society during the 1950's and first applied to the needs of railroads in securing rolling stock. Under this arrangement, the insurance company purchased railroad equipment directly from the manufacturer, and then leased it to the railroad on a fifteen-year contract without requiring a down payment. At the expiration of the fifteen years, the railroad was given the option of extending the lease for an additional ten. The insurance company amortized its investment in the equipment during the fifteen-year period of the first lease.

Finance Companies   Where financing cannot be had from the manufacturer of the equipment, purchasers frequently turn to finance companies for credit.   The requirements of finance companies vary in providing intermediate credit for the purchase of equipment.   Almost always a pledge of property is imperative, and the property pledged in most cases is the equipment to be financed.   In general, a finance company will offer lower down payment and longer terms than will commercial banks.   On the other hand, the rates charged by finance companies are usually higher than rates charged by commercial banks.   In many cases, however, the purchaser of equipment does not have a choice between financing from a commercial bank and a finance company.   If the bank in which the purchaser carries his account is unwilling to extend credit for the purchase of equipment, he usually is forced to depend upon finance companies for credit.

Where a loan from a finance company is obtained, the amount borrowed can be repaid on an installment basis, or the equipment may be leased from the finance company until the payments are completed.   The equipment is then turned over to the full possession and ownership of the purchaser.   As a rule, finance companies are more flexible in tailoring their lending policies to the requirements of particular borrowers than are commercial banks.   Furthermore, in intermediate term lending, as in short-term lending, finance companies are willing to lend to borrowers of lower credit standing than most banks are.

INTERMEDIATE CREDIT FROM COMMERCIAL BANKS

Any business loan extended by a bank or other financial institution for a period of more than one year is called a *term loan*.   It is a loan in which the principal in most cases is retired in installments during the life of the loan.   Term loans are a relatively new means of financing.   Although loans running from three to fifteen years have been available from many sources for decades, availability of loans of terms more than one year has not been characteristic of commercial banking until the 1930's.   The demand for loans with a maturity of more than a year has grown very greatly since World War II, particularly among retailers and all types of small businesses, causing commercial banks to move into this area of intermediate financing.

Uses of Term Loans   Since a term loan is a type of intermediate financing, it is generally used for the same purposes as intermediate financing.   It is particularly well adapted to the uses of small businesses, especially since they are not able to take advantage of some of the sources of financing available to large concerns.

Term loans are available from such sources as commercial banks, insurance companies, certain savings banks, and installment finance companies.   Until the 1950's, term loans were available from the Reconstruction

Finance Corporation, a government agency created in 1932 to aid business in recovering from the depression, and from the Federal Reserve Banks. The intermediate-term lending of the Federal Reserve Banks ended in 1950, while the Reconstruction Finance Corporation came to an end in 1953. A new governmental lending agency, the Small Business Administration, was created in 1953 to replace the Reconstruction Finance Corporation in making intermediate- and long-term loans to small business. In 1958, a law was passed by Congress providing for privately owned federally authorized lending agencies, known as Small Business Investment Corporations, to make loans.

Because a term loan covers a period longer than a year, the lender is more concerned with long-term financial qualifications than he would be on a loan of a few months' maturity. The lender will examine earning capacity, quality of management, stability of the enterprise, and the extent of competion in the industry. He may seek the advice of market analysts, management consultants, and other technicians before deciding upon the details of the loan.

The factors to be analyzed will probably include the following:

1. Market analysis of the merchandise or services sold by the company seeking the term loan.
2. Appraisal of the stock of merchandise, if any, that is carried.
3. Investigation of accounting methods, depreciation schedules, reserve policy, and similar matters.
4. Financial analysis of the business covering a period of several years to determine its financial soundness, the trend of earning power, and the projected availability of cash for repayment of the loan.
5. Investigation of the personal finances of the owners or principal officers where they might influence the credit standing and earning capacity of the business.
6. Estimate of the effect of a recession, war, or other contingency on the business.

The lender may restrict the borrower's scope of action in employing the money borrowed, or he may permit him considerable freedom. He may also demand the right to inspect the company books, or require the company to submit periodic reports of its financial condition.

The Loan Contract   Term loans are much less frequently sought than short-term loans. For this reason, each term loan contract is a custom-made contract, and is drawn up by the lender with greater care and preparation than is true of most short-term loans. It will include all the provisions which the lender feels are necessary to assure repayment. The following is typical:

1. Length of loan period and schedule for repaying in installments.
2. Interest and other charges.

3. Provision that the entire balance of the loan be made due and payable immediately if any default is made in repayment.
4. Any warranties that may be necessary. For example, if a small corporation is the borrower, there will be a warranty that the officers signing the contracts have authority to act for the corporation, that the terms of the loan do not violate the charter or bylaws, and that the financial statements furnished to the lender by the corporation are correct and complete.
5. Requirements to maintain working capital at the proper level.
6. Restrictions on other borrowing during the life of the loan.
7. Description of assets, if any, pledged to secure the loan, and the terms under which they are pledged.
8. Restrictions on the payment of salaries and dividends or distribution of earnings during the life of the loan.
9. Miscellaneous restrictions and stipulations, such as prohibiting the sale of certain assets, keeping proper insurance, paying taxes promptly, furnishing periodic accounting statements to the lender, or perhaps inserting a "no penalty clause" stating that there would be no charge or objection if the loan were paid off before the date originally scheduled.

Repayment of the Term Loans   One characteristic of term lending is repayment of the principal in installments during the life of the loan. In addition, each installment will include a charge to cover the interest on the loan and any other expenses that are required by the lender as a condition to making the loan. Interest rates are usually calculated on the outstanding balance rather than the original amount of the loan, and vary from 4 per cent to 15 per cent. Repayment schedules providing for widely varying frequencies of payment are found in term lending. The most common of these provide for monthly, quarterly, semiannual, and annual payments on principal and interest. How often the lender will require repayment will depend upon the character of the borrower's business, the demand for funds, the credit standing of the borrower, and the desires of the borrower with respect to frequency of repayment. For example, the borrower may make income tax payments quarterly and may wish, therefore, to have a schedule providing for payments on the term loan at times other than when the tax payments must be made.

An example may make the use of term loans clearer. Suppose that a retail store with annual sales of $780,000, and profits before taxes of $14,-800, wishes to secure a term loan from a commercial bank. Equipment and fixtures are in need of modernization, and the officers calculate that a thorough renovation, costing $36,000, would boost sales to a level of $975,-000, and yield profits of $24,300. The financial officer recommends financing this through a term loan to run for three years. The bank agrees and sets up a repayment schedule as shown in Table 9-1.

TABLE 9-1. TERM LOAN

Total amount: $36,000.

Interest rate: 5 per cent per annum on unpaid balance.

Repayment Schedule	Outstanding	Interest	Principal	Total
1957—1st Qtr.	$36,000	$ 450.00	$ 3,000	$ 3,450.00
2nd Qtr.	33,000	412.50	3,000	3,412.50
3rd Qtr.	30,000	375.00	3,000	3,375.00
4th Qtr.	27,000	337.50	3,000	3,337.50
1958—1st Qtr.	24,000	300.00	3,000	3,300.00
2nd Qtr.	21,000	262.50	3,000	3,262.50
3rd Qtr.	18,000	225.00	3,000	3,225.00
4th Qtr.	15,000	187.50	3,000	3,187.50
1959—1st Qtr.	12,000	150.00	3,000	3,150.00
2nd Qtr.	9,000	112.50	3,000	3,112.50
3rd Qtr.	6,000	75.00	3,000	3,075.00
4th Qtr.	3,000	37.50	3,000	3,037.50
		$2,925.00	$36,000	$38,925.00

Source: Adapted from Paul G. Hastings, *Term Loans in Small Business Financing,* Small Marketers Aids #22, Small Business Administration, Washington, D.C., 1957, p. 4.

Not all repayment provisions of term loans call for equal installments. One variation is called a "balloon" note. In this type the last payment is a large one. Let us assume that a company wants a term loan for a period of ten years, but a bank is willing to make the loan for a maximum of only five. In such a case, the bank might be willing to set each of the installments at an amount which would repay the loan in ten years, but at the end of five years require a large payment which would actually repay all the remaining balance. However, the understanding between the borrowing company and the bank would be that at the end of the five-year period, a new five-year term loan could be extended to refinance the large last payment. The bank would normally be quite willing to refinance such a loan, even though it might not be willing to bind itself, at the start, to a ten-year one.

Banks generally permit prepayment of a term loan without penalty, while insurance companies extending term loans typically require that a premium be paid if the borrower wants to retire the loan early. Where a prepayment is made, the terms of the loan contract will generally require that the prepayment be applied to the final installments first. The prepayment will thus advance the date of final retirement of the loan.

LOANS FROM INSURANCE COMPANIES

Following World War II, interest yields on long-term bonds were low. This was particularly true of United States Government Securities.

Life insurance companies during World War II had invested heavily in these low yield securities. After the war, they continued to receive large sums in premium payments on life insurance policies, which increased greatly in number and amount. Therefore, the liquid funds of the life insurance companies were a problem to the investment department of each company, prompting the active consideration of term lending by the investment officers of the companies.

The preference of life insurance companies is primarily for long-term investment. Their operations involve long-term contracts (insurance policies), they are experienced in appraising and making long-term investments, and their flow of funds exhibits neither the seasonal nor cyclical variation found in other industries. Furthermore, the larger life insurance companies prefer a few loans of substantial size to many loans of small size. For these reasons, life insurance companies are a less important source of term lending than commercial banks. The ever-expanding funds at the disposal of life insurance companies, coupled with the low yield of bonds in the period immediately following World War II, prompted insurance companies to seek alternative investments and particularly to enter the intermediate term lending area. Although interest yields on long-term bonds have increased during the 1950's, it is likely that insurance companies will remain receptive to profitable opportunities in term lending.

One notable result of the interest of life insurance companies in intermediate lending has been their participation with commercial banks in extending term loans. The advantages to the life insurance company in a joint loan with a commercial bank are considerable. Because life insurance companies are not interested in the liquidity of the loan, but in its security and income, they have entered into loan arrangements with commercial banks under terms which provide for the preparation of a series of promissory notes by the borrower payable separately to the commercial banks and the insurance company. The promissory notes with short maturities are payable to the commercial bank, and the promissory notes of longer maturities are payable to the insurance company. Under such a contract, a loan of fifteen years with promissory notes requiring repayment of the loan in annual installments would provide, for example, that the promissory notes maturing during the first eight years be payable to the commercial bank, and the promissory notes maturing in the ninth year and later would be made payable to the life insurance company. In a joint participation term loan, the commercial bank acts as the collecting agent for the life insurance company. The commercial bank, being more experienced in the problems of handling term loans and more practiced in examining the credit of business borrowers, could more efficiently act as the agent of the insurance company in a term loan contract.

Questions

1. What differences are there in the uses of short-term and intermediate credit?
2. Distinguish between the three alternative methods available in obtaining the use of equipment.
3. If a manufacturer of office equipment does not need intermediate financing, should he be concerned with the availability and cost of intermediate loans? Explain.
4. If a manufacturer controls a subsidiary providing intermediate credit, should the subsidiary be operated at a profit or not? Defend your answer.
5. What are the similarities between leasing and installment purchase of equipment? What are the differences?
6. Under what circumstances might the purchaser of industrial equipment seek financing for the purchase from a finance company?
7. What are the principal characteristics of a term loan?
8. What are some of the uses for which term loans are appropriate?
9. From what sources are term loans available to businesses?
10. What information is sought by a lender in deciding whether to extend a term loan to a company?

Selected Readings

Gant, D. R., "Illusion in Lease Financing," *Harvard Business Review,* March-April 1959.

Hastings, Paul G., *Term Loans in Small Business Financing,* Small Marketers Aids #22, Small Business Administration, Washington, D.C., 1957.

Prochnow, Herbert V., *Term Loans and Theories of Liquidity,* Prentice-Hall, Inc., Englewood Cliffs, N. J., 1949.

Robinson, Roland I., *The Management of Bank Funds,* McGraw-Hill Book Co., New York, 1951, Chap. 10.

Street, Donald M., *Railroad Equipment Financing,* Columbia University Press, New York, 1959.

Part IV

Types of Securities

10

Common Stocks

Ownership of a business corporation is represented by stock. Stock is issued to facilitate the purchase, sale, and transfer of a part ownership of an incorporated business. The problems of multiple ownership are made easier by creating a corporation and issuing ownership certificates. In a proprietorship or partnership there is no distinction between the business and the ownership: the owners have direct title to the assets. The corporation on the other hand holds legal title to the assets on its books, while the shareholders own the corporation, i.e., they have no direct ownership of the corporation assets. Although the corporation as a form of business is particularly well adapted to the association of a large number of owners, it is also used where the number of owners is small. The laws of the states which provide for incorporation of business enterprises require that a minimum of three or more [1] incorporators associate themselves to secure a charter from the state. Nevertheless, the ownership often is later concentrated in a single individual who owns 100 per cent of the stock. This is because one of the most valuable attributes of the corporation is the ease with which ownership can be changed by transferring shares of stock. Since ownership is represented by stock, each share represents a definite proportion of ownership. Thus, if there are 10,000 shares of stock outstanding, each share represents ownership of .01 per cent of the corporation. The charter states the number of shares into which the ownership may be divided, which may be ten shares or ten million or some other number.

The shareholders in a corporation are the owners, the shares they own representing their equity in the corporation. However, different kinds of stock may be issued representing different or varying rights of ownership.

---

[1] Most states require a minimum of three incorporators. An exception is Michigan, which permits a charter to be granted to a single incorporator. (Michigan General Corporation Act, Section 3).

Corporations frequently issue two classes: preferred and common. The holders of most preferred issues receive prior rights to the dividends of the corporation, but are limited in the amount of the dividend to which they are entitled and do not vote for the directors of the corporation. In the event of liquidation the common stockholders are the residual claimants to the corporation's earnings and assets after payment of all liabilities. If the charter authorizes the issuance of several classes of common stock, it sets out the various priorities and rights of participation in earnings, assets in the event of dissolution, and voting power.

THE STOCK CERTIFICATE

The purchaser of stock is issued a stock certificate, which constitutes the legal evidence of ownership of a portion of the corporation's outstanding stock. Although there is a great variety in form and design of stock certificates, they commonly contain at least the following: (1) the name of the corporation, (2) the state under whose laws the corporation received its charter, (3) the date of issue, (4) the statement that the shares are fully paid and nonassessable, (5) the par value of the stock or the statement that it is no-par, (6) the number of shares represented by the certificate, (7) the signatures of the president, treasurer, or other officers attesting to its validity, and (8) an assignment form on the reverse side for the purpose of transferring ownership.

A small corporation with relatively few stockholders that does not expect to issue certificates frequently generally purchases blank stock certificates from a business stationery store. These can be filled out with a typewriter or pen to include all the necessary information to make the stock certificate a valid instrument of ownership. Corporations that have a large number of stock certificates outstanding and whose share transferals require frequent issuance of new certificates generally have stock certificates specially printed. Heavy, high quality paper is used, and it is engraved with complex border designs, which are intended to make counterfeiting difficult. Furthermore, if the stock of a corporation is listed for trading on the New York Stock Exchange or any other major exchange, the design of the stock certificate must be approved by the officials of the exchange. A stock certificate is shown in Fig. 10-1.

STOCK TERMINOLOGY

Authorized Stock The corporation charter states the classes of stock that may be issued and the number of shares of each class authorized. No more stock may be issued than is authorized by the charter, until such time as a charter amendment provides for an additional authorization. To avoid this procedure each time the directors wish to issue stock for additional funds, the charter generally provides for an authorization consider-

Fig. 10-1   A corporation stock certificate.

ably in excess of the amount issued at the time the corporation commences business.

Issued Stock As soon as stock is sold by the corporation for cash or exchanged for goods or services, the stock becomes issued stock. The difference between the number of shares authorized by the charter and the number already issued indicates the extent to which the officers and directors can use stock as a means of additional financing before having to amend the charter. It is rare that subscriptions are received for less than the par value of the stock. The legal complications and the restrictions imposed by the corporation statutes of the fifty states are such that stock is almost invariably issued for par value or more. Once the stock has been sold by the corporation or exchanged for services or property in an amount equal to or greater than the par value of the stock, the shares are no longer subject to an assessment by the corporation. After the stock certificate has been issued as fully paid and nonassessable, it may later be sold or exchanged for any value, which may be above or below the par value.

Treasury Stock Stock that has once been issued by the corporation and has been reacquired is called treasury stock. There are many ways by which this can be done, but the most common are by purchase and donation. As long as the corporation holds treasury stock, no dividends may be paid to such shares and they lose their voting power. Such stock is, however, issued stock. Although unissued stock may only be sold by the corporation at par or more or exchanged for the equivalent value in services, treasury stock may be reissued by the corporation at any price, regardless of the par value printed on the face of the certificate.

There is no legal bar to acceptance by a corporation of a gift of its own stock. But the law does not permit an unrestricted right to a corporation to repurchase its stock. Corporation law contains the theory of the *trust fund,* which states that the capital stock constitutes a trust fund for the protection of creditors of the corporation. The practical application of this doctrine prohibits the corporation from intentionally reducing the net worth (assets minus liabilities) to the point of impairing the ability of the company to pay its debts and meet its other contract obligations. If the corporation purchases its own shares, its assets and net worth are both reduced, but its liabilities are not. If this impairs the position of the creditors, it violates the trust fund doctrine and is an illegal act of the directors. In many instances, however, no violence is done to the doctrine, provided that the remaining net worth amply protects the creditors. Corporations purchase their own stock to put excess cash to use, to support a sagging market price for their stock, to retire preferred shares when they are available at prices favorable to the corporation.[2]

---

[2] During 1963 the repurchase of outstanding shares by companies was particularly heavy. One magazine comments as follows: "Last year such repurchases mounted to what are probably record highs. There are no exact figures available, but estimates are that stock

Outstanding Stock Stock in the hands of stockholders is called outstanding stock. It does not include stock held in treasury by the corporation. All outstanding stock of a particular class is entitled to the full rights to dividends and voting that are accorded to that class of stock by the corporation charter. If the charter authorizes 100,000 shares and if 50,000 shares are issued, of which 20,000 have been repurchased by the corporation, the stock account will show: authorized stock, 100,00 shares; issued stock, 50,000 shares; treasury stock, 20,000 shares; and outstanding stock, 30,000 shares.

STOCK VALUE

Par Value The *par value* of stock is the value printed on the face of the stock certificate and is the value stated in the charter of the corporation for each share of the stock. Par value represents the minimum amount that may be paid for the stock by subscribers to the shares when they are issued by the corporation. If any subscribers to the stock pay less than the par value, they are liable for the difference between what they pay and the par value to creditors of the corporation in the event of bankruptcy. Furthermore, the corporation is prohibited from paying dividends which reduce the excess of assets over debts of the corporation to a point below the figure representing the par value of all the shares outstanding. When stock is issued by the corporation it may be exchanged for cash or for services or property. Courts have permitted directors considerable latitude of judgment in estimating the value of services or property exchanged for stock. The laws of a majority of states prohibit the issuance of stock certificates to subscribers who have not paid in the par value of the stock. If a subscriber has made a partial payment toward the par value of shares for which he has subscribed, he may be issued a receipt until such time as the balance up to the par is paid. When the par value has been paid, he is issued a certificate marked "fully paid and non-assessable." Stock may be issued for more than the par value and frequently is, in the case of banks and other financial corporations. Then, the capital stock account is credited with the par value of the shares issued, and an account called *capital surplus* is credited with the excess received over the par value. Sometimes the par value of the stock is such a small fraction of the price at which the stock is distributed to subscribers that the par value is a purely nominal figure.

Book Value Where there is only one class of stock outstanding, the *book value* is the total of the capital stock account and all the surplus accounts. The book value per share is determined by dividing the book value for the total outstanding shares by the number of shares outstanding. In deter-

---

worth $750 million or more was bought in as companies took advantage of what they considered bargain prices—sometimes less than book value—to reduce shares outstanding—and thus boost earnings per share" (*Business Week,* March 7, 1964, p. 90).

mining the valuation of assets for the purpose of computing book value, it is customary for accountants to subtract from the total of the assets the valuation for patents, goodwill, and any other intangible assets, unless these are carried at nominal figures. If there is more than one class of stock outstanding, each will have a book value determined by adding the par value of each class to the claim each class has to surplus accounts in the event of liquidation. If there are two or more classes of common stock outstanding, all classes generally participate equally in the surplus in the event of liquidation. If there is preferred stock outstanding, its book value is usually computed by adding to its par value an amount equal to any preferred dividends in arrears.

Market Value   The *market value* of the stock has little relation to the book value and bears no relation to the par value. It is the price that can be obtained at any particular time for shares already issued and in the hands of stockholders and is usually expressed on a per share basis. Where an active market exists for the shares of a company, such as stocks that are listed on the New York Stock Exchange, the market constantly changes. The many factors which affect the market price of a stock include the profit prospects for the company and for the industry in which the company operates, the business cycle or stock market cycle, the trend of interests rates, the threat of inflation, political or governmental influences, the demand for the stock for purposes of controlling the company, international considerations, and emotional factors.

NO-PAR STOCK

Prior to 1912 it was necessary for a special act to be passed by the state legislature each time a corporation was given the privilege of issuing stock with no-par value. In 1912, however, New York gave blanket authorization to corporations chartered in that state to issue such stock. Since then nearly all other states have similarly amended their corporation statutes. The main reasons for the passage of these acts were the purported desire of the state legislators to protect stock purchasers, and the recognition that the concept of par value had lost significance. It was argued that the appearance on the face of the stock certificate of a value in terms of money resulted in some purchasers assuming that the value stamped on the certificate indicated the true value of the share of stock. It was further argued that the absence of any dollar figure on the face of the stock certificate would force the purchaser to make an independent appraisal of the value of the stock before risking his money in the investment.

Advantages of No-Par Stock   A fundamental advantage in using no-par stock is that there is no statement in the charter of the corporation nor on the face of the stock certificate indicating the value of the stock. Thus, the corporation directors may issue the stock for whatever price they think they can get. In accounting for the issuance of stock, the directors of the corporation may credit to the capital stock account the entire proceeds from the sale of an issue of stock. Alternatively, they may credit to the capital stock account a portion of the proceeds of the sale of an issue, crediting to capital surplus the balance of the purchase price. These proportions may be changed upon later sales of the same class of stock. For example, if no-par stock is authorized by the charter of the corporation, it may sell an issue for $15, all of which is credited to the capital stock account. A further issue of the no-par stock may be later sold for $15, with $10 being credited to capital stock, and $5 to capital surplus. Because no-par stock may be issued at different times for different prices, it permits a greater degree of flexibility in financing than was previously possible.

The lower limit placed on the price at which par value stock could be issued does not apply to no-par stock. For purposes of accounting, no-par stock is arbitrarily assigned a value by the directors of the corporation at the time that the stock is issued. If no-par stock is used, the total of the capital stock account represents the stated value of the no-par stock. To determine the stated value per share of the no-par stock, it is merely necessary to divide the capital stock account by the number of shares outstanding. In this connection, it should be emphasized that the amount credited to the capital stock account where no-par stock is issued is treated in the same manner as the capital account of par value stock with respect to the responsibility of directors in maintaining the capital of the corporation. The amount that is carried on the books of the corporation as the capital stock of the corporation may not be impaired by voluntary action of the directors, either by reducing this amount by dividend payments or by any other deliberate action. Foresighted directors can, of course, reduce the possibility of later impairment of the capital account by crediting a portion of the proceeds of the sale of an issue of no-par stock to the capital stock and crediting the remainder to capital surplus.

Before no-par stock was available as a means of financing, the directors of corporations sometimes resorted to devious means of avoiding the liability of issuing par stock at less than the par value. For example, this was sometimes accomplished by issuing par stock in exchange for "valuable services" with the understanding that the recipient would donate to the corporation a major portion of the stock so received by him. The stock returned to the corporation, being treasury stock, could be resold by the directors for any price, and no liability was incurred by the purchaser beyond the purchase price. The use of no-par stock in financing corporations obviates the need for such dubious means of avoiding legal liability.

An important advantage stressed by proponents of no-par stock in the period when corporation laws were being changed to permit its issue was that no-par stock reduced the possibility of confusion on the part of investors as to the true value of the stock. It is difficult to measure the degree of naïveté that might be present among investors in corporations.

Manufacturers of products sometimes attach to the article a "list price" which is grossly exaggerated, for the purpose of inducing customers to believe that they are purchasing the article at a bargain when they pay less than the listed price. If persons purchasing common stocks are no more sophisticated than some customers purchasing household appliances, some investors must think that the par value stated on the stock certificate represents the "true" or "normal" value of the stock. Since only a minor proportion of adults in the United States are investors in stocks, it is probable that, as a class, investors are more sophisticated than the general level of consumers.

Disadvantages of No-Par Stock   One of the disadvantages in the use of no-par stock is that it allows a degree of freedom to directors of certain corporations where irresponsibility or poor judgment may proceed unchecked. The issuance of excessive amounts of no-par stock at different prices, part of which is credited to the capital stock account and part to the surplus account, may permit an unwise dividend policy to be followed by the directors. If net earnings retained in surplus are credited to a surplus account to which the capital surplus has also been credited, there is no distinction between the capital surplus and the retained earnings. Under such circumstances, the directors of the corporation may pay out in dividends part of the capital contributed by the investors. While the state law under which the corporation is chartered may permit such action, sound corporate management generally does not. A second disadvantage in the use of no-par stock is that there are even fewer checks on the directors in using stock to pay for services and property given to the corporation than is the case where par value stock is used. The directors are virtually unrestrained in deciding the number of shares of no-par stock which they may transfer to a person for services rendered or property received.

Another disadvantage is the existence of certain taxes which discriminate against the issuance of no-par as compared with par stock. The mechanism of determining the organization tax levied on a corporation upon its origin in some cases makes it more expensive to use no-par stock than that having par value. Another tax sometimes placing a heavier burden on no-par stock than on par stock is the stock transfer tax. It is levied not on the corporation whose stock is being transferred but upon the investor at the time that he sells it. There are cases where the stock transfer tax paid by investors holding a certain dollar value of stocks having no par value is greater than the transfer tax paid by another investor selling the same dollar value of stocks having par value.

After the passage of state laws permitting the issuance by corporations of no-par stock, the laws stating the minimum value of stocks issued for par was in most cases liberalized. Prior to 1912, for example, many states prohibited the issuance of stock for less than $100 par value. Since that time, the laws of the states have been amended to permit par value stock to be issued at such minimum values as $10, $5, or $1. A number of states have provided no limitation whatsoever to the par value that may be assigned to stocks.[3] One result of this liberalization has been a declining popularity of no-par stock and greater use of a nominal par value of $1, $5, or some such figure. The par value in this case is selected mostly for the purpose of reducing the organization tax of the corporation and the transfer tax of investors. Such stocks sometimes are called "low-par" stocks.

RIGHTS OF COMMON STOCKHOLDERS

Voting Rights One of the fundamental rights of the common stockholder is the election of the corporation's directors. There has been some confusion as to the fundamental nature of this right due to the issuance of two or more classes of common stock. Where several classes of common stock are issued by a corporation, generally only one class is given the voting privilege. The other classes of common stock generally, though not invariably, receive compensating benefits or priorities. In such a case, those stocks not carrying the right to vote for the directors should not be called common at all, even though the statutes permit such a label. They are in fact, if not in name, preferred stocks. Sometimes the common stock that does not have the voting privilege is referred to as *weak preferred stock* by traders of such securities.

Typically in a corporation the basis of voting is one vote per share with no limit to the number of votes per shareholder. In some rare corporation charters, voting is restricted.[4] Furthermore, certain circumstances that affect this voting right should be mentioned. If a stockholder should deposit his stock certificates with a lender as security for a loan, who would exercise the right to vote? Actually the borrower would still be the legal owner of the stock, and his name would remain on the stock ledger of the corporation. He would continue to receive the dividends, announcement of stockholders' meetings, and would exercise the right to vote. If a person sets up a trust and transfers his stock certificates to the trustee to be controlled for the benefit of a beneficiary, the trustee exercises the right to vote.

Another problem arises when shares are bought and sold daily. Considerable confusion and delay could develop at the stockholders' meeting in

---

[3] A few corporations taking advantage of this provision have issued stock at a par value of one mill per share.

[4] The charter of Builders and Developers, Incorporated, provided for one vote per share up to a maximum of twenty votes per shareholder. This was a corporation organized by employees of a large aircraft plant in Fort Worth, Texas, for the purpose of investing in and developing real estate. In preparing the charter, the lawyer was instructed to provide a means whereby the control of the corporation could not later fall into the hands of one or a few persons. The charter of the International Lumber and Development Company provided for one vote per shareholder regardless of the number of shares owned. For a detailed exposition of the voting rights of stockholders, see W. H. S. Stevens, "Voting Rights of Capital Stock and Shareholders," *Journal of Business*, The University of Chicago, 11, Nov. 1938, p. 311.

determining the actual owners of the voting shares. Where the shares of the corporation are actively traded, the stockholders' ledger is closed some time in advance of the meeting, and an announcement is made that the stockholders on the official stockholders' list of the corporation on that date shall be entitled to vote at the coming stockholders' meeting. For example, a corporation might announce an annual meeting of stockholders to be held on March 13. The announcement might state, further, that all stockholders of record February 11 are entitled to vote at this meeting. After all the transfers of ownership entered on February 11 are completed, the stockholders listed at the end of business on that date are sent announcements of the meeting and are entitled to attend and participate in the actual meeting or to send their representatives. Persons who become stockholders too late to have their names entered on the stock ledger on February 11 or earlier do not receive an announcement of the meeting and would not be on the official list of stockholders authorized to vote at the annual meeting. There may be many changes in ownership prior to the March 13 meeting. A person purchasing his stock after February 11 and before March 13 may insist as a condition of the sale that he be given the right to attend the meeting. This can be done by having the seller of the stock appoint the purchaser as his proxy, giving him full right to participate and vote at the meeting. Usually, however, the voting right is considered inconsequential, and persons purchasing stock of a publicly held corporation whose shares are actively traded do not attempt to secure the voting privilege when the transfer is made after the stock list of the corporation is closed prior to the annual meeting.

Those voting at a stockholders' meeting receive a ballot indicating the number of vacancies on the board to be filled and the names of the candidates for those vacancies. There is one vote per share for each of the vacancies, a person having ten shares, for example, casting ten votes for each of the vacancies to be filled. Since the vote for each vacancy on the board is considered a separate contest, a person having a bare majority of the shares voted at a meeting can decide each contest. The minority, no matter how large, can be prevented from having any representation on the board of directors.

Another method of voting—*cumulative voting*—is required by the laws of twenty-two states, is permitted but not required in twenty-one states, while seven state laws make no specific provision for it. The most populous state, California, requires cumulative voting, as do the laws of Illinois, Pennsylvania, Michigan, and Ohio. On the other hand, Delaware, one of the most popular states for incorporation, makes cumulative voting permissive but not mandatory. So also do New Jersey and New York.

Under cumulative voting a shareholder has as many votes as he has shares multiplied by the number of vacancies to be filled on the board of directors. If a board of nine directors is to be elected and a shareholder has 50 shares, he will have 50×9 votes, or a total of 450. These he may scatter among the candidates as he chooses, or he may concentrate all 450 votes for a single director. The object of cumulative voting is to make it possible for a substantial minority to get representation on a board, so that its viewpoint may be heard at board meetings. To determine the number of shares necessary to elect a certain number of directors, a formula has been devised:

$$n = \frac{m\,s}{d+1} + 1$$

$n =$ the number of shares needed to secure the election of the desired directors.

$m =$ the number of directors that the group wishes to elect.

$s =$ the total number of shares of voting stock outstanding.

$d =$ the total number of vacancies to be filled in the election.

Suppose that a corporation has 10,000 voting shares outstanding and a board of seven directors, all of whom are standing for election. Suppose, further, that a group of stockholders wants to place two candidates on the board. How many shares are necessary to accomplish this end? Using the formula, the following computation would be made:

$$n = \frac{2 \times 10,000}{7+1} + 1$$

$$n = \frac{20,000}{8} + 1$$

$$n = 2,501$$

Therefore, it would require 2,501 shares out of the total of 10,000 to place two members on the board of seven directors. Similarly, it would take 1,251 shares to place one director on the board of seven. In order to secure a majority of four on the seven-man board, it would take 5,001 shares.

Actually the voting for directors under the cumulative method may take on some of the aspects of a card game. If the vacancies for the board of directors are designated as place one, place two, place three, and so on to place seven, a group of stockholders holding 2,501 shares out of a total of 10,000 may put up candidates for places ones and two, and no candidates for the other five places. In such a situation the majority might concentrate enough votes for its own candidates for places one and two and fewer votes for the uncontested vacancies for places three, four, five, six, and seven. By this means the majority could elmininate representation by the minority on the board. If, however, the minority group puts up candidates for all seven positions on the board, the majority might not know which two candidates out of the seven presented by the minority group would receive the concentrated votes of the group holding 2,501 shares out of the total of 10,000. In such a situation, success could go to the group which outguesses the opposition. As a matter of fact, it would be possible for a minority group to elect a majority to a board under cumulative voting if the majority stockholders distributed their cumulative votes unwisely. To prevent this type of gaming from influencing an election of directors, the laws of some states require that the contending groups vote for the right to name a certain number of their own candidates to the board, rather than vote for specific positions on the board. Under this method, the contending groups would nominate candidates for the total number of positions to be filled on a board. Then the election for the directors would take place. After the counting of the ballots, the number of places on the board awarded to each group would be determined by the percentage of the total vote received by each group.

Many corporations have over 100,000 stockholders, a few have over a half million, and the American Telephone and Telegraph Corporation has

PROXY

KNOW ALL MEN BY THESE PRESENTS, That the undersigned hereby constitutes and appoints THOMAS W. DELZELL and FRANK M. WARREN and WADE NEWBEGIN, or any of them, with full power of substitution, as attorneys and proxies to appear and vote upon all shares of stock standing in the name of the undersigned at the annual meeting of stockholders of Portland General Electric Company, a corporation of Oregon, to be held at the Portland General Electric Company Service Center Auditorium, 3700 S. E. 17th Avenue, Portland, Oregon, on Wednesday, April 17, 1963, at 2:00 o'clock p.m., and any and all adjournments thereof, for the purpose of electing directors, to consider resolutions ratifying and approving the acts of the Directors, and the transaction of such other business as may properly come before an annual meeting, with all the powers the undersigned would possess if personally present at said meeting or any adjournment thereof, and I do hereby revoke all proxies by me heretofore made.

The undersigned hereby acknowledges receipt of notice of annual meeting of stockholders and information accompanying said notice.

This form of proxy is solicited by and on behalf of the management of Portland General Electric Company, a corporation of Oregon.

IN WITNESS WHEREOF, I have hereunto set my hand and seal this_____day of_____, 1963.
(PLEASE INSERT DATE)

_____   _____
        Stockholder   Stockholder
Please sign exactly as your name appears on the reverse hereof. Persons signing as executors, administrators, trustees, attorneys, etc., should so indicate.

44467

(Continued from other side)

P

R

O

X

Y

See

other side

(1) For the election of directors;

(2) For ☐ Against ☐ approval of the amendment by the corporation of its Pension Plan for its employees substantially as outlined in the proxy statement; and

(3) In their discretion on any other matters that may legally come before the meeting.

       The shares represented by this proxy will be voted upon item (2) in accordance with the specification made. Unless otherwise specified this proxy will be voted in favor thereof.

PAUL G HASTINGS
SACRAMENTO STATE COLLEGE
DIVISION OF BUSINESS
SACRAMENTO 19 CAL

Dated:_____ 1961

_____ . (L.S.)

_____
Please Sign and Mail in Enclosed Envelope

Please date and sign exactly as name appears. When signing as an attorney, executor, administrator, trustee, guardian, etc., or for a corporation, please give your full title. For joint accounts, each joint owner should sign.

IBM A59650-0

Fig. 10-2   *A proxy form.*

more than two million. Although invitations are sent to the stockholders soliciting their attendance at the annual meeting, a very small percentage actually attend. It is perhaps fortunate that this is so in the case of giant corporations. If as many as 10 per cent of the stockholders of American Telephone and Telegraph Corporation should be present for an annual meeting, it would tax the hotel facilities of a large city, and a meeting place for such a group could hardly be found even in the largest stadium in the country. In spite of this, the announcement is usually made at such an annual meeting that "85.3% of the shares outstanding are represented at this meeting." Representation is by use of the *proxy,* which refers both to the written authorization for a person to vote the shares of an absent stockholder and to the individual acting as the absent shareholder's representative. See Fig. 10-2.

In order to make the proxy a more effective means of expressing the desires of absentee stockholders, the Securities and Exchange Commission has issued regulation X-14. It requires all corporations with securities listed on a national stock exchange to file a proxy statement containing information useful to the stockholder in deciding how his proxy shall be voted and to whom to give his proxy. The information that must be contained in the statement includes the following:

1. The names of the persons soliciting the proxy.
2. Identification of the source of funds paying for the costs of the solicitation of the proxy.
3. A statement explaining the rights of dissenting shareholders.
4. A reminder to the shareholder of his right to revoke the proxy.
5. A list, with explanations where needed, of all items of business to be brought before the shareholders at the meeting.
6. Provision on the proxy form enabling the shareholder to vote for or against proposals to be put to vote of shareholders at the meeting —if the shareholder returns the proxy form unmarked on any provision, the proxy holder may vote the stock as he chooses on that provision.
7. If the shareholders' meeting is one at which directors are to be elected, the proxy statement must give information on the following: (a) name and occupation of each nominee for the board of directors; (b) amount of each class of stock of the corporation, its parent, or subsidiaries held by each nominee to the board for which the proxy support is solicited; and (c) if the proxy is solicited by current management, the salaries and other remuneration paid during the previous year to directors and to the three highest paid officers, provided each officer received $30,000 or more.

If a corporation has issued two or more classes of stock, usually only one class is given the voting right for directors. The laws of some states require that no stock be issued unless it be given voting rights for the direc-

tors, as is the case in Illinois corporation law. While this is done to protect the interest of each class of stockholder, the protection is more apparent
than real. For example, preferred stock may be issued at $100 per share
and common stock at $5 per share, with each share having one vote. A
purchase of one share of preferred at $100 gives the investor one vote, while
the purchase of twenty shares of common for $100 gives the investor twenty
votes. Thus, the purchaser of common has twenty times as much voting
power per dollar of investment as the preferred. The charters of a few
corporations reserve voting rights for certain classes of security. For example, the preferred stockholders may have reserved for their election one
or two of the directors, the remaining ones being elected by the common
shareholders. This, of course, guarantees that a certain number of directors shall represent each class of voting stock. In rare cases, even bondholders are given the right to elect a director to the corporation.

In addition to the election of directors, there are certain other matters
which must be approved by vote of the stockholders. They include the
following: (1) a proposal to amend the charter of the corporation; (2)
adoption, amendment, and repeal of bylaws of corporations; (3) a proposal
to merge the corporation with another corporation; (4) a proposal to sell
a substantial portion of the assets of the corporation; (5) a proposal to issue
bonds; and (6) a proposal to dissolve the corporation.

The corporation laws of some states require that approval for some of
of these actions be by simple majority vote, while in other cases approval
by a two-thirds, three-fourth, or four-fifths majority may be required. As
a rule, the state law gives the preferred stockholders the right of voting as
a class on matters which affect their position as preferred stockholders, such
as dissolution or issue of bonds. Voting rights of this nature exist even
though the preferred stockholders might not be given the right by the charter to vote for the directors of the corporation.

Right to Transfer Stock   The right to dispose of one's shares is one of the
fundamental rights of stock ownership. It is the right to sell, give away,
bequeath, or pledge the stock as collateral for a loan. However, in some
exceptional corporations certain restrictions do appear. Generally where
restrictions upon the right to dispose of stock are imposed, they are found in
the charter or the bylaws. For example, in preparing the charter of a corporation the promoters may desire to perpetuate the ownership of stock in a
closely knit group tied together by some common bond, such as employment
in a particular company, membership in a particular church, or residence
in a specific community. One way of accomplishing this is to require that
all stockholders offer their stock to the corporation first before it may be
offered to outsiders. Usually, the price at which the stock is to be resold
to the corporation is the book value at the time of the sale. Otherwise,
some other means of arriving at a reasonable price is specified in the charter or the bylaws. Another restriction that is occasionally found is the re-

quirement that a stockholder wishing to dispose of his shares must first offer them to the remaining stockholders on a pro-rata basis at a price determined by provisions in the bylaws.

To facilitate the transfer of stock, an assignment form is provided with the certificate, usually on the reverse side. See Fig. 10-3. In order to dispose of shares, the owner fills out the assignment form and sends the stock certificates to the corporation or its transfer agent. The stock certificate is then cancelled and a new one issued in the name of the new owner. If the owner has instructed a stock broker to sell his stock for him, the stock certificate is generally filled out with the line indicating the name of the new owner left blank. This is filled in after the transaction is completed

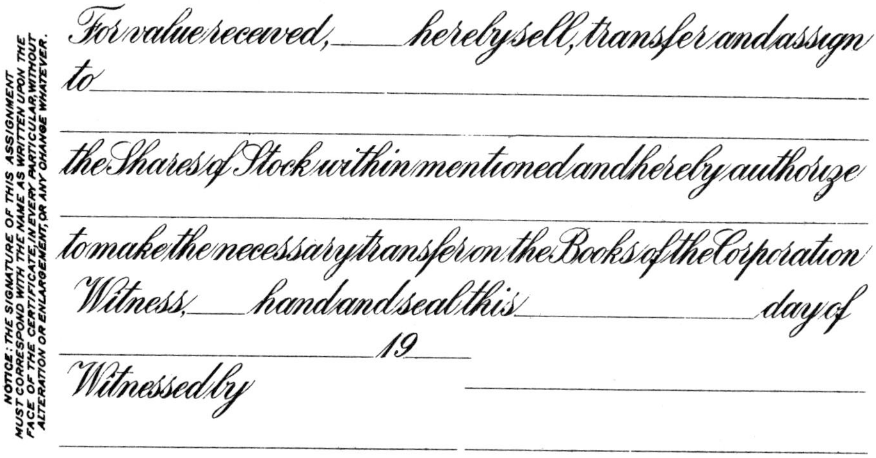
NOTICE: THE SIGNATURE OF THIS ASSIGNMENT MUST CORRESPOND WITH THE NAME AS WRITTEN UPON THE FACE OF THE CERTIFICATE, IN EVERY PARTICULAR, WITHOUT ALTERATION OR ENLARGEMENT, OR ANY CHANGE WHATEVER.

For value received, ____ hereby sell, transfer and assign to ____

____

the Shares of Stock within mentioned and hereby authorize

____

to make the necessary transfer on the Books of the Corporation

Witness, ____ hand and seal this ____ day of

____ 19 ____

Witnessed by ____

____ ____

Fig. 10-3 *Assignment form of stock certificate.*

by the brokers involved in the sale of the stock. Large corporations having many stockholders employ a transfer agent and a registrar to handle the change of ownership in shares of the corporation. The registrar and the transfer agent are in most cases the trust department of a commercial bank. However, a commercial bank may not act both as registrar and transfer agent for the same corporation. After the assignment form is completely filled out, including the name of the new owner, it is sent to the transfer agent where the certificate is cancelled and a new one made out in the name of the new owner. Both certificates are then sent to the registrar, whose responsibility it is to check and authenticate the action of the transfer agent. Finally, the new stock certificate is sent to the new owner, and the corporation is notified of the change in ownership, adjusting its record of stockholders accordingly. If a stockholder having a stock certificate for 100 shares wishes to sell less than 100 shares, he may do so by indicating on the assignment form the number of shares to be transferred. If, for example, he wishes to dispose of thirty shares he will indicate on the assignment form that thirty shares are to be transferred to the new owner. In this case, the certificate for 100 shares is cancelled in the usual way, and two new certificates are prepared. One is in the amount of seventy shares and is sent to the owner previously holding the 100-share certificate; the other in the amount of thirty shares is sent to the new owner of the stock. This ease of transfer of stock ownership is possible because all of the states have enacted legislation making stock certificates negotiable instruments.

Right to Share in Dividends The right of stockholders to receive the profits of the corporation in the form of dividend payments is dependent upon the decision of the directors. Cases are known where stockholders declare dividends to themselves by action taken at stockholders' meetings in accordance with provisions of the bylaws of the corporation. However, such instances are extremely rare and, for practical purposes, these exceptions can be ignored.[5]

Although in the corporation of today, stockholders do not have the right to distribute the profits of the corporation to themselves, a dividend, once declared by the directors, becomes a liability of the corporation. A shareholder may sue the corporation to collect a dividend declared but withheld from him, just as he can sue for payment of any debt. This assumes, of course, that the declaration was legal. For example, dividends may not be paid out of the capital of the corporation unless it is a liquidating dividend following the dissolution of the corporation or is a corporation engaged in the exploitation of property which is depleted in the course of business, such as mining, or is a corporation organized for the purpose of distributing property. If, however, it can be shown by the stockholders that the directors have retained the company earnings for no reasonable or legitimate purpose, the courts have on rare occasions required the directors to make a distribution to the stockholders. Proof in such cases, however, is very difficult to establish. Probably the most celebrated example in which stockholders were successful in forcing a distribution of dividends by means of court action was the case of *Dodge* v. *Ford Motor Company,* 1919.[6]

The Pre-emptive Right If a corporation has 1,000 shares outstanding and Mr. Jones owns 100 shares, his ownership of the corporation is 10 per cent. If the corporation later issues another 1,000 shares and distributes them to various purchasers, Mr. Jones' ownership of the corporation falls to 5 per cent. Furthermore, if the additional 1,000 shares are sold at less than the book value of the first 1,000 shares, Mr. Jones would find that the book

---

[5] During the period in business history when the joint stock company was a common form of organization, stockholders often retained the power of disbursement of their company's profits. One of the characteristics of the development of the modern corporation, however, was the transfer of this control from the owners to the directors of the company.

[6] An account of this case is found in Keith Sward, *The Legend of Henry Ford*, Rinehart & Company, Inc., New York, 1948.

value of his 100 shares is less after the sale of stock than they were before. Thus, by the sale of an additional 1,000 shares by the corporation, Mr. Jones might suffer in two ways: by a reduction in his voting power and a reduction in the book value per share of his stock. If he were given the right to purchase 10 per cent of all additional shares distributed by the corporation and to subscribe to 10 per cent of all bonds or other securities convertible into common stock, he could protect both his voting strength and the book value of his investment. This right is called the *pre-emptive right*. It is not treated uniformly in the laws of all states: some, such as Delaware, provide that the pre-emptive right be given to stockholders unless it is specifically denied in the charter; others do not automatically give the pre-emptive right but permit the charter of corporations to grant it.

The charters of most corporations that have been recently promoted have sought to deny this pre-emptive right, since it reduces flexibility in financing. However, it must be added that it is more in the nature of a minor inconvenience than a major hurdle. The pre-emptive right does not apply to stock issued for property or services rather than for cash. It does not apply to the reissue of treasury stock held by the corporation. And it does not apply to stock that is first offered to stockholders, refused by the stockholders, and then at a later time issued for sale to outsiders. Where the stock is put on public sale, there is, of course, nothing to prevent any shareholder from purchasing as many shares as he can afford.

The Right to Inspect the Books of the Company It is a common law right of stockholders, as owners of the corporation, to protect their investment by examination of the records and accounts of the corporation. The common law holds that the directors are agents of the stockholders, and are, therefore, subject to being held to account for their stewardship. It is, however, a restricted right. The corporation laws of the different states have placed various limits on the right of the owner to look at the books of their corporation. As a generalization the laws of the various states provide that the directors are required to make available to the stockholders upon reasonable demand such books of account and records of the corporation as are necessary for the stockholder to learn the identity of his fellow stockholders and to make reasonable judgment as to the performance of the directors. A right recognized by all of the states is the right to learn the identity of fellow stockholders. Where the state law specifically reinforces the common law right in this respect, it is generally accomplished by requiring that the corporation make available for personal inspection its stockholder ledger for a specified number of hours each working day.

In addition to the register of stockholders, state laws generally reinforce the common law in providing for the stockholder upon reasonable demand the right to inspect the charter of the corporation, the bylaws of the corporation, and the minutes of past stockholders' meetings. Some states (California, for example) provide the right to examine the minutes of directors' meetings and the minutes of the meetings of the executive committees of the directors.

The common law right of stockholders to examine the accounting records and other information concerning the operations of the company has been restricted by state law and by rulings of the courts. The thread of uniformity of court rulings with regard to stockholders' right of inspection of the record books has been that they are entitled to examine accounting records and other records of the corporation when it is necessary to do so to protect their investment and to make a reasonable judgment as to the performance of the directors. Yet some courts have ruled that where the stockholder has demanded of the directors the right to look at the accounting and other records of the corporation, the proof of legitimacy of the demand is a burden resting upon the stockholder. Other courts have ruled that the directors in denying a request by a stockholder for inspection must prove to the court that the stockholder had an ulterior motive in making the demand and that granting it would be damaging to the interests of the corporation and to the other stockholders. In either case proof may be difficult to obtain.

Stockholders have in general been more successful in getting court approval to examine such accounting records as accounts receivable, accounts payable, gross sales, and total expenditures. They have had less success in getting court aid to inspect such records as unfilled orders, salaries and wages of officers and employees, names and addresses of suppliers and customers, unit costs of production for specific items, and information regarding production processes. The courts have generally ruled that these are confidential data, and that divulging such information to any stockholder on demand is detrimental to the interests of the corporation and the other stockholders.

Questions

1. In what respects are common stockholders "residual claimants?"
2. What information is generally found on stock certificates?
3. What is the authorized stock of a corporation? How may it be increased?
4. What is treasury stock? How is it created?
5. Distinguish between par value, book value, and market value.
6. What are the factors that affect the market prices of stocks?
7. What are the advantages to the corporation in issuing no-par stock?
8. What are low-par stocks? What advantages do they have over no-par stock?
9. How does the cumulative method of voting for directors differ from the traditional method?
10. Can a person sign more than one proxy for his stock for the same meeting? Explain.
11. Describe the process of transferring ownership of corporation stock.
12. What restrictions are there on the distribution of profits by the directors of a corporation?
13. How does the pre-emptive right protect shareholders of a corporation?
14. What records of the corporation are subject to examination by any stockholder of the company?
15. What information must be contained on a proxy form sent to stockholders?

Selected Readings

Bogen, Jules I., *Financial Handbook,* The Ronald Press Company, New York, 1952, Sec. 10.

Corporation Course, Prentice-Hall, Inc., Englewood Cliffs, N. J., 1963.

Dewing, Arthur Stone, *The Financial Policy of Corporations,* The Ronald Press Company, New York, 1953, Chaps. 3, 6.

Stevenson, Harold W., *Common Stock Financing,* University of Michigan Press, Ann Arbor, Mich., 1957.

11

Preferred Stocks

ORIGIN OF PREFERRED STOCKS

Preferred stocks are a hybrid type of security, occupying a position between common stocks and bonds. A share of preferred stock represents ownership of a corporation. It offers preferred treatment in some way over common stock, generally in payment of dividends, balanced in most cases by restrictions on the right to vote for directors. In corporation finance preferred stocks offer some of the advantages associated with bonds and some of the advantages associated with common stock. Many preferred stocks originated in the process of reorganization of bankrupt corporations. In such instances the issue of preferred stocks is created to provide a security given to the bondholders in exchange for the bonds which they hold of the bankrupt corporation. By receiving preferred stocks in exchange for bonds, the former bondholders still retain in most cases priority over the common stockholders in the payment of dividends and in any later distribution of assets in liquidation. The reorganized corporation benefits by the retirement of the bonds and the substitution of a type of security which does not carry the legal interest payment requirement and still does not permit control of the corporation to pass to the creditors.

The origin of some preferred stocks is also found in the efforts of corporations to raise funds. In the latter part of the nineteenth century the original financing of many corporations was accomplished largely by means of the sale of preferred stock to the investing public. In such cases, the common stock was sometimes thrown into the sale to provide an added speculative attraction for the purchaser. In other cases, the common stock was retained by the promoters as a means of maintaining control of the enterprise. It was common practice to issue an amount of preferred stock equal in dollar value to the value of the tangible assets of the corporation, and then to issue an equal amount of common stock representing the control of the corporation. The common stock under the doctrine popular with promoters of the day depended for its value upon a claim of any "excess" earnings that might be created by the activities of the company.

At the present time the public utility industry is the principal source of new issues of preferred stocks. The regulation of rates charged by utility companies is intended to permit them to earn a reasonable rate of return and no more on their investment. If part of the long-term funds can be secured by selling preferred stocks and bonds, the cost of the funds may be less than the income generated by their use, thus permitting higher earnings for the common stock. Although funds raised through bond issues normally carry lower interest than the rate of dividends required to sell preferred stock successfully, a public utility company with too high a proportion of debt to equity damages its credit standing. Expansion of preferred stock increases the equity of a company and helps improve the investment quality of its bonds. A further factor encouraging the use of preferred stock by public utility companies is the strong preference of most utility regulatory commissions for capital structures with "balanced" proportions of bonds, preferred, and common stock. Except for public utility companies, the attraction of preferred stock financing has remained low in recent years. With a tax rate on corporate income of 52 per cent until 1964, the use of preferred stock required $1 of net income before taxes to pay 48¢ in preferred dividends. Furthermore, the high prices in relation to earnings and dividends at which common stocks could be sold in the years following the Korean conflict made common stocks the choice for equity financing in all but exceptional cases.

CHARACTERISTICS

The corporation laws of the states generally provide that where two or more classes of stock are issued, the rights and restrictions of the different classes shall be stated in the charter of the corporation. Otherwise, the various classes of stock are given equal treatment under the law. In general, the preferred stockholder enjoys those rights that are given to him by provision of the corporation charter, and he submits to those restrictions that are taken away by provisions of the charter. California law, for example, states that "if the shares are to be classified, or if any class of shares is to have two or more series, the articles shall state the preferences, privileges, and restrictions granted to or imposed upon the respective classes or series of shares or the holders thereof, and the number of shares constituting each series." [1]

The Delaware corporation law states that "preferred stock may be entitled to preferred dividends, cumulative or noncumulative; may be redeemable at par or at a premium; may be preferred in dissolution; may be convertible into or exchangeable for other classes; may have other preferences and participating, optional or other special rights and qualifications, lim-

---

[1] Corporations Code of the State of California, Part 2, Chap. 1, Sec. 304.

itations, or restrictions; all as stated in certificate of incorporation or amendment thereto, or in resolution of the board of directors as authorized by certificate of incorporation or amendment." [2]

Priority over Common   Priority of dividend payments over the common stock is probably the most characteristic feature of preferred stock issues. It is probably the most important feature in making a preferred issue attractive to investors. The priority in dividend, however, usually carries with it a limitation in the amount paid. The dividend on the preferred is stated either in terms of a certain number of dollars and cents or in terms of a percentage of the par value of the stock. For example, a preferred stock having a par value of $100 per share and a dividend of $6 would be known either as a $6 preferred or as a 6 per cent preferred. The $6 dividend per share would have to be paid to the preferred stockholders before any distribution of the year's profits could be made to the common stockholders. In those cases where a preferred stock is no-par, the dividend rate is expressed in terms of dollars and cents. In years of very high earnings, the dividends paid to the common stockholder might be very generous compared to the limited dividends first paid to the preferred stockholder. On the other hand, in years of lean earnings the preferred stockholder might receive the limited dividends and the common stockholder no dividend at all. If the earnings of the corporation were particularly poor, the directors might pay no dividend either to the preferred or common stockholders. Because the corporation does not have a legal liability to the holders of preferred in the declaration of dividends, as in the case of payment of interest to bond holders, the receipt of dividends on the preferred is apt to be less regular than interest on bonds. For this reason the dividend rate on preferred stock is usually higher than the rate of interest on the bonds of the corporation.

Under common law all shareholders are treated equally. In the event of liquidation of the corporation, after payment of all corporation debts, distribution is on a share-for-share basis. If the preferred has been issued at $100 per share and the common at $20, each share of preferred and common would receive the same distribution. In this example, the preferred shareholder would obviously be injured. In most cases, however, where the issue prices of the preferred and the common are different, the preferred shareholder is protected by a clause in the charter stating that the distribution of assets shall be in proportion to the original issue price of the various classes of stocks. Another commonly found provision in the corporation charter is that in the event of liquidation the assets shall be distributed to the preferred shareholder *first* in an amount equal to the original issue price of the preferred shares, any residue after such payments being made to common shareholders. The charters of some corporations provide that the participation per share of the preferred stockholder shall be greater should

---

[2] Delaware Corporation Law, Sec. 151.

the dissolution be voluntary rather than involuntary. An example of this is a preferred stock issue of the E. I. du Pont de Nemours and Company, which provides a payment to the preferred stockholder of $100 per share (the original issue price) in the event that the liquidation is involuntary. A distribution of $115 per preferred share is made in the event the dissolution is voluntary.

Protection from Dilution The position of the preferred with respect to earnings and distribution of assets in dissolution may be jeopardized if the corporation issues bonds, notes, or additional issues of preferred stock having a position either equal or superior to the preferred shares outstanding. Since the common stockholders retain the right to elect the directors, the directors generally reflect the interests of that group. This may result in a program of expansion of the corporation's activities financed by means of bonds and other securities having prior rights compared to the preferred stock. If the policy of expansion results in increased earnings of the corporation, the preferred stockholder generally does not share, but the common stockholder does. If the expansion results in losses or in bankruptcy, the existence of bonds in the financial structure often means the sacrifice of dividends for both the preferred stockholder and the common stockholder. As a generalization, therefore, if the directors undertake financing by means of bonds, the preferred stockholder stands to lose in the event that the decision proves to be disastrous but does not participate in the profits in the event that the decision proves to be wise. For this reason, charters frequently give the preferred stockholder the right to veto a decision (typically, by a vote of two-thirds or three-fourths of shares outstanding) of the board of directors to issue any securities having a position equal to or superior to the existing preferred stock.

Redemption Nearly all preferred stock issues contain a provision in the charter giving the corporation the right to call the issue. The call feature permits the corporation to redeem preferred shares at the call price, which is above the issue price of the stock. By this means, the holder of preferred shares is paid a premium to compensate him for his inconvenience in being required to surrender his shares to the corporation when called. The existence of the call feature places a ceiling on the market price of the preferred stock. For example, if an issue of preferred stock is callable by the corporation at $115 per share, investors would not purchase the stock in the market at a price above $115 and run the risk of having to surrender it to the corporation at the call price. Although the call price places a ceiling on the market price of the preferred stock, it does not follow that the market price tends to remain at or close to the call price. A policy of the board of directors in retiring the preferred stock would be implemented by purchasing as many shares in the open market at less than the call price as the funds of the corporation devoted to redemption would permit. Only if shares of preferred stock were not available at less than the call price would the corporation call in shares.

Preferred stock is frequently considered by corporation directors as a temporary means of financing, similar to bonds. Where a preferred stock has been issued as a means of temporary, although long-term financing, provision is made in the preferred stock contract for retirement of the issue. The redemption of the shares by the corporation may be done haphazardly but, in most cases, is done according to a plan of redemption adopted by the corporation. The redemption clause in many instances obligates the corporation to retire a certain number of preferred shares each year. Alternatively, and this is more common, the redemption clause requires the corporation to set aside a certain percentage of net earnings, for example 10 per cent, to be used to retire preferred shares. A sinking fund, often found in preferred stock contracts, operates in a manner similar to a sinking fund for the retirement of bond issues. Where a sinking fund is provided for preferred stock, the payments into the fund are dependent upon earnings, inasmuch as the preferred stock is an ownership rather than a debt instrument. The existence of a sinking fund, however, exerts a greater degree of discipline in providing for the funds necessary to redeem the preferred stock than would otherwise be the case.

Other Protective Provisions   In addition to the priority over the common stock in the distribution of dividends—and of assets in the event of liquidation—the preferred stock contract often includes additional protective provisions. One type goes beyond merely granting priority; it denies the payment of dividends to the common unless the corporation is in a strong financial position. One type of such a provision prohibits payment to the common unless the surplus of the corporation available for dividends is above a stated dollar figure or is higher than a stated percentage of the preferred stock outstanding. Another type prohibits dividends to the common stock unless the current assets minus the current liabilities are above a stated minimum. In some cases, the total assets minus the total liabilities must be above a given dollar figure, or the total assets divided by the total liabilities must be above a minimum ratio before the directors may distribute dividends to the common stockholders. Although such protective provisions restrict the freedom of the directors in dividend decisions, their inclusion in the preferred stock contract may be necessary in order successfully to sell an issue of preferred, or to make an issue of preferred stock attractive to investors at a price favorable to the corporation. Restriction on dividend payments based on the examples given above, however, can be said to impose financial standards on management that most businessmen would consider quite reasonable.

Voting Rights   The voting rights given to the preferred stockholders fall into three categories: full voting rights, rights to veto certain actions of the board of directors, and contingent voting rights. Most preferred stock issues are given the right to veto certain actions of the board, as well as the right to vote for directors contingent upon nonpayment of preferred dividends. Frequently, both types of voting rights are accorded to the preferred stockholders. Preferred stock issues having full voting rights are comparatively rare.

The corporation laws of Illinois and Mississippi require that preferred stock be given full voting rights equal to the common. The laws of the other states provide that full voting rights be given to preferred unless the charter of the corporation limits the voting rights of the preferred shareholders. The privilege of full voting rights may as noted above, however, be more apparent than real. In the first place, the number of shares of preferred stock outstanding may be quite small compared to the number of shares of common stock. In the second place, the preferred stock may have been issued at a price of $100 per share and the common stock at a price of $20 per share. In such a circumstance, the provision of one vote per share does not accurately equate voting power with the investment of the two classes of shareholders. In the third place, stock splits or stock dividends given to the common stockholders increase the number of shares owned by them, and so increases the number of votes they may cast. The charters of some corporations provide a remedy for the dilution of the voting strength of preferred stockholders resulting from splits and dividends: each share of preferred stock is given additional fractional or full votes in proportion to the increase in common shares resulting from splits or dividends.

Although the preferred stockholder is not usually given the power to vote for the directors of his corporation, he is usually given the right (known as veto rights) to approve or disapprove actions taken by the board that would affect his position as an owner of the corporation. Actions which require the separate approval of both the preferred and common stocks include the following: (1) amendment of the charter, (2) merger or consolidation of the corporation with other corporations, (3) voluntary dissolution of the corporation, (4) sale of a majority of the assets of the corporation, (5) the issuance of bonds, and (6) the creation of additional classes of preferred stock.

Usually, the preferred shareholders vote separately in favor of or against actions of the types listed above. The common stockholders might vote unanimously in favor of a projected issue of bonds, but such action might be rejected by the preferred stockholders, thereby canceling the action.

Where *contingent voting rights* are given to the preferred stockholders, the exercise of this right is contingent upon specifically named developments taking place in the future. In most cases, this means the nonpayment of dividends to the preferred shareholders. For example, the charter of the corporation may state that in the event the directors fail to pay the preferred stock dividend for a period of one year, the preferred shareholders will be given the right to vote for the directors of the corporation. As long as such dividends remain unpaid by the corporation, the preferred shareholders are given the right to elect directors. This right may be restricted to voting for a stated number of directors as, for example, two out of a total of seven directors. Alternatively, the voting right may be given to the preferred shareholders to vote for all the directors along with the common shares also entitled to vote. In the latter case, if the number of votes available to the preferred shareholders is greater than the number of votes available to the common shareholders, the preferred shareholders might elect a majority to the board of directors favorable to their interests. If the number of votes available to the preferred shareholders is small compared to the number of votes available to the common shareholders, the right of the preferred shareholders to compete with the common shareholders for the election of directors may be of little value. Where the number of votes of the preferred shareholders is small compared to that of the common shareholders, generally better protection for the preferred shareholders' interests can be secured by a charter reserving a certain number of positions on the board of directors for election by the preferred shareholders during those years in which the dividends on the preferred are in arrears. The contingent voting rights of the preferred shareholders, of course, expire when the contingency which created the voting rights is eliminated.

Since the contingent voting rights of the preferred shareholders exist only as long as the contingency which created them and since the influence of the directors representing the preferred might be meaningless if such directors were in the minority on the board, preferred stocks are sometimes guaranteed the power to elect a majority of the board. This is accomplished in most cases by giving the preferred shareholders a sufficient number of votes per share so that the total of the votes cast by the preferred shareholders is a majority of the votes cast by the preferred and the common together. There are, unfortunately, cases where boards of directors with preferred stock interest in the majority have abused their position of power, as well as cases where the common stock in the majority have injured the position of the preferred by outvoting the minority directors elected by the preferred. Assuming that boards of directors are mostly composed of men having a sense of responsibility, it would appear that some representation on a board of directors by the preferred stockholders, though a minority, would at least provide a guarantee of careful deliberation of the interests of the preferred stockholders. The provision of the contingent voting rights of the preferred shareholders is considered so important that since 1940 the New York Stock Exchange has refused, with a few exceptions, to list preferred shares which are not given the right to elect directors as a class in the event that preferred stock dividends have been defaulted.

TYPES

In studying the field of preferred shares, one is struck more by the diversity in the characteristics found than by the conformity. There is considerable diversity in the corporation statutes of the various states, in the courts' interpretations of these statutes, and in the charter provisions for the issue of such stock. The types of preferred stocks discussed below include the more frequently found issues; they do not include the unusual types.

Participating Preferred Stock A common shareholder may receive meager dividends in times of adversity and very generous ones in times of prosperity, but the holder of preferred receives a regular payment. To increase the probability of regular dividend payment to the preferred stockholder, the preferred shares receive priority in the payment up to a stated amount. The attractiveness of dividend priority of preferred shares, however, is not always enough for them to be marketed at a price favorable to the corporation unless other attractions are added, such as participation in the earnings of the corporation over and above the regular preferred dividend. A preferred stock carrying this right is known as a *participating preferred stock*. If nothing is said in the charter of a corporation about participation, the preferred stock is *nonparticipating*.

Where preferred stock is participating, the forms that the participation takes are indicated in the charter. One form of participation that is fairly common gives to the preferred and common shares a dividend in the amount that is the same percentage of par value or stated value of the preferred and common shares, respectively, but provides that a stated minimum dividend shall be given to the preferred before any dividend is given to the common. For example, if the par value of the preferred is $100 per share and the stated value of the common is $20 per share, a $3 dividend per share given to the common would require a $15 per share dividend to the preferred. If the regular preferred dividend is in the amount of $6, the participating dividend in this case is $9.

Sometimes the participating dividend is limited. For example, the regular dividend per share on the preferred might be $6, and participation with the common on extra dividends might be granted to the preferred up to an extra $3, but no more than that amount. The inclusion of the participating feature in the preferred stock contract gives a speculative attraction to the stock, which tends to defeat the primary attraction of stability and regularity of income as opposed to a dividend payment dependent on the fortunes of the corporation. Usually, the stronger corporations that issue preferred stocks tend to make them nonparticipating, while the weaker corporations lean more toward the participating stocks. The use of the participating feature is exceptional.

In some instances, the participating feature is applied to the redemption of the preferred shares. For most preferred stock issues, the share of the preferred stockholder in the assets of the corporation upon liquidation is limited to the par value of the preferred shares plus, in some cases, any unpaid dividends which have accrued from prior years. In the event that preferred stock is retired as a result of being called in by the directors, the payment in excess of par is a *call premium*. If a premium is paid to the preferred shareholders out of the assets of the corporation in the event of a voluntary liquidation, the excess payment to the preferred shareholders is usually a *liquidating participation*.

Cumulative Preferred Stocks If a preferred stock is not cumulative, when the board of directors in any one year fails to distribute a dividend to the preferred shareholders, the dividend for that year is lost and cannot be claimed at a later date. There are few issues of noncumulative preferred stocks in existence in this country. Some of them are highly regarded as investments, because of a long record of dividend payments. Where the history of a noncumulative preferred stock indicates that the directors of the corporation probably will scrupulously continue the regular preferred dividend, the noncumulative feature is not likely to reduce the investment standing of the issue. The investment value of such a security is a measure of the confidence of the investor in the good judgment and integrity of the board of directors of the corporation. In a noncumulative preferred stock, the directors are required to distribute the regular preferred dividends before any dividend is distributed to the common. However, if the corporation earns insufficient net income to meet the preferred dividend in one year and the following year earns a large profit, the common stockholder might receive a very substantial dividend in the second year while the preferred stockholder receives only his regular dividend for that year and nothing for the prior year. As a matter of fact, the directors of a corporation are not required to distribute the regular dividend to the preferred shareholder even if the profits are quite sufficient to make such a distribution. In a precedent-establishing case, the Supreme Court in 1930 declared that holders of noncumulative preferred shares could not claim their unpaid dividends in prior years, even if those years were profitable, as long as the directors retained the earnings for expansion or any other legitimate business purpose.[3]

In order to make a preferred stock issue attractive to investors, nearly all preferred stocks provide for dividend assurance that is not subject to the pleasure of the directors of the corporation. This is accomplished by including the cumulative feature in the preferred stock contract, which provides that, where the preferred stock dividend is not declared by the directors in any one year, it must be paid before any dividend can be distributed to the common. Under the cumulative provision, dividends on the

3 *Wabash Railway Company v. Barclay*, 280 U.S. 197 (1930).

preferred may fall in arrears for many years. Nevertheless, all the preferred dividends that are in arrears plus the current dividend must be paid in full before resumption of dividend payments on the common stock. Although the holder of cumulative preferred stock may thus have to wait, he will eventually receive his dividend before the common stockholder does.

Holders of cumulative preferred stocks with dividends in arrears for many years cannot always expect resumption of dividends and the elimination of past arrears when the corporation becomes profitable again. The directors may be anxious to resume payment of dividends on the common but be unwilling to make the considerable outlay of cash necessary to wipe out past arrears on the preferred stock. In such a situation, the directors might offer the preferred stockholders one or more shares of common stock or possibly a new issue of preferred in settlement of the arrears. While the holders of the preferred shares are not required to accept securities instead of cash for the dividends due them, they may be willing to do so if the alternative is considerable further delay in receiving cash payment for their dividends in arrears. The devices by which cumulative dividends in arrears may be eliminated by means other than payment in cash is discussed in Chapter 24, since in most instances it involves a change in the capitalization of the corporation.

Convertible Preferred Stock Securities that are convertible are almost invariably convertible into a junior security. In the case of preferred stocks, the shares are convertible into common stocks. As in the other characteristics of preferred stock issues, the details of conversion vary considerably from one issue to another. In most cases, the convertible feature attached to the stock is designed to attract the speculative instinct of the investor by offering him the conservative features of the preferred and the speculative attractions of common. The application of the convertible feature to a specific stock depends upon the financial requirements of the corporation and the desires of investors at the time of issuing the preferred stock. The conversion clause may be a simple one, giving to the preferred shareholder the right at any time during the life of the preferred the privilege of converting them into a stated number of shares of common. The conversion period may be limited in time, ending, for example, five years after the issue of preferred stock. Alternatively, each share of preferred may be convertible into five shares of common during the first five years, into four shares for the next five years, and into three shares thereafter.

The conversion privilege in nearly all cases is of no value immediately upon the issuance of the preferred stock. For example, if the preferred is convertible into five shares of common, the preferred stock may be issued at $100 per share at a time when the common stock might have a market value of approximately $15 a share. In such a situation, the conversion privilege would hardly be exercised by preferred stockholders unless and until the market price of the common stock rose to $20 a share or higher. Purchasers of convertible stocks entertain the hope that the market price of the common will rise to the point where the conversion privilege will be of value. In the history of convertible preferred stocks, there are many cases where the common stock has never risen to a price that would make the conversion privilege valuable. Nevertheless, there is always hope, and the investor who purchases a new issue of preferred stock usually is willing to pay for the hope that conversion may prove valuable at some future date. A study of preferred stocks with the conversion feature that were marketed in the year 1951 reported that the dividened rate received by the preferred shareholders, and, therefore, the cost to the company of raising funds by selling preferred, was distinctly less than what the dividend rate would have been in the absence of the convertible privilege.[4]

If the preferred shareholder finds that the market price of the common rises to the point where the conversion privilege is of value, he may convert into common or elect to retain his preferred shares. It does not follow, of course, that all shareholders would immediately exercise their option to convert into common stock. Unlike marriage, conversion is irreversible. Once the step of conversion has been taken, it is not possible for the security holder to reconvert back to preferred stock. For this reason, holders of convertible preferred often delay converting it into common as long as possible. Whether they convert or not, they will enjoy approximately the same appreciation in market value enjoyed by holders of common stock. If a preferred stock is issued at $100 per share and is convertible into five shares of common, any increase in the market value of the common above $20 per share would cause an increase in the market value of the preferred at the same rate. If the market price of the common rises to $25 per share, the market price of the preferred would tend to be about $125 per share. If the market price of the common rises to $30 per share, the market price of the preferred would rise to $150 per share. As long as the market price of the common remains above $20 per share, the market price of both the preferred and the common tend to rise and fall together, with the price of the preferred being close to, though not necessarily exactly, five times the price of the common. If the market price per share of the preferred dropped much below $150 a share while the market price of the common was $30 per share, investors wishing to purchase five shares of common could save money by purchasing one share of preferred and then immediately converting into five shares of common.

Since the holder of convertible preferred enjoys the same appreciation in market value enjoyed by the holder of common shares, whenever the conversion privilege is of value, the main advantage that remains in converting into common is the possible payment of larger dividends than received by the holder of the preferred. If there is a possibility that the

---

4 A. S. Dewing, *The Financial Policy of Corporations,* The Ronald Press Company, New York, 1953, p. 262.

market price of the common might collapse, the holders of the preferred shares may prefer to forego the privilege of conversion. In the event that the market price of the common does drop, the market price of the preferred would also go down. However, there would tend to be a resistance to the downward movement of the price of preferred that would not be found in the common. The price of the common might fall well below the point where conversion was of any value to the preferred. In such a case, the market price of the preferred would no longer be influenced by the convertible feature except insofar as potential purchasers of the preferred would consider the possibility of a revival in the price of the common. The market price of the preferred would then reflect the investment value of the issue as a preferred stock, rather than as a vehicle for purchasing common stock.

Sometimes a corporation will issue convertible preferred stock as a means of "deferred common stock financing." Let us suppose that the directors of a corporation wish to finance a program of modernization and expansion requiring approximately $3 million, and that their desire is to use common stock financing. Let us suppose also that an issue of this size can be marketed for the company by an investment banker at a price of $20 per share of common. Thus it would require the sale of 150,000 shares of common stock to raise the $3 million required. Let us further suppose that analysis by the chief financial officer of the corporation shows that the results of the modernization and expansion are likely to increase the market price of the common stock to $25 in five years. At a market price of $25 per share it would require the sale of only 120,000 shares of common to bring in $3 million to the corporation. But the corporation needs the $3 million immediately rather than later. An issue of convertible preferred stock could provide a solution. The corporation might sell 30,000 shares of preferred stock at $100 per share, convertible into common stock at a ratio of four shares of common for each share of preferred. At this ratio the conversion price of the common is $25 per share. The conversion price, therefore, is higher than the market price of the common stock at the time of issue of the preferred, and the preferred shareholders would not exercise their right of conversion until the market price of the common stock rose to the conversion price or higher.

If the projected increase in the market price of the common, as a result of the program of modernization and expansion, is an accurate prediction, the market price of the common stock would rise to $25 per share or higher within the five-year period. If the market price of the common should rise above $25 per share and if all the preferred shareholders should convert their shares into common, the entire preferred issue would be canceled, and the corporation would have outstanding an additional 120,000 shares of common rather than the 150,000 shares that would have been required if common stock financing had been undertaken in the first place. Thus, the corporation would have had the immediate use of the $3 million needed for the modernization program and at the end of five years would have outstanding a smaller additional number of common shares than would have been required by common stock financing originally. To accomplish this, however, requires that all the holders of preferred stock convert into common. This could be accomplished by making the convertible preferred stock callable. If the corporation exercised its call privilege when the market price of the common was above the conversion price, the notification of the call by the corporation would force the preferred shareholders to convert into common before the call date announced by the corporation. For example, if the call price were $105 per share and the market price of the common were $28 per share, the preferred shareholders would receive more value by converting into common than by surrendering their shares to the corporation.

Classified Common Stock In the period from the beginning of World War I until the depression of the 1930's, a new security known as *classified common stock,* became prevalent. This was a period of unbounded optimism in the perpetual growth of business corporations and a limitless rise in the price of stocks. Persons purchased stock on tips from friends and cab drivers without even inquiring what products the corporations made. They also played the stock market without first finding out about the hazards involved. These amateur investors formed a ready market for new securities, and corporations and investment banking houses welcomed their money. In such an atmosphere, it was not preferred but common stock, the security associated with participation in the ever-growing profits of American business, that became the popular investment.

Corporations that wished to raise money by selling stock but did not wish to increase the number of shares with the voting privilege issued stocks which did not give the holder the right to elect the directors of the corporation. Because of the popularity of the term *common stock,* however, these nonvoting shares, regardless of what other preferences were accorded them, were called common stock. In order to distinguish these common stocks from the common shares retaining the voting privilege, the stocks were classified. In nearly every case the nonvoting shares were called Class A common, and the voting shares were called Class B common. As speculation in stocks rose in intensity prior to the collapse of the market in 1929, the number of new issues of classified common stock increased. According to one analysis of 541 issues of classified common stock placed on the market between 1919 and 1932, 37 were marketed in 1926, 45 in 1927, 93 in 1928, and 116 in 1929.[5] After the market crash, the magic attraction of the term *common stock* was no longer potent. It was not surprising, therefore, that

---

[5] J. K. Dow, *Class A Common Stocks,* Harvard Graduate School of Business Administration, 1926, followed by similar studies in 1930, 1932, and 1933, as reported in A. S. Dewing, *The Financial Policy of Corporations,* 5th ed., The Ronald Press Company, New York, 1953, p. 163.

the study of classified common stocks referred to above found only six issues marketed in 1931, and seven in 1932.

The use of classified common stock has been restricted to some extent by the refusal of the New York Stock Exchange after 1936 to list Class A common stock for trading if it differed from the Class B common stock only in a denial of the right to vote for corporation directors. During the 1950's, a new stock market boom, similar in some respects to the 1920's, occurred. The later years of the 1950's witnessed a modest revival in the use of classified common stock.

Sometimes classified common stock has been created for other purposes than selling to the general investing public. For example, upon the death of Henry Ford, the founder of the Ford Motor Company, the virtual ownership of the Company passed to the Ford Foundation, which became the owner of almost all the common stock of the company. The common stock inherited by Henry Ford's heirs represented a small fraction of the ownership of the enterprise. But there was a big difference in that the stock owned by the Ford family members held the voting power. By using two classes of common stock, one voting and the other nonvoting, the *ownership* of the Ford Motor Company passed largely to the nonprofit foundation while the complete *control* of the corporation remained with the family. When the foundation decided to sell part of its holdings of Ford stock in 1956, the Ford family interests held 4.94 per cent of the common stock of the company but had 100 per cent of the voting power.

Questions

1. What are the characteristics of a typical preferred stock? Why are they attractive to some investors and unattractive to others?
2. What are the advantages to the corporation in issuing preferred stock as compared to common stock? Compared to bonds?
3. Does the gradual retirement of the preferred stock benefit the corporation?
4. What voting rights, if any, are usually found in a preferred stock issue?
5. What is meant by contingent voting rights?
6. What kind of participation is provided in participating preferred stock?
7. How does the cumulative feature increase the attraction of preferred stock as an investment?
8. How can dividends in arrears on preferred stock be eliminated without the expenditure of cash?
9. Describe convertible preferred stock. What is its attraction to the corporation issuing it? To the investor?
10. Under what circumstances does a convertible preferred stock and common stock of a company tend to rise and fall in price together?
11. What is the advantage to the corporation in using the call feature in a preferred stock issue?
12. What methods are available to a corporation in retiring shares of preferred stock?
13. Explain how preferred stock may be used as a means of "deferred common stock financing."
14. Explain the term *classified common stock*. Why is it so little used?

Selected Readings

Santow, Leonard J., "Ultimate Demise of Preferred Stock as a Source of Corporate Capital," *Financial Analyst Journal,* May-June 1962, pp. 17-54.
Students Corporation Law Service, Prentice-Hall, Inc., Englewood Cliffs, N. J., 1962, pars. 2144 to 2150.

12

Secured Bonds

THE CHARACTER OF BOND FINANCING

Preferred and common stocks are a means of long-term financing through the use of ownership instruments. Bonds represent a means of long-term financing by using debt instruments. Some business managements have a horror of long-term debt, and avoid it wherever possible, but others use bonds as a permanent part of their financing plans. Utility companies in particular use long-term debt for expansion, modernization, and other purposes. Their capital structures contain a heavy proportion of bonds. The demand for the output of most utilities is reasonably resistant to cyclical and seasonal variations, and franchises give them exclusive rights of operation in their territories. In return for the shelter from competition granted by the franchise, utility companies are subject to rate regulation, sometimes strict and sometimes lax, depending upon the power and independence of the regulatory body. The combination of these characteristics makes bonds an attractive medium for financing utilities.

Bond financing represents an alternative to stock financing as a means of securing long-term funds. Bond contracts can be drawn up to provide advantages over stock financing that may be extremely important in particular situations and to particular businesses. Like preferred stocks, bonds come in a variety of types, which gives the directors the chance to secure long-term funds under terms that are more advantageous to the corporation than would be possible by using preferred or common stocks. Therefore, it is important that business managers be acquainted with the characteristics of different kinds of bonds, and that they understand how different types of bonds can be used to meet the financial needs of their companies.

In general, bond financing permits the corporation to raise long-term funds without diluting the control of the corporation by the present owners, unless, of course, the corporation should go into bankruptcy. Because the payment of bond interest and the retirement of the principal take priority

189

in most cases over any payments to the preferred or common stockholder, bonds can generally be sold at an interest cost that is less than the dividends that would be distributed to the preferred stockholders had preferred stock been used as financing.   The most important advantage, however, of bond financing probably results from the tax laws of the federal government. The payment of interest on bonds is considered a business expense of the corporation, but payment of dividends on preferred and common stock is considered a distribution of income.   The payment of one dollar in dividends to preferred or common stockholders does not reduce the income tax liability of the corporation at all.

In essence a bond is a long term promissory note.   As such it is a contract between the bondholder and the corporation issuing the bond.   It may contain whatever clauses are acceptable to the bondholder and the corporation.   It is not surprising, therefore, that examples can be found of unusual bonds which have characteristics that ordinarily would not be associated with bonds.[1]   Except for unusual issues, a bond contains the following characteristics: (1) a definite promise to pay the principal when due, (2) a definite promise to pay interest when due, (3) a limited life and a maturity definitely stated, (4) a statement as to the means of payment of interest and principal, and (5) a statement as to the rights and powers of the bondholder in the event of default of interest payment or repayment of principal by the corporation.

THE BOND INDENTURE

If a bond issue is to be marketed publicly, a trustee to represent the interests of the bondholders is necessary.   The three parties to the bond contract are: the trustee, the bondholders, the corporation.   The responsibilities of the trustee, the rights of the bondholders, and the obligations of the corporation are stated in a legal document called the *bond indenture*. To define these rights and responsibilities clearly, bond indentures may run to several hundred pages for mortgage bond issues or to only fifty or sixty pages for a debenture issue.   The following list is typical of the items found in an indenture:

Performance of acts necessary to legality
General provisions as to bond certificates
Provisions required by Trust Indenture Act of 1939
Title of bonds
Denomination and numbering of bonds
Authentication of bonds by trustee

---

1 There are bonds, for example, that include one or more of the following provisions: (1) the right to elect one or more of the directors of the corporation; (2) the right to participate in the earnings of the corporation over and above the stated interest payable on the bond; (3) no maturity date, or a maturity date several hundred years in the future; and (4) interest payable only after a stated dividend is paid to preferred and common stockholders.

Registration, transfer, and negotiability of bonds
Replacement of mutilated, lost, stolen, or destroyed bonds
Retirement of bonds
Restrictions on payment of dividends
Use, possession, and disposition of mortgaged property
Payment of interest
Powers of trustee in event of default by company
Procedures for removal of trustee

During the 1930's, many bonds were defaulted by corporations on both interest and principal. Investigation by Congress revealed a number of instances where the interests of the bondholder had not been adequately protected in preparing the bonds for marketing and in providing adequate assurance that the corporation would observe its obligations with respect to the bond contract. In some cases, a trustee had not been provided under the bond indenture; in other cases, the trustee was not competent to provide full protection to the bondholders; and in still other cases, the indenture did not provide adequate power to the trustee to protect the bondholders. In an attempt to correct the abuses uncovered and to provide better protection for investors in corporate bonds, the Trust Indenture Act of 1939 was passed. The Act applies to bond issues that are in excess of $1 million, that are marketed to the general public on an interstate basis, and that are not exempt from the registration provisions of the Security Act of 1933. The indenture of a bond issue must be filed with the Securities and Exchange Commission before the bonds may be distributed to the public. Furthermore, the Trust Indenture Act provides that the following provisions must be fully complied with:

1. There may be no exculpatory clauses in the indenture, clauses that seek to clear the corporation of any guilt or fault in connection with the future actions of the corporation under the indenture.

2. The indenture must include certain protective clauses in order to safeguard the interests of the bondholders.

3. The trustee representing the bondholders may be selected by the corporation issuing the bonds, as was done prior to the passage of the Act. However, the trustee must be a corporation with a minimum capital and surplus of $150,000, it must be financially responsible (usually a bank or trust company), and it must not have any conflict of interest with respect to its responsibilities as trustee under the indenture. The trustee must, in other words, have no affiliation with the corporation issuing the bonds, none of the major officers of the trust company may be associated with the corporation issuing the bonds, and the trustee may not act at the same time under two indentures of the same corporation. Should a conflict of interest develop later, the trustee is required either to eliminate the conflict of interest or to resign as trustee.

4. The trustee must furnish bondholders annually a report indicating

the current status of any sinking fund payments which might be required under the indenture, any financial transactions having taken place between the trustee and the debtor corporation, and any other information of material interest to the bondholder.

5. The corporation must furnish periodically to the trustee a current list of bondholders, up-to-date financial statements of the corporation, and whatever other information is necessary to prove that the corporation is fully complying with the terms of the indenture.

6. The trustee is obligated to notify bondholders within ninety days of any default by the corporation. In the event of any default on the part of the corporation of its financial obligations under the terms of the bond issue, the trustee is required to use the judgment and skill that a "prudent man" would be expected to use in protecting the interests of the bondholder. The duties of the trustee are ordinarily routine. Since the payment to the trustee for his services is made by the corporation issuing the bonds, it is one of the costs to the corporation of raising money by issuing bonds.

REGISTERED AND COUPON BONDS

Bonds may be made out to bearer or registered in the name of the purchaser. If they are bearer bonds, change in ownership may be accomplished as easily as passing a $1,000 bill from one person to another. In the case of bearer bonds the issuing corporation does not know at any time who the owners of the bonds are that are outstanding. Obviously, a $1,000 bearer bond should be guarded with the same care as a $1,000 bill. Generally, such bonds are kept in safes or in safe deposit boxes and are transferred from one place to another by registered mail. Upon maturity, the bond is presented to the corporation or to a designated paying agent for payment.

The payment of interest that corporations make on bearer bonds (usually twice a year) is facilitated by coupons attached to the bond certificate. The coupons operate as a promissory note or a postdated check for the amount of the interest. They are arranged along the side or the bottom of the bond certificate so that they can be easily clipped when they become due.

If a bond is a registered bond, the name of the owner is listed on the books of the corporation, or with a trust company acting as the transfer agent for the corporation and another trust company acting as registrar.[2] If the bond is transferred by the owner to another owner, the same steps must be taken as in transferring a stock certificate, by filling out the assignment form on the reverse side and mailing it to the transfer agent of the corporation, where the bond is cancelled and a new one issued in the name of the new owner. Payment of interest on registered bonds is usually done

---

[2] The function of the registrar is explained in Chapter 16.

by means of a check sent to all bondholders recorded on the books of the corporation or its paying agent. Sometimes registered bonds will be issued with coupons attached. In this case the transfer of ownership of the bond is accomplished in the manner described above, but the collection of interest by the bondholder is done in the same manner as with bearer bonds, by clipping coupons and having the bondholder's local bank send them in for collection.

Corporations sometimes issue bearer bonds and registered bonds under the same indenture, permitting the purchaser of the bond to choose whichever form suits his particular convenience. If a bondholder wishes to change his bond from a bearer bond to a registered bond or vice versa, a small charge is usually made. The market price of both bonds is generally the same, although occasionally there might be some slight variation in price resulting from a greater demand for one form of the bond compared to the other. In the event that registered bonds are to be called by the corporation for retirement, a notice is mailed to those bondholders whose bonds are to be called. Where coupon bonds are to be retired, the holders of the bonds are notified by means of advertisements placed in *The Wall Street Journal* or other financial periodicals. The holder of a coupon bond is obliged to watch carefully for any notices of redemption; should he fail to do so, he would find that payment of interest on his bond would cease after the notification date.

BOND DENOMINATIONS

The traditional denomination for a corporation bond is $1,000, and until the present century it was a very rare bond that was of a denomination either higher or lower. During the two world wars, the federal government marketed a very large volume of bonds to finance the war effort. In order to tap as many sources of investment as possible, the government issued bonds with denominations less than and greater than $1,000. The success of this experiment with bond denominations other than the traditional $1,000 led corporations to do the same. Bonds of less than $1,000 are sometimes known as "baby bonds," and are found in denominations of $500, $100, and even as low as $50. For the convenience of wealthy investors and institutions, bonds with denominations greater than $1,000 are issued both by the federal government and by corporations. Although the federal government issues bonds as high as $100,000, the large denomination bonds of corporations are generally restricted to $5,000 and $10,000.

METHODS OF BOND RETIREMENT

Bond financing is often used as a permanent type of financing by corporations. This is particularly true of public utility companies and railroads. In such cases the main reason that the corporations do not issue bonds with no maturity date is that most investors, both individuals and institutions, are unfamiliar with investment in perpetual bonds. Corporations can have the equivalent of perpetual bonds by arranging in their financing plans for the refunding of bonds (issuing new bonds to replace the old) to provide the funds with which to pay off maturing bonds, an action which can be repeated as often as bond maturities require. Where a corporation plans to use bond financing as a long-term though temporary means of financing, plans for the retirement of the bonds must be made at the time that the bond is first marketed. It is generally difficult for a corporation to raise the money necessary to retire in one lump sum a bond issue at maturity, unless this is accomplished by means of refunding the maturing issue. Two methods are most commonly used by corporations in their planning for the retirement of a bond issue: the *sinking fund* and *serial retirement*.

Sinking Fund   If a $30 million bond issue matures in twenty years, the burden of retirement can be spread over the life of the issue in much the same manner as the cost of depreciation of a building can be spread over the years of its useful life. One method is to provide a sinking fund into which periodic payments are made by the corporation sufficient to pay off the entire bond issue when due. A simple way to do this is to set aside annually a sum of money deposited in an interest bearing investment which would provide the amount necessary to retire the bond issue at maturity. The provision of such a sinking fund increases the security of the bonds held by the bondholders, a security which is stronger if the sinking fund payments are made to a trustee rather than being retained by the corporation.

Because a sinking fund is generally carried on the books of a corporation as an asset account, a balancing account equal in amount to the sinking fund is commonly created. The usual label for such an account is *Sinking Fund Reserve*. As the sinking fund grows, so does the sinking fund reserve. The reserve is an earmarking of a portion of the surplus. When the sinking fund is used to retire bonds the sinking fund (asset) is reduced and the bond account (liability) is reduced. When the entire bond issue is retired, the sinking fund and bond accounts are cancelled. At this point the sinking fund reserve account is also eliminated and the balance transferred to the surplus account. The money paid into the sinking fund can be used to invest in government bonds, municipal bonds, or any investment considered by the trustees of the sinking fund to be reasonably safe. If the payments into the sinking fund are so invested, however, there is always some element of risk that the investment will result in a loss. This explains in large measure the requirements of most bond indentures providing for sinking fund payments that these payments be used to purchase and retire bonds of the issue to be redeemed. By using the sinking fund money to purchase the bonds that are to be redeemed, the bonds that remain out-

standing are gradually reduced during the life of the bond issue.   The use
of sinking fund cash to purchase in the open market the bonds to be retired
has the advantage for the bondholder of providing a demand for the bond
issue, supporting the market price of the bond.   On the other hand, purchases by the sinking fund administrator of the bond to be retired might
be in such volume as to raise the market price unduly high.   To prevent
an undue rise in the market price of the bonds to be redeemed as a result of
the purchases from the sinking fund, the indenture usually provides that
the bond may be callable at par or at a slight premium.   Thus the payment
into the sinking fund can be planned so as to provide for the systematic
retirement of a definite number of bonds each year.   Unless the bonds are
serial bonds, those that are called for retirement are selected by lot.   As
stated above the serial numbers of bearer bonds are published in a newspaper, whereas the holders of the registered bonds selected for redemption
are notified by mail.

Serial Retirement   An alternative to the sinking fund as a method of retirement is the serial bond.   At the time that the bonds are marketed, the date
of retirement of each bond is stated.   There are advantages in such an
arrangement, both to the investor and to the corporation issuing the bonds.
Where a sinking fund is used to retire a callable bond issue, the holder of
individual bonds does not know what time during the life of the issue his
particular bonds may be called.   In other words, the purchaser of a callable
bond has purchased a security with an uncertain maturity date.   The purchaser of a serial bond, however, knows the date of maturity of his particular certificate.   If a twenty-year serial bond issue is marketed, investors
have a choice of maturity ranging from one to twenty years.   In some
instances, the serial bond will be retired beginning with the first year after
the issue of the bond, while in other cases the retirement may begin later.
The serial feature provides under a single indenture the combination of
short-term debt, intermediate term debt, and long-term debt.   The main
disadvantage in such an issue to the corporation is that the obligation to
retire the serial bonds on the date that each of them matures is as legally
binding as the obligation to retire the principal of a bond issue upon the
maturity of the whole issue.
    One advantage to the corporation in issuing serial bonds lies in the
fact that serial bonds represent short-term, intermediate term, and long-
term debt under the same indenture.   Where the prevailing interest rates
on short-term and long-term debts differ, the corporation may take advantage of this difference by offering different interest rates on the bonds that
are to mature early compared to the bonds that have a longer maturity.
If short-term interest rates are lower than long-term interest rates, the interest paid on the serial bonds to be retired early can often be substantially
less than the interest rates that would have to be offered on a sinking fund
issue with bonds to be retired selected at random.   This is illustrated by

the following clause from the indenture of the Serial Debentures of the United States Steel Corporation due August 1, 1955 to 1964:

SECTION 2.01.   The Debentures shall be designated as Serial Debentures and shall mature serially in principal amounts of Thirty million dollars ($30,-000,000) annually on August 1 in each year beginning August 1, 1955, and ending August 1, 1964.

The Debentures maturing on the dates hereafter set forth shall bear interest at the annual rates, which shall be payable semi-annually on February 1 and August 1 in each year, as follows:

Maturity Date	Interest Rate (%)
August 1, 1955	1.30
August 1, 1956	1.80
August 1, 1957	2.05
August 1, 1958	2.25
August 1, 1959	2.40
August 1, 1960	2.50
August 1, 1961	2.55
August 1, 1962	2.60
August 1, 1963	2.65
August 1, 1964	2.65

Another advantage to the corporation issuing serial bonds rather than providing for sinking fund redemption is that the variety of maturities offered to the investing public may tap a wider market than would be possible by offering a bond issue with a single maturity.   Commercial banks and other financial institutions as well as individual investors frequently prefer maturities of a shorter duration than are offered by a particular bond issue.   Often such investors are willing to accept a lower rate of interest in exchange for a bond that is more liquid by reason of its shorter maturity. Another advantage to the corporation is that serial bonds are generally redeemed at par.   When bonds are called for a sinking fund, they ordinarily have to be called at a price including a premium over the par value to offset the disadvantage to investors of the uncertainty as to when their bonds will be called.   Serial maturities are used extensively by railroads to finance the purchase of locomotives and other rolling stock.

Retirement Before Maturity   The call privilege permits the corporation at its option to retire as many bonds as it wishes under the terms of the call clause.   Because the financial requirements of the corporation may change unexpectedly, the flexibility that the call privilege provides is a very important one.   Conditions in the investment market may make preferred or common stock financing more attractive to a corporation than bond financing.   Without the call privilege the corporation might find it difficult to make the shift.   Again, interest rates that were high at the time a particular bond issue was sold to the public might have fallen substantially before the bonds reached maturity.   For example, the call privilege might permit the corporation to retire an issue of bonds with a 5 per cent interest and replace it with bonds paying only 3 per cent interest. As a general rule, circumstances that make it advantageous for a corporation to retire its bonds before maturity are the same circumstances that make it disadvantageous to the holders of the bonds to surrender them. For this reason the voluntary retirement by the corporation through the call privilege of a bond issue almost always requires the payment of a premium to the bondholders. Sometimes the advantage to the corporation of retiring the bond issue through this privilege is not sufficient to pay the call premium. In other cases, the advantage to the corporation of retiring the bonds may be far greater than the cost of the call premium to the corporation. In any case, the existence of the call clause leaves such a decision to the corporation, and is, therefore, a privilege of such importance that most corporations include it in their bond issues.

DIFFERENCES BETWEEN SECURED AND UNSECURED BONDS

Some bonds are secured by the pledge of specifically stated property of the corporation; others depend upon the corporation's general credit for backing. The first group of bonds is known as secured bonds, and the second as debenture bonds. If a bond is secured by the pledge of specific property, the title to the property so designated may be transferred to the trustee representing the bondholder, while the use of the property remains with the corporation so long as the payments of principal and interest are met according to the bond contract. Alternatively, the title to the pledged assets may remain with the corporation, while a lien on the property is given to the trustee to hold until the interest and principal are repaid in full by the corporation. Traditionally, the failure of the corporation to make interest and principal payments when due gave the trustee the right to foreclose on the property pledged by the corporation, to seize it, and to sell it to satisfy the bondholders, with any additional amount needed to pay off the claim in full becoming an unsecured debt of the corporation. However, federal bankruptcy legislation and court interpretations thereof have modified this foreclosure act into one which permits the court in a bankruptcy procedure involving a corporation to keep the whole of the corporate property intact. In bankruptcy proceedings secured bondholders are accorded a position of priority over the unsecured bondholders rather than being permitted to exercise the traditional right of seizure of specific property.

Debentures are not secured by the pledge of any specific property of the corporation but represent an obligation of the corporation having priority equal to the other unsecured debt of the company, such as unsecured notes payable and accounts payable. It is sometimes stated that debentures are "secured by the earnings of the corporation." Short-term unsecured notes depend for payment on the liquidity of the company—the ability of the company to have cash available to retire the notes. Long-term debentures depend for their safety upon the maintenance of the property of the corporation and the continued profitable operations of this property. If the corporation suffers continuous losses, the assets are impaired, and so is the safety of the debenture bonds. In the event of bankruptcy the unsecured creditors are in a position of priority below that of the secured creditors but above that of the stockholders. Where a corporation has both secured bonds and debentures outstanding, the debentures generally provide a higher yield to the investor.

MORTGAGE BONDS

Secured bonds may be divided into two general types: bonds secured by real property and bonds secured by other property of the corporation. Bonds secured by real property are known as *mortgage bonds*. The type of property pledged for mortgage bonds is land, buildings, improvements on buildings, and such heavy equipment and machinery as is permanently attached to the land or buildings. Railroads and public utilities, typically owning large amounts of real estate, use mortgage bond financing to a considerable degree.

Priority of Claims on Fixed Assets If a corporation has a large amount of real property, it may issue several bond issues, each secured by a mortgage on a separate property. In such a case, the bonds would have equal priority in the event of bankruptcy, assuming that the value of any of these pieces of property had not fallen below that of the outstanding bonds secured by the piece. If the value of the specific property mortgaged to secure a bond issue fell below the dollar amount of the obligations secured by the property, the bonds would be unsecured for the difference between the value of the pledged property and the outstanding obligations due on the bonds, including principal and interest. Railroad corporations possessing rights of way, bridges, marshaling yards, terminal buildings, and other real property make considerable use of bonds secured by mortgages on sections of their real estate. Corporations that do not have large real estate holdings, such as most industrial corporations, more commonly mortgage all their real estate to secure a bond issue. These are called *blanket mortgages*.

It is of concern to the bondholder that the amount of the bonds secured by a mortgage on property be safely below the value of the property at the time that the bonds are issued. As stated above, if the value of mortgaged property falls below the dollar value of the obligations outstanding, the bondholders become unsecured creditors for the difference between the property value and the remaining obligation. For this reason the amount of bonds issued secured by mortgage on property of the corporation is below 100 per cent of the value of the property at the time of the issuance of the bonds. In some cases it may be 50 per cent of the value of the mortgage property, while in other cases it may be as high as 75 per cent or more. If the bond issue is retired during the life of the issue, the security offered by the mortgage generally increases. For example, if property with a value of a million dollars is mortgaged to secure a bond issue in the amount of $750,000 to be retired in regular installments over a 15 year period, the amount of the bonds outstanding would represent a declining percentage of the original value of the mortgaged property. If the corporation wished to borrow additional money during the life of the bond issue, it could still offer the mortgaged property as security for a second bond issue. In such a case the second bond issue would have a second mortgage on the property. In the event of liquidation, the holders of first mortgage bonds would be given priority over those holding second mortgage bonds. If there were outstanding at the time of liquidation $500,000 in first mortgage bonds and $300,000 in second mortgage bonds, both secured by the same property having a liquidation value of $600,000, the holders of the first mortgage bonds would be paid in full, while the holders of the second mortgage bonds would be paid $100,000. The holders of the second mortgage bonds would become unsecured claimants in the amount of $200,000 against the corporation. Bondholders having a third mortgage on specific property would hold a claim inferior to that of the first and second mortgage bondholders. The terms *senior* and *junior* are sometimes used instead of first, second, and third mortgages. Where two bond issues are compared, the one designated *senior* has priority over the one designated *junior*.

Closed End and Open End Bonds Where an issue of secured bonds is fully sold at the time of first offering of bonds for sale and the indenture does not authorize any additional issues, the bonds are known as *closed end bonds* and the mortgage known as a *closed end mortgage*. Limiting the amount of bonds authorized under an indenture to the amount originally sold under the indenture protects the bondholders' security against dilution and protects the security of the bondholder in the event of bankruptcy or voluntary dissolution. If the mortgage is a closed end mortgage, any additional bonds secured by the pledged property are necessarily junior to the original issue. In a bond indenture, the closed end clause, which restricts the freedom of financing, is not readily accepted by the corporation, although it may be necessary in order to induce investors to purchase the bonds.

Some measure of financing freedom can be achieved by providing a stated number of bonds in the indenture in excesss of the number needed to finance the funds required by the corporation at the time the bond issue is first sold. Such an issue is called a *limited open end* bond issue. If a corporation has real property in the amount of $100 million available to pledge as security for a mortgage bond issue, the credit standing of the corporation and the conditions of the bond markets might permit a successful bond sale in the amount of $75 million, secured by the $100 million of pledged property.   If the corporation, however, did not require $75 million for its financing needs but needed only $50 million, it would be possible to prepare the indenture to authorize the sale of bonds in the amount of $75 million.   Only $50 million would be issued immediately.   The limited open end feature of the indenture would permit the corporation additional financing under the same indenture in the amount of $25 million.

There can be a greater degree of flexibility in long-term financing by means of the *open end* bond issue.   The open end clause places no dollar limit on the amount of bonds issued under a particular indenture.   Such a clause in the indenture would obviously present the possibility of abuse on the part of some corporation managements, and would thus endanger the security otherwise provided the bondholder in the indenture.   In order to make it possible successfully to sell a bond issue with an open end clause in the indenture, some limitation on the further issue of bonds under the indenture must be included.   The most common limitation is through use of the *after acquired clause,* which provides that any additional property of the type designated by the after acquired clause that might later be acquired by the corporation will be included under the existing pledge of property securing the bond issue.   For example, if a corporation issues $10 million in bonds secured by real estate appraised at $15 million, the open end clause would permit the corporation to issue additional bonds under the indenture.   The after acquired clause would place all land and buildings later acquired under the existing mortgage.   In all likelihood the indenture would require that for every piece of added property bonds of not more than two-thirds of the property's value may be issued.   Thus, if the later acquired property had a value of $6 million, additional bonds could be issued up to $4 million.

Means of Avoiding the After Acquired Clause   The after acquired clause exists to protect the bondholder, and is not inserted in an indenture by choice of the corporation, since it may turn out to be inconvenient for subsequent financing.   There are, however, some ways to avoid the clause.

Creation of a Subsidiary Corporation.   One of the ways of avoiding the after acquired clause is to create a subsidiary corporation, hold all or a controlling part of the stock of the subsidiary, and acquire the needed property through the subsidiary.   Bonds of the subsidiary corporation could be sold to finance the acquisition of the property needed by the parent corporation.   These bonds could be guaranteed by the parent company, unless the bond indenture of the parent company forbade this, to facilitate the sale of the subsidiary's bonds.

Merger or Consolidation.   In a merger or consolidation, any property acquired after the fusion of the companies is not subject to the after acquired clauses of any companies dissolved in the process of fusion, unless the bond indenture specifically states that the after acquired clause binds any corporation successor to the corporation first issuing the bonds. Such a restriction is not often found in indentures, however.

Purchase Money Mortgage. Property may be purchased by a corporation under a contract with the seller providing for payment to be made over a period of time. If the purchase is small, installment payments can be provided under a note held by the seller. If the purchase involves a large sum, a *purchase money mortgage bond issue* may be created to finance the purchase, and sold by the seller of the property, enabling the seller to realize cash immediately. For example, if a corporation purchases equipment, a part payment may be made at the time of purchase. The corporation receives possession of the equipment subject to a lien held by the seller. Payment is then made in installments by the corporation purchasing the equipment to the company selling the equipment. When the payments under the purchase money mortgage are completed, the corporation acquires full title to the property. The purchase money mortgage constitutes a lien on the purchased property which is superior to any other claim, including bonded indebtedness having the after acquired clause. Where the purchase money mortgage is used as a means of avoiding the after acquired clause, any excess of value of the property so purchased over and above the amount of the purchase money mortgage is included under the after acquired clause.

The Use of a Lease. To secure the use of property it is, of course, not necessary to secure title to it. A contract can be negotiated by a corporation with the owner of property to permit the corporation the use of the property for any length of time deemed necessary by the corporation. Long-term leases involving real estate may run to fifty years, seventy-five years, or ninety-nine years. Since the title to the property does not pass to the corporation using it, the after acquired clause does not cover the leased property.

Direct Elimination of the After Acquired Clause. The most direct, though not the easiest, method of elimination of the after acquired clause is to call in the bonds that were issued under the indenture having such a clause. In such an action, presumably a new bond issue would be marketed, replacing the issue called. If long-term interest rates have fallen since the time that a bond issue was sold having the after acquired clause, replacing the old bond issue with a new one not having the after acquired clause might be acomplished at rates more favorable to the corporation. Also, if the credit of the corporation has improved since the time of issuing the bonds with the after acquired clause, the corporation might be able to market a new issue at a lower rate of interest than was paid on the bond issue called.

Another method is to secure the voluntary acquiescence of the bondholders to a change in the indenture eliminating the after acquired clause. Approval by the bondholders of such a change in the indenture would have to be unanimous unless the indenture stated that amendments could be made on approval by 75 per cent, 80 per cent, or some other large percentage of the bondholdings outstanding. To get the necessary approval, the corporation might offer some other amendments to the indenture that would serve to offset the elimination of the after acquired clause.

Another possibility is for the corporation to offer an exchange of new bonds without the after acquired clause to the holders of existing bonds. Some inducement or added attraction would generally have to be included in the new bonds in order to get the bondholders to agree to the exchange. By this method, perhaps all the outstanding bonds could be retired through exchange. More likely, however, a small percentage of bonds would remain unexchanged. If the number of unexchanged bonds is small, the corporation might make a tender of cash for the outstanding bonds in an amount attractive to the bondholders. If through stubbornness or inertia the holders of the few remaining bonds do not exchange their bonds and do not accept the cash tender offered by the corporation, the corporation might have to wait until the issue matures before retiring the remaining bonds. In such a case, some corporations will set aside a portion of the new bonds to be held for exchange in case any of the remaining bonds should be sent in for exchange or to be sold for cash in the event that bonds are sent in acceptance of the cash tender offered by the corporation. As long as the old bonds remain in existence, they would hold a prior lien on the pledged property of the corporation, superior to that of the bonds issued in exchange for them. If the amount of old bonds remaining outstanding is small, it would not significantly affect the safety of the successor bond issue. If, for example, $20,000 in bonds remained unexchanged out of an issue of $1 million, the priority over the succeeding issue held by the unexchanged bonds would be of negligible importance.

Real Property as Bond Security The term *mortgage* under law means literally "dead pledge." Originally, the mortgage instrument made a legal transfer of the pledged property from the *mortgagor* to the *mortgagee,* in return for which the mortgagor received a loan from the mortgagee. To give the mortgagor the continued use of the property pledged, the mortgage instrument usually contains a *defeasance* clause, which provides that the transfer of title to the mortgagee remain "dead" so long as the mortgagor meets all his obligations under the contract. Only if the mortgagor failed to meet interest and principal payments when due, or otherwise violated any terms of the contract, could the transfer of title to the mortgagee become "alive." Upon meeting all the payments of principle and interest to the creditor, the mortgagor would once again regain the title to the pledged property. In the early development of mortgage law, the mortgagee received possession of the pledged property upon default of obligations by the mortgagor under the mortgage contract. Now, however, the legal action of a public sale of the pledged property is usually required. Any excess over the obligation outstanding that is realized in a public sale is given to the mortgagor. In most cases involving the bankruptcy of corporations, the "public sale" becomes a mere formality.

VARIATIONS IN BOND TITLES AND USAGE

As stated before, railroad and public utility corporations make use of mortgage bond financing to a much greater degree than do industrial corporations. Regulation of rates makes bond financing attractive to such corporations. The corporation can "trade on its equity." In other words, the corporation can use bonds to secure funds at a cost that is less than the income generated by the use of the funds. Where rates are regulated, bond financing is a means of possibly increasing the earnings available to the common stock while keeping rates down to the maximum imposed by regulations.

The use of mortgage bonds is usually more attractive to public utilities and railroad corporations than it is to industrial corporations. Mortgage bonds can generally be sold on terms that are more attractive to the corporation than is possible in selling unsecured bonds. Since a large proportion of the assets of a railroad or public utility corporation is in the form of real property, mortgage bonds can be issued in a larger amount than would be possible for an industrial corporation of equivalent size. Utility companies have had, on the whole, little difficulty in meeting the interest and principal payments required under bond contracts. Railroads, on the other hand, have in recent decades had some trouble in meeting obligations under a bond issue. The fact that the demand for electricity, gas, telephones, and other services offered by public utilities have increased while the demand for railroad transportation has declined, particularly in the case of passenger traffic, largely explains the difficulty many railroads have recently had in meeting their bond commitments. Some railroads and public utilities have many bond issues outstanding. In distinguishing among the many issues of bonds distributed by railroads and public utilities, one meets a confusing array of bond titles that are used to identify one issue from others. However, two railroad companies may issue bonds with identical titles except for the name of the railroad, even though the characteristics of the two issues differ in one or more important respects. A specific bond title may be chosen in the hope that it will aid in marketing the bonds, but such a title is not very dependable as a means of indicating the character of the bonds.

Many types of bonds are found in the field of corporation financing. Some are secured by a blanket mortgage, which covers all the property or all real estate of the corporation. Other bonds are secured by a specific mortgage, which grants a lien on a particular piece of property of the corporation. Some bonds are issued through refunding the matured issue. Others are issued to provide funds for corporate financing or improvement of its facilities. Bond titles often indicate the major characteristics of the bond issues. Below is a list of commonly used bond titles and a brief explanation of them:

Bond Titles	Explanation
1. First mortgage bonds.	Bonds having a first claim on either the general property of the corporation or a specific property.
2. General mortgage bonds.	Usually cover a large portion of the company's property. May consist of a number of mortgages with varying positions as to priority of claims. Often means a bond that is partially secured by a first mortgage on certain property and a junior mortgage on other property.
3. Refunding and general mortgage bonds.	A general mortgage bond issued for the purpose of retiring another bond issue.
4. Refunding and improvement bonds.	Issued for the purpose of refunding and expanding or modernizing the property of the corporation.
5. First and refunding bonds.	Secured partially by a first mortgage and partly by junior liens. Issued to refund a previous bond issue.
6. Consolidated mortgage bonds.	Usually issued to replace a number of issues of bonds with a single bond issue.
7. First and consolidated mortgage bonds.	Secured in part by a first mortgage and in part by a general mortgage.
8. First consolidated bonds.	Does not mean a first mortgage but rather means the first issue of bonds by the company for the purpose of consolidating previous issues.

Questions

1. Aside from exceptional issues, what are the characteristics of a bond?
2. What is a bond indenture? What information does it contain?
3. Why was the Trust Indenture Act passed by Congress?
4. What are the provisions of the Trust Indenture Act of 1939?
5. Distinguish between registered and coupon bonds, giving the advantages of each to the corporation issuing the bonds and to the investor purchasing them.
6. How do bondholders receive cash for the bond coupons they clip from coupon bonds?
7. How does a registered bond differ from a coupon bond?
8. If railroads and public utility companies regard bonds as a permanent type of financing, why are bonds with no maturity date so rare?
9. If a sinking fund is established to retire a bond issue, why are the payments into the fund usually used to purchase in the open market bonds of the issue to be retired?
10. What are the advantages to the corporation and to the bondholder of serial bonds compared to sinking fund bonds?
11. Explain why the different maturities of serial bonds often are sold to yield different interest rates.

12. What is a closed end mortgage bond issue and how does it differ from an open end issue?
13. Explain how the after acquired clause in a bond indenture protects the bondholder.
14. By what means can a corporation avoid the after acquired clause?
15. Why are mortgage bonds used more frequently than debentures in railroad and public utility financing rather than in industrial companies?

Selected Readings

Berle, A. A., and W. C. Warren, *Cases and Materials on the Law of Business Organization*, Part IV, The Foundation Press, Inc., Houston, 1948.

Hickman, W. B., *Corporate Bond Quality and Investor Experience*, Princeton University Press, Princeton, N. J., 1960.

13

Bonds Secured by Personal
Property and Unsecured Bonds

For tax purposes, the property of corporations and other businesses is divided into two classes: real estate and personal. Real estate consists of land, buildings, and any improvement or installations that are permanently attached to the land or buildings—all other property of the corporation is personal. From the standpoint of volume of financing, bonds secured by real estate are by far the most important of this type. Although bonds secured by personal property are less important, they are nevertheless often very useful to particular corporations in their total financial planning. Of the bonds secured by personal property, two types are predominant: equipment obligations and collateral trust bonds.

EQUIPMENT OBLIGATIONS

Equipment obligations, developed in railroad financing, were originally used to aid those railroads too weak financially to issue additional bonds to acquire engines and other rolling stock. The generally good record of prompt payment of principal and interest on equipment obligations made them popular as investments for financial institutions. Their popularity in turn was reflected in relatively low interest rates. Thus equipment obligations came to be used as a means of financing the acquisition of rolling stock not only by weak railroad companies but by strong ones as well. Although their use has spread to other industries, equipment obligations remain primarily an instrument of railroad finance.

There are three types of equipment obligations: the equipment mortgage, the conditional sale, and the lease agreement. The rarely used equipment mortgage is a simple chattel mortgage on rolling stock or other equipment. Because of the existence of an after acquired clause in the indenture of a previously issued bond, the equipment mortgage frequently is reduced to a second lien on the equipment purchased. Furthermore, in case of reorganization as a result of bankruptcy, the equipment mortgage bondholders may not foreclose on the property offered as security.

The conditional sale is very similar to the purchase of an automobile by an individual. It came into use during the depression of the 1930's, and is largely confined to railroads. A "down payment" ranging from 15 to 25 per cent of the cost of the equipment is made by the railroad. The balance of the purchase price is paid to the equipment manufacturer from money obtained by serial bonds sold to the investing public. The serial bonds mature in sequence, in much the same manner as the installment payments on an automobile, and are retired at a more rapid rate than the decline in the market value of the equipment. Although the railroad company has the use of the equipment, the legal title to it rests with the trustee representing the bondholders. When all the bonds are retired, the title to the equipment is transferred to the railroad. Frequently, such conditional sales are financed by a single commercial bank or a group of commercial banks. In such a case a trustee is not used, the legal title to the equipment being held by the bank or group of banks. Where the dollar amount of the conditional sale is relatively small, it is more likely to be financed directly by a bank or group of banks than by bonds marketed to the investing public.

The most widely used equipment obligation is the lease agreement.[1] The lease agreement involves three parties: the company using the equipment, the trustee, and the investors holding equipment trust certificates. The lease agreement was first developed by the railroads to finance the purchase of locomotives and other rolling stock, although more recently other transportation industries are sometimes using it to purchase equipment.

Let us suppose that a railroad company wishes to purchase $10 million worth of new locomotives. The specifications for the locomotives are given to a manufacturer, and an order is placed. An arrangement is entered into with a commercial bank or trust company to act as trustee for equipment trust certificates to be issued to finance the purchase. The officers of the railroad and trust companies sign a contract in which the railroad is obligated to pay an advance rental at the time the locomotives are delivered and to make periodic payments of principal and interest to retire the certificates to be marketed by the trustee. Although the locomotives are delivered to the railroad company, the title to the locomotives remains with the trustee. In most cases, a brass plate will be attached to the side of the locomotive stating that this piece of equipment is the property of, for example, the First National Bank and Trust Company of Chicago. In effect, the railroad leases the equipment from the trust company for the

---

[1] This is also known as the Philadelphia Plan. The equipment mortgage and the conditional sale, when used to finance the acquisition of rolling stock by railroads, are both referred to as the New York Plan.

period of the life of the equipment trust certificates. When the certificates are completely paid off, the trust company transfers title to the railroad company. Since the trust company is the legal owner of the locomotives, the railroad's failure to meet lease obligations permits the trust company to take physical possession of the locomotives and sell them to another railroad. There is no red tape or delay comparable to recovering equipment used as security for a chattel mortgage bond issue. From a strict legal standpoint the equipment trust certificates are ownership certificates, and the payments received by the holders prior to the maturity of their particular certificates are frequently called dividends rather than interest. Because the payments are contractual and because the certificates carry a maturity date, the certificates are classed as bonds in the investment market. The railroad incurs a liability to provide money for the payment of interest and for the retirement of certificates serially as they mature. In railroad finance equipment trust certificates are classified as debts on the books of the railroad. In the example in Table 13-1, the value at the time of acquisition of the locomotives is $10 million, the amount of equipment trust certificates issued is $8 million, and the amount of the advance rental or down payment is $2 million. The useful life of the locomotives is estimated at twenty years, and the certificates are retired serially, with the last ones being redeemed at the end of the fifteenth year. It can be seen from this example that the value of the certificates outstanding is always less than the book value of the locomotives, using straight line depreciation. Although methods of charging depreciation might be used by the railroad which would provide for a more rapid reduction in book value during the early life of the locomotives, the retirement of the certificates would always be designed to keep in advance of the decline in the actual market value of the locomotives.

Railroads typically have bonds outstanding in which the mortgage securing the bond issue covers not only property already owned by the railroad but property that might be later acquired by the railroad.[2] If the railroad should purchase the locomotives which it needs and endeavor to recover the purchase price by issuing equipment bonds secured by the locomotives, the railroad company would in all likelihood find that the only bonds it could issue would be second mortgage bonds on the locomotives. Such bonds would be much more difficult to market than would equipment trust certificates. From the standpoint of the investor purchasing equipment trust certificates, the investment value is very high, and the investor, usually a financial institution, is willing to purchase them with a yield lower than that of many bond issues. From the standpoint of the railroad, equipment trust certificates represent a form of financing less expensive than other obligations incurred by the railroad. Typically, the interest rate paid is less than what the railroad would be required to pay on a long-

---

[2] This clause in a mortgage bond contract is known as the "after acquired clause," and was discussed in Chapter 12.

TABLE 13-1. USE OF EQUIPMENT TRUST CERTIFICATES TO
PURCHASE RAILROAD EQUIPMENT

Period	Depreciation (straight line)	Value of Locomotives (20-year life)	Value of Certificates Retired	Value of Certificates Outstanding
At acquisition	―――――	$10,000,000	―――――	$8,000,000
At end of:				
1st year	$500,000	$9,500,000	$530,000	$7,470,000
2nd year	500,000	9,000,000	530,000	6,940,000
3rd year	500,000	8,500,000	540,000	6,400,000
4th year	500,000	8,000,000	530,000	5,870,000
5th year	500,000	7,500,000	530,000	5,340,000
6th year	500,000	7,000,000	540,000	4,800,000
7th year	500,000	6,500,000	530,000	4,270,000
8th year	500,000	6,000,000	530,000	3,740,000
9th year	500,000	5,500,000	540,000	3,200,000
10th year	500,000	5,000,000	530,000	2,670,000
11th year	500,000	4,500,000	530,000	2,140,000
12th year	500,000	4,000,000	540,000	1,600,000
13th year	500,000	3,500,000	530,000	1,070,000
14th year	500,000	3,000,000	530,000	540,000
15th year	500,000	2,500,000	540,000	―――――

term bond issue. Investors who hold equipment trust certificates are protected in a number of ways. For example:

1. The title to the lease equipment remains with the trustee, and does not pass to the railroad until completion of all the obligations under the lease.
2. The dollar volume of certificates issued is always less than the original value of the equipment. Ordinarily, the certificates issued total between 75 per cent and 90 per cent of the original cost of the equipment.
3. The schedule of retirement of equipment trust certificates provides for redemption at a rate more rapid than the wearing out of the equipment, thus increasing the security during the life of the certificates.
4. The corporation using the equipment must pay promptly any taxes, such as property taxes, levied on the equipment.
5. The company using the equipment is obligated to keep it in sound condition.
6. Any default in payments to the equipment trust certificate holders gives the trustee the right to deprive the corporation of the further use of the equipment.
7. Periodic reports, usually annual, must be furnished by the corporation to the trustee giving the financial condition of the corporation, the physical condition of the equipment, and the location of the

equipment in case of rolling stock that changes its location constantly.

8. Each piece of equipment bears a plate indicating the name of the trustee as the legal owner of the equipment.

The investment quality of equipment trust certificates, as stated earlier, is very high. The use of the equipment leased under an equipment trust contract is a necessity to the corporation leasing the equipment. Because of this, the corporation will use every means available to maintain an unbroken payment of obligations under the lease. Equipment trust certificates maintained a far higher record of protection against investor loss during the depression of the 1930's than mortgage bonds and other secured debts.

QUASI-SECURED BONDS

Guaranteed and Joint Bonds Guaranteed bonds involve a double obligation. They are issued by one corporation, being the direct obligation of that corporation, and are guaranteed by a second corporation, in much the same manner as a cosignature on an individual promissory note. The guarantee may be stated explicitly in the indenture, or may be acquired after the indenture was prepared. In the latter case no mention is made of the guarantee in the indenture. In most guaranteed bonds the guarantee involves both the interest and principal. In rare issues, however, the guarantee may be restricted only to the payment of interest or only to the repayment of principal. The guarantee may be instrumental in permitting a subsidiary corporation to borrow money under circumstances more favorable than would be possible without the guarantee, particularly if the subsidiary corporation is not well known in the investment market and the guaranteeing corporation is. The purpose of the guarantee is, in most cases, to permit a subsidiary corporation to borrow at lower cost as a result of the guarantee of its bonds by the parent corporation.

The most common example of joint bonds is the issue of bonds of a corporation created by a number of railroads to construct a terminal to be used by the railroads. To permit the terminal corporation to borrow money at a low rate of interest, several railroads will undertake to guarantee the bonds issued by the terminal company. Because of such multiple guarantee, the investment attraction of the bonds of the terminal company is high. As in the case of guaranteed bonds, joint bonds can be guaranteed as to interest and principal, or be restricted either to interest or to principal. In most cases, the guarantee covers both.

Assumed Bonds An assumed bond is one which is issued by one corporation, but the payment of interest and principal is assumed by another corporation. The fact of such assumption may be stated on the face of the bond issue. Much more likely, however, there will be no statement or indication that the bonds have been assumed by a second corporation as to payment of interest and principal. If such assumption makes it easier to market a bond issue, this fact will be emphasized in marketing the issue. In nearly all cases the assumed bonds are issued by a subsidiary and assumed by the parent corporation. Usually the bonds are issued by one corporation while it is still an independent entity, and are assumed by the parent company when the issuing company becomes a subsidiary. The investment merit of such bonds depends upon two factors: the lien on the property of the issuing corporation and the credit standing of the corporation assuming the payment of interest and principal.

DEBENTURE BONDS

Originally the term *debenture* meant a certificate of debt, and is still usually so defined in dictionaries. In the literature of corporation finance, however, the term debenture has been confined to a bond that has not been secured by the pledge of any specific property of the issuing company. Although unsecured, a debenture obligates the corporation to pay interest and principal when due under the terms of the indenture. Failure to do so is an act of bankruptcy on the part of the corporation. In the event of bankruptcy the debenture bondholders have a position equal to that of the trade creditors, noteholders, and other unsecured creditors.

Reasons for Issuing Debenture Bonds A corporation may use debenture financing because issuing mortgage bonds may be inappropriate or even impossible in a given situation. If a corporation is forced to use debentures instead of mortgage bonds, it may be for one of the following reasons:

1. The corporation may have all its fixed assets already pledged under one or more mortgage bond issues.
2. The assets suitable for mortgage may be scattered in so many states that using them as security for borrowing is difficult.
3. The terms of an existing bank loan or other debt may restrict the corporation in its financing to unsecured borrowing.
4. Suppliers to the corporation may be reluctant to sell on credit to the corporation if bonds having priority over the accounts payable are in existence.
5. The corporation may have property unsuitable for security or have too small an amount of real property to warrant issuing mortgage bonds.

Alternatively, one might examine the reasons that corporations are forced to offer security for their bonds. Many corporations find themselves in a position of being unable to borrow money on a long-term basis except by offering security. If there is a measure of doubt in the minds of the purchasers of bonds as to the ability of the corporation to meet the payment of interest and principal, it is usually necessary for the corporation to secure the bond issues in order to offset the hazard of nonpayment of interest and principal. If the credit standing of a corporation is very high, there is little to be added in the way of protection to the bondholder by having corporate property pledged as security. Besides, in many cases of corporate bankruptcy, the existence of a lien on property to secure a bond issue provides priority in treatment in the reorganization proceedings of the bankrupt corporation rather than a guarantee of payment. The history of corporation bankruptcies does not appear to support the thesis that the pledging of specific property to secure a bond issue constitutes an important element of safety to the investor. Nevertheless, mortgage bonds are still preferred over debenture bonds by many investors. The explanation is probably tradition.

Protective Provisions in Debentures It is sometimes stated that debenture bonds are secured by the general credit of the corporation, which implies that the only safety afforded the holder of debenture bonds is the integrity and good business judgment of the officers and directors of the corporation issuing the bonds. This is true of some debenture bonds. However, most indentures covering debenture bonds place restrictions on the freedom of management of the issuing corporation, so that added protection may be afforded the holder of the debentures. The indenture might state that no securities may be issued having a lien on corporation property as long as any debentures remain unredeemed. The corporation may be restricted from issuing any additonal debentures for long-term debts having equal rights with the debentures outstanding, unless approval is obtained by a stated percentage of holders of bonds. Restrictions may be placed on the corporation with respect to the amount of dividends paid to preferred and common stockholders and may be in the form of a limitation on the extent of borrowing during the life of the debentures. Examples of clauses included in indentures of debenture bonds are the following:

1. SECTION 4.03. If the Company or any Subsidiary shall mortgage as security for any indebtedness for money borrowed any blast furnace facility or steel ingot producing facility, or rolling mills which are a part of a plant which includes such a facility, located in the United States, determined to be a principal property by the Board of Directors in its discretion, the Company will secure or will cause such Subsidiary to secure the Debentures equally and ratably with all indebtedness or obligations secured by the mortgage then being given.[3]

2. SECTION 11.01. The Company covenants that it will not merge or consolidate with any other corporation or sell or convey all or substantially all of its assets to any person, firm or corporation, except that the Company may merge or consolidate with, or sell or convey all or substantially all of its assets to, any other corporation provided that either the Company shall be the continuing corporation, or a successor corporation (if other than the Company) shall be a corporation organized and existing under the laws of the United States of America or a state thereof and such corporation shall expressly assume the due and punctual payment of the principal of (and premium, if any) and interest on all the Debentures.[4]

---

[3] Indenture of Serial Debentures, 1955-1964, United States Steel Company, p. 19.
[4] *Ibid.*, p. 65.

3. SECTION 3.02. (a) On or before April 30 in each year commencing April 30, 1961 and ending April 30, 1975 the Company will make a mandatory sinking fund payment to Bankers Trust Company, as Sinking Fund Agent (or to any successor Sinking Fund Agent as hereinafter provided), of cash in the amount of $13,000,000.[5]

Purposes of Issuing Debenture Bonds

Substitution of Debentures for Preferred Stock. It sometimes happens that a corporation has outstanding an issue of preferred stock with a dividend of 6, 7, or 8 per cent, issued at a time when the corporation was forced to pay dearly for long-term funds. With improved credit standing, the corporation might find it profitable to retire the preferred stock issue and substitute for it a debenture bond carrying an interest rate much lower than the dividend rate on the preferred stock. Another reason for substitution is the changing relationship between the cost of long-term funds raised by debt compared to that raised by equity. The market for investment funds changes constantly. Sometimes interest rates on long-term funds are high and at other times they are low. Some years the demand for equity securities is so high that corporations can raise money by the sale of stock under terms very favorable to the corporation. An astute financial manager can take advantage of the changing cost relationship of debt financing and equity financing so as to raise money needed by his corporation at rates as low as possible at any particular time and under conditions that are most favorable under given circumstances. This may involve the substitution of debt securities for equity securities or the substitution of equity securities for debt.[6]

Debentures Used to Retire Other Debt. If a corporation finds that the terms of an existing mortgage bond are burdensome, it may be able to retire the bond issue by substituting a debenture issue carrying terms more favorable to the corporation. Where an issue of secured bonds matures, it may be better for the corporation to refinance with a debenture bond issue. Sometimes a corporation finds itself saddled with a large volume of short-term debts. If the financial officer of the corporation finds that he is forced to reduce short-term notes constantly as they mature, he might decide that such debt has in fact become "permanent." In such circumstances it might be preferable to eliminate a large portion of the short-term debt by means of funds raised through the sale of a debenture bond issue.

Debentures As a Source of New Capital. Debentures are used most frequently to secure new funds for the corporation. The directors of many companies make it a policy to use unsecured rather than secured debt in raising funds for improvements or expansion. Where the credit standing of the corporation is high, little, if any, is to be gained in lower interest

---

[5] Indenture of General Electric Company, Twenty-Year 3½% Debentures Due 1976, pp. 16-17.

[6] This is discussed more fully in Chapter 24.

costs by issuing mortgage bonds as compared to debentures. The General Motors Corporation 3¼'s of 1979 in the amount of $300 million represents an example of debenture financing at a rate as low as mortgage bonds of high quality. Another example is the issue of General Electric Company 3.5 per cent debentures due 1976.

The Principal Uses of Debenture Bonds Railroads and public utilities are the principal users of mortgage bonds. Debenture bonds, on the other hand, are more frequently used in industrial corporation financing. Debentures also cover the field of municipal and government finance. The federal debt of the United States is an unsecured debt, as are the bonds issued by state governments and other governmental subdivisions. Where the issuing corporation has no mortgage bonds outstanding, the debenture bonds would be junior to no other long-term security of the corporation. In recent years, the acceptance of debenture bonds by investors has been increasing, and the financial operations of corporations both large and small have given increasing importance to unsecured bonds as a means of raising the needed funds of the enterprise.

Subordinated Debentures Subordinated debentures are unsecured debts that rank below secured debt and other unsecured debt as defined in the indenture of the subordinated debenture. For example, the indenture may state that the debentures are subordinated to all senior debts existing or to be contracted in the future. Senior debts may be defined as all secured debts plus any debt maturing within nine months. The latter would include most of the short-term borrowing from banks and other lending institutions. In other indentures the definition of senior debt might exclude trade accounts payable and accrued liabilities.

The use of the subordinated debentures is largely a development following World War II. Their increased use has largely been associated with the consumer finance industry. In the 1960's subordinated debentures have been used as an important tool of financing in the program of the Small Business Administration in providing long-term funds to small businesses.

Although the debentures are subordinated to whatever is defined as senior debt in the indenture, the corporation is obliged to make payments on principal and interest when they are due. Failure to do so is just as much an act of bankruptcy as the failure to pay interest on mortgage bonds. So long as the corporation is solvent, it must make payments when due regardless of rank of the debt. The only exception to this is in the case of income bonds (to be discussed later in this chapter). The treatment to be accorded the holders of subordinated debentures in the event of bankruptcy is defined in the indenture. For example, the indenture of a $100 million subordinated debenture of the Dow Chemical Company contains the following:

Upon any distribution of assets of the Company upon any dissolution, winding up, liquidation or reorganization of the Company, the holders of all Senior Indebtedness shall first be entitled to receive payment in full of the principal thereof and the interest due thereon before the holders of the Convertible Debentures are entitled to receive any payment on the principal (and premium if any) or interest on the Convertible Debentures, but the foregoing does not restrict the Company, except during the tendency of any such dissolution, winding up, liquidation or reorganization proceedings, from making payments of principal, or premium, if any, or interest on the Convertible Debentures.[7]

From the standpoint of the financial officer of a corporation, subordinated debentures are considered an alternative to preferred stock, rather than as an alternative to secured bonds. The existence of subordinated debentures does not impair, but rather enhances, the borrowing power of the corporation. If a corporation issues $10 million in subordinated debentures, it can be assumed that the assets of the corporation are increased by a like amount. Holders of bonds and other debt that is senior to the subordinated debentures are provided additional protection resulting from the increased assets financed by the sale of the debentures but upon which the holders of the senior debts have prior claim. The borrowing capacity of the corporation is increased by the use of subordinated debentures (if the indenture permits additional debt with priority over the debentures) to the same extent as it would be from the use of preferred or common stock in acquiring additional assets. Another benefit to the corporation in using subordinated debentures is that the payment of interest on debentures is an expense, thereby reducing the taxable income of the corporation, while the payment of dividends on preferred stock does not reduce the income tax of the corporation.

The attraction of subordinated debentures to investors can be seen by comparing them to preferred stocks. Like most issues of preferred stock, payments must be made according to the indenture before any distribution to the common stockholders. However, the holders of subordinated debentures have priority over the holders of preferred as well as over the holders of common stock. In addition, the corporation is bound to pay the interest on the subordinated debentures even in those years when the corporation does not earn a net income. Subordinated debentures, therefore, are a more conservative investment than the preferred stock of the same corporation. Although subordinated debentures are given priority over preferred and common stocks, they rank junior to other long-term debts. To offset this disadvantage to the investor, some inducement is provided. Most frequently, the subordinated debentures carry a higher interest rate than the other long-term debts of the corporation. Another inducement is the privilege given to the holder of converting his bonds into either preferred or common stock of the corporation.

---

[7] Dow Chemical Company, prospectus of the $100 million Convertible Debenture issue dated July 14, 1952, p. 18.

SPECIAL TYPES OF BONDS

Collateral Trust Bonds   Where a substantial portion of a corporation's assets are in the form of stocks and bonds, it may offer these securities as collateral for a loan.   If the loan is in the form of bonds issued by the corporation, the issue is called a *collateral trust* bond issue.   The safety of a collateral trust bond issue is indirect.   The collateral offered consists of bonds, stocks, notes, and other intangible assets.   The value of these intangible assets in turn depends upon the strength of their claim upon tangible assets and corporation earnings.   Most issues are secured by the deposit with the trustee of bonds of other corporations, stocks of other corporations, bonds of the corporation issuing the collateral trust bonds, or franchises, leaseholds, and other types of intangible property.

Trustee's or Receiver's Certificates   The conditions under which receiver's certificates and trustee's certificates are issued is discussed in Chapter 25. In this connection, the financial aspects of the certificates are treated.   In both cases, the certificates are issued for the purpose of raising the necessary funds for a corporation while the corporation property is administered by a court appointed manager during bankruptcy.   If it were not possible for funds to be raised to meet the financial requirements of a corporation in financial difficulty, the corporation could not continue to operate as a going concern.   On the other hand, lenders are understandably reluctant to make loans to a corporation that has demonstrated its inability to meet payments on past debts.   To overcome such reluctance and to make the certificates salable, they are given priority over existing debts of the corporation, including mortgage bonds.   To be accorded such priority the certificates may be issued only upon express authority of the court.[8]

For the most part receiver's or trustee's certificates are short-term securities used for the purpose of meeting everyday expenses of the corporation. They are also used, however, to meet long-term requirements of the corporation, such as addition to the plant of the corporation.   The priority of the certificates is determined by the court.   While the practices of different courts vary, the certificates are usually given a priority rating over other debts of the corporation but not over tax payments due, wages unpaid, or court expenses resulting from the proceedings in bankruptcy.   In many instances, the certificates issued under the jurisdiction of a court enjoy a high investment standing due to their position of priority.   If the corporation remains under the jurisdiction of the court for a lengthy period, there may be many issues of receiver's or trustee's certificates.   In such cases, the

---

8 In unusual cases involving lengthy bankruptcy proceedings the volume of trustee's certificates issued has been so great as to equal or exceed the value of the corporation property, leaving nothing to the holders of mortgage bonds and other creditors of the corporation.

court usually gives equal priority to all issues of receiver's or trustee's certificates.

Income Bonds   Income bonds combine some of the features of bonds with some of the features of preferred stock.   As in the case of most bonds, income bonds have a definite maturity date, and the issuing corporation is obliged to pay the principal when due.   Interest payments are usually in a fixed amount, such as 6 per cent.   However, as in the case of preferred stocks, the payment of interest is dependent upon the earnings of the corporation.   Some income bonds make the payment of interest mandatory on the part of the corporation in those periods in which the income of the corporation is sufficient to cover the interest on the bond.   To enforce a payment of interest, however, the trustee acting on behalf of the bondholders may be required to prove that the corporation actually did earn sufficient income during the period in which the interest payment was due.   Some income bonds do not even contain this measure of protection in the payment of interest.   Such bonds make the payment of interest dependent upon the declaration of such payment by the board of directors, in the manner of declaring stock dividends.   As in the case of preferred stock, the payment of interest on income bonds may be cumulative.   The bond may have a mortgage lien on property of the corporation, though in most cases the lien is a second or third claim upon property.   In effect, the income bond is a bond with respect to principal and a preferred stock with respect to interest.

Income bonds are the weakest of the bonds.   In the past they have been used mostly in the reorganization of bankrupt railroads.   Income bonds created as a result of bankruptcy are frequently called *adjustment bonds*, a term which indicates the circumstances of their origin.   Because of the weakness of such bonds, they are not often used as a means of raising money for the corporation.   Income bonds, however, may provide certain advantages to investors over preferred stock.   If the indenture binds the corporation to pay the interest in all periods where the corporation earns sufficient income to cover the interest, such payment is given priority over dividends of the preferred and common stocks.   If the bonds have the cumulative feature, the directors of the corporation may be obliged by the indenture to meet the payments that are past due whenever net income is earned sufficient to do so.   To offset the weak features of income bonds, the interest rate is often a generous one.   Financial institutions that are restricted to investing in bonds may enjoy a higher yield on their investment by purchasing income bonds.

There are several advantages to the corporation in issuing income bonds.   The primary one, of course, is the fact that the corporation is not obliged to pay interest when the net income is too low to do so.   Also, unlike the payment of dividends on preferred and common stock, the payment of interest on income bonds is an expense rather than a distribution of profits.

Bonds with Warrants   A few issues of bonds appeal to the speculative instincts of investors by providing warrants to purchase stock at specified prices.   They are called stock purchase warrants, and should not be confused with stock subscription warrants described in Chapter 18.   For example, each $1,000 bond may have a warrant attached permitting the holder to purchase twenty shares of common stock at a price of $15.   The warrant may be nondetachable, thereby restricting the sale of the stock at the specified price to those investors who hold the bonds.   This restriction permits the corporation to eliminate the warrants through the act of calling in the outstanding bonds.   If the warrant is detachable, the purchaser of the bond may sell the warrant separately while retaining the bond.   Obviously, bonds with detachable warrants provide greater investment appeal than those with nondetachable ones.   The warrants are usually good for the life of the bond.   As a variation, a bond may have two or three warrants attached, each warrant good for a specified period of the life of the bond.   In nearly all cases the subscription price of the stock is higher than the market price at the time the bonds are issued.   For example, the warrant may give the purchaser of the bond the right to buy twenty shares of common stock at $50 a share, with the market price of the stock at the time of the issuance of the bond as $40 a share.   Warrants, therefore, usually have no value at the time of the issuance of the bonds, except for a potential value.   Only if the market price of the stock rises above the subscription price stated in the warrant does the warrant prove valuable.

There are two advantages to the corporation in issuing bonds with warrants attached.   The corporation may be able to borrow at a lower interest cost by providing some speculative attraction through warrants.   The corporation may also receive additional cash in the future through the action of holders of the warrants in purchasing additional shares of stock.   The warrants may be exercised at a time when the corporation needs the money and can put it to profitable use.   Often, however, the warrants will be exercised at a time when it is not convenient to the corporation to receive money in exchange for stock.

"Cost-of-Living" Bonds   The rapid inflation of prices that occurred during and after World War I caused many investors to shun bonds and other fixed income securities.   During a period of rising prices, debtors benefit and creditors lose.   During the 1920's, Rand Kardex Company issued a bond in which the payment of interest was to be adjusted upward by the same percentage as the percentage of any increase in the cost of living as measured by the Bureau of Labor Statistics in Washington, D.C.   This issue did not, however, start a trend in bond financing, for the decline in business activity signaled by the stock market collapse in 1929 made the danger of price inflation remote.

The worldwide inflation of World War II and its aftermath sparked a renewed interest in "cost-of-living" bonds. A large cooperative in Sweden issued bonds whose payment of principal was adjusted to match any increase in the cost of living as measured by government statistics. The adjustment was limited to a maximum of 50 per cent. The indenture provided that if there were to be a decline in the cost of living below the level at the time of the bond issuance, no reduction in payment of principal below par value was to be made. A novel anti-inflation guarantee was included in a bond issue marketed by a government-owned electric power company in France in 1953. A payment of 4.5 per cent interest was guaranteed with another annual payment equal to the cost of 100 kilowatt hours of electric current. This was done to assure bondholders that the return on their investment would keep pace with the cost of living.

In the United States the decade of the 1950's was one of mild but steady inflation. Taking their cue from European practice, issuers of bonds once again gave consideration to cost-of-living features in borrowing money. A recent issue was that of the City of Carlsbad, New Mexico. The city offered a $4 million issue, dated Dec. 1, 1959, maturing in thirty years, paying 6 per cent interest, and carrying a first mortgage on specified property. The announcement of the issue stated the cost-of-living feature as follows: "The redemption value of these bonds is tied to the national consumer price index, and in event of further increases in the cost of living, the redemption and/or the maturity value of these bonds—and the interest paid thereon—will increase proportionately. The redemption value, however, will not decrease below par value of the bonds." 9

As in the case of the Rand Kardex bond issue thirty years earlier, the City of Carlsbad cost-of-living issue did not start a trend. Apparently there continues to be a disbelief in the inevitability of long-term inflation. Should the upward march of prices resume, cost-of-living bonds may become more common. On the other hand, should the fear of inflation become remote, such bonds will once more be classed with rare, unusual issues.

Questions

1. What is the distinction between the real and personal property of a business?
2. Distinguish between equipment mortgage, conditional sale, and lease agreement in financing equipment.
3. What are the protective features in equipment trust certificates that make this type of investment popular with institutional investors?
4. Account for the fact that equipment trust certificates maintained a better record of payment during the depression of the 1930's than bonds and other secured debt.
5. Why might a corporation raise money by means of a collateral trust bond issue rather than sell its pledged securities?
6. What are guaranteed bonds? Under what circumstances are they used?
7. Explain the nature of joint bonds.

9 Announcement of $4 million 6 per cent Thirty-Year Cost-of-Living Bonds, by Investment Sales Corporation, Long Beach, California, January 19, 1960.

8. What are reasons that a corporation might prefer to issue debentures rather than mortgage bonds?
9. What protective provisions are sometimes found in debenture bonds to increase the likelihood that interest and principal will be paid when due?
10. Explain the use of subordinated debentures.
11. What is the attraction of income bonds to the corporation? To the investor?
12. What is the purpose of attaching warrants to bonds? What is the attraction of warrants to the purchaser of bonds?
13. What is the investor appeal of a cost-of-living bond? Why is it more frequently found in European finance?

Selected Readings

Dewing, Arthur Stone, *Financial Policy of Corporations,* 5th ed., The Ronald Press Company, 1953, Chaps. 8 and 9.

Johnson, Robert W., "Subordinated Debentures: Debt That Serves as Equity," *Journal of Finance,* March 1955.

Robbins, Sidney M., "A Bigger Role for Income Bonds," *Harvard Business Review,* November-December, 1955.

Street, D. M., "The Role of Equipment Obligations in Postwar Railroad Financing," *Journal of Finance,* September 1960.

14

Leasing of Long-Term Assets

THE NATURE OF THE LEASE CONTRACT

THE ESSENTIAL FEATURE of a lease is the separation of ownership from control. Each lease is a contract in which the owner of property (known as the landlord or lessor) gives up its use for a stated period to a person or company (known as the lessee or tenant). In return for the use of the leased property, the lessee agrees to pay a rental to the lessor. Aside from the essential features of the lease, there is little conformity in lease contracts. They may run for a few months or as long as ninety-nine years. They may be used to acquire the use of property with a life of a few months or to finance the use of land or other property having either a perpetual life or a long-term existence. The contract may be between a single lessor and a single lessee or may involve several persons or companies.

Leasing may be the only way to secure the use of certain property. Some owners refuse to sell their property but are willing to offer its use by means of leases. The owners of land in choice downtown locations of many cities refuse to sell their property but permit its use on a lease basis. Lease contracts in such cases run for many years, permitting the lessee to erect houses or factories or office buildings to be used by the lessee during the life of the lease. At the expiration of the lease, the land together with all the improvements on it, such as buildings, fences, and roads, revert to the lessor. Some industrial machinery and office equipment is available from the manufacturer either on a lease basis or by outright purchase. However, if the terms of sale are prohibitive, the only practical alternative is a lease.

Those patents that are not for sale at any price may be available on a lease basis. The rental payment for use of the rights is usually called a royalty. In such cases, the lease payments are usually not a fixed sum per month or per year but rather a fixed percentage of the number of units produced by the lessee.

A lease contract involving land may permit the lessee to cut timber standing on the land or to extract minerals from beneath the surface. As in the case of leases involving patents, payments (again, called royalties) to the lessor are usually stated as a percentage of the timber cut or a percentage of the minerals extracted. In some instances, the air space above a piece of land, rather than the land itself, is leased. In cities where a railroad terminal is located close to the center of town, the land on which the tracks approach the station may be very valuable as industrial or office property. Thus, a new office building above the tracks could provide additional income to the railroad through leasing the air space above the railroad tracks.

THE ATTRACTIONS OF LEASING

As we have seen, certain items of machinery and equipment are available *only* on a lease basis. But, for those items that may be purchased or leased, a choice has to be made whether to lease or buy the assets. If this is the choice, it assumes that the company has cash on hand to make the purchase. It is highly unlikely that the corporation or the business has on hand cash sufficient to purchase major industrial equipment, to say nothing of funds to purchase a building or land. As a matter of fact, if a business has on hand cash in amounts sufficient to make major purchases, it is usually evidence not of conservative policy but rather of poor financial management.[1] Therefore, the choice is more accurately stated not in terms of whether to lease or buy but rather in terms of whether to borrow or to lease.

Elimination of Risks of Ownership The ownership of property carries with it risk. Property may suffer damage or be stolen, so the lessor generally insures it. Another risk of owning property is obsolescence, which is not easily adapted to the principle of insurance. Therefore, the risk must be shouldered by the property owner. To what extent a company may avoid the risk of obsolescence by leasing property rather than owning it is a matter of debate. Obviously, the lessor is as conscious of the risk of obsolescence as is the lessee. A charge for the risk of obsolescence will be included in the schedule of rental payments under a lease contract. If the portion of the monthly payment allocated to covering the risk of obsolescence is too small adequately to cover the risk, the lessee benefits and the

---

[1] Cash on hand or in the bank is essential to the running of any business, since cash payments and receipts cannot be perfectly coordinated. Nevertheless, the balance should be kept as low as business operations permit, because cash in a bank checking account or in the money till does not earn any income. However, because it is the one asset that can most easily and quickly be transformed into inventory, machinery, or other productive assets, some managers feel a substantial cash account permits greater maneuverability and speed in business decisions. To meet the needs of such a policy, some financial managers maintain a portfolio of United States Treasury bills, commercial paper, and other investments that can be liquidated rapidly when occasion demands. The interest income on such investments is low, but the price is steady and the marketability very high.

lessor suffers. If the portion is greater than necessary, the company using equipment might better have purchased it instead.

The risk of obsolescence is very difficult to measure accurately. The rate of technological change in some industries is low, while in others it is rapid. In either case, it is difficult to foresee the effects of invention or refinement of processes in the industry. The charge for obsolescence is usually not identified in the monthly payment for leased equipment. Nevertheless, it is included in the total monthly charge, and should be so considered by the lessee in deciding whether or not to accept a lease. There is one aspect of obsolescence, however, that favors leasing rather than buying equipment. A company may need only one electronic computer, and, if it purchases a machine that becomes rapidly obsolete, the loss might be considerable. On the other hand, a company leasing electronic computers may loan many different types. The degree of obsolescence for many machines could perhaps be more accurately determined than for a single one. To reduce this risk, a lessor owning many machines can spread it over the several machines. For this reason, it may be advantageous to a company to lease rather than purchase equipment with a high possibility of obsolescence.

Avoidance of Debt Restrictions The indentures of most bond issues place restrictions of greater or lesser degree on the financing freedom of the corporation borrowing money. The restrictions found in bond indentures typically limit the additional indebtedness which may be incurred by the corporation during the life of the bond issue. Frequently, however, the limitations in a bond issue placed on additional debts incurred by the corporation do not place restrictions on additional lease obligations which the corporaton might incur.[2] Restrictions imposed by lease obligations on the lessee are generally not so formidable in regard to additional indebtedness as are the restrictions imposed in bond indentures. The restrictions found in lease obligations are mainly concerned with limiting the use of the leased property. Examples would be those restrictions on the type of buildings erected on leased land, on the use to which the property is put, on the type and size of advertising signs which may be placed on leased buildings, and so on.

Increasing the Ability to Borrow One of the most frequently stated advantages to leasing over borrowing is that leasing increases the ability of the firm to raise funds on a piece of property. If, for example, a company has a piece of property with a value of $100,000, it may be able to borrow an amount equal to $60,000 or $70,000 on the security of a mortgage on

---

[2] A study of such restrictions stated that only 47 per cent of the agreements that contained limitations on incurring additional debt also have restrictions that are effective against incurring additional lease obligations (R. S. Vancil and R. N. Anthony, "The Financial Community Looks at Leasing," *Harvard Business Review*, November-December 1959, p. 130).

the property. However, under a lease arrangement, it is possible that the corporation could raise $100,000 on the property by means of selling it and leasing its use for a long period of years. This advantage to leasing, however, must be accepted with some reservation. Every action that results in increasing the debts of the corporation or increasing the contractual payments the corporation must make under a lease "uses up" some of the borrowing or contracting capacity of the corporation. Thus, when money received from the sale and leaseback of property is put to use, it generally increases the capacity of the corporation to borrow or to engage in additional contractual payments. If a corporation borrows $70,000 on a mortgage of property with a value of $100,000 and if the $70,000 is used to purchase additional property, it may be reasoned that the borrowing capacity of the corporation has been decreased by $100,000 and in turn increased by $70,000. In effect, the act of mortgaging a piece of property worth $100,000 to secure a loan of $70,000 results in a net decrease in borrowing capacity of $30,000. If the company, on the other hand, sells the property for $100,-000 and leases its use, it could be said that the reduction in borrowing capacity and the increase in borrowing capacity as a result of receiving the $100,-000 neutralize each other. Thus, it could be argued that in the above example the advantage of leasing as compared to borrowing shows a better effect on borrowing capacity through leasing than through mortgaging property for a loan.

On the other hand, it might be reasoned that the advantage of leasing is an illusory one with respect to its effect on borrowing capacity. This argument is that the advantage is a result of the faulty recognition of lenders as to the relative effect on the finances of a company engaging in contractual lease payments compared to the obligation to pay interest and principal on a loan. Both types of payment are contractual obligations that must be met by the business borrower. In any case, from the standpoint of the financial manager of a business, if investigation shows that there is an advantage in a particular instance to leasing rather than to borrowing, it matters little as to the origin of the advantage. The financial manager has fulfilled his obligation to his company if he secures the use of assets under terms that are most advantageous to the corporation. If an advantage of leasing over borrowing in particular circumstances proves to be a temporary one, the opportunity should nevertheless be taken, as long as such advantage remains in existence.

Lower Costs of Financing Lease financing may be less expensive, depending on many factors: the length of the period during which the lease is amortized, the rate of interest included in the lease payments compared to the rate of interest on borrowed funds, and the effect of the rate of taxes on lease payments compared to payments on debts. If obsolescence of leased assets is an important factor, this must be included in any comparison of the cost of leasing with the cost of borrowing. Finally, the residual value of the assets at the expiration of the lease period must also be noted. Considering all these factors together may indicate a lower financing cost through leasing arrangements rather than by means of owning and borrowing, and, if such is the case, the advantage of leasing from a financial standpoint is evident.

Improvement of Financial Ratios   If leasing rather than borrowing is used as a means of acquiring assets, the financial statements and ratios appear to indicate that the company is in a stronger position.   See Table 14-1.   The improved appearance of the balance sheet and the financial ratios is largely a result of the practice of most accountants not to include the company's lease operations in the body of balance sheets.   Custom, however, is changing.   Lease payments are an obligation that are as binding on the company as are payments on debts.   Some leases may be cancelable, and the terms of some may be subject to modification.   However, most leases may not be changed during their lifetime.   In such cases, the lessee must make the payments on the lease when they are due, as he must make the payments on debt obligations when they are due.   For this reason, it is logical to include among the liabilities of a company the capitalized present value of lease payments that may not be altered or canceled.   Similarly, although assets acquired by lease are not usually shown on the balance sheet of companies, they logically should be, since a company generally has as much control over such assets as it has over assets used as security for a loan.   The advantage in renting in improved financial ratios lies in the fact that accounting practice changes slowly.   Therefore, this advantage is apt to prove temporary.

The directors of a corporation may be faced with a choice between leasing and financing the acquisition of assets through the sale of common stock.   If common stock financing is used, it will dilute the equity of the common stock outstanding prior to the sale.   The advantage of leasing in such a choice is that no dilution of equity results.

THE DISADVANTAGES OF LEASING

May Be Costlier Than Borrowing   If a company eliminates the disadvantages of ownership of an asset by leasing it, the lessor assumes the disadvantages.   It is obvious that in the lease payments will be included a consideration for shouldering the risk and disadvantages of property ownership.   It may cost the company more in a particular case to shift the risk of property ownership to another company than it would to shoulder the risk itself. On the other hand, if the lessor owns a large number of similar items of property, the premium for risk of ownership included in the lease payments may be less than what such a cost would be to a company owning only one or two such items.   Thus it might be argued that it is cheaper for a company to lease trucks and automobiles from a lessor owning several hundreds or thousands of such items than it would be to lease a piece of land for a building from a lessor owning only one or two such pieces of property. To determine whether leasing or owning is more costly to a company requires that accurate cost data be available.

TABLE 14-1. COMPARISON OF EFFECTS OF LEASING AND BORROWING

Balance Sheet	Leasing	Owning and Borrowing
Current assets	$1,000,000	$1,000,000
Fixed assets	——	1,000,000
Total	1,000,000	2,000,000
Current liabilities	500,000	500,000
Bonds		1,000,000
Stock and surplus	500,000	500,000
Total	$1,000,000	$2,000,000
Ratios:		
Current ratio	2:1	2:1
Total assets to total liabilities	2:1	2:1½ or 4:3
Liabilities to net worth	1:1	3:1
Income Statement		
Sales	$4,300,000	$4,300,000
Operating expenses less depreciation	3,800,000	3,800,000
Depreciation		200,000
Net operating income	500,000	300,000
Lease payments	250,000	
Bond interest		50,000
Net income before taxes	$ 250,000	$ 250,000
Ratios:		
Return on sales	5.8%	5.8%
Return on total assets	25.0%	12.5%
Times interest earned (net operating income ÷ interest)	not applicable	6 times
Invested capital turnover (sales ÷ total of bonds, stocks, and surplus)	8.6 times	2.87 times

Residual Value of Assets Revert to Lessor Probably the most important disadvantage of leasing is the fact that the property leased remains under the ownership of the lessor after the expiration of the lease as well as during the lease. This may be unimportant for certain types of personal property, such as trucks, automobiles, machinery, and equipment. In many cases, the value of such property at the end of the lease period is very little. Land and buildings are a different matter, however. Buildings depreciate slowly, and land does not depreciate at all in the usual accounting sense. Even if land is leased for a period of ninety-nine years, it will still have value at that time.   As a matter of fact, land frequently has much greater value at the end of a lease period than it had at the beginning.   This is obviously true if the leased land is located in an area of rising values.   It is also true of land and buildings during an inflationary period.   Under some circumstances, if there is a choice between leasing and financing the land by means of borrowing, it would generally appear to be advantageous to the company to borrow in order to purchase the land.   In some cases, of course, a desirable piece of real estate may not be available for purchase at all.   If the company's operations call for certain real estate, regardless of the disadvantages of leasing, it will have to secure the use by that means.

Inflexibility of Lease Contracts   As stated above, a lease contract is a binding obligation both on the part of the lessor and the lessee.   In preparing a lease, the lessor will be attempting to protect in full his interests.   It will be to his advantage to impose restrictions on the use of leased property so that there will be as little risk to him as possible.   Such restrictions may not appear to be burdensome at the time of signing the contract, but the lessee may find the opposite to be true during the life of the lease.   Since contingencies cannot always be foreseen, it is to the advantage of the lessee to have as few restrictions in the lease contract as possible.   Where the bargaining position of the lessee is strong, the restrictions in the lease contract will tend to be minimal.   On the other hand, where the bargaining position of the lessor is strong, the restrictions imposed in a lease contract may be so great as to eliminate the advantages of leasing over borrowing. Where conditions in an industry are subject to rapid change, the restrictions commonly found in lease arrangements may make leasing an undesirable means of acquiring the use of property.   In the broad sense, restrictions are a cost because they impose a sacrifice, just as do money payments.

TAX CONSIDERATIONS IN LEASING

Tax Savings in Leasing   When assets are purchased by funds contributed by the owners of an enterprise, only the depreciation charges may be deducted from income in order to reduce the income tax liability.   If money is borrowed in order to purchase an asset, depreciation charges and interest expenses may be deducted from income.   If the use of property is secured by means of a lease contract, the payments under the lease may be charged against income of the company.   The tax liability of the company can often be reduced by means of leasing rather than by ownership of property. This advantage is particularly evident in the leasing of land and buildings. In the ownership of real estate, no depreciation charges may be made on land.   If the land is leased, however, the lease payments will include the cost to the lessor of land ownership. In effect, leasing permits charges similar to depreciation to be made on land used by a company. This can be clarified by means of a simple example. If a corporation owns a piece of land with a value of $1 million, it may charge no depreciation on the investment it holds in the land. Suppose, however, that the company acquires control of the property by means of a lease running for thirty years, with lease payments totalling $1 million. The lease payments would "write off" the land during the thirty-year period, in the manner of depreciation charges. This would reduce the income tax liability of the corporation by an amount that would be greater than would be possible under ownership of the land. Assuming a tax rate on corporation income of 48 per cent, the company would have "charged to the government" 48 per cent of the cost of the land. In other words, the $1 million in lease payments would have cost the corporation only $520,000. There is an offsetting disadvantage, however. Although only $520,000 would pay for the land, the company does not own the land, despite the fact it has had use of it for thirty years. This disadvantage, however, is not as great as it might appear at first glance. If a company acquires the use of property for a period of thirty years, the fact that it will not own the property at the end of that time, assuming no change in the value of the property during the period, involves a relatively minor burden. If the cost of securing funds is 6 per cent per annum, the present value of $520,000 thirty years in the future is $90,480. In other words, $90,480 invested at a compound rate of 6 per cent per annum equals $520,000 in thirty years. It must be emphasized that the above calculation is based on the assumption that there will be no change in the value of the land. This is unlikely. Because of inflation and population growth, it is reasonable to expect that land values in general will rise. In such circumstances, the lessor, because of his ownership of land, will benefit. The value of land thirty years in the future will in most cases be greater, perhaps considerably greater, than at present.

Tax Requirements in Leasing In order to qualify for the tax advantages of leasing, it is necessary that the lease contract conform to the requirements of the Bureau of Internal Revenue. In summary, they are as follows:

1. If the lease involves a sale and leaseback transaction, the negotiation must represent an arms-length bargaining process between the purchaser and the seller of the property.
2. The leased property must be land, buildings, or the equipment used in the principal business conducted by the lessee.
3. In a sale and leaseback transaction, the price of the property must be a price that is fair in relation to market value of the property. Furthermore, the term of the lease must not be more than thirty years. From a tax standpoint, leases longer than thirty years are considered a sale.
4. The lease payments must represent a reasonable return to the lessor.

5. If the lease transaction involves a renewal option, it must be a genuine option. This is most often met by giving to the lessee an opportunity to meet an equal outside offer for the property.
6. If there is an option to repurchase the property in a sale and leaseback transaction, the option given to the lessee should provide no more than the opportunity to meet an equal outside offer.

SALE AND LEASEBACK ARRANGEMENTS

The sale and leaseback method of financing developed in the United States following World War II. If a company has a piece of property valued at $1 million it can sell this property but retain its use through a lease. Thus the company has both the use of the property sold and the cash realized from its sale. This was a welcome source of funds for many businesses in that period of readjustment. Under the terms of most such leases, the lessee undertook to assume all the operating expenses of the company, including taxes, insurance payments, and necessary property maintenance. The payment to the lessor in most sale and leaseback contracts included only the rental on the property, and the rental covered only the interest and a partial return of the investment. Usually such payments were a fixed amount annually, quarterly, or monthly. However, some rental payments were arranged according to a step plan under which higher periodic payments at the beginning of the lease period were followed by smaller payments toward the end of the lease period. The sale and leaseback method of acquiring funds was made possible by the willingness of financial institutions to purchase property and immediately lease it back to the seller. The sale and leaseback method provided an outlet for investment of institution funds at yields higher than those obtainable on government bonds and other alternate investments following World War II. The first institutions active in the sale and leaseback method of financing were the endowment funds of colleges and universities. Life insurance funds and pension funds were also made available to companies under sale and leaseback arrangements.

Only a few sale and leaseback arrangements provide for a repurchase agreement at the end of the period. Where the lease payments include an amount sufficient to amortize all or nearly all the investment of the lessor in the property, the repurchase price is generally set at a nominal figure. As an alternative to the lease-purchase option, there is sometimes included in a lease contract an option to renew the lease for another period of years. Again, if the lease payments include an amount sufficient to amortize the investment of the lessor during the period of the lease, the option to renew the lease for another period is generally set at a low figure. Types of property used in sale and leaseback financing include hotels, office buildings, retail store buildings, shopping centers, and factories. The most commonly used property in such arrangements is retail store property.

Questions

1. What are the essential features of a lease?
2. In considering a lease, the choice is generally whether to lease or to borrow money rather than whether to lease or to buy. Explain.
3. How can the risk of obsolescence be lessened through leasing equipment rather than buying it?
4. Show how leasing rather than buying fixed assets may improve the ability of the corporation to borrow.
5. Leasing may serve to improve the financial ratios. Explain.
6. Upon the expiration of the lease period, the residual value of the assets revert to the lessor. What is the significance of this in leasing equipment compared to leasing real estate?
7. Compare the effect on the tax liability of a corporation that leases assets and a corporation that borrows money to purchase assets.
8. To qualify for the tax benefits resulting from a lease, what requirements must a corporation meet?
9. Explain the operation of a sale and leaseback transaction.
10. In addition to equipment and real estate, what types of property may be leased?

Selected Readings

Cohen, Albert H., *Long Term Leases,* University of Michigan Press, Ann Arbor, Mich., 1954.

"Fresh Lease on Life," *Barron's National Business and Financial Weekly,* December 31, 1962.

Eiteman, W. J., and C. M. Davisson, *The Lease as a Financing and Selling Device,* Bureau of Business Research, University of Michigan, Ann Arbor, Mich., 1961.

Pratt, Robert A., "Equipment Leasing—A Growing Industry," *The Pittsburgh Business Review,* University of Pittsburgh, Pittsburgh, Pa., July, 1962.

Staats, William F., "Sale—Leaseback of Real Estate as a Financing Device," *University of Houston Business Review,* Winter, 1962.

Part V

Distribution and Trading of Securities

15

Investment Banking

THE NATURE OF INVESTMENT BANKING

INVESTMENT BANKING is essentially a merchandising function. Primarily, investment banking houses purchase securities from corporations and distribute them to investors. As a result of this process, the savings of investors are channeled into the bank accounts of corporations, to be used to purchase plant and equipment for modernization and expansion and to refund maturing obligations, among other purposes. These uses are shown in Fig. 15-1.

Although the primary function of investment banking is the distribution of securities for corporations, the business of investment banking is not confined to distribution. There are many other services provided, as will be seen later in this chapter. Aside from the distribution of securities, probably the most important service of investment banking is the guarantee of the successful sale of securities. This guaranteeing function is called underwriting.

There are about 1,000 investment banking houses in the United States that could be classed as underwriters. Included in this number are the large firms, such as Blythe and Company, First Boston Corporation, Goldman Sachs and Company, Harriman Ripley and Company, Kidder Peabody and Company, Lehman Brothers Company, Morgan Stanley and Company, and Whiteweld and Company. Also included in this number are houses that are much smaller, and that engage mostly in a regional underwriting business. There are perhaps 3,000 houses that could be classed primarily as retailers of securities, and often consist of one or two men plus a secretary in a single-room office. However, these houses do the bulk of their business by purchasing securities from underwriters and reselling them to local investors. Occasionally, such small houses will underwrite a local issue themselves.

The unit cost of distribution of securities varies inversely with the volume of distribution. The spread between the price paid by the investor

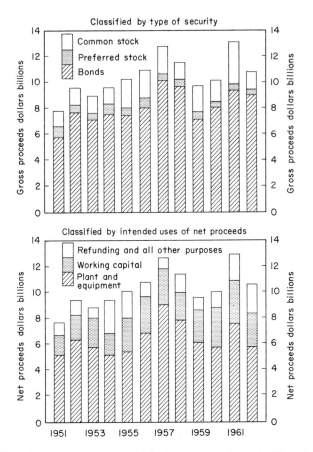

Fig. 15-1 *New corporate securities offered for cash in the United States.*
(*Source:* Securities and Exchange Commission)

and the price received by the corporation for each security distributed is small for large issues and large for small issues. In general, it takes a lot more selling effort on the part of an investment banking firm to market an issue of securities for a small company than for a larger company. Small issues are generally sold to individual investors while large issues are more apt to attract institutional investors that purchase securities in large volume. It is the institutional investors that buy most of the bonds sold by corporations. The amount of their purchases is so large that in most years the volume of bonds distributed is considerably more than the volume of stocks (see Fig. 15-1). In addition to the size of the issue the kind of security offered affects the cost of distribution. It costs more to distribute a common stock issue than it does a preferred stock issue of the same size. In turn, it costs more to distribute a preferred stock issue than a bond issue of the same size. These cost relationships are shown in Fig. 15-2.

The contrast in actual cost between two securities, one large and one

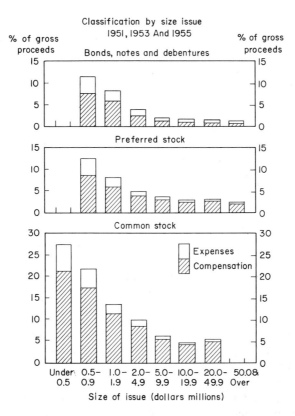

Classification by size issue
1951, 1953 And 1955

Fig. 15-2 *Underwriting spreads of publicly offered securities registered with S.E.C. and sold through investment bankers, 1951, 1953, 1955. (Source: Cost of Flotation of Corporate Securities, 1951, 1953, and 1955,* Securities and Exchange Commission, Washington, D. C., 1957)

small, is illustrative. In 1959 the Southern Company issued 1,300,000 shares of common stock, marketed by a syndicate of underwriters. At a price of $35.50 paid by the investing public the receipts from the total issue amounted to $46,150,000. The underwriting commission agreed upon was $871,000, and the amount received by the company was $45,279,000. In this issue, the underwriting commission amounted to 1.86 per cent of the gross receipts of the sale. The second example is a small issue marketed locally in Texas in 1956 that consisted of 300,000 shares of common stock distributed to the public at a price of $2 per share, for a total price of $600,000. Of this amount, the underwriters retained $120,000, and turned over to the corporation the balance of $480,000. The underwriting commission in this instance was 20 per cent. In some cases, the expenses of preparing an issue for distribution are included in the underwriter's commission. In most of the larger issues, however, such expenses are paid by the corporation. In the case of the Southern Company common stock issue, the expenses were approximately $148,090, which was paid out of the proceeds received by the company. Therefore, they constituted an expense of distribution in addition to the underwriting commission. The Securities and Exchange Commission has estimated the type and amount of such expenses in a typical distribution of bonds amounting to $15,500,000. They are as follows: [1]

Type of Expense	Cost
Legal fees	$16,700
Printing and engraving	30,500
Accounting fees	5,300
Engineering fees	9,100
Federal stamp taxes	16,900
State taxes and fees	4,500
Trustee's fees	16,300
S.E.C. fees	1,600
Miscellaneous	9,900

SERVICES OF INVESTMENT BANKING

The investment banker is a specialist in the distribution of securities. A corporation wishing to market its own securities to the general public would find it necessary to create a marketing organization for the purpose. The techniques involved in successful selling of securities are different from the techniques in selling industrial products. The customers are different, the advertising is specialized, and the body of laws governing the sale of securities is much more complex. A corporation requires the services of an investment banker infrequently. It is generally better for a corporation to have the salesmen, lawyers, advertising men, and other specialists of the investment banker provide their services on the infrequent occasions that a corporation needs them in selling securities.

Certainty   In its planning for the use of funds to be raised by a distribution of securities, the corporation needs some assurance that the funds will be available as planned. There are enough risks involved in the expenses of expansion, modernization, increase in inventory, or other changes in the business resulting from the spending of money raised by selling securities. The directors of most corporations in preferring not to shoulder the additional risk of an unsuccessful distribution can shift this risk to investment bankers. In a typical securities transaction, the investment banking house will contract to purchase the planned issue of securities of the corporation on a particular date for a stated sum of money. Once the underwriting commitment (the guarantee of the successful sale of the securities) has been assumed by the investment banking house, the corporation officers can proceed with their plans for the use of the money and be secure in the knowledge that the funds will be available as agreed upon.

---

[1] Securities and Exchange Commission, *Cost of Flotation of Corporate Securities, 1951, 1953, and 1955*, Washington, D.C., 1957, p. 11.

Advice Some of the characteristics of marketing products, such as product design, careful timing of the introduction of a new item, price determination, and number of units to be marketed, are similar to the characteristics of securities distribution. The securities must be made attractive to potential investors. The time that they are offered to the public bears an important relation to success in a sale. The volume of securities of a particular type that can be successfully absorbed by investors must be carefully gauged. These are decisions that require the knowledge and experience of specialists. Investment banking houses keep constantly in touch with investors, in order to gauge the shifting demands of investors and decide whether the times are favorable for the marketing of a particular issue.

It is especially important in the sale of preferred stocks or bonds that the security be designed to attract investors. As we have seen in the chapters on preferred stocks and bonds, there are many features that can be added to these securities to make them more attractive. The investment banker can give advice as to the form of protective provisions, sinking funds, or other features to be included in an issue. In a particular instance, the investment banker might give advice on the addition of warrants to a bond, on the maturity to be placed on the bond, and on the type of collateral, if any, to be given to the bond issue. He may advise that the conversion feature be included in a projected preferred stock issue. He can give advice as to the price to be asked for the security.

Even after the securities have been distributed, the investment banking house may serve as a source of financial counsel. If it is expected that the corporation will need additional financing in the future, the investment banking house can aid the directors in deciding when additional funds can profitably be used by the corporation. Furthermore, the investment banker has a reputation to maintain in the investment market. He does not wish to be associated with the distribution of securities of a corporation whose directors and officers are not of top quality. While the investment banking house does not guarantee that the price of securities, once issued, will not drop, he does prefer that the customers to whom he has sold securities profit by their investment in the securities. Therefore, the investment banker has an interest in seeing that the corporation continues to be as efficiently operated as it appears to be at the time that the securities were distributed. Sometimes, as a condition to the distribution of securities, an investment banking house will require the privilege of placing one of its officers on the board of directors of the client corporation. Such a director serves as a continuing consultant to the corporation.

Prestige A good reputation is probably the most important asset of an investment banking house. The reputation depends upon thorough investigation of corporations whose securities the investment banking house distributes, skill in designing an issue to make it sell profitably, skill in pricing and timing the issue, and adequate follow-up in maintaining the market value of an issue after it is sold. The foremost investment banking houses can aid in the designing, pricing, and timing of an issue, so that it is sold the first day it is offered. To protect their reputation, the principal investment banking houses select with care the corporations whose securities they are willing to market. To have an issue underwritten by one or more of the principal investment houses lends prestige to the corporation issuing the securities.

Market Protection   After an issue of securities has been sold by an investment banking house, it is under no obligation to prevent a decline in the market price of the stock or the bonds. If, however, the market price of an issue falls shortly after the distribution by an investment banking house, many investors will feel that advantage has been taken of their lack of professional knowledge of securities and that the investment banking house has been guilty of sharp trading. In other words, this decline will reflect back upon the reputation of the investment banker. Furthermore, such a drop in the price of a security shortly after distribution may affect the corporation's public image. In order to prevent the drop, investment banking houses generally support the price of the securities for a period after the distribution has begun. Although the length of time that the market is supported by the investment banker varies, the usual period is thirty days. During this time, the investment banker will stand ready to purchase securities to match any selling pressure that may develop. If the market is relatively steady, the investment banker may be able to peg the price of the stock at a stated figure, by offering to purchase any number of securities at a specified price. If, on the other hand, the investment market is unstable, the investment banker may be able to support the market only to the extent of slowing down a drop in the price. For example, shortly after the stock of the Ford Motor Company was first offered for public sale in 1956 at $64.50 a share, the price rose to $71 in a few days and then began dropping steadily. In this instance, in spite of the support effort of the syndicate of investment bankers that had just distributed the issue, the price continued downward until it reached a level of approximately half what it had been at the time of first issue. The support of the market may take place over the organized securities exchanges or outside of the exchanges. The support of the market, it must be emphasized, is not a legal obligation of the investment banking house. For this reason, although the group of investment banking houses may have agreed to support the price of a security for thirty days after the initial distribution, they reserve the right to discontinue support operations at any time. If such support operations are planned in connection with the distribution of an issue, this intent must be stated in the prospectus describing the issue. For example, the prospectus describing the issue of 1,300,000 shares of the Southern Company, marketed early in 1959, reads as follows:

In connection with this offering, the underwriters may overallot or effect transactions which stabilize or maintain the market price of the common stock of the company at a level above that which might otherwise prevail in the open market. Such transactions may be effected on the New York Stock Exchange, on any other stock exchange on which such stock has been admitted to trading privileges, in the over-the-counter market or otherwise. Such stabilizing, if commenced, may be discontinued at any time.

PROCEDURES IN INVESTMENT BANKING

Investigation   The first step in the process of raising money by a distribution of securities is determining the need for funds. Some corporations prepare a capital budget (discussed in Chapter 19) to determine the needs for long-term funds and to allocate among these needs the funds that can be raised at reasonable cost. Other companies, mostly smaller ones, make no such formal planning for their long-term financial requirements, and seek to raise long-term funds as the need arises. Since the purpose of dealing with investment bankers is to raise funds for the company, it is of paramount importance that the need for the funds be determined with care. In other words, long-term funds should be raised by a company only where there is reasonable assurance that the funds can be put to profitable use by the company.

After determining the need for funds, the corporation officials seek out an investment banker or possibly several investment bankers. Sometimes, it is an officer of the investment banking house that first contacts the corporation, because investment banking houses are constantly on the search for additional business.

During the preliminary conferences between the investment banking house and the corporation, only the broad outline of the security to be issued will be tentatively decided on. Since the investment value of the security to be distributed will depend upon the profitability of the corporation, the investment banker will seek to determine the probability of the funds to be raised enhancing the profits of the corporation. No investment house valuing its reputation with investors will voluntarily engage in the distribution of securities for a corporation unless the investors purchasing these securities are likely to benefit from their investment. Acting under its responsibility to investors, the firm will make a thorough investigation of the corporation. If the funds are to be used to modernize plant and equipment, the firm will engage engineers to make a technical appraisal of the company's operations. Lawyers engaged by the underwriting firm will examine the proposed issue of securities with respect to its legality, to make sure the charter of the corporation authorizes the issue, and to make sure the proposed issue does not conflict in any way with the contract provisions of previous securities issued by the corporation. Accountants will examine the financial records of the company to determine the completeness and accuracy of these records. Consultants on marketing may be called in to appraise the methods of distribution of products, advertising, and other marketing techniques of the corporation. Perhaps an economist will be retained to make a broad-scale investigation of the corporation, its relative standing in its industry, and the strength of its competitive position.

The investigation by the underwriting house has to be more detailed and extensive if it has not had any previous dealings with the client corporation. In such a case, the investment banking house will also delve into its past history. It will examine the quality of the products of the company, the rapidity of expansion of the company, any past financial difficulty, the extent of control of the corporation by one or a few stockholders, whether or not the management is basically aggressive, the labor relations of the company, and the opinion held of the company by suppliers, competitors, and customers.

Perhaps during the early stages of these investigations, the investment bankers become convinced that the prospects of profitable use of the funds do not warrant the raising of the funds. In that event, the firm will probably inform the corporation that it is no longer interested in further negotiation with respect to the proposed distribution of securities. In such a case, if the officers of the corporation still feel that there is a need for the funds, another house can be approached. There are, after all, many investment banking houses in competition with each other. If the preliminary investigations appear to justify more extensive analysis, the investigation will proceed. During the investigation, the corporation officials are expected to give full cooperation to the representatives of the house. The officials are expected, for example, to provide information, sometimes confidential, with the assurance, of course, that the investigators will not disclose it to competitors. During the investigation, the corporation officials are expected not to open negotiations with another house. Should they do this, they would find in the future that it would be very difficult to secure the services of any reputable investment banking house. The investment banking house will bear the cost of the investigation to the extent that the wages and salaries of its own officers and staff are involved. However, any additional expenses, such as traveling expenses and the cost of engineers or other specialists not on the regular payroll of the banking house, are borne by the corporation.

Negotiations If the investment banking house is satisfied with the results of its investigation and if it feels that the proposed issue will be favorably received by investors, the terms of the underwriting agreement will be negotiated by officers of the house and of the corporation. The agreement is reached in a negotiating conference, where most of the details of the proposed issue are determined. One important detail, however, is agreed upon only in approximate terms: the price at which the proposed issue will be sold to the public. The price of the proposed securities will determine the proceeds available to the corporation. Therefore, the corporation officials at the negotiation conference will not know exactly the amount of the funds raised by the proposed distribution. The approximation of the amount, however, will usually be sufficient for the corporation's planning. The decision on price is often postponed until a few days before the issue is actually put on sale.

After agreement is reached, a letter is prepared by the investment banking house and sent to the corporation. This letter sets forth in detail the understanding between the corporation and the house with respect to the proposed issue of securities. The letter serves as notice that the investment banking house is committed with respect to its agreed responsibilities relative to the issue of securities.

The Registration Statement The Securities Act of 1933 requires that, with certain exceptions, all corporations distributing securities to the general public in interstate commerce and in an amount of $300,000 or more file a statement with the Securities and Exchange Commission.[2] The specific information demanded by the act is given in Chapter 17. In this connection, it is sufficient to say that the statement must contain all the facts necessary to a prudent man in making an investment decision. If any statement of fact is incorrect or if any material information is omitted as the result of a willful intention on the part of the officers or directors, they may be held criminally liable for the misstatement or omission. Futhermore, this liability extends to directors who may not have signed the registration statement, to the investment banking house managing the distribution of securities, and to any consultants or experts aiding in the preparation of the statement. It is probably small wonder that registration statements tend to be long (some are more than 100 pages). In order to avoid the charge of willful withholding of facts, the persons preparing a registration statement tend to be verbose. Much information is usually included in registration statements which is not really necessary, but is put in just to be safe. As a matter of fact, the Securities and Exchange Commission generally does not institute criminal proceedings in the event that a registration statement appears to be faulty. In such cases the statement is returned to the corporation officers with a note stating the omissions or deficiencies in the original statement. The additional information required at the request of the S.E.C. is then filed in the form of an amendment to the original statement.

The S.E.C. is not concerned with the degree of risk to the investor in purchasing securities. The securities may be highly speculative common stocks of brand new corporations or mortgage bonds of old and conservative public utilities. In approving a registration statement, the S.E.C. merely attempts to insure that the prospective purchaser of securities will be reasonably well informed if he reads the prospectus derived from the registration statement.

---

[2] Exempt issues include those of federal, state, and local governments, banks, savings and loan companies, insurance companies, and certificates issued by receivers in bankruptcy.

The Prospectus At the time that the registration statement is drawn up, a *prospectus,* which is a summary of the registration statement, is prepared. Being a summary, it is shorter than the registration statement, although it is often not much shorter. The shorter prospectuses run about twenty pages, while longer ones will be fifty pages or more. A prospectus, however, designed for securities that are exempt from the registration require‑ ment of the S.E.C. may be very brief. For example, the prospectus describing the common stock offering of the Allstates Life Insurance Company of Texas consisted of a four-page pamphlet: the cover page, two pages of pictures and biographical descriptions of the directors, and a highly summarized balance sheet. The cover page of a prospectus is shown in Fig. 15-3.

Although registration statements are public information and may be read by anyone in the reading rooms of the S.E.C., few people take the time and expense to do so. Photostatic copies of the statements are available at moderate cost and are purchased by some institutional investors. The prospectus, on the other hand, is printed and widely distributed for most issues. In general, the prospectus is written in less technical language than that used to prepare the registration statement, so that it can be understood by the average investor. A copy of the prospectus must be offered to every buyer at the time a solicitation is made to purchase the securities.

In order to speed the sale of securities when they are offered for sale at the expiration of the waiting period imposed by the S.E.C. requirements, a preliminary prospectus is usually prepared. This contains about the same information that is contained in the regular prospectus, with the exception of the price at which the securities are to be sold to the public. In addition, the preliminary prospectus must not contain any promise or statement indicating that the securities will actually be offered for sale, for the reason that there is always the possibility that the S.E.C. will disapprove the preliminary statement or require extensive modification of it before the securities can be sold.

As an aid to marketing the issue, the investment banking house will generally place advertisements in financial newspapers. Such advertisements give little more information than the name of the issuing corporation, the number of shares of stocks or bonds to be sold, and a list of the principal underwriting firms handling the issue. If the advertisement is to be run after the completion of the waiting period imposed by the S.E.C., it may also state the price at which the securities may be bought. Because such an advertisement contains very little information, it is popularly known as a "tombstone" advertisement.

The Underwriting Syndicate The investment banking house that conducts the primary investigation of a proposed security issue, thereby being the "originator" of the issue, will act as the sole underwriter only in distribu-

1,300,000 Shares

The Southern Company

Common Stock

($5 Par Value)

THESE SECURITIES HAVE NOT BEEN APPROVED OR DISAPPROVED BY THE
SECURITIES AND EXCHANGE COMMISSION NOR HAS THE COMMISSION
PASSED UPON THE ACCURACY OR ADEQUACY OF THIS PROSPECTUS.
ANY REPRESENTATION TO THE CONTRARY IS A CRIMINAL OFFENSE.

	Price to Public(1)	Underwriting Discounts(1)	Proceeds to Company (2)
Per Share	$35.50	$0.67	$34.83
Total	$46,150,000	$871,000	$45,279,000

(1) The Company has agreed to indemnify the several Underwriters against certain civil liabilities, including liabilities under the Securities Act of 1933.

(2) Before deduction of expenses estimated at $148,090.

It is expected that delivery of the Stock, in definitive form, will be made in New York, N. Y., on or about February 11, 1959.

Among the Underwriters named herein are:

Eastman Dillon, Union Securities & Co.   **Blyth & Co., Inc.**

Equitable Securities Corporation

Bear, Stearns & Co.   **Francis I. duPont & Co.**   **R. W. Pressprich & Co.**

Johnston, Lemon & Co.   **Shields & Company**   **G. H. Walker & Co.**

The Johnson, Lane, Space Corporation   **McDonnell & Co.**
Incorporated

F. S. Smithers & Co.   **Stroud & Company**   **Sutro Bros. & Co.**
Incorporated

The date of this Prospectus is February 4, 1959.

Fig. 15-3   *The cover page of a prospectus.*

tions that are relatively small. If the issue is large, a syndicate of underwriters will be formed by the originating house. The number of underwriters in a large issue may run well above two or three hundred. The purpose of forming a syndicate of investment houses is to spread the risk of an unsuccessful sale, which could bankrupt a house handling the issue alone. The syndicate so formed exists for the purpose of underwriting a single issue. Each time a new issue is to be marketed, a new syndicate is formed. In forming a syndicate, the number of banking houses invited to join is roughly proportionate to the size of the issue. There is, naturally, an eagerness on the part of investment banking houses to participate in the distribution of those securities where the risk is small and where the issuing corporation is highly regarded. In forming a syndicate to distribute a popular issue, the originator must select the other investment banking houses with care. Invitations to join syndicates tend to be reciprocal. In other words, the originating investment house will issue invitations to houses that offered invitations to them in previous distributions. Sometimes the size of the underwriting syndicate appears to be larger than necessary to spread the risk. In such cases, probably a larger number of investment banking houses are issued invitations than are considered necessary to spread the risk in order to maintain cordial business relations with as large a group as possible. Generally, just before filing the registration statement with the S.E.C., the originating investment banking house issues the invitations, which are usually tendered by phone or telegram, and acceptance or rejection by each is expected within a day or two. After the registration statement has been filed with the S.E.C., copies of it are sent to each member of the syndicate along with copies of the agreement among underwriters and other contracts covering the underwriting of the issue. Typically, the originator subscribes to between 5 and 10 per cent of the issue to be sold, offering smaller portions to the other members of the syndicate. For example, the originating house (Morgan Stanley and Company) of a $150 million debenture bond issue of General Motors Corporation, marketed in 1954, subscribed to $8,800,000 of the issue. The rest of the issue was distributed among 234 investment banking houses, with each subscribing to between $100,000 and $900,000 in bonds.

Marketing the Issue   The investment banking houses distributing an issue work on a very small margin, frequently 1 per cent or even less in the case of a large issue of bonds. In order to reduce the risk involved in operating on such a small margin, the members of the underwriting syndicate attempt to distribute the issue as quickly as possible. If an issue sells slowly, there is danger that the underwriters may have to sell it at a price lower than planned. Since even a small reduction in selling price wipes out the entire profit on an issue, every effort is used to speed up the process of distribution of securities. One means of providing rapid distribution is by forming a *selling group,* which consists of securities dealers and brokers in various parts of the country. The number of such dealers included in the selling group is usually three or four times the number of underwriters participating in an issue. A diagrammatic representation of the distribution of an issue is shown in Fig. 15-4. The members of a selling group do not bear

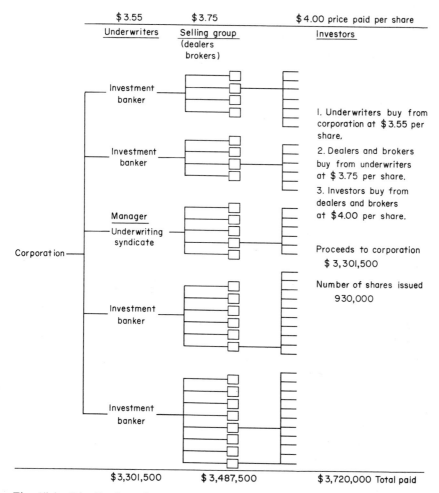

Fig. 15-4 *Distribution diagram of an issue of 930,000 shares of common stock.*

any risk of unsuccessful sale as do the underwriters of the issue. Securities remaining unsold by the selling group are returned to the investment bankers underwriting the issue, and must be sold by them.

Those underwriters selling directly to the investing public receive the full spread of the price paid to the issuing corporation and the price paid by the investors to the underwriters. Those securities that are given to members of the selling group are sold to them at a slight discount from the price paid by the public, which enables the public to purchase at the same price from either the underwriters or the selling group.   One prospectus gives the terms of distribution by the selling group as follows:

> The Underwriters propose to offer the Debentures, subject to certain conditions, in part directly to the public at the initial public offering price set forth under "Price to Public" in the table on the cover page hereof, and in part, through the Representatives, to certain purchasers at such price and to certain security dealers at such price less a concession of not in excess of one-half of 1%, out of which a concession of not in excess of one-eighth of 1% may be allowed to any dealer who is a member of the National Association of Securities Dealers, Inc.   The public offering price and concessions to dealers may be varied after the initial public offering, by reason of changes in general market conditions, upon determination of the Representatives.[3]

Although the Securities Act forbids a formal offer of securities to members of the selling group until after the designated waiting period, the underwriters can have an informal understanding with members indicating the number of securities that will be offered them after the registration statement has become effective.   In the meantime, the members can inform their own customers of the forthcoming issue by means of the preliminary prospectus, which is distributed to the selling group.   However, no offers to sell may be made until the effective date of the registration statement, usually at the completion of the normal twenty-day waiting period required by S.E.C. regulations.   Just prior to the effective date, the originating investment banking house and the corporation issuing the securities reach an agreement on the price at which the securities are to be offered to the public.   The other members of the underwriting syndicate are notified, and all members of the syndicate then sign "The Agreement Among Underwriters" to send to the originating house, which is now called the manager of the underwriting syndicate.   A purchase agreement is then signed by the corporation issuing the securities and by the manager of the syndicate.   At this point, the preliminary prospectus is discarded, and the regular prospectus, containing the names of the underwriting syndicate and the price of the securities to the public, is distributed to all members of the underwriting syndicate, the members of the selling group, and the investors considering purchase of the issue.

On the effective date, the manager of the underwriting syndicate sends by telegram a formal offer of securities according to the preliminary agreement between the dealers comprising the selling group and the manager of the underwriting syndicate.   The members of the selling group are expected to indicate their acceptance by telegram within a few hours.   The terms of the selling contract are then confirmed by a signed contract sent through the mails.   Actual selling can then proceed, with delivery of the securities to be made later.   After a period lasting usually one or two weeks, the members of the underwriting group are required to make payment for the securities in the amount that they have subscribed.

---

[3] Prospectus of Household Finance Corporation, $40 million 5 per cent sinking fund debentures due 1982, dated July 1, 1957, p. 22.

The date on which the payment for the securities purchased from the issuing corporation is to be made is called the closing date for the issue. In every distribution of securities, it is the hope of the underwriting group that the entire issue will be sold by the closing date. Even if the issue is not sold by that time, the members of the underwriting syndicate are obligated to make payment in full for the amount of their contractual commitment. The manager of the underwriting group then usually draws a single check to the order of the corporation issuing the securities, and the check is formally exchanged for the securities delivered by the corporation manager. If the securities have not been sold by the closing date, those underwriters that have not sold the amount for which they have subscribed are nevertheless still obligated to purchase that amount. In this circumstance, the underwriters generally borrow from commercial banks the amount necessary to make payment for the securities purchased, with the securities themselves pledged as a guarantee for the bank loan. Every effort is, of course, made to sell the securities as quickly as possible, even selling them at a loss, if necessary, in order to complete a rapid distribution.

METHODS OF CONTRACTING FOR THE SERVICES OF INVESTMENT BANKERS

The Bid Plan   Under this plan, the securities to be sold by a corporation are advertised for sale, and investment banking houses then make bids. They are either in the form of a price for the securities issued or of a dividend rate or an interest rate. If the bids are on the basis of price, generally the highest bid is the one that is accepted by the corporation. If the bids are in the form of interest or dividend rates, the lowest interest or dividend is the one that is accepted. Each bid may be for the entire issue or for only a part. If the bids are for only a part of a large issue, they are ranked from the most favorable to the least, and the awards are made through the number of bids necessary to clear the issue. In addition to investment banking houses there are sometimes financial institutions, such as pension funds, insurance companies, and commercial banks, bidding for an issue. Such institutions place bids for securities to add to their own investment portfolio rather than to resell them to the investing public. The advantage of competitive bidding in distributing securities is apparent. It brings competition among financial institutions and investment houses to aid the corporation issuing securities to raise money on terms most favorable to itself. Competitive bidding has long been used in the distribution of state and local bonds. In the field of railroad securities, the rules of the Interstate Commerce Commission have required since 1926 the distribution of equipment trust certificates by means of the bid plan. In 1944, the Interstate Commerce Commission required all debt issues of railroads to be distributed on the bid basis. In 1941, the Securities and Exchange Commission issued Rule U-50, which required all holding companies and their subsidiaries that were subject to the regulations of the S.E.C. to use competitive bidding as a means of distribution of their securities. Although exceptions to this rule are sometimes granted by the S.E.C., about 90 per cent of all bonds distributed by public utility companies are sold under the bid plan. Competitive bidding is not required by regulation for industrial corporations.

The bid plan, which is not often employed by industrial corporations, is primarily restricted to railroad and public utility financing, where regulations require its use. There are several reasons why the bid plan has not been more extensively adopted. For one, its use has been opposed by the Investment Bankers Association, which questions the validity of the argument in favor of competitive bidding. The association denies the charge that there are monopolistic tendencies in the investment banking industry, that investment bankers dominate the policy of railroad and utility companies, and that genuine bargaining is absent between the corporations issuing securities and the investment banking houses marketing them.

There is also the charge that in competitive bidding the close advisory relationship between a client corporation and an investment banking house marketing its securities is lost. In competitive bidding the corporation must decide for itself when to raise money by selling securities, how much money to raise, and the type of security to distribute. In other words, companies that engage in competitive bidding require financial officers of wider experience and greater financial sophistication than is needed by companies that engage in negotiation with a single investment banker. In their opposition to competitive bidding, investment bankers place considerable stress upon the importance and benefit of a permanent relationship between a corporation and its investment banker. A corporation's frequent change of investment banking house is considered by investment bankers to be as unwise as a change of commercial bank or law firm. Those who oppose the practice of competitive bidding for securities also contend that it places an undue emphasis on price rather than on the quality of the investment banking service. The widely diversified character of companies in the industrial field, compared to utility or railroad companies, makes the competitive bid plan seem impractical for industrial companies.

The Purchase Plan Under this plan, the investment banking house assumes the role of security merchant, and purchases the securities from the corporation at an agreed price. Under competitive bidding, the corporation issuing the securities does not know exactly the amount that it will receive or the cost to it in terms of interest or dividends of the particular financing until all the bids are received and the most favorable bid accepted. Under the purchase plan, the amount to be realized from the sale of the securities and the cost to the corporation in terms of interest or dividends are decided in negotiation between the investment banking house and the corporation issuing the securities.

The Commission Plan   Under this plan, the investment banking house or syndicate of houses acts as a selling agent for the corporation rather than as a merchant purchasing the issue for resale to investors.   Payment for services of distribution in this case is not in the form of a profit from the sale of the securities but in the form of a commission for each share or each bond sold.   It is used both in the sale of highly speculative common stock and in the sale of conservative bonds.   Where it is used to distribute common stock of a corporation unknown to the public, the cost of underwriting the issue may be so great that the directors of the corporation would prefer to assume the risk of an unsuccessful issue themselves in order to reduce the cost of distribution.   In some cases, a corporation unknown to the public may find that the "best efforts" plan of distribution is the only one which will interest investment bankers.   The Lexa Oil Company, for example, engaged the services of an investment banking house to sell common stock on a best efforts basis at a price to the public of 20¢ per share, with a commission to the investment banker of 5¢ a share for each share sold.   At the other extreme, the directors of a corporation may be convinced that an issue of securities will prove so popular with investors that there is no need to have it underwritten by investment bankers.   In this case, the best efforts basis of distribution is used to decrease the cost of distribution by eliminating the underwriting fee.   If the corporation directors know that a sizable portion of an issue will be purchased by institutional investors, they may feel that it is cheaper to distribute the issue on a best efforts basis.   Of course, it must be remembered that if the issue is unsuccessful, the corporation may find that at the end of the contract period a sizable portion of the issue remains unsold.   In such an event, the corporation would receive a smaller amount of money than it had expected to receive.   In the case of an unsuccessful issue, the underwriters would lose nothing except the indirect expenses incurred in the distribution of the issue.   Sometimes a mixed understanding is used.   In such a case the underwriters contract to purchase and resell a fixed portion of an issue, and to use their best efforts in distributing the rest.

PRIVATE PLACEMENT

During the 1930's, a corporation, notably in the public utilities field, sometimes negotiated a sale of securities directly with a single investor or a few investors.   In this case the investors were financial institutions with the capacity to purchase large blocks of securities.   This practice came to be known as *private placement,* which can be defined as the sale of an entire issue of securities by a corporation directly to one or a few financial institutions.   Although private placement is undertaken occasionally by industrial or railroad corporations, the bulk of such placements are done by public utilities.   Insurance companies are the most important purchasers, in some years accounting for nine-tenths or more of total purchases.   Other financial institutions purchasing issues of securities directly from corporations include pension funds, trust accounts, and endowment funds.   Private placement of securities is largely confined to bond issues, with stock issues accounting for approximately 5 per cent of the total.   Private placement of bonds was rare prior to 1933, increased during the depression, and increased still further following World War II.   Since the end of that war, of the total volume of bond financing, approximately half has been placed with financial institutions and half distributed to the public by investment bankers.

The private placement of securities is feasible only for large, well-known corporations having a high credit standing.   For such corporations the chief attraction of private placement is the reduction in financing costs.   In many cases the services of an investment banker can be dispensed with entirely, thereby saving the costs of distribution.   In those instances where an investment banking house is retained to negotiate between the corporation and the institution purchasing the securities, the fee charged by the investment banking house is relatively small.   Legal costs and printing costs are also reduced in private placement.

Another attraction of private placement is the reduction of risk.   No matter how carefully a public distribution of securities is planned, there is still an element of risk that the security will not be sold.   On the other hand, in a private placement there is no risk that the issue will not be sold.   There may be uncertainty during the process of negotiation between the corporation and the financial institution, but once the agreement has been reached the entire issue is sold without any other selling effort.

If a corporation sells a bond issue to the general public, it is usually difficult to secure the assent of the bondholders to any later change in the terms of the bond contract, because the agreement of many individuals is required.   If only one or a few financial institutions hold the bonds, their assent to any reasonable change in the bond contract is much easier to obtain, a factor that is emphasized in Chapter 20 in the context of long-term financial planning.   Private placement makes financing more flexible in meeting unforeseen contingencies arising during the life of the issue.

Still another advantage of the private placement of securities lies in the avoidance of registration requirements.   There is no need to prepare a prospectus, to file a registration statement with the S.E.C., or to wait twenty days for the registration to become effective before selling the issue.   Furthermore, the officers and directors of the issuing corporation are not liable for misstatements or incomplete data as they are in preparing a prospectus and registration statement for a public sale of securities.

On the other hand, there are some disadvantages to private placement. A public sale of securities generally provides favorable publicity for the issuing corporation. If the corporation wishes to market additional shares of the same issue or if it wishes to market a new issue similar to the one just marketed, it will generally find in a public sale of securities a body of investors favorably disposed to purchasing additional shares in the corporation. In other words, through a public sale of securities the corporation acquires an investment standing. Another disadvantage to private placement lies in the absence of an active market for the securities of the corporation. If, for example, a corporation has its bonds only in the portfolios of institutional investors, the absence of an active market for the securities makes it difficult for the corporation in its later financing efforts to determine at what price future securities may be sold. The absence of an active market for the securities privately placed by the corporation prevents it from buying back a portion of the issue during those periods when the market price might fall below the original issue price. A publicly distributed bond or preferred stock permits the corporation to take advantage of periods of low prices to purchase some of the securities for retirement.

DIRECT SALE OF SECURITIES TO THE PUBLIC

If the corporation finds itself unable to secure the services of an investment banker, it may be forced to sell securities itself in order to raise funds. Such a situation may be encountered by a small, locally owned corporation that has few prospects of collecting anything more than local investor interest. In such a case, the financial officer of the corporation and the board of directors must decide on the type of security to be sold, the total size of the issue, and the price at which it is to be marketed to the public. If the issue amounts to less than $300,000, it is unnecessary to register it with the S.E.C. It is likely that the issue would have to be registered with the State Commissioner of Securities, whose requirements under most state laws are considerably more lenient than those of the S.E.C. After complying with the legal requirements for distribution of securities within the state, the issue is usually advertised by the corporation. The advertisement probably will state that investors interested in purchasing the issue may write to the offices of the corporation or visit them to secure a copy of the prospectus. If the company employs product salesmen, they usually double as securities salesmen. The distribution of an issue of securities directly to the public through the efforts of officers and employees of the company may appear to entail little cost. This is usually because the time spent by the officers of the company in preparing the issue for sale and the efforts of the salesmen or officers of the company in contacting the public and trying to induce investors to purchase are usually not measured in terms of dollars nor charged against the cost of distribution of the securities. If the cost of the time spent by company officials in marketing the issue were calculated, they undoubtedly would appreciate that selling securities takes time and money. If a company has decided to distribute securities directly to the public in order to save the fees charged by an investment banking house, the company officials may discover that it is cheaper to retain an investment banker to distribute the securities than to attempt to market them directly.

CURRENT STATUS OF THE INVESTMENT BANKING INDUSTRY

In our economy the function of investment ranks equally in importance with that of consumption.   Investment involves the channeling of savings either directly or through financial institutions, such as banks and insurance companies, into expanding and improving our productive capacity.   To some extent, the importance of investment banking has been reduced during the last twenty years, partly due to the increasing reliance on internal financing that is characteristic of many companies, and partly to the increased importance of private placement of securities in raising funds for industrial purposes.   One result of this has been that the range of functions of investment banking have expanded.   It is no longer confined, as it largely was in an earlier age, to the distribution of securities for corporations.   The investment banker serves as a "finder" in locating financial institutions seeking to purchase large issues of securities and corporations willing to issue their securities on such a basis.   He acts as a catalytic agent in promoting mergers and consolidations.   Investment bankers serve on the boards of directors of many companies, thereby providing their experience and counsel to the companies that they serve.   They aid in the reorganization of bankrupt corporations and serve as a guide to small corporations during their early critical years of existence.   Because the industry of investment banking is highly competitive, it changes with the times to provide solutions for new financial problems facing corporations.   Although an ancient industry, investment banking shows considerable vigor and adaptability to new demands and conditions.   *Fortune* magazine has said of one of the large investment banking houses, Lehman Brothers, as follows:

> Indeed it would be a good bet that long before this second century in Lehman's history is completed, Lehman Brothers will have developed many radically new investment techniques to keep pace with an era of profound technical, social, and economic change.   For whenever the technical skill of the scientist creates some new tool for man's use, the banking skill of a Rothschild, a Morgan, or a Lehman is required to bring it to economic life.[4]

Questions

1. What is the primary function of investment bankers?   How does it differ from the services of commercial bankers?
2. How does the cost per bond or share vary with the size of the issue?   What are the reasons for this?
3. What are the expenses that must be covered in a distribution of securities to the general public through investment bankers?
4. Define underwriting as it applies to securities distributions.

----

4 T. A. Wide, "The House of Lehman," *Fortune*, December 1957.

5. What is the nature of the market protection provided by investment bankers in connection with a distribution of stocks or bonds?

6. How does an investment banker investigate the corporation before undertaking a distribution of securities?

7. Describe the negotiations between corporation officers and investment bankers prior to distribution of securities.

8. Registration statements filed with the S.E.C. tend to be lengthy. Why?

9. What is the prospectus? What is its purpose?

10. How is an underwriting syndicate organized?

11. Why does it appear that the number of underwriters in a syndicate is often larger than necessary to spread the risk?

12. Sometimes the price at which a bond issue is sold to the public is only one per cent higher than the price at which the syndicate purchases the bonds from the corporation. How can investment bankers work on such a small margin?

13. What is a selling group? What function does it perform in the distribution of an issue?

14. At what point in the distribution of a securities issue is the decision made as to the price? Why?

15. What is the bid plan of using the services of investment bankers? Why is it used more often in financing public utility rather than industrial companies?

16. What is the purchase plan? What are its advantages to the corporation over the bid plan? What are its disadvantages?

17. Describe the advantages and disadvantages of the commission plan in distributing securities.

18. What is meant by private placement of securities? How does it differ from a public distribution?

19. Under what circumstances might a corporation attempt directly to distribute securities rather than use investment bankers?

20. "To some extent the importance of investment banking in raising funds for corporations has declined." Explain.

Selected Readings

Clark, F. G., and R. S. Rimanoczy, *Where the Money Comes From,* D. Van Nostrand Company, Inc., Princeton, N.J., 1961.

Facts You Should Know About Investment Banking, Better Business Bureau, Educational Division, 1947.

"The New Flurry in Private Placement," *Business Week,* September 29, 1962.

Prochnow, H. V., *American Financial Institutions,* Prentice-Hall, Inc., Englewood Cliffs, N.J., 1951, Chaps. 14 and 15.

The Role of the Investment Banker in Arranging Private Financing, The Investment Bankers Association of America, 1961.

16

Trading in Securities

THE SECURITIES MARKET

THE SECURITIES MARKET comprises all the places where buyers and sellers of stocks and bonds or their representatives undertake transactions involving the sale of securities. Some are organized with a trading floor open only to members. The New York Stock Exchange, the American Exchange, the Mid-West Stock Exchange, and the Pacific Coast Stock Exchange are leading examples. The over-the-counter market, on the other hand, is nationwide, with buyers and sellers contacting each other by telephone, telegram, or letter. Securities exchanges are older than the Industrial Revolution. The Royal Exchange, for example, opened in London in 1570, and aided in the financing of trading companies, voyages of discovery, and other ventures.

The New York Stock Exchange Prior to 1792, the securities market in the United States was an unorganized one. Persons having stocks or bonds to sell generally had to seek purchasers by their own efforts. On May 17, 1792, however, twenty-four merchants in securities met to organize the first formal exchange in the United States. Meeting under the branches of a buttonwood tree in lower Manhattan, only a few blocks away from the present location of the New York Stock Exchange, they created the Exchange. The bulk of trading was in issues of the newly created federal government of the United States, securities which were then called government stocks but are now called government bonds. In addition to these, a few issues of insurance companies and commercial banks were traded. The stock of the United States Bank, chartered by the federal government in 1791, the stock of the Bank of North America, and the stock of the Bank of New York were among the issues actively bought and sold. Later, as the exchange expanded, securities of canal, mining, and manufacturing companies were added. When railroad companies came into existence, their securities were also traded.

The New York Stock Exchange is a voluntary association providing a convenient place for its members to trade. The exchange itself does not buy or sell securities.

The membership is limited, and the only way a person can become a member is to buy a seat on the exchange (i.e., membership from an existing member). The price of a seat varies according to the volume of stock market activity. The highest price was $625,000, paid in 1929, and the lowest in recent decades was $17,000, paid in 1942. Any American citizen twenty-one years of age or older may purchase a membership provided his character, integrity, and reputation are satisfactory to the membership committee.

Most of the exchange members are partners or employees of brokerage houses and execute the orders to buy or sell for the customers of their firms. Some of the small brokerage firms employ a single member; the larger firms have several floor operators. Some of the members, called *floor brokers,* spend most of their time assisting the *commission brokers* employed by brokerage firms in executing orders at those times when commission brokers have too many orders to handle themselves. Some members are *odd lot dealers.* Since the unit of trading, with a few exceptions, is 100 shares each, the odd lot dealers provide the service of buying or selling shares in units of one to ninety-nine. They carry an inventory of stocks, thus providing a market for purchases and sales of less than 100 shares. They will adjust their inventories in various stocks as needed by purchasing and selling in 100 share lots, known as *round lots.*

Another type, the *specialist,* deals in a selected group of stocks, stationing himself at one of the trading posts on the exchange to do his work. He buys and sells either for his own account or as agent for the commission brokers employed by the stock exchange firms. One of the important responsibilities of a specialist is to maintain an orderly market in the securities he specializes in. To prevent a runaway rise or a catastrophic drop in the prices of securities, the specialist judiciously places buy or sell orders for his own account to stabilize the market. A few of the brokers specialize entirely in the bonds listed for trading on the New York Stock Exchange. The bond room is separate from the main trading room in the exchange, and activity is not nearly so hectic as it sometimes is on the stock exchange floor.

Finally, a small number of members, the *floor traders,* are persons who do not carry out orders for customers but buy and sell on their own account. Because they have no commission to pay in executing orders, they can profit from very small changes in the price of stocks, in conjunction with a rapid turnover of the stocks that they own. For example, they will purchase a stock at 10 A.M. and perhaps sell it a half an hour or an hour later at a slightly higher price. Although their activity has been condemned by some as being needless speculation, it does have the effect of broadening the market for securities.

The primary function of the exchange is to permit brokers more effectively to execute the orders of their customers to buy and sell securities. Suppose, for example, a customer in New Orleans wishes to buy 100 shares of Du Pont stock. Most often the order is given *at the market,* obligating the brokerage firm to purchase the stock at the lowest price available at the time the order is executed on the floor of the exchange. The New Orleans office will send the customer's order by private wire to its New York office, where the order is transmitted by phone to a clerk on the exchange floor. The phone clerk in turn transmits the order to the commission broker employed by the firm, who goes to the trading post where Du Pont stock is traded to execute the order. He may find very active trading of the stock, leading him either to engage in the auction, waiting briefly if he feels the market trend is downward, or place his bid immediately if he thinks the trend is up. If there is no activity in Du Pont stock at the moment, the broker will purchase 100 shares from the specialist at the lowest price then attainable. The details of the transaction are reported back to the customer in New Orleans within a few minutes after the order is placed. Several days later, he will receive his certificate of Du Pont stock. If the customer in New Orleans had placed an order to purchase less than 100 shares of Du Pont stock, the order would have been relayed to the floor of the stock exchange as before. However, the shares would have been purchased from the inventory of the odd lot trader dealing in Du Pont stock. The price per share in this case would be fractionally higher than the price per share for a round lot transaction.

The American Stock Exchange and Regional Stock Exchange   The American Stock Exchange was formerly the Curb Market, so-named because from the Civil War era until June 27, 1921, the members comprising the exchange operated out in the street in New York City. The organization and operation of the American Stock Exchange is similar in all respects to that of the New York Stock Exchange. No securities, however, that are listed on the New York Stock Exchange are also listed on the American Stock Exchange. The latter has listing requirements less severe than those of the New York Stock Exchange, although the character of the requirements are the same. For the most part, the companies listed on the American Stock Exchange are smaller, younger, and less well known than those listed on the New York Stock Exchange. In addition to the two stock exchanges in New York City, there are those in the following cities: Boston, Cincinnati, Detroit, New Orleans, Pittsburgh, Salt Lake City, Spokane, Colorado Springs, Honolulu, Richmond (Virginia), Chicago, Philadelphia-Baltimore, and San Francisco-Los Angeles. Each exchange serves its own region, listing mostly stocks of local interest, although some securities listed on the New York or American Stock Exchange are also listed on some of the regional ones. The organization and operation of the regional exchanges are patterned on those of the New York Stock Exchange, but listing requirements are less severe. Often a company is listed first on one of the regional exchanges, and, as it grows in importance, is listed later on the American Stock Exchange, and finally on the New York Stock Exchange after still more growth.

The Over-the-Counter Market Stocks that are not traded on the organized security exchanges are often sold *over-the-counter*. This market exists anywhere that stocks and bonds are sold in the United States. It consists of dealers who maintain an inventory of unlisted stocks and bonds and are always ready to buy and sell securities, making a profit on the difference between the buying and selling price. In this respect, dealers in the over-the-counter market are somewhat similar to dealers in used cars. Both maintain inventories, and both stand ready to buy and sell. In the over-the-counter market, the number of securities that are traded actively numbers about 3,000. Many more are traded intermittently, perhaps between 30,000 and 40,000 issues. The stocks of most banks, insurance companies, mutual funds, and companies having fewer than 2,500 stockholders are traded over the counter. Although federal government bonds are listed on the New York Stock Exchange, most trading in federal securities is over the counter. This is also true of corporation bonds, even those bonds of large, well-known companies that have stocks listed on the securities exchanges.

If an investor wishes to purchase some bonds or shares of stock that are not listed on an exchange, he places the order with a stock broker just as he does with an order to purchase a listed security. If the broker is also a dealer in the desired security, he will sell directly to his customer. If the broker does not have an inventory of the requested security, he will telephone one of the dealers that does maintain an inventory in the desired stock or bond. Although there might be some haggling over the price between the buyer and the seller of securities, it is not common. If the price asked by a dealer for securities carried in inventory is too high, he will find sales low and will reduce his price to increase his inventory turnover. If he finds the inventory of a particular security being depleted by an excess of purchase orders over sell orders, the dealer will raise the price of his securities. The price at which the more actively traded issues are bought and sold are quoted in the financial sections of the major newspapers. Lest some investors take the quoted prices as actual offers to buy or sell, *The Wall Street Journal* places this cautioning statement above its listings of over-the-counter securities: "These bid and asked prices, from the National Association of Securities Dealers Incorporated, do not represent actual transactions. They are a guide to the range within which the securities could have been sold (indicated by the 'Bid') or bought (indicated by the 'Asked') at the time of compilation."

There are over 4,000 dealers in the over-the-counter market, including commercial banks handling federal and municipal bonds and investment banking houses dealing in securities. Some dealers specialize in bonds, some in the stocks of insurance companies, and some in mutual fund securities.   Others deal almost exclusively in speculative issues of new, untried corporations.   The large brokerage houses having memberships in the major securities exchanges usually have a department handling over-the-counter trading.

CONTRIBUTIONS OF THE SECURITIES MARKETS
TO THE FINANCIAL SYSTEM

Directing the Flow of Capital   The stock exchanges are considered by many to be a very sensitive barometer of business activity.   Events or rumors unfavorable to business tend to drag the market down.   The expectation of increased profits, the hope of favorable tax legislation, or the fear of inflation tend to pull the market up.   The stock exchanges are often called the consensus of informed opinion on future business developments.   Because of the rapidity with which orders to buy or sell can be completed on the stock exchange, any shift in the prevailing opinions of investors is immediately reflected on the stock exchanges.

Whether the stock market is going up or down as a whole, many individual securities do not follow the prevailing trend.   While the stock market as a whole may be rising rapidly, securities of railroad companies may show little tendency to rise.   During a period when the stock market is declining, some industries may remain steady or even show a tendency to rise.   The stock market, in other words, reflects the changing profit prospects and growth potentialities of different industries as they are estimated by investors.   The action of the market, available for all to see, helps to guide the flow of investment funds toward those industries that show more favorable prospects.   Although the rise in the market price of securities does not immediately or directly benefit the company financially, since prices on the securities exchanges represent transactions between investors and not transactions between a company and investors, a price rise in securities considerably aids the company in any attempt to raise funds by selling securities.   Therefore, the stock market aids the financing efforts of those companies with promising prospects and makes more difficult the financing of those with poor prospects.   If we can assume that those companies with promising growth are most deserving of investors' attention, we can conclude that the stock exchanges serve to channel investment funds in the most socially useful directions, benefiting efficient, dynamic companies at the expense of less efficient, sluggish ones.   It must be emphasized that since the markets deal in securities already in the hands of investors, the flow of funds to dynamic, vigorous companies is indirect.   The prices at which securities are traded serves as a barometer of investor sentiment, which would indicate to company directors whether it will be easy or difficult to raise funds through the sale of securities at prices favorable to the company.

Aid in New Financing   Having a market place where investors can buy and sell securities is of considerable importance to a company in raising additional capital for any modernization or expansion program.   For one thing, the costs of underwriting an issue of securities are lessened if the issue is already listed for trading on one of the major exchanges.   Investors, knowing that listing on an exchange provides a ready place for liquidation of their securities should the occasion arise, are much more receptive to the selling efforts of investment bankers in marketing an issue.   If a security is listed, the selling problems of the investment banking house are eased and the risk of an unsuccessful sale is less.   As a result, investment banking houses are more willing to market a listed issue for a corporation at low cost than an unlisted one.   Furthermore, listing broadens the market for additional issues of a security.   Not only is the security attractive to the investor wishing to purchase and hold for a long time, but also the speculator is attracted to the security, confident in his ability to liquidate promptly his investment in the active market on the exchange.   Therefore, listing helps raise the price of additional issues of a security being sold.

An Active Market for Investors   Buying and selling in a security tends to concentrate on those exchanges where the security is listed for trading. The volume of trading of a particular security on an exchange is far greater than the volume of trading at any one spot, if trading in the security were scattered all over the United States.   This concentration of trading is particularly valuable to those investors who have a large amount of securities to sell or wish to purchase a large amount.   Securities exchanges also are responsible for a steadier market: by concentrating purchases and sales of securities, the market price is not likely to be upset by relatively large orders to buy or sell as would be the case if trading were thin and widely scattered. The marketability of a security on one exchange or on several exchanges is therefore greatly enhanced.   Investors can more easily dispose of their investments, should they need the cash, with reasonable assurance that individual transactions will have little effect on the market price of the securities.

Trading on the stock exchanges is recorded by a ticker tape, which permits the immediate publication of prices throughout the nation.   Each day the major newspapers of the country publish reports of the opening price, the highest price, the lowest price, and the final price at which sales of each major stock took place on the stock exchange the previous day. Brokerage houses can provide an interested investor with up-to-the-minute reports of the prices of securities on the major exchanges at any time during the trading day.   Purchases and sales of securities not listed on a major exchange are not reported except by the dealers specializing in the securities.   These prices are also given in the financial sections of the major newspapers.   In most cases, they are less accurate indicators of the prices that the securities could be bought or sold than the prices of actual transactions of securities listed on an exchange.

THE MECHANICS OF TRADING

The most common type of order to buy is "at the market." Such an order specifies that the broker will purchase the security at the lowest price available at the time the purchase order is executed on the exchange. This order is completed in a matter of a few minutes, and the price, unless the market is unusually erratic, will be very close to the price of the previous sale of the stock. An order to sell at the market is completed at the highest price available when the order is executed.

A customer may wish to limit the price at which he wishes his order executed. In the case of a *limit order* to buy, the customer specifies the maximum price he is willing to pay for the security. For example, the customer may place an order to buy 100 shares of North American Aviation stock at $60 a share. When the order was placed, the price of the stock might have been $66 per share. Only if the market price drops to $60 or less, will the customer's order be executed. Such an order may not be executed for a considerable time. Limit orders may be placed for one day, one week, one month, or an indefinite period until countermanded. In the last case, the broker will check with the customer periodically to reconfirm the order. While a limit order to buy is placed below the current market price, the limit order to sell is placed above the current market price. For example, if the current market price for Magnavox common stock is $38 per share, a limit order to sell may be placed at $43 per share. The sale would be made by the broker only if it could be made at $43 per share or higher. According to *The Wall Street Journal,* some limit orders to sell in 1929 were carried on the books of the brokerage houses through the stock market collapse, the depression of the 1930's, the war years of the 1940's, and were finally executed in the 1950's when the rapid rise in the stock market brought stock prices up to the limit price placed a generation earlier.

Another type of order is a *stop loss* order. If Diamond Alkali stock is selling at the market for $50 a share, the customer may wish to limit his loss in the event that the price of the stock should begin to drop. To do so, he could place an order with his broker to sell his holding of Diamond Alkali at a stop loss order of $47. If the price of the stock should decline, reaching $47 a share, the stop loss order would immediately become an order to sell *at the market.* Such an order will prevent a further loss to the customer in the event the price of the stock continued its downward trend. Stop loss orders are frequently placed with brokerage houses by customers who do not have the opportunity or the desire to watch the market daily.

Most customers pay in full for the stock that they purchase, but they can *buy on margin*. If a stock is so bought, part of the purchase price is paid by the customer, and the balance is borrowed by the broker from a commercial bank. The customer in this case does not receive the stock certificate purchased. Instead, the certificate is deposited with the bank making the loan, and serves as security for the loan until such time as the balance is paid.

If a customer is convinced that the price of a stock is bound to fall, he may take advantage of the decline by placing with his broker an order to *sell short*. In an order to sell short, the investor does not have the stock to sell. He arranges with the broker to have the securities borrowed for him in order to complete delivery of the stock sold. The customer placing the order to sell short obligates himself to deliver the shares to the broker at some future date. If the customer's conviction that the price of securities will fall proves accurate, he may complete the transaction by buying the shares in the open market at a lower price than that at which the earlier sale was made. His profit is the difference between the price of the short sale and the price at which the stock was later bought to replace the shares borrowed from the broker. If the price of the stock sold short rises rather than falls, the customer will suffer a loss by having to replace the borrowed stock at a higher price than the price of the short sale. One other use of the short sale can be illustrated by the following example. Suppose a customer takes a three-month trip around the world. While he is in Bombay, he is convinced that he should sell his shares of International Telephone and Telegraph stock. If these shares are in a safe deposit box in a bank in the United States, the customer could not deliver the shares for sale until he reached home. In such a situation, he can wire his broker to sell short the number of shares which he has in his box. After the customer completes his cruise, he can remove his shares from his safe deposit box and deliver them to his broker who borrowed the stock at the time that the sell order was made.

LISTING OF SECURITIES FOR TRADING ON AN EXCHANGE

From 1792 until 1869 there were relatively few stocks that were traded on the New York Stock Exchange, and the procedure of listing was very informal. In 1837, for example, there were only thirty-one issues of stocks and eight issues of government and state bonds traded on the New York Stock Exchange. All that was necessary to add a security to the trading list was for a member of the exchange to move that the issue be added to the list. The motion was then put to a vote, and a majority vote in favor of adding the security was sufficient. Its name was then read by the presiding officer each day, as were the other securities listed, to signal the time allotted during the day for trading in the new security. In 1869, the New York Stock Exchange established its first standards for the listing of new stock. As the years passed, the standards became more numerous and stringent. Eligibility for listing at the present time is based on the company's size, age, demonstration of earning power, distribution of securities, and history of successful operation. Eligibility for listing also requires publicity of those facts necessary to investors in determining whether or not to purchase shares in the company. In particular, this requires that a company with securities listed make available to its stockholders, the exchange, and the general public accurate, up-to-date, and complete financial information. For the corporation to be eligible for listing, it must show average yearly earnings of $1 million or more, a market value of shares outstanding of $10 million or more, and a minimum of 500,000 shares of stock owned by at least 1,500 stockholders. There must not be any undue concentration of outstanding stock in a few hands. The application for listing must include the following:

1. A brief description of the company's business, the products it produces or the services it renders, its date of organization, and a brief biographical sketch of the officers.

2. Financial data, with balance sheets for several years and income statements for the same period in the past. These statements must have been audited by independent reputable auditing firms. Any major contractual arrangements, patent licenses, or leases must be completely explained. Relationships with subsidiary companies or affiliated corporations must be indicated.

3. A copy of the bylaws and charter of the corporation.

4. The amount of stock outstanding and the number of shareholders holding the stock. If there is more than one type of stock, the rights of the various classes must be indicated. The method of conducting annual meetings and the means of voting must be disclosed. The names and amounts of stock held by the largest stockholders must be stated.

5. Approval of the stock certificate form by the stock exchange. The engraving must be of such a quality as to minimize the danger of forging certificates.

6. A registration statement must be filed with and approved by the Securities and Exchange Commission, as explained in Chapter 18.

7. A transfer agent and a registrar acceptable to the stock exchange must be provided by the corporation. Usually, the trust department of one bank is designated as the transfer agent, and the trust department of another bank as the registrar.

ADVANTAGES TO THE CORPORATION OF LISTING

A company's name is given useful publicity when its securities are listed on a major stock exchange. This is of particular value to the company whose goods are sold to the general public, for, as transactions in the company occur on the exchange, the company's name is recorded on the ticker tape and in the financial sections of the nation's newspapers. Constant mention in the stock reports of the larger newspapers increases investors' interest in the securities of the company. This in turn tends to widen the distribution of the company's stock and to increase the number of stockholders. A listed security will receive more attention from investment advisory services than an unlisted one. Through this medium the name of the company is also brought before investors. There is also a prestige value attached to listing on a major exchange, particularly on the New York Stock Exchange, where listing requirements are known to be strict. Some investors refuse to purchase any but listed securities. Also some financial institutions purchasing in large quantities are limited by their charter or by an investment policy adopted by the board of directors or trustees to invest only in stock listed on a major stock exchange.

Since many investors will not purchase a stock unless it is listed on an exchange, listing aids a corporation in its financing efforts. If an issue of securities to be marketed is not already listed, the prospectus frequently states that an application for listing will be made following the distribution of the securities. Listing, or the promise of future listing, aids in the distribution of securities. Because listing increases the number of investors that could be interested in a security, the broader market may make it possible for the shares to be sold at a higher price. As stated earlier, the auction market on an organized exchange accurately reflects the price at which the securities can be sold. In selling additional shares of an issue already listed, the company is largely guided by the market action of the shares on the exchange. Since the price at which additional shares may be successfully distributed can be more confidently determined if the company is listed on an exchange, the underwriting fees charged by investment bankers are generally less. Also, listing could simplify the process of preparing an issue for distribution. For example, most states have laws requiring that all securities offered to residents of the state be registered with a state official. Many of these states, however, exempt from the registration requirements those issues that are listed on the New York Stock Exchange, American Stock Exchange, or one of the regional exchanges. Finally, listing frequently reduces the expenses of legal, accounting, and clerical work involved in distributing an issue.

If a corporation wishes to raise funds by issuing rights to its stockholders (discussed in Chapter 18), listing could further the success of such an effort. When stock rights are issued on listed stock, the rights are traded at the same trading post at which the stock is bought and sold. Whenever rights are issued to stockholders, some investors prefer to sell their rights rather than exercise them. Thus a market develops in the rights as well as in the stock. Where the stock is listed (giving the rights the privilege of trading on the exchange), it makes it easier for those investors wishing to dispose of their rights to do so by using the same facilities of the stock exchange. Frequently, stock rights are more actively traded than is the stock itself. On the other hand, where rights are issued on stock that is not listed on a major exchange, disposing of them is sometimes difficult.

If the common stock of a company is listed, it makes it easier for the corporation to raise funds by selling bonds or preferred stocks that are convertible into the listed common stock. The purchaser of such a convertible issue has the assurance of knowing the market price of the securities into which his holdings may be converted. The fact that the bond or preferred stock can be converted into a listed common stock makes it possible in most cases to sell the securities at a higher price and also reduces the underwriting fee which must be paid to investment bankers.

Since it can be justifiably assumed that listing increases the investor interest in a stock and, therefore, tends to raise its price in the market, it improves the position of a corporation during a merger negotiation. The market price of a company's stock is a very important element in determining the value placed on the company's shares in the bargaining preceding a merger.

One aspect of the prestige accorded listed stock is the improvement in the credit standing of the corporation. The financial standard imposed upon a corporation having stock listed on the New York Stock Exchange or other major exchanges is a favorable factor usually taken into account by a lending institution in making a loan to the corporation. If a corporation wishes to raise long-term funds through the sale of a bond issue, the listing of the bond on a major exchange increases its marketability. Financial institutions, as previously indicated, furnish a large portion of the demand for corporation bonds. Many of them as a matter of policy will not purchase bonds that are unlisted. Some are restricted by law to investing in bonds that are listed on a major exchange.

DISADVANTAGES OF LISTING

Publication of Information   The regulations of the New York Stock Exchange require that corporations with listed securities send their stockholders quarterly financial statements in summary form and detailed annual statements. The exchange also requires the publication of data about the corporation which the exchange deems to be necessary to permit an intelligent investor to make a reasonable decision concerning the buying or selling of the stock. Such information as the sales volume, the gross and net profit earned by the corporation, salaries of principal officers, stock options or bonuses offered to them, and changes in the stockholdings of the company by the principal officers and directors must be made available to the exchange and the stockholders. This information could also be useful to competitors. Disclosure of such information may not put a company in a disadvantageous position if its competitors are also listed on a major exchange, because they must furnish similar information to investors. Such disclosure may, however, injure the competitive position of a company with respect to those competitors with unlisted stock. They could withhold much information from the public and their stockholders by providing only sketchy financial data. The validity of this disadvantage is open to question, however.

The amount and character of information required by the New York Stock Exchange to be made available annually to investors is comparable to the amount and type of information required by the S.E.C. in registering an issue for public sale. Although a corporation registering an issue of securities with the S.E.C. prior to a public offering must provide extensive and detailed information about the company and its financial affairs, it is publicized only once. After the distribution of securities registered with the S.E.C., disclosure of such information at future dates is required only if the securities are listed. Disclosure requirements of the American Stock Exchange and regional exchanges are similar, except as we emphasized before, they are not as strict as those of the New York Stock Exchange.

Effect Upon the Credit of the Corporation   A rising trend in the price of a company's stock reflects the conviction of investors that the prospects of the company are good, and the reverse is equally true. Such a decline, particularly if it is not part of a general market decline, may affect the credit standing of the corporation. Long-term financing efforts will not be so successful under such circumstances. A drop in the market value of a company's securities may also affect its efforts in short-term financing. Indeed, the market action of a company's stocks influences lenders in their decision. The credit reputation of a corporation with unlisted stock is not affected by the frequent volatile action of prices on the exchanges.

Restrictions Imposed on Companies with Listed Securities   In compensation for the advantages of listing, corporations are subject to certain regulations imposed by the exchange on which the stock is listed. Some of these regulations imposed by the New York Stock Exchange are as follows:

1. All the common stock listed on the New York Stock Exchange must be voting stock.

2. Preferred stock listed on the New York Stock Exchange need not have the power to vote for directors. However, the exchange requires that if six quarterly dividends on the preferred shares have not been met, the preferred shareholders must then be given the right to elect at least two of the directors.

3. The corporation must furnish quarterly statements to its stockholders and detailed annual statements prior to the annual meeting.

4. In the proxy statement sent out by the corporation to stockholders, there must be provision for the stockholders to indicate on the proxy form whether their vote is yes or no on specific issues to be brought to a vote at the annual meeting.

5. Any substantial acquisition of assets or disposal of assets or other information of importance or interest to the stockholders must be made available to them.

Volatility of Market Prices   The market action of the price of a company's stock on an exchange tends to reflect the quality of the corporation's management.   If the market price of the stock shows a steady rise, investors will credit management; on the other hand, if the market price shows a downward trend, they may blame management to some extent.   There are many influences which tend to raise or lower the price of a particular stock on a stock exchange.   Factors completely independent of management action may be very important in raising or lowering the price of the stock.   A rumor concerning a company, whether true or false, frequently causes a sharp increase or drop in the company's stock.   The effort of a group of speculators to gain control of a corporation may drive up the price of the stock.   On the other hand, the unloading of a sizable amount of stock by a group of large shareholders may depress the market considerably.   Although manipulation of the market price of stock in order to gain a speculative profit is forbidden by law, there appears to be evidence that such actions occasionally take place.   Since, as stated before, the credit standing and reputation of the corporation are somewhat dependent upon the market action of its listed securities, listing may sometimes be detrimental to the company's reputation.

Excessive Interest of Managers in Fluctuations of Their Company's Stock
Company directors sometimes fail to take action which would be beneficial to the company in the long run but which might have the immediate effect of depressing the common stock.   Increasing depreciation allowances, disposing of obsolete inventory or equipment, changing a model design or product line, or modernizing the plant may result in lower earnings as reported at the time that these changes were instituted, even though the benefits in the long run might be considerable.   The effect of such actions on the earnings of a corporation may have an initial effect of depressing the market price of the stock.   As a result, corporation directors might postpone such action as long as possible.   Also, company directors and officers having knowledge of the effect on company stock resulting from corporate action are in the position to profit thereby.   The Securities and Exchange Act of 1934 seeks to eliminate the temptation of company officers and directors to decide on a policy that would benefit themselves.   Profits made by officers and directors resulting from transactions in the company stock must in most circumstances be transferred to the corporation itself.   Furthermore, profits made by officers and directors as a result of a purchase and sale of company stock completed within six months is subject to recovery by the corporation if a suit is instituted within two years of such a transaction.

Questions

1. What is the organizational structure of the New York Stock Exchange?
2. Since the unit of trading in most stocks is 100 shares, how can an investor purchase less than 100 shares of a security traded on the New York Stock Exchange?

3. What is a specialist on the New York Stock Exchange? What does he do?
4. Describe how an order of a customer of a brokerage firm to buy 100 shares of Ford stock is executed.
5. What is the over-the-counter market? How does its operation differ from that of the New York Stock Exchange?
6. Why is it easier for a company to raise money through a sale of additional common stock if it is already listed on an exchange?
7. List the advantages to an investor of having the securities he holds traded on one of the major exchanges.
8. How does the American Stock Exchange differ from the New York Stock Exchange? How do the regional exchanges differ from the two in New York?
9. Explain the term *limit order* and show how it is used.
10. What is meant by buying on margin? Why is such buying regulated by the government?
11. Explain the mechanics of short selling.
12. In general terms, what are the qualifications for listing a security on the New York Stock Exchange?
13. What are the advantages to a corporation in having stock listed on an exchange? What are the disadvantages?
14. What is a stop loss order? How can it be useful to an investor?
15. What factors influence the market price of a company's stock?

Selected Readings

Kimmel, Lewis H., *Share Ownership in the United States,* The Brookings Institution, Washington, D.C., 1952.

Leffler, George L., *The Stock Market,* The Ronald Press Company, New York, 1951.

Loeser, John C., *The Over-the-Counter Securities Market,* National Quotation Bureau, New York, 1940.

Morgan Stanley & Company, published by Morgan Stanley & Company, New York, 1958.

Robinson, Ronald I., Erwin W. Boehmler, Frank H. Gane, and Loring C. Farwell, *Financial Institutions,* Richard D. Irwin, Inc., Homewood, Ill., 1960, Chap. 11.

Wall Street, 20th Century, The Investment Association of New York, 1955.

17

Regulation of Securities Distribution and Trading

In the not-too-distant past, a company was formed to drain the Red Sea in search of gold and jewels left by the Egyptians in their unsuccessful pursuit of the Israelites escaping from Egypt. Although the purpose of this enterprise was preposterous, shares were offered to the investing public. During much of the long history of securities distribution, the investor has had to protect himself from solicitation by promoters of dubious honesty, since the doctrine of *caveat emptor* was generally applied by the courts. During the present century, however, public opinion has generally changed from one of the unaided investor protecting himself to a feeling that government responsibility is necessary to give protection to the investor. As time passed, nearly all the state governments set up laws providing some degree of protection to investors against unscrupulous promoters of securities. More recently, the federal government also has taken the responsibility of investor protection. In addition to state and federal governments the securities industry itself has undertaken a commendable amount of self-policing. In spite of the efforts of state governments, the federal government, and the responsible members of the securities industry, stock frauds and stock manipulation still occur on occasion. Nevertheless, at the present time the investor is protected to a far greater degree by the securities industry and by government than he was a few decades ago. The regulatory agencies must be ever watchful, for dishonest manipulators annually concoct schemes for extracting investment funds from unwary individuals. Louis Loss, formerly the associate general counsel for the S.E.C. has stated that "the problems at which modern security regulation is directed are as old as the cupidity of sellers and the gullibility of buyers." [1]

---

[1] *The Exchange,* New York Stock Exchange, October 1954, p. 1.

STATE REGULATION OF SECURITIES DISTRIBUTION

The first legislation to regulate the distribution of securities was made by the state governments. The first of these laws was passed by Kansas in 1911. Since that year, all the other states have passed securities laws of some sort except the state of Nevada. The popular name given to these state laws is *blue sky* laws. The origin of this term is obscure. One explanation is that the laws are so named because they are intended to protect the public against promotions having no more substance than so much blue sky. One of the earliest mentions of the term *blue sky* was made in an opinion delivered in a federal court decision in Alabama in 1914. In this decision the judge stated, "We take notice of the common understanding that this 'blue sky law' was intended, as is said by the Attorney General, to stop the sale of stock in fly-by-night concerns, visionary oil wells, distant gold mines, and other fraudulent exploitations." [2]

The blue sky laws vary considerably from state to state. Delaware, Maryland, New Jersey, and New York have very liberal laws. The Attorney General of each of these states may order the immediate stoppage of the distribution of a security if he suspects fraud on the part of the promoters. However, the registration requirements are very lenient with respect to the type of information that is to be made public. Rhode Island, Pennsylvania, Massachusetts, Maine, and Connecticut require the registration with the state administrator of the blue sky laws of each broker, dealer, and salesman connected with a distribution of securities within the state. Although the registration requirements are stronger and the amount of information required is greater than in the case of the more liberal states mentioned above, the requirements are lenient compared to federal laws.

State legislation has in general proved inadequate. In those states where the laws have been deficient, the administration of the laws, however conscientiously done, has not protected investors. In those states having stronger blue sky laws the enforcement has been on the whole rather spotty. Some administrators have vigorously enforced the laws while others have been negligent. The fear, imagined or real, that strict enforcement of blue sky laws will hamper the efforts of states to attract industry has been partly responsible for the lack of enthusiasm on the part of officials in enforcing the security laws of their states. The lack of uniformity of the state laws, the many registrations required, and the variability of administration serve to make the laws in some states at least as much a hazard to the honest promoter as they are a deterrent to the dishonest operator. The experience of securities distribution under state laws from 1911 until 1932, a period during which a large number of dishonest and questionable promotions were recorded, indicated the need for federal legislation in this area.

---

2 *Ibid.*

FEDERAL LEGISLATION TO PROTECT THE INVESTOR
BEFORE CREATION OF THE S.E.C.

The Postal Act of 1909 The first federal regulation of securities distribution was the Postal Act of 1909, which forbade the use of the mails for fraudulent purposes, including attempts to promote fraudulent security issues. This provided a limited amount of protection to the investor. However, only cases of outright fraud were barred from the use of the mails. Where means other than the post office were used to promote the sale of securities, the federal law did not apply.

The Transportation Act of 1920 The Transportation Act of 1920 gave power to the Interstate Commerce Commission over distribution of the securities of railroads. The power given to the Commission, however, was not extensive, and was used by it in an advisory manner. In general, the Commission urged railroads to be more conservative in their issue of bonds to raise money for capital purposes.

The Background of the Securities Act of 1933 There was very little public interest during the decade of the 1920's in federal regulation of securities distribution. The stock market enjoyed the greatest boom in its history, and it appeared to many investors that regardless of the securities purchased a profit was bound to be made if the securities were held long enough. Any interference by the federal government in the securities market was thought by many to endanger the upward march of stock prices. The public attitude underwent a sharp change, however, following the historic collapse beginning in October 1929. Many investors found that the promotions which they had so eagerly participated in became practically worthless in a matter of a few months. They discovered, too, the meager protection afforded by state regulation. An investigation of securities distribution by a committee headed by Ferdinand Pecora uncovered a large number of promotions of very dubious honesty, and was largely responsible for passage by Congress of the Securities Act of 1933.

In this Act the intent of Congress was to force those distributors operating on an interstate basis to provide full and accurate information on the securities that they were marketing. The Securities Act is, in fact, sometimes known as the "Truth in Securities" law. It was not the intent of Congress, however, to protect investors from unwise investments. The Act was not intended to pass judgment on the quality of securities distributed but to make full disclosure and provide accurate information to the investor to enable him to make an intelligent decision.

PROVISION OF THE SECURITIES ACT OF 1933

Exemptions Provided in the Securities Act of 1933 The Securities Act provided for a number of exemptions from the registration requirements of the Act: (1) Private offerings of securities to a limited number of persons or institutions who do not propose to redistribute the securities are exempt. (2) Those offerings are exempt from the registration requirement that are restricted to the residents of the state in which the company issuing the securities is organized and is doing its business.   (3) Exemptions from the Act are provided for securities of municipal, state, federal, and other governmental instrumentalities, and of charitable organizations, commercial banks, and building and loan associations.   (4) The securities of railroads and other transportation companies are exempt, inasmuch as the issuance of securities of such companies is subject to regulation by the Interstate Commerce Commission.   (5) The securities of farmers' cooperatives are exempt.   (6) An exemption applies to certificates issued by a trustee or receiver in the course of bankruptcy proceedings.   (7) An exemption applies to endowment policies and issues of insurance companies that are subject to control of a state insurance commissioner.   (8) An exemption involves the exchange by a corporation of one issue of securities for another issue already held by the securities holders of the company.

The Securities Act gives discretionary power to the commission to exempt from registration requirements individual distributions involving the sale during one year of a total of securities of less than $300,000.   A company planning a public interstate distribution of securities of less than $300,000 in one year must file a statement of information with the S.E.C. providing basic facts about the company and about the proposed security distribution.   For securities of this size, the S.E.C. does not require filing the comprehensive registration statement that is required of larger distributions.   If the statement of information and the financial data provided by the corporation planning a distribution of below $300,000 is deemed insufficient by the S.E.C., it may require additional data.   After filing the information with the S.E.C., the waiting period before the securities can be marketed is ten days—a period, however, which may be shortened at the discretion of the S.E.C.

Registration Requirements   The Securities Act of 1933 requires a registration statement to be filed with the S.E.C.   The statement must be prepared with care by the principal members of the corporation, and it must be signed by the principal executive officers of the corporation and by at least a majority of the board of directors.   Any intentional omission or misstatement of fact subjects not only those officers that signed the registration statements but also the directors, officers, consultants, and investment bankers concerned in any way with the preparation of the statement to possible criminal or civil penalties.

In general, the registration statement must describe such matters as:

1. The names of persons who participate in the direction, management, or control of the issuer's business;
2. Their security holdings and remuneration, options, or bonus and profit-sharing privileges allotted to them;

3. The character and size of the business enterprise;
4. Its capital structure, past history, and earnings;
5. Its financial statements, certified by independent accountants;
6. Underwriters' commissions;
7. Payments to promoters made within two years or intended to be made;
8. Acquisitions of property not in the ordinary course of business, and the interest of directors, officers, and principal stockholders therein;
9. Pending or threatened legal proceedings; and
10. The purpose to which the proceeds of the offering are to be applied.[3]

The Prospectus   At the time the registration statement is filed, a *prospectus* is prepared. This is a comprehensive summary of the information contained in a registration statement. It is prepared, however, not to inform the members of the commission but to inform potential purchasers of the securities. For that reason, the language in the prospectus is apt to be less legalistic than that contained in the registration statement. The law requires that a prospectus be offered to each potential purchaser of the security at the time the solicitation is made or before it is made. Although the registration statement is available to any member of the interested public at the time that it is filed, few investors bother to read the statement. The prospectus being the major source of information on which an investment decision is made, the commission requires that a copy of the prospectus be included with the registration statement at the time of filing. The commission rules on the adequacy and accuracy of information in the prospectus as well as that in the registration statement. Because the registration statement and the prospectus accompanying the statement become available for inspection by the public at the time of filing with the Securities and Exchange Commission, copies of the prospectus are generally made in sufficient number to distribute to potential investors interested in the issue. Since changes may be required by the commission before the expiration of the waiting period, such a prospectus is a preliminary one. Warning of the fact that the preliminary prospectus may differ from the prospectus distributed after the effective date for distribution of securities must be stated on the cover page prominently in red lettering. For this reason, the preliminary prospectus is usually called a "red herring" prospectus. After the effective date of the registration, when the securities may actually be offered for sale, the warning is eliminated.

THE NEED FOR REGULATION OF THE EXCHANGES

Prior to 1934 the organized exchanges of the United States were free from regulation by the federal government. It was the feeling of most of the people of the United States during the 1920's that the regulations the exchanges imposed on the activities of their own members and the requirements for listing securities of corporations for trading were sufficient protection for the general public. Many of the states exempted from registra-

---

3 From the *Annual Report,* Securities and Exchange Commission, 1957, p. 34.

tion under the blue sky laws those securities listed on a major exchange. However, the collapse of the stock market in 1929 and the deepening depression culminating in the near collapse of the financial system in 1933 changed the mood of investors to one of critical hostility toward the exchanges and the brokers and dealers trading in securities. It was not surprising, therefore, that the passage of the Securities Act of 1933 regulating the activities of the investment banking industry was followed by the Securities Exchange Act of 1934 to regulate the trading of securities already in the hands of investors.

In addition to bringing under federal regulation the trading of securities, the Securities Exchange Act of 1934 created the Securities and Exchange Commission. The law provides for the appointment of five members to the commission by the President with the approval of the Senate. The terms of appointment are five years, and may be renewed. The expiration of the term of office of the five members is arranged so that one term expires each year. In an attempt to keep a political balance of commission members, the law provides that not more than three members could be appointed from the same political party. The headquarters of the commission is located in Washington, D.C., with regional offices in nine other cities. The commission operates with the aid of about 800 employees on an annual budget that averages between $7 and $10 million. The appointments to the commission have generally been of a high order, and the actions taken by the commission have, on the whole, been considered just and reasonable by the financial community. In addition to being given the authority to administer the Securities Act of 1933 and the Securities Exchange Act of 1934, the commission has been given additional regulatory power through the Public Utility Holding Company Act of 1935, the Trust Indenture Act of 1939, the Investment Company Act of 1940, the Investment Advisers Act of 1940, and the Bankruptcy Act of 1938.

THE FEATURES OF THE SECURITIES EXCHANGE ACT OF 1934

The basic purposes of the Act of 1934 were:

1. To prevent unfair practices on the securities exchanges and to control other practices which might be injurious to investors;
2. To control the use of credit to finance speculation in the market;
3. To compel corporations to provide adequate information about their securities sold in these markets;
4. To prevent corporate officials and persons having inside information about companies from using their positions unfairly for their own profit; and
5. To establish regulatory machinery to prevent the wild gyrations of stock prices characteristic of the stock market in the 1920's.

The Prevention of Manipulative Practices   Until 1934, it had been fairly common practice for directors, officers, and major stockholders to speculate in the movement of prices of the stock of their corporation. With the knowledge they could gain from inside information about the changing prospects of their company, it was a fairly simple matter to predict accurately the upward or downward movement of the stock prices of their company. In an attempt to remove some of the advantage to persons having inside information of corporations from unfairly profiting by such knowledge, the Securities Exchange Act of 1934 provided that each officer, director, or stockholder owning more than 10 per cent of any class of stock outstanding must file a report of his holdings of the stock. Monthly reports were required of such persons in each month in which any change was made in their holdings of company stock. Any short-term profits (those realized within a six-month period) could be recovered either by the corporation or by the stockholders through action initiated (by the corporation or any stockholder) in the United States District Court having jurisdiction in the area where the action was taken. But action to recover such short-term profits was not made automatic by the law. Corporations and stockholders were required to take the initiative in instituting action in the federal court. Furthermore, stockholders owning more than 10 per cent of any class of stock, directors, and principal officers are forbidden by the law from short-selling the stock of their own company.

Not all manipulation of stock prices is forbidden by the Securities Exchange Act. Investment banking houses are permitted in the process of marketing an issue to maintain a stable price in the security which is being distributed. In such a case the maintenance of stability of price during the period of distribution of the issue is considered to be entirely legitimate. The Act gives considerable discretion to the Securities and Exchange Commission in determining when the activities of professionals in the stock market are legitimate in intent or are intended to defraud the public. The commission investigates suspected manipulations on its own initiative and on the complaints received from investors who have suffered losses. If persons are convicted of manipulation to defraud the public as a result of court action initiated by the Securities and Exchange Commission, the violators are subject to civil and criminal liabilities. The intent of the commission is, however, to prevent such manipulation from occurring rather than bring court action after it has occurred. In these actions the commission is aided by the governing bodies of the national securities exchanges and by associations representing securities dealers, particularly the National Association of Securities Dealers.

Registration of the Exchanges   The law requires that all National Securities Exchanges be registered with the Securities and Exchange Commission. In 1963 there were thirteen exchanges registered. The commission, however, does have the power to exempt small exchanges from registration requirements. Under this authority, the commission has exempted exchanges having a small volume of trading.

The registration requirement provides that the exchange must have an organization complying with the provisions of the Securities Exchange Act and the regulations of the S.E.C. under the Act. A copy of the constitution of the exchange, its bylaws, its rules of organization, and a list of its active members must be furnished the commission. Any changes in the constitution, bylaws, or rules must be reported to the commission. Each registered exchange must have adequate rules for the expulsion, suspension, and disciplining of its members for conduct that is inconsistent with fair trading operations and of possible injury to investors. The emphasis of the commission in this aspect of its regulations is to encourage self-discipline on the part of the exchanges. Generally, the New York Stock Exchange, the American Exchange, and the other major exchanges have been found by the commission adequately to police their own members. There have been exceptions, however, and in such cases the commission has intervened to require changes in operations to protect investors and members of the exchange. From time to time, as its resources in money and personnel permit, the commission makes a study of the operations of the registered exchanges, in order to be satisfied that the operations of the exchanges are consistent with current needs.

The Registration of Securities Traded on the Exchanges Not only must the exchanges themselves be registered, but the securities traded on the registered exchanges must be registered with the Securities and Exchange Commission. The registration statement must contain detailed information about the character of the securities and the company issuing it. The type of data required and the completeness of information in a registration statement is similar to that required by the commission prior to the distribution of such securities through investment bankers. The purpose in both instances is the same. The commission attempts to provide the investor with information adequate to make a reasoned judgment, whether he purchases securities on an original distribution or through trading on an exchange.

Not all listed securities must be registered with the S.E.C. Exemption from registration requirements may be granted by the S.E.C. for securities of corporations in bankruptcy, and for bonds of the federal, state, and local governments. Where registration statements are required, they must be kept up to date by filing annual financial reports and interim quarterly reports with the commission. The reports and information filed with the S.E.C. sometimes contain data of a confidential nature, the public disclosure of which might be embarrassing to the corporation. In such cases, the commission has the authority to use its judgment in deciding whether or not to require the publication of the information. Decisions by the commission to withhold information from the general public are rare, however.

Regulation of Brokers and Dealers The large amount of trading in securities over the counter escapes the regulatory authority exercised by the S.E.C. over securities traded on the organized exchanges. Some regulation of over-the-counter trading, however, is accomplished indirectly, through registration of brokers and dealers. All brokers and dealers in securities, except those concerned exclusively with intrastate transactions, must be registered with the S.E.C. Registered dealers and brokers must conform to the requirements of the Securities Exchange Act and to the regulations of the S.E.C. No brokers or dealers may make use of the mails or of any instrumentality of interstate commerce for any deceptive, fraudulent, or manipulative purpose. They are required to conduct their business in a highly responsible manner. The Securities Acts leave to the judgment of the S.E.C. the definition of manipulation, deception, and fraud as it applies to acts of brokers and dealers. As conditions change and new means of manipulation or deception are invented, the S.E.C. broadens its definition of manipulation and fraud. Any broker or dealer applying for registration may be denied such registration if the S.E.C. finds that there is any intentionally false or misleading information in the application made by the applicant, or that the broker or dealer was convicted at any time during the preceding ten years of a felony or misdemeanor involving the trading of securities, or that one or the other is enjoined by a court order from engaging in any practice connected with securities distribution, or that one or the other has willfully violated any provision of the Securities Act of 1933 or the Securities Exchange Act of 1934.

Annual reports of financial conditions must be filed by each registered broker or dealer. Furthermore, all registered brokers and dealers are subject to periodic inspection by the staff of the Securities and Exchange Commission.

Proxy Rules Stockholders own the corporation, and the directors are their agents in administering the policies of the corporation in a manner of benefit to the stockholders. The corporation charter provides that the stockholders elect the directors according to the rules of the charter. The privilege of voting for the directors of the corporation, however, are in many cases almost meaningless. The stockholders may be widely scattered and rarely attend stockholders' meetings. The only knowledge of the affairs of the corporation which they receive may come from the directors, who may or may not give information reflecting unfavorably on their management. The participation of stockholders in the affairs of their corporation is usually confined to signing the proxy form sent once a year by the corporate directors. Until the creation of the Securities and Exchange Commission, the proxy sent out by the management was generally in the form of a carte blanche, giving the management unrestricted power to vote the shares of the absent stockholder as the management pleased. In an effort to make the proxy a more useful instrument in reflecting the wishes of absent stockholders, the Securities Exchange Act gave to the S.E.C. the authority to prescribe rules under which the proxies for securities listed or on exchanges regulated by the S.E.C. were to be prepared and distributed to stockholders.

Proxy forms must be filed with the Securities and Exchange Commission in advance of being sent out to stockholders. This is done so that the S.E.C. can require any changes in the form that are needed to protect the stockholders' interest. Where directors are to be elected at the stockholders' meeting, the proxy form must be sent to the stockholder either at the same time as the annual report of the corporation or after the report has been sent to them. Either the proxy form or a separate form accompanying the proxy form must state information concerning the directors in behalf of whom the proxy is solicited. Such information must be included as the remuneration of each candidate on the board of directors, the stock he holds in the company, and any transactions between him and the corporation that may recently have been made.

As far as it is practical, the commission seeks to make the proxy a ballot rather than a "blank check." Questions of importance to be brought up at the stockholders' meeting must be stated on the proxy form, with an opportunity given to the stockholder to have his vote recorded in favor of or against the proposed action. For example, if an amendment to the constitution of the corporation is proposed, the stockholder is given the right to have his stock voted for or against the amendment. Another example is a proposal to merge the corporation with another corporation, with the proxy form giving the right to the stockholder to vote for or against the merger. Some proxy forms may have half a dozen or more propositions on which the stockholder is given the right to vote for or against. In most cases of this sort, the proxy form solicited by management urges the stockholder to have his proxy recorded in favor of the management position. However, the proxy form must make it absolutely clear that the stockholder has the right to have the stock voted either for or against the wishes of the management soliciting the proxy. Furthermore, the stockholder must be informed that his proxy is revocable by him at any time either before the meeting or at the meeting, should he decide to attend in person. An example of a proxy form is given in Fig. 10-2, p. 166.

Restrictions on Margin Trading It is generally conceded that one of the contributing factors to the collapse of stock prices in 1929 was the overextension of credit to speculators purchasing stock. It was common for speculators during the 1920's to purchase stock with a payment of only 10 per cent of the purchase price, also known as a margin of 10 per cent, borrowing the remainder from commercial banks through arrangements made by securities brokers. The stocks were kept by the bank as security for the loan, and could be sold by the bank if the price of the stock began to fall. When stock prices began declining in October 1929, the fall of prices was accelerated by the dumping of large numbers of securities for sale on the stock market by banks holding these stocks as collateral for loans to speculators in stock. To prevent a repetition of the 1929 collapse, Congress felt it necessary to provide for federal control of credit used in stock speculation. The Securities Exchange Act of 1934 gives this power to the Board of Governors of the Federal Reserve System. This act gives the Board of Governors the power to specify the minimum amount of margin which must be required in arranging a loan to purchase securities, to specify the classes of securities to which the margin requirement applies, and exempts certain transactions from the required margins. The board was given authority to change the minimum margin from time to time and to increase or decrease the classes of securities to which the margin requirement applies. Margin requirements were raised as high as 100 per cent in 1946 (in effect, making it illegal to use any bank credit in the purchase of stock), and at other times have been reduced by the board to 50 per cent and lower. The regulations governing the purchase of stock on margin applies to the market price of the stock at the time of purchase. What the lender does in the event that the stock drops in price is decided by him. The lending institution may require that part of the loan be repaid if the price of the security drops. However, in those cases where the margin paid by the purchaser at the time of the security transaction was high, the lender may permit a considerable drop in price before requiring payment of part of the loan.

The Board of Governors does not require any minimum margin on the purchase of bonds; the amount of margin is determined entirely by the bank or other lender. Banks commonly lend 90 per cent of the purchase price of the bond, requiring only a 10 per cent margin payment by the purchaser. If the credit of the purchaser is unusually high and the customer is one valued by the bank, the bank may lend 95 per cent, or, in rare cases, even 100 per cent of the purchase price of the bond. Bond prices, of course, do not move up or down as rapidly as do stock prices.

SELF-REGULATION BY THE INDUSTRY

It has been the policy of the Securities and Exchange Commission to encourage self-regulation wherever possible in the securities industry. Where self-policing has been well developed and adequately enforced by associations of investment bankers, securities dealers, the exchanges, and others, the S.E.C. has interfered very little. Where self-discipline on the part of the industry has appeared to be inadequate to protect the interests of the investing public, the S.E.C. has taken a more active role in the industry's affairs. The success of self-regulation by the industry has been partly due to the conviction that, if vigorously carried out, it is more effective than government regulation. Also, the S.E.C. encourages self-regulation because it has insufficient money and staff for effective policing of the activities of the securities industry.

The New York Stock Exchange   All the exchanges have rules of conduct to which their members must submit.   Those exchanges registered with the S.E.C. generally have regulations more stringent than those that are exempt from such registration.   The New York Stock Exchange is generally conceded to have the most extensive regulations governing the activities of its members.

The rules of the New York Stock Exchange have two purposes: to protect the members of the Exchange and to protect the investing public.   The regulations governing the conduct of members on the floor of the exchange, such as that all trade in a particular security may take place only at an assigned trading post and that all bidding be in a clearly audible voice, will not concern us here.   Of more importance is the regulation by the exchange of the activities of member firms, which are those firms that have one or more of their officers as members of the New York Stock Exchange.

There are approximately 600 member firms of the New York Stock Exchange, and each is subject to close exchange supervision.   Each member firm doing business with the public is required to have sufficient capital to undertake the volume of business it does with the public.   Each firm must also fill out a detailed questionnaire and submit it to the exchange at least three times a year.   In addition, each firm is required to submit to a surprise audit by a reputable independent public accounting firm at least once a year.   Furthermore, examiners from the stock exchange can make surprise audits of their own on the records and policies of each member firm.   More than 700 surprise examinations by the New York Stock Exchange are made of member firms in an average year.   Weekly reports are required of each member firm to be made to the exchange of participation in underwriting, trading in securities, and amount of money loaned to customers.

The exchange handles complaints against member firms received from customers of the firms.   In 1957, for example, 296 complaints were received by the exchange.   Of this number, 180 were the result of misunderstandings which were cleared up by adequate explanation to the customer.   The remainder were more thoroughly investigated and cleared up by arbitration or other means acceptable both to the firm and to the customer.   If partners or officers of member firms are found guilty of having violated regulations of the New York Stock Exchange they are subject to punishment by fine, suspension, or expulsion from the exchange.

The National Association of Securities Dealers   An amendment to the Securities Exchange Act of 1934 (the Maloney Act of 1938) provided, through the help and encouragement of the S.E.C., for a self-policing body composed of over-the-counter brokers and dealers.   The amendment authorizes the registration with the commission of such an association of brokers and dealers so that, in the words of the amendment, it will "prevent fraudulent and manipulative acts and practices, promote just and equitable principles of trade, provide safeguards against unreasonable rates of commission or other charges, and in general protect investors and the public interest, and remove impediments to and protect the mechanism of a free and open market."

Out of this legislation came the National Association of Securities Dealers. It is a trade association representing over 4,000 brokerage and dealer firms. However, it is not an ordinary trade association. Much of the activity and most of the reason for existence of the N.A.S.D. is enforcing its own rules and the policies and rules of the Securities Exchange Commission.

The N.A.S.D. employs a staff of examiners that are sent out to audit without advance notice the affairs of each member of the N.A.S.D. Any suspected violation of regulations are reported by the examiner to the main office of the association. The association also investigates complaints received from customers of association members. Any suspected violations require a hearing before a panel of N.A.S.D. members. In an average year, approximately 300 cases are investigated by panels of N.A.S.D. members acting on a complaint lodged by a customer or examiner. If a panel finds the member guilty, the member is disciplined. In minor cases, a reprimand coupled with a warning is given to the offending member. In more serious cases, fines, suspension, or expulsion from the association are handed down. In 1959, ten member firms were suspended and thirty member firms expelled from the association.[4] The punishment assessed by a panel of N.A.S.D. members may be appealed to the governing board of the N.A.S.D. If the governing board upholds the discipline imposed by the panel, the member may appeal to the Securities and Exchange Commission. If the S.E.C. upholds the punishment, the disciplined member may take his appeal to the federal courts. One member of the N.A.S.D. appealed his expulsion from the association through the governing board of the N.A.S.D., the S.E.C., and the federal courts all the way to the Supreme Court of the United States. The expulsion was upheld at every step.

The policing powers of the N.A.S.D. overlap those of the S.E.C. The two bodies, however, coordinate their activities as closely as possible to prevent unnecessary duplication. The examiner of the N.A.S.D. has a greater discretionary power in dealing with questionable activities of member firms. The S.E.C. must limit its investigations to possible violations of the federal law. The examiners of the N.A.S.D., on the other hand, can also report cases of questionable ethics. In practically all its actions, the N.A.S.D. is upheld by the S.E.C. Sometimes, when an examiner from the N.A.S.D. uncovers evidence of serious legal violations, he will report his findings directly to the S.E.C. for more speedy prosecution than would be possible if the violation were first reported to the governing board of the N.A.S.D.

On the whole, the N.A.S.D. has a most creditable record in enforcing a reasonable standard of ethics on its members, while at the same time pro-

---

[4] *Barron's Financial Weekly,* December 28, 1959, p. 6.

moting the public relations of the association.   In addition to its promotional and policing activities, the association takes responsibility for the quotations carried in newspapers of the more actively traded over-the-counter securities, thus providing a guide to the investing public of the value of those securities.

OTHER LAWS ADMINISTERED BY THE S.E.C.

As we noted earlier, Congress has given additional responsibility to the S.E.C. through the passage of several acts: the Public Utilities Holding Company Act of 1935, the Trust Indenture Act of 1939, the Investment Company Act of 1940, and the Investment Advisers Act of 1940.   In addition, Congress gave the S.E.C. responsibility in bankruptcy proceedings of corporations held in federal court.   (This will be discussed in Chapter 25.)

The Public Utilities Holding Company Act of 1935   The passage in 1935 of the Public Utilities Holding Company Act followed a comprehensive nine-year study of the public utilities industry made by the Federal Trade Commission.   A number of abuses was uncovered, the chief of which included the following: [5]

1. Inadequate disclosure to investors of the information necessary to appraise the financial position and earning power of the companies whose securities they purchase.
2. Issuance of securities against fictitious and unsound values.
3. Overloading of the operating companies with debt and fixed charges, and thus tending to prevent voluntary rate reductions.
4. Imposition of excessive charges upon operating companies for various supplies and equipment.
5. The control by holding companies of the accounting practices and rate, dividend, and other policies of their operating subsidiaries so as to complicate or obstruct state regulation of rates charged to consumers.
6. The control by holding companies of subsidiaries through disproportionately small investment.
7. The extension of holding company systems without relation to economy of operations or to the integration and coordination of related properties.

The broad purpose of the Act was to protect consumers and investors from the abuses and evils facilitated by the excessive pyramiding of the financial structure of public utility empires.   Particularly, the Act was intended to free the operating electric and gas companies from the control of absentee and uneconomic holding companies.   It was felt that if a greater degree of freedom of operations could be given to the operating companies, their rates and services could better be regulated by state regulatory agencies.

The Securities and Exchange Commission is given control over the issuance of securities by holding companies and their subsidiaries.   The

---

[5] *The Work of the Securities and Exchange Commission,* November 1, 1954, U. S. Government Printing Office, Washington, D.C., p. 11.

law provides that the security issue must be reasonably adapted to the structure and earning power of the company, that it must be necessary and appropriate to the efficient operation of the company, that the fees, commissions, and other payments made in connection with the issue must be reasonable, and that the terms and conditions of the issues of the securities must not be detrimental to the interests of investors or consumers.   Where the utility company plans to distribute an issue through an investment banking house, the company must invite competitive bids from investment banking houses to obtain the lowest cost of distribution of securities to the investing public.   Exceptions may be made by the Securities and Exchange Commission from the requirement of securing competitive bids in those cases where the commission is convinced that there is reasonable cause for exemption.

The law gives the S.E.C. the power to regulate dividend payments where such payments might be subject to abuse by the directors of the company.   Intercompany loans (loans by one company to another company in the same holding company structure), the soliciting of proxies, and trading in company stock by directors and officers are also subject to control by the S.E.C.   To eliminate the abuse common during the 1920's of excessive service charges levied upon operating companies by the parent holding company, the Act forbids holding companies from charging their subsidiaries unreasonable fees for services rendered.

One of the most important provisions of the Act is the authority it gives to the S.E.C. to require the physical integration and corporate simplification of holding company systems.   If, in the judgment of the S.E.C., the combination of several small operating units into a single operating company would improve the services and reduce the cost of operation, the commission has the authority to require such integration.   Furthermore, the commission was given the authority to reduce the number of layers of holding companies on top of holding companies, if such simplification of the holding company structure would result in reduced cost, improved services, and better protection to investors.

Trust Indenture Act of 1939   This Act is intended to protect the purchasers of bonds, debentures, notes, and similar debt securities.   It applies to securities in the amount of $1 million or more outstanding at any one time.   It requires that the trustee under the indenture be free of any conflicting interests that might interfere with the trustee's responsibility toward security holders.   The law requires that the trustee be a corporation with capital and surplus satisfactory to the S.E.C.   In administering this Act, the S.E.C. imposes a high standard of conduct and responsibility on the part of the trustee, requires the trustee to secure evidence of compliance by the corporation issuing the securities of all terms in the indenture, and requires financial reports to be periodically issued by the trustee to the holders of the securities.

The Investment Company Act of 1940   This Act provides for the registration and regulation of companies engaged primarily in the business of investing, reinvesting, or trading in securities.   It requires that the company must disclose its finances and investment policies to the holders of its own securities.   All investment companies, with certain exceptions permitted by the S.E.C., must be registered with the commission.   The investment company must file information describing its policies, and submit to control by the S.E.C. of its investments, contracts, capital structure, loans, and other phases of operations.

Investment Advisers Act of 1940   All persons who are in the business of advising others with respect to securities matters and charge a fee for their services must be registered with the S.E.C. under the Investment Advisers Act.   Advisers are required to give information concerning their education, experience, the manner of giving advice, and the method of collecting fees from clients.   The commission has the authority to revoke, suspend, or deny registration of any adviser, if the adviser fails to measure up to the high standards of conduct required by the Act.   Each adviser is required to file annual and special reports of his operations.

SUGGESTED CHANGES IN REGULATIONS

On the whole, the general philosophy and regulatory practices of the S.E.C. have been commended by the members of the securities industry. Two studies recently have been made, one of the S.E.C. and one by the S.E.C.   The study *of* the S.E.C. was made by a private firm of management consultants under a contract with the Budget Bureau of the federal government and was generally complimentary.   However, a number of criticisms were made, the chief one of which was the large number of delays in processing registration statements submitted by companies wishing to issue securities.   The study, completed in 1961, showed that in the previous year only about 10 per cent of all registration statements were reviewed by the S.E.C. within twenty days.   More than one-third of the registration statements were not reviewed by the S.E.C. before fifty-one days or more had passed.   The cause of the delays, according to the study, was the rapidly rising number of registration statements filed with the S.E.C. and lack of personnel for processing the applications.   The study strongly recommended that Congress increase the budget of the S.E.C. to enable it to add to its staff.

The study made *by* the S.E.C. was prompted by Congress and encouraged by the President.   Its purpose was to determine the effectiveness of existing legislation in the securities field and the possible need for additional laws to be enacted by Congress.   This study, started in 1961, was completed in 1963 and submitted in three installments to Congress.

One recommendation to Congress would, if enacted into law, separate firms into either brokerage or dealer houses. The idea is similar to the enforced separation of investment banking from commercial banking by Congress early in the 1930's. Practically all securities firms in the United States at the present time are both brokers and dealers. The chances for an inherent conflict of interests detrimental to the investing public have caused concern to the S.E.C.

A second possible change would replace the N.A.S.D. by the S.E.C. in taking primary responsibility for policing the over-the-counter market. The following recommendations were made in the report: [6]

> 1. It is an essential role of government [the S.E.C.] to assure that there is no gap between the total regulatory need and the quantity and quality of self-regulation provided by the recognized agencies.
> 2. In the present statutory scheme there are marked differences between the provisions defining the Commission's powers in respect of exchanges and those applicable in respect of the N.A.S.D. Re-examination of these differences and of related Commission responsibilities is now warranted.
> 3. The present statutory pattern applicable to exchanges, under which the Commission has comprehensive power to adopt its own rules as to major substantive matters and to amend or supplement exchanges' rules as to other matters to assure fair dealing and protection of investors, has no direct counterpart in respect of over-the-counter markets. The Commission does have very considerable rule-making power, but has no authority to amend or supplement N.A.S.D. rules on substantive matters [as it has with respect to rules of the organized exchanges].

A third recommendation would reduce or entirely eliminate the exemptions from present disclosure requirements of publicly owned corporations. At the present time, those corporations that are not listed on any major exchange are exempt from making periodic reports to the S.E.C. In addition, commercial banks enjoy an exemption from the disclosure requirements of the Securities and Exchange Commission.

A fourth recommendation would extend the margin requirement rule, and possibly give the authority to set the margin requirement to the S.E.C. rather than the Board of Governors of the Federal Reserve System. This suggestion of the S.E.C. would provide that the margin requirement imposed on commercial banks be extended to other sources of loans as well, and apply to all securities transactions involving stock, whether over-the-counter or on organized exchanges.

Questions

1. What is the meaning of *caveat emptor?*
2. What is the purpose of laws regulating the distribution of securities?
3. What are *blue sky* laws? Do they adequately protect investors? Explain.
4. Why is it more difficult for an individual to judge for himself the value of a share in a company than the value of a suit of clothes?

---

[6] Excerpts from the *Special Report of the Securities Markets,* submitted by the S.E.C. to Congress in 1963.

5. Securities of a highly speculative character, so long as they are not fraudulent, are not barred from distribution under federal and state statutes. Do you think legal action should be taken in such distributions? Why or why not?
6. What securities distributions are exempted from the registration requirements of the Securities Act of 1933?
7. Is any manipulation of stock prices permitted by the S.E.C.? Explain.
8. The privilege of voting for the directors of a corporation is for many stockholders almost meaningless. Why?
9. How do the requirements of the S.E.C. regarding proxies make voting at annual meetings of stockholders something more than a "blank check"?
10. How are stock purchases on margin regulated? What are the purposes of these regulations?
11. How do the S.E.C. and the N.A.S.D. cooperate to provide some regulation of securities dealers?
12. It has been the policy of the S.E.C. to encourage self regulation by members of the securities industry. Why?
13. What are the purposes of the rules adopted by the New York Stock Exchange on securities trading?
14. How was the N.A.S.D. formed, and what was the reason for its creation?
15. What rights of appeal does a member of the N.A.S.D. have if punishment is imposed by the governing board of the N.A.S.D.?

Selected Readings

Choka, A. D., *An Introduction to Securities Regulation,* Twentieth Century Press, New York, 1958.

Frey, A. H., "Federal Regulation of the Over-the-Counter Securities Market," *University of Pennsylvania Law Review,* November 1957.

History of National Association of Securities Dealers, Inc., Its Membership, Activities, etc., U.S. Government Printing Office, Washington, D.C., 1959.

Loss, Louis, *Securities Regulation,* Little, Brown and Company, Boston, 1961.

Walter, J. E., *The Role of the Regional Security Exchanges,* University of California Press, Berkeley, Calif., 1957.

The Work of the Securities and Exchange Commission, Securities Exchange Commission, Washington, D.C., 1954.

Work of the Securities and Exchange Commission, U.S. Government Printing Office, Washington, D.C., 1960.

18

Raising Funds by Special Distributions of Securities

SALES TO EMPLOYEES AND EXECUTIVES

Stock Purchase Plans for Employees

STOCK PURCHASE plans for employees are a product of the twentieth century, although Pillsbury Mills instituted such a plan as early as 1882. It was not, however, until after World War I that plans for employees became widespread in the United States. This was a decade characterized by a stock market boom, and workers in factories began taking an interest in buying stock. This was also a decade in which management sought by a variety of means to diminish the influence of organized labor and to reduce the loyalty of workers to their unions. Largely as a result of these two factors, the number of companies instituting stock purchase programs for their employees increased rapidly. By 1929, many of the largest corporations, such as United States Steel, Standard Oil Company of Indiana, American Telephone and Telegraph, Procter and Gamble, and about 200 other large companies, had some type of plan in operation for their employees.

Most of these plans had little effect on the financing policies of the company, because the amount of money raised by a corporation through the sale of stock to its employees was too small to be much of a factor in the company's financing operations. The purpose was not to raise money but to raise morale. The argument was that the purchase of stock by an employee made him an owner of the company and would make him sympathetic to management's point of view. As a part owner in the business, the employee was expected to become less wasteful, more diligent, and more responsible in his work. As a stockholder, the employee was entitled to attend the annual meeting of the owners of the company, and some corporations encouraged this.[1]

The stock market crash in 1929, not surpisingly, put to an end many of the plans that had been instituted just a few years earlier. Employee loyalty to the company was hardly improved when the employee purchased stock at $200 a share and saw it drop to $20 a share. Following World War II, however, a revival of interest in employee stock purchase plans took place. These, on the whole, were more carefully planned than those in the 1920's. The generally rising trend of the stock market during the 1950's, as during the 1920's, is one explanation for the revival of interest. Most of the plans included some safeguard to prevent heavy losses to the employee in the event the prices of the stock should drop. Furthermore, the employee was usually cautioned concerning the risks of stock ownership as well as the benefits. The emphasis of recent stock purchase plans is to make the employee not just an owner of the company but a well-informed capitalist as well.

Advantages of Stock Ownership Plans to the Employee. Investment in common stock carries with it the risk that the dividend rate may be reduced or eliminated or that the market value of the stock may fall. On the other hand, common stock is one of the investments that provides some protection from the danger of inflation. To an employee, a stock purchase plan combined with a savings bond plan can present an investment program for him that provides dollar security through the purchase of bonds, and inflation security through the purchase of the company's stock.

Price concession is the second advantage. If the company offers its employees company stock at prevailing market prices, they might just as well have purchased the stock through a brokerage house. The only saving would be the brokerage fee. Stock ownership plans that provide for a purchase price below the prevailing market price do so as an inducement for employees to participate in the plans. Such a plan offered to American Telephone and Telegraph Company employees in the 1950's provided for a purchase price of $20 below the prevailing market price, subject to the limitations stated in the offering.

A third advantage is the convenience of buying stock through a company plan. A common feature of these plans is the installment purchases. Thus, the employee pays a small amount on each payday until he owns one share. A further convenience is that the installments are deducted from his paycheck. The company undertakes all the bookwork and record keeping necessary in installment purchasing with no cost to the employee. Some companies make a small interest payment to the employee while his installments are building up to the point necessary to purchase one share.

---

[1] The reports of annual meetings of stockholders of the Standard Oil Company of New Jersey revealed that sharp and pointed questions are occasionally asked of management by employee stockholders during the time when the chairman throws open the meeting to questions from the floor.

A fourth advantage is found in the cancellation or repurchase provisions of the stock purchase plan of many companies. Usually an employee has the option of canceling his participation in the plan at any time, with a full refund of any installments paid toward the purchase of stock. Furthermore, some companies agree to repurchase stock sold to employees in the event that the market price of the stock should fall below the purchase price paid by the employee. Some companies permit the employee to resell his shares to the company at the price he originally paid. Other companies, in the event that the market price drops, permit the employee to resell to the company at a price at which both the employee and the company share part of the loss.

Disadvantages to the Employee. Probably the greatest disadvantage is the concentration of investment risk and job risk. If, as the result of participation in an employee stock purchase program, a substantial portion of the savings of an employee are invested in his company's stock, his income from invested savings will be dependent on the success of the same company that furnishes him wages. Furthermore, the average savings of a typical employee will be relatively small. Conservative investment practices would in such cases dictate a policy emphasizing government bonds, savings and loan deposits, and similar investments. It is probably safe to say that the average rank-and-file worker is unsophisticated in investment matters, and should steer clear of common stocks. Opinion is, however, divided as to the extent of fiscal wisdom possessed by the average factory worker, and it might be argued that investment knowledge is increasing along with the rise in education and training of the average company employee.

Another disadvantage to the employee is the limitation placed in some plans on the resale of stock acquired by him. Most companies place no restrictions on the resale of this stock. However, some companies, because they sold the stock at less than the market price, require that, if the employee wishes to sell it, he must first offer it back to the company at the price at which he purchased it.

Advantages to the Corporation. The company's principal goal in starting a stock purchase program is to increase the loyalty of the worker toward his company. The success of a program is thus measured by the improvement in employee morale that it generates, rather than by the amount of money it raises for the corporation. If labor turnover is reduced, absenteeism brought down, and cooperation increased, the program can be called a success. However, such programs are not always successful due to the existence of many other factors which affect the workers' morale. A second benefit to the corporation sometimes credited to employee stock purchase programs are their educational value. Ownership of stock may bring better understanding to the employee of the company's financing problems: he becomes aware that company profits were not as high as he had supposed.

Some employee stock programs are justified on the ground that they encourage the workers to be thrifty, because many are unable to undertake a savings program unless it involves some deduction from their wages. A stock purchase program, like a savings bond program, financed by deductions from the employee's paycheck, builds up his savings. Such employees tend to be relatively more stable workers. Occasional financial crises can be met by the thrifty employee without resort to high cost personal loans that might cause worry, and, therefore, inefficiency on the part of the employee at his job.

Most of the benefits claimed for an employee stock purchase program can be achieved by other means as well. Increase in loyalty to the company can be fostered by fair wages, clean and safe working conditions, and recognition of each employee as a human being rather than as an item of expense. An understanding, as management sees it, of the economics of American industry can be fostered through articles in the company magazine, items on plant bulletin boards, and classes at the high school or college level offered to workers. Thrift can be encouraged by promoting a savings bond buying program and by supporting a company credit union. The credit union can, of course, also serve to emancipate the employee from dependence upon high cost personal loans from other sources. Those companies that have stock purchase programs for employees generally have the other programs mentioned above, hence the difficulty of measuring the stock purchase program in accomplishing the objectives sought by the company.

Disadvantages to the Corporation. Probably the major disadvantage to the corporation is the risk to employee morale that is involved. If the market price of the stock drops or its dividends are cut, the employee is likely to blame the company. It was this factor that led to the abandonment of so many stock purchase programs after the crash of 1929. Management could meet this risk to morale in two ways: (1) It could provide a means by which the company would either absorb the entire loss or at least part of the loss the employee might suffer as a result of selling his stock at less than the price at which he bought it. (2) It could try to make it absolutely clear to the employee upon signing up for the stock purchase program that there are risks involved in the ownership of capital. While this may not console the employee suffering a loss as a result of purchasing the company's stock, it might lessen the tendency to blame the company.

Another disadvantage to the company is the expense involved. In order to induce employees to participate in a stock purchase program, usually the shares are offered at less than the market price, causing the company to receive less money for its stock than would be the case in sales to the public. There is also a bookkeeping expense involved, which may or may not be significant, depending upon the methods used by the company in distributing stock to its employees. Another cost disadvantage to the company is involved if the company agrees to repurchase the stock sold to the employee in the event that the market price drops. In this case, the company purchases its own stock at a higher price than would be required in the open market.

There may be still another disadvantage in that existing stockholders have a pre-emptive right in the further distribution of shares. A waiver of this pre-emptive right may be included in the articles of incorporation of the company, in which case there is no problem. The instituting of a stock purchase program for employees is sometimes put on the agenda of the stockholders' meeting to be approved by the stockholders before being put into effect.

Stock Compensation Plans for Management Prior to the 1930's, the methods of paying the top ranking executives for their services to the corporation were relatively simple. Since income tax rates were low, an executive's salary was his chief payment for services. During the 1930's, tax rates on individual incomes became sharply progressive; that is, the rates increased more rapidly than the increases in income. This led to a search for other ways to compensate employees. The income tax laws as amended and administered have provided numerous means of avoiding the high rates of income tax, encouraging the use of stock options, deferred compensation, pension plans, and the many fringe benefits given to executives at company expense. The last-mentioned include free medical checkups, free or low cost insurance, country club dues paid for by the company, company-owned yachts, airplanes, hunting lodges, and vacation facilities, liberal travel and expense allowances, and many others. The result is that, although income tax rates remain high, much of the compensation that executives receive is not subject to these high rates. Devising means of exempting executives' income from high income tax rates has become an important business in itself. In connection with business finance, however, we shall confine our attention to stock options and stock bonuses, since these two affect the financial structure of the corporation.

Stock Option. A stock option is an option to purchase a stated number of shares of the company's stock at a stated price. Such a privilege is generally good for a number of years. The appeal of the stock option to the executive is that it can be drawn up in a manner to escape the income tax. For example, a company may give its top ranked executives the option to purchase a stated number of shares of stock over a period of five years at a price of $20 a share. If the option is exercised when the market price of the stock is $30 a share, the option gives the executive a discount of $10 a share for every share he purchases. Should he later resell the stock at $30 a share, he would pay a long-term capital gain tax instead of the personal income tax on his profits. The capital gains tax is one-half of the income tax or 25 per cent of the capital gain, whichever is the lower figure. A highly paid executive might be taxed at 80 per cent for any additional salary he might receive. If, instead of an increase in salary he is given its equivalent in stock options, he would be taxed only 25 per cent on his profits resulting from his stock option rather than 80 per cent. To qualify for the lower tax on capital gains, care must be taken. The plan should be drawn up by an expert well versed in tax matters. Some of the important ingredients of a stock option include the following: (1) The option price at the time of first offering to the executive must not be less than 95 per cent of the fair market value. (2) The term of the option must not exceed ten years. (3) The executive must keep the stock he purchases under the option plan for at least six months before he resells it. (4) Stocks purchased under the plan during the first two years of the option must not be sold for two years after the granting of the option by the company, in addition to having to be held at least six months before resale.

Where stock option plans are presented to stockholders at a stockholders' meeting for approval, it is usually stated to the stockholders that the plan will increase the incentive of the executives in making their company prosper, so that the market price of the stock will rise, increasing the value of the option. This is a lot of sentimental nonsense. An executive, like any employee, gives his services to a company in exchange for compensation, primarily in the form of salaries, but it can take on many other forms. If an executive earning $75,000 a year from his company needs some additional incentive in order to give his best effort, it would appear that the company should allow the executive to seek employment elsewhere. The purpose of the stock option is to enable the corporation to pay its executives in a way that will escape the high rates of income taxation. It also benefits the corporation in that stock option plans for executives can reduce employee turnover at the higher levels.

A method of compensation similar to the stock option is the issue of stock subscription warrants to executives. Like stock options, warrants permit the executive to purchase a stated number of shares at a stated price at any time during a stated number of years, and can be transferred or sold as easily as a stock certificate. The value of the warrant at the time it is given to the executive must be reported by him as income received subject to income tax rates. If an executive receives a warrant to purchase 1,000 shares of the company's stock at $20 a share while the market value is $21 a share, the executive must report the receipt of $1,000 as income. If the value of the stock drops, the warrant may become worthless. However, if the market price of the stock rises, the market price of the warrant will rise more rapidly. Furthermore, the profit on the sale of the warrant could qualify as a capital gain, subject to the relatively low capital gain tax rate.

Stock Bonuses. A stock bonus is a bonus payable in stock of the corporation rather than in cash. The value of the stock received as a bonus must be reported as ordinary income by the recipient and is subject to the personal income tax. For this reason, it is not as popular among executives as the stock option.   Its main advantage to the corporation is that it permits it to pay part of the compensation of executives in a form that does not reduce the cash account of the corporation.   The executive getting the stock bonus may sell it immediately, receiving cash not from the corporation but from the stock market.   The payment of bonuses in stock increases the number of shares outstanding, and so dilutes to some extent the ownership of the corporation by each stockholder.   Because of this, stock bonus plans are often criticized at stockholders' meetings.

SALES TO EXISTING STOCKHOLDERS

The owner of a business constitutes an important source of funds for company needs whether the company is a small partnership or a large corporation.   Primary dependence upon owners for additional funds may be a necessity in a smaller business but is usually not so in a large corporation. In the case of corporations, when the owner first purchased or received the stock, he presumably had faith in the future of the company.   This faith, of course, may be shaken by later developments.   Those stockholders that have held onto their shares, however, have presumably done so because of a belief that the value of the stocks would rise again as a result of improved company fortunes.   It can therefore be generally concluded that at any one period of time there exists a source of funds from stockholders who are sympathetic to the company and have faith in its future.   The importance of stockholders as a source of funds is stressed in a study made by the Securities and Exchange Commission.   Of the $4 billion raised by the sale of common stock in the period studied, more than two-thirds was raised by the sale of stock to stockholders of the company, and less than one-third was raised by sales to the general public.

The Pre-emptive Right   The pre-emptive right is a right that gives to the existing stockholders of the company the first option to purchase additional shares that might be offered for sale by the corporation.   The purpose of the pre-emptive right is to assure each stockholder the opportunity to retain the percentage ownership of the corporation that he had prior to the offering of additional stock.   A stockholder owning 10 per cent of the common stock of a company would, under the pre-emptive right, be given the chance to purchase 10 per cent of every subsequent common stock distribution before the stock was offered to others.

The pre-emptive right used to be guaranteed by state law more often in the past than it is now.   At the present time, only two states require in their corporation laws that the pre-emptive right be preserved in the charter of the corporation.   More than two-thirds of the corporation laws of the states give the pre-emptive right to existing stockholders if there is no mention of such rights in the charter of the corporation, but permit corporation charters to deny the pre-emptive right.   In the remaining states, there is either no mention of the pre-emptive right or the right is denied unless specifically granted by the charter of the corporation. The charters of most of the large, publicly held corporations contain a paragraph denying the pre-emptive right to their stockholders.

Purpose of Stock Rights   A *stock right* is an option to purchase an additional number of shares at a stated price during a stated period. Stock rights have some similarity to the stock options given to management as discussed above. The term *stock rights,* however, applies to options given to stockholders rather than options given to management. Furthermore, the stock right, unlike the stock option given to management, remains good for a very limited time, generally less than one month. Although the purpose of issuing stock options is to provide a tax-protected compensation to management, the purpose of issuing stock rights to stockholders is usually to raise additional funds for the company. Stock rights are quite frequently used by corporations as a means of financing, and are used by large corporations having many stockholders as well as by small corporations having very few stockholders. Although the pre-emptive right is generally not a factor in the decision to issue stock rights, the raising of funds by means of stock rights does permit stockholders to preserve their proportionate ownership of the corporation by exercising the rights issued to them.

Techniques of Issue   The process of issuing stock begins with the board of directors. If it decides to raise funds by an issue of rights, a resolution to that effect must be passed at a meeting of the board. If the amount of stock authorized by the corporation charter but as yet unissued is sufficient to raise the funds desired, there is no additional need to amend the charter of the corporation. If, however, the stock to be distributed by the exercise of stock rights exceeds that authorized by the charter, an amendment to the charter is necessary. Such an amendment, of course, must be approved by the stockholders. Since the exercise of the right involves a sale of stock, the issue must be registered with whatever securities commission of the state has jurisdiction. In addition, the issue is subject to the same registration requirements imposed by the Securities Act on interstate distribution of securities. Thus, it is usually necessary to prepare a registration statement and a prospectus to be filed with the S.E.C. A copy of the prospectus sent to each stockholder notifies him of the details of the issue. If the stock is listed on a stock exchange, that exchange must be notified by the corporation, since the stock rights will be traded at the same trading post where the stock is traded.

For a corporation having a large number of stockholders, the names of these stockholders are changed constantly as the stock of the company is bought and sold. It is necessary to set a specific date and to announce that the names on the stockholders' ledger on that date will be the ones to whom the rights will be subsequently sent. This date is known as the record date. As in the distribution of dividends, an investor purchasing stock too late to get his name on the stockholders' ledger on or before the record date will not receive the rights. They will be sent instead to the stockholder listed on the record date who subsequently sold his stock. The rules of the New York Stock Exchange provide that stock transactions be settled on the fourth business day following the transaction. Therefore, stock purchased up to and including the fourth day before the record date will receive the stock rights when they are issued. Stock purchased on the New York Stock Exchange on the third day before the record date or later does not receive the rights. In the nomenclature of the market the stock is traded *cum rights* (or *rights-on*) until the close of the fourth day prior to the record date, and after that date sells *ex-rights*.

Where an issue of rights must be registered with the S.E.C., no trading of the rights is permitted until the registration statement becomes effective. The rights may be bought and sold on a "when issued" basis on the exchange where the stock is listed, or, if the stock is unlisted, the rights are traded over the counter. Following the record date, the rights are mailed to the stockholders of record. Thereupon, the rights are bought and sold in the same way that stock is bought and sold, until the rights expire.

The price at which the new stock is to be issued as a result of the exercise of the rights may present a problem to the directors of the corporation. Suppose the company wishes to raise $2 million by issuing rights, at a time when the market price of the outstanding stock is $55 a share. The rights would have to provide the privilege of purchasing at less than the market price, otherwise they would have no value. Subject to the exercise of rights, the corporation could issue 40,000 additional shares at $50 a share or 50,000 at $40 a share. In both cases, the company would receive $2 million as a result of stockholders exercising the rights. The advantage to the corporation of issuing the additional stock at $50 a share is that a smaller number of shares will be issued, and that there will be less dilution of existing stockholdings and a smaller number of additional shares distributed to which dividends must be paid. On the other hand, there is a danger in pricing stock subject to purchase through rights at a figure too close to the existing market price. There would be a greater possibility of their becoming worthless if the subscription price of the new stock were set at $5 below the market price than if it were set at $15 below. If the market price of the stock drops to the subscription price or lower, the rights become worthless and will not be exercised. In that event, the corporation would not receive the money that it expected through the rights offering. In determining the price of the stock at which the rights are to be exercised, the risk of a market drop must be balanced against the advantages to the corporation in limiting the number of additional shares issued to raise the required sum of money. To reduce the risk resulting from a drop in the market price of the stock, the corporation may pay a fee to an investment banking house to guarantee the successful sale of the issue by purchasing any unsold shares at the end of the subscription period. The underwriting of rights issues is discussed below.

Valuation of Stock Rights   The right to buy additional shares at prices below the market price is a privilege that will not be exercised unanimously by the stockholders of the corporation. In order to keep their ownership of the corporation unchanged, each stockholder must use the right given to him by purchasing the additional shares the rights provide. This, of course, requires an additional cash investment in the corporation. If the stockholder does not exercise his right, his proportionate ownership of the corporation will drop. The primary interest of the corporation in issuing rights is to raise funds. In order that the financing plans of the corporation will not be upset, it is essential that all or nearly all the rights be exercised. To facilitate this, the rights are made assignable, permitting them to be sold by the stockholder receiving them. Thus a market is established in the rights, and they are traded along with the stock of the corporation.

Since the subscription price of the new issue is set below the market price of the existing stock, the rights, when issued, have a market value. The value of the rights depends upon the subscription price of a new share and the market price of the existing shares. Any increase in the spread between the market price and the subscription price will raise the market value of the rights, and any fall in the market value of the shares will depress the value of the rights. When the stock is selling *rights-on,* the purchaser of the stock will not only receive his stock certificate but will also receive his share of the rights when issued. He is, in other words, purchasing a share and a right for each share of stock he buys. When the stock is traded *ex-rights,* however, the purchaser of the stock will receive the stock but not the rights. Therefore, when the stock is first traded ex-rights, the price of the stock, in the absence of other market influences, will drop in price by the value of one right.

The value of a right can be determined from the difference between the market price of the stock and the subscription price at which new shares can be bought through exercise of the right. Since the market price of the stock will drop when the stock goes ex-rights, two formulas have been derived, one for use when the market price of the stock is rights-on and the other when the market price is ex-rights. When the stock is selling rights-on, the value of one right is computed from the following formula:

$$V = \frac{m - s}{r + 1}$$

$V =$ the value of one right
$m =$ market price of one share of old stock

$s =$ subscription price of one share of new stock
$r =$ the number of rights needed to subscribe to one new share

For example, if the market price of the old stock, rights-on, is $180 a share, the subscription price for each new share is $100, and the number of rights needed to purchase one new share is 4, the formula gives the following value for one right:

$$V = \frac{\$180 - \$100}{4 + 1} = \$16$$

Thus, the value of one right in the above example is $16. When the old stock is sold ex-rights, the following formula is used:

$$V = \frac{m - s}{r}$$

As explained above, when the old stock is first traded ex-rights, the price of the stock, in the absence of other influences, drops by the value of one right. In the above example, stock selling rights-on at $180 a share would tend to drop to $164 a share. Using the second formula, the value of one right would be calculated as follows:

$$V = \frac{\$164 - \$100}{4} = \$16$$

Changes in the market price of stock cause changes in the value of the rights. The change in the value of the right is, however, relatively much greater than the change in the value of the market price of the stock. This is particularly true when the market price is very close to the subscription price of the stock. This opens an opportunity for speculation in the rights which appeals to the gambling instinct many people have. Table 18-1 shows different market prices of a share of stock with the corresponding formula values of one right. Using the example in Table 18-1, one could invest $100.04 in one share of stock expecting that it would rise in the next few days. If the market price rose to $102, the purchaser would realize an increase in his investment of approximately 2 per cent. If, on the other hand, he had spent $100.04 to purchase rights at 1¢ each, he could purchase 10,004 rights at 1¢ a right, ignoring brokerage commissions. If, as in the previous case, the market price of the shares went up to $102, the formula value of the rights would be 50¢ each. The 10,004 rights the speculator held would then be worth $5,002. On the other hand, an extremely small drop in the market price of the stock would cause the formula value of the right to become worthless.

Although the market price of the right rises and falls with the changes in the market price of the stock, the rights do not change in price exactly as would be indicated by the formula. In Table 18-1, at a market price of $100 for the stock, the formula value of one right would be zero. If the life of the right still had several days or weeks to run, the rights would, nevertheless, command a price in the market. The possibility that the market price would rise above $100 a share would give the rights a specula-

TABLE 18-1.   EFFECT ON VALUE OF RIGHT AS MARKET VALUE CHANGES

Subscription price of stock $100
Number of rights needed to buy one share   4

Market Price of Old Stock (Ex-rights)	Formula Value of One Right
$108.00	$2.00
104.00	1.00
102.00	.50
101.00	.25
100.40	.10
100.00	.00
100.08	.02
100.20	.05
100.04	.01

tive appeal in spite of the fact that they would have no value in the event that the price of the stock failed to rise. Buying and selling activity in rights is sometimes far more active than it is in the stock associated with the rights. Although the market value of the rights is usually close to the formula value, occasionally the difference is considerable. As the life of the right approaches its end, the market price and the formula value tend to converge.

Table 18-1, for the sake of clarity, uses dollars and cents figures for the prices of the stocks and the rights. Stock is usually quoted in fractions of an eighth of a dollar, while rights are quoted in 16th's, 32nd's, 64th's, or 128th's of a dollar. For example, ex-rights prices for General Motors stock and General Motors rights issued in 1955, with a subscription price of $75 and a conversion ratio of twenty rights for one new share, are given below for selected dates:

Date	Market Price of Stock	Market Price of Right
February 10	99 3/8	1 14/64
February 14	93 1/2	58/64
February 25	92 1/4	55/64
March 1	94 3/8	61/64
March 7	97 3/4	1 9/64

Effect on Stockholders   The effect on stockholders of the issue of rights can be seen by looking at the effect of rights on a single stockholder in the example given in Table 18-2. Suppose a shareholder has ten shares in the X corporation. The book value of his investment in the company is $2,200. When the rights are issued, he will receive ten rights, which give him the option of buying two new shares at a price of $100 each. If he should exercise his rights, he would send them to the corporation or to its designated agent for issuing stock, enclosing a check for $200. He now has twelve shares in the company. The book value per share, however, after the issue of rights is $200. His twelve shares, therefore, have a total book value

TABLE 18-2.   THE X CORPORATION

Assets	Liabilities $ 400,000
$2,600,000	Stock and surplus $2,200,000
Total $2,600,000	$2,600,000

Stock outstanding   10,000 shares
Book value per share $220
Number of rights issued   10,000
Subscription price for new shares $100
Number of new shares to be issued   2,000
Number of rights needed to buy one new share   5

Balance sheet after exercise of all rights

Assets	Liabilities $ 400,000
$2,600,000	Stock and surplus $2,400,000
200,000 (cash received)	
Total $2,800,000	Total $2,800,000

Stock outstanding   12,000 shares
Book value per share $200

of $2,400. The book value of his investment in the company has been increased by $200, exactly the amount of additional cash given to the corporation by exercising his rights. Although it appears superficially that the purchase of stock at a "bargain" price through exercise of rights gives something of value to the stockholder, the only value the stockholder receives by exercising his right is what he pays for.

Alternatively, the stockholder could have sold his rights. The value per right given by the formula is $20. If he had sold his rights, he would have received $200 for his ten rights. His ten shares in the company after the offering of rights would have a total book value of $2,000, which is exactly $200 less than the book value of the ten shares before the rights were issued. The drop in the book value of his investment in the corporation is exactly the amount of cash he received through the sale of his rights. The offering of rights gives the stockholder the choice of increasing his investment in the company in the amount of the value of the rights or withdrawing part of his investment in the company by selling the rights.

The announcement that an issue of rights is to be made by a corporation, nevertheless, is usually greeted with enthusiasm by stockholders. The purpose of issuing rights is to raise money for the corporation, and this is taken to mean by most stockholders that the corporation directors feel that additional investment in the company will be profitable. Also, rights are usually offered in a rising stock market when economic conditions for the country as a whole appear to be favorable for the immediate future. For these reasons, the market price of the stock following an offering of rights often rises in spite of the reduction in book value per share resulting from the exercise of the right.

To be successful, an offering of rights must generally be supported by nearly all the company's stockholders. If a large portion of the stockholders sell their rights rather than exercise them, this action generally depresses the price of the stock. Large-scale disposal of rights by stockholders may depress the price of the stock to the point where it falls below the subscription price. In this case, the corporation is not likely to receive the money it expected when the decision was made to raise money by issuing rights. Before deciding upon the issue of rights, the directors of a corporation having several large stockholders usually ascertain the action these stockholders will take in the event that rights are issued.

Underwriting of Rights Issue   In the decision to issue stock rights there is always some element of risk that the rights will not be exercised and that the corporation will not receive the money it expects from the exercise of the rights. The risk primarily derives from the possibility of the market price of the stock dropping below the subscription price for the new shares to be issued. This risk can be reduced by making the subscription price so far below the existing market price of the stock that the possibility of the market price dropping to the subscription price is remote. However, this strategy has the disadvantage of requiring a larger number of shares to be issued to raise a given sum of money than would be necessary if the subscription price were closer to the existing market price.

Another means of reducing the risk to the corporation in raising money by issuing rights is to have the issue underwritten by an investment banking firm or syndicate of firms. Where rights are distributed to holders of stock registered with the Securities and Exchange Commission, a majority is underwritten by investment bankers.

The assumption of risk in a rights offering is an agreement to purchase whatever number of shares has not been subscribed for through the exercise of rights at the subscription price or lower. The fee charged for the assumption of risk is generally in two parts. One is a flat fee based on the total amount of the issue, and the other a fee per share for all shares purchased by the investment banker as a result of rights not being exercised. The investment banking house may limit its participation in the offering of rights solely to the underwriting of the success of the issue. On the other hand, it may aid the corporation in the preparation of the issue, the composition of the prospectus, and the registration of the statement with the Securities and Exchange Commission and may also prepare and send circulars to the stockholders on behalf of the corporation urging them to subscribe to the new issue of stock. If these services are undertaken by the investment banking house, an additional fee is charged.

Since the degree of risk in the offering of rights depends upon the possibility of the market price dropping below the subscription price, the decision on the subscription price is of vital importance to the investment banker underwriting the issue. If the market price of the stock has been unsteady, the risk is, of course, greater than if the price has been stable. In any case, it is to the interest of the investment banker to set a low subscription price, while it is to the interest of the corporation to set a relatively high subscription price. Determining on the subscription price in most cases requires much discussion between the corporation and the investment banking house. In preparing the registration statement for the Securities and Exchange Commission in those cases where the stock issue is subject to registration requirements, all the information about the issue is included except the price at which the stock is issued. The decision on the subscription price is usually made just before the registration statement becomes effective, and is filed as an amendment to the registration statement. Where a stock issue subject to rights is registered with the S.E.C., the decision on the subscription price is also delayed until just before the rights are to be issued. One of the final acts in the issue of stock rights is the concluding of the agreement between the investment banking house and the corporation on the subscription price for the new stock to be issued.

The degree of risk in underwriting an issue of stock distributed through rights may be greater than underwriting a sale of stock to the general public. If a sale of stock to the general public is successful, all the stock is usually sold on the first day or a very few days thereafter. Where an investment banking firm underwrites an issue of stock subject to rights, it is not known until the end of the rights period how many shares the firm will be obligated to buy at the contract price. The rights may be good for two weeks, three weeks, a month, or even longer in some cases. During this period, there may be a sudden and unexpected drop in the stock market as a whole or in the stock of the corporation issuing the rights. Hence the length of life of the rights and the stability of price of the company's stock are important elements in the risk of underwriting an issue of rights. If the stockholders sell their rights in unusually high volume, this action may depress the market price of the stock. To prevent the market in rights from depressing the trading price of company stock, the underwriter will usually support the price of the rights by purchasing them as they are brought to the market. It frequently happens that the house underwriting an issue will have bought up a substantial portion of the rights by the end of the subscription period. In this case the investment banking house must exercise the rights, buy the stock, and undertake to sell the shares at the best price obtainable. If the offering of rights has been successful, the number of shares that the investment banking house is required to purchase will be small and will be resold at a price higher than the subscription price. The contract between the corporation and the investment banking house will determine what is to be done with the profit, if any, realized from the house's sale of unsubscribed stock. In some cases, all the profit is returned to the corporation; in some cases, all of it is retained by the investment banking house; and in other cases, it is shared by both.

An example of financing by means of rights is the General Motors

Corporation issue of 1955, one of the largest ever undertaken in the United States.   On January 3, 1955, an announcement was made that the board of directors of the General Motors Corporation had decided to raise $325 million through the sale of common stock.   It was intended that the money be raised by issuing rights to the stockholders of the company, giving them the privilege of purchasing one additional share at the subscription price in exchange for twenty rights.   At the time of the announcement, no subscription price was stated, but it would be announced just prior to the distribution of the rights.   At the time of the announcement, there were 88,513,817 shares of common stock of General Motors outstanding.   The market price of General Motors stock then was approximately $100 a share. In order to guarantee the success of the issue, a syndicate of investment banking houses, headed by Morgan Stanley and Company was formed to underwrite the issue.   The syndicate was made up of 330 banking houses. The registration statement was filed with the Securities and Exchange Commission on January 20, having been prepared with the joint cooperation of the financial officers of General Motors and Morgan Stanley and Company.   Over 550,000 copies of the preliminary prospectus were printed. Most of these were mailed to the approximately 460,000 stockholders of General Motors Corporation, and the remainder was made available to brokerage houses and other interested persons.   On February 7, the day before the effective date of the registration permitting the issue of rights, the board of directors of General Motors Corporation and Morgan Stanley and Company partners agreed on a subscription price of $75 a share.   The rights were to have a life of four weeks.   At noon on February 8, trading in the rights began on the New York Stock Exchange at the post where General Motors stock was traded.   The following day the rights were mailed to the stockholders, who were cautioned that the rights would expire at 6 P.M. on March 7.

During the four-week period that the rights were "alive," the market price of General Motors stock fluctuated between $92 and $100 a share.   At all times, the market price of the shares was comfortably above the subscription price.   This was due partly to the decision of the directors of E. I. du Pont de Nemours & Co., holder of twenty million shares of General Motors stock, to exercise its rights rather than to sell them.   As a result, the Du Pont Corporation purchased one million additional shares of General Motors stock at a price of $75 million.   Of the rights mailed out by General Motors Corporation, 98.5 per cent were either exercised by the stockholders or sold by them and exercised by the purchasers of the rights.   One and one-half per cent of the rights, for which 66,427 shares could have been purchased at the subscription price, were presumably carelessly discarded by the stockholders who received them.   The underwriting contract provided that any unsubscribed shares were to be purchased by the syndicate at a price of $75 a share.   Under this commitment, Morgan Stanley and Company and the other members of the syndicate purchased 66,427 shares at $75 a share. Most of the shares were promptly resold by the members of the syndicate at the market price which then prevailed—about $95 a share. According to the underwriting agreement, any profit from the resale of shares by the syndicate was to be kept by General Motors Corporation. The underwriting fee paid by General Motors to the syndicate was $2,803,637. The proceeds of the sale received by General Motors was $325,760,411.

Taxation The effect on the tax position of the stockholder receiving rights is of considerable importance to him, but is of no direct importance to the corporation in its financing plans. Whether to exercise the rights or to sell them, when to exercise the rights, and how to report the transaction on the income tax are questions which each stockholder must decide for himself, since such decisions depend upon the individual stockholder's tax position. These are questions which can best be answered by each investor with the advice of an accountant well versed in income taxation. In any case, they are beyond the scope of this book. In general, the rights received by a stockholder are not taxable income but represent a return of a portion of the original investment by the stockholder in the corporation. This applies in most cases not only to the rights to purchase additional stock but also the receipt by the stockholder of warrants to purchase bonds or preferred stock convertible into common stock. Warrants to purchase bonds or preferred stock that are not convertible into common stock generally must be reported by the stockholder as income to the full extent of the value of the warrant.

STOCK SALES TO CUSTOMERS

Programs for selling stock to customers of a corporation are comparatively rare. Nevertheless, they have occasionally been undertaken. The manufacturer or distributor may require the purchase of stock in the company as a requisite to obtaining a franchise permitting the local dealer to use the corporation's name and to have exclusive rights within an area to distribute the corporation's product. For example, the use of the "Rexall" name as a right to distribute Rexall products was originally given only to local druggists willing to purchase stock in the United Drug Company, the owner of the Rexall trademark. Another type of customer purchase of company stock, of which there are several examples, is the creation of a wholesale company by a group of retailers financed by the sale of stock to the retailers.

Questions

1. Account for the fact that employee stock purchase plans increased rapidly during the 1920's.
2. For what purposes do companies institute stock purchase plans for their employees?
3. Give the principal characteristics of employee stock purchase plans.

4. What disadvantages may result from stock purchase plans to the employee? To the company?
5. Explain the growth of stock compensation plans for executives during the 1950's.
6. How does the stock option benefit the executive receiving it?
7. Compare stock options, stock warrants, and stock bonuses as to advantages and disadvantages to the executive receiving them.
8. How important in terms of money raised is the sale of stock to existing stockholders of the company?
9. What is the pre-emptive right? What is the purpose of giving this right to stockholders?
10. What is a stock right? Compare the use of stock rights in raising money to the public sale of stock through investment bankers, giving the advantages and disadvantages to the corporation of each.
11. Why is the decision concerning the price at which rights are to be issued an important as well as a difficult one to make?
12. Describe the nature of the choice faced by stockholders receiving rights to buy additional stock.
13. Why does a share of stock tend to drop in price by the value of one share when it is first quoted ex-rights in the market?
14. Why does the market price of rights frequently differ from the price of rights calculated by formula?
15. Why is the sale of stocks by issuing stock rights sometimes underwritten by investment bankers?

Selected Readings

Brooks, John, "The Adventure," *The New Yorker,* April 23, 1955, pp. 84-111. This article describes the offering of rights by General Motors Corporation to stockholders to raise approximately $325 million.

Evans, George H., "The Theoretical Value of a Stock Right," *Journal of Finance,* March 1955.

Griswold, E. N., "Are Stock Options Getting Out of Hand?" *Harvard Business Review,* November-December 1960.

Holland, D. M., and W. G. Lewellen, "Probing the Record of Stock Options," *Harvard Business Review,* March-April 1962.

"Rights Prove Profitable," *The Exchange,* New York Stock Exchange, April 1960.

"Stock Rights—An Analyst Weighs the Question of When to Sell," *Barron's Business and Financial Weekly,* September 16, 1957.

Part VI

Long-Term Financial Planning

19

Capital Budgeting

APPRAISING THE DEMAND FOR CAPITAL EXPENDITURES

Capital budgeting is the planning of those expenditures that will yield a return over a long period of time and a means of financing such expenditures. The purchase of land, buildings, equipment, and similar expenditures are involved in capital budgeting. It may also include a decision to absorb a subsidiary, purchase a patent, expand a product line of the company, or engage in an advertising program with expected benefits that will continue over a period of several years.

The problem of capital budgeting can be divided into two parts: the demand for capital expenditures, and the supply of funds for long-term financing. On the question of demand for capital funds, the following decisions must be made:

1. What funds will be available for capital expenditures during the coming budgetary period.
2. What total amount of funds are needed for capital expenditures.
3. On what basis should available funds be rationed among the proposed capital expenditures.

The supply aspect of capital budgeting concerns the following three considerations:

1. What amount of funds can be raised from internal sources for capital purposes.
2. How much can be raised at reasonable cost through outside financing.
3. By what means should the outside funds be raised.

Significance of Capital Budgeting It is a rare business that is not continuously confronted with opportunities for capital spending. Decisions to increase plant capacity, to modernize equipment, to acquire control of a competitor, or to expand the product line are typical of the questions that must be discussed and decided at the top managerial levels of a company. Because the amount of money involved in a capital expenditure is usually large, considerable care must be taken before a decision to spend is made. The securing of capital funds involves sacrifice. Funds are not available for all of the possible capital expenditures that might appear to be justified. A decision in favor of one capital expenditure means a decision against another capital expenditure. Furthermore, there is the danger that a decision in favor of a capital expenditure that appears to be profitable today may mean a lack of funds for an expenditure that appears in the following year to be far more profitable. Opportunities for capital expenditure today can be considered with some degree of confidence. Profitable opportunities that develop in the future, however, may be only vaguely foreseen, if at all.

The availability of capital funds determines the extent to which capital expenditures can be met. The cost of funds, furthermore, varies with the sources from which the funds are derived. In deciding which expenditures to make, it is necessary not only to estimate the profitability of each expenditure but also the sacrifice involved in raising the funds to make the expenditure. The preparation of a capital budget organizes and systematizes the process of decision-making. It aids in deciding two fundamental questions which must be answered if the company is to be operated successfully: (1) How much in total should be raised for capital expenditures? (2) What priority should be established in allocating funds for capital expenditures?

Presumably the goal of capital budgeting is to maximize the return on the funds invested by the owners of the business. This return takes two forms: a distribution of the earnings of the company as dividends or otherwise, and an increase in the market value of the owners' investment in the company. One basic budgeting decision is whether to sacrifice a generous distribution of earnings so that earnings can be reinvested in capital expenditures. Some highly prosperous companies have not paid any dividends for years, because the directors decided that reinvestment of the earnings would result in a sufficiently high rate of market appreciation in the stock price to satisfy the stockholders.

The adaptation of budgeting techniques to capital decision-making is comparatively new; theories in the area of capital budgeting are still relatively undeveloped. As a result there is a lack of uniformity among economists and businessmen with respect to the theory of capital budgeting. However, businessmen are becoming increasingly aware of the importance of capital budgeting, recognizing capital budgeting as a foundation on which financial decisions are based.

The Scope of Capital Budgeting   There is considerable variation in the length of the time interval for which a capital budget is prepared—from one year to ten years or more. Although there is this wide gap, five years is a commonly used figure. Where a capital budget is prepared for a period of several years, it is common practice to review the budget annually. The purpose of the annual review is to make whatever revisions, deletions, or modifications appear to be necessary as the passage of time changes the assumptions on which the capital budget was originally prepared. Sometimes a yearly capital budget is constructed in addition to a long-term budget. A capital budget prepared on a yearly basis is similar to the budget prepared for raw materials, wages, or sales. The budget will indicate the monthly expenditures for capital purposes and the monthly receipt of funds to pay for these expenditures. If an annual capital budget is prepared in addition to a long-term capital budget, the purpose of the annual budget is to facilitate reaching the goals indicated in the long-term budget. If the long-term budget is complex and involves many types of expenditures, an annual capital budget is likely to prove useful. If a long-term budget is relatively simple, the preparation of an additional annual budget is not as likely to be needed. For this reason, the preparation of an annual capital budget in addition to a long-term capital budget is confined mostly to large businesses.

CLASSIFICATION OF CAPITAL EXPENDITURES

The Bases of Classifying Capital Expenditures Classification is an aid in organizing the decision-making process on a logical basis. Among the bases used in classifying proposed capital expenditures are the following:

Profitability. It might appear that the only justifiable basis on which to classify capital expenditures is the relative profitability expected of each. If an expenditure on Project A is calculated to yield a higher return than expenditures on B or C, it might appear that no other consideration should be used in deciding to allocate capital funds to Project A. Project A, however, may be risky, and the estimate of profitability of Project A may be less definite than the estimates on B and C. Possibly, the profitability on Project A may be short-lived, while that of Projects B and C might expect to yield a slightly lower rate of profit but for a much longer period. Furthermore, expenditure of capital funds on Project A might reduce the profitability of existing company operations. For these and other reasons, it is usually dangerous to consider profitability alone as a basis for making capital budgeting decisions.

Aggressive or Defensive. Projects can be classified according to whether they are aggressive or defensive. An aggressive project is usually defined as one that is expected to increase the earnings of the company. A defensive project, on the other hand, is designed to combat any tendency that might develop to reduce the earnings of the company. A defensive project, in other words, is one undertaken to defend the existing profits of the company.

Postponability. Projects may be ranked according to the degree to which each may be postponed. The scrapping of old machinery and its replacement by new machinery may have a very low degree of postponability. On this basis, such a project would be ranked high. The construction of a parking garage or the purchase of land for a parking lot might be rated highly postponable, if the lack of parking space did not appear to affect the efficiency of employees.

Replacement or Addition. Projects may be classified according to whether they are replacements of existing facilities or additions to existing facilities. Replacement of a worn-out machine with a new one would be classified as a replacement expenditure. An entirely new machine, providing a service or operation not previously used by the company, would be classed as an addition.

Relation to existing operations. Proposed capital expenditures may be classified according to the degree with which they are related to the existing operations of the company. The decision of a company making cameras to produce photographic film would be much more closely related to the existing operations of the company than would a decision to produce textile fibers. In general, capital projects that are highly unrelated to the existing operations of a company tend to be riskier than those that are closely related, because unfamiliarity increases as relativeness decreases.

Pitfalls in Analyzing Capital Expenditures   It may clarify the process of selection of capital projects to list what is to be avoided. The seven items listed below are among the most important.

Simple replacement. Some companies work on a policy of simple replacement of certain capital assets according to a prepared schedule. The schedule might call for the automatic replacement of each truck that has been used for six years or the automatic replacement of a certain machine on reaching the age of ten years. This has the advantage of making certain capital budgeting decisions routine. The profitability of the company would be enhanced, however, if instead of automatic replacement, examination were to be made of the effect on profits when a new machine or truck is substituted for an older item.

Absolute necessity. In all capital investments there are alternatives that can be considered. In some cases, the alternatives may be so poor that they may he rejected with very little consideration. For example, the alternative to replacing the roof of a building damaged by a storm may be to permit the machinery in the building to suffer damage. In this example the alternative can be rejected without a time-consuming analysis of the effects of replacing the roof compared to not replacing the roof. Choices, such as the above one, that are obvious are not as common as is assumed by the management of many companies. In a larger number of situations than is generally recognized, alternatives are available that deserve consideration. As a general rule, it is unwise to assume that there are "no alternatives available."

The effect of taxes. It is sometimes assumed that the effect of corporate income taxes is uniform on capital investment, and, therefore, can be ignored in capital budgeting decisions. If there is a difference in time in which the investment in the project is returned, the effect of income taxes must be considered. Furthermore, depreciation schedules may be different for different capital projects. This, too, will affect taxes. Therefore, taxes should be included in the calculations for the probable profitability for different projects that are being considered.

Book Value. Valuation of property in considering capital expenditures is frequently necessary to determine the worth of an asset owned by the company. For example, one proposal for an expenditure may be to spend $50,000 to repair an existing machine. If the cost of the repairs are considered as expenses, there is no increase in the book value of the machine, and, therefore, no capital expenditure. If, however, the expenditure for repairs increases the useful life of the machine, it could justifiably be considered a capital expenditure, to be considered with other capital expenditures competing for the funds available to the company. Book value is often not a dependable guide in capital budgeting decisions. What the company can get for the asset or what the asset is worth to the company in its next best use is a better basis for valuation of those assets that are included in capital budgeting decisions.

Consideration of overhead. In determining the costs of a capital project, a portion of existing overhead expenses is sometimes allocated to the new project. Sometimes no consideration of overhead expenses is included in calculating the profitability of the capital project. Both methods are in error. For the sake of accuracy it is necessary to calculate the *increase* in overhead expenses resulting from the adoption of a particular capital expenditure. This will permit more accurate determination of the profitability of alternative capital expenditures.

Strategic necessities. It is sometimes argued that a capital expenditure must be made for reasons of business strategy regardless of the rate of return expected on the investment. For example, competing stores may be air-conditioned. It might be argued, therefore, that business strategy requires that all stores owned by a company be air-conditioned. If a decision to air-condition a group of stores is made on the basis of business strategy rather than on the basis of cost and profitability, funds available for capital expenditures may not be spent in the direction most beneficial to the company. Capital expenditures should be justified on an economic basis rather than on a basis of competitive strategy alone, particularly since strategic considerations are difficult to measure on any meaningful basis.

Difficulty of prediction. Since prediction is increasingly difficult the longer the period of time predicted, some managers use only short-term predictions in classifying proposed capital expenditures. For example, projects may be classified according to their effect on company profits only over the coming three-year period. In some cases, the effect of proposed capital expenditures on profits for the next single year are used as a basis for selection. It is clear that such an insistence on short-range considerations may lead to a faulty classification of alternative capital expenditures. Predictions of the effect of capital expenditures on company profits should be made for the expected useful life of the project, even though such predictions are made for several years in the future. Predictions covering many years in the future, however low the accuracy, are better than no predictions at all in making a choice between capital projects.

Preparing the Capital Budget In preparing the capital budget, the first step is generally the compilation of proposals for capital expenditures. Although most will originate at the higher officer levels, useful ideas for capital expenditures can sometimes come from individuals at the lower ranks of the company.

Suggestions for capital expenditures usually go through a number of screening processes. There may be a capital budget committee in each department of the company. Such a committee considers suggestions originating in the department, rejecting those considered defective, and recommends for further consideration those thought promising. In some cases, the department manager undertakes to screen suggestions originating in his department. The form that suggestions for capital expenditures must take varies considerably from one firm to another. In some cases, the first screening process is highly formalized, whereas, in other cases, it is rather informal. The degree of detail required for each proposal to be considered by the first screening committee again differs considerably from one firm to another. If a departmental screening committee exists, the next step may be for the screening committee to submit to the department manager those projects approved by it. The department manager may send back certain proposals to the screening committee for further evaluation or additional data. The approval of the department manager is generally required of all proposed capital expenditures affecting his department.

Proposals surviving the screening process of the departmental budget committee and the scrutiny of the department manager are then usually forwarded to a capital budgeting committee representing the company as a whole. An alternative is to submit proposals for capital expenditures from all departments to a budget director. In such a case, the budget director has the responsibility of eliminating any duplications that might be found in expenditure proposals submitted by various departments and of coordinating all the proposed expenditures into a single proposed capital budget for the company. A budget director coordinates and consolidates the proposals received from various departments so that the company's budget committee can save time in its deliberations. Because capital expenditures are generally large, affect the company for a relatively long period of time, and have an important bearing on the profits of the company, a company's capital budget committee generally includes the president, the treasurer, and other high ranking officers. The company capital budget committee considers the proposals received from each department in the light of the effect of such proposals on the company as a whole. Proposals will also be examined with respect to their effect on any policy directives received from the board of directors with respect to capital expenditures.

The proposals that survive the committee of company officers are submitted to the board of directors. Decisions on capital expenditures are among the most important decisions considered by the directors. The directors are concerned not so much with details as with the broad objectives of each proposal. It is the responsibility of the board to decide what departments are to receive emphasis. If the capital expenditures have not been ranked according to some basis dictated by the board, it will be the function of the board to determine the relative importance or priority of the proposals. The board may pare the list of proposals down to a number considered to be within the company's financing capacity. The board will also be concerned with the timing of the proposed capital expenditures. It must consider the stage of the business cycle in relation to the period of the proposed budget. If the economic conditions of the country and the industry are expected to be poor in the immediate future, the board of directors is likely to reduce the capital budget to a much smaller size than would be likely if the expectation were for a favorable economic outlook. Projects included in the budget submitted to the board of directors may be rejected, postponed, or adopted. The capacity of the company to raise the necessary funds for capital expenditures and the cost of such funds will also determine the size of the capital budget approved by the directors. Furthermore, the philosophy of the board of directors, whether cautious and conservative or otherwise, will be reflected in the deliberations.

The policy of the board might be to give tentative approval to projects submitted for its consideration in a capital budget. Those items that are given such approval are then returned to the department managers for detailed analysis of cost and expected benefits. The projects given tentative approval by the board may again be sent through the same screening process from department managers to budget director, to company committee and back to the board of directors. Arrangements are then made to secure funds for the approved capital projects. Finally, authorization is given by the board of directors for money to be spent to implement each approved capital project.

MEASURING THE RETURN ON CAPITAL EXPENDITURES

One of the most important aspects of the capital budgeting process is the identification of alternatives. One obvious alternative is not to make the capital expenditure. When the available alternatives are identified, it is necessary to appraise them as well as the proposal. This involves consideration of initial cost of each of the alternatives, the useful life of the proposal and each of the alternatives, the effect on earnings, and the effect on existing operations of the company. Precise answers to these considerations may not be available in all cases. What, for example, is the effect on the company's earnings of the installation of air conditioning in a factory building, or the purchase of land to be used as a recreational area for employees? In some cases, particularly in small businesses, decisions of this nature are made on the basis of what might be described as business intuition. Although business intuition may serve satisfactorily in some businesses as a basis for capital budgeting decisions, more sophisticated analytical techniques are generally advisable.

Ascertaining the Desirability of Capital Expenditures Most businesses are faced with more capital expenditure opportunities than can be financed with the funds available to the company. Capital funds must be rationed. In order that the rationing process may be intelligently applied to the available investment opportunities, the benefits expected from each proposed capital expenditure must be measured. Among the means for measuring prospective benefits are payback, average rate of return, time-adjusted rate of return and present worth of future cash flow.

Payback. One of the most important measures is *payback,* also known as *payout.* This measures the length of time needed to repay the investment of capital through the extra cash flow that is generated by the capital expenditure. The cash flow is calculated by adding the after-tax profit generated by the capital expenditure to the depreciation allowances set up for the capital expenditure. For example, a capital expenditure of $1 million for which an annual depreciation allowance of $150,000 is made, and one which generates income after taxes of $50,000, has a payback of five years. Because of the uncertainty of the future, it is understandable that businessmen seek to recover their investments as rapidly as possible. Hence a short payback period is attractive. In the above example, if the capital expenditure of $1 million has earned nothing beyond the cash flow of the first five years and had to be abandoned at that time, the company would at least have recovered its investment in the project, although it would have received no income from it. The payback setup is widely used in industry in America as a means of rating capital proposals. In some cases, payback is used as the initial means of screening various capital proposals. For example, expenditures for equipment may not be made by a company unless the payback period is no longer than three years. On the other hand, the proposed purchase of a subsidiary may not be further considered unless the payback period is six years or less. Payback is also used to choose between projects having equal desirability as determined by other measures.

The use of the payback as a means of choosing among investment possibilities is essentially a defensive mechanism. The actual useful length of life of the project is ignored, and no calculation of income beyond the payback period is included in this test. If an industry is one of high risk, its calculations of income decrease rapidly in accuracy for future years; or if political or economic conditions in the country are unstable, the use of the payback is justified. Furthermore, if shortages of cash plague a company, emphasis of rapid recovery of cash invested in capital projects may be a necessity.

The payback method can, however, lead to decisions that are not the best for a company. The payback is not a direct measure of earning power. The calculation of cash flow for two alternative capital expenditures is given in Table 19-1.

TABLE 19-1. CALCULATION OF CASH FLOW FOR TWO ALTERNATIVE
CAPITAL EXPENDITURES

Investment in each project: $1,000,000

	Cash Flow	
Year	Project 1	Project 2
1	250,000	100,000
2	250,000	150,000
3	200,000	150,000
4	175,000	200,000
5	125,000	200,000
6	100,000	200,000
7	50,000	200,000
8	–––––	200,000
9	–––––	200,000
10	–––––	200,000

The estimated cash flow for Project 1 results in a payback period of five years. The payback period in Project 2 is six years. However, Project 1 ceases to generate any cash flow after the seventh year, while Project 2 continues to generate $200,000 a year after the investment has been paid back through the added cash flow. The payback test would dictate the choice of Project 1 rather than Project 2. Probably the most serious weakness of the payback period as a test of investment alternatives is that it ignores the useful life of the asset for which the expenditure is being considered. Another weakness is that it ignores the cost of money. This is illustrated in Table 19-2.

TABLE 19-2. COST OF MONEY

Investment in each machine: $28,000

Year	Machine A	Machine B
1	10,000	4,000
2	8,000	6,000
3	6,000	8,000
4	4,000	10,000

The estimate of cash flow for both Machine A and Machine B indicates a payback period of four years. The recovery of investment in Machine A is, however, more rapid than is the recovery of investment in Machine B. From the standpoint of the cost of money, investment in Machine A is preferable to investment in Machine B.

A refinement of the payback measure is illustrated in Table 19-3. If a businessman wishes to divide his cash flow between a return on his investment and the recovery of the principal, he may use the calculation shown in this figure. Here the cash flow is divided between return on the investment at 10 per cent and recovery of the principal, which is accomplished in the ninth year. This measure is subject to the same criticism directed to the rough payback discussed earlier—receipts after the payback period are ignored.

TABLE 19-3. RETURN APPLIED TO CASH FLOW

(a) Year	(b) Investment (first of each year)	(c) Annual Cash Flow	(d) Return on Investment at 10%	(e) Annual Recovery of Investment (c minus d)	(f) Balance of Investment Unrecovered (end of year) (b minus e)
1	$1,000,000	$100,000	$100,000	-----	$1,000,000
2	1,000,000	150,000	100,000	50,000	950,000
3	950,000	200,000	95,000	105,000	845,000
4	845,000	200,000	84,500	115,500	729,500
5	729,500	200,000	72,950	127,050	602,450
6	602,450	200,000	60,245	139,755	462,695
7	462,695	200,000	46,270	153,730	308,965
8	308,965	200,000	30,897	169,103	139,862
9	139,862	200,000	13,986	186,014	-----

Average Rate of Return. The rate of return measures the relationship between the anticipated earnings of a capital investment and the amount of funds invested in the capital project. Unlike the payback method, the rate of return measure uses net earnings after allowance for depreciation. There are two methods that are in general use in applying the rate of return as a yardstick in comparing capital projects. One is the average rate of return, and the other is a time-adjusted rate of return.

The average rate of return method consists of adding all the projected earnings generated during the expected life of the project, after making allowances for depreciation, and dividing the total by the number of years comprising the life of the project. This gives a figure representing the average annual earnings of the project. By applying this figure to the average investment in the project during its life, the average rate of return can be calculated. Table 19-4 illustrates this method.

TABLE 19-4. AVERAGE RETURN ON INVESTMENT

Project A Useful life: 5 years Initial investment: $1,000,000			Project B Useful life: 8 years Initial investment: $1,000,000		
Income before Depreciation	Depreciation Allowance	Earnings after Depreciation	Income before Depreciation	Depreciation Allowance	Earnings after Depreciation
$400,000	$200,000	$200,000	$100,000	$125,000	$ 25,000 deficit
400,000	200,000	200,000	150,000	125,000	25,000
300,000	200,000	100,000	175,000	125,000	50,000
300,000	200,000	100,000	200,000	125,000	75,000
250,000	200,000	50,000	250,000	125,000	125,000
		$650,000	300,000	125,000	175,000
			300,000	125,000	175,000
			300,000	125,000	175,000
					$775,000

Average investment * (assuming no scrap value): $500,000

Average earnings: $\dfrac{\$650,000}{5} = \$130,000$

Average rate of return: $\dfrac{\$130,000}{500,000} = 26\%$

Average investment (assuming no scrap value) : $500,000

Average earnings: $\dfrac{\$775,000}{8} = \$96,875$

Average rate of return: $\dfrac{\$ 96,875}{500,000} = 19.375\%$

* One method of calculating average investment is to subtract the estimated scrap value at the end of the useful life from the initial investment and divide by 2.

Table 19-4 shows two projects each of which require an initial investment of $1 million. The useful life of Project A is calculated to be five years, and that of Project B eight years. The earnings pattern during the life of Project A shows a declining trend, while that of Project B shows a rising one. Using straight line depreciation and no scrap value gives an average investment for each project of $500,000. Calculating the average rate of return on the average investment of each project indicates a return of 26 per cent per annum on the life of Project A and of 19.375 per cent during the life of Project B. This method of comparing projects is superior to the payback method, because it takes into consideration the earnings generated by each project over the useful life of the projects.

The main disadvantage of this method is that money received in the future is treated with equal importance as is money in the present. This method is also criticized because it deducts depreciation expenses in measuring rate of return. Although from the standpoint of accounting principles this is correct, it is obvious that a capital investment once made cannot easily be unmade. Money sunk into a capital project cannot usually be recovered except through cash flows generated by the project. By this criterion it may be argued that the payback is preferable because it does not account for depreciation.

Time-adjusted Rate of Return. Money to be received in the future is worth less than money available in the present. Therefore, calculating the present value of a future receipt of money is useful to capital budgeting. To understand this concept, assume that a person is to be given $10,000 ten years from the present date. What is the present value of the future receipt of money? To answer this one must decide upon a rate of return. If 6 per cent is selected, the present value is that sum of money which invested at 6 per cent compound interest will equal $10,000 at the end of ten years, a figure calculated by use of the formula below. Although the formula provides a precise answer, the use of a table of present values of future receipts of $1 is sufficiently accurate for most purposes. Such a table is given in Appendix A. In this example one reads from the table that the figure for $1 to be received at the end of ten years discounted at 6 per cent is .558. This is multiplied by 10,000 to get the answer $5,580.

FORMULA FOR PRESENT VALUE OF FUTURE RECEIPT OF MONEY

$$p = \frac{s}{(1+i)^t}$$

where p = present value of future receipt of money
s = amount to be received in future
i = interest rate per period (usually annual)
t = number of periods (usually years) interest is compounded.

Using the example in the paragraph above,

$$p = \frac{\$10,000}{(1+6)^{10}} = \$5,584$$

If a person expects to receive a sum of money annually for a given number of years, the present value of the future stream of dollars is that sum of money which invested at a selected rate of interest will yield the given stream of dollars. Appendix B provides a table giving approximate values for this purpose. Suppose a person expects to receive $1,000 annually for twenty years. What is the present value of this annuity discounted at 6 per cent? Appendix B gives the value of $1 annually for 20 years discounted at 6 per cent as 11.470. Multiplying by 1,000 gives the present value at 6 per cent of $1,000 received annually for 20 years as $11,470.

The officers of a company may examine capital proposals by determining the present value of the net cash receipts discounted at a rate representing the cost of acquiring the funds necessary for the investment. A table can be prepared presenting the expected annual cash expenses (including taxes but not depreciation) of a particular investment as well as the expected annual cash receipts from the investment. The stream of expected expenses can be subtracted from the stream of expected receipts and the difference discounted at the rate representing the cost of acquiring the funds necessary for the investment to indicate the present value of the net stream of income. If a machine having an initial cost of $100,000 is expected to have a useful life of four years during which it is expected to generate a net cash flow above maintenance and other expenses amounting to $40,000 each year, the following calculations are made:

Initial investment	$100,000
Salvage value at end of four years	10,000
Selected discount rate	8 per cent
Net cash flow annually (expected cash receipts less expenditures)	40,000
Present value at 8 per cent of $40,000 received annually for four years	132,480
Present value at 8 per cent of net receipts for four years minus original investment	32,480
Present value at 8 per cent of $10,000 salvage to be received at end of four years	7,350
Difference between initial investment and present value of net cash receipts plus present value of anticipated salvage (this is the sum of the last two items)	$39,830

If alternative investment proposals are being examined, each of which requires $100,000, the above calculations can be made of each proposal to determine which is the most promising in terms of present value. The selection of the 8 per cent discount rate is arbitrary. If the money for the investment is borrowed, the cost of the loan usually determines the discount rate. If the investment is made from internal funds, the discount rate selected is usually the assumed cost of retained income, the estimating of which is discussed later in this chapter.

Present Worth of Future Cash Flow. Adjustment for the time value of money required the selection of a discount rate. In the example above at the rate of 8 per cent the present value of the future stream of cash of $40,000 annually for four years was $132,480. It is obvious that at lower discount rates the present value is higher; at higher discount rates it is lower. If two projects each requiring the same initial investment are compared on the basis of discounted cash flow, a low discount rate may favor one project and a high discount rate the other. In the example below, the present values of the cash flows of two projects at various rates of discount are given.

	Project A	Project B
Initial Investment	$100,000	$100,000
Anticipated cash flow		
Year 1	40,000	10,000
2	35,000	20,000
3	30,000	30,000
4	20,000	40,000
5	10,000	50,000
	$135,000	$150,000

6% Discount

		Project A		Project B	
	1	2	3	4	5
Year	Discount Factor (from 6% column of Appendix I)	Cash Flow	Discounted Value (Column 1 x 2)	Cash Flow	Discounted Value (Column 1 x 4)
1	.943	$40,000	$ 37,720	$10,000	$ 9,430
2	.890	35,000	31,150	20,000	17,800
3	.840	30,000	25,200	30,000	25,200
4	.792	20,000	15,840	40,000	31,680
5	.747	10,000	7,470	50,000	32,350
			$117,380		$121,460

10% Discount

		Project A		Project B	
		Cash Flow	Discounted Value	Cash Flow	Discounted Value
Year	Discount Factor				
1	.909	$40,000	$ 36,360	$10,000	$ 9,090
2	.826	35,000	28,910	20,000	16,520
3	.751	30,000	22,530	30,000	22,530
4	.683	20,000	13,660	40,000	27,320
5	.621	10,000	6,210	50,000	31,050
			$107,670		$106,510

12% Discount

		Project A		Project B	
		Cash Flow	Discounted Value	Cash Flow	Discounted Value
Year	Discount Factor				
1	.893	$40,000	$ 35,720	$10,000	$ 8,930
2	.797	35,000	27,895	20,000	15,940
3	.712	30,000	21,360	30,000	21,360
4	.636	20,000	12,720	40,000	25,440
5	.567	10,000	5,670	50,000	28,350
			$103,365		$100,020

14% Discount

		Project A		Project B	
		Cash Flow	Discounted Value	Cash Flow	Discounted Value
Year	Discount Factor				
1	.877	$40,000	$ 35,080	$10,000	$ 8,770
2	.769	35,000	26,915	20,000	15,380
3	.675	30,000	20,250	30,000	20,250
4	.592	20,000	11,840	40,000	23,680
5	.519	10,000	5,190	50,000	25,950
			$ 99,275		$ 94,030

16% Discount		Project A		Project B	
Year	Discount Factor	Cash Flow	Discounted Value	Cash Flow	Discounted Value
1	.862	$40,000	$ 34,480	$10,000	$ 8,620
2	.743	35,000	26,005	20,000	14,860
3	.641	30,000	19,230	30,000	19,230
4	.552	20,000	11,040	40,000	22,080
5	.476	10,000	4,760	50,000	23,800
			$ 95,515		$88,590

If the cash flows of Projects A and B are discounted at 6 per cent Project B is preferable.   At 10 per cent there is little difference between the two.   At rates of 12 per cent and higher, Project A is preferable.   Therefore, the choice between the two projects depends upon the discount rate selected.   If this is the estimated cost to the company of the funds to be invested in A or B, the company's cost of capital will determine the choice of the project.[1]   If the cost of capital is below 10 per cent, Project B is selected; if the cost is 10 per cent or above, Project A is selected.   The point of indifference between the two projects is between 9 and 10 per cent, as shown in Fig. 19-1.

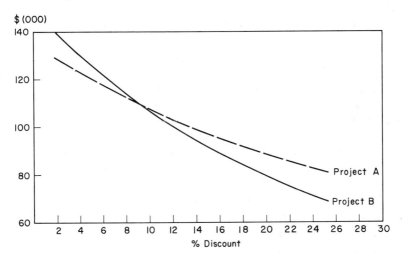

Fig. 19-1   *Effect of discount rates on present value of cash flows of two projects.*

From the data given above it can be seen that at a discount of 12 per cent the cash flow from Project B is $100,020.   At a discount of 14 per cent the cash flow from Project A is $99,275.   This analysis gives us the discount rate at which the anticipated cash flow equals the initial investment.   It is called the rate of return on the investment.   For Project A the time ad-

---

[1] Cost of capital is discussed later in this chapter.

justed rate of return (of the anticipated cash flow) is about 14 per cent; for Project B it is 12 per cent. The time adjusted rate of return on investment is sometimes used to rank alternative capital projects, which would favor Project A in this example. However, if the cost of capital is ignored, a company may not make the most profitable choice among capital projects, since at rates below 10 per cent Project B is preferable to A and at rates of 10 per cent and above Project A is preferable. The cost of capital funds changes frequently, and when it does it may change the relative attraction of alternative capital projects.

Recognizing Uncertainty In comparing the value of future receipts and expenses, the present value of a dollar to be received in the future is discounted at whatever rate of interest is considered appropriate by management. Tables showing the discounted value of a future receipt of dollars do not take into consideration the risk factor. Any decision involving the future involves risk. In comparing different proposals for capital expenditures, the choice should involve some consideration of the different degrees of risk involved in each proposal. In general, the risk becomes greater the larger the number of years in the future involved in the decision. It is partly for this reason that a rapid payback of investment is very attractive to businessmen. It was shown above, however, that an undue insistence on an avoidance of risk by making capital budgeting decisions on the basis of rapidity of payback of the investment could lead to unprofitable choices among capital investment alternatives. Adjustments in the figures representing future expenses and receipts on alternative capital expenditures may be made. However, such adjustments for risk may be challenged on the ground that they are merely guesses. Possibly, such adjustments are merely a reflection of intuitive judgment. On the other hand, they may represent guesses based on experience relevant to the choices being made among capital expenditure proposals. In all capital budgeting decisions, risk is considered, either explicitly or implicitly. The degree of risk involved in capital budgeting decisions can be reduced by using the techniques used for measuring returns on capital expenditures and by using more sophisticated techniques than can be presented in this book. Although risk can be reduced by the use of such techniques, it cannot be entirely eliminated.

In order to give management some basis on which to include risk in a capital budgeting decision, some estimate of the range of possible error in computing the rate of return on proposed projects may be included. Two projects might each have an estimated rate of return of 20 per cent. The range of possible rates of return for one might be from 15 per cent to 25 per cent, and for the other from 10 per cent to 30 per cent. The second project obviously involves the greater risk. There is the possibility of a lower rate of return, but also the possibility that the return might be higher than the estimate. The choice between the two projects would reflect the degree of willingness of the management to undertake risk. In most cases, however, where the most probable rate of return of two projects is the same, management will choose that project which involves the least range of error in estimating the return. To simplify the problem of choosing between two alternative capital investments, a bar chart may be prepared indicating the most probable return for each project and the range of possible error. See Fig. 19-2. Let us assume that there are four projects requiring capital expenditures of $10 million each. The most probable rates of return for

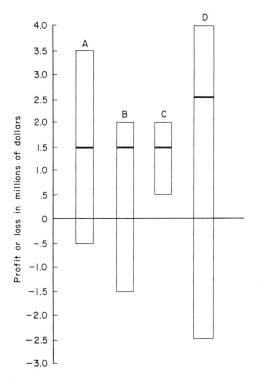

Fig. 19-2 *Probable return and range of possible error on capital projects.*
Most probable estimate (or modal estimate of profit on projects A, B, and C is $1.5 million; on project D is $2.5 million. Range of estimated possible profit or loss is indicated by length of bar.

Projects A, B, and C are estimated to be $1.5 million. Both Projects A and B entail the possibility of loss. The possibility of loss is greater for Project B than it is for Project A. Furthermore, the possibility of a higher rate of return than the most probable calculated return is greater for Project A than for Project B. Therefore, in choosing between Projects A and B, management would undoubtedly choose Project A. In comparing Projects A and C, management must choose between varying degrees of error in estimating the probable return. Although the most probable return for

A and C is $1.5 million per year, there is calculated to be no probability of loss on Project C, whereas there is a possibility of loss in Project A. In most instances, management would choose Project C in preference to Project A because of the greater degree of certainty in estimating the profits.

Project D promises a probable return of $2.5 million, but the range of error in calculating the probable return is considerable. Although the return on Project D may run as high as $4 million, it is also possible that a loss as great as $2.5 million might be suffered. A choice between Projects C and D would indeed test the gambling instincts of management. If the worst possible loss calculated for Project D proved to be true, management would have to consider the effects of such a loss on the company as a whole. If such a loss would bankrupt the company, would it be worth the risk in order to receive a probable return of $2.5 million and the hope of receiving a return as high as $4.5 million? A probable return of $2.5 million is considerably better than a probable return of $1.5 million. In this respect Project D is more attractive than Project C. The higher probable rate of return on Project D can be considered a premium for the risk involved in Project D. In this example, the premium for the risk involved in Project D amounts to $1 million, the difference between the probable return on Project D and Project C. Is the premium for risk worth the hazard involved in suffering a possible loss? This is a choice similar to the one faced by a young man who reportedly asked Baron Rothschild his advice on choosing between a safe investment and a speculative one. The Baron is reported to have replied, "Young man, do you wish to eat well or to sleep well?"

In addition to calculating the upper and lower limits of the estimated profits for each project, it is useful to know the skewness of the dispersions of estimated profits above and below the figure representing the most likely estimate of profits. On Projects B and D in Fig. 19-2, it appears that there is greater likelihood that the actual profits will be less than the most probable profit than that it will be more. For Project A, a profit greater than the most probable profit appears to be equally likely as a profit less than the most probable. The forecast of income from a capital project may be arranged in the form of a frequency distribution, as indicated in the example below:

> There are three chances in 100 that the annual profits will be $6 million.
>
> There are twenty chances in 100 that the annual profits will be $4.5 million.
>
> There are forty chances in 100 that the annual profits will be $3 million.
>
> There are thirty chances in 100 that the annual profits will be $1.5 million.
>
> There are seven chances in 100 that the annual profits will be zero.

In the above examples, the modal (most likely) forecast of annual profits is $3 million. The distribution also indicates that there is a greater likelihood that the annual profits will be less than $3 million than that it will be more than $3 million. In other words, the above distribution of chances of annual income is skewed in a downward direction rather than in an upward direction from the modal point. The calculation of a frequency distribution for possible profits to be earned from a project enables management to judge the degree of accuracy of the forecast of profits. If the variation of possible profits is large, as it is in Project D in Fig. 19-2, the greater is the uncertainty of the forecast of profits, and hence the greater the risk.

CONSIDERATIONS OF THE COST OF CAPITAL

The sources of funds for capital expenditures are long-term debt, preferred stock, common stock, retained earnings, and depreciation allowances. Each of these sources has its uses, and each has its disadvantages. In one sense the disadvantages of each of these sources represent the cost of each. Some of the methods used to measure the cost of these sources are discussed below. These should be considered as approximate methods of measuring the cost of capital. Some of the costs, in the form of disadvantages or sacrifices, of using specific sources are not readily apparent. It is difficult, therefore, to evaluate all the costs inherent in these sources of capital. For example, interest rates are not the sole measure of the cost of long-term borrowed funds. An increase in long-term indebtedness of a corporation affects the value of the common stock of the corporation. It may also affect the relative ease with which a company can borrow short-term funds. The contracts under which long-term funds are borrowed may include restrictions on the financial operations of the company. Furthermore, the cost of raising capital funds may depend to some extent upon the use to which the funds are to be put. It would be an oversimplification to assert that a company would improve its earning capacity if it applied funds to a capital project expected to yield a return in excess of the visible cost of acquiring the funds. Studies are being made to develop more refined methods of determining all the costs of acquiring capital funds. As these studies yield usable results, they will enable businessmen to decide capital budgeting questions systematically and precisely. In the meantime, businessmen must use the best information available in particular situations and let judgment, intuition, or guesswork apply where information is unavailable.

Cost of Long-Term Debt Some businessmen have an aversion to using debt as a means of financing capital projects. This aversion is found to exist not only in the minds of those who own and manage small and unincorporated businesses, but also in the minds of those who sit on the boards of directors of large corporations. No matter how profitable the capital expenditure might appear to be, a rigid policy exists in some companies not to spend any money for the project if it requires going into debt. Aversion to debt financing is actually one aspect of the unwillingness to undertake additional risk. This aversion to debt financing is to some extent explained by memories of the unfortunate consequences of debt financing during the depression of the 1930's. It was the conviction of some that a serious depression was inevitable after World War II.[1]

The financial costs of raising funds by borrowing is the amount of interest expense that must be incurred in raising the funds. If the proceeds of a bond issue of $10 million face value is $10 million and the interest payments are 4.5 per cent per annum, the interest cost to the company is 4.5. If the bond issue is sold at a discount, however, the calculation of interest costs is somewhat more complicated. An approximation of the interest costs can be illustrated by the following method. Suppose a bond issue with a face value of $10 million is marketed at a price which yields a net amount to the company of $9,800,000. Let us assume that the life of the bond issue is ten years, and that the interest payments each year are $400,-000. The amount of funds available to the company is $9,800,000, and the amount which must be repaid at the end of ten years is $10 million. The average between these two figures is found through the following calculation:

$$\frac{\$9,800,000 + \$10,000,000}{2} = \$9,900,000.$$

Since the corporation must pay $200,000 more upon the redemption of the bond issue than it received upon the original sale of the bond, the discount of $200,000 represents additional interest cost to the corporation. One-tenth of the amount of this discount is added to the interest payment each year. The approximate annual interest cost is $400,000 plus $20,000, or $420,000. Dividing $420,000 by $9,900,000 (representing the average amount of the loan) gives a figure of .0424. Expressed as a percentage, the interest cost is approximately 4.24 per cent per annum. To get a more accurate figure one can refer to bond tables that are used by investment analysts, banks, and others in calculating to a high degree of accuracy the interest cost of bonds of various maturity, discount and premium, and interest payments.

If the cost of raising funds through long-term debt is to be compared to raising funds by an increase in equity, the effect of income taxes must be considered. Interest payments on bonds are considered an expense, while

---

[1] Probably the most celebrated example of this type of thinking was reflected in the management policies of the board of directors of Montgomery Ward and Company during the ten years following the end of World War II. In this case, the board was so convinced that an economic collapse was inevitable that the company was kept in a position of liquidity, which cost it many opportunities for profitable expansion during the prosperous postwar years. It was not until the composition of the board of directors was changed with the removal of its chairman that the unseemly emphasis on liquidity was modified and opportunites for capital expansion exploited.

dividend payments on stock are considered a distribution of profit. If the tax rate on corporation income is 48 per cent, each dollar paid in interest can be considered to reduce taxable income by the same amount. Expressed in other terms, for each dollar paid in bond interest, the income tax liability of the company is reduced by 48¢. It follows from this reasoning that only 52 per cent of the amount paid in bond interest represents a reduction of net income of the company. Applying this percentage to 4.24 per cent, representing the pre-tax cost of the loan, the after-tax cost of the bond issue in the above illustration is 2.205 per cent. It should be emphasized that the interest cost represents only the visible cost of raising funds by means of the sale of bonds. As the discussion in the previous paragraph suggests, the total cost in the sense of the total burden in raising funds by means of bonds cannot readily be reduced to figures.

Cost of Preferred Sock Preferred stock, unlike most bonds, are perpetual securities. Unless the corporation intends to retire the preferred stock, no adjustment need be made, as in the case of bonds, for the difference between the issue price and the redemption price. The cost of raising funds by issuing preferred stock can be calculated by dividing the annual dividends by the price per share received by the company at the time of issue. For example, if a preferred stock is sold by a company at $90 a share and pays a dividend of $4.50 per annum, the visible cost to the company of the funds is 5 per cent. This is the cost after taxes, since the payment of dividends on preferred is not considered an expense of the corporation. The cost including corporation income tax of 48 per cent is $8.65, or 9.6 per cent.[2] This means the corporation must earn 9.6 per cent on the investment financed by the preferred stock issue to "break even." If the corporation plans to retire the preferred stock at a price different from the issue price, this difference must be considered in calculating the cost of funds raised by the sale of preferred stock. If the preferred stock is retired at a price higher than the issue price, as is commonly done, the cost of the funds raised by the sale of preferred stock is higher than the dividend rate. To approximate the cost of funds raised by a preferred stock issue which is to be retired at a price different from the issue price, the method of approximation used in the case of bonds can be applied to the preferred stock.

Cost of Common Stock Because the market price of common stock rises and falls sharply, it is difficult to predict the cost of securing funds by the sale of common stock. The simplest measure of the financing cost of a

[2] When including the corporation income tax in the comparison of costs of bond and equity financing, care must be taken not to include the effect of taxes twice. Comparing the preferred stock above with the bond in the previous paragraph, we find that the pre-tax cost of the bond financing is 4.24 per cent and of the stock is 9.6 per cent. The after tax cost is 2.205 per cent and 5 per cent, respectively. Comparison of each of these pairs of figures shows that the cost of preferred stock financing in this example is 2.2 times as high as bond financing.

capital project by means of common stock is based on the current returns of the common stock. If the market value is $40 per share and the most recent financial statement shows that the net earnings of the corporation amount to $8 per share before taxes, the cost of financing (including the expense of the corporate income tax) by means of common stock is calculated to be 20 per cent per annum. The earnings after taxes (at 48 per cent) amount to $4.16, or 10.4 per cent. The use of this measure implies that those capital expenditures financed by common stock and expected to bring in a return of less than 20 per cent should be rejected, and that only those projects expected to yield a return of more than 20 per cent should be considered.

There is considerable variation in the stock market in the price of common stock relative to earnings. The stocks of some corporations sell at a price at which the earnings represent a 20 or 30 per cent return after corporate income taxes, while other stocks sell at a price at which the earnings represent only a 4 to 5 per cent return. In 1961, the earnings per share on the common stock of International Business Machines Corporation was $6.12, while the stock sold at prices close to $600 a share. Why were investors willing to pay such sums for a share of IBM stock at a time when the current rate of earnings amounted to approximately 1 per cent return on the price paid? It is clear that frequently the price at which common stock sells on the market bears little relation to the recent earnings per share of the company. In the case of IBM stock, the purchasers were expecting a considerable increase in earnings per share in the relatively near future. The price at which common stock can be sold on the market, therefore, depends more on the expectation of future income than it does on past income. A better measure of the cost of raising funds by selling additional common stock results from an estimate of probable future earnings of the corporation. Two calculations should be made: (1) an estimate of the future earnings per share if the contemplated capital expenditure is not made, and (2) an estimate of the future earnings per share if the contemplated capital expenditure is made. If these calculations show that an increased return per share can probably be made by the company if the expenditure for the capital project is made, then there is reason to make the expenditure and finance it by common stock. Included in the estimate of the cost of financing by means of the sale of common stock, and this is true of preferred stock and bonds as well, is the cost of distributing the issue. If the issue is small, the cost can be relatively high, running to 15, 20, or even 30 per cent of the dollar amount of the issue. If the issue is a large one, the cost of distribution is a relatively small percentage of the total amount. The invisible costs must also be considered, as they must in the case of preferred stock and bonds. The contract with the investment banking house distributing the issue of common stock may require that the banking house name one or two members to the board of directors of the corporation. As part of the payment to the investment banking house for distributing the issue of common stock, an option to buy common shares at stated prices, which may prove to be far below the future market price, may be included. These and other disadvantages or limitations on management freedom are "costs" that must be considered in capital budget decisions. If the cost of raising funds by common stock is compared to the cost of raising funds by bonds, it should be remembered that the payment of interest on bonds is considered an expense that reduces the taxable income of the corporation, an advantage not enjoyed in raising funds by the sale of common stock.

When an issue of common stock is sold on the market where existing shares of the stock are traded, the price at which the new issue of stock is offered must be less than the market price of the outstanding stock at the time that the offer is made. Placing a block of common stock on the market increases the supply of the common stock available for sale on the market. The effect of this is to depress the market price of the existing stock. As to how much the market price will be depressed by the offer of a new issue of stock depends upon various factors. If the size of the new issue of common stock is small relative to the amount of stock outstanding in the market, the depressing effect of the additional supply will be small. If stock prices in general are rising, an additional issue may be absorbed by the market without depressing the price of the existing stock at all. If the issue of new stock is announced at the same time as the release of favorable news about the company, such as an increase in the dividend rate or a promising new product or development in the company, the favorable announcement may so increase the demand for the stock that the additional supply put on the market is absorbed at the existing market price or even at rising market prices.

The guide mentioned above under which capital projects are expected to earn a rate of return on common stock greater than would be earned by the common stock in the absence of the expenditure requires modification if used by a company with a considerable growth potential. If investors are willing to pay $600 for a share of IBM stock that has earned slightly over $6 in the previous year, it does not follow that the corporation should consider all the capital expenditures to be financed by the sale of common stock that yield a rate of return in excess of 1 per cent. If many such projects with a low yield were financed by the sale of common stock, investors would be disillusioned as to the growth prospects of the company, and the market price of the stock would drop. In the case of IBM and other companies with high prospects for growth, the market price of common stock is of almost no value in guiding the decisions as to what capital projects to finance by common stock. In such cases, some other measure must be used. Possibly, an arbitrary minimum rate of return may serve to eliminate low yield projects from consideration. For example, those projects expected to yield a return of less than 20 per cent on the investment may be eliminated from further consideration.

Cost of Retained Earnings   Earnings that are not paid out in dividends to the stockholders are available to the corporation for investment. As a matter of fact, if earnings cannot be profitably invested by a company, there is no justification for withholding them from the stockholders. Since retained earnings are made available to the company without any increase in debt or securities outstanding, they are sometimes considered to be a cost free source of capital. Because, however, the retention of earnings reduces the amount of dividends paid to the stockholders, retained earnings represent a sacrifice on the part of the owners of the business. Hence, the retention of earnings involves a cost.

Unfortunately, the measurement of the cost of retained earnings is not a simple matter. If there were no costs of distribution of securities and if there were no personal income taxes, the amount of money paid out by a corporation in dividends could be reinvested in the corporation by the stockholders, and the amount returned to the corporation would be equal to the amount distributed in dividends. Under such conditions, the cost of retained earnings could be assumed to be the earnings per share of the stock. If $1 million is paid out in dividends by a corporation, stockholders receive $1 million in income. The receipt of this income must be reported by the recipients on their personal income tax returns. The part of the $1 million that is paid in personal income taxes would depend on the income tax liabilities of each of the stockholders. Wealthy stockholders might pay more than half of what they receive in dividends in their tax payment. Stockholders in the lower income tax bracket would pay a smaller percentage of their dividend income in taxes. Some stockholders, including financial institutions, might not be required to pay any portion of dividends received in taxes. In any case, some of the $1 million distributed by the corporation would not be available for reinvestment in the company. Furthermore, the mechanics of reinvestment by stockholders would involve some expense, which would further reduce the amount that might be returned to the company. These expenses and the payment of personal income taxes on the dividends distributed can be avoided by the company through retention of earned income. It is justifiable, therefore, to consider that the cost of retained earnings is less than the cost of raising additional funds through the sale of common stock.[3] But how much less? What the company saves in the retention of earnings by avoiding the cost of distribution of earnings can be estimated with accuracy. But the amount of personal income tax not paid by stockholders due to the retention of earnings by the company cannot be accurately measured unless the taxable income of every stockholder of the company is ascertained. This is ob-

---

[3] There is disagreement on this issue in the literature of finance, with some writers taking the position that the cost of retained earnings is less than the cost of common stock financing and others arguing that for capital budgeting purposes the cost of both should be considered equal. The latter position is presented in Ezra Solomon, "Measuring a Company's Cost of Capital," *The Journal of Business,* University of Chicago Press XXXVIII, No. 4, October 1955, pp. 240-252.

viously not feasible where a large number of stockholders is involved. The average income tax liability for dividends received can perhaps be estimated roughly by the directors of the corporation. Suppose that 40 per cent of dividends distributed by the corporation are paid out in personal income taxes by the stockholders. The stockholders would be able to return to the company only 60 per cent of what they received in dividends. The retention of earnings by the corporation in this case saves from the personal income tax 40¢ for every $1 distributed in dividends. The stockholders would have to earn $1.67 in an alternative investment for every $1 earned by income retained by the corporation before retention of earnings would become uneconomic to them. Assume also that the costs of distribution of common stock is estimated to be 10 per cent for a particular corporation. Using these assumptions, the cost of retained earnings would be 50 per cent of the cost of raising funds through the sale of common stock. Thus it would appear that the directors could justify the retention of earnings even where the investment of the retained earnings would yield a lower return than the rate currently earned on the market price of the common stock. Such an action, of course, has the result of diluting the rate of earnings on the common stock, a result deplored by nearly all stockholders. It is an article of faith generally accepted by investors that directors should strive to limit retained earnings to an amount that can be invested to yield a return equal to or greater than the current rate of return on the stockholders' investment in the company.

The dividend policy adopted by a corporation generally involves considerations other than its effect on the income tax liability of the stockholders receiving the dividends. Directors typically have a dividend policy which guides them in determining what portion of earnings will be paid out in dividends each year. Corporations generally try to maintain a stable pattern of dividend payments; they commonly do not vary the amount of dividends paid year by year in accordance with calculations as to the relative cost of retained earnings for capital purposes and the opportunities available for such investment of retained income. Although the directors are reducing some of the burden of the income tax of stockholders by retaining the earnings of the corporation, the retention of earnings deprives the stockholders of the choice to invest income in other channels. The retention of earnings by the directors of the corporation, in effect, is a forced increase in the investment in the company by the owners.

Cost of Depreciation Funds Depreciation represents an estimate of the amount of investment in capital assets used up during a particular period of business. Depreciation is not a cash expense. It reduces the earnings reported for a period, but is not a charge against the funds for the period. Therefore, the allowance for depreciation represents an amount of funds generated internally that is available for reinvestment in the business. The retention of funds represented by the allowance for depreciation may be used in a variety of ways. The funds may be deposited in a bank account to accumulate a sum sufficient to purchase assets to replace the ones worn out. They may be used to retire indebtedness of the corporation, thus putting the corporation in a better position to borrow money when purchasing assets to replace those worn out. It is not necessary, of course, for a corporation to replace worn-out assets with similar assets. The character of the business may change over a period of years, making other uses for funds retained in the business more profitable than a simple replacement of worn-out assets. Funds derived from depreciation allowances may appear to be costless. This is not so. The cost of funds retained as a result of depreciation allowances may be assumed to be the same as the cost of funds obtained as a result of retention of net earnings of the corporation.

The Average Weighted Cost of Capital   It was stated above that an increase in the long-term indebtedness of a corporation affects the value of the common stock of a corporation. A corporation with a low level of debt relative to equity may be able to borrow money by issuing bonds yielding 4 per cent. The same company with a higher level of debt already outstanding may have to offer a yield of 5½ per cent in raising money for capital purposes. The capacity of each company to borrow is limited. It is limited in the sense that as the debt of a company increases, its cost of borrowing rises, perhaps slowly at first and then steeply as the amount of outstanding debt approaches what lenders consider safe borrowing limits. A company cannot, therefore, depend upon debt alone as a source of capital funds. Other sources must be used even though they may appear to be more costly.

Measurement of the cost of each of the sources of capital funds was discussed above. Since capital funds are derived from a variety of sources, it is necessary to determine the average cost of funds derived from these sources. This figure is a valuable guide in deciding the total capital expenditures to be approved.

The first step in measuring the average cost of capital is estimating the cost of each of the sources the company uses in long-term financing. It does not matter whether the before income tax or after income tax cost is used, so long as one or the other is uniformly applied to the sources of capital. In the illustration below we shall use the before tax cost. Assume the following cost of sources of capital are estimated:

Bonds	6 per cent per annum
Preferred stock	13 " " " "
Common stock	20 " " " "
Retained earnings	15 " " " "

The next step is the assigning of weights to the sources of capital. The weights commonly selected are the percentage of each source in the existing structure of the firm. If the directors feel that the present structure is not the best for the company and that a different proportion of stocks to bonds or retained earnings would improve the financial position of the company, the weights assigned may be the proportions of each source in the "ideal" structure determined by the directors for the corporation under current conditions. Let us assume that the weights assigned by the directors are as follows:

Bonds	30 per cent or	.30
Preferred stock	15 " " "	.15
Common stock	35 " " "	.35
Retained earnings	20 " " "	.20
	100 " "	1.00

The final steps are to multiply the cost of each source of capital by its weight and add the results. The computation is shown below:

Source of Funds	Cost %	Weight	Weight X Cost
Bonds	6	.30	1.80
Preferred stock	13	.15	1.95
Common stock	20	.35	7.00
Retained earnings	15	.20	3.00
Average Weighted Cost of Capital			13.75 per cent

The importance of the concept of the average weighted cost of capital is based on the obvious fact that companies do not raise capital funds from one source alone. Some companies may confine their capital sources to common stock and retained earnings. Most, however, will use long-term debt occasionally or regularly, and many will use preferred stock as well. If a company sells bonds yielding 6 per cent to finance one project and common stock at a cost of 20 per cent to finance another, it is an error to assume that the first project need earn a return of 6 per cent to cover its cost and the second project 20 per cent to cover its cost. The fact that the financing of the first project increased the debt of the company may have forced the financing of the second project through common stock rather than through additional bonds. In approving capital projects it is a mistake to tie individual sources of funds to individual projects. If a proposed capital expenditure will not yield a return of at least the average cost of capital for a firm, it should ordinarily be rejected. The average weighted cost of capital can serve as the cutoff point in considering capital proposals. In the above illustration, the cutoff point is 13.75 per cent. Only those capital proposals expected to yield more than 13.75 per cent would be given consideration by the board of directors. After estimating the average weighted cost of capital, some companies place the cutoff point at a higher level. In the above example it might be placed at 15 or 20 per cent.

IMPLICATIONS FOR MANAGEMENT

Capital expenditures are sometimes required as a result of governmental regulations. Some expenditures are made with employee safety as a primary reason. Others may be made to improve community welfare or good will rather than profits. Management must consider not only financial factors but also nonfinancial ones. In making capital budgeting decisions, many factors are considered. A few will be discussed below.

Government Regulation and Taxation The effect of income taxes on the choice of capital expenditures has been discussed above. The effect of the federal income tax was noted in connection with the choice between bonds and stocks in financing. For the sake of illustration, a corporate income tax rate of 48 per cent was assumed.[4] In bringing income taxation into consideration in comparing costs of alternative sources of funds, it is usually assumed that the current income tax rates will continue in the future. Is this assumption a reasonable one? The possibility of change in rates of taxation on corporate income is always present. It is necessary for management to consider the possibility that the tax may be raised or lowered. Yet, unless political considerations at the time of making capital budget decisions indicate the probability of a change in tax rates, it is safest for management to assume that the existing rates will continue.

Stockholders' Attitudes The body of stockholders of a company are a very important potential source of funds. It will benefit a company to cultivate this source of funds with care. This is particularly true when a company wishes to raise funds through a sale of common stock. Frequently, this can be accomplished with least cost to the company by offering the stockholders rights to buy additional shares at a price slightly below the existing market price. Although the directors of a corporation have the obligation to manage the company for the benefit of the owners, there is considerable variation among boards of directors in carrying out this obligation. The trend since World War II has been in the direction of recognizing the importance of cultivating the good will of stockholders. Furthermore, since World War II, stockholders have taken an increasingly strong interest in the affairs of the corporations they own. The implications for management have been twofold: (1) to consider the effects of proposed capital expenditures from the standpoint of the stockholders' benefit, and (2) to recognize that a body of satisfied stockholders is a valuable source of funds for the financing of capital expenditures.

Significance of Market Price of Common Stock If a corporation undertakes capital expenditures whenever it can raise the necessary funds for less than the expected return from the expenditure, it might be led to depend

---

[4] In 1965, the tax on net corporate income was 22 per cent on the first $25,000 of net taxable income and 48 per cent on income in excess of $25,000.

heavily upon debt financing to cover most of its capital expenditures. The excess of earnings over the cost of borrowed funds would increase the total profits available for distribution to the stockholders or for reinvestment in the business. But any increase in indebtedness increases the risk of insolvency resulting from an unexpected decline in business activity.

Social Aspects The direction of capital expenditures by management and the methods used to finance these expenditures have a very important effect on the economic health of a country. It might be assumed that funds available for investment in capital projects will be directed to those projects that promise the greatest reward in terms of profit. If corporations paid out all their earnings in dividends and then competed with other businesses for funds to finance proposed capital projects, funds would tend to flow to those corporations whose proposed capital expenditures promised the greatest return on investment consistent with the degree of risk involved. In other words, the market place would direct the flow of investment funds in those directions considered by investors to be most likely to yield the greatest benefits to them. A large proportion of funds invested in capital projects, however, are not derived from the market place for investment funds. Rather, they are financed by funds retained by corporation management. The result is that funds retained by directors of a corporation and used for capital expenditures may be used to finance projects of less benefit to investors than would be the case if the investors were given the opportunity to choose among competing corporations in placing their funds. Obviously, the choice of capital projects financed by depreciation allowances and retained earnings is not effectively subjected to the test of the market place.

As was mentioned above, the retention of earnings by corporation management is partly a result of tax considerations. If taxes were eliminated from influencing directors in setting their dividend policy, the choice of capital expenditures might be different. In any case, solid evidence to back up any conclusions in this area is lacking.

If a company is large and has a diversified range of activities, it also has a diversified list of capital projects from which to choose in making its capital budget. Within large, diversified corporations, a rationing mechanism is at work allocating capital funds among competing demands for capital expenditures. To some extent, therefore, capital projects must stand the "test of the market" within a company when competing for scarce capital funds, and presumably the allocation of the available funds is made to capital projects largely on the basis of what will most benefit the owners.

Questions

1. How does capital budgeting differ from annual budgeting?
2. What are the goals of capital budgeting?

3. How is risk taken into consideration in evaluating proposals for capital expenditures?
4. If a truck or machine used by a company wears out, it seems obvious that it must be replaced. Is there any choice available to management? Explain.
5. "In all capital investments there are alternatives that can be considered." Are there exceptions to this statement? Explain.
6. From what sources are suggestions for capital expenditures derived?
7. What is the payback or payout method of choosing between alternative capital expenditures? Why is it sometimes called a defensive method?
8. Distinguish clearly between net income and cash flow.
9. Describe average rate of return as a standard to measure capital projects.
10. What are the sources of funds for capital expenditures?
11. How is the cost of long-term debt measured?
12. How is the cost of equity funds for capital purposes measured? What is the effect of income taxes in comparing the cost of bonds with that of stocks in financing?
13. Can the current market price of the common stock of a corporation be used as a guide to deciding whether or not a project should be financed by a sale of common stock? Explain.
14. Do earnings retained by the company cost anything? Why or why not?
15. If the allowance for depreciation is not accumulated in the form of cash, can it be considered as a source of funds for capital projects? Explain.

Selected Readings

Bailey, M. J., "Formal Criteria for Investment Decisions," *Journal of Political Economy,* October 1959.

Baldwin, R. H., "How to Assess Investment Proposals," *Harvard Business Review,* May-June 1959.

Barish, Norman N., *Economic Analysis,* Part IV, McGraw-Hill Book Co., Inc., New York, 1962.

Chamberlain, Neil W., *The Firm: Micro-Economic Planning and Action,* McGraw-Hill Book Co., Inc., New York, 1962, Chap. 12.

Dean, Joel, *Managerial Economics,* Prentice-Hall, Inc., Englewood Cliffs, N.J., 1951, Chap. 10.

Haeberle, William L., "Profits and Managers: Key Factors in Business Stability," *Indiana Business Review,* February 1962.

Haynes, William Warren, *Managerial Economics,* The Dorsey Press, Inc., 1963, Homewood, Ill., Chap. 13.

Helfert, E. A., "Checkpoints for Administering Capital Expenditures," *California Management Review,* Spring 1960.

House, William C., "The Optimal Capital Investment Strategy Under Conditions of Risk and Uncertainty," *The Business Review,* University of Houston, Summer 1961.

Másse, Pierre, *Optimal Investment Decisions,* Prentice-Hall, Inc., Englewood Cliffs, N.J., 1962, Chap. 2.

Nemmers, Erwin Esser, *Managerial Economics,* Part VI, John Wiley & Sons, Inc., New York, 1962.

Shubin, John A., *Managerial and Industrial Economics,* The Ronald Press Company, New York, 1961, Chaps. 11 and 12.

Waterman, Merwin H., "The Numerator and Denominator of Profits," *Michigan Business Review,* May 1962.

20

Planning the Capital Structure

ALTERNATIVE SOURCES OF FUNDS

Variations in Capital Structure of Industries

THE ASSET side of a balance sheet lists the materials, equipment, real estate, and other items of value, tangible and intangible, that the company uses in its business operations. The liabilities and net worth side of the balance sheet lists the various sources of financing of the assets. These sources consist of short-term debt instruments, long-term debt instruments, and the investment of the owners in the business. We are concerned in this chapter with the long-term financing of the firm, which is shown by the capital structure. The *capital structure,* known also by the term *financial structure* or *financial plan,* is composed of the long-term debt and the owners' equity. For a corporation, this comprises bond issues and other long-term debt, preferred stock, common stock, and retained earnings. For many companies, particularly small ones, the capital structure is unplanned, except at the beginning, and develops as the company expands largely on the basis of decisions made without reference to any existing financial plan. Many companies prosper in the absence of any financial plan for securing funds for the company. It is becoming increasingly recognized, however, that a carefully planned capital structure will permit the company to adjust more easily to meet changing conditions.

There is considerable variation among industries and among individual companies in each industry in the proportion of debt and equity used in financing the acquisition of assets. This variation reflects differences in individual judgment on the part of boards of directors, differences in degree of risk from one industry to another, and variations in growth rate of individual companies.

At first glance, it might appear odd that such a wide degree of variation exists between corporations in the use of debt and equity in financing the

337

acquisition of assets. Even in cases where the characteristics of two firms are very similar with respect to age of the company, products or services sold by the company, and size, there might be considerable difference in the capital structure. Although the facts on which decisions are made by the board of directors can be very similar for two firms, individuals differ in their judgment of the importance of various factors, in their estimate of future economic conditions for their industry and for the country as a whole, and particularly in the degree of financial conservatism guiding the thinking of each.

Formulation of Objectives   In formulating policies, whether in the field of advertising, sales, production, personnel administration, or finance, the goals that the policies are expected to reach must be clearly indicated. If the goals formulated by the board of directors are unclear, planning to reach the goals will be haphazard and uncoordinated. The goal of business planning is not necessarily a simple one of maximizaton of profit alone. Other objectives, such as maximization of sales, diversification of products, maintenance of control, and avoidance of possible antitrust action may be subsidiary goals of company operations. Financial planning must be tailored to fit the overall objectives of a company. If the overall objectives of a company are kept clearly in mind, the directors can better establish the goals of financial planning. For most companies, the financial objectives would include the following:

1. To include a degree of flexibility so that the financial plan can be adapted with a minimum of delay to meet changing conditions in the future.
2. To take advantage of different rates of interest and costs of using equity funds so as to reconcile the conflicting objectives of raising funds at the least cost and keeping risk at a minimum.
3. To provide funds when they are needed and in the amount they are needed, so as to assure financing of capital expenditures without undue delay.
4. To reduce the risk of loss of control of the company.

In addition to the above general requirements of good financial planning, there may be specific requirements reflecting a company's particular situation. The emphasis given to each of the above overall objectives will differ from one company to another. For some companies, keeping the capital structure simple may be considered to be an important objective. In many other companies, it may be considered advantageous in raising funds to use a variety of preferred stock, mortgage bonds and debentures, and perhaps more than one class of common stock. Furthermore, the relative importance of these objectives will change with shifting conditions. To survive in an economy that is constantly changing, it is necessary for the policies of a company to be adaptable. In a competitive industry, the principle of survival of the fittest is constantly at work eliminating those companies that are financially weak or unable or unwilling to adapt to changing conditions. In a rapidly expanding industry, the growth in sales may be enough to permit the continued existence of companies both well managed and poorly managed. Such a situation, however, does not continue indefinitely. Inevitably, the time comes in every industry when growth rates slow down. In the years immediately following World War II, for example, demand for services and products of all kinds was so intense that nearly every business, however managed, could survive. This happy situation, happy from the standpoint of producers, did not last long. The decade of the 1950's was one of a relatively slow rate of growth of the economy as a whole, interrupted by several recessions of business activity. It is during such times that the difference between weak and strong management and between effective financial planning and ineffective planning is made evident.

The Problem of Maintaining an Optimum Capital Structure The optimum capital structure for a corporation is that combination of bonds, preferred stock, and common stock that provides the ideal amount of funds needed at any given time at terms most advantageous to the company. It is usually difficult to determine the ideal amount of funds that should be invested in a company, and it is even harder to determine the ideal mix of securities and internal sources of financing to achieve the desired amount. Nevertheless, the concept of this goal, however difficult to determine in quantity and structure, must be kept in mind in making decisions involving long-term financing.

Since it is not possible to determine with precision the total amount of long-term funds representing the ideal investment at any given time for a company, the best that can be done is to set a rather broad range within which the optimum volume of investment is presumed to lie. If a company has difficulty in finding proper uses for retained earnings, it could be argued that there is too much investment in the company. Presumably, the easiest way to correct this overinvestment would be to reduce some of the surplus through a distribution of dividends. Yet, if a company has insufficient funds on hand to finance a profitable project, it can be argued that there is too little capital invested in the company. If the projects requiring capital investment are indeed worthy, the remedy for the condition of underinvestment is to retain a larger portion of earnings, sell additional common stock, or increase the long-term debt of the company. As business conditions change, the ideal volume of investment in a company will change also. To some extent, adjustment to these changing conditions can be made by changing the volume of intermediate credit secured by the company, or even by changing the amount of short-term debt.

Underinvestment in a company is usually indicated by one or more of the following:

1. Inability to take advantage of cash discounts on purchases, and hand-to-mouth buying of materials and supplies.
2. A cash level too low to maintain the volume of payments made by the company without danger of overdrawing the account of the company in its bank.
3. A level of raw materials inventories too low to assure uninterrupted operations or a volume of finished goods too low to meet customers' demands without undue delay.
4. Vulnerability to seasonal or minor declines in business activities.

Companies in a condition of underinvestment are undoubtedly much greater in number than those companies facing the problems of overinvestment. Many small businesses are opened by individuals starting out on a "shoestring," which is another way of saying that the initial investment in the enterprise is dangerously low. Enterprises begun in a condition of underinvestment must be successful from the very start in order to survive. They are not in a position to wait out a slow buildup of sales to a profitable level nor to suffer an unexpected decline in income.

It is possible, on the other hand, for too much investment to be tied up in an enterprise. The condition that signals too high an investment is usually excessive liquidity. A company that has a larger volume of cash in the bank than is needed for efficient operations is not managing its cash efficiently. Although a large amount of cash in the bank may give a feeling of security to the owners of the business, the cash is not earning any income for the owner. A level of cash in excess of the amount needed to support a given volume of business should be changed into some other form of asset or distributed to the owners of the company. The company that carries an unusually large investment in low yield marketable securities, such as United States Treasury securities, probably has a larger investment than can profitably be handled by the business. Investment of excess funds temporarily in short-term, low-yield securities does not indicate a position of overinvestment. However, a large investment in low securities continued for a long period signals the probability of overinvestment. If the stockholders of a company wish to invest in high-safety, low-yield government bonds, they could better do so directly rather than investing in the stock of a company the assets of which include a "permanent" investment in government securities.

Correcting a condition of overinvestment, contrary to the problem of finding a solution to underinvestment, is relatively easy. One of the solutions is to liquidate the investment in low-yield securities and distribute the excess cash to the owners of the company. Another is to use the excess liquid assets for expansion or modernization. However, caution should be exercised before a decision is made to use surplus funds. A condition of excess liquidity may tempt the managers of a business to embark on a program of expansion that is not economically justifiable. Where money is available, it is easy to argue that it should be spent. Overinvestment may lead to an uncritical acceptance of opportunities for capital expenditures.

Size and Its Bearing on Financial Planning   The size of a company has an important bearing on the availability of funds from different sources. A very small company, whether a partnership, proprietorship, or a corporation, must depend almost exclusively for its long-term funds upon the owners of the company. As emphasized in an earlier chapter, it is very difficult for small companies to secure long-term loans from any source, although the existence of small business investment companies has reduced this difficulty somewhat. The capital structure of small companies consists almost entirely of owners' investment plus retained earnings. A small corporation has greater flexibility than has an unincorporated business in raising long-term funds. Common stock can be sold to the public where the total amount needed is $100,000 or even less. However, the sale of such a small amount of stock is expensive, unless it can be sold by the corporation directly to investors. This is frequently done by corporations locally owned and well known in their community. But where stock must be sold to the general public through the services of an investment banker, the cost for small issues is often prohibitive.

In using common stock to raise long-term funds, there is a greater danger to a small company than to a large company in the possible loss of control of the corporation. The distribution of $100,000 of common stock cannot be scattered as widely as can a distribution of $10 million in common stock. The possibility of a dissident group of stockholders organizing for the purpose of getting control of the corporation is generally greater for a small corporation than it is for a large one in those cases where the block of shares exercising control is less than 50 per cent of the shares oustanding. As a result, the owners of businesses in the form of small corporations frequently prefer to limit the rates of growth of their companies to what can be financed by means of retained earnings.

The larger company generally has a greater degree of choice in planning its capital structure. It is not limited to retained earnings and additional investment by the owners. The larger company can sell common stock to the general public, preferred stock, or any of a wide variety of bonds. The cost of distribution of a large dollar volume of securities is low compared to the costs of a small distribution. A large issue of common stock can be scattered widely by a group of investment banking houses, thereby making loss of control unlikely. The percentage of the total receipts of a large distribution that represents the cost of distribution is low. If the amount to be raised is large enough, it is not necessary, in order to lower the costs of distribution, to limit the issue to one type of security. To raise $300 million, it is entirely feasible to use a combination of common stock, preferred stock, and bonds. As a matter of fact, the raising of a very large sum of money for a corporation may necessitate the use of a variety of securities rather than limiting the securities to a single type. Thus, the existence in the capital structure of a large corporation of a variety of long-term instruments is a result partly of choice and partly of necessity.

CONSIDERATIONS OF RISK AND CONTROL

Nature of Risk   There are two general types of risk that must be considered in planning the capital structure of a firm.   One risk inherent in financing the corporation is the risk of loss of control of the company in cases where control is held by less than 50 per cent of the voting stock.   In such cases, the planning of each security issue gives considerable attention to this risk.   The distribution of more than $600 million in stock held by the Ford Foundation required a syndicate of investment bankers to use every effort to insure a wide distribution of the stock in small lots.   The use of non-voting common stock in the capital structure of the corporation is another means of reducing the risk of loss of control.

One of the attractions of using preferred stock as a means of raising capital funds is that it does not generally carry with it the privilege of voting for the directors of the corporation.   If preferred stock is included in the capital structure of a company, it generally carries some voting rights, such as the right to vote for or against a change in the charter of the corporation.[1]   The use of preferred stock in the financial plan of the corporation reduces the assurance of regularity of dividend payments to the common stockholder, since one of the privileges associated with most preferred stock issues is the prior claim on the earnings of the corporation.   Furthermore, the preferred stockholder is generally given a prior position in liquidation in assets of the corporation.

Another risk that must be considered in planning the capital structure of the corporation is bankruptcy.   All debts, except for some rare cases of bonds with a perpetual life, have a maturity date.   Payment of the principal amount of the debt must be made on this date or according to a schedule of retirement provided in the contract.   Failure of the company to pay the principal of a debt when it is due constitutes an act of bankruptcy.   Failure to pay interest on a debt when it is due is also an act of bankruptcy, except in the case of income bonds.   Payment of short-term debt, such as accounts payable and bank loans, can usually be coordinated with the receipt of income from sales.   Payment of interest and retirement of principal on long-term debts, however, requires careful budgeting on the part of company officials.   In planning the capital structure of a corporation, a fundamental decision must be made regarding the proportion of long-term debt in the total capital structure.   In the public utilities field, many companies raise more than half of their long-term funds by means of bonds.   In mining companies, on the other hand, one-third or less of the total capital struc-

---

[1] The voting characteristics of preferred stocks are discussed in Chapter 11.

ture is in the form of bonds., The regularity of income enjoyed by most companies in the utility field reduces the risk of inability to meet interest and principal payments on debts when due.   Partly for this reason and partly because the rates charged by most public utilities are subject to some governmental regulation, bond financing plays an important part in the capital structure of public utilities.

Within each industry, of course, there is considerable variation in the capital structure of corporations.   A company well established in its field can generally forecast receipt of income with a greater degree of accuracy than can a newcomer.   There is less risk, in other words, to an established company in any industry in using long-term debt than there is to a company recently organized.   To some extent, the variation from one company to another within an industry in the proportion of debt in the capital structure can be explained by variations in the degree of risk the boards of directors of different companies are willing to assume.   Boards, except in rare cases, are elected only by the common stockholders.   The policies adopted by the directors are usually designed to reflect the best interests of the common stockholder rather than the preferred stockholder or bondholder.   If a company enters a period of adversity, it is generally the common stockholders that will suffer first, usually in the form of declining market prices of their stock.   Therefore, under ordinary circumstances directors will not raise funds by the sale of preferred stock or bonds unless the added risk resulting from the sale of the securities is compensated by the expectation of added benefits to the common stockholder.   The added benefits hoped for ordinarily take the form of increased income available for the common stockholder.

Trading on the Equity   Most organizations have a larger amount of assets employed in the business than are secured by the owners of the company. In other words, most businesses acquire a part of their total assets by going into debt.   The degree to which debt is used in acquiring assets in a business is called *trading on the equity*.   The degree to which debt and preferred stock is used in the total financial structure we shall call *capital leverage*.   Trading on the equity is measured by using one of the two following ratios: the ratio of total debt to total assets or the ratio of total debt to net worth.[2]   In our treatment of the subject we shall measure trading on the equity by dividing total debt by total assets.   We shall measure capital leverage by dividing total debt plus preferred stock outstanding by total assets. These results are usually presented as percentages.   Table 20-1 shows the computation of the figure representing trading on the equity and the figure representing the capital leverage.

---

[2] In some books on finance, short-term debt is excluded from this measure.   It seems appropriate to include short-term debt, however, because, like long-term debt, it permits the acquisition of assets without an increase in the investment of ownership capital.

TABLE 20-1. BALANCE SHEET OF X CORPORATION

Assets	Liabilities and Net Worth	
$10,000,000	Short-term debt	$ 2,000,000
	Bonds	3,000,000
	Preferred stock	1,600,000
	Common stock	3,000,000
	Surplus	400,000
$10,000,000		$10,000,000

$$\text{Trading on the equity } \frac{2{,}000{,}000 + 3{,}000{,}000}{10{,}000{,}000} = 50\%$$

$$\text{Capital leverage } \frac{2{,}000{,}000 + 3{,}000{,}000 + 1{,}600{,}000}{10{,}000{,}000} = 66\%$$

If a company is able to secure assets through use of debt, it may be able to increase earnings of the corporation without increasing owner investment. If the assets acquired by use of debt increase earnings by an amount greater than the cost of the debt, the return on owners' investment is increased without an increase in owners' equity. If, by using capital leverage, assets acquired by debt and preferred stock raise the income of the corporation by more than the cost of debt and preferred stock dividends, the return on common stock investment is increased.

Some companies use capital leverage to a considerable degree in their financial structure. This is particularly true of companies in the public utilities field. Any increase in the use of leverage, however, carries with it an increase in risk. Because interest payments and preferred stock dividends have priority over common stock dividends, a small decline in sales may eliminate any income available for common stock dividends. If the proportion of bonds to total assets is high, a relatively small decline in gross income may result in eliminating net income entirely. On the other hand, the use of leverage can be very attractive. A small increase in gross income may increase the net income available to the common stockholder by a considerable amount. Where an increase in gross income can be predicted with confidence, the risk involved in the use of leverage may appear to be worth taking in order to enjoy the expected increase in income after payment of interest and preferred stock dividends.

The effect on the earnings available to the common stock of using bonds and preferred stock in the capital structure of a company is illustrated in Table 20-2. Here three different structures, each totaling $20 million, are compared. If income before interest and taxes amounts to $2 million, a capital structure composed entirely of common stock would yield a return of 5.2 per cent after payment of federal taxes. The capital structure of Company Y, which includes $8 million in bonds with an interest payment of 4 per cent, yields a return of 7.28 per cent on the common stock after payment of interest and taxes. In Company Z, the capital structure con-

TABLE 20-2. EFFECT ON EARNINGS THROUGH USE OF BONDS AND PREFERRED STOCK

Liabilities and Net Worth	(X)	(Y)	(Z)
Bonds 4%	―――――	$ 8,000,000	$ 8,000,000
Preferred stock 5%	―――――	―――――	7,000,000
Common stock	$20,000,000	$12,000,000	$ 5,000,000
Total	$20,000,000	$20,000,000	$20,000,000
Income before interest and taxes	$ 2,000,000	$ 2,000,000	$ 2,000,000
Interest on bonds	―――――	320,000	320,000
Income before taxes	2,000,000	1,680,000	1,680,000
Federal income tax (48%)	960,000	806,400	806,400
Income after taxes	1,040,000	873,400	873,400
Dividends on preferred stock	―――――	―――――	350,000
Earnings on common stock	1,040,000	873,400	523,400
Return on common stock (%)	5.2%	7.28%	10.47%
Income before interest and taxes	$ 1,000,000	$ 1,000,000	$ 1,000,000
Interest on bonds	―――――	320,000	320,000
Income before taxes	1,000,000	680,000	680,000
Federal income taxes (48%)	480,000	326,400	326,400
Income after taxes	$ 520,000	$ 353,600	$ 353,600
Dividends on preferred stock	―――――	―――――	350,000
Earnings on common stock	$ 520,000	$ 353,600	$ 3,600
Return on common stock (%)	2.6%	2.95%	.072%

sists of $8 million in bonds at 4 per cent, $7 million of preferred stock at 5 per cent, and $5 million in common stock. Here an income of $2 million before interest and taxes results in a return on the common stock of 10.47 per cent after payment of taxes. The increased yield of Y and Z is a result of the use of financial leverage. However, the risk involved is indicated in Fig. 20-2 if income falls to $1 million before interest and taxes. In this case, the return on the investment amounts to 5 per cent before payment of interest and taxes. This results in a return on the common stock of Company X of 2.6 per cent after payment of income taxes. In Company Y, since the payment of interest is an expense deductible before income taxes and since the bond interest amounts to 4 per cent, the yield on the common stock of Company Y after payment of income taxes is higher than for Company X. However, Company Z has preferred stock outstanding on which $350,000 dividends are due. The income after payment of taxes is the same for Company Y and Company Z. In Company Z the preferred stock has first claim on this income. After payment of preferred stock dividends, there is very little left for the common stock of Company Z. If an income tax of 52 per cent (the rate prior to 1964) had been in effect, the tax for Company Z would have been $353,600, leaving income after taxes of $326,-400. The result would have been income insufficient by $23,600 to pay the dividends due on the preferred stock. Thus the 1964 tax law, which reduced the 52 per cent tax rate on income of corporations to 48 per cent beginning with 1965 income, had the effect of changing for Company Z a "deficit" after payment of preferred stock dividends to a positive figure for income available to common stock.

By determining the income on common stock after payment of interest, taxes, and preferred stock dividends on several levels of income before interest and taxes, a graph can be prepared showing the effect at different levels of earnings of different methods of financing. Table 20-2 illustrates three methods of financing the acquisition of assets totaling $20 million, and Fig. 20-1 shows the effect on earnings available to the common stock of these three methods of financing through a wide range of income before interest and taxes. As income before interest and taxes increases, the increase in the percentage return on common stock rises at the slowest rate where common stock alone is used in the financial structure (Company X), at a more rapid rate if bonds are used in the financial structure (Company Y), and at a still more rapid rate if both bonds and preferred stock are used (Company Z).

There is a point of intersection for each pair of lines. Each point of intersection marks the indifference point in comparing the two methods of financing; at each of these points the return on the common stock will be the same for both methods of financing used. The indifference point between X and Y is $799,231 in income before interest and taxes. At this level of income before interest and taxes the return on common stock will be 2.08 per cent, whether common stock alone is used or whether $8 million in 4 per cent bonds and $12 million in common stock constitutes the capital structure. At any level of income before interest and taxes below $799,231 the return on the common stock is greater for the capital structure of Company X than it is for the capital structure of Company Y. At levels of income before interest and taxes above $799,231 the return on the common stock is greater for structure Y than it is for structure X. Similar conclusions can be drawn for the indifference point at which X and Z intersect and the point at which Y and Z intersect. This graph shows the value to a company in accurate forecast of future income. If future income can be forecast with confidence, the capital structure can be changed to maximize the return on common stock. The degree of probability that earnings will fall below any of the three indifference points indicated in Fig. 20-1 measures the degree of risk involved in using bonds and preferred stock in the capital structure. Because the income of a company in the public utilities field can usually be forecast with a greater degree of accuracy than for a manufacturing or mining company, the use of bonds and preferred stock in the capital structure of public utility companies is much more common than it is for companies in the field of manufacturing and mining.

In 1964, the Congress of the United States reduced the maximum rate on taxable corporate income (the rate applying to income in excess of the first $25,000) from 52 per cent, the rate in effect for a decade, to 50 per cent on 1964 income and to 48 per cent on income of 1965 and later years. The effect of this reduction on planning the financial structure of corporations is illustrated in Fig. 20-1. At every level of income before interest and taxes the return on common stock is higher at the 48 per cent rate of taxation· than at the 52 per cent rate. Furthermore, the leverage principle applies to make the return on common stock higher at the reduced rate of taxation if more leverage is used. Most important is the shift in the indifference

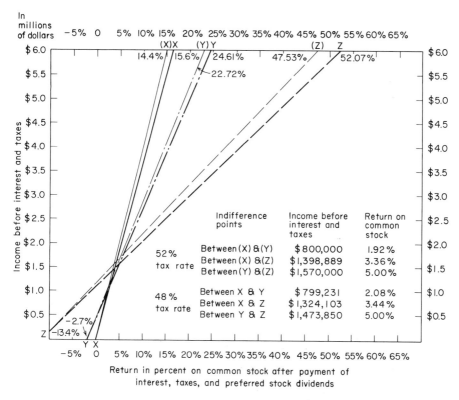

Fig. 20-1 *Illustration of principle of leverage.*

points caused by the reduction in taxes. In comparing a capital structure including bonds with one not using bonds, the indifference point is a lower dollar figure and the rate of return at the indifference point is a higher percentage with the 48 per cent tax rate than with the 52 per cent rate. The tax reduction enacted in 1964 reduced slightly the risk in using bonds. Stated in other terms, at the 48 per cent tax rate a larger proportion of debt could be used in the capital structure with no increase in risk than could be used at the 52 per cent tax rate. It would appear, therefore, that one result of the reduction in corporate income taxes should be some increase in long-

term debt relative to common stock in corporate financing. The indifference point between Y and Z in Fig. 20-1 is a lower dollar figure at the 48 per cent tax rate than at the 52 per cent rate. It is important to note, however, that the rate of return is the same percentage at either tax rate. The rate of return on common stock at the indifference point of two capital structures differing only in that one includes preferred stock and the other does not is the dividend rate on the preferred stock. The preferred stock dividend in Table 20-2 and Fig. 20-1 is 5 per cent. The rate of corporate income taxation does not influence the choice between financing by means of preferred or common stock, since the tax is levied on the income prior to payment of dividends on preferred or common stock. The reduction in the tax rate on corporate income from 52 per cent to 48 per cent merely made it possible to achieve a 5 per cent return on the sum of the preferred and common stock at a lower dollar figure representing income before interest and taxes, as illustrated in Fig. 20-1.

The points of indifference can also be calculated by means of formulas. The formulas are given below, together with the application of the formulas to the information on Table 20-2 for the capital structures X, Y, and Z.

FORMULAS FOR DETERMINING INDIFFERENCE POINTS

X = Income before interest and taxes
C = Dollar amount of capital with common stock alone
C_y = Dollar amount of common stock where financing includes common stock and bonds
C_p = Dollar amount of common stock where financing includes common and preferred stock
C_z = Dollar amount of common stock where financing includes common stock, preferred stock, and bonds
I = Dollar amount of interest on bonds
P = Dollar amount of dividends on preferred stock
T = Corporate income tax rate

1. The point of indifference in comparing common stock alone with common stock and bonds is found by the formula,

$$\frac{X(1-T)}{C} = \frac{(X-I)(1-T)}{C_y}$$

Applying the formula to structures X and Y in Fig. 20-2,

$$\frac{X(1-.48)}{20,000,000} = \frac{(X-320,000)(1-.48)}{12,000,000} \qquad X = \$799,231$$

If earnings before interest and taxes are $799,231, the return on common stock is 2.08 per cent, whether the capital structure is as in X or as in Y.

2. The point of indifference in comparing common stock alone with common and preferred stock is found by the formula,

$$\frac{X\,(1-T)}{C} = \frac{X\,(1-T) - P}{C_p}$$

3. The point of indifference in comparing common stock alone with common stock, preferred stock, and bonds is found by the formula,

$$\frac{X\,(1-T)}{C} = \frac{(1-T)\,(X-I) - P}{C_z}$$

Applying the formula to structures X and Z in Fig. 20-2,

$$\frac{X\,(1-.48)}{20,000,000} = \frac{(1-.48)\,(X-320,000) - 350,000}{5,000,000} \qquad X = \$1,324,103$$

If earnings before interest and taxes are \$1,324,103, the return on common stock is 3.44 per cent, whether the capital structure is as in X or as in Z.

4. The point of indifference in comparing common stock and bonds with common stock, bonds, and preferred stock is found by the formula,

$$\frac{(X-I)\,(1-T)}{C_y} = \frac{(1-T)\,(X-I) - P}{C_z}$$

Applying the formula to structures Y and Z in Fig. 20-2,

$$\frac{(X-320,000)\,(1-.48)}{12,000,000} = \frac{(1-.48)\,(X-320,000) - 350,000}{5,000,000}$$

$$X = \$1,473,850$$

If earnings before interest and taxes are \$1,473,850, the return on common stock is 5 per cent, whether the capital structure is as in Y or as in Z.

5. The point of indifference in comparing common stock and preferred stock with common stock, preferred stock, and bonds is given by the formula,

$$\frac{X\,(1-T) - P}{C_p} = \frac{(1-T)\,(X-I) - P}{C_z}$$

Control As mentioned above, one of the risks involved in business operations is the risk of loss of control of a company. The degree of this risk varies with circumstances. For proprietorships and partnerships, the question is not one that enters into the long-term financing plans for the company unless, in the case of a partnership, it is necessary to add one or more new partners to secure the desired long-term funds. For a small, locally owned corporation it may be necessary for a person or group of persons wishing to assure control of the corporation to own at least one share more than 50 per cent of the voting shares outstanding. In the case of large corporations with stock widely scattered among many stockholders, control can be assured with a block of stock considerably less than 50 per cent of the voting shares.   The assurance of maintaining control may be considered of such importance in the financial planning of a company that it may slow the rate of growth which could otherwise be achieved.   By depending entirely upon internal sources of funds for expansion, the proportion of equity held in the hands of the controlling group can be maintained unchanged.   Similarly, if debt is used to finance expansion, there is no dilution of voting control held by the controlling group of stockholders.   Increasing debt, however, increases the possibility of loss of control to the creditors as a result of bankruptcy.   In financing expansion by means of issuing additional voting shares, the risk of loss of control of the corporation can be lessened if the investment banking firm distributes the shares widely and in small lots.   In any case, one of the best assurances of maintenance of control of the corporation is for those in control to operate the company with a high degree of efficiency, with an adaptability to changing conditions, and in a vigorous competitive spirit.   If a company is so managed, the stockholders, large and small, are likely to maintain their loyalty toward the existing management against the efforts of other groups that may try to seize control.

MARKETABILITY AND COST OF DISTRIBUTION

The economic law of supply and demand determines the price for the securing of funds.   When long-term funds are scarce in relation to demand, the cost is high, and vice versa.   The supply of investment funds for business is available on a variety of terms.   Some investors demand security for their funds.   Others are willing to lend money to business on an unsecured basis if the interest payment is higher than for a secured loan.   To meet the differing conditions demanded by the owners of funds, some large businesses must offer bonds, preferred stocks, and common stock.   Furthermore, they may have to offer a wide variety of bonds and preferred stocks, and on rare occasions a variety of common stocks.   Thus, instead of considering investment funds as a single large homogeneous supply, one should consider a large source of funds available to business under different conditions.

Good financial management requires that those officers given the responsibility for determining the long-run financial needs of the company plan the security issues to raise the required funds in accordance with the best estimate of the trend of interest rates and stock prices.   The popularity of common stock as a hedge against inflation of prices since the middle 1950's has meant that the raising of long-term funds by the sale of common stock has been relatively cheaper than it was earlier.   During the 1950's, interest rates on bonds rose steadily.   This meant that raising long-term funds by bond issues was more expensive to corporations than it was earlier.

Thus the decade of the 1950's was a time during which the raising of long-term funds by corporations through the sale of common stock became more favorable relative to the sale of bonds. It should be emphasized, of course, that costs in terms of interest or dividend yield is by no means the sole consideration in determining the type of issue to use in raising funds. It remains, however, an important one.

To a corporation, the cost of distributing an issue of bonds or stocks to raise capital funds is a very important part of financial planning. Because the cost of distribution of an issue of securities in terms of percentage of the issue declines rapidly as the size of the issue increases, good financial planning requires that long-term funds not be raised on a piecemeal basis but rather be raised in as large amounts as possible for each issue. It may sometimes be advantageous for the financial officer of a corporation to use short-term debt to finance the acquisition of long-term assets. From time to time, when market conditions are favorable, an issue of bonds, preferred stock, or common stock may be marketed to consolidate a portion of the short-term indebtedness and to provide additional funds for long-term purposes. Another advantage resulting from long-term financial planning that permits financing infrequently in relatively large amounts is the greater willingness of most investment banking houses to handle a large issue than to distribute a small one.

TIMING THE ISSUE

The time that the issue of stocks or bonds is marketed has a very important bearing on the cost of the issue to the corporation. The fluctuation of bond yields from 1943 to 1962 are shown in Fig. 20-2. The cost of raising money by means of long-term bonds to corporations whose bonds were rated Aaa by Moody's Financial Series was less than 3 per cent per annum in 1954 and over 4.5 per cent per annum at the end of 1959. The cost of long-term funds to corporations with lower ratings, indicated as Baa by Moody's Financial Series, rose from 3.5 per cent per annum in 1954 to 5.5 per cent per annum in 1959. The cost of raising funds through the sale of preferred stock has shown a degree of fluctuation comparable to that of raising funds through the sale of bonds. Since World War II, the yield on preferred stock has varied from 3.5 per cent to 4.5 per cent per annum, as shown in Fig. 20-3. The cost of raising funds through the sale of common stock has fluctuated very widely. This is true of past decades and of recent years as well. In 1949 the market price of common stock was low relative to the earnings of corporations. In that year, common stock could be sold at a price which would yield the investor more than 15 per cent if all earnings of corporations had been paid out in dividends. Also in that year, the payment of dividends by corporations yielded a return of slightly more than 6 per cent per annum of the market price of common stock. In 1949, therefore, raising funds through the sale of common stock was relatively ex-

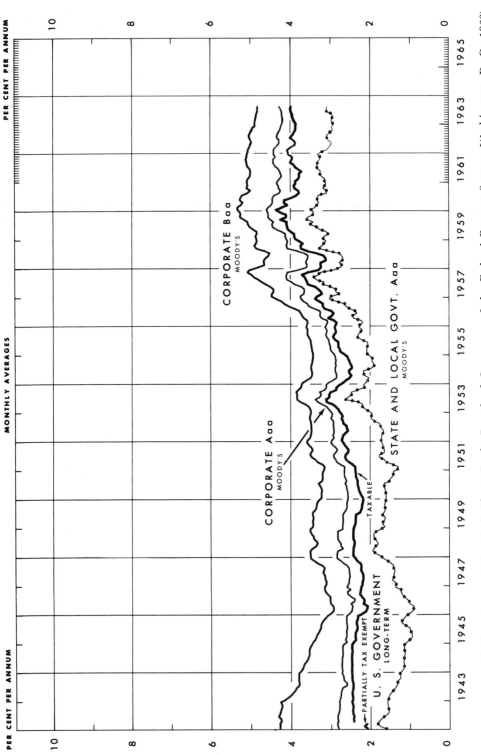

Fig. 20-2 *Bond yields.* (*Source: Historical Chart Book*, Board of Governors of the Federal Reserve System, Washington, D. C., 1963)

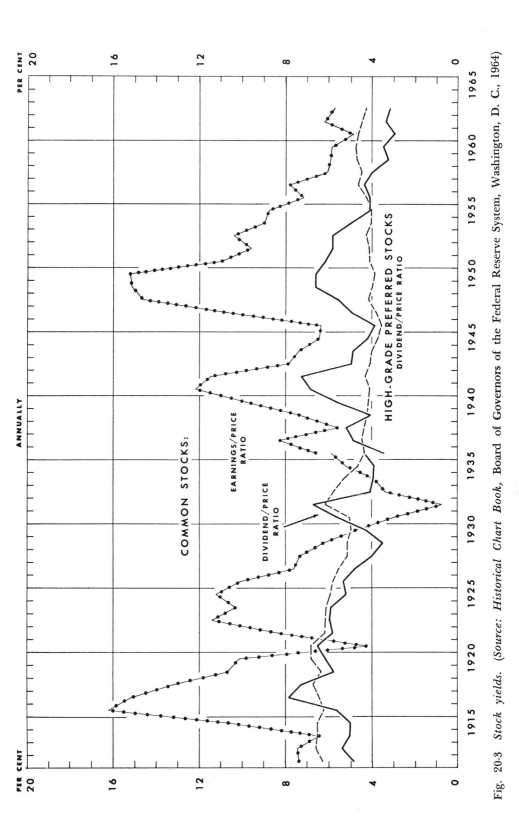

Fig. 20-3 *Stock yields.* (*Source: Historical Chart Book,* Board of Governors of the Federal Reserve System, Washington, D. C., 1964)

pensive. From 1949 to 1961, however, the price of common stock rose very rapidly, a rise that enabled corporations to sell common stock at much higher prices in terms of the income earned by the corporation than had been possible in 1948 and 1949. The investor buying common stock during the 1950's was willing to pay a price yielding a low return to him in terms of the income of the company and in terms of that portion of the income paid out in dividends. In 1961, for example, dividend yields dropped below 3 per cent per annum for the first time in decades.

Because the cost to the corporation of raising funds by means of bonds, preferred stock, or common stock changes from year to year and from month to month, the timing of an issue of bonds or stock can save or lose substantial sums to the corporation. From the standpoint of the financial manager of the individual corporation, the importance of timing the sale of an issue is expressed by *Fortune* as follows: [3]

> In any kind of economic weather, the job of raising funds for a company is difficult, and without a nice sense of timing a financial officer has always been able to lose money for his company quite easily. The Spring of 1956, however, was something extra special. A severe money pinch and a peak rise in interest rates turned the capital market bewilderingly turbulent, and week by week corporate financial officers worried over what might have been. If only, some wondered, they had gone to market just a few weeks earlier. Or should they have waited a while—and how long? The questions were not academic. Tidewater Oil called off $50,000,000 of a proposed $100,000,000 debenture issue and substituted five-year bank credit instead. The company found it would have to pay 3.5% on the debentures, not 3.25% or less originally estimated by its investment bankers.
>
> Whirlpool-Seeger sold $30,000,000 in March. Had the company moved just two weeks earlier, it could have shaved its interest charges by $60,000 a year. General Electric's $300,000,000 issue of 3.5% debentures sold out completely in one day in May. But General Electric could have sold it in January for 3.25% and saved $750,000 a year in interest. Had General Electric anticipated its needs even earlier—as early as United States Steel for example, which sold debentures in the summer of 1954—the savings would have been in excess of $1,500,000 a year.
>
> A two week delay cut $67,500 a year from Niagara Mohawk Power's interest bill on a $30,000,000 issue, and about $22,000 on a $16,000,000 issue of California Oregon Power. Columbia Gas, which on April 10 issued $40,000,000 of 3⅞% debentures, had the unhappy experience of seeing the underwriters syndicate disband on April 23 with less than half the issue sold. Less than a month later, however, investors were bidding over 102 for the debentures. Had Columbia Gas waited until then, it would have been able to sell its debentures above par.

Economic Factors To answer questions regarding the timing of the sale of an issue of securities to take maximum advantage of fluctuating interest rates and stock prices, a forecast of the future is essential. The particular aspects of forecasting that are of interest to the financial officer of the corporation in raising the long-term funds needed by the corporation are the

[3] Charles E. Silberman, "The Fine Art of Raising Capital," *Fortune,* July 1956.

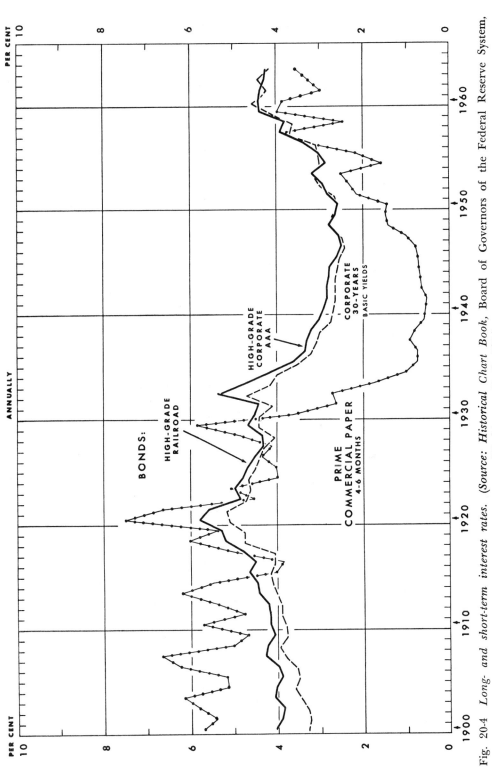

Fig. 20-4 *Long- and short-term interest rates.* (*Source: Historical Chart Book*, Board of Governors of the Federal Reserve System, Washington, D. C., 1964)

expected future movement of rates of interest on short-term and long-term funds and yields on common and preferred stocks. The cost of borrowing money tends to rise during periods of vigorous business activity. Stock prices also tend to fall with an actual decline or the expectation of an imminent decline in business activity, and stock prices tend to rise when business activity is expected to increase. One of the characteristics of a recession of business activity is the low level of capital expenditures by business, and one of the measures of a high level of business activity is a high level of capital expenditures. The rise and fall of long-term financing tends to be closely associated in time with the rise and fall of expenditures for capital purposes. In other words, capital funds are to a considerable extent spent as the funds for them are received. To some extent, it is true that, when businessmen want to raise funds for capital expenditures, money is expensive, and, when they do not need money for capital expenditures, money is cheap. From the standpoint of the cost of long-term funds alone, the company should undertake its raising of funds during economic recessions and spend them during periods of recovery. In practice, it is not possible to raise capital funds much in advance of the need for them. It is possible, however, to use short-term borrowing to finance capital expenditures, with the expectation of replacing the short-term loans with long-term financing when the market conditions for long-term issues become favorable to the company. A forecast, therefore, of interest rates on short-term loans and on long-term loans is helpful to the financial officer in deciding which to use in particular cases. Until the 1930's, except for occasional periods, interest rates on short-term loans remained higher than interest rates on long-term loans. From 1930 to 1957, however, interest rates on short-term loans remained lower than for long-term loans, as shown in Fig. 20-4. As a result, the total financial planning for many corporations included efforts to use short-term financing as much as possible. Since 1957, the interest cost of short-term loans to businesses with the highest credit ratings has sometimes been higher than the interest cost for long-term loans, and at other times it has been lower.

Industry Factors The characteristics of the industry that a company is in has an important bearing on this question of proper timing of an issue of securities. Many public utility companies have very little seasonal variation in the sale of their services. Furthermore, the sales of many public utilities show little influence from the business cycle. The sales of such companies frequently rise in depressions as in prosperity, the growth in their services being more a function of increase in population than of the fluctuating rate of economic activity. Such companies can more easily take advantage of changing interest rates in timing the sale of a bond issue and in changing stock prices in timing the distribution of a stock issue. Companies with a sales pattern subject to the rise and fall of business activity over the course of a business cycle have much less freedom in timing the distribution of securities to take maximum advantage of favorable rates of interest and stock yields.

The rapidity of the rate of growth of an industry also is a factor in timing.   In an industry with a relatively slow rate of growth, companies need to go to the capital markets less frequently for financing than an industry with a rapid rate of growth.   In an industry with a slow rate of growth, the choice of the particular time at which an issue is marketed may range over a period of months or years.   On the other hand, an industry with a rapid rate of growth is almost constantly in need of additional capital funds.   Some of these funds can be made available through retained earnings.   In many cases, however, the company must use outside financing to secure the volume of capital funds necessary to keep up with the increasing sales of the company.   In such an industry, the period within which the choice of the actual time that an issue is marketed is relatively narrow. Postponing the procurement of capital funds in order to take advantage of an expected decline in the price of such funds may seriously hamper the expansion of a company in a rapid growth industry.

Governmental Factors   The philosophy of *laissez faire* with respect to government policy toward the business cycle was dealt a heavy blow with the near collapse of the American economy from 1929 to 1933.   With the advent of the Roosevelt administration, government action to lessen the amplitude of the recurring swings between depression and boom became accepted as a legitimate and necessary responsibility of the federal government and the Federal Reserve System.   Attempts to introduce a measure of stability into the business cycle are confined largely to two categories of activity: (1) monetary policy, which is largely the function of the Federal Reserve Board of Governors, and (2) fiscal policy, which is largely controlled by the administration in power.

To counter a decline in business activity, the actions of the Federal Reserve System are intended to expand the capacity of commercial banks to make loans to business and to exert a downward force on interest rates to reduce the costs of business loans.   With a decline in the level of business activity comes a reduction in the demand for loans by business.   By encouraging commercial banks to make loans more attractive to business, through lower interest rates and other means, the Federal Reserve Board attempts to stimulate a revival of business activity.   Because of the decline in the demand for business loans during a recession and because of the action of the Federal Reserve System in making loans to business cheaper and more attractive, there are obvious advantages in borrowing to raise funds during a recession.   At such times stock prices are generally low, though they sometimes rise in advance of the business recovery.   Therefore, if financing is contemplated by a corporation during a recession, the cost of raising funds generally favor debt securities over equity securities.

If the recovery from a recession appears to be endangering the stability of the price level, the Federal Reserve System generally reacts by restricting the capacity of commercial banks to expand their loans to business. As a result, costs of borrowing money rise, and loan contracts impose more restrictions on the borrowing company. The reactions of the Board of Governors to changing economic conditions are predictable, and should be included in the financial plan of a corporation, particularly in timing its borrowing. Although the action of the Federal Reserve System in attempting to control the business cycle is directed largely toward short-term loans, the cost and availability of long-term loans are also affected. Figure 20-4 illustrates the decline in interest rates on short-term loans, as indicated by prime commercial paper, and also the decline in the yields on high grade corporate bonds during the recessions of business activity in the decade of the 1950's. It should be noticed that the fall during recessions of short-term interest rates is considerably greater than the fall of long-term interest rates.

The fiscal policy of the federal government is used to some extent to combat the business cycle. During recessions, tax collections decline, either as a result of reduced receipts from income taxes at existing rates or as a result of a reduction in income taxes. The expenditures of the federal government during recessions frequently are kept as high as they were previously, or are increased. Although the reason is often explained in terms of national defense or other important factors, the fact that federal government expenditures remain above receipts during a recession or are consciously increased above receipts exerts a stimulating effect. The pattern of business cycle movements since the end of World War II has been a curious one, not following the pattern of business cycles prior to World War II. Recessions since World War II have been more frequent than they were prior to the war. However, they have also been less severe and of shorter duration. Whether this pattern will continue in the future is a matter of speculation among economists. It is also a matter of disagreement among economists as to the causes of this pattern of business activity, particularly the extent to which the monetary policy of the Federal Reserve Board and the fiscal policy of the federal government are responsible for the more frequent but shallower recessions. In any case, the financial officer of the corporation in meeting the need for funds of his company can better decide the timing of a security issue by recognizing the role of the Federal Reserve System and the federal government in attempting to counteract the fluctuations of the business cycle.

MAKING THE PLAN FLEXIBLE

No matter how carefully a company prepares its forecast of the future, events will not occur exactly as expected. In predicting sales, for example, the actual sales may be relatively close to the forecast in some years. In other years, they may vary considerably from the predicted volume. Other predictions on which the company bases its present plans may vary considerably in accuracy from year to year. Unforeseen developments occur frequently. It is, therefore, wise management policy to make allowances in planning for unforeseen contingencies, and to keep planning flexible. Or, stated another way, the financial planning of the company should leave as much room as possible for maneuver in adapting the plan to changing future conditions.

In providing room for maneuver in financial planning, the following points should be given consideration:

1. If a company borrows to the limit of its capacity at reasonable rates, it will not be in a position to borrow additional money to finance unforeseen demand except at excessive rates. Therefore, prudence would dictate that the company keep available some capacity for additional borrowing in its financial plan.

2. In the preparation of bond indentures and other contracts for long-term debts, a company should keep to a minimum restrictive clauses that prevent it from taking financial action that may in the future be advisable. Companies often find themselves saddled with restrictive covenants in long-term debt contracts that place a severe burden on the company in its financial activities.

3. The company should anticipate its long-term financing requirements as far in advance as possible. This will permit the company to take the time necessary to raise funds on terms that will provide as much freedom of future action as possible.

4. The company should maintain relations on a cordial basis with commercial banks, its principal investment banker, and other potential sources of funds, such as insurance companies and other financial institutions. Even though there may be no prospect for the need of the services of the members of the financial community in the near future, conditions may change. An atmosphere of mutual confidence between the company and sources of supply for short-term and long-term funds is a wise precautionary measure.

5. A program of actively cultivating the goodwill of the stockholders of the corporation is always a good investment. The body of stockholders of a corporation constitute a source of equity funds that the corporation can use in its financing plan. By providing the stockholders with quarterly reports on the company's activities and its financial condition, by providing adequate and attractively presented annual statements, and by extending cordial treatment to those stockholders that attend annual meetings the corporation can increase considerably its stature in the eyes of its owners. Although the value of such a policy in dollars and cents is difficult to measure, the value exists nevertheless.

In its financial planning, a company should attempt to achieve three kinds of flexibility. These might be called upward, downward, and sideways flexibility. A company should attempt to keep itself in a position that will enable it to borrow additional funds or sell additional equity securities, without undue delay, so as to be able rapidly to take advantages of profitable investments when they occur. A company should also attempt to maintain flexibility in a downward direction by providing in its financial planning means of advance repayment of debt or retirement of preferred stock should future conditions make such a reduction in debt or equity advisable. A company should also attempt to keep itself in a position of flexibility with respect to changing the composition of its capital structure. If possible, it should keep itself in a condition to decrease short-term debt by increasing long-term debt, or vice versa. It should keep itself in a position to reduce long-term indebtedness by increasing the amount of preferred or common stock outstanding.

A company should take particular care in accepting obligations to retire debt on a serial basis or by means of sinking fund payments. Mandatory retirement by means of repurchasing a stated proportion of the outstanding debt issue each year or mandatory payment of money into a sinking fund for retirement of the debt issue are burdens that, in addition to the mandatory payment of interest on debts, may make it difficult for the corporation to meet its obligations in years of low business activity. If sinking fund payments can be made contingent upon earnings sufficient to meet the payments, a degree of flexibility is achieved that may prove very useful in the future.

Although flexibility in financial planning is very valuable, it can usually be secured only at a price. Flexibility in tying sinking fund payments to income of the company may be achieved at the price of a higher rate of interest on the bonds than would otherwise be required. Flexibility in the form of repayment of debt in advance of the maturity date may be obtainable only by paying a premium in addition to the payment of the principal. Achieving the desired goal of flexibility, as in the case of achieving other desirable goals, nearly always involves some cost. The sacrifices in achieving flexibility are commonly those of a higher interest or dividend rate in acquiring the funds, a reduction in the amount of funds that can be raised, or added restrictions in one form to balance the increased flexibility given to the corporation in some other form. The amount of flexibility attainable must be balanced against the cost of attaining the desired degree of flexibility.

The stage of development of the industry in which a company operates has a bearing on the degree of flexibility desirable in the company's financing plans. The railroad industry, for example, has passed the stage in its life cycle characterized by growth. The need to include flexibility in the financing plans of a railroad is, it would appear, not as necessary as the advantage of obtaining funds at lowest cost. A company in the railroad industry would find in most cases that achieving a high degree of maneuverability in changing its financing plans in the future would probably not be worth the higher cost of financing or restrictions in other forms that would be required to "pay" for the flexibility. A company in the electronics industry, characterized by a rapid rate of technological change, would be likely to find that the cost of keeping its financing commitments flexible in raising funds would be worth the cost involved in attaining the flexibility.

A company in an industry characterized by stability of earnings over the business cycle does not require as much flexibility in its financial plans as does a company in an industry characterized by unstable earnings. Most companies in the public utilities industry have a pattern of steady earnings. Even if a public utility company serves an area of growing demand for its services, the rate of increase is generally steady and can be predicted with accuracy. In such circumstances, a company does not require as high a degree of flexibility in its financing commitments as companies in manufacturing or distribution.

Flexibility is generally achieved as a result of care in negotiating with the sources of loans or equity funds or with the investment banking house distributing an issue of bonds or stocks. It may also be achieved through selection of the source of funds. If an issue of bonds is marketed to the general public through an investment banking house, any later request by the corporation for a change in the provisions of the indenture will be granted only with the approval of the bondholders. If an issue of bonds, on the other hand, is privately placed with one or two insurance companies, a later request by the corporation for a change in the indenture is much more likely to be approved. In a private placement of securities, the entire issue is distributed only to a small number of financial institutions. If a request by the corporation to take an action prohibited by the indenture is a reasonable one, the executives of the financial institution can usually be more easily persuaded than can a scattered group of small bondholders.

It must not be assumed, of course, that the managers of insurance companies, pension funds, endowment funds, and other institutions are equally willing to accommodate the directors of the corporation wishing to make a change in the provisions of the bond issue held by them. The experience of a financial officer of a corporation in dealing with financial institutions will reveal that the managers of some institutions are reasonable from the standpoint of the corporation and others are unreasonable. Furthermore, what appears to be a reasonable request to the financial officer of the corporation may appear to be unreasonable to the manager of the investment portfolio of a financial institution. However, an officer of a financial institution is sophisticated in financial matters. He is more likely than a typical member of the general investing public to recognize that the quality of the investment held in the portfolio which he manages depends to a considerable extent upon the prosperity of the corporation having issued the bonds. If a change in the indenture provisions of an issue of bonds held in the portfolio of a financial institution will improve the position of the corporation, it follows that it will strengthen the security of the bond issued by the corporation. For this reason, some corporations prefer to raise funds wherever possible by placing their security issues with financial institutions. They feel that it is easier to "talk" to a few officers of financial institutions than it is to "talk" to several hundred bondholders.[4]

Questions

1. What is the distinction between capitalization and capital structure?
2. What overall objectives do companies typically adopt to guide their financial planning?
3. What is meant by the optimum capital structure of a firm?
4. What are some of the evidences of underinvestment in a company?
5. What signs indicate that a level of investment is too high?
6. What actions can be taken to correct a condition of overinvestment?
7. How does the size of a business affect its ability to raise long-term funds from different sources?
8. What are the two general types of risk of loss of control of a company associated with long-term financing? How can they be minimized?
9. Distinguish between *trading on the equity* and *financial leverage*.
10. What are the advantages and risks involved in trading on the equity?
11. What is meant by "indifference points"? How do they aid in financial planning?
12. What explanation is there for the continued high price-earnings ratio for common stocks since 1950?
13. Discuss the importance of timing in the successful sale of an issue of securities.
14. What types of information does a financial officer seek in using forecasts to plan a securities issue?
15. Why is the economic policy of the federal government an important factor in planning a security issue?

Selected Readings

Childs, J. F., *Long-Term Financing*, Prentice-Hall, Inc., Englewood Cliffs, N.J., 1961.

Dewing, Arthur Stone, *Financial Policy of Corporations*, 5th ed., The Ronald Press Company, New York, 1953, Chap. 10.

Dobrovolsky, S. P., "Economics of Corporate Internal and External Financing," *Journal of Finance*, March 1958.

Geraci, Joseph J., *Financial Planning in Closely Held Businesses*, Management Aids for Small Manufacturers #156, Small Business Administration, Washington, D.C., September 1963.

Hunt, Pearson, "A Proposal for Precise Definitions of 'Trading on the Equity' and 'Leverage'," *Journal of Finance*, September 1961.

Kuznets, Simon, *Capital in the American Economy: Its Formation and Financing*, Princeton University Press, Princeton, N.J., 1961.

Lore, M. M., *Thin Capitalization*, The Ronald Press Company, New York, 1958.

---

[4] Expressions from corporate financial officers of a viewpoint contrary to that expressed above, as well as concurring expressions, may be found in Charles E. Silberman, "The Fine Art of Raising Capital," *Fortune*, July 1956.

21

Surplus and Dividend Policy

LEGAL ASPECTS OF DIVIDEND DISTRIBUTION

Business exists primarily to make a profit. If profits are realized by a corporation as a result of business operations, the board of directors is faced with the problem of what to do with them. This problem constitutes one of the happier ones; nevertheless, it requires careful deliberation and may cause disagreement on the part of the members of the board. Essentially, two things can be done with profits earned by a corporation: they may be retained in the surplus accounts, or they may be distributed to the stockholders in the form of dividends. The questions of how much to pay out, when to pay the dividends, and in what form dividends shall be distributed are not always easy to answer. The decision of what to do with profits is relatively simple in the case of unincorporated businesses. In a proprietorship, the net earnings of the business belong to the proprietor, and may be withdrawn by him at will. In a partnership, the net earnings are credited to the drawing accounts of the partners in accordance with the partnership agreement, and each partner's share may be withdrawn by him in accordance with that agreement. In a corporation, however, the owners do not control the distribution of the income of their company. The directors determine the distribution of net earnings or their retention as surplus. In deciding the distribution of earnings of the corporation, the directors must balance the needs of the company with the desires of the stockholders.

Most corporations operate at a profit. The amount of profit varies from year to year with changes in the business cycle and changes within the industry. Figure 21-1 shows the net profits after taxes for corporations in various industries in the years 1962 and 1963.

The typical dividend policy of most directors of corporations is to retain part of the net earnings in surplus and distribute part to the owners in dividends. This pattern is shown clearly in Fig. 21-2. Only during the 1930's did the directors of corporations as a whole fail to divide the incomes

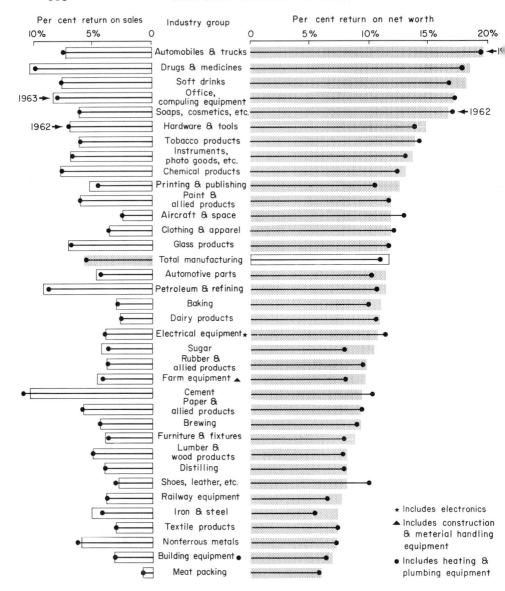

Fig. 21-1 *Profits after taxes of leading manufacturing corporations, 1963* vs. *1962. (Source: Road Maps of Industry,* No. 1477, copyright 1964 by National Industrial Conference Board, Inc.)

of corporations between retained earnings and dividends. During some years of the 1930's dividends were distributed out of past earnings accumulated in surplus, in spite of the fact that in depression years net profits were sometimes a negative figure. The pattern during the prosperous years following World War II have, for corporations as a whole, been one of ap-

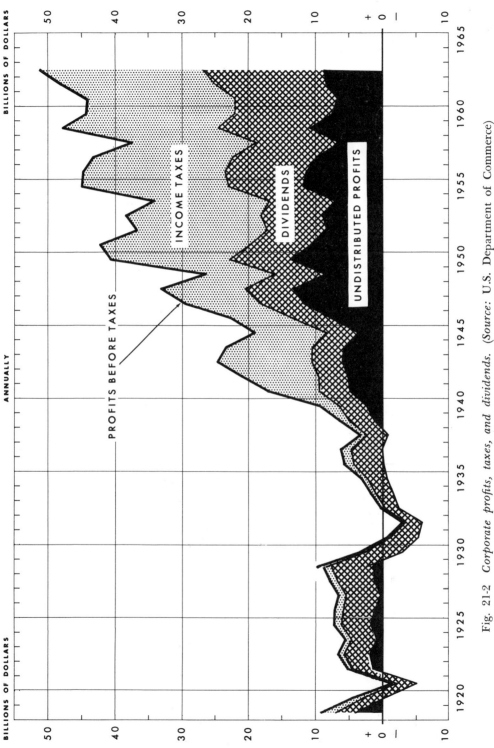

Fig. 21-2 *Corporate profits, taxes, and dividends.* (*Source:* U.S. Department of Commerce)

proximately equal division of net profits between retained earnings and dividends distributed.

Steps in the Process of Dividend Distribution   Authority to distribute dividends is contained in the charter and the bylaws of the corporation. If there is more than one class of stock authorized in the charter, the rights and preferences to dividends of each class of stock will be stated in the charter. In practically all corporations the authority to declare dividends or not to declare dividends is given explicitly to the board of directors. Such authority is in most cases found in the bylaws of the corporation. Where there is more than one class of stock outstanding, the distribution of dividends by the director must conform with the provisions of the charter with respect to dividend priority and payment to the various classes of stock.

Although the priority of various classes of stock in the participation of dividend payments is stated in the charter of the corporation, there is usually no limitation on the judgment of the directors in deciding whether or not to issue a dividend to any of the classes of stock.

The first step in the distribution of a dividend is taken at the board of directors meeting. Board meetings to decide upon dividends may occur once a year or as often as the directors decide. If, for example, the policy of the board with regard to dividends is to distribute them quarterly, the directors' meeting for the purpose of declaring a dividend is held after each quarterly profit and loss statement of the corporation is made available to the directors. After examination of the financial condition of the corporation as determined by the most recent financial statements, the directors determine the amount of dividend, if any, to be distributed to the stockholders. A resolution declaring the dividend must be adopted by the board. The resolution will state the amount in dollars and cents of the dividend payable per share to each class of stock, the date on which the list of stockholders to receive the dividend will be compiled, and the date on which the dividend checks will be distributed to the stockholders. The stockholders are then notified, either by publication of an announcement in a newspaper or by a letter sent to each stockholder.

The declaration of a dividend constitutes a formal obligation on the part of the corporation to pay the dividend according to the terms of the declaration. The declaration, in other words, creates a debt which the corporation is legally liable to pay in the amount stated and on the date stated. The stockholders eligible to receive the dividend are those whose names are on the stock ledger on the record date stated in the dividend declaration. The actual mailing of dividend checks takes place two or three weeks after the record date. If a stock is listed on the New York Stock Exchange, the rules of the exchange provide that the seller must deliver his stock certificate within four working days following the date of sale on the exchange, and that the purchaser must make payment for the stock within the same period.

Thus, for a purchaser to receive a declared dividend, the purchase of the stock must be made at least four days prior to the record date.

Payments can be made in two ways. Under one method the payment of the dividend is handled by the corporation itself. The secretary of the corporation compiles a list of the stockholders on the record date, giving the address and the number of shares owned by each. Dividend checks are then prepared in the accounting department and signed by the officers authorized to sign checks. These are then mailed to the stockholders. This procedure is followed by small corporations and by some large corporations having a relatively small number of shareholders. The second method, resorted to by corporations having a large number of stockholders, uses the services of the trust department of a commercial bank to act as transfer agent for the stock of the corporation. Among the services performed for a corporation by a transfer agent are the compilation of the list of stockholders on the record date, the preparation of the dividend checks, and the distribution of the checks to the stockholders.

Legal Limitations The extent and character of the legal limitations on the payment of dividends imposed by the laws of different states show considerable variation. In Arizona, for example, the state law is silent with respect to dividend payments of business corporations. The most common limitation in state law is that dividends may not be paid when the corporation is insolvent or when the payment of a dividend would render the corporation insolvent. A typical example of such a restriction is found in the corporation law of Ohio, which states that "no corporation shall declare or pay a dividend in cash or other property when there is reasonable ground for believing that it is unable or, by the payment of the dividend, may be rendered unable to satisfy its obligations and liabilities." Often the position of the preferred shareholder, as well as the creditor, is protected by state law. For example, California corporation law states that dividends may not be paid "if the value of the net assets amounts to less than the aggregate amount of stated capital attributed to shares having liquidation preferences." It should be emphasized that the above limitation of California law seeks to protect the position of holders of preferred shares having priority in liquidation, and to prevent any payment of dividends that might impair the liquidation position of the holder of preferred stock. State law generally does not specify that holders of preferred shares shall have preference in the payment of dividends. Nebraska law is typical in this respect, stating that "the holders of preferred or special stock of any class or of any series thereof shall be entitled to receive dividends at such rates, on such conditions and at such times as shall be stated and expressed in the articles of incorporation, or any amendment thereto, or in the resolution or resolutions provided for the issue of such stocks adopted by the board of directors." In other words, the priority of the preferred shareholder in participation in dividends must be expressly stated in the corporation charter, bylaws, or express action taken by the board of directors at the time of issuing such stock.

A modification of the rule that dividends may not impair the capital of the corporation is found in the laws of some states, to permit corporations organized for the purpose of extracting mineral wealth or exploiting other types of wasting assets to distribute dividends that are in part a return of capital. Where state law permits such modifications, it is required that the dividend containing a return of capital may not at the same time endanger the ability of the corporation to meet its debt and other obligations.[1]

There is also a lack of uniformity in the laws of the states with respect to the position of stockholders receiving illegal dividends. In general, the courts will order stockholders to return dividends illegally received, if the distribution of the dividend is found to be a principal factor in making the corporation bankrupt. Recovery of illegal dividends is also generally ordered if the stockholders receiving the dividend were in full knowledge of the fact that the dividend was illegally distributed by the directors. On the other hand, if stockholders receive dividends in good faith, the courts will generally not order a return of the dividend unless the distribution of the dividend was a direct cause of making the corporation bankrupt.

If a dividend is declared which any creditor believes to be illegal, he may bring action in court to stop the payment of the dividend. The distribution of cash of the corporation to the stockholders would thereby be prevented, and probably no further court action would be needed against the directors. Such an action is generally taken by a creditor or group of creditors in cases where the corporation has failed to meet interest or principal payments on debts when due. Creditors would obviously prefer to take legal action to prevent a distribution of cash in the form of dividends where such action would impair the ability of the corporation to meet its debts, than to initiate court action to recover payments already made to the stockholders. If, on the other hand, the cash has already been distributed to the stockholders, the creditors may initiate court action for the amount of cash so distributed either by recovering it from the directors declaring the dividend, from the stockholders receiving the dividend, or from both.

Resort to legal action is undertaken only with reluctance in most business dealings, due to the expenses of court costs and attorney fees, the delay in securing satisfaction that is a result of the slow progress of most court cases, and the uncertainty involved whenever a court must make a decision.

---

[1] An example of such a modification is found in California state law, as follows: "A wasting asset corporation is a corporation engaged solely or substantially in the exploitation of mines, oil wells, gas wells, patents or other wasting assets, or organized solely or substantially to liquidate specific assets.

"A wasting asset corporation may distribute the net income derived from the exploitation of such wasting assets or the net proceeds derived from such liquidation without making any deduction or allowance for the depletion of the asset incidental to the lapse of time, consumption, liquidation, or exploitation, if adequate provision is made for meeting debt and liabilities and the liquidation preferences of outstanding shares and notice is given to shareholders that no deduction or allowance has been made for depletions."

Some creditors try to improve their position, or at least to increase their chances in the event of a court action, by placing in any loan contract with a corporation restrictions on the payment of dividends by the directors until the loan is repaid. The loan contract may entirely prohibit or severely restrict the payment of dividends in cash or other property of the debtor corporation except out of earnings generated by the corporation subsequent to the loan. Restrictions similar to the above may state that the surplus of the corporation must be maintained at least at the amount existing at the time that the loan was made. Loan contracts sometimes prohibit or limit the payment of dividends if such payment reduces the current ratio of the corporation below a figure stated in the loan contract. Prohibitions or limitations in loan contracts on the payment of dividends are generally restricted to dividends paid in cash or other property of the corporation. The declaration of stock dividends is usually not limited in loan contracts, since the distribution of such dividends does not impair the ability of the corporation to meet its debt commitments. Long-term loans requiring sinking fund payments or serial retirement of bonds are in themselves a restriction on the payment of dividends by corporations, since such obligations must be met by corporations before dividends in cash or property may be declared.

FORMS OF DIVIDENDS

Cash Dividends are commonly paid in cash. It is obvious that a corporation declaring a cash dividend must have enough cash in its bank account at the time that the dividend checks are mailed to cover the dividend paid in addition to the cash requirements of the corporation. The dividend policy of a corporation obviously must take into consideration that the payment of a cash dividend requires increase of the cash balance in the bank. Receipts from customers may be allowed to accumulate in the bank account of the corporation prior to the payment of the cash dividend, or cash may be borrowed in order to build up the cash account to the level necessary to meet the dividend and other cash requirements of the corporation. If a corporation maintains regularity in its dividend payments as to time and amount, the cash budget prepared for the coming year can indicate the steps necessary to meet the regular dividend payments of the corporation. If the dividend policy of the board is to pay a dividend of $1 per share on March 31, June 31, September 31, and December 31, the planning for cash can include the requirements of building up the cash account on the dates when the dividend checks are mailed. An irregular dividend policy makes cash planning in anticipation of dividend needs difficult.

The distribution of a cash dividend reduces the cash account of the corporation by the dollar amount of the dividend distributed and reduces the surplus account of the corporation by a like amount. The payment of the cash dividend, therefore, reduces both the total assets and the total net worth of the corporation. The book value per share of the stock is reduced by the amount of the dividend. The market price of the stock on which the cash dividend is paid is similarly affected. The price of the stock drops, in most cases, by the amount of the cash dividend distributed.

Other Assets A distribution to stockholders of assets of the corporation other than cash is rare. Nevertheless, circumstances do sometimes occur to make it seem expedient for the directors to declare a dividend which distributes some asset other than cash. The asset that is most often distributed in lieu of cash is securities held by the corporation as an investment. During World War I, for example, some corporations accumulated a sizable portfolio of government bonds. The boards of directors of a few corporations reduced their holdings of government bonds by distributing them rather than cash to stockholders of the company. Corporations holding stock in other corporations sometimes distribute a portion of these holdings to their own stockholders. Such a distribution may be a voluntary action on the part of the directors. In other cases, however, it is forced on the directors by court order, usually in implementing an antitrust decision against the corporation. A recent example of such a dividend is the distribution of General Motors stock held by the Du Pont Corporation to Du Pont stockholders. This distribution was required in compliance with the federal court decision declaring that the holding of General Motors stock by the Du Pont Corporation constituted a violation of the antitrust laws. If a corporation holding stock of another corporation for the purpose of control decides to eliminate its control, the stock of the subsidiary is sometimes distributed to the stockholders of the parent corporation in the form of a dividend.

A distribution to the stockholders of some of the products of the corporation is occasionally made. Dividends in the form of inventory of the company appear to have been fairly common during the seventeenth century. The East India Company, for example, made frequent distributions to its stockholders of such products as spices and calico imported by the company in its trade with the East Indies. The distribution of inventory items of a company to its own stockholders has been rare in recent decades, however. During the nineteenth century, a few railroad companies in the United States distributed to their stockholders title to parcels of land donated to the railroad under the generous land grants given by the federal government to subsidize the construction of railroads. Whiskey has also been distributed by a few distilleries to their stockholders.

Where the amount of property distributed to the stockholders is in proportion to the amount of stock held by each, the property dividend is a true dividend. Corporations sometimes distribute samples of company products to their stockholders, giving the same amount to each stockholder regardless of the number of shares held by each. Such a distribution is more in the nature of a sales promotion than a dividend. During a period of war, when certain items, such as cigarettes, may be in short supply, stockholders may welcome the receipt of inventory items rather than cash as dividend payments. In normal times, however, stockholders generally prefer to receive cash than to receive property. The value to each individual stockholder of the item in the inventory of the corporation varies considerably. And if the inventory items are distributed in proportion to stock held by each shareholder, there may be a problem of dividing the inventory item for purposes of distribution. Most inventory items are not divisable into small units as is the cash of the company.

As far as the corporation laws of the states are concerned, there is no prohibition in distributing property of the corporation. In the event that a shareholder refuses to accept a dividend in the form of property, there are no uniform precedents to guide the corporation directors in handling such a refusal except to rule that the stockholder is not entitled to demand cash from the corporation in lieu of the distribution of properties. The corporation may hold the property in trust for the stockholder refusing it, or may sell the property and distribute to the stockholder the cash received from the sale. Such action by directors in handling the refusal by stockholders to accept a distribution of property of the corporation has been upheld by the courts.

Scrip As was stated in Chapter 4, keeping cash in the bank in excess of current needs indicates poor financial management. In the payment of a cash dividend, however, it is necessary to increase the cash in the bank in order to pay the dividend checks. A profitable year may have added considerably to the assets of a corporation but not to its cash in the bank. One of the ways of increasing cash is to borrow from the bank the necessary amount to meet the payment of dividend checks. A bank loan must, of course, be repaid later, and involves a cost to the corporation in the form of interest. Such a loan is usually repaid out of cash receipts expected in the future in excess of the cash disbursements of the corporation. If it is the policy of the directors to pay dividends on regular dates, it may be willing to borrow frequently from the bank in order to increase the cash account to meet the dividend payments. An alternative is available, however. This, in essence, is for the corporation to go into debt to the stockholders by distributing dividends in the form of *scrip*. If a corporation has insufficient cash in the bank to pay a dividend when the regular dividend payment date approaches, the directors may declare a scrip dividend instead. The stockholder receives a promissory note from the corporation payable at a date in the future when the corporation expects its cash account to be sufficiently high to redeem the promissory notes. Because the failure to declare dividends when the policy of the directors is to pay them on regular dates may be interpreted by stockholders as evidence of the inability of the corporation to pay the dividend, a scrip dividend is sometimes a useful alternative.

A scrip dividend merely postpones the cash drain of the corporation in meeting the dividend payment. In anticipation of the approaching maturity of the promissory notes distributed to the stockholders, the corporation must plan to increase its cash account in the bank to redeem the scrip. For this reason, scrip dividends are generally issued by corporations only on infrequent occasions.

In very rare cases, corporations have issued bonds in lieu of cash as dividends to their stockholders. The principal advantage to the corporation in doing this is that it postpones the day of reckoning (payment in cash) to a future date more distant than the maturity date of scrip. Such a use of bonds is considered by financial authorities to be a misuse of the bond as an instrument of long-term finance. With a few exceptions, no large, well-known corporations use bonds as a means of paying dividends.

Stock Dividend   A stock dividend is a distribution to the stockholders of the same kind of stock that they are holding. A 10 per cent stock dividend, for example, distributed to the common stockholders gives each one share of common for every ten shares he already holds. In the distribution of a stock dividend, the problem of fractional shares is always present. This difficulty is generally handled by giving the stockholder cash. Thus, if a stockholder has thirty-three shares at the time the corporation declares a 10 per cent stock dividend, he would receive three additional shares plus cash in the amount of 30 per cent of the market value of one share. Alternatively, the shareholder might be given the option to purchase one additional share with a payment amounting to 70 per cent of the market price of the share. For purposes of handling fractional payments in stock dividends, market valuation at the close of business on a stated day is generally the basis for the cash distribution. Occasionally, a corporation will issue fractional shares rather than pay cash in distributing its stock dividends. In such a case, the holder of thirty-three shares of stock receiving a 10 per cent stock dividend would receive a fractional share amounting to three-tenths of one share.

The effect of a stock dividend on the accounts of a corporation is to increase the capital stock by the amount of the dividend and decrease the surplus by the same amount. The total net worth is unaffected by the declaration of a stock dividend. If a corporation has issued all the common stock authorized by the charter, it will be necessary to amend the charter to provide for an increase in the authorized stock before the stock dividend may be declared. If the possibility of the declaration of stock dividends is included in the long-term financial planning of the corporation, the directors will secure a revision of the charter, if necessary, to permit stock dividends to be declared in future periods.

One of the advantages to stockholders, particularly large stockholders, in the receipt of stock dividends is in the beneficial treatment of such dividends with regard to income taxes. If a stockholder receives $100 in cash as a dividend from a corporation, this constitutes income and must be reported on the income tax return of the individual. If the distribution of the stock dividend does not change the proportionate ownership of the corporation by stockholders, the receipt of the stock dividends by the stockholder is not taxable as income.   If in distributing the stock dividend, the corporation does not distribute fractional shares but distributes cash instead, the receipt of the cash must be reported as income subject to taxation in the same manner as the receipt of a regular cash dividend.   Furthermore, if the declaration of a dividend permits the shareholder to receive either stock or cash for the full amount of the dividend, the dividend is taxable as income received, even if the stockholder in such a case elects to receive the dividend in the form of stock.   The declaration of a dividend giving the stockholder the option of stock or cash is comparatively rare.   It is inconvenient to the corporation, because corporation officials cannot easily determine what number of stockholders will elect to receive the dividend in cash and what number will elect to receive it in stock.   Such a dividend is generally unpopular with stockholders, particularly large stockholders, because the dividend is treated as ordinary income for tax purposes, regardless of the choice made by the stockholders between stock and cash.

A stock dividend, obviously, increases the shares outstanding.   Therefore, future dividend payments must be divided among a larger number of shares.   If there were no other factors influencing the market price of the stock, the distribution of a stock dividend would have the effect of lowering the market price for the stock.   The distribution of a cash dividend has the same effect of reducing the market price, in the absence of other market influences, by the amount of the cash dividend per share.   If a stock dividend is regularly declared, the market price of the stock often drops by the dollar amount representing the value of the stock distribution per share.   If, on the other hand, the stock dividend is used only occasionally, it tends to be regarded as a "special" or "extra" dividend.   In other words, the declaration of a stock dividend is frequently interpreted by investors as an indication that the corporation is more profitable than in the past or that the directors expect an expansion of sales and income of the corporation.   Unless a stock dividend is a regular feature of the dividend policy of the corporation, the declaration is usually made during periods of rising business prosperity.   The announcement of a stock dividend in a period of rising stock prices often has the effect of accelerating the rise in the price of the stock rather than depressing it.[2]   One result of the increase in shares outstanding caused by the distribution of a stock dividend may be a wider distribution of the stock, as some recipients of the dividend sell their shares. The resulting increase in the number of shareholders of the company may increase the market interest in the stock and exert an upward pressure upon its market price.

---

[2] A study of the market effects of stock dividends concludes that in general the declaration of stock dividends, while often producing temporary increases, generally does not produce lasting gains in the market price (from C. A. Barker, "Evaluation of Stock Dividends," *Harvard Business Review*, July-August 1958).

In arriving at dividend decisions, directors must consider the financial welfare of the corporation and the desires of the stockholders. Often the needs of the two are in conflict. The use of stock dividends represents a compromise which in many cases enables the directors to satisfy the requirements of the corporation and the desires of the stockholders. In some cases, they may be the only means by which the directors can satisfy the wish of stockholders to receive dividends. This is true in situations where loan contracts are in existence forbidding the corporation to distribute cash dividends. Stock dividends have the advantage of permitting the corporation to retain and reinvest earnings and, at the same time, of distributing to the stockholders some tangible evidence of the existence of the earnings and the fact of their reinvestment. By distributing an additional stock certificate, each stockholder can conveniently sell it if he prefers to spend his dividend rather than reinvesting it. The distribution of a stock dividend may mean higher cash dividends to the stockholder. If the corporation maintains a regular cash dividend, it usually continues to pay dividends at the previous rate per share after the distribution of the stock dividend. As a result, the total cash received in dividends each year by the stockholders is often increased after the distribution of the stock dividends.

Stock dividends are accepted unquestioningly by most investors as a valuable contribution from the corporation. Stockholders are practically unanimous in their delight in receiving stock dividends. But most shareholders do not realize that stock dividends in themselves are of no value except as a formal recognition of something the stockholder already owns. They merely divide ownership of the corporation into a larger number of certificates. As one writer has put it, stock dividends "represent simply a division of the corporate pie into a larger number of pieces." [3] Actually, stock dividends give to the stockholder no benefits which he could otherwise not have gotten without stock dividends. Stock dividends can be sold for cash, but, if a stockholder sells his stock dividends, he reduces his percentage ownership of the corporation from what it was before he received the dividend. He could have accomplished the same result in the absence of a stock dividend by liquidating part of his holdings. If the stockholder retains his stock dividends, his percentage ownership of the corporation is not increased. Perhaps the chief benefits, both to the corporation and to the stockholder, in the distribution of a stock dividend is the betterment of public relations. The declaration and distribution of a stock dividend serves as an advertisement of the corporation's growth. Thus the publicity resulting from the announcement of a stock dividend benefits both the corporation and the stockholder to the extent that favorable publicity strengthens the position of the corporation.

---

[3] James T. S. Porterfield, "Dividend, Dilution, and Delusion," *Harvard Business Review*, November-December 1959.

DIVIDEND POLICIES

The limitations imposed on directors in distributing earnings of the corporation were discussed above. Within these limitations, the directors have considerable freedom of judgment in determining the disposition of earnings. They may distribute all the net profit earned during the year, they may distribute earnings accumulated from previous years, they may distribute part of the earnings earned during the year, or they may distribute no earnings at all. They may attempt to maintain a fixed dollar amount of dividends each year, regardless of fluctuating earnings of the corporation, or they may distribute a fixed percentage of the profits earned each year. They may distribute dividends once a year, twice a year, four times a year, or more often. There may be several different classes of stock outstanding, each of which has a different priority in claims upon the earnings of the corporation.

In the case of some corporations, the history of dividend payments appears to follow no pattern. The directors of most corporations, however, have adopted a dividend policy of some sort to guide them in making dividend decisions. The policies may be rigid or elastic. In the choice of dividend policies, the directors of a corporation are faced with a number of factors that must be considered. The needs of the corporation for retained earnings, the degree of fluctuation of corporate earnings, the conflicting desires of wealthy stockholders as compared to lower income stockholders, the effect of changes in the dividend rate on the market price of the stock, the availability of surplus cash for distribution as dividends—these and other factors must be considered in determining dividend policies.

REGULARITY

Regularity of dividend payments is considered an important part of dividend policy by the directors of most corporations. In dividend policy, two types of regularity can be distinguished. The policy of many corporations is to pay some dividend annually, even though the amount of the dividend may fluctuate from year to year. Lists are published of corporations that have maintained a dividend payment each year for an unbroken period of twenty years, thirty years, or longer. To have a record of many years of consecutive dividend payments, even though the amount may have varied, is considered by many investors to be an important factor in choosing a stock for investment. The Pennsylvania Railroad, for example, has a record of more than 100 consecutive years of dividend payments. To maintain this record in 1960, when the railroad suffered a net loss, dividends were paid out of past accumulated income.

Regularity of payments also refers to the amounts paid out. The policy of some corporations is to pay the same dollar amount at each dividend payment, even though the net earnings of the corporation may rise and fall from year to year.   If such is the policy of the directors, the amount of the regular dividend may be low compared to the average earnings of the corporation.   The policy of some corporations is to set the regular dividend at a low amount, supplementing it with an extra dividend in years of high earnings.   An example of regularity with respect to amount of dividend is furnished by the American Telephone and Telegraph Corporation.   This company paid a dividend of $2.25 per share four times a year for several decades, including the depression years of the 1930's and the war years of the 1940's.   Indeed, the record of regularity of dividend payment on the common stock of American Telephone and Telegraph was superior to the regularity of interest payments on many bond issues during the 1930's.

Regularity in the payment of dividends tends to make the common stock of a company an investment rather than a speculation.   Persons purchasing stock for investment generally intend to keep it for long periods of time.   A stock paying an irregular dividend is rated by most investment analysts as a speculation, and the tendency is for such a stock to be attractive to persons hoping for a short-run rather than a long-run profit.   In other words, an irregular dividend pattern tends to attract stock purchasers whose intention is to hold the stock for relatively short periods of time.   Stocks that have had a history of unbroken dividend payments for many years in the past are given considerable publicity by brokerage firms, stock exchanges, and investment rating services.

The importance of regularity in dividend payments is probably given undue emphasis in rating the stock of a company as an investment.   Nevertheless, regularity is an advantage to the corporation in its financing.   It probably increases stockholder loyalty and good will toward the corporation.   Investors holding the stock as an investment rather than as a speculation tend to be more receptive to an offer by the corporation of further issues of stock.   The success of a stock distribution by means of stock rights issued to stockholders is more likely if the stock is primarily held by investors rather than by speculators.   A history of regular dividend payments serves to spread the ownership of outstanding stock more widely among small investors, and thereby reduces the chance of loss of control.   Stocks with such a history of dividend payments are more often recommended as investments for persons having a limited amount of money to invest.

A history of regular dividend payments helps not only in the sale of additional issues of common stock but in the sale of preferred stock and bonds as well.   Since one of the features of a preferred stock is a priority in the payment of dividends over the common stock, a record of regular payment of dividends on common serves as an assurance of dividend payments on the preferred stock.   In all issues of bonds except extremely rare ones dividend payments may not be made on the common stock unless interest payments are made on the bonds outstanding.   A long record of regular dividend payments is one of the attributes qualifying the bonds of a corporation to be included in lists drawn up by state regulatory commissions of bonds eligible for investment by pension funds, commercial banks, insurance companies, and other financial institutions, whose investments are regulated by many states. The fact that the bonds of a corporation are eligible for investment by these institutions considerably widens their market, and permits the corporation to raise funds through bonds at a lower interest cost than would be possible if the bonds were not eligible for investment by regulated institutional investors.

If the income pattern of a corporation shows little variation over the years, it is easy to follow a policy of regularity in dividend payments. Where income from year to year is highly variable, however, a policy of regular dividends is more difficult to maintain. With a variable pattern of income, it is essential for a company wishing to maintain regularity of dividend payments to build up surpluses in years of higher than average income in order to maintain dividends in years of below average income. Some companies earmark a portion of the surplus retained in years of good earnings as a reserve for dividend equalization. This reserve is then reduced in years of lean earnings to maintain the regular dividend. Since dividends are payable for the most part in cash, it is usually necessary in the years of higher than average earnings to increase the volume of assets easily convertible into cash with the intention of liquidating these assets in years of poor earnings to meet the regular dividend payment. Some companies accomplish this by increasing their investment in marketable securities in years of high earnings, and reducing this investment in years of low earnings by selling the securities to meet dividend requirements.

When a policy of a payment of regular dividends is adopted by the board of directors, it should be maintained under all normal circumstances. The expectation of the receipt of the regular dividend by investors holding the company's stock will form an important part of the financial planning of these investors. If a regular dividend is passed after many years of regular payments, the break in the pattern has a more severe effect on investors than the failure to pay a dividend in the case of a company with an irregular pattern of dividend payments. The regular dividend should be set at a figure conservative enough in relation to the earnings of the corporation so that it can be maintained during several years of depressed earnings. If for any reason the directors of a corporation wish to make increased dividend payments, a distinction should be made between the regular dividend and the extra payment, which is usually labeled an extra dividend. The failure to pay an extra dividend does not have as depressing an effect on investors as the failure to pay a regular one.

The chief danger in establishing a policy of regular dividend payments is that once the pattern is established, it becomes difficult to change it without seriously affecting investor attitudes and the financial standing of the corporation. Investors come to consider the regular dividend as part of their dependable income. A stockholder considers a cut in the regular dividend to be as serious as a cut in salary. If a period of lean years occurs greater than that expected by the directors of a corporation in setting up a reserve for dividend equalization, there is a strong temptation to continue the regular dividend payment even though financial prudence would indicate that the dividend should be cut or eliminated. Even in situations where directors realize that it is essential for the corporation to reduce its dividend payment, directors are usually reluctant to omit the payment of a regular dividend entirely. A cut in the regular dividend rate, however, does not remove a corporation's name from lists of corporations having maintained dividend payment for an unbroken number of years in the past.

The Point of View of the Stockholder   An appropriate dividend policy is one in which the financial needs of the corporation and the desires of the stockholders are both taken into account. In small, closely held corporations, the body of stockholders frequently consists of a homogeneous group of persons. Giving consideration to the desires of such a group is a relatively easy matter in determining dividend policy, because the desires of each stockholder are generally similar to the desires of the other stockholders. In such a case, a dividend policy can be adopted which equally satisfies the desires of all the stockholders. In corporations having many stockholders, on the other hand, no dividend policy can be adopted that will equally satisfy all the owners. Some stockholders will prefer a liberal distribution of earnings; others will prefer that most or all the earnings be reinvested in the company. Some stockholders will wish a distribution in cash; others will want a distribution of stock dividends.

In considering the desires of stockholders in shaping dividend policy, it is necessary that the directors analyze the makeup of the body of stockholders for whom dividend policy is being determined. The composition of the body of stockholders can be analyzed by determining the proportion of the total number of stockholders of each group and the total number of shares held by each class of stockholders. The stockholders may be divided, for example, into four groups: small, retired, wealthy, and institutional stockholders. If a corporation has a stock purchase program for its employees, stockholder-employees may be included in the classification of stockholders.

Small stockholders, holding but a few shares of stock in a limited number of companies, usually follow a program of infrequent purchase of stock. They generally make their choices of stock on the basis of advice received from brokerage houses or friends. Trading the shares of one company for those of another is infrequently done. For the most part, the investment policy of small stockholders is one of acquisition of stock when savings permit, and the holding of such shares for long periods of time.

To retired persons dividend income may be an important part of the total income or it may be negligible, depending upon the wealth of the individual. Unless a retired stockholder is in a high income bracket, a policy of liberal payment of cash dividends is apt to be more popular to him than to young stockholders.

Wealthy persons typically have a large proportion of their wealth invested in common stocks. They are generally sophisticated in financial matters, and are more concerned with the dividend policy followed by the board of directors than are less wealthy individuals. The dividend income that they receive generally is taxed at a high rate, if the dividends received are in the form of cash. They are more apt to prefer a dividend policy emphasizing retention of earnings and distribution of stock dividends. Because they hold relatively large blocks of shares or sit on the board of directors of corporations, their influence in shaping dividend policy is apt to be felt.

Institutional investors purchase stock in large blocks. Their decisions to purchase are generally made on the basis of committee action. They tend to hold shares for relatively long periods of time. Unlike wealthy investors, institutions are not concerned with personal income taxes on investments. Most institutional investors avoid speculative issues, seek diversification in their investment portfolio, and favor a policy of regular cash dividend payments.

If the ownership of stock is widely scattered, the directors have little fear of being replaced by other persons as a result of voting at a stockholder's meeting. The directors themselves are likely to be persons of considerable wealth. A dividend policy emphasizing retention of earnings may be favorable to the personal interests of the directors in such a situation, and may run counter to the best interests of the majority of stockholders. Often the dividend policy adopted by directors in such a case is a compromise between the desires of the large body of small stockholders and the personal interests of the directors. If the welfare of the majority of the stockholders is completely ignored by the directors, the possibility of a contest for control of the corporation through solicitation of proxies is increased. Contests for control of corporations with stock scattered widely and in small units are rare. When they do occur, however, one of the best defenses for the existing board of directors in facing a challenge for control is a loyal body of stockholders. For this reason, even though there are no large blocks held by individual stockholders and the obstacles faced by a group attempting to wrest control from existing directors are formidable, it is to the interest of directors carefully to consider the desires of stockholders in formulating dividend policy.

If most of the stock of a corporation is held by a few wealthy stockholders, the dividend policy generally reflects the interests of this group alone. In this circumstance, the wealthy stockholders would in all likelihood be on the board of directors. The dividend policy in such a situation is usually one of retaining most of the earnings and severely limiting the distribution of cash dividends.

If a corporation has been in existence for a considerable period, if it is listed on one of the major exchanges, and if the securities of the corporation have high investment ratings, it is likely that the stock will be held by a heterogeneous group of stockholders. How do the directors of a corporation reconcile the conflicting interests of small stockholders, wealthy stockholders, institutional investors, and other groups in considering stockholder welfare in dividend polices? There is no simple answer. Two points need to be mentioned, however. One is that a policy should be adopted giving some consideration to the interests of each of the groups comprising a substantial proportion of the stockholders. The other is that the dividend policy, once established, should be continued as long as it does not interfere with the financing needs of the corporation. A definite dividend policy, whether it be one of reinvesting nearly all the earnings of the corporation or one of liberal dividends, tends to attract those investors that consider the dividend policy in accord with their investment requirements. As time passes the continuance of an established dividend policy tends to become the policy which holds the approval of the majority of the stockholders. A sudden change may work to the disadvantage of most of the existing stockholders of the corporation, who presumably were attracted by the previous policy. Thus whatever the policy of the board of directors, any change should be made only after considerable analysis and discussion as to its probable effect on the existing body of stockholders. Furthermore, it probably would be considerate of existing stockholders for the board of directors, in changing established dividend policy, to do so gradually over a period of years, rather than abruptly.

The Point of View of the Company   In establishing dividend policy the directors frequently find the financial needs of the corporation are in conflict with the desires of the stockholders. In general, the directors will give priority to the financing needs of the corporation. In most instances, this is prudent dividend policy. However, the directors should have clearly in mind the nature of the needs of the corporation for retained earnings and the extent to which retained earnings can profitably be employed by the company. The directors are elected to their position to establish policies which will benefit the owners. The owners, however, are residual claimants to the earnings of the corporation. Except for liquidating dividends, the directors must establish policies for the corporation that will maintain the company as a solvent enterprise, fully capable of meeting its debt commitments and other contractual obligations. Furthermore, there are other groups that must be considered by the directors in establishing policy for the disposition of corporation earnings. The employees of the corporation depend upon the continued existence of the company for their livelihood. Suppliers selling to the company, customers buying from the company, and the communities in which company facilities operate depend in varying degree upon the continued existence of the company for their welfare. The obligations of the directors to such groups may not be a contractual one, but the moral obligation is increasingly recognized as time passes.

Taxation   One of the important factors in determining dividend policy is taxation. The taxes with which the directors will be concerned are those placed on undistributed profits of the corporation, on cash dividends reported as income of stockholders, and on stock dividends.

The first attempt to tax undistributed profits of corporations was made in 1936. A certain portion of retained income was exempt from the tax, and all retained income in excess of the exemption was taxed at rates rising from 10 per cent to 27 per cent. Retained earnings were taxed regardless of the purpose for which the earnings were retained, whether for a legitimate business purpose or for the purpose of reducing the taxable income of wealthy stockholders. This act was repealed two years later.

The Internal Revenue Code of the federal government now attempts to tax only earnings retained by a corporation for no reasonable business purpose. The application of the law does not question the retention of earnings until the amount exceeds $100,000. Earnings in excess of $100,-000 that are retained by the corporation for no legitimate business reason are taxed at a rate of 27.5 per cent on the first $100,000 of earnings unreasonably retained and 38.5 per cent on anything in excess of that amount. A corporation retaining $500,000 of earnings in one year for which a legitimate business purpose can be shown for only $300,000 is taxed for $200,-000 of unreasonably retained earnings. The burden of proof rests with the taxing authority in determining whether earnings are unreasonably retained or not. In most cases, it is not difficult for directors of a corporation to show that the retention of earnings is to retire debt, to expand operations, to modernize plant and machinery, or to build a reserve for unforeseen contingencies.

The effect of the Federal Personal Income Tax on dividend policy of the corporation depends upon the characteristics of stock ownership of the corporation. The receipt by individuals of dividend income is accorded a tax benefit not enjoyed by the receipt of cash in the form of interest on corporation bonds. Under the 1964 tax law, for example, the first $100 of dividend income received by an individual is tax free. Although one of the purported reasons for easing the income tax on dividend income was to encourage the distribution by corporations of dividends, it appears to have had little effect on the dividend policies of directors. If a corporation is owned by a small number of individuals, however, the tax on personal income may be of considerable importance. Beginning in 1959, the owners of a corporation may, if certain conditions outlined in the law are met, elect to have the corporation income taxed as if it were the income of an unincorporated business. Each stockholder's share of the corporation's income, whether it is distributed in dividends or retained by the corporation, will be taxed according to the personal income tax liability of each shareholder. This is of considerable benefit to the owners of corporations having few stockholders and wishing to distribute most of the income of the corporation in dividends. In such a case the income of the corporation would not be taxed first as corporate income and later as personal income when paid out in dividends. For tax purposes the corporation is, in effect, treated as a partnership.[4]

Stock dividends were taxed to the same extent as cash dividends from 1913 until 1920. In 1920, the Supreme Court ruled that the receipt by common stockholders of a stock dividend in the same kind of stock as that already held by the stockholder did not constitute taxable income. Since that time, stock dividends received by stock owners have generally been exempt from income taxation. One important exception, as mentioned before, exists if the holder of common stock is given the option by the corporation of receiving a stock dividend or its equivalent in cash. In this case, the dividend, in either form, must be reported by the stockholder as taxable income.

EARNINGS RETENTION VERSUS EARNINGS DISTRIBUTION

The most important decision faced by the directors of a corporation in determining the disposition of profits is to decide what proportion of net earnings to pay on dividends and what proportion to retain for investment in the company. Some corporations have depended heavily on retained earnings for expansion. One of the most spectacular examples of rapid expansion through retained earnings is that of the Ford Motor Company, which expanded from an original investment of $28,000 to well over $2 billion in 1960. Henry Ford, the founder of the company, was well known for his prejudice against outside financing. In deciding what proportion of net earnings to retain, the directors must satisfy themselves that the retained earnings can be profitably used by the corporation. Retained earnings are a favorable means of financing under the following conditions:

1. If retained earnings are at a rate sufficiently high to permit the corporation to finance most or all its needs for expansion out of earnings;
2. If the sale of additional common stock is rejected for any reason;
3. If the sale of preferred stocks or bonds is for any reason considered unwise;
4. If stockholders prefer a rising market price for their stock to liberal dividend payments; and

---

[4] In the Internal Revenue Act of 1954, Congress permitted partnerships with fifty or fewer members and proprietorships to be taxed as corporations, if the owners so desired. For a partnership or proprietorship to qualify as a corporation for tax purposes, the business must be devoted largely to manufacturing or to distribution, or at least half of its gross income must be obtained from purchasing and selling securities, real estate, or commodities.

5. If there is a possibility that increasing the number of shares outstanding may result in loss of control of the corporation.

If a company is in a position of not needing additional financing, the policy of paying out a large proportion of the net earnings in dividends is logical. If, on the other hand, there is a need of additional financing for expansion or modernization of equipment, the question arises whether the stockholder interest would best be served by retaining earnings to provide for expansion or paying liberal dividends and raising the needed funds by other means. The failure by the board of directors to pay dividends when earnings are sufficiently high to do so imposes a sacrifice on the stockholders. The sacrifice may be worthwhile, and the stockholders may be willing to bear it, if they are convinced that the retention of earnings will benefit them either as a result of more liberal payments in the future or through an increase in the market price of their stock.

Directors generally prefer not to pay out a large proportion of earnings in dividends unless they are reasonably sure that the corporation will continue to be profitable in the future. If there is uncertainty on this point, it would be prudent for the directors to use the earnings to put the corporation in a better position to meet possible financial reversals. This ordinarily means using the income to reduce the outstanding debt of the corporation. If a period of financial difficulty can be predicted, it would be advisable for the directors to put the corporation into as liquid a position as possible. It is easy, of course, for the directors to be entirely too pessimistic in their estimate of the future, thus losing opportunities for profitable investments in their desire to put the corporation in a condition to meet an expected depression.

The segregation or earmarking of part of the surplus for specifically stated purposes is often done, as explained above. This has no effect on the book value per share of the common stock, since the various surplus accounts are included in the net worth of the corporation. It does, however, indicate to the readers of the financial statements the purpose of retained earnings. The bookkeeping entries appropriating portions of the surplus to the reserve accounts debit the general surplus account and credit each of the surplus reserve accounts. Asset accounts and liability accounts are unaffected by such bookkeeping entries. Furthermore, the creation of such reserves does not reduce the liability for income tax of the corporation, since the accounts represent an allocation of the surplus. The amount transferred from the general surplus account to the surplus reserve accounts is determined by the judgment of the directors of the corporation. The policy of the directors may be to transfer as far as possible the same dollar amount each year to each of the surplus reserve accounts of the corporation. Under such a policy, the amount remaining in the general surplus account might show a higher degree of variation than the variation in the earnings of the corporation. In some years the earnings of the corporation might fall below the dollar amount to be credited to each of the surplus reserve accounts according to the policy of the directors. In such years, either a smaller amount will be credited to each of the surplus reserve accounts or the general surplus account will be reduced from the level of the previous year in order to credit the required dollar amount to each of the surplus reserve accounts.

Another policy is to allocate a fixed percentage of net earnings after payment of taxes each year to each of the surplus reserve accounts created. Under such a policy, each of the reserve accounts and the general surplus account are credited with a portion of the net earnings of the corporation each year. The dividend policy of the board of directors should, of course, be coordinated with the policy allocating portions of the net earnings to surplus reserve accounts.

Questions

1. How is the distribution of profits decided in a proprietorship, a partnership, and in a corporation?
2. What is the nature of the obligation, if any, of the corporation to pay a dividend declared by the board of directors?
3. Describe the mechanics of the two methods of distributing a cash dividend.
4. What limitations on the payment of dividends are found in state legislation?
5. What liabilities, if any, are found in state legislation of stockholders receiving dividends distributed in violation of state law?
6. Why are restrictions on the payment of dividends sometimes found in loan contracts? Why do the limitations usually exempt stock dividends?
7. What are the advantages to the corporation and to the stockholder in a policy of dividend distribution on regular dates?
8. What assets other than cash may be distributed to stockholders? Why are such distributions rare? Are all such distributions dividends? Explain.
9. What is a scrip dividend? Under what circumstances might a corporation distribute such a dividend?
10. What is a stock dividend? How is the problem of fractional shares handled?
11. How does a stock dividend affect the accounts of a corporation? The proportionate ownership of the corporation by stockholders?
12. What is the effect on the income tax of individuals of receiving stock dividends?
13. Describe the effect of stock dividends on the market price of shares. What is the effect on market price of a cash dividend?
14. What is the advantage to the corporation of a policy of regular payment of dividends? What possible disadvantages are there to a corporation in a policy of regular dividend payment?
15. Under what general conditions are retained earnings a favorable means of financing expansion?

Selected Readings

Brown, H. G., "Division of Retained Earnings to Reflect Business Needs," *Accounting Review,* April 1957.
Miller, M. H., and Franco Modigliani, "Dividend Policy, Growth, and the Valuation of Shares," *Journal of Business,* October 1961.

Porterfield, J. T. S., "Dividends, Dilution, and Delusion," *Harvard Business Review*, November-December 1959.

Sussman, M. Richard, *The Stock Dividend*, Bureau of Business Research, University of Michigan, Ann Arbor, Mich., 1962.

Walter, James E., "Dividend Policies and Common Stock Prices," *Journal of Finance*, March 1956.

Part VII

Promotion and Expansion

22

Promoting New Business

THE WORD *promotion* has a number of different meanings. In this chapter, it means the exploitation of a business opportunity by creating a new business company, the reorganization of an existing enterprise, or the consolidation of existing companies. On the average day in the United States, more than 1,300 new businesses are born, about 1,000 existing businesses change ownership, and somewhat more than 1,000 businesses are discountinued either because they failed or were absorbed into another company. Approximately 40 per cent of new enterprises have a precarious existence for a few months or a few years and die without having experienced any period of profit. The high degree of risk involved in promotion does not appear to discourage the activity of promoters. Even where the chances for success are small, adventurous individuals are willing to undertake the risk in the hope of success. Promotion is the beginning phase in the history of an enterprise and includes all the activities from the time the promoter thinks of the project to the point at which the enterprise begins actual operations.

STAGES IN PROMOTION

Some promotions are complicated and lengthy, whereas others are simple and brief. Each promotion is faced with its own set of problems. How these problems are met depends upon many factors, including the size of the promotion, the phase of the business cycle during which the promotion is undertaken, the degree of originality of the promotion, the amount of financing required, and the personality, experience, and resources of the promoter. To simplify the analysis of promotion, the subject has been divided into four stages: inspiration, investigation, financing, and assembly.

Inspiration Promotion begins with an idea. The idea may have very little originality. It may be the opening of a new service station or the building of an apartment house, in which the only bit of originality is the selection of the location.   In such promotions the probability of success can be estimated by measuring the degree of profitability of existing service stations or apartment houses in the community.   On the other hand, the idea may be highly original, such as the sale of one-foot square pieces of land in Texas to persons living in other states but wishing to become owners of Texas property for sentimental reasons.   The idea may involve long and costly experimentation before it is ready for profitable exploitation. Thomas Edison experimented many months with a large variety of filaments for his incandescent electric light before he found one that had a long enough life to make an electric light commercially practical.   The idea may be a single brilliant inspiration, such as Benjamin Franklin's decision to put two different pairs of lenses in a single frame to create bifocals.   The idea may be a result of an accident.   For many decades, rubber was severely limited in utility, because in cold weather it became hard and brittle and in warm weather sticky and odoriferous.   In 1839, Charles Goodyear put a batch of rubber mixed with sulphur on the stove in his home.   This was not done by design but entirely by accident.   Nevertheless, the application of heat to the mixture of sulphur and rubber made it flexible in cold weather and durable in warm weather.   It marked the beginning of the modern rubber industry.

A dynamic economy is one that is ever undergoing change.   In such an economy, opportunities for promotion abound.   In fact, the promoter is the key individual in making the economy dynamic.   Men with imagination, daring, and dissatisfaction with the existing way of doing things are the men who are largely responsible for progress.

Investigation   It would appear obvious that careful investigation is a necessary step in any business promotion.   Nevertheless, many promotions are carried to the assembly stage with no adequate investigation having been made as to the practicality and profitability of the venture.   Most of these are small-scale promotions.   The enthusiasm of the promoter and the impatience to get the business started often interfere with adequate investigation.   Investigation, undertaken to determine practicality and profitability, consists of determining the potential demand, analyzing the availability of resources, and estimating the profitability.

Determination of the demand for a product may be a relatively simple matter or a highly complex one.   If a person is considering erecting a service station at the intersection of two highways, he might take a count of the number of cars passing the corner in each direction on both streets. For maximum effectiveness, such a count should be taken on an hourly basis from early morning until late evening for a period of seven days.   The number of service stations already at the intersection should be noted, and, if possible, the number of cars turning into each of the service stations should be tabulated on an hourly basis.   This probably represents the minimum investigation that should be undertaken. In addition, it would be useful to the promoter to count the number of service stations within a five- or ten-block radius of the intersection under consideration. The number of houses within a one-mile radius of the intersection would also be useful information as would an estimate of the number of cars per family and the average income in the neighborhood. The ease of entry to and exit from the corner should be noted, particularly from the opposite side of each street.

Determining the potential market or demand for a product that is new may be more difficult. The promotion of a hearing aid disguised in the frame of a pair of glasses might require estimating potential demand through determining the number of persons wearing glasses who are also hard of hearing. An estimate of this number may already be available, but the difficulty would be in locating the information from government or trade sources. As part of the study of demand for such a pair of eyeglasses, it would be necessary to estimate the number of partially deaf persons willing to pay for a hearing aid that hides the fact of deafness.

Evaluating the availability of resources to put the idea into operation is the next step in determining the practicality of a promotion. If the promotion involves manufacturing, the availability of machinery and factory space should be considered, the availability of labor with the necessary kinds of skills determined, and the availability of managerial and technical talent investigated. Some products require a large amount of clean water in their manufacture, and others require a large amount of cheap electricity. In some, the disposal of waste materials must be considered. In others, the waste materials can be used as raw materials for by-products of the company or for sale at a profit to other companies. In the field of manufacturing, determining the availability of resources is generally a more complex problem than it is in the promotion of a wholesale establishment, retail store, or other nonmanufacturing company.

As part of the problem of determining the practicality of a promotion, the methods of distributing the product or selling the service must be investigated. For success in promotion, it is not sufficient merely to make available the new service or new product. "If you build a better mouse trap, the world will beat a path to your door"—this maxim may be true, but it has never actually been tested. It is certainly true that if a product or service is clearly superior to existing ones, it will be easier to promote and much more likely to succeed. Nevertheless, distribution is a very important factor in the successful promotion of any product or service. In many consumer items the cost of distribution exceeds the cost of manufacture. A careful evaluation of methods of distribution is therefore extremely important.

In investigating the probability of success of a promotion, an estimate of profitability must be made. In addition to analyzing the demand for the product or service, the availability of resources, and the methods of distribution, an estimate of the costs of production must be made. The costs of operation of a service station, grocery store, or apartment house can be estimated within a relatively high degree of accuracy. For a new service or a new product, however, estimates for the cost of operation are necessarily less reliable. Costs of manufacturing will vary according to the methods of production used, the amount of skilled labor needed, the degree of precision required, and the volume of production. The volume of production will depend upon the estimate of the demand for the product. Production volume is one of the factors determining the method of production to be used, particularly the use of automatic machinery. In cases where a product is entirely new, the estimates of the costs of production are particularly difficult. The methods of producing an item in a laboratory can rarely be expanded and applied to production on a commercial basis. New techniques must be used, both for production and control of quality. A pilot plant may be built as a means of testing the practicality of using various techniques, before full-scale commercial production is attempted. The number of different sizes, styles, or models to be offered will affect the costs of manufacture. If the product has a seasonal demand, the volume of production must vary during the year, or provision must be made for excess production during the season of slack demand to provide for the expected volume of sales during the selling season.

Financing Without optimism, there would be very few promotions. Optimism is, however, a source of danger because it frequently leads to an overestimate of future receipts and an underestimate of expenses. An experienced promoter knows, probably as a result of bitter experience, the pitfalls of overoptimism. A person organizing a business for the first time is more likely to err in this respect.

In studying the financial aspects of promotion, the first step is to determine the financial requirements. This can best be divided into two parts: (1) The amount of assets required to begin business should be determined. (2) An estimate should be made of the excess of expenses over receipts during the initial period of operation at a loss that is experienced by the typical new business.

The listing of original assets required can be arranged according to the way they would appear on a balance sheet, in the following manner:

1. Current assets.
   (a) Cash.
   (b) Accounts receivable.
   (c) Inventories.
   (d) Other current assets.
2. Fixed assets.
   (a) Machinery and equipment.
   (b) Furniture and fixtures.

(c) Buildings and land.

(d) Other fixed assets.

3. Promotional and organization expenses.

4. Patents, franchises, and goodwill, if bought for cash.

A detailed schedule for each of the classes of assets listed above should be prepared by the promoter. For example, the schedule of furniture and fixtures required to open a flower shop as given by the Small Business Administration is shown in Fig. 22-1.

Schedule of furniture, fixtures, and equipment

Item	If cash purchase, enter full amount below and in last column	If installment purchase, enter below and also enter in last column the down payment plus at least one installment			Estimate of initial cash requirements for furniture, fixtures, and equipment
		Price	Down payment	Amount of each installment	
Display refrigerators					
Supplemental storage case					
Display stands, shelves, tables					
Window display fixtures					
Wrapping counter					
Cash register					
Lighting					
Workroom tables					
Delivery equipment					
Safe					
Outside sign					
Miscellaneous equipment					
Total furniture, fixtures, and equipment					$

Fig. 22-1 *Worksheet for estimating initial capital requirements for a flower shop.* (*Source:* Wendell O. Metcalf, *Starting and Managing a Small Business of Your Own,* Small Business Administration, Washington, D. C., 1958)

The preparation of the estimate of initial asset requirements should be made with as great care as possible. The investment in assets will depend upon the expected volume of sales, the character of the business (retail store, factory, motel, and so on), and the method of obtaining the assets. In any case, the available financial resources for the new company should exceed by a safe margin the initial investment in the venture. What constitutes a safe margin must be judged by the promoter but should be enough to absorb the losses from operation that most new enterprises experience during the early months of existence.

To conserve capital resources, various steps may be taken. Some examples are given below:

1. Rent, rather than purchase, all buildings needed.
2. Lease the machinery, trucks, and other equipment needed rather than purchase them.
3. Make sales on a cash only basis to eliminate the investment in accounts receivable.
4. Keep the number of products, lines, sizes, and colors to a minimum, so as to reduce the initial investment in finished goods inventory.

More suggestions could be added to the above list, depending upon whether the new business is in retailing, manufacturing, or some other industry, what services competitors offer, and other factors. All the above means of conserving capital will permit the new enterprise to have a better chance of survival if the financial resources of the owners are limited. In addition to absorbing the losses that may be expected during the initial period of operations of a new enterprise, the owners' resources should be sufficient to withstand an unexpected decline in business activity. Safety is a relative matter, however. Promoters can be overcautious as well as reckless. All the means of conserving capital resources involve sacrifice. Renting buildings rather than purchasing may be more expensive, as is true of leasing equipment. Limiting sales to a cash only basis may lose many customers to competitors selling on credit. Limiting the number of sizes and product lines may offer too limited a choice to clients, with a resulting loss of patronage. The promoter must balance the advantages and disadvantages of the means of conserving capital resources and make his decisions as they apply to a particular promotion. To enhance the likelihood of success, the promoter should have a good measure of judgment, experience, and luck.

A very important factor in determining the asset requirements for a new business is the estimated volume of sales. Assume the promotion involves a factory making an automobile accessory. Assume further that a sales volume annually of $500,000 is considered necessary in order to operate at a profit. If the accessory is to be sold at a price of $10 per unit, 50,000 units must be produced and sold each year. If production can be spread evenly throughout the year, the production rate will be 1,000 units per week for fifty weeks. Given a rate of production of 1,000 units per week, the promoter must estimate the number of machines of each type needed to attain this production, the amount of storage space needed for raw materials, supplies, and finished items, the average investment in accounts receivables necessary in order to obtain the sales, the average cash balance in the bank that must be maintained, the investment in office machines necessary, and the investment in other assets required to attain the projected rate of production.

If the promotion involves the creation of a new business rather than the consolidation of existing businesses, it generally takes a period of time after business operations are begun to build up a volume of sales sufficient to cover all expenditures. In estimating the financial requirements for a new business, a certain period of unprofitable operations should be assumed. The promoter cannot expect cash receipts to equal cash expenditures during this time. Financial planning should include sufficient funds to pay salaries, purchase materials, and pay the rents, installments, and other expenses of doing business. In introducing a new retail store, expenses of promotion, such as free balloons, searchlights shining in the night sky, and introductory bargain prices, may be needed to attract the first customers. The length of time that a new business can expect to be unprofitable before it begins covering total expenses depends upon the type of business, the extent of competition, and many other factors. Some promotions can reasonably be expected to cover all costs after a period of two to three months of operation. In other instances, it may take a year or longer before a new promotion becomes profitable. In determining initial financial requirements, it is essential that an estimate be made of the length of time necessary for operations to run at a loss before becoming profitable, and the amount of funds necessary to carry the business through the unprofitable period must be determined. Failure to do this is one of the most important causes of bankruptcy in new businesses. Specifically, the lack of adequate funds during the probable initial period of unprofitable operations will result in the following:

1. Inability to hire sufficient numbers of employees to keep the business operating and to serve customers adequately.
2. Inability to obtain required equipment, or if needed equipment has been obtained, inability to maintain it in proper condition.
3. Difficulty in maintaining an adequate supply of merchandise or materials to serve customers effectively.
4. Inability to take advantage of discounts offered by suppliers.
5. Difficulty in granting credit to customers where that is necessary to meet the competition.

After having analyzed the financial requirements of a new company, it is necessary to determine the availability of the needed funds and the related cost of financing. Availability of funds is a relative problem. Funds are available for almost any type of promotion if the promoter is willing to pay the price demanded. The problem of availability of funds, therefore, becomes a problem of securing the necessary funds at a reasonable price. Perhaps funds can be secured by the sale of a bond issue or through other debt instruments, but the cost in terms of interest may be prohibitive. Alternatively, funds may be secured through the sale of common stock to the general public, but the investment banker distributing the stock may require 30 to 35 per cent of the receipts from the sale of stock as his commission. This may be higher than the promoter is willing to pay. If the funds deemed necessary by the promoter are not available at a cost which is considered reasonable by him, the promoter may decide to drop the promotion entirely, or postpone it until a future time in the hope that funds may be available at lower cost than at present.

Of the many factors that affect the cost of financing, the following are most important:

Form of business organization. The availability of funds and the cost of financing will depend upon whether the promotion is organized as a corporation, a partnership, or a proprietorship. The initial financing of a proprietorship or a partnership generally is limited to the funds that the owner or owners can contribute plus money borrowed from friends. A corporation has a greater degree of flexibility, since common stocks, preferred stocks, and bonds may be used to raise funds.

Size of financing. The studies of the Securities and Exchange Commission mentioned in Chapter 15 show that the cost of raising funds in small amounts by a corporation are proportionately much greater than the cost of raising a large sum by a corporation.

Industry. The promotion of a new company in the field of mining is a much riskier proposition than a promotion in the public utilities field. Costs of financing will vary according to the industry in which the company is promoted. Where risk is greater, financing costs are higher.

Extent of demand for funds in relation to supply of funds for investment. It is axiomatic that the demand for funds and the supply of funds seeking investment vary from one period to another. These changes will affect the cost of investment funds. If there are many companies seeking funds for expansion, modernization, or promotion of new enterprises, the demand for investment funds can be expected to rise. As a result, the cost of raising funds for new promotions will tend to increase. On the other hand, a decline in the demand for funds will tend to make investors and lenders willing to accept a lower yield for their funds. If individual savings, investments of financial institutions, and other sources of funds increase, the cost to promoters of funds for new businesses will tend to decline. The opposite will be true, if the supply of funds for investment decreases. The effect on the cost of financing for new businesses of changes in supply and demand follow the same pattern as in other economic areas.

Assembly If the inspiration which initiated the promotion has survived the tests of investigation and availability of financing, the process of assembling the necessary factors to begin operations is undertaken. The details that must be taken care of in the final stage of promotion prior to beginning operations vary considerably from one promotion to another. Nevertheless, they are usually many. If the new business is organized as a corporation, the charter must be secured, the stock issued, and the other necessary steps taken to make the corporation an operating reality. Buildings must be constructed or leased, machinery, equipment, and supplies secured, materials for production or resale ordered, and personnel hired. If a license or franchise is needed, it must be secured.

After the assembly of the factors required by the business, the promotion function is terminated. The managers of the business take over the responsibility of operations. Frequently, the promoter remains as one of the managers of the company, often as the proprietor, a partner, or president of the corporation.

LEGAL ASPECTS OF PROMOTION

In the process of creating the business, the promoter must, in the stages of financing and assembly, enter into agreement with other persons and business concerns. Otherwise, the stages of financing and assembly could not be accomplished. If the business being promoted is a partnership or proprietorship, the legal problems are simplified, inasmuch as the promoter remains as proprietor or partner. In the promotion of a corporation, however, the legal status of the promoter is not so clearly defined. The difficulties faced by the promoter of a corporation in entering into agreements during the stages of promotion are that he cannot bind the corporation to a contract entered into before the corporation comes into existence. He can, however, enter into agreements with other parties on the understanding that these agreements will be replaced by formal contracts after the corporation has come into existence. Should the corporation fail to assume such contracts, the law generally will hold the promoter personally liable. In drawing up the articles of incorporation, the promoter may include the assumption of contracts and other agreements made by him, thus binding the corporation by its charter to assuming commitments made prior to the company's origin. The legal position of the promoter has proved one of the most difficult areas of corporation law. In his dealings with other parties during the stages of promotion, the promoter acts as an agent even though he cannot legally be in an agent's position, for the simple reason that his principal (the corporation) is not yet in existence. Some courts have taken the position that the promoter acts in the capacity of a trustee prior to the origin of the corporation. Under this theory, courts hold the promoter to the exercise of reasonable good faith and prudence in all dealings with other parties in connection with the promotion of a corporation. Although court decisions involving promotion are far from uniform, the general trend is in the direction of requiring the promoter to act with the honesty and prudence expected of a trustee in protecting the interests of the unborn corporation and its future owners.

The promotion of a new business frequently involves the use of options, leases, and patents.   If a piece of real estate is needed for the operation of a projected company, it must be made certain that its use will be available if and when the company begins operations.   If there is some uncertainty as to whether a promotion will proceed to the point of bringing into existence a company or if the funds available for property acquisition are low, the promoter may purchase an option to buy the property.   An option is an agreement whereby the owner of property gives the exclusive right to the holder of the option to purchase the property at a price stipulated in the option and at a time no later than the date of expiration of the option. Where the option is purchased in the name of the promoter but is to be used by the corporation if it should come into existence, the promoter will include in the option contract the right to assign the option to the corporation.   As an alternative to purchasing an option, the promoter may enter into a lease arrangement with the owner of the desired property so as to secure its use for the company.[1]   If the promotion of the new enterprise involves the exploitation of a patent, it is necessary that the rights to the patent be secured by the company.   If the promoter is the inventor, he may simply assign his patent rights to the corporation after it comes into existence.   If another person acts as a promoter to exploit the invention, it is necessary that an agreement be made between the inventor and the promoter as to the assignment of the patent to the corporation after its birth.   In order to conserve the cash of the new company, the holder of a patent desired by a company may be paid with the stock of the company rather than in cash.   Another means open to the company in securing the rights to a patent is to get its use on a royalty basis.   Such a contract generally requires the company to pay the patentholder a certain sum of money for each unit produced under the patent.   Copyrights on a book, a play, or other literary or artistic work, like a patent, may be secured by outright purchase, fixed annual payment, or a royalty based on the number of items sold each year.   The main legal difference between the two is that a patent may be secured for a period of seventeen years and is not renewable except by act of Congress, whereas a copyright has a life of twenty-eight years and may be renewed for another twenty-eight-year period.

THE PROMOTER

Characteristics   Promotion is probably more of an art than a science.   Furthermore, it is an art that cannot readily be analyzed or taught.   Each promotion involves problems that are unique in some measure.   It may be easier to analyze the promoter than the promotion.   There are certain characteristics that appear to be common to promoters.   Probably the most important is optimism.   Without optimism, a person is unwilling to take the risk involved in promotion and is unable to convince others to associate

---

1 Leasing is discussed in Chapter 14.

with him in a venture. In addition to optimism, all promoters must have the willingness to take initiative. Many persons are able to come up with ideas for new services or products, but few are willing to translate their ideas into action. An important ingredient in the personality of a promoter that distinguishes him from his fellows is his willingness to act. The professional promoter, as distinct from the occasional promoter, is usually a nonconformist to some degree. He has a restless imagination which makes him dissatisfied with the existing structure of an industry, the existing process of production, or the existing pattern of distribution. The habitual promoter must be a man of daring. There are many persons that have considerable intelligence and breadth of knowledge of business affairs who find it difficult to make important decisions. The essence of promotion is taking a course of action whose results cannot be known with certainty.

The promoter must, however, also be a practical man. He must be able to analyze all the information available about a particular proposed venture. The success of a promotion will depend to a considerable degree on the skill with which he analyzes the factors involved.

The promotion of a new business involves working with other people. To be successful, the promoter must be convincing and persuasive. If he has the qualities of a good salesman, he will need to use these to secure the cooperation of the persons necessary in any successful promotion. Like a successful salesman, he must inspire confidence. He must be able to cooperate with others and in turn secure their cooperation. He must be a good organizer and be able to bring together men, materials, and money in such a way that these factors are directed toward a single goal. Few men are blessed with a large measure of all the qualities described above. Nevertheless, the success of a promoter will depend in large measure upon how well endowed he is with the proper characteristics.

Types of Promoters

Professional promoters. The professional promoter is an individual who engages in promotions but does not continue in the management of the companies that he promotes. Such promoters appear to be somewhat similar in nature to the prospectors who spend most of their lives climbing over hills, descending into canyons, or scouring desert areas, always in search of undiscovered deposits of ore. The professional promoter, like the prospector, is always on the search for that which has not yet been discovered. Like the hardened prospector, the professional promoter, having discovered a business opportunity and brought it into being, leaves it to the management of others and renews his search for new opportunities. Professional promoters are rare at the present time. Probably this is true for the same reason that individual inventors are comparatively rare today. In the last century, scientific discoveries and important inventions were commonly the result of an individual working in his own laboratory or machine shop.

At the present time, scientific discoveries are increasingly made by teams of scientists working in the laboratories of government, industry, and universities. The same trend has taken place in the field of promotions of business enterprises. The lone individual promoter has largely been displaced by organizations. A few, however, still survive.

Entrepreneurial promoters. J. A. Schumpeter developed the theory of innovation as a determinant of economic conditions. In his analysis of innovation, Schumpeter created the image of the entrepreneurial promoter. Such a promoter has the following qualities:

1. An innovation is always involved in the promotion.

2. Much of the work of the promotion is changing the customs or habits of individuals so that the public will accept the innovation. This may mean that the promoter will have to create a demand for the innovation through publicity, advertising, and any other means of persuasion available to him.

3. Habit and custom die hard. In order to change habit and modify existing customs, a long slow process of education is usually necessary. The entrepreneur introducing an innovation must be prepared to cope with the long, discouraging process of changing customs before the innovation is accepted by the public.

4. Entrepreneurial promoters remain with the company introducing the innovation rather than leave the enterprise to the management of others and move on to new promotions.

5. These promoters are by nature iconoclasts. Because the innovations that they introduce change or modify existing customs, they are not very popular with the general public or with existing businessmen until after the innovation has become accepted by a large proportion of society. Entrepreneurial promoters must be prepared to incur the opposition, sometimes mild and sometimes violent, that is directed toward changing "our way of life," whatever the way of life happens to be at the particular point of time chosen by the entrepreneur to introduce his innovation. [2]

Investor promoters. Investor promoters are those who engage in a promotion primarily to create a means whereby they can invest funds at their disposal. It is the hope and expectation of an investor promoter that the funds that he invests in the company he promotes will yield a greater return than could be had in alternative investments. Such promoters do not usually invest in innovations. Rather, they promote companies that offer the same type of service or product that is already available to the general public. A person who has worked as a buyer for a department store for a number of years and has saved up money may decide to open his own retail

---

[2] The promoters of the early railroads in the nineteenth century were accused of preventing cows from giving milk, frightening farm animals, and of using a satanic power to drive the trains. When the airplane was in its early stages of development, the attitude of many persons was that "if God had intended man to fly, He would have provided him with wings."

store, using the savings that he has accumulated. A salesman working for a company for a number of years may feel that he has enough experience and funds to create his own company, and "to work for himself." An executive working for a large company may decide that he has saved enough money to start his own company. Like the entrepreneurial promoter, the investor promoter usually engages in only one promotion during his life.

The firm as promoter. The primary function of an investment banking house is to sell securities for client corporations. However, investment banking houses have sometimes initiated the creation of a new company or the consolidation of existing companies. In such cases the investment bankers have acted as promoters. Recently companies have been formed to finance the exploitation of new ideas or projects. Individuals with ideas for commercial exploitation, such as the distribution of frozen orange juice or the manufacture of plastic pipe for residential plumbing, may secure financing from one of these firms to create a new company. Such companies make a thorough investigation of the practicality and profitability of each venture they finance. In the process of investigation, they generally add the ideas of their executives to those of the original promoter, and in so doing help to shape the promotion into a form that is most likely to be commercially successful. In this capacity, they act not only as financiers but as co-promoters. The payment of companies participating in the promotion of new ventures is generally in the form of stock in the new company that they help to create.

Liabilities of the Promoter On all the contracts and agreements made by the promoter prior to the establishment of a corporation, the promoter is liable until the contracts and agreements are accepted by the corporation. Upon acceptance of the contracts by the corporation, the promoter ceases to become liable, provided at the time of making the contract the promoter clearly stated his position as promoter rather than as principal in the contract. If the other parties to the agreements entered into by the promoter acted under the belief that the promoter was acting in his own personal capacity, the later ratification of the agreements by the corporation does not relieve the promoter from personal liability.

In a promotion involving the sale of securities to the general public, the promoter must be very careful not to transgress any of the laws of the state governing the public distribution of securities. If any violations are discovered, the promoter can be held personally liable. If the promotion involves the sale of securities subject to the registration requirements of the Securities Act of 1933, the promoter is subject to the requirements of the federal law and the regulations of the Securities Exchange Commission in preparing the securities for public distribution.

Some of the negotiations during a promotion are best kept secret. If the promotion requires the purchase of land, the public knowledge of this may cause a rise in the price of the land sought by the promoter. Secrecy may also be necessary in the early stages of promotion of some enterprises, if knowledge of the promotion is likely to result in competitors copying the idea. Although secrecy may be necessary during most or all the stages of promotion, the law holds that the promoter may not make secret profits at the expense of the corporation being promoted.

Compensation for the Promoter   Many promotions are suspended before completion. In those cases where a promotion does not proceed to completion, the promoter generally loses all the time and money he spent in the promotion. As a matter of fact, the majority of promotions that are begun are not carried through to the point where the company is formed and actually begins operations. Because of the high likelihood of loss of time and money in promotions, a promoter is usually willing to undertake the risk involved in promotion only in return for generous profits if the promotion is a success. Generally, the payment for the promoter's services is in two forms. The first is direct payments of cash. These cash payments might be for the services of promotion, or may be in payment for properties sold by the promoter to the corporation. If a promoter has title to a valuable patent, a lease on land under which oil might be found, or a franchise to undertake a particular type of business activity, the promoter may create a corporation for the purpose of exploiting the asset which he owns. His compensation for the promotion of the new corporation might be in the form of the profit which he receives on the sale of the asset to the corporation created by the promoter. If payment for the promotional services is in the form stated above, the amount of the profit realized from the promotion does not depend upon the future success of the corporation.

The promoter may also be paid with the stock of the company he created. If so he may sell the stock immediately, transforming his payment into cash, or he may retain the stock as an investment in the hope of making a greater profit as the result of an increase in its market price. If the promoter elects to keep the stock of the corporation, the compensation for his efforts will depend upon the economic soundness of the promotion and the skill with which the company is managed after its creation. In other words, the profitability of the corporation will determine the value of the compensation to the promoter.

Sometimes the promoter is paid in warrants of the company. Generally, this is not used as a sole means of payment for the promoter's services but is frequently given to promoters in addition to other forms of compensation. Since the warrant is a contract binding the corporation to sell securities to the holder of the warrant at a price stated in the contract, the value of the warrant may be zero at the time that it is received by the promoter. However, if the corporation proves profitable, the market price of the stock is likely to rise. In such a case, the exercise of the warrants will permit the holder to purchase stock from the company at less than the market price.

If the corporation proves to be very profitable, the warrants paid to the promoters may become very valuable.   If stock or warrants are given to the promoter as the principal payment for his services, he is often also paid in cash for the amount of out-of-pocket expenses incurred by him in the course of the promotion.   Such an arrangement is eminently sensible, since it permits the promoter to recover the cash payments incurred by him during the promotion and makes the payment for the time he spent contingent upon the financial success of the company he created.

There is no uniformity in the amount of payment for promotional services.   Whatever the payments made to the promoter for his services, they must not be secret, a fact that is brought out above.   The Securities Act of 1933 requires full disclosure of all pertinent facts in connection with a distribution of securities subject to registration under the act.   This law does not dictate the amount of payment to the promoter for his services. It merely requires that the amount so paid be clearly stated in the prospectus prepared for distribution to potential purchasers of stock.

RISKS IN PROMOTION

The burden of risk to the promoter is considerable, because such a large proportion of promotions never reach the stage of completion.   The losses in money and time suffered by a promoter in those promotions that are not completed were mentioned above.   There is, perhaps, a risk that cannot be measured in terms of money spent.   In every promotion undertaken by a professional promoter, the risk to his reputation is present.   This may be unimportant to nonprofessional promoters, but the person who expects to engage in a number of promotions during his lifetime has a considerable stake in maintaining a successful reputation.   As in the fielding average of a baseball player, every error of a promoter can be costly.   To be successful, a promoter must instill confidence in those investors, investment bankers, and other parties with whom he deals during the stages of promotion.   Every unsuccessful promotion with which a promoter has been associated makes it that much more difficult for him to create the necessary confidence in future promotions.

If a new corporation is highly profitable, the common stockholders are the ones that receive the major benefit.   It is for this reason that in the promotion of a new corporation the long-term funds are secured largely or entirely through the sale of common stock.   Because the return on bonds is in practically every instance a fixed return, it is generally difficult to find a market for bonds of a newly created corporation, unless the corporation is a consolidation of established companies.   If the promotion is a success, the bondholder receives a limited return.   If the promotion is a failure, the bondholder is likely to suffer a loss in spite of the protective features that might be found in the bond contract.   The protection to the bondholder of a mortgage on the property of a new industrial corporation is liable to prove insubstantial. Factory buildings, for example, are likely to be designed for maximum utility of one type of operation. Unlike retail store buildings, factory buildings are generally specialized structures and often are not easily adapted to other uses. For this reason, bonds secured by the mortgage of the factory building of a corporation often do not protect the bondholder against loss as a result of the failure of the corporation soon after its promotion. The purchasers of preferred stock of a new corporation are in a position somewhat similar to that of the bondholders of the corporation. If the corporation should succeed, their participation in the profits is generally limited. If the corporation should fail, they are likely to lose what they have invested in the company. Furthermore, the preferred stockholders do not have the priority in dissolution of assets enjoyed by bondholders.

In view of the considerations mentioned above, it is not surprising that in the promotion of most new ventures common stock alone is the source of long-term financing. An exception is found in the case of public utility promotions. Electric light and power companies, gas companies, and other public utilities have heavy investments in fixed assets, which are generally suitable for mortgaging to protect the holders of bonds. Most utility companies enjoy a relatively stable income. Also, the future demand for their services can be more accurately estimated than can the demand for the products or services of other industries. For these reasons, the promotional plans for public utility companies generally include bonds and preferred stocks.

If the services of investment bankers are used to raise funds for a new corporation, they undertake some of the risk involved in promotion. If the investment bankers agree to underwrite the distribution of common stock of a new company, they undertake the financial risk of an unsuccessful sale. Even in cases where an investment banker agrees to distribute the securities of the new corporation on a "best efforts" basis, there is risk to the investment banker. To a much greater extent than to the promoter, the reputation of an investment banker is his most valuable asset. The association of an investment banker with the promotion of a corporation that proves to be unprofitable is damaging to his reputation. If the investment banker fails to sell all the securities at the price originally proposed, it tends to reflect unfavorably on his ability to sell securities. If the securities are successfully sold to the public and the corporation is brought into being, the failure of the corporation to earn a profit on its stock will oftentimes be blamed on the inability of the officers of the investment banking house to recognize an unprofitable venture or, even worse, on the willingness of the investment banker to unload the securities of a dubious venture on a trusting public. Some investment bankers are, however, willing to undertake these risks to their reputation, if the payments to them for their participation in a promotion are sufficiently high.

All parties associated with the promotion are interested in reducing the risk to themselves as much as possible and increasing their share of the rewards of success as much as possible. The negotiations undertaken during the various stages of promotion involve jockeying for positions of better advantage, attempting to outguess the strategy of others, and using bargaining tactics similar to those found in an oriental bazaar. Promotions involve human beings, and the emotions and instincts of humans are evident in the history of every promotion. Promotions often contain dramatic moments. Dewing describes the human aspects of promotion in the following words:

> The struggles, defeats, and misrepresentations, the play of primal human emotions, the unrestrained anger caused by the sudden conflict of different types of personalities—all these are the undercurrent of every promotion. They seldom reach the open light, for in the end the only thing the public knows is the prosaic and unemotional registration statement and prospectus filed with the Securities and Exchange Commission. But behind the veil is a lurid background of human victory and defeat, of overmastering personalities and thwarted ambitions. No phase of our modern industrial world, unless it is that of reorganization, reaches deeper into the elemental forces of the human personality. [3]

PROMOTION OF THE REYNOLDS INTERNATIONAL PEN COMPANY

Many new companies were formed following World War II to exploit the tremendous unsatisfied demand for goods and services that had been building up during the war years when scarce goods were rationed. Some of the new companies were involved in promotions in already developed fields. Others involved the exploitation of innovations. Two highly publicized promotions were financial failures. One was the Tucker Corporation, formed to manufacture and sell a radically new automobile. Another was the Lustron Corporation, formed to manufacture on a mass production basis houses made almost entirely of metal. Many promotions, however, did not fail. Probably the most spectacularly successful one was that of the Reynolds International Pen Company, formed to introduce the ball-point pen. The course of this promotion illustrates the problems involved in promoting a new product and a new company.

Career of a Promoter The Reynolds International Pen Company was formed by Milton Reynolds, a promoter with a shrewd sense for recognizing profitable opportunities. Born in 1892, he became a millionaire by the time he was twenty-six years old. He accomplished this with an investment of $25 of his own money in organizing a chain of tire stores handling manufacturers' seconds. Four years later most of his fortune had been lost in unwise speculation in the stock market. With borrowed money, he promoted a company during the land boom in Florida in the mid-1920's to build prefabricated houses in Louisiana, shipping the unassembled parts by

---

[3] Arthur Stone Dewing, *The Financial Policy of Corporations*, 5th ed., The Ronald Press Company, New York, 1953, p. 451.

barges to the coast of Florida. This promotion also made him rich. His second fortune, however, was lost when a string of barges carrying a load of his unassembled houses disappeared in a hurricane. During the 1930's, he promoted an oversized typewriter designed to type display cards for retail stores. In 1944, he purchased silver cigarette lighters in Mexico, shipped them by air to department stores in the United States, and made a profit of a quarter of a million dollars during the Christmas selling season of that year.

This diversity of business activity is typical of the character of a true promoter. Reynolds was not a specialist in the tire industry, the house-building industry, the manufacture of typewriters, nor the distribution of cigarette lighters. His genius lay in sniffing out profitable opportunities much as a bloodhound would search a trail. His most spectacular and most profitable promotion, however, was the ball-point pen.

Inspiration The inspiration for the ball-point pen promotion came to Reynolds in June 1945, when he was in Buenos Aires. The German army had surrendered the month before, and the Japanese forces in the Pacific were being pushed back to their homeland with increasing ferocity. It appeared possible that Christmas of 1945 would be the first postwar one. Reynolds was looking for some novelty that could help satisfy the demand of people with plenty of money in their pockets but a scarcity of things to buy. The ball-point pens that he saw in some stores in Buenos Aires gave him his inspiration. Pens of this type had not yet been introduced into the United States, and he thought they would be just the novelty that would sell well during the Christmas trade.

Investigation The first thing that Mr. Reynolds did was to call on the manufacturer of the pens in Buenos Aires. He found that they were made by László Biro, whose company, Eterpen, had sold the distribution rights in the United States to the Eberhard Faber Company, which subsequently entered into an agreement with the Eversharp Corporation to manufacture and distribute the pens in the United States. Reynolds bought a number of the pens, anyway, and took a plane to Chicago as soon as he could.

The next step in the investigation was to determine the patent position of the ball-point pen. He found that a pen with a ball point had been patented as early as 1888, but had been commercially unsuccessful. The patents held by Biro covered the mechanism of feeding a gelatinous ink to the ball bearing by making use of the principle of capillary attraction. Since the patent on the idea of using a ball bearing as a writing point had long since expired, Reynolds knew he would be safe from patent infringement if he could devise a new method of feeding the ink other than that of capillary action.

At this stage in his investigation, he enlisted the services of an engineer. Both of them experimented with a variety of ways of feeding the ink to the ball point, and finally succeeded in getting a working model constructed that used a gravity feed.

At this point in the promotion, in August of 1945, Japan surrendered. Since he was convinced that success depended upon his exloiting the pent-up demand during the first Christmas following the end of hostilities, he speeded up his promotion. Partly because of the lack of time and partly because he thought it was unnecessary, he did not undertake an investigation of the potential demand. He still had to arrange for the manufacture of the pen, determine the costs of manufacturing, decide upon a selling price, and arrange for the distribution of his pens to the public.

Aluminum was plentiful and was used for the pen barrel. He arranged for a manufacturer of ball bearings to supply him with the tiny steel spheres needed for his pens. He arranged with a machine shop in Chicago to manufacture the parts for the pen and estimated their cost of manufacture at 80¢ apiece. Since wartime price controls were still in effect, it was necessary for him to get approval from the Office of Price Administration for the retail price he desired. His request for a retail price of $12.50 a pen (entered as a bargaining device with the hope of receiving a ceiling price of at least $5) was, astonishingly, granted. He then took a sample pen to one of the large department stores in New York City, Gimbel Brothers, hoping to get an order on the basis of the sample alone. He succeeded in making an initial sale of 2,500 pens, and very shortly later was surprised with an additional order totaling 50,000 pens. All of this was accomplished before the manufacture of pens was begun. But with these matters out of the way, he was in a position to finance and organize his company.

Financing Financing the promotion was a relatively simple problem. Since the pen parts were to be made by a machine shop, since the only part in the production of pens undertaken by Mr. Reynolds' company was the assembly of the parts, and since it was obviously unnecessary to finance an advertising campaign to promote demand for the pens, the amount of funds required to get the business started was little. The idea of a public stock offering was rejected because of the delay involved and because the funds needed were small. The individual financial resources of Mr. Reynolds appeared to be easily sufficient to organize the company and begin operations. He was compensated for his promotional services with stock ownership of the company.

Assembly The Reynolds International Pen Company was chartered in 1945 at a capitalization of $26,000. The original manufacturing "plant" of the company was a corner of the factory making the pen parts for Mr. Reynolds. The parts were assembled in this corner largely by hand operated machines. In view of the 50,000 pen order from Gimbel Brothers in New York, it was apparent that no sales force needed to be assembled. The main problem was making the pens. Production began as soon as the necessary tools for assembly were available and workers hired to operate them.

At the beginning, Mr. Reynolds' wife and daughter were among these workers. Finished pens were shipped to New York as rapidly as possible in order to complete the Gimbel Brothers order as early in the Christmas selling season as could be done.

Gimbel Brothers Department Store put the pens on sale for the first time on the morning of October 29, 1945, after first announcing the "miraculous pen that will revolutionize writing" in the city newspapers. More than 5,000 people were waiting at the department store when it opened in the morning, and fifty policemen were dispatched to handle the crowds. The demand for pens was so great that sales counters were set up in many departments in the store, including the umbrella counter, the clock department, and the silverware department. In response to frantic orders for more pens, the Reynolds plant shipped them to New York by plane. The first day's sale of pens at Gimbel Brothers store exceeded 10,000. Orders from stores all over the United States began flooding into the Reynolds office in Chicago at a rate so great that it swamped communications facilities. Store managers trying to reach Reynolds by telephone had to wait five days to get a clear signal. Mail orders piled up more rapidly than the hastily organized office staff could handle them. Even telegrams lay unopened for days. By the first of December the backlog of unfilled orders reached more than one million pens. The net profit after taxes for the first month's operation was $541,000.

Although this promotion was meant to capitalize on the tremendous demand for consumer products during the first postwar Christmas season, the demand for pens showed no signs of receding at the end of December. By February 1946, 800 people were working for the company in a factory building formerly used to manufacture parts for aircraft engines. A profit and loss statement prepared in February 1946 showed net profits after taxes of $1,558,607.81.

As the year 1946 progressed, many companies began manufacturing and selling ball-point pens, including Eberhard Faber and Eversharp Company. At the beginning of the Christmas selling season of 1946, the number of ball-point pen manufacturers was over 300, and the net profits of the Reynolds International Pen Company had dropped to approximately $350,000 a month. Competition knocked down the retail price of pens at a more rapid rate than the increased volume of production reduced manufacturing costs. By 1948, Reynolds pens costing 8¢ to manufacture were selling at 39¢ retail. In that year, Mr. Reynolds closed his manufacturing facilities, dismissed his workers, and ended his career as a fountain pen tycoon. Like a true promoter, his interest in fountain pens faded after the industry became established, and his energies were diverted to seeking other profitable promotions.

Questions

1. In the field of finance, what is meant by the word *promotion?*
2. The origin of promotion is an inspiration. Several examples are given in this chapter. List five examples of your own.
3. How can the potential demand for a product or service be determined? Explain by means of examples.
4. If the product or service to be promoted is not similar to existing ones, how may the potential market for it be estimated?
5. "Without optimism there would be very few promotions." Explain. Is optimism a source of danger in promotion? Why or why not?
6. How can a promoter determine the financing required to open a new furniture store? A radio and television repair shop? A restaurant?
7. Why is the early operation of a new business frequently at a loss, although later it may be very profitable? What implications does this hold for financing new businesses?
8. What factors affect the cost and availability of funds for business promotions?
9. What is the nature of the legal difficulties encountered by the promoter of a new corporation when entering into agreements with others during the promotion? Why are these difficulties avoided in promoting a partnership or proprietorship?
10. What characteristics are apt to be found in a professional promoter?
11. What are the qualities of an entrepreneurial promoter?
12. How is a promoter paid for his services of promotion? Why are two or more methods of payment sometimes combined in compensating a promoter?
13. Discuss the risks of promotion to the promoter, to the owners, and to the creditors of a new company.
14. In the promotion of a company in a new field, the funds are derived usually from the sale of common stock. Why?
15. Distinguish the nature of the hazards of promotion of a new product and promotion of a product similar to those already produced by established companies.

Selected Readings

Donham, Paul, and J. S. Day, *Getting Ahead in Small Business,* Dun & Bradstreet, Inc., New York, 1954.

——, *New Business and Small Business Management,* Richard D. Irwin, Inc., Homewood, Ill., 1959.

Kelley, P. C., and Kenneth Lawyer, *How to Organize and Operate a Small Business,* Prentice-Hall, Inc., Englewood Cliffs, N.J., 1961.

Metcalf, Wendell O., *Starting and Managing a Small Business of Your Own,* Small Business Administration, Washington, D.C., 1958.

Murphy, T. P., *A Business of Your Own,* McGraw-Hill Book Co., Inc., New York, 1956.

Weston, J. F. (ed.), *Readings in Finance from Fortune,* Holt, Rinehart and Winston, Inc., New York, 1958.

23

Expansion and
Intercorporate Relations

THE URGE TO EXPAND

IN A DYNAMIC SOCIETY, it is difficult for an enterprise to "stand still." This is particularly true of a company in an industry characterized by vigorous competition. The essence of competition is the fight for the customer's dollar. If a company is successful in this struggle, it enjoys an increase in its share of industry sales. If it is unsuccessful, its share of industry sales drops. In a vigorously competitive industry the share of each company in the industry is constantly changing. Some expand and become giants in the industry. Others contract and eventually disappear. If the economy of the country as a whole is expanding, it is easier for companies to remain alive and to expand. It is also easier for a company to remain alive or to expand during a period of increasing prosperity than during a declining phase of the business cycle. In a period of recession, the failure rate increases, and the number of companies expanding is reduced. In this chapter, we are concerned with the problems of expansion and the effects that these problems have on business finance.

Psychological Factors

Ambition and Status. The drive to achieve recognition and status is very important in human beings. This drive is seen in the effort to excel in sports, the importance attached to titles in business, and the pride of being favorably mentioned in newspaper articles. The desire to achieve recognition is one of the important factors in business expansion. Practically every businessman is ambitious to have his enterprise become larger. In business, recognition is generally accorded in proportion to the size and

410

number of enterprises a businessman controls. "The bigger the business the bigger the man," is the way this fact is often stated. To some businessmen, of course, the management of an enterprise is merely a means of earning enough income to enjoy a comfortable home, world travel, security for a family, or an expensive hobby. A businessman who has achieved the level of income necessary to finance these desires may have no ambition to expand his enterprise further. Most business owners, however, and most executives of companies, have a consuming desire to see their businesses expand. This is probably more common in the United States than in most other countries.

Achievement in business endeavors is more often accorded recognition in the United States than in most other countries. Trusteeships of college boards, chairmanships of charity drives, and positions of importance open to laymen in religious organizations are most often given to businessmen. Acceptance into the higher circles of society is based largely upon wealth achieved in business.[1]

The Desire for Power. With an increase in the size of business there is an increase in power. To some extent, large businesses represent empires, and are often referred to as such. If a person does not get satisfaction from wielding power, he will not find himself in a position of authority in a large enterprise, unless his position was achieved by inheritance. It is a normal human ambition to enjoy power, even though some powerful men may deny it. Among the explanations for the growth in the concentration of control in railroads and other industries is the desire to wield power. For those who enjoy wielding power, business is one of the best avenues to achieve it. The instinct of conquest can find expression in the expansion of business by swallowing up competitors or by making them smaller relative to one's own enterprise. While Alexander the Great sought new worlds to subdue, the modern Alexander is likely to seek new markets to conquer or additional businesses to absorb.

The Desire to Create. Human life is short. After a man is dead, he is remembered by his children and perhaps less distinctly by his grandchildren. After that, his name is forgotten, or, if it is remembered at all, it is usually just a name. But what man creates may endure long after he is dead. The creative impulse, like the instinct for power and the desire for status, is strong. One of the reasons for writing a book, for example, is the author's hope that copies of it may survive long after he is dead. The joy of creation can also be experienced by businessmen. They can create corporations. The satisfaction of being the founder of a business enterprise is an important reward for promoters. It is also an important reward for

---

[1] This does not mean that the individual who created a fortune is accepted into society. As a matter of fact, he is generally not. Acceptance into society is based largely upon inherited wealth rather than earned wealth, particularly in the older states of the East. Although a businessman may not expect to gain entrance into society by becoming rich himself, he can set the stage for acceptance of his children or grandchildren by bequeathing his wealth to them.

those who expand or combine existing businesses. Although he may not originate an enterprise, the creative urge of a businessman can be satisfied by molding an existing business to his desire. The act of creation puts the image of one's individuality on the thing created, which partly explains the expansion and combination of business enterprises.

Economic Factors   In a country with a rising population, there must be an increase in capital goods, which includes such items as railroads, buildings, machine tools, factories, highways, schools, bridges, and anything else that helps to produce or distribute goods and services consumed by the population. If the increase in capital goods is at the same rate as the increase in population, the standard of living would remain static, unless there were a more even distribution of goods or a more efficient use of capital goods. In order for society to enjoy a rising standard of living, it is necessary that the production of capital goods increase at a more rapid rate than the rise in the population. In the United States, the production of capital goods is undertaken both by the various levels of government and by private industry. Nearly all the roads, bridges, schools, and port facilities are created by government or financed by government. Most of the factories, tools, locomotives, and other items of this nature are created by private business. The economic philosophy supported by most of the public places primary reliance on private industry for increases in the production of capital goods, and thus also upon the achievement of higher living standards. The public expects small businesses to become larger and large businesses to become still larger.

Of primary importance as an explanation for expanding business operations is the hope for increased profits. A farmer doubles the number of acres under cultivation with the hope that he can make more profitable use of his time, farm machinery, barns, and so on. The owner of a motel increases the number of his rooms from 50 to 100 with the expectation that his gross receipts will rise more rapidly than his total expenses. The owner of one of two newspapers in a town may buy out the other one with the expectation that the combining of operations will result in a reduction in cost, and that the elimination of competition will permit larger profits to be earned. Profit is a prime motive for expansion. It can be achieved by reducing competition, by exploiting the advantages of large-scale operations, and by using other factors that will be discussed below.

Reduction of Competition.   If competition in an industry can be reduced, it permits the remaining companies a greater control over their selling prices. It may also permit a reduction in advertising expenses, selling expenses, and the other expenditures associated with the endeavor of each company to maintain its share of the market or to increase it. The development of the industrial trusts during the last century is explained by the desire to increase profits by eliminating competition. If a position of monopoly is achieved in an industry, the monopolist can set his prices at the level calculated to yield the greatest profit. Furthermore, he can bargain more effectively with suppliers of materials and so probably reduce the prices of many of the materials purchased. Any reduction in the number of competitors in an industry permits the remaining members to benefit to some degree from the shift in the direction of monopoly.

Lessening the number of competitors in an industry can be achieved by tactics that will drive some out of existence. It can also be achieved by absorbing competitors through merger or consolidation, or by reducing them to the status of subsidiaries. These methods were all used during the period following the Civil War when the steel, petroleum, tobacco, sugar, and other industries rapidly developed into monopolies. As a result of public indignation toward the means used to achieve monopoly in some industries, the passage of the antimonopoly laws, beginning with the Sherman Antitrust Act of 1890, made "combinations in restraint of trade" a violation of the law. Where the number of competitors in an industry have been reduced to a few rather than to a single monopolist, it is difficult to measure the degree of concentration of power achieved. This has made enforcement of the antimonopoly laws difficult for the federal government and has created uncertainty in business. The uncertainty in merging, consolidating, or absorbing a competitor by means of purchasing control of its outstanding stock is that there are no easily defined guides to indicate at what point of concentration in an industry the federal government will take antimonopoly actions.

Advantages of Large-Scale Operations. There are many economies that can be achieved through large-scale operations. Those costs not related to volume of operation can be reduced per unit if they can be spread over a larger number of units. Expenses of overhead, for example, can usually be reduced per unit of output by increasing the output. Or, to take another example, two or three dentists can reduce their office expenses by sharing a common reception room, reception clerk, and billing facilities. They can also reduce their costs by sharing an X-ray machine. Not every firm, of course, can reduce its unit cost of operation by the simple process of expanding the number of units produced. A company may already be so large as to be unwieldy; expansion of a particular enterprise may have gone beyond the point of most efficient size. Nevertheless, most firms, because of their small size, can realize economies through expansion. The areas in which advantages can be achieved through large-scale operations are discussed briefly below.

(1) *Specialization of Labor and Production.* The savings that can be achieved in labor and production through large-scale operations depend upon the type of industry and the character of the production process. In some types of business enterprise, little, if any, advantage can be achieved through expanding the size of the operations. One example is the barber shop. Since haircuts must be done by hand, a barber shop with twelve

chairs has little advantage over one with only three. Any operation depending largely upon hand labor or individual service cannot expect to achieve much reduction in operating costs through expansion of the volume of production. At the other extreme are those enterprises that can hardly be conducted at all unless the scope of operation is large. Steelmaking, shipbuilding, and automobile manufacturing are examples. Where production can largely be undertaken by machines, where machines can be operated largely automatically, where labor can be specialized, or where assembly line techniques can be used, expansion of operations generally results in reducing the unit cost of operation.

(2) *Purchasing.* Considerable savings may be achieved through purchasing in large quantities. Purchasing agents with expert knowledge of the materials needed by a company cannot be efficiently used unless the volume of operations is large. Quantity discounts and a stronger bargaining position make the large company better able to purchase materials at a lower price than can its smaller competitors. Transportation costs on materials purchased may also be less if the volume is large.

(3) *Financing.* The advantages available to a large company in the area of financing may be considerable. Small firms, for example, are restricted in their choice of lenders for short-term loans. Large companies, on the other hand, can raise short-term funds through the commercial paper market, a means not available to small businesses, and can bargain more effectively with commercial banks, financial institutions, and other sources of loans. In raising long-term funds, the larger company also has an advantage over its smaller competitor. The larger company's bargaining power in dealing with investment bankers is generally greater than is that of the smaller company. In general, the cost of distributing stocks and bonds is a smaller percentage of the amount raised if the issue is a large one in terms of funds than if it is a small one. The larger company generally can collect its accounts receivable more successfully than can a small company, for the reason that a large company can employ persons specialized in credits and collections where small companies may not be able to do so. A large company faced with the problem of investing excess funds for a short or a long time has an advantage over the smaller concern. Where the amount to be invested is relatively large, the cost involved in selecting and making the investments is generally a smaller percentage of the funds invested than if the amount is small.

(4) *Research.* In some areas of business activity, research is an essential ingredient of success. In industries undergoing rapid technological change research is not only important, but essential to success. Unfortunately for the small company, research can be very expensive. *The Corporate Director* states the problem of supporting research by small business in the following terms: [2]

---

[2] *The Corporate Director,* American Institute of Management, May 1957, p. 1.

About fifty to sixty per cent of an annual research allotment is spent for salaries. The average salary of a research scientist is between $8,000 and $10,000, and each scientist must be supported by one other employee (laboratory worker, technician, librarian, stenographer, etc.) whose salary is about half that of the researcher's.

It costs at least $10,000 to equip each scientist to carry out his work—although in specialized fields this figure can be much higher. Added to that figure would be the initial investment in a research building or facility.

A research team of, say, five scientists and five other personnel would, therefore, need a budget of about $100,000 to $140,000 per year plus the initial cost of the building and a minimum of $50,000 for equipment. A company can spend a lot less of course—down to the cost of supporting a single researcher. But the *practical* minimum is not much below a budgeted $120,000 a year. One research consultant advises: "If a company can't spend at least $100,000 a year for five years it can't afford its own research department."

The research budget of a large company in the chemical and some other industries runs into the tens of millions of dollars, employing teams of research specialists engaging largely in group research rather than individual efforts. E. I. DuPont de Nemours and Company spends close to $100 million a year to finance the research activities of its 2,000 scientists working at over thirty laboratories.

(5) *Management.* Money and prestige attract executive talent. It can hardly be denied that the large company can offer more of both than can the small company. Furthermore, the large company can afford to employ a greater number of highly paid executives than can a small company, thereby permitting a specialization of executive functions according to the talents of each executive.

(6) *Marketing.* In the area of marketing large-scale operations permit advantages that are not available to small-scale operators. If many salesmen are employed by a company, they may be specialized according to territory or product. If marketing is undertaken on a nationwide rather than a local basis, all the national media of advertising are available to the company, which would be inefficient and too expensive for a smaller company marketing on a regional or local basis. Costs of transportation per unit can be reduced and speedier deliveries to customers made by a large company shipping its products in considerable volume to regional distribution centers, permitting rapid delivery of customers' orders. Finally, a large company generally finds it easier to get into export sales than does a small company.

(7) *By-Products.* In general, a larger company can exploit by-products of its operations more easily than can a small company. A large meat packing company, for example, can make profitable use of the bristles, intestines, blood, and other parts of the animal. A small company, on the other hand, would find it difficult to process the intestines into animal feed, the blood and bones into fertilizer, and the bristles into brushes in large enough volume to make processing and marketing of these products commercially profitable.

High stock prices.   Studies have shown that periods of high stock prices have coincided with periods of increased activity in mergers and consolidations of corporations.[3]   In a period of rising stock prices, mergers and consolidations are easier to complete, since the marketing of new shares to the general public or the exchange of shares for those held by the stockholders of companies prior to the merger or consolidation can be more successfully accomplished.   During the 1920's and again in the 1950's, stock prices rose rapidly, and the number of mergers was large.   During the depression of the 1930's, when stock prices were low, mergers and consolidations were comparatively infrequent.

Taxes.   The corporation income tax law permits the losses suffered in one year to be offset against profits of the last three years or against profits of the succeeding five years in determining the tax liability of the corporation.   For example, if a corporation suffered a net loss of $10 million from operations in the year 1959, it could deduct this loss against income earned during the years 1960 through 1964, and so reduce its tax liability during those five years.   Alternatively, the corporation could apply the $10 million loss of 1959 against profits earned through the years 1956, 1957, and 1958. If profits during the years 1956 through 1958 amounted to $10 million or more, the corporation could claim a refund of past tax payments amounting to $5,200,000, as a result of suffering the $10 million loss in the year 1959, since the corporation income tax during those years was 52 per cent of net income.   The corporation income tax law permits companies consolidating or merging to consolidate their incomes for tax purposes.   This means that a corporation with a $10 million loss for the previous year's operations could bring to the merger a potential tax refund amounting to $5,200,000. A corporation with a net loss can, therefore, be very attractive as a partner for mergers.   In such a situation, the loss suffered by one company is of considerable value to it in merger negotiations, since the loss can be used to reduce the tax liability of the other partner or partners to the merger.

Keys to Recent Business Growth.   In a dynamic economy, changes in consumer taste, changes in the tax structure, changes in the direction and volume of government spending, the commercial exploitation of scientific discoveries, and changes in other factors affecting business present increased profit opportunities in some industries and reduce the profit prospects of others.   Companies in those industries where a shift in the economic climate has increased demand for the industry can often take advantage of the change to expand their operations and their profits.   A recent analysis comparing companies with a high growth rate with those companies having a slower growth rate reveals the following characteristics of high growth firms: [4]

---

[3] One such study is that of the Federal Reserve Bank of Chicago, covering the period from 1920 to 1955, and published in *Business Conditions*, Federal Reserve Bank of Chicago, July 1955.

[4] From Robert B. Young, "Keys to Corporate Growth," *Harvard Business Review*, November-December 1961.

(a) Twenty-two per cent of the sales of high growth companies are to the federal government, compared with about 2 per cent for slow growth companies.

(b) Sixty-three per cent of the sales of rapid growth companies are to industry compared with 41 per cent for slow growth companies.

(c) For rapidly growing companies manufacturing consumer products 20 per cent of the sales are accounted for by recreational products, such as boats, sporting equipment, and camping products. For slow growth companies in the consumer product field less than 2 per cent of the sales of consumer products of such companies are in the form of recreational products.

(d) Approximately 52 per cent of the sales of rapidly growing companies are of highly technical products, such as electronics, chemicals, drugs, missiles, and automatic machinery and office products. Only 10 per cent of the sales of slow growth companies are in highly technical products while 50 per cent of the sales of such companies are in nontechnical products, such as foods, apparel and textiles, home furnishings, and building materials.

Changes in the business environment present both a hazard and an opportunity to business management. The hazard is that the demand for the products of a company may decline, or that changes in the pattern of production or distribution in the industry in which a company is located may

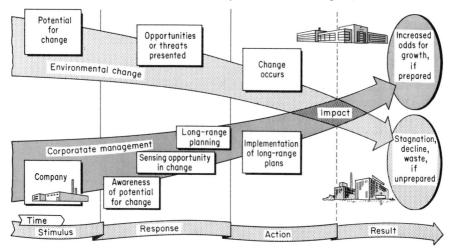

Fig. 23-1 *The seeds of business growth and decline.* (*Source:* Robert B. Young, "Keys of Corporate Growth," *Harvard Business Review,* November-December 1961, p. 60)

be such as to require drastic changes in either the product or the methods of manufacture and distribution previously used by the company. The opportunity presented by environmental changes is that those companies that can adapt or adjust rapidly to take advantage of the changed environment may enjoy an increase in sales and a rise in profits. Awareness of a change in business environment permits companies to adjust before it is too late to do so. And, as seen in Fig. 23-1, awareness of change and ability to adapt to it are characteristics of growth companies.

Disadvantages of Large Size   As an organization increases in size, it develops certain weaknesses that are associated with large-scale operations. If expansion is applied to a small-scale operation, the inefficiencies associated with large-scale operations may be negligible in comparison to the advantages of expansion. However, with continued growth, the inefficiencies associated with size become more important and the efficiencies less so. If expansion continues, a point is reached in the growth of any organization where the inefficiencies of size surpass the efficiencies. Expansion beyond this point—the point of optimum size of operations—results in the company becoming less efficient. It is difficult for the management of any company to recognize the point of optimum scale of operations, particularly in view of the likelihood that the optimum point changes with any change in competitive conditions in an industry, changes in technology, and development of the arts of management.

The Law of Diminishing Returns.   Much of what has been said above about the increasing inefficiencies resulting from continued expansion is an application of the economic law of diminishing returns. The application of this law is found to limit the size of factories, the number of employees a single person can direct, and other aspects of production and distribution. Executive efficiency declines as it is applied to ever-increasing volume of production or distribution. Speed of adjustment to new situations in business declines rapidly as size increases. To some extent, the inefficiencies associated with huge size can be reduced by organizing a large company into departments or subsidiaries, each of which is given considerable freedom of action. Nevertheless, complete freedom is not given to the divisions or subsidiaries, and, therefore, some flexibility is inevitably lost.

Legal Limitations to Expansion.   The dominant economic philosophy that has prevailed throughout most of American history is founded on the belief that competition acts as a controlling force to protect consumers against abuses of monopoly power. This belief is in turn based on the assumption that firms compete with each other by better satisfying the customer as to price, quality, and service—an assumption not always borne out by the facts. Numerous exceptions to the philosophy of unrestrained competition are found in federal, state, and local laws, most of them having been enacted as a result of the demand of some industry or group of businessmen. The exceptions to the belief in competition are so numerous that a student may get the impression like Hamlet, "It is a custom more honour'd in the breach than the observance." Nevertheless, the philosophy persists, and has found expression in numerous statutes. The most important of these are the federal antimonopoly laws, beginning with the Sherman Antitrust Act of 1890. These federal laws are intended to preserve and promote competition in interstate trade. They have sometimes been enforced vigorously and laxly at other times. Some states also have antimonopoly statutes intended to preserve competition within the state. However, most of such laws are either unenforced or loosely enforced.

The existence of antimonopoly laws inhibits the growth of a firm when it becomes so dominant in its industry as to pose a threat to the existence of its competitors. If a company is already the largest in its industry, its continued growth, accompanied by the disappearance of most of the competitors in the industry, will probably bring the company to the attention of the antitrust division of the Department of Justice of the federal government. Continued expansion of the company in such a situation may result in a court ruling breaking up the dominant firm into a number of smaller companies. Under the provisions of the federal antitrust laws, the Standard Oil Company, the Du Pont Corporation, and the American Tobacco Company were broken up into several smaller companies.

Bureaucracy. Bureaucracy is associated in the public mind with inefficiencies of large government operations. It connotes red tape, delayed decisions, a tremendous amount of paperwork, sluggishness in responding to changes in environment, a multitude of regulations stifling the initiative of persons at the lower levels of the chain of command, and poor communications between divisions and departments. These aspects of bureaucracy are not confined to big governmental units, however; they are also found in large business units. Steps may be taken by an expanding business to counter these manifestations of bureaucracy, but their elimination is almost impossible. The larger a corporation becomes the more likely are the manifestations of bureaucracy to be found.

FORMS OF EXPANSION

In order to analyze business expansion and to shed some light on the reasons for expansion the various forms that expansion takes are grouped together into four categories: vertical, horizontal, complementary, and heterogeneous.

Vertical Expansion Vertical expansion adds additional steps or stages in the process of production and distribution to those steps already undertaken by the company. A steel company may expand into the production of coal and the extraction of iron ore, a manufacturer of rubber products may purchase a rubber plantation, or a chain of grocery stores may acquire canning plants or a bakery to produce the foods sold by the chain. All of these are examples of expansion in the direction of sources of raw materials or products required by the company. Expansion in the direction of the raw material is called backward expansion. Expansion in the direction of marketing the product or service is called forward expansion. Examples of forward expansion are the building of a fence-making plant by a steel company, the manufacture of aluminum products by a company formerly making aluminum ingots and sheets, and the opening of grocery retail stores by a canning plant. Some companies have expanded their activities until they have an integrated operation starting from the extraction of the raw material until its final distribution to the consuming public.   One example is the United States Steel Company, which extracts iron ore from its own iron mines, transports the ore on its own oreboats, combines the iron ore with limestone and coal from its own mines, refines the iron produced in its own furnaces to form various types of steel, fabricates the steel into a variety of finished products, such as wire, rails, and structural shapes, and, finally, distributes these products through its own outlets.   Some oil companies own or control through subsidiaries a completely integrated operation from the exploration for petroleum, through extraction and refining, to the sale of gasoline by company owned service stations.   In the field of manufacturing, vertical integration has rapidly developed during the present century.

Horizontal Expansion   If a company increases its volume of operations in one stage of production or distribution, it is known as horizontal expansion. This is the most common form of expansion.   For example, a bank may open a new branch office, a chain of retail stores may add new outlets, a textile company may add additional looms, or an airline may extend its routes to additional cities, add additional flights to its schedule, or increase the capacity of each flight by purchasing larger airplanes.   The larger companies in each industry have achieved their present size largely through horizontal expansion.

Complementary Expansion   Complementary expansion is similar to horizontal expansion.   It involves, however, not the addition of units of the same type already in existence, but the addition of products or services that complement the products or services already offered by a company.   Complementary expansion generally involves the same type of production processes, the same type of raw materials, the same channels of distribution, or perhaps all three.   For example, the manufacture of trucks by a company formerly making only passenger cars utilizes the same production processes, perhaps the same machines, that are already used in the manufacture of passenger cars.   A manufacturer of radios may add television sets to his product line.   The owner of a motel may add a restaurant.   A publishing house specializing in books for high schools and grade schools may acquire a subsidiary selling college textbooks.   In all these examples of complementary expansion, the activity added is related in some way to the activities already undertaken by the company.   This type of expansion is often necessary if a company wishes to survive in a rapidly changing field. The Studebaker Corporation began as a maker of wagons, added automobiles, and later dropped wagons from its production line.   The R.C.A. Victor Company has a history of originally producing phonographs and records.   It added the production of radios as the demand for phonographs declined during the 1920's, and then a line of television receivers after the market for radios had become saturated.

Heterogeneous Expansion Heterogeneous expansion is the addition of products or services bearing 'little or no relation to those already undertaken by a company. One of the reasons heterogeneous expansion is undertaken is to diversify operations. If a company expands into several different fields of endeavor, its fortunes will not be at the mercy of shifts in demand in any one field. By this means, a company may be able to reduce risk. Another reason for heterogeneous expansion is to reduce the instability caused by operating in an industry characterized by seasonal or cyclical fluctuations. If a company expands by entering into an industry with a seasonal or cyclical pattern different from that of the company's original operations, the fluctuation in business activity may be lessened. A company in an industry faced with an expected decline in profits may expand into an industry that promises rapid growth. For this reason, a company in the textile industry may acquire a subsidiary in the growing field of electronics. A company may also enter a new industry by merging with a company having suffered net losses in the last two or three years, which may reduce the income tax liability of the other party to the merger. The attractions of such a merger were discussed earlier.

In addition to the reasons for heterogeneous expansion given above, there are some expansions that appear to defy logical explanation. In such instances, probably the most reasonable explanation is that a subsidiary corporation can be acquired at a bargain price or expansion into a new field of activity promises a greater return to invested capital than expansion of the existing activities of the company.

METHODS OF COMBINATION

There are many methods of achieving concerted action in an industry. Some of these depend upon formal agreements between the members, and others upon an understanding as informal as a handshake. Some may be entirely legal under our antitrust laws, others may have dubious legality, and still others may be patently illegal. New methods of achieving a concert of action among members of an industry are devised as rapidly as older methods become obsolete. Here we shall discuss only some of the more commonly used devices.

Gentlemen's Agreements Gentlemen's agreements are among the more informal methods of achieving a reduction in competition between members of an industry. Their purpose is to provide some of the benefits of monopoly for all the members to the agreement by determining the extent and character of competition that each of the members may use in their attempt to expand sales. The agreement may be to adopt a common price for the products and services of the industry. The agreement might provide for a division of markets among members, the establishment of quotas on production by each member, or to submit identical bids to government agencies when bids for government contracts are announced. There usually is no mechanism provided for securing compliance to the agreement except the knowledge of each member that violation of the agreement will result in retaliation by the other members. For example, an agreement to keep the retail price of gasoline in a particular city at a stated level may be effective in keeping gasoline prices high because of the experience of distributers of gasoline that a reduction in price at the service station by one distributer will be followed by price cuts from other distributers. Because most gentlemen's agreements depend upon voluntary compliance, they often break down. Because most such agreements are illegal under our antitrust laws, the agreements are almost always secret. One type of gentlemen's agreement that is almost customary is the policy of not making derogatory remarks about competitors' products through identifying them by name. However, the code of "gentlemanly competition" permits a company to advertise that its product is superior to all other products or to publish the "results of laboratory tests" indicating that the advertiser's product is superior to that of companies X and Y.

Interlocking Directorates The term *interlocking directorates* refers to the seating of the same individuals on the board of directors of two or more companies. Two companies may have one individual serving on the board of both or may have several individuals serving on the board of each. If a majority of the members of the board of one company also serve as the majority of the board of another company, the two companies operate as if they were divisions of a single company. Where one or two persons serve on the board of directors of two or more companies, there may be no evidence of a concert of action between the companies. In such cases, the persons serving on the board of the separate companies act as a contact between the companies involved. This might result in each company purchasing from the other company whenever possible. It is very common for a person to serve on the board of directors of several corporations when each company is in a different industry. Because companies in different industries are not direct competitors, the sharing of common directors does not run counter to the antitrust laws. It is very common for a commercial bank to have on its board of directors several persons also serving on the boards of corporations not in the field of banking. Where a person serves on the board of directors of two companies that are competitors, it is almost certain that some limitation of competition will result. To prevent the use of interlocking directorates as a device to limit competition, the Clayton Act of 1914 forbids interlocking directorates among industrial corporations operating in interstate commerce where the effect is substantially to reduce competition and where any one of the companies shows a net worth of $1 million or more. The Banking Act of 1933 forbids interlocking directorates among commercial banks that are members of the Federal Reserve System. In the railroad industry, interlocking directorates are permitted only by approval of the Interstate Commerce Commission. In the field of electrical power and in holding companies in the public utility field, interlocking directorates are forbidden except by permission from the Federal Power Commission.

Cartels A cartel is a formal association of companies organized for the purpose of entirely eliminating or extensively controlling competition among its members. Its purpose is the same as that of the gentlemen's agreement. However, the cartel is more highly organized. Provision is usually made in a cartel to discipline members violating any of the clauses of the agreement. Prior to World War II, cartels were frequently formed in Germany, Great Britain, and other Western European nations. Some of the cartels were international in scope and included most of the large members of the industry throughout the world. Although most of the cartels have been formed by the initiative of the members of an industry, a few cartels have been organized by governmental action. One example is the cartel of producers of natural rubber, organized after World War I through the encouragement of the British government.

Most cartel agreements have been temporary in nature. The cartel agreements existing between companies in Germany, France, and Great Britain were suspended with the outbreak of World War I, although some of them were revived after the end of hostilities. The Great Depression of the 1930's spurred the creation of international cartels in an effort to raise prices from the depths to which the depression had driven them. Most of these were dissolved with the outbreak of World War II. Until 1918, participation of American companies in cartels was considered generally to be a violation of the antitrust laws of the United States. However, the Webb-Pomerene Act of 1918 gave legal permission to American companies to join in cartels, providing that the agreement did not restrict competition by American companies within the United States market. The act permitted American companies to enter into cartel agreements among themselves or with companies in other nations so long as the participation of the United States companies was restricted to their foreign operations.

Trusts In a trust, the shares of corporations are surrendered to trustees by stockholders who receive trust certificates in exchange. The holders of the trust certificates have no voting rights in selecting the trustees, but do receive dividends on the certificates that they hold when the earnings of the trust permit such distribution. The shares of the corporations included in the trust are held by the trustees. The trustees, a self-perpetuating body, whose original members are named in the trust agreement, determine the policies under which the companies comprising the trust are administered by the boards of directors of the companies. The trustees exercise the voting power of the shares of the corporations held in the trust. By this device, competition among corporations whose shares are held by the trust can be completely eliminated.

The trust was commonly used to achieve monopoly power in industries in the United States during the nineteenth century. After the Civil War, trusts were formed in many industries, including sugar refining, tobacco products, the distillation of whiskey, and linseed oil. Probably the most famous trust was that formed by John D. Rockefeller in 1879—the Standard Oil Trust, which achieved a monopoly of petroleum refining and marketing in the United States, and came close to achieving a world monopoly a few years later. The trust is no longer used as a device for expansion in an industry, having been superseded by the holding company as a means to effect combinations. However, the importance of the trust in the history of monopoly is reflected in the use of the term *antitrust* to describe antimonopoly activities. The division of the federal government concerned with enforcing the antimonopoly laws, known better as antitrust laws, is the Antitrust Division of the Department of Justice.

Community of Interest Although the Clayton Act of 1914 made interlocking directorates illegal among competing companies in interstate trade, it did not prohibit a person from owning shares of voting stock in several companies in the same industry. By this means, it was possible for a few persons to own enough stock in two or more companies in an industry to control the election of directors to each of the companies. Where a small group of persons sharing common interests and following a common policy achieve voting control of two or more companies in an industry, the grouping is referred to as a community of interest. A community of interest can be tightly organized or it may be a very loose association.

MERGERS AND CONSOLIDATIONS

Mergers and consolidations are means by which two or more companies are combined into one. In a merger, one company retains its charter and its unbroken existence as a corporation, while the other corporations go out of existence. In a consolidation, all the companies are dissolved, and a new corporation is formed to take over the assets and liabilities of the corporations going out of existence.

The Steps in a Merger or Consolidation The corporation laws of the states indicate the steps that must be taken in consolidating a group of corporations or in merging one or more corporations into another corporation. The first step requires the calling of a meeting of the board of directors of each of the corporations considering the merger or consolidation. A majority of the board of directors of each of the corporations must approve the terms of the merger or consolidation. After the merger or consolidation agreement has been adopted by the board of directors of the separate corporations, it must be submitted to the stockholders of each of the corporations for approval. In most states an approval of two-thirds of the voting stock of each of the corporations is necessary to ratify the agreement. The details under which a meeting of the stockholders must be called to consider the approval of a merger varies from state to state. The laws require, however, ample notice to each of the stockholders having voting power, so as to give them time to attend the meeting in person or to appoint a suitable proxy to vote their shares.

If the merger agreement submitted to the stockholders of each corporation is approved by the necessary majority of each of them, a copy of the agreement is forwarded to the Secretary of State of the state in which the corporations have received their charter. If corporations having charters from different states are to be merged or consolidated, the approval by the board of directors and ratification by the stockholders of each corporation must be in accordance with the laws of the state under which each corporation received its charter. The surviving corporation in a merger continues its existence under the charter of the state which gave it birth. In a consolidation, the charter for the new corporation is secured by application to a state in the same manner as the creation of any new corporation. After filing a copy of the agreement with each of the secretaries of state of those states from which the corporations involved in the merger or consolidation received their charters, the assets of the corporations are transferred to the surviving corporation in a merger or to the new corporation created in a consolidation. In the same manner, the debts and other obligations of the separate corporations are assumed by the surviving corporation or the newly created one.

The Problem of Valuation of Shares In a merger, the shares of the surviving company are exchanged for the shares of the corporations dissolved by the merger. In a consolidation, the shares issued by the newly created corporation are exchanged for the shares of the companies dissolved. The shares surrendered by the stockholders in a merger or consolidation are then retired. But what of the basis of exchange? This is probably the most difficult question to be solved in a merger or consolidation. In a consolidation, should one share of the new corporation be exchanged for one share of each of the corporations to be dissolved? Or, if two corporations are to be consolidated, should the stockholders of one corporation receive two shares of the new corporation in exchange for each share they hold, while the stockholders of the other corporation receive one share of the new corporation for each share that they hold? Since the shareholders of the companies to be dissolved are paid in stock of the corporation surviving in a merger or created in a consolidation, the price in terms of the shares of the new corporation that the stockholders receive for the shares they surrender is of vital concern to them. On what basis shall the exchange value of the shares of each company be determined? Possible bases for determining the valuation of shares are discussed below.

Book Value. The book value per share is calculated from the information given on the balance sheet of a corporation. If only common stock is outstanding, the book value per share is found by subtracting the total liabilities from the total assets as shown on the books of the corporation and dividing the remaining figure by the number of shares of common stock outstanding. If the balance sheet of the corporation lists intangible assets, such as patents, goodwill, or franchises at more than a dollar or some other nominal figure, the total value of these assets is generally subtracted from the total assets in calculating the book value per share. If a corporation has outstanding preferred stock, the calculation of the book value per share of the common is a little more complicated. The preferred stock must be subtracted from the net assets (total assets minus total liabilities) and the remainder divided by the number of shares of common stock outstanding. Determining the value to place on each share of preferred stock, however, may require some judgment. If the preferred stock was originally sold by the corporation at its par value, this figure plus accrued dividends is generally used in determining the value per share of the preferred stock. If, on the other hand, the preferred stock was sold at a price higher than the par value, the issue price is commonly used instead of the par value. At the time the preferred stock is created, it may have been given a stated redemption price in the event of involuntary dissolution and a higher redemption price in case of voluntary dissolution, as was described in Chapter 11. Financial analysts, in estimating the book value of the common stock of such a corporation, generally use the voluntary liquidation price in calculating the value of the preferred stock. To whatever figure is used in determining the value of the preferred stock, any accrued unpaid dividend would be added.

The weakness in using book value as a basis for determining the exchange of shares stems from the wide variation of accounting practices used in determining the value of assets. One corporation may use straight line depreciation for some of its long-term assets, while another may use the sum-of-the-years' digits method in setting up depreciation schedules for the same type of items as the first corporation. Some corporations use acquisition cost in valuation of capital assets, while other corporations use replacement cost. Some corporations clearly distinguish between expenses and capital expenditures on their books, while other corporations do not. Some corporations use nominal values in listing intangible assets, such as goodwill, while other corporations list such assets at substantial values. Where there is uniformity in accounting methods used by two corporations, there is justification in using book value as a basis for exchange of shares. Where there is not uniformity in accounting procedures, it must be achieved if book value is to have any significance in determining the basis of exchange. Where two corporations use different methods in determining the value of intangible assets, uniformity must be achieved by eliminating the value of intangible assets from the balance sheets of both corporations. Where uniformity of accounting procedures cannot be easily achieved, book value is generally given little consideration in determining the ratio of exchange of shares.

Capitalization of Earnings. Capitalization of earnings is the placing of a dollar value on a stream of earnings. In capitalizing the earnings of a corporation, one must select a capitalization rate and multiply the earnings of the company by the inverse of the capitalization rate. To capitalize earnings of $6 per share at 5 per cent, the following computation is made:

1. Express the capitalization rate in the form of a fraction: 5 per cent is expressed as 1/20.
2. Divide the earnings of $6 per share by the fraction 1/20 to get the capitalized value per share.
3. The value per share based on capitalization of earnings at 5 per cent is 6 ÷ 1/20 = $120.

If the earnings of a single year are used to determine the value of stock by capitalization of earnings, the value per share may not be representative of the true earning capacity of the assets of the corporation. If the earnings of a company fluctuate from year to year, the average annual earnings per share for several years in the recent past are generally used. Thus, if the average earnings of Corporation A are $1 million and the average earnings of Corporation B are $1,200,000, and if 10 per cent is the agreed rate of capitalization, the value of the stock of Corporation A is $10 million and that of Corporation B is $12 million. In a consolidation based on capitalization of earnings, Corporation A would receive five shares of stock for every six shares distributed to Corporation B. In selecting the rate of capitalization, reference is usually made to the market price of stock of similar companies expressed in terms of the price-earnings ratio. If the stocks of steel companies are being traded in the stock market at a price that is approximately twenty times earnings after taxes, the earnings of two steel companies contemplating consolidation would be capitalized at 5 per cent. If the stocks of airline companies are being traded at a price ten times average earnings, the earnings of two airline companies contemplating merger would be capitalized at 10 per cent.

Market Value. The market price of the shares of companies contemplating merger or consolidation is often used as a basis for determining the ratio of exchange. If the shares of Corporation A are selling at $24.50 and the shares of Corporation B at $37, the stockholders of Corporation A would receive two new shares for each share surrendered, and the stockholders of Corporation B would receive three shares for each share surrendered.[5] Market value strongly influences the determination of the basis for exchange of shares in most mergers and consolidations. Stockholders

---

[5] For the market price of the stock of B to be exactly at a three-to-two ratio with the price of stock A, the stock of B would be $36.75. Since most stock prices fluctuate constantly, the market price at any moment is in the range of the figure representing the ratio of exchange, but not often exactly on it.

tend to accept the market price as an accurate indication of the investment worth of a stock. Furthermore, it is generally accepted that the market price of a stock reflects the considered judgment of investors as to the probable future earning capacity of the corporations.

It is usually easier for the directors of a corporation to persuade the stockholders to accept a proposed merger or consolidation if the exchange of shares is based on market value rather than book value or capitalization of past earnings. Any stockholder can compare the market price of his shares with the market price of the shares of the other corporations to be merged or consolidated. The market value seems to be "real" value, while capitalization of earnings and book value appear to many stockholders to be based on theoretical rather than on factual considerations. To the average stockholder, the market price represents an impersonal valuation, while book value, capitalization of earnings, or appraisal value depends upon the judgment of individuals. The proposed consolidation of Capital Airlines and Northwest Airlines in 1952 used market prices as the basis of the exchange of shares of the two companies.[6]

Appraisal Value. When the value of real estate is to be determined for tax purposes, an appraisal of its value is made by the taxing authority. Similarly, an appraisal can be made of the assets of those corporations considering merger or consolidation to use as a basis in determining the exchange value of the shares of the corporations. Real estate experts can be hired to estimate the value of land and buildings, engineers can be used to estimate the value of machinery and equipment, and other experts can be called in to estimate the value of investments, patents, and other properties owned by each corporation. At first glance, it would appear that this method of determining the value of the property of corporations and, therefore, the value of the shares in exchange, would be more accurate than other methods. However, this is not necessarily true. Appraisal of certain assets, such as accounts receivable, cash, and other current assets, may be simple. Appraisal of land, buildings, and machinery is more difficult. The market price of adjacent land and similar buildings may be used as a guide in appraising real estate owned by corporations. But industrial land is less frequently sold than is residential property, and industrial buildings are often so specialized in construction as to make it difficult to find similar buildings that have recently been sold. The value of such equipment as trucks and typewriters can readily be appraised, but the value of specialized machinery cannot so easily be estimated. Determining the value of intangible property, such as patents, is still more difficult, and appraisals of these assets is largely guesswork. As a result, the appraisal by two different experts of the assets of a corporation may differ widely.

---

[6] The directors of the two companies announced that the closing prices on January 31, 1952, formed the basis of valuation for exchange. On that day, Capital Airlines closed at $16\frac{1}{2}$ and Northwest Airlines at $16\frac{5}{8}$. The exchange agreed upon was one for one for each company.

Bargaining in the Valuation Process   In negotiating an agreement to merge or consolidate, the representatives of the corporations engage in bargaining. The basis for exchange of shares in a merger or consolidation generally represents the relative strength of the bargaining position of the representatives of each company and their relative skill in bargaining.   If two companies are considering a merger and the bargaining position of one is strong while that of the other is weak, the basis of exchange of shares will almost always favor the company with the stronger position.   For example, if two newspapers compete for circulation in a city, and the circulation of one is large and growing but that of the other is small and declining, the alternatives faced by the representatives of the smaller newspaper may be a choice between merger and ultimate extinction.   In such a situation, the book value per share of the weaker company, its capitalization of past earnings, the market value of its stock, or a valuation of its assets based on expert appraisal will have little effect in determining the basis of exchange of shares. The owners of the weaker newspaper may be forced to accept a valuation of their shares at considerably less than the value as determined by any of the means discussed above.   If, on the other hand, the bargaining strength of two companies is approximately equal, the basis finally agreed upon on which the shares will be exchanged will very often be based on one of the methods of valuation discussed above.   In the bargaining process, the representatives of each company will emphasize the strong points of the company they represent and attempt to minimize any weaknesses their company may have.   One company may be able to offer engineering or scientific talent to the proposed consolidation, another company may have a long record of profitable operations, and a third may have valuable patents to contribute.   Often, the disagreements among the negotiators in a proposed merger or consolidation are so great that it is impossible to resolve them, and the negotiations are broken off.   Where negotiations are successful and an agreement is reached on the terms, it is usually as a result of compromise, with the representatives of each company making concessions in order to get an agreement acceptable to all.   In nearly every merger, it is the expectation of the representatives of each company that the combination will be competitively stronger than the separate companies were before.   If the combination does produce this result, the profits of the combination should be greater than the sum of the profits of the formerly independent companies.   Therefore, with the expectation that combining the companies will benefit the owners of each, there is an advantage to be gained in the success of the merger or consolidation negotiations.

Treatment of Minority Stockholders   It often happens, particularly if a corporation has a large number of stockholders, that the directors fail to get a unanimous vote of the stockholders in approving a merger or consolidation.   In such cases, what are the rights of the minority?   If the dissenting stockholders suspect that there is fraud or violation of any statute (for example, one of the antitrust laws), any stockholder may seek a court injunction to void the merger or consolidation. If there is no evidence of fraud or illegality in the action taken by the directors, the laws of about half of the states make provision for payment to the dissenting stockholders of the value of their shares. Although these laws differ considerably in detail, they indicate the means by which the value of the shares of dissenting stockholders shall be appraised, the means of settling any disagreement between stockholders and appraisers as to the value per share, the time within which payment must be made by the corporation, and the form and manner of making such payment.

In those states where no statutory provisions exist outlining a procedure for settlement of the dissenting stockholders' claims, these stockholders have no recourse but to accept the exchange of shares as provided in the merger or consolidation agreement. This assumes that the merger or consolidation is not in violation of any laws, is not fraudulent in any respect, and was negotiated in good faith. In those states where statutes exist providing for payment of the shares of dissenting stockholders in cash according to their appraised value, the amount of cash required to do so may be so large as to prevent the merger or consolidation. Where dissenting stockholders must be paid off in cash, the directors will generally not proceed with the merger unless the vote of the stockholders is nearly unanimous. To illustrate, the plan of Industrial Rayon Corporation to absorb the Texas Butadiene and Chemical Corporation was dropped when 10 per cent of the stock of Industrial Rayon Corporation voted against the proposed merger, because the dissenting shareholders would have had to be paid the appraised value of their shares in cash.[7]

Bondholders and Other Creditors   In general, the surviving corporation in a merger or the newly created corporation in a consolidation assumes all the outstanding obligations of the companies prior to the fusion. The debts, both long-term and short-term, of the companies going out of existence are assumed by the company existing after the fusion. Mortgage bondholders continue to hold a lien on the property specified in the mortgage contract after the transfer of the property to the corporation in existence following the consolidation or merger. Unsecured creditors of the individual companies prior to the fusion become unsecured creditors of the company remaining after the fusion. If, however, there is an after-acquired clause in an issue of bonds of a dissolved company, the clause no longer has any effect, and cannot be applied to property acquired after fusion by the corporation remaining in existence. The same is true of a convertible clause in a bond issue of a company going out of existence in a merger or consolidation. The bonds cannot be converted by the bondholders into the stock of the corporation existing after the merger or consolidation. An after-acquired clause or a convertible clause in a bond issue of the surviving

---

7 *The Wall Street Journal*, May 3, 1960.

company in a merger continues in force, since the surviving company suffers no interruption in its corporate existence.

Purchase of Entire Assets of Another Company A fusion may be accomplished by the simple process of one company purchasing the entire assets of another. Under the laws of more than forty states, the sale of the entire assets of a corporation must be approved by the stockholders. The laws vary—from a simple majority to as much as four-fifths of the outstanding stock—as to the proportion that must approve such a sale. A fusion by this means requires negotiations between the boards of directors of the companies involved, as in the case of a merger or consolidation. The agreement to sell the assets to another corporation is then submitted to the stockholders of the selling corporation for approval. If the approval is secured, the assets are transferred to the ownership of the purchasing company, and payment is received by the selling company. The selling company then pays all the debts owed by it, settles any other obligations outstanding, and may distribute any remaining amount to the stockholders. The corporation usually is voluntarily liquidated, according to the laws of the state under which the corporation received its charter. Approval by the stockholders of the corporation purchasing the entire assets of another corporation is not required, unless it is necessary to issue securities in order to pay for the assets purchased. The payment usually is in cash but may be in the form of securities of the purchasing company or a combination of cash and securities of the purchasing company. The purchase agreement may require the purchasing corporation to assume liability for bonds of the selling corporation and perhaps of short-term debt as well.

HOLDING COMPANIES

The definition of holding company in business usage today is a corporation that owns enough stock of another corporation to exercise control of the other corporation.[8] In order for control to be certain, it is necessary for the holding company to have a majority of the voting stock of the controlled corporation. However, if the stock not held by the holding company is widely scattered and in small amounts, it is usually unnecessary to hold more than half of the stock to insure control. Ownership of as little as 10 per cent of the voting stock may be sufficient to control the election of the directors of the subsidiary corporation. A company that undertakes no business operations under its own name but exists merely to hold controlling stock in subsidiary corporations is called a *pure holding company*. A company that undertakes business operations in its own name in addition to controlling subsidiary corporations is called an

---

[8] In some legislation and in the decisions of some courts, the term *holding company* includes other forms of business, such as trusts and joint stock companies, owning enough voting stock of other corporations to control elections to the boards of directors of the corporations.

operating holding company. The holding company is often referred to as the parent company. If a holding company controls another holding company, the latter may be called the parent and the former called the grand-parent.

Comparison of Holding Companies with Mergers and Consolidations

Advantages of the Holding Company. Probably the most important advantage of the holding company is that control of the operating assets of subsidiary corporations can be maintained with a small investment on the part of the holding company. To secure control of the assets of a subsidiary corporation, it is only necessary to purchase a fraction of the voting stock of the corporation, as illustrated in Table 23-1.

TABLE 23-1. USE OF THE HOLDING COMPANY TO MINIMIZE THE AMOUNT
OF INVESTMENT REQUIRED TO CONTROL OPERATING ASSETS

Company X

Assets, operating	$100,000,000	Bonds 4%	$ 40,000,000
		Preferred stock 6%	30,000,000
		Common stock	30,000,000
	$100,000,000		$100,000,000

Company Y

Assets, stock in X	$ 15,000,000	Bonds 5%	$ 6,000,000
		Preferred stock 6%	5,000,000
		Common stock	4,000,000
	$ 15,000,000		$ 15,000,000

Company Z

Assets, stock in Y	$ 2,000,000	Preferred stock 6%	$ 1,000,000
		Common stock	1,000,000
	$ 2,000,000		$ 2,000,000

Assuming an investment of 50 per cent in the common stock of Company X (purchased at book value), control of Company X can be had by Company Y through purchase of $15 million of the common stock of Company X. Control of Company Y in turn can be had by Company Z by investing $2 million in the common stock of Company Y (purchased at book value), again assuming that 50 per cent ownership of voting stock is sufficient for control. An investment of $500,000 in the common stock of Company Z, again assuming that 50 per cent ownership of voting stock is sufficient for control, will secure control of Company Z. Therefore, with an investment of $500,000 in common stock of Company Z, operating assets in the amount of $100 million may be controlled.

Another attraction of the holding company is that it makes possible a greater return on the common stock of the holding company than is earned by the common stock of the subsidiary company. If earnings are sufficient to cover interest on debts and dividends on preferred stocks, the return on common stock may be multiplied through the holding company device. If, however, the earnings of the subsidiary are insufficient to cover interest on debts and dividends on preferred stock, the return on the common stock of the holding company is sharply reduced or becomes a deficit. The multiplication of earnings can be increased by using intermediate holding companies, but the losses resulting from a decline in earnings of the operating company or companies are similarly increased. This is illustrated in Table 23-2, where the holding company structure of Fig. 23-2 is used. The effect

TABLE 23-2. USE OF THE HOLDING COMPANY DEVICE TO INCREASE RETURN ON COMMON STOCK INVESTED

Percentage return on operating assets of $100,000,000	16%	10%	5%
Income before bond interest on operating assets	$16,000,000	$10,000,000	$5,000,000
Bond interest, Company X	1,600,000	1,600,000	1,600,000
Income before taxes	14,400,000	8,400,000	3,400,000
Income taxes at 48%	6,912,000	4,032,000	1,632,000
Income after taxes	7,488,000	4,368,000	1,768,000
Preferred stock dividend, Company X	1,800,000	1,800,000	1,800,000
Income available to common stock	$ 5,688,000	$ 2,568,000	none
Percentage return on common stock of Company X	18.96%	8.56%	
Income before bond interest of Company Y	$ 2,844,000	$ 1,284,000	none
Bond interest, Company Y	300,000	300,000	
Income before taxes	2,544,000	984,000	
Income taxes at 48% on 15% of dividends received from subsidiary	202,848	92,448	
Income after taxes	2,341,152	891,552	
Preferred stock dividend, Company Y	300,000	300,000	
Income available to common stock	$ 1,041,152	$ 591,552	
Percentage return on common stock of Company Y	26.03%	14.79%	
Income before preferred stock dividend of Company Z	$ 520,576	$ 295,776	
Income taxes at 48% on 15% of dividends received from subsidiary	37,481	21,296	
Income after taxes	483,095	274,480	
Preferred stock dividend of Company Z	60,000	60,000	
Income available to common stock	$ 423,095	$ 214,480	
Percentage return on common stock of Company Z	42.31%	21.45%	

on the net income of the intermediate holding company and of the primary holding company of rates of return on operating assets of Company X amounting to 16 per cent, 10 per cent, and 5 per cent is shown. In some of the utility company empires created during the 1920's, numerous layers of intermediate holding companies existed. Control of vast operating as-sets was secured by a very small investment in the holding company at the top of the pyramid, and the rate of return on the common stock of the top holding company was extremely high as long as the earnings of the operat-ing subsidiaries at the bottom remained relatively steady.

The holding company makes the acquisition of control of another com-pany a simple process. All that is required is that the holding company acquire enough stock of another corporation to exercise effective control. This may be done by purchasing stock over a period of time as it is offered for sale on the stock market. Usually, a holding company wishing to ac-quire control of another company purchases the block of stock held by the person, group of persons, or company that controls the corporation. Often, the price charged for the block of shares exercising control is considerably higher than the market price of the shares traded in small lots in the stock market. The reason, of course, is that the block of shares representing con-trol constitutes not merely an investment in the corporation but the acqui-sition of control. To secure control through purchase of the voting stock does not require approval of the remaining stockholders, of the creditors, nor of the officers of the corporation. Stockholders not having control of a corporation may object to the control passing from one group to another or from one holding company to another. However, they have no recourse, since they do not exercise voting control. It is possible, for example, that control of a corporation may be maintained by means of ownership of 15 per cent of the voting stock, and that control may frequently pass from one holding company to another holding company. The remaining stockhold-ers, although widely scattered and holding stock in small amounts, may on rare occasion be sufficiently aroused against the shift in control to organize and elect a board of directors in opposition to those selected by the com-pany holding the 15 per cent block of stock. If a holding company wishes to eliminate its control of an operating subsidiary for any reason, control by means of the holding company device makes the action easy. All that is necessary is to sell the block of shares representing control of the subsidiary, a procedure far simpler than the liquidation of a division of a corporation.

Since the subsidiary companies of a holding company are corporations, the debts of the subsidiaries are not obligations of the holding company, except for those debts that may be guaranteed by the holding company. Therefore, the bankruptcy of a subsidiary company is less of a disaster than the failure of a division or department of a company to meet its expenses. If a company wishes to engage in diverse fields, it can to some extent reduce the loss that might result if one of the industrial areas in which the com-pany is active becomes depressed, by operating each of its diverse activities through subsidiaries. If a decline is anticipated in an industry in which a holding company has an operating subsidiary, the shares of the subsidiary owned by the holding company can more easily be sold than could the assets of a division or department of a company operating in the area. It must be realized, of course, that creditors are aware of the limitation of liability involved in a holding company organization. In extending credit to a subsidiary, suppliers or lenders will do so only if they are convinced that the subsidiary is financially strong. If creditors feel there is some danger in making loans or selling supplies on credit to the subsidiary, they may require some guarantee from the parent company. For a subsidiary corporation to get credit on reasonable terms, it may be necessary for the parent company to guarantee the debts of the subsidiary. The reduction in risk made possible by a holding company-subsidiary relationship is, therefore, not automatic.

The corporation laws of some states confer certain advantages on corporations with charters issued by the state that are not granted to corporations with charters from other states. A foreign corporation (a corporation with a charter granted from another state) can avoid the discrimination imposed in the laws of certain states by conducting its operations through a subsidiary incorporated in the state. The legal benefits to be gained by conducting operations through a subsidiary are particularly marked in connection with international operations. If an American company should wish to undertake operations in a foreign nation, other than merely selling, it will find in many cases that it is highly advantageous to undertake such operations through a subsidiary operating with a charter issued by the government of the foreign nation. Furthermore, the tax levied by a foreign nation on the profits of a subsidiary corporation controlled by an American holding company is frequently less than the tax on an American corporation doing business in the foreign nation.

An important legal advantage to the use of the holding company is obtained in the event of a lawsuit against the operating subsidiary. A claim for damages, for example, against a division or a department of a company is a suit against the entire corporation. A claim for damages resulting from a defective product or because of patent infringement resulting from actions of a subsidiary is limited to the subsidiary corporation, and the other units of the holding company system are not affected by the suit.

If two or more companies wish to share control of a business activity, the holding company device is particularly useful. The usual example given to illustrate this is a railroad terminal. Here, two or more railroads being served by the terminal may control its activities by owning the stock of the terminal corporation.

Disadvantages of the Holding Company. Nearly every large corporation in the United States is a holding company as well as an operating company. The attractions of the holding company discussed above explain its popularity among large corporations, but there are also disadvantages. One of the major ones is taxation. Each corporation must pay a franchise tax annually to the state from which the corporation received its charter. Fees must be paid for the incorporation of the company, for increases in the authorized capital stock, for certificates of consolidation or merger, and for certificates of dissolution. In addition, there are other fees that may be charged by the state for the privilege of doing business as a corporation. Most of these taxes and fees are small in amount, however. Of more importance is the federal income tax. Eighty-five per cent of the income received by a corporation in the form of dividends from another corporation is exempt from the federal income tax levied on the income of the company receiving the dividends. This means that a holding company must pay the full corporate income tax of 48 per cent (except for a tax of 22 per cent on the first $25,000 of net income) on 15 per cent of the dollar amount of dividends it receives from subsidiaries. The holding company may avoid the payment of the tax on dividends received from subsidiaries by filing a consolidated return covering income and expenses of the holding company and its subsidiaries as if all were divisions of one corporation, provided the holding company owns at least 80 per cent of the voting stock and 80 per cent of the nonvoting stock of the subsidiaries. In such a case, the consolidated return comprising the operations of the holding company and the subsidiaries is subject to the corporate income tax as if it were a single company.

Another disadvantage is the possible increase in overhead costs resulting from organizing operations on a holding company-subsidiary basis rather than on a basis of divisions or departments of a single corporation. Each subsidiary corporation must have a board of directors, a president, a secretary, and a treasurer. There can, of course, be some duplication in these offices. For example, the office of secretary and treasurer is often combined. The other members of the board of directors of subsidiary corporations may be, and usually are, officers of the holding company. Each corporation must hold an annual meeting of stockholders in order to reelect the board of directors. Special meetings of the stockholders must be called whenever any change in the charter is sought or other action taken requiring the approval of the stockholders. If the subsidiary is owned 100 per cent by the holding company, such meetings are an empty formality. However, holding them does entail expense. The financial records of the subsidiary corporation must be kept separately from those of the parent corporation. Intercompany loans, dividend payments, payments for services rendered by one company to another within the holding company system, and other financial transactions between companies in the holding company system generally require more bookkeeping than is needed for similar transactions between divisions or departments of a company.

Supervision and control of operations of the subsidiary may be weaker than would be the case where the subsidiary were made a department of the parent corporation. If autonomy of the separate operations of an organization is considered an advantage, the parent-subsidiary relationship can provide the autonomy required. On the other hand, if close control of operations of a company is desired, this may better be achieved by organizing operations as divisions and departments of a single corporation.

If a holding company owns less than 100 per cent of the stock of a subsidiary corporation, it must consider minority stockholders in its dealings with the subsidiary. Every stockholder, even those owning a single share, has the right to inspect some of the records of the corporation whose stock he owns. (The extent of this right to look at the records of a corporation is discussed in Chapter 10.) A stockholder may get a court order to enjoin an action (for example, the payment of a dividend, the purchase of services or property from the parent company, or the extension of a loan to the parent company) taken by the board of directors of a subsidiary, if any of these are considered detrimental to the minority stockholders. Some transactions between the subsidiary corporation and the parent company may appear to be entirely proper and businesslike to the officers of the parent company, but may appear otherwise to the minority stockholders. In such a situation, a minority stockholder may delay the consummation of the transaction, pending examination of its legality. If a holding company owns most of the stock of a subsidiary, it can outvote minority stockholders in cases where approval of the stockholders is required before action can be taken by the subsidiary. If a corporation owns at least 80 per cent of the stock of a subsidiary, it already commands the necessary majority for those actions on which a vote of three-fourths or four-fifths of the stock is required. To control the election of the directors, only a bare majority of stock must be held by the parent corporation. If, however, the holding company owns less than 50 per cent of the stock, it must be much more careful in initiating transactions with the subsidiary that require stockholder approval, because in such cases the parent company will have to convince enough of the public stockholders to vote with the holding company to secure the necessary majority required.

Acquiring Control of Subsidiary Corporations The quickest means of acquiring control of another corporation is to negotiate with the person or company holding the block of stock constituting control. The block of shares thus purchased may be paid for either in cash or in securities of the holding company. Control can also be sought by purchasing as many shares as possible in the stock market. Orders by the corporation may be placed with one or several brokerage houses to buy all shares purchasable at a price not to exceed a stated figure. If the order is placed with several brokerage houses, a large number of shares may be secured before it becomes obvious that the increased demand for the stock in the market is originating from one purchaser seeking control. As soon as such knowledge becomes general, the price of the stock may rise rapidly, since the holders of the stock become aware of its value as a means of securing control as well as an investment. Acquiring control by means of purchases in the open market generally takes considerable time, particularly if the purchasing corporation desires to secure at least 50 per cent of the stock outstanding. If the group of stockholders controlling the board of directors wishes to fight the possible loss of control as a result of purchases by another corporation of publicly held stock, a proxy battle may result. If a proxy battle must be fought to secure control of another corporation, the cost to the company seeking control may be prohibitive, since the company seeking to acquire control must bear all the costs of the proxy campaign itself. The group having control at the time of the proxy battle charges the expenses of its campaign to retain control to the treasury of the corporation.

Another means of seeking control through purchasing stock held by the public is to announce in financial newspapers or in letters sent to each stockholder of the corporation of which control is sought, a tender to purchase shares at a stated price, usually substantially above the market price at the time of the offer. Such an action may raise the price of the stock above the tender price if stockholders feel that by holding their stock they may force an offer of a higher price. In an effort to prevent the market price from rising too high, the announced offer to purchase shares may be made contingent upon the acceptance by enough shareholders at the price offered to secure control of the corporation. Frequently, such an offer is made after the company seeking control has purchased a substantial number of shares quietly through orders given to brokerage houses. To secure additional shares, an announcement is then made to the stockholders still owning shares, offering an exchange of their shares for the shares of the corporation seeking control. If the offered exchange rate is attractive, many additional shares can be secured.

The Public Utility Holding Company Act of 1935 This Act brought under the jurisdiction of the Securities and Exchange Commission all utility holding companies and their subsidiaries engaged in the distribution of electricity and gas on an interstate basis. The principal provisions of the Act follow:

1. The Act gave the S.E.C. authority to approve or disapprove the issuing of securities of a holding company or of any of its subsidiaries. In exercising its authority, the S.E.C. seeks to simplify the financial structure of the holding company and its subsidiaries and to prevent the overissue of senior securities, such as bonds and preferred stocks. The terms of the sale to the general public of any securities of a holding company must be such as not to be detrimental to the investors, consumers purchasing utility services, or the general public. The S.E.C. was given authority to prohibit the issue by a holding company of no par stock, nonvoting stock, preferred stock, or debenture bonds. The S.E.C. could make exceptions to this general requirement if the needs of a particular holding company appeared to justify the exception. The payment of dividends by holding companies and by operating subsidiaries also was put under the jurisdiction of the

S.E.C. to approve, disapprove, or require a change in the amount of dividends distributed.

2. If any holding company subject to the jurisdiction of the Act wishes
to acquire shares of stock in another company or purchase the assets of another company, approval from the S.E.C. must be obtained.

3. The lending of money by a subsidiary to a parent in the holding
company structure is prohibited by the Act, since the "upstream loan" was
considered one of the worst abuses in the public utility field prior to the
passage of the Act.   On the other hand, loans from a parent to a subsidiary
were permitted if approved by the S.E.C.   Intercompany transactions involving services rendered by one company to another in the holding company structure, sale of products, fees for management services, and contracts
for construction of generating or distributing facilities were made subject
to approval by the S.E.C.

Questions

 1. Explain the relationship between ambition and status and the expansion of
    business.
 2. What are the economic factors in growth of size of business units?   Why is
    there less rapid growth in size of banks than in other industries?
 3. What are the advantages in large business units compared to small units?
 4. What incentive to unite separate companies into a single corporation is there
    in the tax laws?
 5. List and discuss some of the disadvantages of large size in business units.
 6. What are the reasons for legal limitations to the size of business units?
 7. What are "Gentlemen's Agreements" and what is the purpose of making them?
 8. What is a cartel?   By what means are the objectives of a cartel achieved?
 9. Explain the growth of trusts following the Civil War.   Why is this device
    seldom used now?
10. Some companies have expanded vertically from the control of raw materials
    obtained from the ground to distribution of the finished product to the con-
    sumer.   Give a few examples of companies of this kind.   Why does competi-
    tion not result in all companies in an industry becoming completely integrated
    vertically?
11. Complementary expansion is very common in business.   In what ways might
    it improve the competitive position of a company?   What problems might it
    create for a company?
12. For what reasons does a company enter into heterogeneous expansion?
13. In calculating the book value per share for purposes of exchange of shares in
    a merger or consolidation, the value of goodwill, patents, and franchises are
    usually eliminated or listed at $1, regardless of the value on the company
    books.   Why?   Is this justifiable or not?   Support your answer.
14. What are the steps in valuation of shares by capitalization of earnings?   How
    should the capitalization rate be chosen?
15. Market value strongly influences the choice of a ratio of exchange of shares in
    a consolidation or merger.   Why?
16. Is valuation of shares based on appraisal of value of assets by engineers, ac-
    countants, or other authorities more equitable because it is more "scientific"?
    Explain your answer.

17. Under what circumstances might a company considering merger accept a valuation of its shares at less than the value as determined by any of the means discussed above?

18. What is the treatment of minority stockholders voting unsuccessfully against a merger or consolidation? What is the treatment of bondholders and other creditors of the individual companies?

19. What is a holding company? What percentage of stock is required to exercise control? Explain your answer. Distinguish between pure and operating holding companies.

20. List the advantages and disadvantages of the holding company as a means of achieving expansion compared to the merger or consolidation. Critically evaluate each item on your list.

Selected Readings

Bosland, C. C., "Valuation of Public Utility Enterprises by the SEC," *Journal of Finance,* March 1961.

"Burnt Fingers, Penn-Texas Points Up the Risks of Over-Expansion," *Barron's National Business and Financial Weekly,* December 2, 1957.

Christopher, Albert, *Growth: Implications for Small Marketers,* Small Marketers Aids #86, Small Business Administration, Washington, D.C., December 1962.

Dewing, Arthur Stone, *Financial Policy of Corporations,* 5th ed., The Ronald Press Company, New York, 1953.

Kaplan, A. D. H., *Big Enterprise in a Competitive System,* Brookings Institution, Washington, D.C., 1954.

McCarthy, G. D., "Premeditated Merger," *Harvard Business Review,* January-February 1961.

McGuire, Joseph W., *Factors Affecting the Growth of Manufacturing Firms,* Bureau of Business Research, University of Washington, Seattle, Wash., 1963.

Martin, David D., *Mergers and the Clayton Act,* University of California Press, Berkeley, Calif., 1959.

Nelson, Ralph L., *Merger Movements in American Industry,* Princeton University Press, Princeton, N.J., 1959.

Young, Robert B., "Keys to Corporate Growth," *Harvard Business Review,* November-December 1961.

Part VIII

Changing the Structure of Firms

24

Recapitalization, Refinancing, and Dissolution

In order to survive in a dynamic economy, it is necessary for a business to adapt to changing conditions. It must be able to change its marketing operations, its manufacturing processes, its employment policies, and its capital structure to meet the varying economic conditions under which the business must operate. In plant life and in animal life, those species unable to adapt to changes in environment disappear while those organisms that are able to adapt are the ones that survive. The principle applies equally well to business. Practices successful in one decade may be disastrous in another. Under changing economic conditions, business managers are faced with opportunity and danger—opportunity to take advantage of changing conditions to improve their competitive position and danger in recognizing the changed conditions too late to effect alterations in business practices.

In this section, we are concerned with changes in the capital structure of business enterprises. Figure 24-1 shows diagramatically the principal changes in capital structure that may better prepare a company to meet new conditions. *Refinancing* involves the marketing of bonds or stocks to eliminate existing obligations of the business. If a corporation wishes to reduce its volume of current debt, it may market an issue of bonds to raise the money necessary to reduce the current debt. In effect, the corporation exchanges long-term debt for short-term debt. This operation is known as *funding*. Another type of refinancing is *refunding*, which involves the marketing of a new issue of bonds to retire an existing issue of bonds.

Recapitalization describes a shift in the proportion of bonds, preferred stock, and common stock comprising the long-term capital of the corporation. It may be accomplished by inducing holders of bonds to exchange them for preferred stock or vice versa. It may involve a change in the par value of common stock, or a change from no par to a nominal par value.

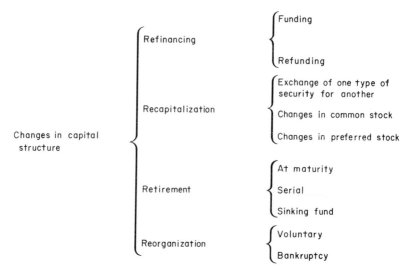

Fig. 24-1 *Types of capital structure change.*

It may involve a stock split or reverse split, and it may involve a change in the volume outstanding or the composition of the preferred stock.

Changes in the capital structure may be brought about by the *retirement* of securities outstanding. This usually involves retirement of bonds that may be paid off in full at the maturity date, may be retired serially, or may be retired by means of a sinking fund. The capital structure may also be changed as a result of a *reorganization* of the corporation to provide relief from financial distress. The reorganization might be achieved by voluntary agreement between the corporation in difficulty and its creditors. It might be accomplished by a court acting under the authority of bankruptcy legislation.

REASONS FOR CHANGING THE CAPITAL STRUCTURE OF CORPORATIONS

There are many possible reasons for changing the capital structure of a company. As a result of financial success continued for a long period, the retained earnings may have accumulated to the point where the surplus account of the corporation is far out of proportion to the capital stock account. On the other hand, the corporation may have suffered repeated and substantial losses to the point where any accumulated surplus is completely wiped out and the capital stock account is impaired. Two of the most important reasons for change, however, are to relieve financial stress and to improve the financial structure of the corporation.

To Relieve Financial Stress

Readjustment of Long-Term Debt. Practically all readjustments of the terms of any debt contract between a debtor company and its creditors will take place as a result of bankruptcy proceedings in court or a voluntary agreement with creditors as an alternative to bankruptcy. Creditors are often willing to modify the terms of the debt contract in favor of the debtor, if the modification might help to eliminate the necessity for bankruptcy proceedings. Probably the most common voluntary modification in a debt contract is an extension of the time within which payment of principal or interest is due. Although this means that the creditor will have to wait a longer period of time than the contract provided to receive payment for the debt owed to him, it may increase the likelihood that he will eventually be paid in full. Other modifications of debt contracts are the reduction of principal, reduction of interest payments, or modification of any provisions in the contract that appear to place an undue burden on the debtor. The problem of modifying long-term debt contracts to relieve the financial stress of the debtor company is discussed in more detail in Chapter 25.

Elimination of Preferred Stock Dividends in Arrears. When the preferred stock is cumulative, the dividends must be paid in full before any distribution of earnings may be made to the common stockholders. Because of financial stress, corporations sometimes have dividends in arrears from past years amounting to a considerable sum. Although the payment of dividends on preferred stock is not a contractual obligation as is the payment of interest on bonds, the accumulation of dividends in arrears affects the credit standing of the corporation. It particularly affects the success of any attempt on the part of the corporation to raise additional funds through the sale of preferred or common stock. Investors are reluctant to purchase an issue of preferred or common stock marketed by a corporation that has dividends in arrears on existing preferred stock, unless the price at which the issue is offered represents a depressed price.

The elimination of dividends in arrears may be accomplished in a number of ways. One is by negotiating an agreement with the holders of the preferred stock to accept securities in lieu of cash for the dividends in arrears. Thus, if dividends in arrears on a preferred stock issue amount to $38 per share, the corporation might offer common stock to the holders of the preferred stock as partial payment of the dividends in arrears. If at the time the offer is made to the preferred stockholders the common stock is selling for $10 a share, the corporation might offer three shares of common stock plus $8 in cash to eliminate the accumulated dividends. Another possibility is for the corporation to create a second preferred issue junior to the first preferred issue, having an issue price at $30 per share. One share of the junior preferred stock plus $8 in cash might be offered to the holders of the first preferred stock in the example above. In rare cases, the corporation might offer promissory notes maturing in two or three years or bonds maturing in several years as compensation for unpaid dividends. If at the time that such an offer is made to the preferred stockholders, the corporation is in no better financial position than it was when the dividends were falling into arrears, the wisdom of offering promissory notes or bonds in settlement of the dividends is highly dubious.   However, the dividends on the preferred stock may have fallen into arrears during a period of depression. If the earnings of the corporation increase substantially during the economic recovery following the depression, it might be justifiable for the corporation to issue promissory notes in settlement of the unpaid dividends, so as to permit the corporation to resume immediate payment of dividends on the common stock. Whatever settlement is offered by the corporation for payment of dividends in arrears, it must be unanimously accepted by the holders of preferred stock, or whatever proportion of the preferred stock outstanding is required by the state law or the corporation charter to approve any change in contractual provisions between the corporation and the holders of preferred stock. Securing the assent of the holders of the preferred stock is not always as difficult as it would appear. The board of directors of any corporation normally represents the common stockholders. The directors can exert pressure on the holders of preferred stock to accept an offer of settlement for the dividends in arrears, particularly if the offer is a reasonable one. If such an offer is rejected by the preferred stockholders, the directors may point out to them that regardless of the earnings of the corporation the directors will not resume payment of cash dividends on the preferred stock, allowing the profits to be retained in the business rather than distributing them first to the preferred stockholders and then to the common stockholders. If the holders of preferred stock are widely scattered and are numerous, it is likely that they will assent to the offer of the directors rather than attempt to match them in a test of strengh.

Change in Stated Value of Common Stock to Eliminate a Deficit. A corporation that has suffered losses to the point where it shows a negative surplus or deficit may find its financial operations seriously curtailed. The existence of a deficit on the balance sheet of the corporation will undoubtedly lower its credit standing in the eyes of creditors. It will be difficult for the corporation to raise additional funds through the sale of common stock because of the reluctance of investors to purchase stock of a company showing a deficit. The problem of selling additional common stock may be further complicated if the par value of the stock is higher than the price at which it can be sold to the public, because of the existing deficit. If the deficits are likely to continue and there is no prospect of profitable operation, it might be better to liquidate the company before it becomes bankrupt. If, however, the corporation begins earning a net profit on its operations, the elimination of the deficit may enable the corporation to speed up its recovery from the period of deficit operations. The process by which this may be done is shown in Table 24-1. If it is necessary to reduce the par value per share, this may be done through an amendment to the corporation charter, an action which will require approval by the majority stated in the corporation law of the state from which the corporation received its charter.   In the example in Table 24-1, the par value of the stock was changed from $100 to $50 per share.   This action created a capital surplus equal in amount to the reduced value of the capital stock account.   The existence of the capital surplus resulting from this operation permitted the deficit to be offset against the capital surplus, thereby eliminating the deficit.   Any earnings of the corporation following the elimination of the deficit are available for distribution to the stockholders, but dividends are not usually paid out of the newly created capital surplus.   This enables the corporation to sell additional shares if it feels that it needs additional capital, and increases the probability to the purchasers of the stock that they will be paid dividends out of the earnings of the corporation, which would not have been possible as long as a deficit remained on the books of the corporation.   Actions similar to the example given in Table 24-1 were taken by a number of corporations during the depression of the 1930's as a means of eliminating a deficit.

To Improve the Financial Structure   Just as the investment manager of a financial institution constantly reviews the portfolio of investments of the institution, so should the financial officer of a corporation scrutinize the financial structure of his company.   The purpose in either case is the same, to make improvements wherever they may be accomplished.   Changes in the financial structure may be necessary because of financial difficulties, as we have discussed above, or they may be made in the absence of financial pressure, to adapt the structure to any changes in the economic environment.

Effect of Changes in Interest Rates.   In Chapter 20, we discussed the timing of the marketing of a new issue of securities.   Favorable timing for the marketing of an issue was seen to be an important factor in the success of the distribution.   Where changes in interest rates occur, they affect not only the timing of the distribution but also make it advisable to consider whether an existing issue of securities should be exchanged or retired. Figure 20-2 shows the changes in interest rates that have occurred in recent years.   These changes make certain types of financing more expensive and other types less expensive.   If interest rates are low and are expected to rise in the future, a bond of a long maturity can provide financing for a lengthy period at low cost to the corporation.   On the other hand, if interest rates are high and are expected to drop in the future, borrowing should be restricted as far as possible to a short-term basis so as not to saddle the corporation with high cost financing for a lengthy period.   However, short-term interest rates and long-term interest rates do not always move in the same direction at the same time.   An astute financial manager may be able to take advantage of such changes by increasing the proportion of long-term debt comprising the total debt of the corporation during those periods when long-term interest rates are lower relative to short-term interest rates, and vice versa.

TABLE 24-1. ELIMINATION OF A DEFICIT

Corporation with Deficit

Assets	$500,000	Accounts payable	$ 40,000
		Note payable	200,000
		Capital stock, $100 par	
		3,200 shares	320,000
		Deficit	(60,000)
	$500,000		$500,000

Recapitalization to Create Capital Surplus

Assets	$500,000	Accounts payable	$ 40,000
		Note payable	200,000
		Capital stock, $50 par 3,200 shares	160,000
		Capital surplus	160,000
		Deficit	(60,000)
	$500,000		$500,000

Absorption of Deficit into Capital Surplus

Assets	$500,000	Accounts payable	$ 40,000
		Note payable	200,000
		Capital stock, $50 par 3,200 shares	160,000
		Capital surplus	120,000
	$500,000		$500,000

Effect of Changes in Stock Prices. If the stock of a corporation is publicly owned, the price of the stock will probably fluctuate considerably during the life of the firm. If the corporation grows and earns substantial profits, the price might increase tenfold, twentyfold, or fiftyfold during a decade. The stock of a financially profitable corporation issued at $100 a share might be quoted at $2,000 a share a few years later. Such a high price per share for the stock of a corporation would severely restrict the market for any additional shares sold by the company to raise funds. To expand the market for the shares of a company, the directors will generally adjust the price of the stock to a convenient figure. If a stock is selling at too high a price, the adjustment takes the form of either a stock dividend or a stock split. Although there is very little uniformity of opinion as to what constitutes a convenient range of prices for a stock, a price range between $50 and $100 appears to be the most popular. Thus, if the stock of a company were selling for $300 a share, a stock split of three to one, four to one, or five to one would be the most probable choice. The sale of additional securities at a price range between $50 and $100 would attract more buyers than the sale of securities at a price of $300 or $400 per share.

As one of the necessary steps in assuring the success of the sale of Ford Motor Company stock by the Ford Foundation in 1955, the stock held by the Ford Foundation was split (by action of the board of directors of the Ford Motor Company) fifteen to one, thus multiplying the number of shares held by the Ford Foundation by fifteen. After the stock split, part of the shares held by the Foundation were sold to the public at a price of $64.50 per share. The sale was highly successful. However, it is dubious whether it would have been as successful if the price per share had been fifteen times $64.50.

Not all companies, of course, subscribe to the general belief that stocks selling at high prices should be split so as to bring their prices down below $100 per share. The directors of some companies permit their stocks to rise well above that figure. Although a high price per share restricts the extent of the market for the stock of a company, it may carry a connotation of high quality. The extent to which investors associate quality with price, as they might associate quality and price in the goods that they buy, is open to dispute. Nevertheless, a few companies refrain from splitting their stock even though the price is so high that many investors find it difficult to purchase a single share. For example, the common stock of Superior Oil Company sold above $1,700 a share in 1964, and the stock of International Business Machines Corporation reached $600 a share during 1962. On the other hand, during a depression the price of the stock of some companies might sell at a figure so low as to reflect adversely upon the stability of the company. During the depths of the depression of the 1930's, many stocks sold at less than $1 a share. To bring the price of such stocks up to a respectable figure, a reverse stock split is sometimes used. Thus, a stock selling for 75¢ a share could be increased in price to $7.50 a share by means of a one for ten reverse split.

Funding of Short-Term Debt. The credit rating of a company depends to a considerable extent on its current ratio—the ratio of its current assets to its current liabilities. A rise in the current liabilities without an offsetting rise in the current assets of the company may make it more difficult for the company to raise short-term funds when needed. If the short-term debt of a company is kept at a conservative figure in relation to the current assets, the company will be in a better position to take advantage of opportunities to purchase raw materials, increase its investment in accounts receivable, or take other actions financed by means of an increase in short-term debt. Part of the short-term debt of a company is "permanent" in the sense that there is always a minimum volume outstanding at any given time. In order to reduce the current liabilities of a company, thus putting it in a better position to borrow funds quickly, the financial officer may advise funding a portion of the short-term debt. *Funding* is a process of replacing short-term debt with long-term debt. Funding is often done even where the rate of interest on long-term borrowing is higher than the rate of interest on short-term borrowing, since funding of short-term debt improves the current ratio and makes it easier for a business to borrow short-term funds as needed.

Reclassification of Stock. Reclassification of stock is the action of issuing one class of stock to replace another class already in existence. Additional shares of common stock may be issued to replace outstanding preferred stock. A new preferred stock may be created to replace another preferred stock. Occasionally, a preferred stock is exchanged for part of the common stock outstanding. If the directors of a corporation consider it advisable to simplify the financial structure of a corporation, they may retire an existing issue of preferred by replacing it with common. If the preferred is convertible into common and also callable, the retirement of the preferred can be accomplished simply by announcing a call for the preferred at a time when it would be more profitable to the holders to exercise their option to convert into common rather than surrender their stock to the corporation at the call price. If an outstanding preferred issue contains features that restrict the freedom of financial action of a company, the retirement of the preferred might be considered necessary by the directors of the corporation. For example, the preferred stock contract may contain a clause giving to the holders of the preferred the right to vote for the directors in the event that two or more dividends have been passed. To reduce the possibility that control of the corporation may shift from the holders of common to the holders of preferred, the directors may decide to retire the preferred stock. If it is not feasible to retire an unwanted issue of preferred by forcing a conversion into common, it may be necessary to create a new class of preferred stock to replace the existing one. The newly created preferred may be sold for cash to be used to purchase the existing issue. Another possibility is to offer the newly created preferred stock to the holders of the existing preferred for exchange. To get rid of the objectionable feature of the existing preferred stock, such as the contingent voting right for the directors of the corporation, it may be necessary to include in the newly created preferred a higher dividend than that being paid to the existing preferred.

In Anticipation of Merger or Public Offering of Shares A change in the capital structure of a corporation is sometimes made in anticipation of a merger. If there is considerable disparity in the market prices of the stocks of two corporations contemplating a consolidation, a recapitalization which will bring the price of the common stock of each company to approximately the same figure may simplify the process of consolidation and make it more likely that the plan will be accepted by the stockholders of both companies. This was done in the case of the consolidation of Packard Motor Company and Studebaker Corporation. A recapitalization might also be advisable if the directors of a closely held corporation are contemplating a public distribution of stock. If the appraised value per share of the stock to be offered to the public is either very low or very high, it may increase the likelihood of successful distribution of the stock if the price is adjusted by means of changing the number of shares outstanding. A case in point is the fifteen for one stock split, mentioned above, made by the Ford Motor Company to enable the Ford Foundation to market part of its holdings of common stock at $64.50 a share. If the appraised value of the stock of a closely held corporation is less than $1 per share, a reverse split bringing the valuation to $10 or $20 a share may make the stock more acceptable to purchasers.

CHANGES IN THE STRUCTURE OF DEBT

Refunding Refunding, the process of replacing a bond issue that has matured or is about to mature with a new bond issue, is an action frequently taken by a corporation. If no sinking fund has been created to provide the means to retire a bond issue, most corporations will not be in a position to spare the amount of cash necessary to pay off the individual bonds when they fall due. In such a situation, about the only thing that a corporation can do is to refund the maturing issues. This can be done by selling a new bond issue for cash, which is then distributed to the holders of the maturing bonds. It is likely that some of the holders of the maturing bonds will wish to continue their investment in the bonds of the corporation. That being the case, corporations often offer an exchange of new bonds for the maturing bonds. The corporation may find that most of the bonds held by investors will be returned to the corporation for exchange for new ones. This, of course, will simplify the process of redemption considerably. If most of the bonds of the old issue are sent in for exchange for new bonds, the number of new bonds that must be marketed to the public to raise the cash necessary to redeem the remaining old bonds will be a relatively small number. If the general level of interest rates has not changed since the maturing bonds were first issued and if the credit of the corporation is the same as before, it is likely that the new bonds issued to replace the maturing ones will carry the same rate of interest and have the same general features as the maturing bonds. It is more likely, however, that both the credit rating of the corporation and the general level of interest rates will change during the life of the maturing bonds. Change is also likely in the financing needs of the corporation. Therefore, a new issue of bonds distributed to replace a maturing issue is likely to carry a different rate of interest and to contain different features from the maturing issue. A refunding operation provides an opportunity to the corporation to eliminate those characteristics of the maturing bonds that have proven inconvenient to the financing operations of the corporation. If the closed end feature of the maturing bond issue has proved restrictive, the new bonds may have the open end feature. The maturing issue may be a mortgage bond issue, possibly because the corporation at the time of issuance of the bonds was forced to provide the security offered by the mortgage. If such security is no longer necessary to assure the successful sale of bonds at a reasonable rate of interest, the refunding issue may be a debtenture bond. It is also likely that the refunding bonds will be larger in total amount or smaller in total amount than the maturing issue, depending upon whether the requirement for funds of the corporation is larger or smaller than it was at the time that the maturing bonds were first distributed. Efficient financial planning requires that the officers of the corporation make plans for refunding well in advance of the maturity of the old issue, so that the refunding issue can be designed without haste.

Convertible Bonds Bonds convertible into preferred or common stocks provide a simple means of changing the structure of debt of a corporation. Because the exercise of the conversion is at the option of the bondholder, the reduction in long-term debt resulting from conversion may or may not take place at a time convenient to the corporation. Some control over the timing of conversion can be retained by the corporation if the bonds are callable as well as convertible. As long as the stock into which the bonds are convertible remains above the price at which conversion is profitable to the holder of the bonds, the corporation can force conversion into stock by announcing a call of the bonds. If the corporation wishes to use bonds as a temporary means of financing, eventually to be replaced by preferred or common stocks, including a convertible feature in the bonds will make it possible for the corporation to exercise some choice regarding the timing of the elimination of the bond issue. If, on the other hand, the price of the stock into which the bonds are convertible remains below the point at which it is profitable for the bondholders to convert, the announcement of the call by the corporation will result in the bonds being sent to the corporation for cash rather than for conversion into stock. In such a situation, it would be prudent for the directors of a corporation to provide a sinking fund to retire the bonds when due or to plan a refunding operation.

Repayment and Retirement Practically all bond issues have a maturity date. It is, therefore, necessary to plan for the retirement of a bond issue at or prior to maturity. Retirement can be accomplished by refunding, conversion into stock, or repayment. If a corporation retires a bond issue by means other than refunding, the proportion of debt to equity in the capital structure is changed. Some corporations look upon bonds as a means of temporary financing, and plan a reduction in the total long-term debt outstanding when a bond issue matures. If a corporation expects to expand its operations during a coming ten- or twenty-year period, it may speed up the process of expansion by purchasing assets from the funds made available through a sale of bonds. The expansion is presumed to increase earnings and to permit a retirement of the bond issue out of the increased earnings. If the bonds are indeed a temporary means of financing, their retirement by use of a sinking fund, by serial retirement, or by other means will not prove burdensome, provided the expansion increases the earnings of the company as expected.

In the field of industrial enterprises, the prevailing philosophy is that bonds should be considered a temporary means of financing. In the public utility and railroad fields, however, bonds are more generally accepted as a legitimate means of permanent financing, in spite of the fact that individual bond issues must be refunded as they mature. Furthermore, bond issues with long maturities, such as 50 or 100 years, are found mostly in railroad finance and to a lesser extent in public utility financing. In industrial corporations, the maturity of bonds is generally shorter—typically between ten and thirty years.

In financial matters, it is generally accepted that conservatism is equivalent to wisdom. In the management of debt, conservative policy dictates retirement as soon as it can be accomplished without undue strain on the resources of the company. For industrial corporations particularly, such a course is considered wise, since fluctuation of earnings from year to year is generally greater than it is in the field of public utilities. Conservatism dictates that earnings in excess of those needed to pay a reasonable dividend on the stock of the company be used to reduce the debt of the corporation. During a period of profitable operations, however, there is a temptation to use retained earnings for expansion rather than debt reduction. Such a use of retained earnings will prove to be astute if demand for the company's products increases and conditions of prosperity continue, but it increases the risk of financial difficulties in the event of a downturn in business activity. If a decline in demand for the company's products occurs, the income of the company may shrink. In such an event, the decision to use retained earnings for expansion rather than for debt reduction may prove disastrous. During a long period of prosperity, there is a tendency for the directors of many companies to underrate the risk resulting from a decline in business. The level of economic activity does not remain stable either at a high or a low point for very long. Inasmuch as the length of a period of prosperity cannot easily be predicted in advance, the importance of debt reduction during such periods is obvious. During World War II, railroad traffic increased tremendously over what it had been during the depression decade of the 1930's. It was obvious to the management of railroads that the large volume of traffic would drastically decline following the cessation of hostilities. Because the management of most railroads wisely used this opportunity to reduce their indebtedness, the war years constituted a period of spectacular debt reduction out of earnings.

RECAPITALIZATION OF EQUITY SECURITIES

Preferred Stock There are two principal reasons for the recapitalization of preferred stock. One is to get rid of any features in an existing preferred issue that prove unduly restrictive to management. The other is a desire for simplification of the capital structure of the corporation. Probably the feature that is most restrictive is the cumulative one, which is found in most preferred issues. If unpaid preferred dividends are permitted to accumulate for many years, the corporation will find it difficult to raise money by selling bonds, by issuing additional preferred stock, or by marketing common stock. The problems created by the existence of dividends in arrears and the methods available to eliminate the arrearages were discussed above. Other restrictive features in preferred stock that may prove unduly burdensome to management include the right to vote for directors when a stated number of preferred dividends have been passed, the participating feature, and the right to approve or disapprove the issue of bonds by the corporation. To eliminate burdensome provisions in preferred stocks, voluntary agreement by the stockholders is necessary or the preferred issue must be eliminated. The state law under which the corporation received its charter will indicate what percentage of the preferred stockholders will be required to give their assent before a change in the privileges given to them under the preferred stock contract may be made. Commonly, this percentage is two-thirds of the outstanding preferred shares. If approval by the required percentage can be obtained, the elimination of the objectionable features of the preferred stock is usually accomplished either through an exchange of a new preferred for the old preferred issue or an exchange of common stock for the old preferred issue. However, to secure the necessary approval by the persons holding the old preferred shares, some compensating privilege must be offered, inasmuch as a provision that is considered objectionable by the corporation is generally considered a privilege by the stockholders. Thus, if the new preferred issue eliminates the cumulative feature found in the old issue, the new preferred might carry a higher dividend rate, or might give the privilege of conversion into common stock.

In addition to offering an inducement in the form of a new privilege to compensate for the sacrifice of a feature objectionable to management, persuasion or even threats are used on occasion by the directors to get the preferred stockholder to accept the exchange of new preferred for the old preferred. Letters will, of course, be sent to each holder of preferred stock explaining the desire of the directors to retire the old preferred and replace it with new preferred, emphasizing the advantage to the shareholder of the features in the new preferred stock and minimizing the importance of the attractive features of the old stock to be eliminated. It may be necessary to send not one letter but several letters to each holder of preferred stock. If there should be a few persons or institutions holding a substantial number of shares of the issue, a visit to each of these stockholders by an officer of the corporation might be advisable. Generally, the preferred stockholder will not receive any letters in opposition to those sent out by the management of the corporation. The reason is that in most cases the holders of the preferred shares will not be sufficiently aroused to spend the time and money necessary to correspond with the other holders. If the proposed exchange appears to a stockholder to be unfair, he has the right to inform other stockholders of his reasons for urging them to vote against the exchange urged by the corporation. To do this a stockholder must secure the names and addresses of the other holders of preferred stock, which is his right. However, the cost of contacting his fellow stockholders will have to be paid out of his own pocket, whereas the law permits the cost of sending letters and making personal visits on behalf of the directors of the company to be charged to the corporation.

If persuasion does not appear to be sufficient to secure the necessary acceptance by the preferred stockholders of an exchange, a threat might work. Any threat made by the directors of a corporation to secure assent by the stockholders is of dubious legality. However, a threat may be made in a form which does not appear to be a threat. In one instance, the chairman of the board of directors of a corporation announced to the holders of preferred stock that if they did not approve of an exchange, the directors might not find any incentive in the future to resume payment of dividends on the preferred stock. Just as the preferred stockholder is at a disadvantage compared to the directors of a corporation in seeking to persuade his fellow stockholders to vote against an exchange of shares desired by management, so is the preferred stockholder at a disadvantage in any legal contest with the directors of his corporation. Should a holder of preferred stock be convinced that the pressure exerted by the directors to secure approval goes beyond the permissible limits of the law, in testing this conviction in court the stockholder would have to hire a lawyer with his own money and bear any other expenses connected with the case, while the directors could charge all legal fees and court costs to the corporation. Furthermore, the uncertainty, the delay, and the expenses of a court case make it unlikely that any stockholder or group of stockholders will seek to contest an abuse of power by the board of directors unless the action is a flagrant violation of corporation law.

Where preferred stock is used for permanent financing, no provisions are made for its retirement. If it is deemed advisable to retire the preferred stock, several courses are open. An exchange into common stock may be offered, an exchange into bonds may be offered, or the stock may be repurchased. Ordinarily, the directors are unable to retire a preferred stock issue unless the holders of the preferred shares can be persuaded to give them up voluntarily. Most preferred stocks, however, have the call feature. If this is so, the directors of the corporation may announce their intention of calling in the outstanding preferred stock at the call price stated in the preferred stock contract. The call feature is found in those preferred issues where the directors of the corporation consider the preferred as a means of temporary financing. As in the case of bonds, the call feature in preferred stocks is often coupled with the convertible privilege, permitting the shares to be exchanged for common stock at a stated exchange rate. To simplify the capital structure of a corporation through elimination of the preferred stock outstanding, a callable, convertible preferred stock issue may be eliminated by announcing a call at a time when it is more advantageous to the holders of the preferred to convert into common than to accept the call. If the preferred shares are convertible into five shares of common stock and the call price is $105, the preferred shareholders will exercise their right of conversion into common rather than accept the call of the corporation whenever the common stock is selling above $21 a share.

If the preferred stock does not have the call feature and it is not possible to secure voluntary exchange of the securities for common stock or for a newly created preferred stock issue, an existing issue of preferred stock may be gradually retired through repurchase by the corporation. The corporation can place a standing order with one or more brokerage houses to purchase as many shares of the preferred stock of the company as can be purchased at a price less than the maximum authorized by the directors of the corporation. Generally, such an operation will not require the selling of additional common stock or the sale of a bond issue to secure money with which to purchase the preferred shares. The number of preferred shares purchased at any one time will in most cases be small, and the purchases will be spread over a number of years. A corporation will generally depend upon its net income to provide the means to purchase the outstanding preferred stock. In some cases, all the preferred shares outstanding may be retired by this means in a few years. In most cases, however, there will remain some shares that the holders refuse to surrender at any reasonable price. If the number of these shares outstanding is small, the directors of the corporation may prefer to leave them outstanding. If the purpose of retiring a preferred stock issue is to eliminate the priority in payment of dividends held by the preferred stock, the existence of a few shares outstanding will in most cases be insignificant. If, however, the directors wish to eliminate a preferred issue because the holders of preferred must approve any long-term borrowing, the directors may find that the continued existence of a few shares of preferred to be inconvenient. To eliminate all the preferred shares, the directors may offer tenders (offers to purchase securities at a stated price) to the holders of the remaining preferred shares. The tenders may have to be at a price considerably higher than the original issue price of the preferred. The directors may offer a tender to purchase preferred originally issued at $100 a share at a purchase price of $120 a share. In addition to offering a generous premium for repurchase of outstanding shares, the directors may use persuasion or veiled threats, as mentioned earlier.

Common Stock   If the directors of a corporation wish to increase the number of common shares outstanding, they may do so either by a stock split, discussed above, or by declaring a stock dividend. A stock split affects only the common stock account, and does not change the surplus account. A stock dividend, on the other hand, involves a bookkeeping transfer of a portion of the surplus to the capital stock account. A stock dividend does not change the book value of the common stock account.   However, because it increases the number of shares outstanding, a stock dividend reduces the book value per share.   Because a stock dividend transfers a portion of the surplus to the common stock account, the action is sometimes called capitalization of surplus.

If the surplus account is so large that it gives the impression of excessive earnings or unreasonable retention of earnings by the corporation, the distribution of stock dividends will reduce the surplus account.   This capitalization of surplus is evidence of the channeling of earnings into permanent investment in the corporation.   Companies with a rapid rate of growth generally prefer to retain as large a proportion of earned surplus as they can without making the stockholders restless because of nonpayment of cash dividends.   It is sometimes difficult for the directors to make the stockholders understand that a policy of nonpayment of cash dividends is compatible with a rapid increase in earned surplus.   Capitalization of surplus by means of distribution of stock dividends generally silences the opposition of stockholders to a policy of retention of earnings for expansion or other purposes.

If the directors of a corporation maintain their position through ownership of a minority of the shares, and wish to strengthen their position without increasing their investment in the company, they can accomplish this by a stock split or stock dividends.   Since both actions increase the number of shares outstanding and reduce the market price per share, the result is to increase the likelihood that the shares not held by the directors of the corporation will become more widely scattered than before.   Another means of strengthening the control of the corporation by the board of directors is to reduce the number of voting shares in the hands of the general public.   This may be done by purchasing shares of company stock in the open market and holding them in the treasury.   A means of strengthening the position of the board of directors, which does not require a change in the capitalization of the company, is to institute a retirement plan for employees of the company involving the purchase in the open market of common stock with the money credited to the retirement fund.   As the amount in the fund increases, the number of shares purchased will rise, and the voting power of the shares in the pension fund will increase.   If the directors appoint themselves the trustees of the pension fund or retain for themselves the power to select the trustees, the number of voting shares directly controlled by the board of directors will increase as the number of shares held by the general public decreases.

The directors of a corporation may seek approval from the stockholders to change the par value of the common stock.   In nearly every case, the change is to a lower par value or to no par.   If the dividend paid by the directors amounts to a substantial sum per share, such as $20 or $30 per share, it will be taken as evidence by some members of the public or by members of a regulatory commission that the earnings of the corporation are excessive. A reduction in the par value of the stock accomplished by a stock split may make the corporation appear to be less profitable. A change in the capitalization by means of a ten for one stock split and a reduction in the dividend rate to $2 per share will permit the corporation to disperse the same dollar amount of earnings as before, but the payment will appear to many members of the general public to be a modest distribution of earnings. Regulated public utilities have occasionally used this device to avoid the appearance of excessive earnings while mantaining generous dividend payments to the owners of the corporation. Changes in par value are also sometimes made to reduce the corporation franchise tax levied by the state from which the corporation charter was secured. In the case of no par stock, some states value such stock at $100 per share for the purpose of levying the state franchise tax. By changing the value of the stock from no par to a nominal par, such as $1 or $5, the total annual franchise tax paid by a corporation may be reduced. A change from a no par to a purely nominal par figure may reduce the burden of transfer taxes imposed by some states on the sale or gift of stock from one person to another. The existence of franchise taxes and taxes on the transfer of shares among stockholders has made no par stock less popular than low par stock in recent decades.

Retirement of common stock is associated with liquidation of a corporation. However, partial retirement is sometimes undertaken when there is no thought of imminent liquidation. A company may be faced with a declining demand for its services. If it has a substantial amount of cash or investment in securities and little or no debt or preferred stock, the directors might undertake a program of repurchase of a portion of the common stock outstanding. Assuming that the declining demand for the services of the company is translated into declining income for the company, using the cash or marketable securities owned by the company to reduce the number of shares of common stock outstanding rather than to maintain or increase the dividend rate would appear to be a wiser course. Such an action reduces both the assets of the corporation and the number of ownership certificates outstanding. In effect, it is an acknowledgment of the fact that the demand for the services of the company has shrunk, and that in consequence the corporation should be reduced in size. The corporation may purchase common stock by placing orders with brokerage houses in the same manner as was indicated in connection with the retirement of preferred stock. This will serve the purpose of reducing the number of shares outstanding and supporting the market price of the stock as well, inasmuch as the shares of those persons most eager to sell will be acquired by the corporation first. As the earnings of the corporation decline, therefore, the gradual reduction in the number of shares outstanding may enable the directors to maintain the dividend rate on common stock characteristic of the earlier period when the demand for the company's services was higher. If the demand for the services of a corporation have disappeared entirely, the directors might consider dissolving the corporation and distributing a liquidating dividend to the stockholders. A liquidating dividend is not taxed as ordinary income to the stockholder. If the corporation, however, wishes to liquidate partially a corporation so as to reduce both its assets and net worth by distributing a large dividend to stockholders, such a dividend would not be considered as a partial liquidating dividend for tax purposes. From the standpoint of the stockholders it is preferable for the directors of their corporation to adjust to a lower demand for the services of the company by gradual purchases of shares of common stock rather than by distribution of a large "partially liquidating" dividend.

It is part of human nature to prefer advance to retreat, to go forward rather than backward, and in the case of business to prefer expansion to retrenchment. Even where it is obvious that the market for the products or services of a corporation have declined, and that the decline appears to be permanent, both the directors and the stockholders are reluctant to admit the fact. Rather than reduce the size of the corporation as discussed above, the directors and stockholders of many corporations prefer other means of adjusting to a decline in demand. A shift into another line of activity is often undertaken. Companies that have started out in one field have gradually shifted their operations out of the field and into an entirely different one. Sometimes the name of the company indicates the earlier business activity and is not changed even though that activity no longer is performed by the company. The Adams Express Company, for example, originally did an express business. Shortly after World War I the company went out of this business entirely and became an investment company instead, although the name was not changed. One of the reasons that companies expand their operations into a variety of lines is to guard against the possibility of retrenchment if the demand for their original products or services declines in the future.

SPIN-OFF

One means of reducing the scale of operation is by a *spin-off,* which is a distribution of the shares of a subsidiary to the stockholders of the holding company. The distribution of the subsidiary shares is made to each holder of the holding company stock in proportion to the number of holding company shares held. The spin-off may also be used to eliminate a department or division of a company. In this case, however, it would be necessary to create a corporation, transfer the assets of the department or division to the corporation, and distribute the shares of the new corporation to the holders of shares of the parent company. Such a distribution is in the nature of a property dividend, and may be taxed at personal income tax rates. It is possible, however, for such a distribution to escape the income tax. In order to escape being taxed as ordinary income to the recipient, a spin-off must meet the following requirements:

1. The amount of stock of the subsidiary held by the parent must be at least 80 per cent of the stock of the subsidiary.
2. There must be no attempt to use the spin-off as a device to disguise the distribution of earnings of the corporation.
3. All the stock of the subsidiary held by the parent must be distributed in the spin-off.
4. The subsidiary corporation and the parent corporation must have conducted business as separate entities for at least five years *prior* to the spin-off.
5. Both the former subsidiary, now an independent company, and the parent company must conduct an active separate business for at least five years after the spin-off.[1]

The spin-off accomplishes a reduction both in the assets and in the net worth of the corporation distributing the shares of a subsidiary. The spin-off reduces the book value per share of the parent company and the market value per share. However, unlike a repurchase of the company's stock, a spin-off does not reduce the number of shares of the parent company outstanding. The stockholders receiving a spin-off find themselves holding shares in two companies rather than in one. Ordinarily, the combined market value of the shares of the two companies held by each stockholder will be approximately equal to the market value of the shares of the single company before the spin-off. However, a spin-off may result in the total holdings of each stockholder increasing in market value compared to the value of parent company shares before the spin-off. A spin-off is similar in some respects to a stock split. In both cases the market price per share is reduced and a larger number of shares is put in the hands of the investing public. If, as in the case of most stock splits, the increase in the number of shares outstanding and the lower market price per share after the spin-off result in an increased market for the shares, both of the former parent company and of the newly independent corporation, the market price of the stock holdings of each stockholder may be higher than before.

A spin-off is also sometimes made with the conviction that two entirely separate companies will be more efficient and operate more profitably than if they were divisions of a single company. The creation of an independent company as the result of a spin-off may lead the new company to compete more vigorously (perhaps against its former parent as well) than it was able

---

[1] In response to a ruling by the Supreme Court that the ownership of 23 per cent of the stock of General Motors by E. I. du Pont Nemours & Company constituted a violation of the antitrust laws, a federal district court in 1961 ordered a distribution of General Motors stock to the Du Pont shareholders. Inasmuch as the Du Pont Corporation did not hold 80 per cent of the stock of General Motors, the distribution of GM stock to Du Pont stockholders could not qualify as a tax-free spin-off under existing tax laws. In order to save Du Pont stockholders from the pain of paying full personal income taxes on the market value of the General Motors stock received, a bill was introduced in Congress to provide relief for the Du Pont stockholders. In news reports this bill was aptly named "The Du Pont Stockholders' Relief Bill."

to prior to the spin-off.   New production techniques, new marketing devices, and new inventions or laboratory discoveries made by the independent company may be more vigorously exploited and more rapidly put into operation than would be the case if the company were a subsidiary.

A spin-off is sometimes required by federal courts in antitrust cases or by federal regulatory commissions.   The Securities and Exchange Commission required spin-offs in a number of instances to simplify the structure of holding company empires in the public utility field under the authority of the Public Utility Holding Company Act of 1935.   Since a spin-off requires no sale of assets or of securities, it simplifies the divestment of a subsidiary or a division of a company, because there is no problem involved in determining fair valuation for assets or for securities.   In cases where the spin-off has been used as a court ordered device to counter monopoly in an industry, its effectiveness in increasing competition has sometimes been questioned.   Obviously, the ownership of the companies following a spin-off remains in the same hands that owned the single company prior to the spin-off.   Each stockholder simply owns shares in two or more corporations after the spin-off rather than in one company prior to the spin-off.   It appears, however, from the history of companies following a court-ordered spin-off that the passage of time finds the shares of the separated companies falling into the portfolios of many new investors.   The stockholders of each of the separated companies become more and more distinct, and, therefore, the companies themselves become more and more independent of each other.

DISSOLUTION OF COMPANIES

Reasons for Business Terminations   Most businesses that cease operations do so for reasons other than failure; liquidation usually occurs before the business becomes insolvent.   To illustrate, one study of business terminations in the state of Washington during 1957 indicated that only one out of every fifty was due to financial failure.[2]   The reasons reported by the owners for terminating their enterprises are given in Table 24-2.   Approximately half of the firms in the study had less than $5,000 in average annual sales, one-third had sales of less than $2,500, and one-fifth had sales less than $500 a year.   The large number of business owners in Table 24-2 giving no reason for terminations undoubtedly found low sales volume a prime reason for the decision to quit, since 40 per cent of those giving no reason for termination had average annual sales of less than $500.

Two other characteristics are found in the majority of business terminations: age and type of enterprise.   The first months of any enterprise are the most critical.   If it survives a few years, its chances of continued life are greatly improved.   The Washington State study found more than a third of the terminations were of businesses created less than a year earlier.

---

2 Warren W. Etcheson and James F. Robb, *A Study of Business Terminations,* Bureau of Business Research, University of Washington, Seattle, Wash., 1959.

TABLE 24-2. REASONS FOR BUSINESS TERMINATIONS OF 2,369
WASHINGTON STATE FIRMS IN 1957

Reason Given	Number of Firms	Per Cent of Total Group	Per Cent of Those Giving Reason
Succeeded by another business	653	27.6	48.5
Illness, disability, or death	130	5.5	9.7
Moved from the State or city	115	4.8	8.5
Tax warrant issued	112	4.7	8.3
Business absorbed	110	4.6	8.2
Bought out by partner	70	2.9	5.2
Formed partnership or corporation	42	1.8	3.2
Lack of business ability	31	1.3	2.3
Bankruptcy	24	1.0	1.8
Retirement	23	1.0	1.7
Changed to other work	12	.5	.9
School or military service	8	.3	.5
Contract expired	4	.2	.3
Lease expired	4	.2	.3
Place of business destroyed	4	.2	.3
Supplier went out of business	4	.2	.3
No reason given	1,023	43.2	——
Total	2,369	100.0	100.0

Source: Warren W. Etcheson and James F. Robb, *A Study of Business Terminations,* Bureau of Business Research, University of Washington, Seattle, Wash., 1959.

Half of the terminated businesses had been in existence less than three years. The type of enterprise also had a bearing on the rate of termination. Approximately 70 per cent of the terminations in the study were retail enterprises. It is in the field of retailing that the bulk of new businesses are born and die each year. Persons with limited business experience and limited capital find retailing easy to enter. But they then find it a slow, difficult process to build up a volume of sales necessary to cover all expenses.

Not all terminations are the result of disappointing sales, as Table 24-2 shows. Often a successful proprietorship is sold to a new owner, thereby terminating one business and creating another. Sometimes a business is terminated to transform a proprietorship or partnership into a corporation, or a corporation into a proprietorship or partnership. In any case, because the number of businesses created usually exceeds the number terminated, the business population increases nearly every year. This is shown in Fig. 24-2 and Fig. 24-3.

Dissolution of Unincorporated Businesses A proprietorship may be terminated at the will of the proprietor. He remains personally liable for unpaid debts, completion of contracts, and any other valid claims against the proprietorship. If the proprietorship is solvent, its ending is a simple affair. The usual announcement of termination is a statement inserted

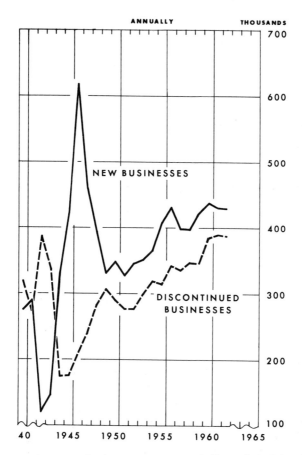

Fig. 24-2 *Annual rate of businesses created and discontinued in the United States.* (*Source: Historical Chart Book,* Board of Governors of the Federal Reserve System, Washington, D. C., 1964)

either in a local newspaper or in a window of the place of business. The death of the owner automatically terminates a proprietorship.

A general partnership is ended if any of the following events takes place: (1) death of a partner, (2) bankruptcy of a partner, (3) withdrawal of a partner, (4) insanity or other disability of a partner, (5) expiration of the time period specified in the partnership agreement, (6) bankruptcy of the partnership, (7) outbreak of war between two nations of which one partner is the citizen of one nation and another partner the citizen of the other, or (8) mutual agreement of the partners to dissolve the partnership. A partnership interest cannot be transferred by one partner to his son or any other person by will or sold without the permission of the remaining partners, which would, in any case, dissolve the old partnership and create a new one. If the partners desire the continued existence of their business, they must make an agreement among themselves on the terms under which

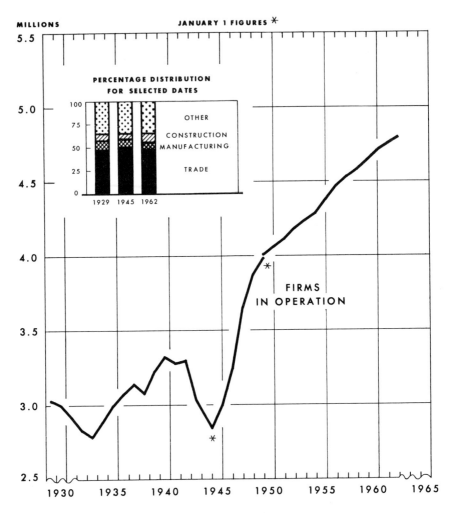

Fig. 24-3 *Business population.* (*Source: Historical Chart Book,* Board of Governors of the Federal Reserve System, Washington, D. C., 1964)

a successor partnership will be created, including the means of purchasing the investment of a withdrawing partner.

The termination of a partnership does not alter the liability of the partners for the business' debts and other obligations. Because the death of a partner requires the creation of a new partnership if the business is to continue, partnership life insurance is sometimes bought which pays the amount of the investment of any deceased partner to the partners remaining. With this money the surviving partners may pay the estate of the deceased partner the amount of his interest in the firm and continue the business without any dislocation caused by the change in ownership.

Involuntary Dissolution of Corporations   The dissolution of a corporation is governed by the legislation of the state that issued the charter.   It is not affected (unless the law of the state says otherwise) by a failure of the corporation to use the powers authorized in the charter, by suspension of business activity, by sale of all its assets, by the appointment of a receiver to administer the business of the corporation, or because all the stock has been concentrated into ownership by a single person or company.   To dissolve a corporation, it is necessary that the charter be extinguished, the business affairs wound up, its debts liquidated, and any remaining property distributed to the stockholders.

State corporation laws define the conditions necessitating involuntary dissolution.   Involuntary dissolution is most commonly brought about by bankruptcy proceedings in court, expiration of the time stated in the charter as the life of the corporation, court order, or forfeiture of the charter.

Bankruptcy.   As described in Chapter 25, proceedings in bankruptcy dissolve the bankrupt corporation, either liquidating the properties or transferring them to the successor corporation.

Expiration of the Term of Existence Stated in the Charter.   Most corporations are granted a perpetual life, as stated in the charter, by authority of the laws of the state.   The laws of a few states place a maximum limit on the life granted in the charter issued by the state, but provide for renewal of the charter if requested by the directors and if such request is ratified by the stockholders.   If, after the expiration of its charter, the corporation continues to conduct business, the courts may hold the corporation exists *de facto* and is liable for payment of property bought by it or services furnished to it.

By Court Order.   A court order may dissolve a corporation.   Examples of circumstances under which a court may dissolve a corporation are the following:

1. As the result of a suit brought by a stockholder alleging fraud on the part of the majority stockholders, gross mismanagement by directors or officers, or dissension among stockholders of such magnitude as to render the continuation of the business impossible.

2. Failure to file the annual report with the Secretary of State of the state giving information required by the laws of the state on the previous year's operations, and failure to pay fees and franchise taxes to the state.

3. If the articles of incorporation or amendments were procured fraudulently.

4. The corporation has continuously transacted business not authorized in the charter.

5. The corporation has failed to maintain a registered agent in the state of its incorporation.

6. Misrepresentation is found in any reports, affidavits, or other documents submitted by the corporation.

Forfeiture of the Charter. The state gives life to the corporation; it may also take that life away. An act of the state legislature may dissolve a corporation existing under a charter granted by the state, if the charter resulted from a special act by the legislature and contained a clause permitting the legislature to dissolve the corporation. Failure to begin business operations under the charter within a specified period after its issuance can result in the forfeiture of the charter.

Voluntary Dissolution Voluntary dissolution may be accomplished under the procedures provided by the laws of the state that granted the charter. Those laws differ in the details of the steps required in voluntary dissolution. The following procedure is typical, however:

Dissolution by Unanimous Consent. Upon receipt by the Secretary of State of a statement that it is the will of the stockholders to dissolve the corporation, which statement is signed by the president, secretary, and every stockholder, the Secretary of State may issue a certificate of dissolution and appoint agents (usually the directors or officers of the corporation) to wind up the affairs of the company, pay the claims of the creditors, and distribute the remaining assets to the stockholders.

Dissolution Without Unanimous Consent. The following steps are followed if unanimous consent of the stockholders is not obtained:

1. A meeting of the board of directors is called. Each director must be served notice of the time and place of the meeting and the purpose for which it is called. A majority of the board must vote to dissolve.

2. A stockholders' meeting is called. The purpose of the meeting must be stated in the notice sent to each stockholder, and must be sent sufficiently in advance of the meeting to permit attendance or naming of proxies. The meeting may be held anywhere in the United States. At the stockholders' meeting, at least two-thirds of the stock entitled to vote must be voted in favor of dissolution.

3. If approval by the stockholders is obtained, a statement to that effect must be sent to the Secretary of State and must be properly signed by the president and secretary of the corporation.

4. The Secretary of State examines the documents attesting to the actions to dissolve taken by the board of directors and the stockholders of the corporation. He then issues a statement of dissolution, filing one copy in his office, sending a second copy to the county records office where the corporation's principal office in the state having granted the original charter is located, and sending a third copy to the corporation secretary.

5. The directors and officers are usually designated by state law as

trustees or agents of liquidation of the property of the corporation. They must notify in writing each known creditor and claimant and those parties with which the corporation has entered into contracts that have not been completed. Some states accept a notice in a newspaper as sufficient notification to creditors and claimants.

6. The trustees complete or settle contracts outstanding, collect debts due the corporation, pay debts owed by the corporation, and discharge all other obligations of the corporation. This may take a few days or a few years.[3]

7. After the payment of all corporate debts and settlement of all obligations of the company, the trustees liquidate the property of the corporation. The proceeds are then distributed to the stockholders. If there is more than one class of stock, each class is treated in liquidation according to the laws of the state and the provisions of the corporation charter. The distribution takes the form of a liquidating dividend, which is exchanged for the stock certificates of each stockholder. The stock certificates are canceled by the trustees. Such cancellation is usually the final act of dissolution. Some states require that the Secretary of State wait until receiving notice from the trustees that all obligations have been settled, the liquidating dividend paid, and the stock certificates canceled before issuing the statement of dissolution described in step 4 above.

Questions

1. Distinguish between refinancing, funding, refunding, and recapitalization.
2. Why is it important for a corporation to eliminate dividends in arrears on cumulative preferred stock? By what means may this be acomplished?
3. If the balance sheet of a corporation shows a deficit or negative surplus, how can this be eliminated? What is the advantage of doing this?
4. Why, since it does not change the totals of assets and liabilities plus net worth on the balance sheet, does a change in the common stock account to absorb a deficit aid a corporation in future financing?
5. For what reasons might a corporation split its common stock? Why might it engage in a reverse split?
6. Why might a·corporation fund its short-term debt even if the interest rate paid is higher than before the funding operation?
7. How may a recapitalization of the stock of a corporation aid in effecting a merger?
8. If a corporation has a convertible bond issue outstanding, under what circumstances does it exercise some control over the timing of the conversion by the bondholders?
9. If bonds are considered by a corporation as part of its plan for permanent financing, how can this be accomplished if all bonds of the corporation have

---

[3] Texas law states, "The existence of every corporation may be continued for three years after its dissolution from whatever cause, for the purpose of enabling those charged with the duty, to settle up its affairs." A court may extend the period beyond three years if "it is necessary suitably to settle the affairs" (Texas General Corporation Law, Article 1389).

maturity dates? Can the corporation issue bonds with no maturity dates? Why or why not?

10. What are the principal reasons for recapitalization of preferred stock? Explain.

11. For what reasons are stock dividends declared?

12. What are the advantages in stock of a low or nominal par value compared to stock of a higher par value, if the total capital stock account is the same? What is the advantage in a nominal par value compared to no par stock?

13. What is a spin-off? Suggest circumstances under which it might be used.

14. Why might the directors and stockholders of a corporation wish to dissolve a corporation that is profitable?

15. Outline the steps in voluntary dissolution of a corporation.

Selected Readings

Barker, C. A., "Effective Stock Splits," *Harvard Business Review*, January-February 1956.

Fergusson, D. A., "Preferred Stock Valuation in Recapitalizations," *Journal of Finance*, March 1958.

Gordon, Myron J., *The Investment, Financing, and Valuation of the Corporation*, Richard D. Irwin, Inc., Homewood, Ill., 1962.

Jamison, C. L., "How Good Are the Reasons for Stock Splits?" *Michigan Business Review*, January 1956.

25

Treatment of Financial Failure

The problems of financial failure are a primary concern of the financial officer and other executives of a business in financial difficulty. The treatment of such failure is, however, not limited to those businesses in difficulties. Most businesses extend credit to customers as well as receive credit from suppliers and lenders of money. To any business that extends credit the treatment of financial failure is an important aspect of financial management. The financial manager must be aware of the legal rights of his company in the event that a customer to which credit has been extended goes bankrupt. He must be able to judge whether it is best for his company to accept an out-of-court settlement, or whether it is better to go through the time-consuming and uncertain process of bringing suit for nonpayment of debts. In the event that his company is involved as a creditor in a bankruptcy suit, the financial manager must know how to protect his company's position. He must be aware of the signs of impending failure of any companies to which his company has extended credit.

The principal officers of a company in financial difficulty must, first of all, be acutely aware of the early signs of approaching crisis, so that, if possible, they may change their policies to avoid financial failure. The financial officer must be able to reason well enough with creditors to secure concessions for his company to carry it through times of temporary financial stringency. If bankruptcy cannot be avoided, he must be aware of the rights of employees and owners and know whether it is best to seek dissolution or reorganization of the company.

There are various degrees of financial difficulty. A few companies may have a long history of annual profits, regardless of depression or prosperity. Others have had a history of unbroken annual losses. Between these two extremes lies the majority of firms. Some companies may occasionally experience an inability to pay their debts on time. The financial difficulties of other firms may be greater, requiring an agreement with creditors for an extension of the time during which payment of debts is to be made, or an agreement on a reduction in the amount due. Still others may have to be reorganized in bankruptcy, even though the goods they produce or the services they perform may continue uninterrupted. Some railroads have maintained an unbroken service although they have been reorganized in bankruptcy more than once. Statistics of business failure usually include only those cases that involve court proceedings or out-of-court actions in

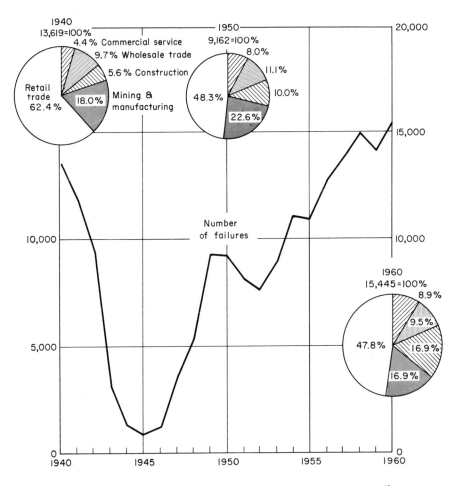

Fig. 25-1   *Total number of business failures, 1940-1960. Business failures represent a small portion of all business discontinuances, including only those cases involving court proceedings or voluntary actions in which creditors are likely to sustain a loss. The distribution of failures, which totaled 15,445 in 1960, has changed over the years, with retail trade establishments showing proportionately fewer failures and construction and commercial service businesses relatively more failures in 1960 than in 1940. (Source:* Dun & Bradstreet, Inc., *Road Maps of Industry,* No. 1314, copyright 1961 by National Industrial Conference Board, Inc.)

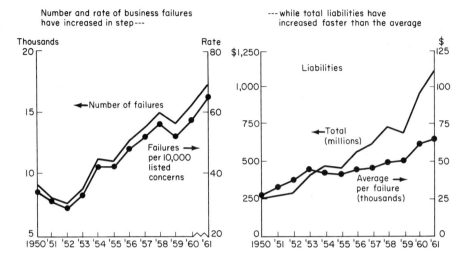

Fig. 25-2 *Increase of business failures and total liabilities, 1950-1961.* (*Source:* Dun & Bradstreet, Inc., *Road ,Maps of Industry,* No. 1396, copyright 1962 by National Industrial Conference Board, Inc.)

which creditors are likely to sustain losses. As a result, the number of failures each year exceeds the number reported in most statistics on failure.

During the depression of the 1930's, the annual number of business failures was high. The outbreak of World War II, however, sharply reduced the rate of failure in American business. In 1940, the number of failures was less than 14,000, dropping to about 1,000 in the year 1945. Since 1945, the number of failures has been on the rise, interrupted by a decline during the Korean Conflict, but rising again since 1953. In 1960, the number of business failures was in excess of 15,000.

The proportion of the total number of business failures classified according to different areas of business activity has changed during the last twenty years. In 1940, almost two-thirds of all business failures took place in retail trade. In 1950 and again in 1960, retail trade accounted for slightly less than half of the total number of business failures. This is shown in Fig. 25-1. Figure 25-2 shows the number of business failures from 1950 to 1961 and the rate of business failures per 10,000 firms. Both have increased in about the same proportion.

CAUSES OF FAILURE

Financial failure is generally defined as the inability to pay debts in full when due. Such a condition rarely develops suddenly. Rather, it is one of the final stages in a period of declining financial fortunes of a company. Usually, there are earlier signals that indicate the approach of the inability to meet debts. One such signal, which immediately alerts the credit manager of a company selling to customers on credit, is the failure of a customer to take cash discount in paying its bills. As was discussed in Chapter 7, the cost to a customer in terms of interest per annum of a failure to pay invoices within the cash discount period is so great that it constitutes strong evidence of financial difficulty. Other signals of approaching financial failure are the inability to maintain adequate inventories, to keep equipment in repair, and to retain capable employees. In a corporation the failure to pay dividends on preferred stock is generally an indication of financial difficulty. A cut in the dividend rate on common stock or the failure to declare dividends on common stock on several successive regular payment dates may alert creditors to give stricter attention to extension of

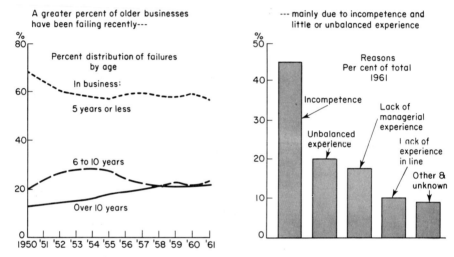

Fig. 25-3 *Age distribution and reasons for business failures, 1950-1961.*
Source: Dun & Bradstreet, Inc., *Road Maps of Industry,* No. 1396, copyright 1962 by National Industrial Conference Board, Inc.)

credit to the company, but does not necessarily indicate impending failure. In any case these are symptoms and not causes of financial failure. The causes are generally complex, deep-seated, and in particular cases sometimes difficult to identify. The failure of particular concerns may be caused by forces beyond the control of the company's officers. In other instances failure may be identified with particular policies or decisions made by company officers. In a few cases a single cause is dominant, but mostly the causes are many. The reasons for failure of a particular company can usually be divided into principal causes and contributory or minor causes. In some industries certain hazards are important factors in the failure of businesses that may be unimportant in other industries.

It is a commonly accepted belief that newly organized businesses are more likely to fail than older businesses. However, the failure rate among recently organized businesses has been declining in recent years. Although businesses less than five years old that fail comprise most of the failures—

as is shown in Fig. 25-3—the failure rate among new businesses has shown a declining trend. On the other hand, the failure rate of businesses older than ten years has been slowly increasing since 1950.

The reason for business failures can be classified in a number of ways; one of them is shown in Fig. 25-3. For 1961, this classification gives primary importance to incompetence as a cause of business failure. Unbalanced experience and lack of experience are other reasons given in the analysis in Fig. 25-3. Incompetence and inexperience are certainly found to some degree in every failure of business. The designations are, however, broad. There are often other factors that should be considered in determining causes of business failure. In our analysis of these causes, factors beyond the control of business managers as well as the quality of management itself will be covered.

Competition Under our economic philosophy, competition is the dominant regulating force modifying and adapting production and distribution to conform to the changing demands of consumers. Those companies that produce a superior product, sell at a lower price, provide better service, or in other ways better satisfy their customers, find the demand for their products and services increases. Those companies making an inferior product, at a higher price, providing poorer service, or in other ways not meeting the desires of customers, find their sales declining. In this way, competition is expected to shape production and distribution to the best interests of consumers. This assumes, of course, that competition among businesses is based largely upon quality, price, and service. It also assumes that the average consumer is a capable and discriminating judge of the thousands of products and services he purchases each year. It is beyond the scope of this book to discuss the effectiveness of competition in warranting the faith placed in it as a protector of consumer welfare.

In a number of industries competition appears largely to be in styling or in the intensity of advertising. In some industries, competition, whatever its form, is intense; in others, it is on a "gentlemanly basis." In some industries, competition is restricted by governmental regulations demanded by the companies in the industry. In classical economic theory, competition weeds out the inefficient and rewards the efficient producer. Since one of the aspects of depression is an increase in business failures and another is a decline in business activity, during depressed periods a smaller volume of business must be shared by the same number of competitors. Since no management passively accepts a decline in sales, a decline in total industry sales generally intensifies competition in an industry. Those companies in a strong competitive position can survive; those in a weak competitive position are likely to fail. Thus, competition is one of the underlying causes of business failure.

Business Cycles During the declining phase of the business cycle, business activity becomes slower. To resist falling sales, each company is likely to

intensify its efforts to combat the decline in orders. As stated before, competition tends to increase during the falling phase of the business cycle.
Defects in product design, personnel policies, inventory practices, pricing
policies, and other aspects of business management are likely to become
more apparent. Pressure on management increases. Although one could
not blame competition or the business cycle for a business failure where
management policies were found to be weak, one can conclude that depression subjects business decisions to a severer test than in prosperous times.
If the prosperity phase of a business cycle is long, the managements of many
businesses tend to become a bit lax and "soft." If the management of a
company can foretell the onset of a depression, the company can adjust its
policies and strengthen its financial condition as a ship captain prepares
his ship in anticipation of a storm. Depressions are, however, very difficult
to predict, and management can be overcautious as well as reckless.

Changing Public Demand A changing consumer demand creates both an
opportunity and a hazard for businesses. It tests the sensitivity of businessmen to shifts in consumer desires and the speed with which they can adapt
their product or policies to satisfy the changes in demand. During the last
half of the 1950's, there was a substantial increase in consumer demand for
smaller, lighter cars. American Motors Company, by pushing the sale of
its "compact car," and importers of smaller European cars, increased their
sales rapidly during this period. The Ford Motor Company, made a decision in 1955 to produce a new car to be called the Edsel. Designed as a
large, heavy car, the Edsel was first sold in 1957. It was a failure from the
start, because sales fell far below the point necessary to return a profit on
the venture. Before the Edsel was finally eliminated from the line of Ford
cars, the Ford Motor Company had absorbed losses of over $450 million.
This was the cost to the company of incorrectly estimating consumer demand in 1955. In response to the demonstrated demand for smaller cars,
the Ford Company, General Motors, and Chrysler Corporation introduced
a line of compact cars in 1960 and earned substantial profits from the sale
of these cars. A weaker company than the Ford Motor Company could not
have survived the error made in 1955 in forecasting the public demand for
cars. Many other companies have failed to adapt to changing public taste
and have disappeared as a result.

Natural Catastrophies Catastrophies of nature, known in law as "acts of
God," are responsible for some business failures. Included in this category
are fires, tornadoes, hurricanes, floods, earthquakes, and landslides. Insurance is available for most of these hazards, but the coverage might not
be adequate. Furthermore, insurance might cover the cost of damage to a
building caused by earthquake or fire, but may not cover the loss in sales to
the company resulting from the interruption in production caused by the
damage to the building.

    Another hazard, associated particularly with small businesses, is the injury to a business resulting from the death of a key member of the firm. To reduce this hazard, a life insurance policy is often taken out by the company, with the company paying the premium and being named as beneficiary, so that compensation may be received to offset partly the loss to the firm during the period of transition to new management. Life insurance of this type is found both in corporations and in unincorporated businesses.

Acts of Government An act of government may be a primary or a contributing cause of the failure of a company. A court award of damages for injury as a result of a product defect, patent infringement, or violation of antimonopoly laws may be so large as to contribute to the failure of the enterprise. The lowering of tariff barriers reduces government intervention in business and increases competition in the industry. The results are generally beneficial to consumers, but the increase in competition may be a contributing factor to the failure of the weaker companies in the industry.[1] The passage of acts by government may cause previously legal activities to become illegal. The passage of the Eighteenth Amendment to the Constitution made the beverage alcohol industry illegal. Some breweries and distilleries shifted to the production of other products. Others claimed that the passage of the amendment caused the failure of their companies. The awarding of government contracts may save a company from imminent bankruptcy, and the failure to get a government contract may be a contributing cause to the failure of other companies.

Labor Relations Unreasonable wage demands by a labor union may be one of the causes of failure of a company. If the union is strong and the company weak in bargaining, the wage costs of the company may rise to the point where it injures the competitive position of the company. The interruption in operations resulting from a strike, whether caused by unreasonable demands by labor or unreasonable demands by management, may result in loss of customers and eventual failure. A work stoppage in the plant of the supplier of an essential item may cause a shutdown in a company not directly concerned with the labor dispute. Nevertheless, the interruption in the supply of the essential material may be a contributing factor to the failure of the company.

Deficient Management A deficient management is probably responsible in some degree for all business failures. The factors discussed above, as being partly responsible for the failure of businesses, are faced by nearly all firms.

---

[1] In claiming that foreign competition causes failure of domestic businesses, the charge is generally exaggerated. Businesses do not welcome competition whether is is from domestic or foreign companies, since an increase in competition from whatever source forces management to "keep on its toes" in order to survive. Vigorous competition is the cornerstone of the philosophy of free enterprise. Companies that demand government interference to restrict competition indicate to that extent their lack of faith in free enterprise as an effective regulatory force when applied to their industry. In some instances, this may be warranted. In many instances, it represents a demand for government interference to protect inefficient business management.

Many companies not only survive intensified competition, a downturn in the business cycle, or changes in consumer demand, but, through foresighted, aggressive management policies, capitalize on these changes. Factors that contribute to the failure of some companies provide the opportunity for success of other companies. Success or failure is to a considerable extent a measure of management efficiency. Types of managerial deficiency are discussed briefly below.

Production. Deficiency in production may be caused by deficient product design, poor production techniques, or obsolete machinery. One of the reasons for the success of Andrew Carnegie in the steel industry was his policy of scrapping obsolete but usable machinery in favor of more efficient machinery. Layout in the factory may be faulty, supervision of workers may be inadequate, lighting might be bad, or quality control may be deficient.

Unwise Expansion. It was brought out in Chapter 23 that expansion entails problems for management. A company may operate successfully at a small scale but be unable to cope with the problems of large-scale operation or distribution. Management may pick the wrong time to expand its operations, a time when demand for the products of the industry are on the decline rather than on the increase. Management may expand into new lines of operation that are unfamiliar. Expansion may deplete the cash resources of a company, require borrowing, or otherwise create difficulties in financing. If expansion is not carefully planned, properly timed, or adequately financed, the expansion may result in disaster.

Purchasing. Purchasing policies are particularly important in the success of any retail or wholesale enterprise. Carefully selecting items, purchasing from dependable sources of supply, and buying at prices that will permit profitable resale are essential to the success of a mercantile company. In manufacturing industries purchasing is somewhat less important but may be a contributing factor to the failure of the company. In some manufacturing industries the cost of materials used is a large proportion of the cost of the finished product. In other industries the cost of the raw material is much less important. Obviously, where the cost of materials is significant, careful and efficient purchasing policies are essential.

Maintenance and Depreciation. The property of an enterprise must be kept in good condition in order to make efficient use of it. There must be adequate maintenance and repair, as well as provision for depreciation and obsolescence. Failure to do so may result in distribution of cash representing earnings that are nonexistent under proper accounting procedures.

Inventory Policy. Inventory management, like purchasing, is of particular importance to companies in the merchandising field. If inventory is too large, there is the danger that it may move slowly with the additional possibility that items may go out of season or out of style before they can be sold. If inventories are too low, there may be inadequate selection available to customers, or delivery to customers may be delayed. In either case sales may be lost. Inadequate supervision of inventories may entail such severe losses, because of employee theft or pilferage by customers, as to be an important factor in failure. For manufacturing companies this problem may be somewhat less critical but is, nevertheless, important.

Selling. Failure is sometimes the result of ineffective sales policies. Whatever the method of distributing one's products the methods of generating sales must be carefully chosen and efficiently applied. If a company fails in attracting new customers and retaining old ones, it will soon go out of business. Where the demand for a product or service is elastic and competition in the industry is intense, successful selling techniques are essential to the continued existence of a firm.

Credits and Collections. The extension of credit by a company may be entirely too liberal and collection policies too lax. For small businesses, particularly retail stores, the desire to increase sales may lead management to an unwise expansion of accounts receivable and failure to collect accounts when due. A slow turnover of accounts receivable and a high rate of credit losses will cause financial strain to any company.

Too Much Debt. A company should borrow only an amount within the capacity of the firm to repay without strain on the finances of the company. However, it is sometimes very difficult to determine capacity to pay. In addition an amount of debt well within the capacity of the company to carry during good times may be excessive if business conditions take a turn for the worse. Payment of interest and principal must ordinarily be made regardless of the financial fortunes of the company. To avert failure, therefore, management must take into consideration the possibility that sales may decline, expenses mount, or other developments occur to make it difficult to meet payments on debts. Receipts and expenditures of cash must be carefully budgeted so as to make provision for meeting interest and principal payments when due. Poor planning to meet debt payments and excessive indebtedness are two important causes leading to business failure, particularly among smaller concerns.

Dividend Policy. It is characteristic of most companies to pay out only a portion of the net earnings generated by operations. If a conservative dividend policy is followed, a company may be able to maintain a regular rate of dividend payments during periods of low activity as well as during periods of high activity. In periods of low activity there might be a temptation to maintain dividend payments that would have been conservative in the past but become dangerously high in the face of a decline in earnings that proves to be permanent. If a company is held by a few stockholders, the payment of excessive dividends in the face of declining earnings may be fraudulent, if such disbursement prevents the company from meeting debt payments on time.

OUT-OF-COURT SETTLEMENT OF CREDITOR CLAIMS

The primary concern of a creditor in dealing with a company in financial difficulties is to secure full payment of the debts owed to the creditor. If it is not possible to collect payment when the debt is due, the concern of the creditor is to reduce his loss to a minimum. Under the terms of most loan contracts and credit agreements, the failure to pay interest or principal when due permits the creditor to sue the debtor for payment. It does not follow, however, that it is always to the advantage of the creditor to sue. Court actions usually involve delay, expense, and uncertainty. For these reasons, it is often better for a creditor to secure an out-of-court agreement if this can result in a reasonable settlement. Out-of-court arrangements between debtors and creditors generally take one of three forms: extension, composition, or creditors' committee.

Extension   Where there are few creditors and the debtor company is small, an *extension* of the payment terms is frequently used. Generally, all the creditors will arrive at a common understanding as to the terms of the extension permitted the debtor, so that no creditor will be favored over others. To be binding, the agreement must be written and signed by all the creditors. If any creditor refuses to sign the extension agreement, he is not forced by law to do so, and the extension is not binding on him. Creditors with relatively large amounts owing may permit the debtor to pay in full those claimants having a small amount unpaid, so as to prevent the small claimants from upsetting the extension agreement by instituting suit in court for repayment. In order to secure the acceptance of the agreement by the creditors, interest payments may be added to the principal due in those cases where the credit originally extended did not include interest. Suppliers to a company typically make sales on a credit basis on which interest is not charged, although often an inducement for immediate payment in cash is made in the form of a cash discount. If such creditors are to accept a delay in payment beyond that allowed by the credit terms, interest is often added. Another inducement to accept an extension is the pledging of specific assets as security on debts previously unsecured.

If the financial difficulties causing the default in payment by the debtor are considered to be temporary, a simple extension of time often proves the most satisfactory solution. It is seldom practical, however, for a debtor dealing with a large number of creditors, such as a corporation unable to meet payments on a bond issue held by many bondholders. There have been occasions where corporations unable to meet the payment of principal on an issue of bonds have offered an exchange of bonds of a later maturity in lieu of cash payment for the maturing bonds. As an inducement the new bonds might carry a higher rate of interest or additional security or both. If the corporation is successful in retiring most of the maturing bonds by means of such an exchange, it may be able to pay off in cash those bondholders refusing to accept the exchange. Since the extension agreement is a voluntary one, bondholders unwilling to accept an extension offered by the corporation have a legal right to sue for immediate payment of bonds overdue.

Compositions If it appears that an extension is not sufficient to solve the inability of a debtor to meet maturing obligations, a composition might be used. A *composition* is a voluntary acceptance on the part of the creditors of a stated percentage of the debt owed each of them in full settlement of the debt.[2] As in the case of the extension, the appeal of the composition to creditors lies in the belief of each creditor that he will receive a larger percentage of the debt owed him than he could hope for in a bankruptcy settlement. Since the composition involves not just a postponement of payment in full of the debt but also a reduction in the amount to be paid, the acceptance by creditors of a composition agreement depends upon their conviction that the financial difficulties of the debtor are not temporary.

In most compositions the reduction accepted by each creditor is a uniform percentage of the debt due. In some cases, however, there may be an unwillingness on the part of certain creditors to accept the uniform reduction. If these creditors have claims in small amounts, perhaps less than $100 each, the creditors having larger amounts owing to them may accept a composition in which creditors with claims of less than $100 each will be paid in full, and all amounts in excess of $100 owed to each creditor will be settled for 70 per cent, 75 per cent, or some other percentage. Creditors with small amounts owing them will sometimes exploit the desires of the larger creditors to conclude a composition agreement by insisting on full payment of the small amount owing to them.

A composition may be suggested originally by the debtor upon realization of his inability to pay the full amount of his debts due. In other cases the initiative may rest with one or more of the creditors, usually those having large amounts owing to them. Sometimes a loan officer of a commercial bank, holding an overdue note of a debtor, will draw up a composition agreement. The composition, like the extension, is confined mostly to small companies dealing with a small number of creditors. Because of the difficulty of getting agreement from a large number of creditors, such as a group of bondholders, a composition is not often attempted in the case of a large debtor corporation.[3]

The composition agreement may provide for an immediate payment of cash. For example, if the settlement is to be 60¢ on the dollar, each creditor may receive immediate payment in cash of 60 per cent of the loan owed by the debtor. A debtor company in difficulties, however, is generally short

---

[2] If a debtor negotiates with a single creditor an acceptance of a portion of the debt owed the creditor as full settlement of the debt, the agreement is called an *accord*.

[3] An exception is the composition involving the Studebaker-Packard Corporation in 1958 with three insurance companies and twenty banks, where debts totaling $22 million were settled by payment from Studebaker-Packard of $16,500,000 in preferred stock.

of cash.   If such is the case, the composition settlement may provide for an immediate payment in cash of a stated percentage of the outstanding debt and the signing of short-term notes by the debtor, maturing at different intervals in the future, in payment of the balance in the composition settlement.   Such a settlement combines the extension and the composition in one agreement.   The willingness of creditors to accept an extension in combination with a composition depends, obviously, upon the confidence creditors have in the ability of the debtor to pay the notes maturing in the future when they become due.   If it seems likely that the debtor company will be in worse condition in the future than it is at the present, creditors may prefer to take a smaller amount of cash in full settlement of their claims than a larger amount in the form partly of cash and partly of notes maturing in the future.

Creditors' Committees   If the creditors feel that the inability of a company to meet its debts is caused largely by management weakness, they may feel that an extension or a composition is not the best solution to the problem. In such a situation a creditors' committee may be formed for the purpose of rehabilitating the company and putting it back into profitable condition. As in the case of the extension and the composition, the use of a creditors' committee is most likely to be successful if the number of creditors and the business are both small.   The owners of the company in financial difficulties are asked to turn over the operation of their business to the creditors' committee or to a manager selected by the committee for a specified period of time.   The agreement may provide for a period stated in terms of a definite number of months or one to end when the overdue debts are paid. Since the alternative to acceptance of a creditors' committee arrangement is usually the instituting of bankruptcy proceedings in court, the owners of a business in financial distress generally prefer to turn over management of the enterprise to the temporary committee to avoid the possible permanent loss of the business through reorganization or liquidation in bankruptcy. If the business is unincorporated, an agreement signed by the proprietor or the partners and the principal creditors is the basis for the creation of the creditors' committee.   If the business is a corporation, the usual procedure is for the owners to deposit their stock with the creditors' committee under a voting trust agreement.   By this means the creditors' committee is assured of effective control of the corporation.

The creditors' committee may represent all the creditors of the company or only the principal ones.   In the latter case the committee usually seeks an extension or composition of the claims of the remaining creditors. Failing that, the committee may liquidate the debts owing to the remaining creditors by payment in full, even if this requires the extension of an additional loan to the company.   Such a liquidation of the small debts is often necessary to prevent the creditors holding claims of small amounts from precipitating bankruptcy proceedings by demanding immediate payment.

One of the first acts of the creditors' committee may be to appoint one of its members as manager of the debtor company. If a commercial bank is one of the principal creditors represented on the committee, an officer of the bank frequently is selected for this responsibility. An alternative is for the committee to hire a management consultant or other person with recognized managerial ability and experience in the line of business of the debtor company. Usually the first step taken by the manager is a complete audit of the affairs of the company and a critical examination of the business policies followed by the owners. Generally this results in an overhauling of business policies, an elimination of wasteful procedures, possibly a reduction in the number of workers employed, and an attempt to institute measures to increase sales. In short, the new manager seeks to improve the efficiency of the company. If the business is fundamentally sound, the improvements instituted by the new manager should put the company on the road to profitable operations. If the existence of the firm serves no economic function in the community, this should become obvious to the creditors' committee after a short period of operation under the new manager. If the latter is the case, the committee may conclude that the only solution is to liquidate the firm before continued unprofitable operations further deplete the assets of the company.

The use of creditors' committees to rehabilitate distressed businesses was frequently used in the first depression following World War I (the years 1920-1922). The creation of creditors' committees were usually sponsored by one or more commercial banks holding overdue notes of the distressed company. An officer of the bank was usually selected as manager of the company during the process of rehabilitation. The amendments to the Bankruptcy Act that were made during the depression of the 1930's provided speedier and more satisfactory solutions to financial distress than were available through legal means in 1920. As a result the use of creditors' committees has been less frequent in recent decades.

One illustration of the use of a creditors' committee came to the attention of the author during the 1950's. An automobile agency organized as a corporation and owned in full by three stockholders, who also constituted the board of directors and the chief officers, was unable to meet payments on debts. The apparent cause of the financial difficulty of the corporation was the inability to sell enough vehicles to meet all expenses, and the chief reason for the low level of sales was the intensive competition of older and better established automobile agencies in the city. The number of the corporation's creditors was small, one of the principal ones being a commercial bank. A creditors' committee was formed to take over management of the corporation until such time as the overdue debts were paid. The three owners of the corporation agreed to the temporary surrender of their control, inasmuch as the choice they faced was management by the creditors' committee or bankruptcy. An officer of the commercial bank was selected by the committee as manager of the company. The three owners continued to work at the agency in their capacity as officers of the company, but all actions taken by them were made subject to approval by the manager. Under the creditors' committee agreement, the manager collected compensation for the time he spent on the affairs of the company.

After eliminating certain weaknesses and inefficiencies, the manager sought a solution to the principal cause of the financial difficulty of the firm, which was the small gross income. It was soon determined that there was no immediate improvement likely to the low level of sales. The agency had been recently established, was not in a good location of the city, and was not franchised to sell as wide a variety of vehicles as most of the other automobile agencies carried. Because efforts to increase the volume of sales appeared to have no early solution, the manager sought other means of increasing the income of the corporation. Through the connections that his bank had with government agencies in the area and through the personal acquaintanceship of the officers of his bank with the commanding officer of a large airbase operated by the United States Air Force, the manager was able to secure for the corporation a contract for repair and maintenance of trucks used at the airbase. This contract proved very profitable. The income from the repair services made it possible for the corporation, after the passage of several months, to pay off in full all the overdue debts. Having restored the corporation to a sound financial position, the manager turned over control of the corporation to the owners. The creditors, having been paid in full on their overdue debts, dissolved the committee. The corporation had been rehabilitated, the creditors had been paid in full on the debts owed to them, and a customer for future credit had been kept in being.

BANKRUPTCY LEGISLATION BEFORE 1938

The Bankruptcy Act of 1898 Prior to 1898, except for three brief periods, there was no federal bankruptcy statute. The Bankruptcy Act of 1898 provided for a uniform treatment of persons and companies unable to meet their debts. The Act provided means for liquidation of the assets of bankrupt companies and persons. However, it was obvious that the liquidation of railroads, public utility companies, and other business firms providing services to the public would severely injure the welfare of the general public in attempting to meet the debt obligations of the company. In such cases the court modified the common law principles applying to insolvency by developing a body of rules under which companies could continue in existence to provide services for the public while a plan of reorganization was worked out under court supervision. Such reorganizations were called equity reorganizations.

In an equity proceeding the court appointed a receiver to operate the property of the company during its reorganization. The receiver was responsible for the efficient operation of the company, but did not participate in the reorganization. Plans for reorganization were drawn up by the owners of the company, the officers and directors of the company, or investment bankers that had previously distributed the issues of the company. Stockholders, bondholders, trade creditors, and others having an interest in the reorganization plans generally formed protective committees to guard their interests. In some cases many protective committees were organized. Rather than have each protective committee draw up its own plan of reorganization, favoring the particular group represented by the committee, the court usually organized a reorganization committee, composed of one or two representatives from the protective committees, to draft a plan of reorganization. The reorganization plan was submitted to the court for examination and approval. It was the responsibility of the court to see that the plan was fair and equitable to all parties concerned. If this was the case, the assets of the bankrupt company were "sold" to the company created by the plan of reorganization. Payment was made not in cash but in securities issued by the newly created corporation. These securities were then distributed according to the reorganization plans to the owners and various classes of creditors of the bankrupt corporation. The claims made by the members of the protective committees and of the reorganization committee to the courts for payment for services rendered were often excessive, and depleted further the liquid assets of the company, even though the courts might reduce the amounts claimed. The main weaknesses of equity reorganizations were as follows:

1. *Delay.* The process of reorganization was lengthy, in some cases running more than a score of years.

2. *Scattered authority.* If equity proceedings were brought under state courts and the property of the bankrupt company was located in several states, a separate reorganization was required in each state where property of the debtor was located. In equity proceedings instituted in a federal court, separate actions had to be undertaken in other federal courts if the property of the bankrupt company was located in more than one federal court district.

3. *The power of the protective committees.* The courts had little control over the formation and actions of the protective committees. In some cases the number of members on each committee was higher than necessary to protect the group represented by the committee, and, in many cases, it appeared that the principal interest of the members serving on such committees was to enrich themselves by demanding high fees rather than protecting the group they represented.

4. *The reorganization plan.* The reorganization committee had extensive authority in drawing up the reorganization plan. Although the courts could rule a plan unfair, it had almost no authority to participate in drawing up the plan. Rather than continue reorganization proceedings indefinitely, courts sometimes accepted reorganization plans that favored some groups to the detriment of others concerned with the reorganization. The

committee was sometimes dominated by one group, such as the bondholders or the stockholders of the bankrupt company.

5. *The right of dissent.* Any persons dissenting from a plan of reorganization were completely without restriction in doing so. The courts could not force dissenters to accept a plan considered fair by the court. Often it was necessary to pay off in full the claims of dissenters in order to put into effect a plan of reorganization.

6. *Raising funds for operations during the period of reorganization.* To continue the services needed by the public during the reorganization of a company, it was usually necessary for the receiver to borrow money from time to time. Funds were raised by the receiver by issuing receivers' certificates to which the court could grant priority. Since the court did not have clear authority to subordinate the claims of old creditors to those of new creditors, the granting of priority to the purchasers of receivers' certificates was based on dubious legality.

7. *Excessive cost.* The number of protective committees, the number of members on each committee, the number of lawyers providing advice and services, and the delay in drawing up and putting into effect reorganization plans resulted in excessive costs of reorganization under equity. The authority of the court was weak in reducing the expenses of reorganization except in those cases where claims for payment of services were clearly exorbitant.

Amendments During the Early 1930's   The increase in the number of bankruptcies in 1930 and 1931 emphasized the weaknesses of equity reorganization procedures. To correct these weaknesses, Congress enacted a series of amendments to the Bankruptcy Act of 1898. In March 1933, an amendment, known as Section 77, was designed for the relief of railroad corporations. It provided that a federal district court could accept a petition from a railroad claiming inability to meet its debt obligations and assume custody, if the petition were approved, of the property of the railroad located both within and without the federal court district. A trustee appointed by the court was given authority to bring in a plan of reorganization within six months, unless the court granted an extension of time. The new law provided that the reorganization plan be submitted to the Interstate Commerce Commission for approval, and gave to the court specific authority to impose upon a dissident minority a reorganization plan accepted by a large majority of the creditors.

In June 1934, Congress passed a similar amendment known as Section 77B, providing, with a few exceptions, reorganization procedures for corporations other than railroads. Reorganization procedure under Section 77B was parallel to that under Section 77, except that approval by the Interstate Commerce Commission was not required. Weaknesses in the new amendments soon became evident. Congress, therefore, requested the Securities and Exchange Commission, created in 1934, to study the bankruptcy legislation in force at the time and to suggest possible improvements. Most of the changes suggested by the S.E.C. were enacted by Congress in 1938. The bankruptcy legislation of 1938 applying to business corporations was entitled Chapter X and Chapter XI of the Bankruptcy Act, but the legislation was more popularly known as the Chandler Act. Chapters X and XI constitute the legislation under which reorganization of companies other than railroads have been accomplished since 1938, and will be discussed below.

BANKRUPTCIES OF PROPRIETORSHIPS AND PARTNERSHIPS

The failure of proprietorships and partnerships generally involves a smaller number of creditors and a smaller dollar amount of claims than is involved in the failure of a corporation. The advantages of handling such failures by friendly action between creditors and debtor are particularly important where the visible assets of a company constitute a relatively small dollar value. A court administered proceeding in bankruptcy is expensive, including court costs, lawyers' fees and those of other experts. It happens all too frequently that the amount realized from the liquidation of the property of a small company is less than the total expenses of the bankruptcy proceedings. In such a case, the creditors get nothing. It is for this reason that bankruptcy is initiated by creditors only as a last resort in the case of small debtor firms.

Either the bankrupt company or the creditors may initiate bankruptcy proceedings. A bankruptcy proceeding initiated by the debtor is termed a *voluntary* bankruptcy. If the action is initiated by creditors, it is termed an *involuntary* bankruptcy. The debtor begins a bankruptcy proceeding by filing with the federal court serving his district a petition indicating that he is unable to meet his debts and requesting that the court declare him bankrupt. A petition from the debtor is not subject to dispute by his creditors. In the case of voluntary bankruptcy, upon receipt of the petition from the debtor the court is required to declare him bankrupt. If the petition is initiated by creditors, the debtor will be served with a notice of the petition, and a hearing will be held by the court to determine whether evidence indicates that the debtor is in fact bankrupt. At the hearing the debtor is privileged to dispute the charge brought by the creditors and request that the court deny the allegation of the creditors. If the court decides that the evidence is sufficient to support the petition of the creditors, the court will overrule the objections of the debtor and declare him bankrupt.

If there are fewer than twelve creditors, any creditor or group of creditors having claims of $500 or more in excess of the fair value of specified security for the claim may file a petition for involuntary bankruptcy. If there are twelve or more creditors, the total outstanding debt of the debtor must be $1,000 or more, and the involuntary petition must be filed by at least three creditors having claims totaling $500 or more in excess of the fair value of security pledged for the claim. A petition for involuntary bankruptcy must state that an act of bankruptcy has been committed within four months prior to the time the petition was filed and that the total assets of the debtor are insufficient to meet the claims of creditors. The following list comprises the most common acts of bankruptcy:

1. The debtor conveyed, transferred, concealed, or removed property with intent to hinder, delay, or defraud creditors.
2. The debtor, while insolvent, transferred a portion of his property to a creditor with the intent of giving him preferred treatment over other creditors.
3. The debtor, while insolvent, permitted one creditor to obtain a lien through legal proceedings, and did not discharge the lien within thirty days or at least five days before the date set for the sale of the property.
4. The debtor made a general assignment for the benefit of creditors.
5. The debtor, while insolvent, permitted the appointment of a receiver or trustee to take charge of his property.
6. The debtor admitted in writing his inability to pay his debts and his willingness to be adjudged a bankrupt.

After the filing of the petition, the court, if it considers it necessary, may name a *receiver in bankruptcy* to take charge of the property of the debtor and operate his business until such time as the court dismisses the petition for lack of evidence of bankruptcy or declares the debtor bankrupt and appoints a *trustee*. In the latter case, the trustee takes over operation of the enterprise from the receiver.

If the debtor is adjudged bankrupt, the court will appoint a referee to administer the bankruptcy proceedings for the court. The *referee* is an officer of the court, serving an appointment running for several years, to administer bankruptcy cases for the particular court. Usually, the first action of the referee is to call a meeting of the creditors in the case, examine the validity of their claims against the debtor, and determine the financial condition of the debtor company. The creditors usually recommend an individual to act as trustee (they may, if they choose, nominate three trustees, and the court may appoint the three to act as a board of trustees in a particular bankruptcy case) to take over the property of the bankrupt company for continued operation or liquidation. If the person nominated by the creditors is acceptable to the referee, he will recommend that the court appoint the nominee as trustee. If the person nominated by the creditors for the position of trustee is unacceptable to the referee and to the court, or, if the creditors do not nominate any person, the referee or the court may select the trustee.

If a reorganization is chosen by the court, the trustee will supervise the drawing up of the plans. In the case of partnerships and proprietorships, however, the remedy sought is usually through liquidation. Title to the partnership assets or the assets of the proprietor pass to the trustee, who proceeds to convert them into cash, pay the costs of the bankruptcy case, and distribute the remainder to the creditors.

One of the principal disadvantages of the partnership as a form of business organization is that each of the general partners is financially responsible for the acts of the other general partners undertaken in the operation of the firm. In a partnership, each general partner has unlimited liability for the debts of the partnership. A partner, however, is not liable for any personal debts incurred by the other partners. If one of the partners becomes insolvent as a result of inability to pay personal creditors, these creditors may seek to collect from the partnership but only to the extent of the equity that the partner has in the firm.[4] In the event of the insolvency of a partnership, any creditor of the firm could seek payment for the amount owed to him from the assets of the firm or from the personal assets of any or all the partners. If the firm is being liquidated under bankruptcy proceedings or if partnership creditors and personal creditors file for payment at the same time, the rule of *marshaling of assets* must be observed. Under this rule, the personal creditors of each partner are accorded priority in their claims on the personal assets of each partner and a claim subordinated to that of the partnership creditors on the property of the firm. The creditors of the partnership are given priority in their claims on the assets of the firm and a claim subordinate to the personal creditors on the personal assets of the partners. Since a bankruptcy is instituted through a belief on the part of the debtor or the creditors of insufficient property to pay debts, it is very unlikely that the liquidation of the assets will realize a sum sufficient to pay in full all the claims to be met. Federal bankruptcy legislation provides the following priority of payment of claims in bankruptcy proceedings:

1. The cost and expenses of the bankruptcy proceedings, including court fees, reasonable payments to the trustee, referee, lawyers, and others assisting the court during the bankruptcy proceedings.
2. Wages, salaries, and other payments due to persons employed by the firm. The priority of this claim is limited to $600 per person and to wages and salaries earned within three months of the filing of the petition for bankruptcy.
3. Taxes.
4. Secured creditors. The priority is limited to the amount realized from the liquidation of the specific assets as security for each secured loan.
5. Rent due and unpaid on property. The priority is limited to rent

---

[4] The laws of some states require that before the personal creditors of a partner may seek recovery from the equity of the partner in the firm, the debts owed to the creditors of the firm must first be liquidated.

accrued within three months prior to filing the petition for bankruptcy.

6. Unsecured creditors.   Secured creditors are treated equally with unsecured creditors for that portion of the debt owed each secured creditor remaining after liquidation of the asset pledged as security for each secured loan.

In the unlikely event that after payment of all the claims listed above there should remain funds from the liquidation of the assets of the firm, the owner or owners of the firm would receive a distribution of the remaining funds.

The laws of the states specify certain property that is exempt from seizure and liquidation to satisfy debt.   Most states exempt the equity up to the maximum stated in the law in the homestead where the debtor maintains his residence.

A proceeding in bankruptcy relieves the debtor of obligation for payment of outstanding debts.   However, there are certain exceptions.   Only those debts that can be proven and that were contracted before the bankruptcy are liquidated in the bankruptcy proceeding.   If a creditor had no knowledge of the bankruptcy proceeding and did not have time to schedule his claims for examination as to their authenticity, the claim of the creditor is not extinguished by the bankruptcy proceeding, provided that the debtor had full knowledge of the existence of the debt at the time bankruptcy proceedings commenced.   This emphasizes the importance to a debtor of listing all outstanding debt obligations at the time that the bankruptcy proceedings are initiated.   Moreover, the following debts, unless they are paid off in full by the trustee, are not discharged by the bankruptcy action:

1. Taxes.
2. Unpaid wages or salaries earned within three months prior to the filing of a petition for bankruptcy.
3. Money paid by an employee to the owner or owners of the firm to insure adequate performance of the employee's responsibilities.
4. Debts created as a result of any kind of fraud or illegal activity by an officer of the firm acting on behalf of the firm.
5. Claims resulting from injury to the person or property of other individuals.
6. Claims resulting from obtaining any item of value through false pretenses or misrepresentations.

CHAPTER XI OF THE BANKRUPTCY ACT

Chapter XI was enacted for the relief of small companies, incorporated or unincorporated, and was designed to handle unsecured debts only.   This piece of legislation provides for an *arrangement* with creditors rather than for a formal organization or liquidation of the assets of the company.   The nature of such an arrangement involves either an extension or a composition or a combination of the two. The arrangements and compositions discussed earlier as examples of out-of-court settlement were voluntary. Arrangements under Chapter XI, on the other hand, are carried out under court authority. Although Chapter XI was designed for the relief of debtors, it was also intended to provide more equitable treatment for unsecured creditors than was sometimes experienced under simple compositions and extensions. It was adopted by Congress at the urging of the National Association of Credit Men.

Under Chapter XI the petition is filed by the debtor company and not by any of the creditors. Although the petition is ordinarily filed in the federal district court where the main office of the debtor company is located, it may be transferred to another district court if the convenience of creditors and other parties to the settlement can thereby be better served. The information contained in the petition filed by the debtor company must include the following:

1. The name of the company, address of the main office, and nature of the business conducted.
2. A statement that the company is insolvent or that it is unable to meet its debts when due.
3. An affirmation that bankruptcy proceedings have not begun under any other section of the bankruptcy laws.
4. An arrangement or plan for liquidation of debts drawn up by the owners or officers of the debtor company.
5. A statement or schedule listing completely all assets and all debts of the company.
6. A description of the type of business of the debtor including all contracts entered into by the debtor company.

The arrangement drawn up by the debtor may provide for equal treatment of all debts owed to each creditor, or it may set up a classification of claims against the company and provide for different treatment for each class. It may provide for a termination or modification of certain contracts entered into by the company. It may suggest a reduction in the amount of debt owed or an extension of time for payment of the debt or a combination of extension and reduction. After the debtor's petition has been filed, the court may permit the owners to continue operation of their business during the court's action, or appoint a receiver, a trustee, or a committee of the creditors to take over operation from the directors or owners. In most instances the court permits the directors or owners to continue the operation of the company after the filing of the petition. If, however, the creditors feel that they would be better protected through operation of the company by a court-appointed receiver or trustee or by a creditors' committee, they may petition the court to take such action. They may also petition the court to appoint an appraiser to make an independent appraisal of the assets of the debtor company.

The court, or the referee, if one is appointed by the court, calls meetings of the creditors and the debtor. At the first meeting the court or the referee usually examines the claims of each of the creditors to determine their validity. At one of the early meetings the arrangement suggested by the debtor is examined by the creditors. Changes in the plan proposed by the debtor may be demanded by the creditors. Any modifications suggested by the creditors are examined by the debtor, and may be accepted or rejected by him. If disagreements exist, they are generally settled by compromise. The arrangement finally worked out must be accepted by the debtor and both by a majority in number of the creditors and by creditors representing more than half of the debts outstanding. If the arrangement is unacceptable to a majority of the creditors and to the debtor, relief under Chapter XI is deemed to be a failure, and liquidation of the firm through bankruptcy proceedings is instituted.

If the plan suggested by the debtor in the original petition and modified in the meetings held between creditors and debtor is accepted by the debtor and by a majority of the creditors, the court must then examine the plan to determine whether it is feasible and fair to all parties concerned. If the court determines that the plan is equitable to all and feasible in operation, the plan is made binding on all creditors including any minority creditors that disapproved of the plan. The court states the time when the plan is to be put into effect, and when under the plan any payments are to be made by the debtor for disbursement to the creditors. Upon distribution of money, promissory notes, or other securities by the debtor to the court for distribution to the creditors, the court discharges the debtor from further liability for all debts or contracts covered by the plan. If, within six months following confirmation of the plan by the court, any creditor discovers an element of fraud in the preparation of the arrangement or concealment of property in any reports by the debtor, or any other irregularity, the creditor may petition to nullify the arrangement. In such an event, the court may order the reopening of action under Chapter XI or may declare the debtor bankrupt and arrange for liquidation of the assets of the debtor.

If only a few creditors are involved and if agreement between the debtor and all the creditors can be reached without much difficulty, an out-of-court settlement is generally preferable because it saves court costs and eliminates publicity unfavorable to the debtor. However, if agreement cannot be reached easily by the debtor with all his creditors, proceedings under Chapter XI offer an alternative to bankruptcy and liquidation, and is therefore generally sought by the debtor.

Although Chapter XI was designed for the relief of small companies, in recent years large concerns have used this Chapter to secure a court enforced arrangement with creditors. This development has disturbed the members of the Securities and Exchange Commission. The contention of the commission is that Chapter X of the Federal Bankruptcy Act gives shareholders of corporations more protection against loss than is afforded them under Chapter XI. Subject to the exceptions indicated below, under Chapter X the officers of a corporation are replaced by a court-appointed referee, and a financial audit is conducted by the court. Under Chapter X the company may be liquidated, sold as a unit, or reorganized. Under Chapter XI the officers of the debtor company in most cases remain in charge pending court proceedings, and the arrangement is originally drawn up by officers of the debtor company. The S.E.C. has the authority under the Federal Bankruptcy Law to recommend to the federal district court the dismissal of proceedings under Chapter XI and the institution of new proceedings under Chapter X. The recommendation is not binding upon the court, and in some cases is rejected by the court.

CHAPTER X OF THE BANKRUPTCY ACT

Initiation of Proceedings Chapter X provides a means for reorganization of corporations in which the public interest is involved through investment in stocks and bonds of the corporation. Corporations excluded from· the use of Chapter X include railroads, commercial banks, savings and loan associations, and municipal corporations. Initiation of proceedings may be voluntary or involuntary. If voluntary, a petition is filed in the name of the corporation with a federal district court. If involuntary, the petition is filed by at least three creditors having claims amounting to $5,000 or over or by a trustee representing bondholders. Most of the petitions filed in federal courts have been voluntary.

A petition from the corporation must state the name of the corporation, the nature of the business undertaken by it, a list of assets and liabilities, the amount and kind of each type of capital stock outstanding, and a statement that the corporation is insolvent. A petition from three or more creditors or from the trustee named in the indenture of a bond issue must give the name of the corporation, the nature of its business, and a detailed description of the act or acts of bankruptcy charged to the corporation. If the petition is received from creditors or a bond trustee, the court must serve notice on the corporation of the filing of the petition. The corporation is permitted ten days to file an answer. After receiving the petition and denial, if any, from the corporation, the court may appoint a temporary receiver to oversee operations of the corporation until the court has determined the validity of the petition from the creditors and the denial by the corporation. If the petition is initiated by the corporation or if the charge brought by the creditors is admitted by the corporation, the court may appoint a receiver to administer the property of the corporation until a trustee can be named by the court.

If the petition is approved, the court must appoint a trustee or trustees to take over administration of the property of the debtor from the receiver. The schedules of property of the corporation, lists of creditors and the claims of each, the list of stockholders, details of contracts undertaken by the corporation, and other information furnished by the corporation and by creditors are examined for their validity.

The Trustee   In cases where the indebtedness of the company is less than $250,000, the court may appoint an officer of the corporation, one of the creditors, or any other person who is considered by the court to be capable and reliable.   If the claims of creditors amount to $250,000 or more, the law requires the court to appoint a disinterested trustee.   Chapter X defines a disinterested trustee as one who has not been a creditor, stockholder, director, or underwriter of any distribution of securities for the corporation during a period of five years preceding the filing of the petition; nor may the trustee have been a director, officer, or employee of the company within two years of the filing of the petition.   To qualify as a disinterested trustee, there must be no evidence of any direct or indirect relationship between the trustee and either the debtor company, underwriter having dealt with the company, or creditor within the preceding five years.
    The duties of the trustee under Chapter X are as follows:

1. To gather all the information regarding the property, operations, liabilities, and financial conditions of the company and submit this information to the court, to the creditors, to the stockholders, and to the S.E.C.
2. To investigate the conduct of the directors and chief officers of the company for the purpose of discovering any fraud or illegal action that might have been taken, for the purpose of discovering if any legal action should be instituted against individual officers or directors.
3. To examine the plans for reorganization, whether there be one or several, submitted by creditors, preferred stockholders, or common stockholders.
4. To recommend to the court either the desirability of continued operation of the property of the company as a unit or the liquidation of the property and distribution of proceeds to satisfy the claims outstanding.
5. If, in the opinion of the court, it is to the interest of all parties concerned that the bankrupt company continue in operation, the trustee must present a plan of reorganization to the court.

The Protective Committee   As was noted above, under Chapter X the trustee has the primary responsibility for drawing up the plan of reorganization.   However, it is usually advisable for the general creditors, stockholders, and bondholders to form committees to aid the trustee in the preparation of the reorganization plan and to protect the interest of the groups they represent. They are known as *protective committees*. In most re-organizations under Chapter X, at least two protective committees are created, one representing the creditors and the other representing the stockholders. More, however, may be formed. In the case of the reorganization of a railroad or large industrial corporation, there may be outstanding several issues of bonds, different classes of preferred stock and common stock, and general creditors. The committee representing the common stockholders is generally formed by the directors of the corporation. The strategy of this committee during the preparation of the reorganization plan is largely a defensive one. It seeks to retain an interest for the common stockholders in the reorganization plan and, if possible, to retain voting control of the reorganized corporation. If this is not possible, the committee seeks to prevent the exclusion of the common stockholders from the reorganization plan. The bondholders' protective committee is usually formed by the investment banking house that distributed the issue. Its strategy is largely an offensive one. It is to seek as favorable a settlement for the bondholders in the reorganization plan as possible, and to seek exclusion of the stockholders from the reorganization plan when necessary. Although there is usually only one protective committee formed for each class of creditors or stockholders, there may in some cases be more than one. If, for example, a substantial portion of the common stockholders feels that the protective committee formed by the former directors of the company will not adequately protect their interests, a minority stockholders' committee may be formed independent of the stockholders' committee formed by the directors.

Any group of persons seeking to form a protective committee may do so.[5] The usual process of forming a protective committee is to announce in letters to each security holder (or creditor) or through advertisements in financial newspapers the formation of the protective committee and to request authorization from each person to represent him in the court proceedings. Security holders are generally requested to send in their securities to a designated bank or trust company for deposit under a trust agreement, an agreement giving power to the protective committee to act on behalf of the persons having deposited their securities. An alternative method is to send out forms designating the members of the protective committee as representatives for the group and request that they be signed and returned. They give a power of attorney to the members of the committee to act on behalf of the persons in the group. As soon as a committee receives the support of at least 50 per cent of the outstanding security, the committee seeks recognition by the court as a representative of the particular class of security holders. The agreement signed by each security holder authorizes the members of the committee to hire lawyers, to speak

---

[5] In the case of the railroad reorganizations, it has been unlawful since 1935 for any group to form a protective committee and seek the support of security holders until permission to do so has been obtained from the Interstate Commerce Commission.

for the security holders in all matters during the court proceedings, and to receive compensation for their services.

Because corporation bonds have tended increasingly in recent years to be held by institutions rather than by individuals, an institution having a substantial investment in bonds of a corporation will often send one of its own officers to act in its behalf during the court proceedings. If, for example, all the bonds of a particular issue are held by an insurance company, the company's own officers will represent its interests in court. If the insurance company does not own the entire issue but owns a substantial investment in a class of bonds, it may take the initiative in forming the protective committee for the bondholders, or, if a committee has been formed independent of the insurance company, the insurance company may prefer to have its interests protected by one of its own officers rather than by the protective committee.

The Reorganization Committee   Any of the protective committees may draw up a plan of reorganization. Sometimes several plans are drawn up by various committees and submitted to the trustee for consideration. If there are several protective committees representing a variety of classes of creditors and stockholders, a reorganization committee is often formed. The reorganization committee includes one or two members from each of the protective committees. This committee seeks to resolve the differences of interest of the various classes of security holders and creditors and to draw up a plan of reorganization that will have a reasonable chance of acceptance by all of the groups involved. If a reorganization committee is formed, the trustee will be an active participant in the deliberations of the committee, because the trustee is given the primary responsibility under law of drawing up the reorganization plans to be submitted to the court. However, the law does not restrict the court only to considering the plan of reorganization submitted by the trustee. In some cases the plan of reorganization prepared by the reorganization committee or the trustee will be considered unsatisfactory to the members of one of the protective committees. The dissenting committee may prepare a plan of its own and present it to the court for consideration.[6]   For a reorganization plan to be

---

[6] The following recommendation to the court by the Securities and Exchange Commission on two proposed plans of reorganization for the Inland Gas Corporation, Kentucky Fuel Gas Corporation, and American Fuel and Power Company (interconnected companies treated as a unit for the purpose of reorganization) illustrates this point: "The Commission's supplemental report concludes that the trustee's plan should not be approved since it would accord a smaller cash distribution to Kentucky Fuel Gas Corporation security holders than the security holders' plan. The security holders' plan is deemed to be fair and equitable subject to certain recommendations regarding preemptive rights for the new common stock. The security holders' plan is also deemed to be feasible provided it is revised to provide for court supervision of the use of cash working capital for distribution to security holders at the time of consummation and provided the terms and amounts of a possible bank loan are delimited within a suggested area in order to assure a sound capital structure" (S.E.C. Release No. 93, April 7, 1955, The Securities and Exchange Commission).

approved by the court, Chapter X provides that certain elements be included. The required provisions include:

1. A prohibition in the proposed charter of the reorganized corporation of the issuance of stock without voting power and assurance of equitable distribution of the power to elect directors among the classes of stock to be issued by the reorganized corporation.
2. The rejection of executory contracts except those in the public authority.
3. Provision for the execution of the reorganization plan so that the plan may be carried out with a minimum of difficulty.
4. A clear statement of the changes in the rights of trade creditors, bondholders, and stockholders provided in the reorganization plan held by such groups prior to the reorganization proceedings.
5. Provision for the payments of reasonable and just expenses of members of committees, legal firms, and others participating in the drawing up of the reorganization plan and for other expenses of the court proceedings approved by the court.

Although bargaining between protective committees may affect the treatment of various security holders, certain characteristics are common to reorganization plans. Those creditors having a preferred status by law, such as taxing agencies and employees, are usually paid off in full while the company is operated by the trustee during the bankruptcy proceedings. If the continued operation of the business requires additional funds, *trustee's certificates* are issued to raise the needed funds. These certificates enjoy whatever priority the court gives them. In order to raise money through the sale of trustee's certificates, it is usually necessary that the court give the purchasers of these certificates priority ahead of all claimants except the preferred creditors stated immediately above (the investment position of trustee's certificates was discussed in Chapter 13). Except in rare instances, holders of secured bonds are given priority in the reorganization plan over unsecured creditors. The holders of debenture bonds, trade creditors, and other unsecured creditors generally are required to accept some reduction of their claims. To the secured bondholders may be distributed a "package" containing a secured bond of the reorganized corporation, several shares of preferred stock of the new corporation, and several shares of common stock of the new corporation, all of which will generally total the par value plus unpaid interest of each secured bond. The reorganization plan might provide for the unsecured creditors a "package" consisting of a debenture bond, shares of preferred stock, and shares of common stock. This may add up to 60 or 70 per cent of the claim of the unsecured creditors. The number of shares of common stock distributed to the bondholders and unsecured creditors might constitute 10 per cent, 30 per cent, 50 per cent, or some other proportion of the issue of common stock of the reorganized corporation. The balance of the common stock might be divided between the holders of the preferred stock and common stock of the old corporation, with the preferred stock generally being given preferred treatment.

The reorganization plan might give an opportunity to the unsecured creditors to purchase a stated number of preferred or common stock of the reorganized company as a condition to receiving debentures of the new company. The court may rule that the common stockholders be eliminated entirely in the reorganization plan and that the preferred stockholders also be eliminated. Generally, however, they are not entirely eliminated. The common stockholders, having held 100 per cent of the common stock of the old corporation, may be given only 10 per cent of the common stock of the reorganized company. Another alternative is for the reorganization plan to provide an assessment of a certain amount of money to be paid by the common stockholders, or by the common stockholders and preferred stockholders, to qualify for inclusion in the distribution of the reorganized company's stock. The stockholders may not agree to such an assessment. However, if they do not, they may be excluded entirely from the reorganization plan.

The Securities and Exchange Commission   After the trustee has drawn up a reorganization plan, a hearing is held by the court. At the hearing the trustee's plan, and any plans that might be submitted by other groups, is examined by the court for fairness, equity, and feasibility. Objections to the trustee's plan are registered by any persons desiring to do so. Criticism of alternate plans, if any, are also heard. Following the hearing, the court submits the plan or plans to the Securities and Exchange Commission in all cases where the liabilities of the old corporation exceeded $3 million. The court may, at its discretion, also submit reorganization plans to the S.E.C. for comment where the liabilities are less than $3 million. The Securities and Exchange Commission examines the plans submitted to it and returns them to the court with recommendations, advising the court to accept, modify, or reject the plans. Although the court may accept or reject any or all of the S.E.C. recommendations, it generally gives them careful consideration.

Securing Approval from Creditors and Stockholders   After receiving the comments of the S.E.C. on the plan or plans for reorganization, the court gives its approval in most cases to one of the plans. In rare instances, more than one plan is given approval by the court. The plan or plans approved by the court as being fair, equitable, and feasible are transmitted together with the comments of the S.E.C. and of the court to the creditors and stockholders of the old corporation. If the plan approved by the court eliminates the old preferred and common stock entirely from consideration (by ruling that the corporation is insolvent), the plan is only submitted to the creditors for approval. If two-thirds of each class of creditors and at least 50 per cent of each class of stockholders approve the plan, the plan becomes binding on all creditors and stockholders. If the plan does not receive the required approval by each class of creditors and each class of stockholders, a new plan of reorganization must be drawn up. The process of creating a plan which is finally approved by all groups determined by the court to have authority to approve or disapprove may take many years in some cases. Plan after plan is drawn up and submitted for approval. In exceptional cases ten years or twenty years may pass before the reorganization is finally completed.

The court has the authority to deal with those creditors disapproving a plan of reorganization "by such method as will equitably and fairly provide such protection" as the court deems fair in each case.[7] The court has the power to treat dissenting creditors differently from those creditors assenting to the plan of reorganization, or it may treat assenting and dissenting creditors alike.

Following a favorable vote on the reorganization plan, the court calls a final hearing to consider confirmation of the plan. This provides a last opportunity for any person or group of persons to present criticisms or recommendations for modification. If the court is satisfied as to the fairness and workability of the plan, it will issue a final decree which discharges the company from all its debts existing at the beginning of the reorganization, terminates the rights of ownership of all stockholders as they existed in the old company, establishes the title of ownership of property in the name of the newly created corporation, and closes the proceedings.

Compensation for Services Rendered during Reorganization In some reorganization cases prior to 1938, the fees presented to the court by committee members, trustees, legal firms, and others were exorbitant. One example is the Paramount-Publix reorganization beginning in 1935 and lasting two and one-half years. The total fees presented to the court for services rendered during reorganization amounted to $3,500,000. Of the amount demanded, the court ordered payment (out of the estate of the bankrupt company) of $1,500,000, and disallowed the rest. The receivers and trustees were awarded $279,799, of which amount one person was paid $112,433. Six protective committees presented bills for $248,500, and were awarded $19,500 by the court. Forty-eight lawyers and law firms presented fees for services totaling $2,050,606 and for these the court ordered payment in the sum of $555,032.

Chapter X gives authority to pay fees and provide allowances out of the estate of the bankrupt corporation only if the services rendered have, in the judgment of the court, made contributions of value to the reorganization plan. If the court is uncertain as to the value of the contributions of a particular individual, it may refuse any compensation to him. It is, of course, difficult to determine the value in terms of money of the services

[7] Chapter X of the Federal Bankruptcy Act, Art. VII.

of each of a varied group of persons acting on committees and/or giving legal counsel or expert advice to the court or to the trustee in drawing up the plan. The court can, however, throw out claims that are patently unreasonable.

Comparison of Reorganization under Chapter X and Equity Receivership
The most important difference between reorganization under equity receivership and reorganization under Chapter X is the treatment of individuals rejecting the plan of reorganization. In an equity receivership individuals dissenting from the reorganization plan have the legal right to demand full payment of their claims. This has made it possible for some creditors, particularly if the amount of their claim was small in comparison to the total indebtedness of the company, to demand and get full payment of their claims, while creditors having larger claims received less than full payment. If under Chapter X the plan is accepted by two-thirds of each class of creditors, the court has the authority to force the settlement on dissenting creditors.

Under Chapter X the plan of reorganization is subject to greater scrutiny than reorganization plans under equity receiverships. The reorganization plan must be critically examined for fairness to all parties concerned and feasibility of operation by the trustee, the court, and the Securities and Exchange Commission. Reorganizations under Chapter X are more likely than are reorganizations in equity receiverships to be equitable to all parties and to be feasible in operation, thereby making it more likely that the company as reorganized will be profitable.

BANKRUPTCY UNDER STATE LAWS

Receiverships in equity are rarely brought in state courts. If a creditor brings suit against a debtor in a state court, a judgment may be rendered by the court against property of the debtor identified in the judgment. If the property listed in the judgment is insufficient to satisfy the claim of the creditor and if it is discovered that additional assets of the debtor are available, the court may appoint a receiver to liquidate the remaining assets to satisfy the claim of the creditor. However, the appointment of a receiver for the property of a corporation, partnership, or proprietorship by a state court constitutes an act of bankruptcy as defined in the Federal Bankruptcy Act. If any creditor of the company files a petition of bankruptcy in a federal court within four months after the appointment of the receiver by the state court, the federal court takes over exclusive jurisdiction of the proceedings and control of the company property. A state receivership may discharge a debtor from continued liability of existing debts, but only if all creditors agree to the discharge of the debts. If unanimous agreement of the creditors of a composition cannot be achieved either through proceedings in a state court or an out-of-court settlement, the only way in which the debtor may be discharged from further liability of his debts is through bankruptcy proceedings in a federal court under the Federal Bankruptcy Act.

Questions

1. Why is it that statistics on financial failure do not reflect the full extent of financial difficulties of businesses?
2. What are the signals that serve to alert a creditor that a customer is in financial difficulties?
3. Competition is one of the underlying causes of business failure. What is meant by this statement? How can competition be considered a useful force if it is a cause of business failure?
4. Explain how changing public demand, natural catastrophies, and acts of government sometimes contribute to business failure.
5. Deficient management is a factor in nearly all business failures. Discuss the forms that management deficiencies may take, in production, purchasing, selling, finance, and other areas of business operations.
6. What is the distinction between an extension and a composition? What are the advantages of each to the debtor? To the creditor?
7. What is a creditors' committee? How does it aid in the settlement of overdue debts of a business?
8. What did the Bankruptcy Act of 1898 attempt to accomplish?
9. What is an equity reorganization? Under what circumstances did it develop in the United States? Outline the steps in an equity reorganization. What were the weaknesses of equity reorganizations?
10. Why is it generally advantageous both for the creditors and the debtor to settle overdue claims out of court where the debtor is a proprietorship or partnership?
11. What acts of bankruptcy are most commonly committed?
12. Distinguish between the responsibilities of the receiver in bankruptcy, the trustee, and the referee.
13. Explain the rule of marshaling of assets as it applies to partnerships.
14. Under federal bankruptcy legislation, what is the priority of claims of various groups?
15. What is the procedure under Chapter XI of the National Bankruptcy Act? For what types of financial failures is it intended?
16. To what types of businesses is Chapter X of the National Bankruptcy Act applied? How are proceedings under this chapter initiated?
17. What restrictions are imposed by Chapter X in the appointment of a trustee? What are the responsibilities of the trustee under this chapter?
18. What are protective committees, how are they formed, and what functions do they serve in a reorganization?
19. Under what conditions is a reorganization plan referred to the Securities and Exchange Commission? What is the authority of the S.E.C. in such cases?
20. After a plan of reorganization has been prepared, what steps are required to put it into operation?

Selected Readings

"Business Failures," *Dun's Review and Modern Industry,* September 1961.

Deran, Elizabeth Y., *The Successful Shopkeeper: A Study of Retailer Survival in Nine Communities,* Bureau of Business and Economic Research, University of Illinois, Urbana, Ill., 1963.

The Failure Record Through 1958: A Comprehensive Failure Study, Dun and Bradstreet, Inc., New York, 1959.

Halzman, R. S., *Corporate Reorganizations,* The Ronald Press Company, New York, 1955.

A Handbook on Chapter XI of the National Bankruptcy Act, New York Credit and Financial Management Association, New York, 1955.

MacLachlan, James A., *A Handbook of the Law of Bankruptcy,* West Publishing Co., St. Paul, Minn., 1956.

Warren, Charles, *Bankruptcy in United States History,* Harvard University Press, Cambridge, Mass., 1935.

Part IX

Financing Small Business

26. THE FINANCING OF SMALL BUSINESS

26

The Financing of Small Business

THE PROBLEM OF SMALL BUSINESS FINANCING

THE ESTABLISHMENT of the Small Business Administration by Congress in 1953 was based on the assumption that a need existed for financial aid to small businesses that was not required by larger businesses. Since that time, there have been numerous studies attempting to show whether financial aid was particularly needed by small businesses, and, if it were needed, the extent of the needed aid. The existence of a number of competitors sufficient to provide vigorous competition in industry has been one of the important goals of government antimonopoly policy. It is for this reason that the government has shown concern for the small businessman.

Although the findings of the many studies on small business are perhaps not conclusive, they do appear to indicate that small firms generally have a harder time in securing short-term and long-term funds. Small business needs for working capital appear to be reasonably met. They tend to rely more often on bank loans and trade credit in financing working capital than do larger enterprises. Nevertheless, during periods when bank loans are in short supply, banks generally favor large borrowers over small ones. The period from 1955 to 1957 was a stringent one for short-term bank loans. During these years, bank loans to businesses with assets of $100 million or over increased by 66.4 per cent. During the same period, loans to business borrowers with assets less than $50,000 declined by 3 per cent.[1] It is an understandable tendency of banks to favor their larger business borrowers when the demand for loans seems to outstrip the supply of available credit. The larger businesses are generally older, better established, and often have a higher credit rating. Furthermore, it is cheaper for a bank to make a single loan in the amount of $100,000 than it is to make ten loans each in the amount of $10,000.

---

[1] *Financing Small Business*, Reports of the Federal Reserve System to Congress, 1958, p. 375.

While periods of stringency of short-term credit appear to injure smaller concerns more than larger ones, there is also considerable evidence that smaller businesses have greater difficulty in satisfying their demand for long-term funds than their demand for short-term funds. One writer states that "though personal savings of the small business enterprise are still available for investment, many small businesses complain that heavier personal and corporate income taxes and banking and securities regulations have subtly shifted the economic odds against them." [2] Another writer states "Changes in individuals' savings habits and investment preferences have restricted the scope of such traditional external sources of small business capital as the entrepreneurs' friends, debenture-capital investors, and business associates." [3] Small firms do not use the established securities market channels nearly as much as do larger enterprises in tapping investors' funds. (See Chapter 15 for an explanation.) For these reasons they must use the expedients treated in this chapter.

The conclusion can tentatively be drawn that small firms with possibilities for growth are hampered in their search for adequate long-term financing funds. "Small manufacturers with good credit records can usually get short term loans at a price. Intermediate loans are harder to get, and long term loans harder still." [4] Small companies appear to be more dependent upon retained earnings to finance increased investment in fixed assets. At the same time there is considerable evidence that the retained earnings available to most small businesses are entirely inadequate to meet the needs for expansion. Some small companies attempt to meet the need for long-term loans by expanding their trade credit and short-term borrowing from the bank. Whenever short-term loans are used for long-term financial requirements, a company is placed in a vulnerable financial position. If meeting the needs for long-term finance imposes greater problems on small rather than large businesses, it follows that small businesses need expert financial talent. Unfortunately, most small businesses are in a poorer position to hire financial talent than are larger businesses.

NONGOVERNMENT SOURCES OF FUNDS

Commercial Banks The commercial bank is the logical starting point for the small businessman in search for short-term, intermediate-term, or long-

---

[2] T. T. Murphy, "The Big Worry of Small Business: Money," *Fortune*, July 1957, p. 188.

[3] Charles Schmidt, "Meeting the Long-Term Capital Requirement of Small Business," *Journal of Finance*, Vol. 6, 1951, p. 143. Although studies of the availability of the long-term funds for small business in recent years are inadequate, one made shortly after World War II indicated that small companies, with 20 per cent of invested capital, 30 per cent of sales, and 21 per cent of profits during the years 1947 to 1948, accounted for only 11 per cent of the capital expenditures of all businesses during those years (William F. Buttler and Robert P. Ulin, "Business Needs for Venture Capital," *Harvard Business Review*, July 1950, p. 68).

[4] Murphy, *op. cit.*, p. 190.

term funds. A number of studies [5] indicate that the commercial bank is a primary source of loans for small businessmen.

The commercial bank is primarily a source of short-term funds. Banks do, however, make available a wide variety of types of credit, including accounts receivable loans, installment credit, loans secured by warehouse receipts, equipment loans, and loans secured by mortgages on real estate. Some banks, of course, are more aggressive than others in promoting the principle that the first place to turn for credit is the commercial bank. If a banker feels that he is unable to grant a request for a loan from a small businessman, he frequently expends considerable effort to locate a source of funds suitable to the requirements of his customer. The banker often contacts other loan agencies on behalf of his customers, provides recommendations and credit references for his customer, introduces his customer to other loan sources, and in other ways acts as a financial godfather to small businessmen. Efforts of this nature on the part of commercial bankers is not confined to small banks. As a matter of fact, some of the most aggressive programs particularly designed to aid small businessmen are found in the larger commercial banks.[6]

Commercial banks as a source of loans appear to be most important for construction firms, particularly with respect to long-term loans. Manufacturers, wholesale companies, and retailers depend to a lesser degree on bank financing than on other sources of credit. Furthermore, small firms that are already established and have a credit history of several years find bank financing more readily available than newer firms do, as Table 26-1 indicates.

Wholesalers and Suppliers For many small firms wholesalers and suppliers form a very important source of credit. The balance sheets of many small businesses show a current ratio of less than two to one, resulting in most cases from a large volume of accounts payable. Because the credit made available by both wholesalers and suppliers is tied in with purchases from them, these firms are usually more generous in their extension of credit than are the sources of cash loans. New enterprises in particular depend upon credit from wholesalers and suppliers in financing their purchases. Such credit is usually restricted to short-term credit. Intermediate-term financing, where needed to finance the purchase of equipment, is usually available

5 *Financing Small Business,* Economic Policy Series No. 35, National Association of Manufacturers, 1950, p. 25. This study shows that a representative sample of small businessmen obtained approximately 80 per cent of all their loans from their commercial bank. A later study by the National Association of Manufacturers in 1955 and studies by other organizations confirm the findings of the earlier Report.

6 Two outstanding examples discussed in *Dun's Review* of large commercial banks having programs especially designed to aid small businesses are the Bank of America in California and the National City Bank in New York. See E. B. George, "Can Small Businesses Get the Capital They Need?" *Dun's Review,* Supplement, October 1952, p. 118.

TABLE 26-1. DISTRIBUTION OF NUMBER OF LOANS OBTAINED BY SMALL BUSINESSES
BY SOURCE OF LOANS, IN PER CENT 1954

Type of Firm	All Sources	Source of Loans		
		Bank	Individual *	Other †
All Firms:	100.0	78.3	9.1	12.6
Established firms	100.0	79.3	8.4	12.3
Newer firms	100.0	68.8	15.7	15.5
Established Firms:				
Construction	100.0	83.1	3.5	13.4
Manufacturing	100.0	80.3	8.5	11.2
Wholesale trade	100.0	79.3	10.1	10.6
Retail trade	100.0	76.8	9.2	14.0
Newer Firms:				
Construction	100.0	70.5	13.4	16.1
Manufacturing	100.0	67.9	12.2	19.9
Wholesale trade	100.0	70.6	16.4	13.0
Retail trade	100.0	67.7	18.7	13.6

* Partner, corporate official, acquaintance, or relative.
† Insurance companies and other financial insitutions, suppliers, equipment dealers, factors, government, and others.
SOURCE: Office of Business Economics, U.S. Department of Commerce.

from suppliers, but long-term credit is not available from such sources except in rare cases.

Insurance Companies   Insurance companies are primarily a source of intermediate- and long-term financing for small businesses. As a source of long-term funds they rank second to the commercial bank, as Table 26-2 shows.

TABLE 26-2. SOURCES OF LONG-TERM FUNDS FOR SMALL MANUFACTURERS, 1954

Respondents' Views	Percentage Distribution
Respondents not in need of optional funds	38.5
Primary sources mentioned by respondents needing funds:	
Bank loans	20.8
Insurance companies	9.2
Retained earnings	9.0
Mortgages	7.9
Stocks and bonds	5.4
Loans from stockholders and friends	4.6
Other	4.6

SOURCE: National Association of Manufacturers, *Financing Small Business,* Economic Policy Series No. 70, 1955, p. 16.

Some insurance companies, including two of the largest, have consciously made an effort to expand their loans to small businesses.[7] For the most part, however, insurance companies prefer to confine their lending to large businesses. Furthermore, because of legal restrictions and the desire for safety, insurance companies generally restrict their loans to small businesses that are well established and have a relatively long history of successful operations.

Small Loan Companies and Industrial Banks Small loan companies and industrial banks exist primarily as a means of financing the purchase of consumer durable goods. Their operations have, however, expanded into business financing. Their rates are relatively high, and they usually are approached by small businessmen who find that they are unable to get adequate financing from less costly sources, and turn to small loan companies in desperation. For example, a company unable to get financing from banks or insurance companies, borrowed $200,000 from a finance company by mortgaging $600,000 of plant and equipment for a loan at an interest cost of 13 per cent per annum.[8]

Community Development Organizations Community development organizations exist primarily for the purpose of reducing unemployment in a community by expanding industry. They seek to accomplish this by attracting branch plants of existing companies to their localities and by aiding in the promotion of new companies. Most community development organizations are chartered as corporations with capital subscriptions by citizens of the community, with additional funds being raised chiefly through debenture issues. Some are operated to make a profit for their investors, while others are nonprofit companies. These organizations may receive loans from the Small Business Administration, if the purpose of the organization is to aid small businesses financially or otherwise. In addition, these organizations aid businesses in securing loans from local banks or other sources of funds.[9]

---

[7] The Metropolitan Life Insurance Company made an active effort to promote term lending to small business companies in participation with commercial banks. A program to implement this desire was announced on February 7, 1950, by the company. The maximum amount of each term loan to a particular business was fixed at $250,000. The life of these loans was to vary from three to ten years. Commercial banks were invited to participate in these loans in the amount of 10 per cent of each loan, with the Metropolitan Life Insurance Company assuming 90 per cent of each loan. The bank participating in each loan was to act as the loan agent, and to receive a fee for making the credit investigation and for handling the collections. Although several thousand commercial banks were informed of this plan, it enjoyed limited popularity. During the first seven years, only about 200 loans were actually extended. Other life insurance companies did not follow the example of this ambitious effort in term lending (Saul B. Klaman, *Life Insurance Company Financing of Small Business*, Federal Reserve System, Washington, D.C., 1958, pp. 522-523).

[8] Murphy, *op. cit.*

[9] In some states the number of such organizations is considerable. In Minnesota, for example, there were in 1962 approximately 200 community development corporations in existence. Approximately half were operated on a nonprofit basis, while the other half sought to earn a profit for their investors. As of the beginning of 1962, twenty-six loans had

Local Capital Pools and Chambers of Commerce   In some cities an informal organization of investors exists for the purpose of making investments in high risk but potentially profitable companies seeking to organize or locate a branch in the community.   Local chambers of commerce or banks sometimes act as intermediaries to bring together promoters of businesses willing to locate in a particular community if financing can be found to aid in the development of the business.   In return for the willingness to undertake a high risk, such investors generally insist on an investment in stock of the new corporation and a probability of growth at a rate of 15 to 20 per cent per annum.   Such investors are interested primarily not in generous dividends, but in the possibility of an increase in the value of their investment.

INVESTMENT BANKERS' AIDS TO SMALL BUSINESS

Most businessmen hope that their enterprises will grow.   Growth, however, takes money, and it may be difficult, particularly for a small company, to obtain the necessary financing.   It is paradoxical that a company with a good record of profits and prospects of a rapid rate of expansion may find its financial problems far more difficult than a company which is static and has poor prospects for profitable expansion.   In spite of a high rate of profit, the money left after payment of taxes is frequently much too small to meet the amount needed for expansion.   To finance expansion, money is needed to purchase additional equipment, to increase raw materials and other inventories, to enlarge the plant capacity, and to meet all the other necessities of an expanding enterprise.

Large corporations finance their expansion in most cases by selling securities to the general public.   Small firms, on the other hand, find this to be a costly means of securing funds.   Figure 15-2 shows the cost of selling an issue of stock of less than $500,000 to be between 25 and 30 per cent of the gross proceeds of the issue.   This cost covers the compensation and expenses of the investment banker.   If stock options are offered as part of the compensation of the investment banker, if he is given the privilege of naming one or two men to the client's board of directors, or if various restrictions on the financial freedom of the client corporation are included in the agreement between the corporation and the investment banker, the cost of distribution of a small issue might be reduced to between 15 and 20 per cent of gross proceeds.   The cost of flotation of bonds is generally less than for stock, regardless of the size of the issue.   According to the Securities and Exchange Commission, the cost of flotation of a small bond issue is between 10 and 11.5 per cent in most cases.   For example, a small corporation sell-

---

been made to the community development organizations in Minnesota by the Small Business Administration (Harold W. Stevenson, *Sources of Equity and Long Term Financing for Small Manufacturing Firms,* Research Summary of the Small Business Administration, June 1962, pp. 2-3).

ing $300,000 in bonds to the general public through an investment banking house would realize about $270,000. The commission received by the investment banker in this instance is $30,000, or 10 per cent of the amount paid by the public.[10]

In addition to the greater cost to a small corporation of raising funds through a public sale of securities, there is generally less flexibility in the choice of the type of security to use. Although the average cost of flotation of bonds by a small corporation is considerably less than the cost of flotation of common stocks, many small businesses encounter a much greater reluctance on the part of an investment banker in agreeing to market a bond issue as compared to a stock issue. The institutional investors, such as insurance companies, banks, pension funds, and charitable foundations, prefer to purchase bond issues of large rather than of small corporations. The market for bond issues of small companies, therefore, is rather restricted. Small firms depend to a greater extent on the sale of common stocks to the general public than on the sale of bonds in financing expansion. The opposite is true of large corporations. The sale of bonds in most years is greater in dollar volume than the sale of stocks sold to the general public, as Fig. 15-1 shows.

If a small businessman is forced to secure funds from others, equity funds are the safest and, according to many writers, the soundest method of raising long-term funds. Nevertheless, there is a reluctance on the part of many owners of small businesses to sharing the ownership of their enterprise. Sometimes this reluctance borders on the pathological. Rather than sell stock in a company which they own, some small businessmen prefer to juggle short-term loans and long-term debt in an effort to keep 100 per cent control of their company at all costs. As a result, an enterprise which could be adequately financed by sharing ownership with others is sometimes put on a financial starvation diet. Furthermore, the effort expended in meeting or trying to prevent constantly recurring credit crises could better be directed toward the other areas of business management, such as sales and improvement of products and services. If a business is well managed and profitable, the principal owner can expect freedom of action whether he owns 25 per cent of his company or 100 per cent. On the other hand, if his company is so inadequately financed that it cannot meet its obligations without recurring crises, his freedom of action will be more strictly curtailed by means of restrictive covenants in his loan contracts than it might be from dissatisfied fellow owners.

If the owner of a small corporation considers issuing stock through an investment banking house, thought should be given to three areas of preparation prior to the distribution of stock: a management audit, the possible

10 For comparison, General Motors Corporation sold an issue of bonds through a syndicate of investment banking firms for a price to investors of $301,500,000. The commission received by the syndicate was $3 million, and the amount received by General Motors Corporation was $298,500,000. The cost of flotation was approximately one per cent.

issuance of stock to management personnel of the company, and the psychological attitude to the change in status from a wholly owned company to one with ownership shared with others.

A management audit is a detailed analysis of the operational history and experience of a company. Included in such an audit will be a critical survey of the product line, changes in the market positions of the firm, the trend of profits, the relation between the company and its suppliers and the company and its customers, and changes in the credit standing of the company. Such an audit is not often undertaken by the owners of small businesses. It would, however, enable businessmen to negotiate with underwriters much more effectively than is possible when presenting financial statements alone as a basis for negotiation. The potential purchasers of common stock in a small company are interested in the growth possibility of the company. A managerial audit will indicate such possibilities. It will better enable the business owner to bargain with the underwriter with respect to his fee and such requirements of the underwriter as naming a member of the underwriting firm to the board of directors of the company. A well-prepared management audit will also simplify the task of preparing a prospectus.

If a business owner considers selling shares to the public, it is an excellent time to explore the possibility of giving key personnel a share in ownership of the company for which they work. It is common practice for large corporations to offer their employees stock at less than the market price as a means of giving workers a more direct stake in the profitability of the company. Such a program can be confined to the top executives or extended to all the employees of the company. The privilege of purchasing a limited number of shares each year may serve to increase the loyalty of workers, increase their thrift, and reduce labor turnover. Also, options to buy stock may be given to executives of the company. If the option to buy is made good for several years and the increasing profits raise the market price of the stock of the company, the option may prove to be a valuable tool in spurring the effort of key personnel in contributing to the rise in profits. In negotiating with underwriters, a program of stock purchasing, either in existence or planned, is a favorable factor.

If a corporation has been owned entirely by a businessman for many years, the sharing of ownership may be psychologically painful. The businessman is apt to consider his fellow stockholders as "outsiders." Nevertheless, he will have to share with these "outsiders" information about the company which he probably considers to be nobody's business but his own. Reports will have to be furnished to fellow stockholders concerning the profits, dividend policy, changes in management, and product developments. Stockholders' meetings must be held. At these meetings the businessman is frequently called upon to justify his actions during the past year. The questions put to him by his fellow owners may be searching and sharp. Even if he retains 51 per cent ownership of the company, he will have to secure approval of his fellow owners on such matters as changes in the charter or the issue of preferred stocks or bonds. At times he may feel like a politician holding public office, having to justify his actions to voters. To sum up, the businessman must become reconciled to the loss of absolute control, recognize the need for a conscious effort to win and hold the good will of his fellow owners, and recognize the necessity of considering the effects of management decisions not only on the financial situation of the company but also on the company image in the minds of stockholders.

Of crucial importance in the successful marketing of an issue of common stock for a small company is the choice of an underwriter. As in the choice of a bank, the choice of an underwriter should be made with care and after some shopping around. A small company that has good growth possibilities will probably require the services of an investment banker on numerous occasions. Once a careful choice has been made of an investment banking house, the advantages of remaining with the same house on future occasions of financing are as great as the advantages in maintaining a steady banking connection with one commercial bank. An investment banker can serve as financial counsel for long-term financing needs as a commercial banker can serve as counsel for short-term requirements. Some investment bankers are eager to assist small firms in their long-term financing needs, while others prefer to handle issues of larger companies. Some investment bankers are willing to handle an issue that is to be sold entirely within a state, a restriction requested by some small businesses. Investment bankers who operate nationally, on the other hand, will usually not touch an intrastate issue. Some provide their services with care and skill, and demand only reasonable compensation. A few, unfortunately, show little concern for either the company or the investing public, and demand fees as exhorbitant as the situation will permit. Because of the importance of wise selection of an investment banking connection, the choice should not be hurried.

While a good investment banker will offer valuable suggestions in planning an issue of securities, it is useful for the owner of a small business to have clearly in mind the basic financing requirements which prompted the approach to the investment banker. Reputable investment bankers that are willing to handle the issues of small corporations generally cannot afford the time necessary to assist businessmen in all the steps in the process of planning a long-term issue. A carefully chosen management consultant can be of considerable aid to the small businessman in the initial stages of planning a security issue, particularly if it is the first one that a businessman is proposing for his company. Such a consultant will aid in diagnosing the need for funds and in preparing the necessary data to support an issue of securities. The consultant may be of valuable aid in selecting the best investment banking firm for the businessman. Whether a management consultant is retained or not, a carefully thought out long-term financing proposal will save the time of the investment banker and may be reflected in a lower cost of distributing the issue.

As in all financial transactions, the small businessman should be aware of all the costs involved in marketing an issue of stocks or bonds. These costs are not confined to the fees charged by the investment banking firm. They also include expenditures for the development of a registration statement for the Securities and Exchange Commission, if the issue is subject to regulation by the federal government. A prospectus must be prepared, fees for legal services must usually be met, and fees to state regulatory agencies may have to be paid.

GOVERNMENT SOURCES OF LOANS

The federal government has directly and indirectly aided in financing of business both large and small for many years. The Reconstruction Finance Corporation, chartered in 1932 and dissolved in 1953, was principally a source of loans for larger enterprises, but it made loans to small companies as well. The Export-Import Bank, chartered in 1934, confines its activities largely to aiding in financing of foreign trade operations. The twelve Federal Reserve Banks were authorized by Congress in 1934 to make loans directly to proprietorships, partnerships, and corporations for periods up to five years. The bulk of the lending activity of the Federal Reserve Banks was confined to the years immediately preceding World War II. They were mostly of the term variety, with average maturity of three years. The business loan activities of the banks terminated in 1950. The primary federal agency in the business loan field of importance to small businessmen is the Small Business Administration. Two other federal lending agencies that also deserve mention are the Rural Electrification Administration and the Area Redevelopment Administration.

Rural Electrification Administration The Rural Electrification Administration was created to spur the use of electricity on farms and in small towns not previously enjoying electricity. During the thirty years of its existence, it has made primarily low cost loans to electrical cooperatives to create power production and distribution facilities. In recent years, however, the locally owned electrical cooperatives have, with funds supplied by the Rural Electrification Administration, made loans to businesses. The purpose of these business loans has been to speed the industrial development of towns in farming areas. Loans by rural electrical cooperatives are made to companies that are customers or potential customers for the electricity distributed by the cooperatives. For example, Chestnut Hills Resort of Hanover, Illinois, borrowed $30,000 from a local electrical cooperative to finance the purchase of a snow-making machine. This loan negotiated in 1961 was at the rate of 4 per cent per annum. The electrical cooperative, in turn, borrowed the money from the Rural Electrification Administration at the rate of 2 per cent per annum. Other recent examples of loans from electrical cooperatives to businesses are a $250,000 loan to equip a lumber plant in Minnesota and a $25,000 loan to a North Dakota company to purchase electric gravel-and-crushing equipment.

Area Redevelopment Administration The Area Redevelopment Administration was created in 1961 for the purpose of aiding in the revival of unemployment areas. Neither the Rural Electrification Administration nor the Area Redevelopment Administration is restricted as to the size of loan made. However, in practice the loans are made mostly to small business. Unlike the lending activities of the Rural Electrification Administration, which aid electrical cooperatives in making loans to businesses, the Area Redevelopment Administration makes loans directly to business borrowers. One example is a loan for $145,685 for twenty years at 4 per cent per annum to a meat packing company in Alabama. Another is a loan of $572,000 to a newly established furniture corporation in West Virginia to permit it to begin operation.

The Small Business Administration When the Reconstruction Finance Corporation was dissolved in 1953, Congress created a new agency to take over its lending activities. The agency was called the Small Business Administration. Its loan activities were to be confined to small business.[11] In addition to making loans, the Small Business Administration participates in loans made jointly with local commercial banks. Under the terms of such participation agreements, the Small Business Administration shares the risk in making loans of a term nature, and makes it possible for commercial banks to extend credit running beyond one year in amounts larger than would be possible without this participation. Loans from the S.B.A. are available only to borrowers that are unable to secure financing at "reasonable rates" from private loan sources.

The loans made by the S.B.A. to individual business borrowers are limited to $250,000 for each borrower. Loans may be made for periods as long as ten years. If the applicant company is in an area struck by a natural disaster, the S.B.A. is permitted to make loans for longer than ten years. The longer term loans made by the S.B.A. are usually secured by the pledge of assets of the borrowing company. In general, the S.B.A. has been much more cautious and conservative in its lending activities than was the Reconstruction Finance Corporation.

Lending is not the only activity of the Small Business Administration. It aids small businesses in securing contracts for materials purchased by the federal government, it publishes a wide variety of pamphlets and books to aid businessmen in their managerial problems, it cooperates with colleges and universities in sponsoring seminars on business management, and it

---

11 Among the qualifications set up by Congress in defining a small business for the purpose of the Act was that recipients of financial aid from the Small Business Administration could not be companies dominant in their field nor have more than 1,000 employees.

serves as a source of advice and counsel. During the first decade of its operations, approximately 30 per cent of the loans made by the S.B.A. was to
manufacturers, approximately 30 per cent to retailers, and the balance was
made to companies in mining, service, and other areas of business activities.

SMALL BUSINESS INVESTMENT COMPANIES

Congress passed a bill in 1958 providing for the establishment of a new
type of lending institution for small businesses. They are called *Small Business Investment Companies*. The law provides that a Small Business Investment Company may be chartered under the corporation laws of the state in
which it is located and be organized by a group of local citizens. The
minimum capitalization for a Small Business Investment Company is $300,-
000, of which at least one-half must be subscribed by the local stockholders
and an amount up to one-half may be borrowed from the Small Business
Administration. Borrowing from the S.B.A. is in the form of subordinated
debentures. In addition to the corporation charter, the Small Business
Investment Company requires an authority to proceed from the S.B.A.
Such a company may also borrow from sources other than the S.B.A. The
limit to such borrowing is an amount equal to four times the capital stock
and surplus plus the debentures held by the S.B.A.

S.B.I.C.'s are permitted considerable latitude in their operations.
They may make loans to small businesses or they may invest in stocks of small
businesses. The financing operations are for the most part, however,
limited to the purchase of convertible debentures from the enterprises seeking funds from the investment company. The interest charge usually varies
from 6 to 8 per cent. The maximum which may be legally charged is 15
per cent per annum. Where convertible debentures are purchased by the
investment company, the option to convert into common stock of the borrowing company provides a possible advantage in participating in the
growth of the business. This option is an attraction to the investment company because it serves to offset the disadvantage of the high risk involved
in making such loans.

Some businessmen are reluctant to borrow money from S.B.I.C.'s under convertible debentures, because of the fear of losing control of their
corporation if the debentures held by the investment company are converted into common stocks. The attitude of some small businessmen toward S.B.I.C.'s has been roughly as follows: "If you fail, you lose control of
your company to your creditors; if you are successful, you lose control of
your company to the S.B.I.C." If the amount of stock into which the convertible debentures held by the S.B.I.C. can be converted is less than half
of the common stock outstanding after conversion, the risk of loss of control
would appear to be little. As indicated earlier, some small businessmen
are very reluctant even to share control of their companies with anybody
else. Such businessmen prefer not to borrow from S.B.I.C.'s in spite of the

attitude of most S.B.I.C.'s that control of corporations borrowing under convertible debentures is not sought. Where the conversion privilege is exercised by the S.B.I.C., it appears that the purpose is to market at a profit rather than to control the corporation. It is, however, common practice for an S.B.I.C. to require that, as a condition in making a loan to a small corporation, the directors of the S.B.I.C. be permitted to name one director to the board. If the person chosen to act as director has experience in business management, he can contribute immeasurably to the management of the borrowing corporation. Some S.B.I.C.'s retain a staff of management consultants to aid borrowing corporations in such matters as marketing, manufacturing, financing, and inventory control.

To the financial manager of a small company, the selection of an S.B.I.C. should be carefully done. In most towns and cities, several S.B.I.C.'s are operating. If no S.B.I.C.'s are available in the vicinity of a small company, the financial manager can contact a number of S.B.I.C.'s in other towns. There is considerable competition among S.B.I.C.'s, and shopping around is good advice to the financial manager of a company seeking a loan. Furthermore, it is important that the financial manager of a small company seek an S.B.I.C. with policies compatible with the requirements of the borrower. Some S.B.I.C.'s will make loans only in large amounts, such as $50,000 or more. Some S.B.I.C.'s specialize in certain industries, such as electronics, or retailing, or manufacturing. Some S.B.I.C.'s require that each borrower subscribe to consulting services of a consulting firm associated with the S.B.I.C., whenever the directors of the S.B.I.C. feel that such services will improve the operation of the borrower.

Because a loan from an S.B.I.C. is long term, running from five to fifteen years in most cases, the preparation by the financial officer of the borrowing company of a long-term forecast is advisable. Such a forecast should be for a period of years equal to the length of the loan, if possible. If not, the forecast should run five years at least. Such a forecast should include the predicted sale of products or services, the financing needs of the company during the period, any contemplated expansion of production facilities together with the cost for such an expansion, expenses of production, expected profits, and probable tax liabilities. If the loan is to be an installment loan, a schedule of repayment should be included in the forecast. During the life of the loan, the forecast prepared at the time the loan was negotiated should be revised whenever necessary to meet the changing conditions of the company as time passes.

One of the serious mistakes made by the financial managers of small companies is to ask for a minimum amount of funds. It is true that the larger the loan the larger the loan payments in interest and principal. To keep these payments to a minimum there is a strong temptation to request the estimated minimum amount needed. In many situations this is a mistake, since it often results in undercapitalizing the company. Operation on a shoestring is rarely advisable, and is not to be recommended in seeking a loan from an S.B.I.C. If it can be avoided, the company should not be niggardly in financing such things as product research and development, advertising, modernization of plant and equipment, and maintenance of adequate inventories.

OTHER SOLUTIONS TO THE NEED FOR FUNDS

Sale of Unneeded Assets   In the search for funds for long-term financing, the possibility of selling assets not currently needed is often overlooked by the financial manager of a small company.   A critical examination of the assets belonging to a firm will often uncover some that have a marginal utility to the function of the business.   There may be equipment which is not needed and for which a future use is dubious.   There may be some land acquired by the company for possible future expansion, for which expansion plans in the immediate future find no use.   A company might own a parking lot, convenient for its employees but not essential to the company operations.   In planning the long-term financing needs of a company, the possible sale of such assets should always be considered as one of the alternatives.   Even assets that are needed by the company may be sold to raise cash and then immediately leased for company operations.   Thus, a factory building might be sold for cash under an agreement to lease it from the purchaser for a specified number of years.   Such an operation in effect transforms the building into needed cash, while preserving the use of the building for a stated number of years in the future.

Merger or Sale   A company that has favorable growth prospects is always a candidate for a merger.   It is a commonly used means of effecting an expansion.   Furthermore, the merger may provide not only a means of expansion but also a means of diversification.   Such diversification may be in the form of product, market, or managerial talent.   The choice of continued growth or merger presents a typical decision to most small businessmen.   Many factors must be considered, including new product development, competitive forces, the depth of the market, an allowance through the merger for a full line of products, and the effect of the merger on the ease of raising additional funds.   The merger generally provides a more rapid means of expansion than is otherwise possible.   It also involves a sharing of ownership.   If the merger terms offered to a particular company are very favorable, such a means of expansion may be more attractive than the slower rate of expansion to be expected through the resources of a single company.   On the other hand, the merger may be the only means of avoiding threatened bankruptcy.   In the latter case the terms of merger offered to a company cannot be expected to be particularly favorable, although the alternative of probable bankruptcy may be considerably worse. In any case it is best for the owners of a small business to keep an open mind with respect to possible merger offers.   The growth of some enterprises has been extremely rapid as a result of mergers. On the other hand, the merger route may be the quickest road to loss of identity and loss of control of a company.

Use of Financial Consultants A company having difficulty securing adequate financing should consider the possibility of retaining a financial consultant. This is particularly true for small businesses that do not have a financial officer on the staff on a full-time basis. As in the case of other management specialties that are not available in sufficient degree within the firm, financial skill can be hired from without.

When a small company expands, its financing problems do not merely increase in size but also in the nature of the problems. Small companies, as we have seen, depend to a much greater degree than do larger companies upon bank financing. As a small company grows, it will in most cases make more use of sources other than bank financing than it did when it was small. The financial operations that are commonplace to a medium or large business are frequently beyond the experience and knowledge of small businessmen. For this reason retaining a financial consultant experienced in those financial operations with which the management of a small company is not familiar is generally a wise move.

A financial consultant may confine his services to offering advice, or he may act as a middleman. In his capacity as a middleman he may actively negotiate for loans with lending sources not previously contacted by the small business. Because of his greater experience and specialized knowledge, a good financial consultant can be a much tougher negotiator in securing favorable loan terms than would be possible for a small businessman bargaining for himself.

Obviously, the choice of a financial consultant must be very carefully made. As in the case of a lawyer or an accountant, the manager of a small business must recognize that there are good financial consultants and poor ones. A small businessman must investigate carefully before entrusting the fate of his enterprise to the advice or negotiating skill of a financial consultant. If the choice is carefully made, the services of financial consultants can be beneficial not only to the small businessman but to the lender of the funds as well. In speaking of a highly successful financial consultant, *Business Week* describes his services as follows: "[His] unique contribution is his ability to act as a catalyst between a well-run small business and big lenders—and to refine the agreement so that the lender gets safety without putting the borrower in a strait jacket." [12]

Questions

1. Why is it that when availability of bank credit is low, commercial banks restrict their loans to small businesses much more than to larger ones?

12 *Business Week,* June 16, 1962, p. 48.

2. Small companies tend to depend upon retained earnings to finance growth to a greater extent than larger firms. Why?

3. Why is it that newly organized firms depend to a greater extent upon credit from wholesalers and suppliers in their total financing plans than do older firms?

4. What is the purpose of community development organizations? How do they help small businesses in their financing?

5. Why is the sale of securities to the general public a less attractive means of financing for small companies than for large ones?

6. Account for the reluctance of owners of small businesses to share ownership of their companies.

7. What is a managerial audit? How can it be useful to a small company where the owners are contemplating selling stock to the public?

8. How has the Rural Electrification Administration aided in the financing of small businesses?

9. List the activities of the Small Business Administration that aid small businesses.

10. Describe the lending activities of Small Business Investment Companies.

Selected Readings

Carson, Deane, *The Effect of Tight Money on Small Business Financing,* Brown University Press, Providence, R.I., 1963.

Equity Capital for Small Business Corporations, Investment Bankers Association of America, Washington, D.C., 1955.

Finn, Gene Leroy, *The Availability of Credit to Wisconsin Small Business,* University of Wisconsin Press, Madison, Wisc., 1962.

Flink, Salomon J., *Equity Financing of Small Manufacturing Companies in New Jersey,* New Jersey Bureau of Commerce, Trenton, N.J., 1962.

Hastings, Paul G., *Term Loans in Small Business Financing,* Small Marketers Aids #22, Small Business Administration, Washington, D.C., 1957.

Jolivet, Vincent M., *Sources of Credit and Capital for Washington State Business,* Bureau of Business Research, University of Washington, Seattle, Wash., 1962.

Money Management in Small Business, Monthly Letter of the Royal Bank of Canada, September 1955.

Small Business: Its Role and Its Problems, Chamber of Commerce of the United States, Washington, D.C., 1962.

Years Hence	1%	2%	4%	6%	8%	10%	12%	14%	15%	16%	18%	20%	22%	24%	25%	26%	28%	30%	35%	40%	45%	50%
1	0.990	0.980	0.962	0.943	0.926	0.909	0.893	0.877	0.870	0.862	0.847	0.833	0.820	0.806	0.800	0.794	0.781	0.769	0.741	0.714	0.690	0.667
2	0.980	0.961	0.925	0.890	0.857	0.826	0.797	0.769	0.756	0.743	0.718	0.694	0.672	0.650	0.640	0.630	0.610	0.592	0.549	0.510	0.476	0.444
3	0.971	0.942	0.889	0.840	0.794	0.751	0.712	0.675	0.658	0.641	0.609	0.579	0.551	0.524	0.512	0.500	0.477	0.455	0.406	0.364	0.328	0.296
4	0.961	0.924	0.855	0.792	0.735	0.683	0.636	0.592	0.572	0.552	0.516	0.482	0.451	0.423	0.410	0.397	0.373	0.350	0.301	0.260	0.226	0.198
5	0.951	0.906	0.822	0.747	0.681	0.621	0.567	0.519	0.497	0.476	0.437	0.402	0.370	0.341	0.328	0.315	0.291	0.269	0.223	0.186	0.156	0.132
6	0.942	0.888	0.790	0.705	0.630	0.564	0.507	0.456	0.432	0.410	0.370	0.335	0.303	0.275	0.262	0.250	0.227	0.207	0.165	0.133	0.108	0.088
7	0.933	0.871	0.760	0.665	0.583	0.513	0.452	0.400	0.376	0.354	0.314	0.279	0.249	0.222	0.210	0.198	0.178	0.159	0.122	0.095	0.074	0.059
8	0.923	0.853	0.731	0.627	0.540	0.467	0.404	0.351	0.327	0.305	0.266	0.233	0.204	0.179	0.168	0.157	0.139	0.123	0.091	0.068	0.051	0.039
9	0.914	0.837	0.703	0.592	0.500	0.424	0.361	0.308	0.284	0.263	0.225	0.194	0.167	0.144	0.134	0.125	0.108	0.094	0.067	0.048	0.035	0.026
10	0.905	0.820	0.676	0.558	0.463	0.386	0.322	0.270	0.247	0.227	0.191	0.162	0.137	0.116	0.107	0.099	0.085	0.073	0.050	0.035	0.024	0.017
11	0.896	0.804	0.650	0.527	0.429	0.350	0.287	0.237	0.215	0.195	0.162	0.135	0.112	0.094	0.086	0.079	0.066	0.056	0.037	0.025	0.017	0.012
12	0.887	0.788	0.625	0.497	0.397	0.319	0.257	0.208	0.187	0.168	0.137	0.112	0.092	0.076	0.069	0.062	0.052	0.043	0.027	0.018	0.012	0.008
13	0.879	0.773	0.601	0.469	0.368	0.290	0.229	0.182	0.163	0.145	0.116	0.093	0.075	0.061	0.055	0.050	0.040	0.033	0.020	0.013	0.008	0.005
14	0.870	0.758	0.577	0.442	0.340	0.263	0.205	0.160	0.141	0.125	0.099	0.078	0.062	0.049	0.044	0.039	0.032	0.025	0.015	0.009	0.006	0.003
15	0.861	0.743	0.555	0.417	0.315	0.239	0.183	0.140	0.123	0.108	0.084	0.065	0.051	0.040	0.035	0.031	0.025	0.020	0.011	0.006	0.004	0.002
16	0.853	0.728	0.534	0.394	0.292	0.218	0.163	0.123	0.107	0.093	0.071	0.054	0.042	0.032	0.028	0.025	0.019	0.015	0.008	0.005	0.003	0.002
17	0.844	0.714	0.513	0.371	0.270	0.198	0.146	0.108	0.093	0.080	0.060	0.045	0.034	0.026	0.023	0.020	0.015	0.012	0.006	0.003	0.002	0.001
18	0.836	0.700	0.494	0.350	0.250	0.180	0.130	0.095	0.081	0.069	0.051	0.038	0.028	0.021	0.018	0.016	0.012	0.009	0.005	0.002	0.001	0.001
19	0.828	0.686	0.475	0.331	0.232	0.164	0.116	0.083	0.070	0.060	0.043	0.031	0.023	0.017	0.014	0.012	0.009	0.007	0.003	0.002	0.001	0.001
20	0.820	0.673	0.456	0.312	0.215	0.149	0.104	0.073	0.061	0.051	0.037	0.026	0.019	0.014	0.012	0.010	0.007	0.005	0.002	0.001		
21	0.811	0.660	0.439	0.294	0.199	0.135	0.093	0.064	0.053	0.044	0.031	0.022	0.015	0.011	0.009	0.008	0.006	0.004	0.002	0.001		
22	0.803	0.647	0.422	0.278	0.184	0.123	0.083	0.056	0.046	0.038	0.026	0.018	0.013	0.009	0.007	0.006	0.004	0.003	0.001	0.001		
23	0.795	0.634	0.406	0.262	0.170	0.112	0.074	0.049	0.040	0.033	0.022	0.015	0.010	0.007	0.006	0.005	0.003	0.002	0.001			
24	0.788	0.622	0.390	0.247	0.158	0.102	0.066	0.043	0.035	0.028	0.019	0.013	0.008	0.006	0.005	0.004	0.003	0.002	0.001			
25	0.780	0.610	0.375	0.233	0.146	0.092	0.059	0.038	0.030	0.024	0.016	0.010	0.007	0.005	0.004	0.003	0.002	0.001	0.001			
26	0.772	0.598	0.361	0.220	0.135	0.084	0.053	0.033	0.026	0.021	0.014	0.009	0.006	0.004	0.003	0.002	0.002	0.001				
27	0.764	0.586	0.347	0.207	0.125	0.076	0.047	0.029	0.023	0.018	0.011	0.007	0.005	0.003	0.002	0.002	0.001	0.001				
28	0.757	0.574	0.333	0.196	0.116	0.069	0.042	0.026	0.020	0.016	0.010	0.006	0.004	0.002	0.002	0.002	0.001	0.001				
29	0.749	0.563	0.321	0.185	0.107	0.063	0.037	0.022	0.017	0.014	0.008	0.005	0.003	0.002	0.002	0.001	0.001	0.001				
30	0.742	0.552	0.308	0.174	0.099	0.057	0.033	0.020	0.015	0.012	0.007	0.004	0.003	0.002	0.001	0.001	0.001	0.001				
40	0.672	0.453	0.208	0.097	0.046	0.022	0.011	0.005	0.004	0.003	0.001	0.001										
50	0.608	0.372	0.141	0.054	0.021	0.009	0.003	0.001	0.001	0.001												

Source: R. N. Anthony, *Management Accounting: Text and Cases* (Homewood, Illinois: R. D. Irwin, Inc., 1960), p. 656.

I. Present Value of $1 Received at End of (N) Number of Years

Years (N)	1%	2%	4%	6%	8%	10%	12%	14%	15%	16%	18%	20%	22%	24%	25%	26%	28%	30%	35%	40%	45%	50%
1	0.990	0.980	0.962	0.943	0.926	0.909	0.893	0.877	0.870	0.862	0.847	0.833	0.820	0.806	0.800	0.794	0.781	0.769	0.741	0.714	0.690	0.667
2	1.970	1.942	1.886	1.833	1.783	1.736	1.690	1.647	1.626	1.605	1.566	1.528	1.492	1.457	1.440	1.424	1.392	1.361	1.289	1.224	1.165	1.111
3	2.941	2.884	2.775	2.673	2.577	2.487	2.402	2.322	2.283	2.246	2.174	2.106	2.042	1.981	1.952	1.923	1.868	1.816	1.696	1.589	1.493	1.407
4	3.902	3.808	3.630	3.465	3.312	3.170	3.037	2.914	2.855	2.798	2.690	2.589	2.494	2.404	2.362	2.320	2.241	2.166	1.997	1.849	1.720	1.605
5	4.853	4.713	4.452	4.212	3.993	3.791	3.605	3.433	3.352	3.274	3.127	2.991	2.864	2.745	2.689	2.635	2.532	2.436	2.220	2.035	1.876	1.737
6	5.795	5.601	5.242	4.917	4.623	4.355	4.111	3.889	3.784	3.685	3.498	3.326	3.167	3.020	2.951	2.885	2.759	2.643	2.385	2.168	1.983	1.824
7	6.728	6.472	6.002	5.582	5.206	4.868	4.564	4.288	4.160	4.039	3.812	3.605	3.416	3.242	3.161	3.083	2.937	2.802	2.508	2.263	2.057	1.883
8	7.652	7.325	6.733	6.210	5.747	5.335	4.968	4.639	4.487	4.344	4.078	3.837	3.619	3.421	3.329	3.241	3.076	2.925	2.598	2.331	2.108	1.922
9	8.566	8.162	7.435	6.802	6.247	5.759	5.328	4.946	4.772	4.607	4.303	4.031	3.786	3.566	3.463	3.366	3.184	3.019	2.665	2.379	2.144	1.948
10	9.471	8.983	8.111	7.360	6.710	6.145	5.650	5.216	5.019	4.833	4.494	4.192	3.923	3.682	3.571	3.465	3.269	3.092	2.715	2.414	2.168	1.965
11	10.368	9.787	8.760	7.887	7.139	6.495	5.938	5.453	5.234	5.029	4.656	4.327	4.035	3.776	3.656	3.544	3.335	3.147	2.752	2.438	2.185	1.977
12	11.255	10.575	9.385	8.384	7.536	6.814	6.194	5.660	5.421	5.197	4.793	4.439	4.127	3.851	3.725	3.606	3.387	3.190	2.779	2.456	2.196	1.985
13	12.134	11.343	9.986	8.853	7.904	7.103	6.424	5.842	5.583	5.342	4.910	4.533	4.203	3.912	3.780	3.656	3.427	3.223	2.799	2.468	2.204	1.990
14	13.004	12.106	10.563	9.295	8.244	7.367	6.628	6.002	5.724	5.468	5.008	4.611	4.265	3.962	3.824	3.695	3.459	3.249	2.814	2.477	2.210	1.993
15	13.865	12.849	11.118	9.712	8.559	7.606	6.811	6.142	5.847	5.575	5.092	4.675	4.315	4.001	3.859	3.726	3.483	3.268	2.825	2.484	2.214	1.995
16	14.718	13.578	11.652	10.106	8.851	7.824	6.974	6.265	5.954	5.669	5.162	4.730	4.357	4.033	3.887	3.751	3.503	3.283	2.834	2.489	2.216	1.997
17	15.562	14.292	12.166	10.477	9.122	8.022	7.120	6.373	6.047	5.749	5.222	4.775	4.391	4.059	3.910	3.771	3.518	3.295	2.840	2.492	2.218	1.998
18	16.398	14.992	12.659	10.828	9.372	8.201	7.250	6.467	6.128	5.818	5.273	4.812	4.419	4.080	3.928	3.786	3.529	3.304	2.844	2.494	2.219	1.999
19	17.226	15.678	13.134	11.158	9.604	8.365	7.366	6.550	6.198	5.877	5.316	4.844	4.442	4.097	3.942	3.799	3.539	3.311	2.848	2.496	2.220	1.999
20	18.046	16.351	13.590	11.470	9.818	8.514	7.469	6.623	6.259	5.929	5.353	4.870	4.460	4.110	3.954	3.808	3.546	3.316	2.850	2.497	2.221	1.999
21	18.857	17.011	14.029	11.764	10.017	8.649	7.562	6.687	6.312	5.973	5.384	4.891	4.476	4.121	3.963	3.816	3.551	3.320	2.852	2.498	2.221	2.000
22	19.660	17.658	14.451	12.042	10.201	8.772	7.645	6.743	6.359	6.011	5.410	4.909	4.488	4.130	3.970	3.822	3.556	3.323	2.853	2.498	2.222	2.000
23	20.456	18.292	14.857	12.303	10.371	8.883	7.718	6.792	6.399	6.044	5.432	4.925	4.499	4.137	3.976	3.827	3.559	3.325	2.854	2.499	2.222	2.000
24	21.243	18.914	15.247	12.550	10.529	8.985	7.784	6.835	6.434	6.073	5.451	4.937	4.507	4.143	3.981	3.831	3.562	3.327	2.855	2.499	2.222	2.000
25	22.023	19.523	15.622	12.783	10.675	9.077	7.843	6.873	6.464	6.097	5.467	4.948	4.514	4.147	3.985	3.834	3.564	3.329	2.856	2.499	2.222	2.000
26	22.795	20.121	15.983	13.003	10.810	9.161	7.896	6.906	6.491	6.118	5.480	4.956	4.520	4.151	3.988	3.837	3.566	3.330	2.856	2.500	2.222	2.000
27	23.560	20.707	16.330	13.211	10.935	9.237	7.943	6.935	6.514	6.136	5.492	4.964	4.524	4.154	3.990	3.839	3.567	3.331	2.856	2.500	2.222	2.000
28	24.316	21.281	16.663	13.406	11.051	9.307	7.984	6.961	6.534	6.152	5.502	4.970	4.528	4.157	3.992	3.840	3.568	3.331	2.857	2.500	2.222	2.000
29	25.066	21.844	16.984	13.591	11.158	9.370	8.022	6.983	6.551	6.166	5.510	4.975	4.531	4.159	3.994	3.841	3.569	3.332	2.857	2.500	2.222	2.000
30	25.808	22.396	17.292	13.765	11.258	9.427	8.055	7.003	6.566	6.177	5.517	4.979	4.534	4.160	3.995	3.842	3.569	3.332	2.857	2.500	2.222	2.000
40	32.835	27.355	19.793	15.046	11.925	9.779	8.244	7.105	6.642	6.234	5.548	4.997	4.544	4.166	3.999	3.846	3.571	3.333	2.857	2.500	2.222	2.000
50	39.196	31.424	21.482	15.762	12.234	9.915	8.304	7.133	6.661	6.246	5.554	4.999	4.545	4.167	4.000	3.846	3.571	3.333	2.857	2.500	2.222	2.000

Source: R. N. Anthony, *Management Accounting: Text and Cases* (Homewood, Illinois: R. D. Irwin, Inc., 1960), p. 657.

II. Present Value of $1 Received Annually at End of Each Year for (N) Years

Index

Deficit, elimination from balance sheet, 447-448
Depletion, 36
defined, 30
Depreciation
cash flow, 44-45
concept of, 28
income tax effects, 37-39
methods of calculating
compound interest, 34
contingent upon earnings, 35
fixed percentage of declining balance, 31
inspection, 35
straight line, 31
sum-of-the-years' digits, 33
use or wear, 34
price inflation, 40
revenue act of 1962, 39
source of funds, 43
Depreciation allowances as source of funds, 69-71
Diminishing returns, the law of, 418
Dissolution of companies, 461
corporations, 465
partnerships, 463-465
proprietorship, 462-463
Dissolution of corporations
involuntary
bankruptcy (see bankruptcy)
court order, 465-466
expiration of charter, 465
forfeiture of charter, 466
voluntary
by unanimous consent, 466
without unanimous consent, 466-467
Distribution of securities (see securities distribution)
Dividend policies
effect on company finances, 380-381
regularity, 375-378
stockholder attitudes, 378-380
tax consideratons in, 381-382
Dividends
forms of
cash, 369-370
other assets, 370
scrip, 371-372
stock, 372-374
in cash budget, 61
legal limits on, 367-369
reserve for, 383-384
steps in distributing, 366-367
Dividends as a use of funds, 75-77

Dividends earned ratio, 24
Du Pont Company, 460n
Dun & Bradstreet, Inc., 118

Employee purchase of stock, 286-288
Equipment obligations, 206-210
Equipment trust certificates, 206-210
Equity receivership compared with Chapter X of the Bankruptcy Act, 498
Equity reorganizations, 482
Equity to debt ratio, 20
Expansion, forms of
complementary, 420
heterogeneous, 421
horizontal, 420
vertical, 419-420
Expansion, methods of
cartels, 423
community of interest, 424
gentlemen's agreements, 421-422
interlocking directorates, 422-423
trusts, 423-424
Expansion, reasons for
economic factors, 412-417
psychological factors, 410-412
Ex-rights, 294
Extension (in debt), 478-479

Factor, defined, 133
Factoring
advantages of, 134-135
costs of, 134
defined, 130
example of, 133-134
services to clients, 136
Factor's lien, 136
Failure
causes of, 473-477
signals of impending, 471-472
Federal Deposit Insurance Corporation, 90
Federal Reserve Banks, 512
Federal Reserve System, 89, 357
term lending, 148
Field warehousing, 138-140
Finance
defined, 3
organization for, 7
place in the economy, 3
Finance companies in financing equipment purchases, 147
Financial leverage, 345 (see also capital leverage, trading on the equity)
Financial plan (see capital structure)